INNOVATION FOR THE 21ST CENTURY

INNOVATION FOR THE 21ST CENTURY

HARNESSING THE POWER OF

INTELLECTUAL PROPERTY AND

ANTITRUST LAW

MICHAEL A. CARRIER

OXFORD UNIVERSITY PRESS

OXFORD
UNIVERSITY PRESS

Oxford University Press, Inc., publishes works that further Oxford University's objective
of excellence in research, scholarship, and education.

Oxford   New York
Auckland   Cape Town   Dar es Salaam   Hong Kong   Karachi   Kuala Lumpur   Madrid   Melbourne
Mexico City   Nairobi   New Delhi   Shanghai   Taipei   Toronto

With offices in
Argentina   Austria   Brazil   Chile   Czech Republic   France   Greece   Guatemala   Hungary   Italy
Japan   Poland   Portugal   Singapore   South Korea   Switzerland   Thailand   Turkey   Ukraine
Vietnam

Copyright © 2009 by Oxford University Press, Inc.

Published by Oxford University Press, Inc.
198 Madison Avenue, New York, New York 10016

Oxford is a registered trademark of Oxford University Press
Oxford University Press is a registered trademark of Oxford University Press, Inc.

Library of Congress Cataloging-in-Publication Data
Carrier, Michael A.
    Innovation for the 21st century: harnessing the power of intellectual property and antitrust law/
Michael A. Carrier.
        p. cm.
    Includes bibliographical references and index.
    ISBN 978-0-19-534258-1 (hardback : alk. paper) 1.   Intellectual property--United States. 2.   Antitrust
law--United States. I. Title.
    KF3116.C37 2009
    346.7304'8--dc22

                                                                                    2008042087

First printing in paperback, 2010

ISBN 9780199794287 (paperback : alk. paper)

Printed in the United States of America on acid-free paper

Note to Readers
This publication is designed to provide accurate and authoritative information in regard to the subject
matter covered. It is based upon sources believed to be accurate and reliable and is intended to be current
as of the time it was written. It is sold with the understanding that the publisher is not engaged in rendering
legal, accounting, or other professional services. If legal advice or other expert assistance is required, the
services of a competent professional person should be sought. Also, to confirm that the information has
not been affected or changed by recent developments, traditional legal research techniques should be used,
including checking primary sources where appropriate.

(Based on the Declaration of Principles jointly adopted by a Committee of the
American Bar Association and a Committee of Publishers and Associations.)

CONTENTS

Acknowledgments vii
Introduction 1

I. PRIMER

Chapter 1. Innovation 19
Chapter 2. Intellectual Property 35
Chapter 3. Antitrust 55
Chapter 4. Antitrust and IP: 20th Century 71
Chapter 5. Antitrust and IP: 21st Century 87

II. COPYRIGHT

Chapter 6. Pioneering Peer-to-Peer and Other Disruptive
  Dual-Use Technologies 105
Chapter 7. Damaging Copyright Damages 147
Chapter 8. The Digital Millennium Copyright Act: From
  Pirates to User Innovators 163

III. PATENT

Chapter 9. Better Patents: A Post-Grant Opposition Procedure 205
Chapter 10. Less Dangerous Patents: A Framework for Relief 231
Chapter 11. Biotechnology Dilemma 1: Patented Research
  Tools and Experimental Use 253
Chapter 12. Biotechnology Dilemma 2: Material Transfer Agreements 279

IV. ANTITRUST

Chapter 13. Innovation Markets: Saving Lives and Money in the
  Pharmaceutical Industry 295
Chapter 14. Supporting Standard-Setting Organizations 323
Chapter 15. Unsettling Drug Patent Settlements: A Framework
  for Presumptive Illegality 345

Conclusion 383

Index 385

ACKNOWLEDGMENTS

No book of this scope can be accomplished single-handedly. I received helpful comments from Chris Anderson, Jon Baker, Jonathan Band, Mike Carroll, Perry Dane, Don Dodge, Harry First, Bert Foer, Shubha Ghosh, Rich Gilbert, Scott Hemphill, Renata Hesse, Gwen Hinze, Stephen Horowitz, Herb Hovenkamp, Mark Janis, Greg Lastowka, Anne Layne-Farrar, Mark Lemley, Christopher Leslie, Gail Levine, Jason Mendelson, Michael Meurer, Joe Miller, Joe Milowic, Brian Nester, Sean O'Connor, Mark Popofsky, Tony Reese, Bill Rosenblatt, Pamela Samuelson, Josh Sarnoff, F.M. Scherer, Dave Schwartz, Ephraim Schwartz, Greg Sidak, Katherine Strandburg, Jay Thomas, Eric von Hippel, Dave Weisberg, Phil Weiser, Kevin Werbach, and Christopher Yoo. In addition, students in seminars I taught at Rutgers Law School in the 2007–2008 year offered useful feedback on my proposals.

I have also benefited from the excellent work of many research assistants. Assisting in the early stages of research were Alex Gonzalez, Philip Jon, Mike Koptiw, Jon Marshfield, Ryan Murphy, Jon Pentzien, and Dave Tseng. Giving up even more of their time to add impressive contributions in later stages were Lionel Cassin, Katie Coyne, Llewy Davis, Erin Fitzgerald, Brian Fitzsimons, Sean Neafsey, and Ryan Strauss.

A scholar can ask for no better law school dean than Ray Solomon, who has consistently and enthusiastically supported my work in so many indispensable ways. Jay Feinman and Dennis Patterson have been generous mentors throughout this project as well as my academic career. Lori Rowland cheerfully kept on top of my personal library of interlibrary loans. Fran Brigandi reliably kept on top of everything else, providing sterling administrative support and never letting any of my thousands of sources slip through the cracks.

Going back further in time, I would like to thank my parents, Judy Carrier and Peter Carrier, who taught me so much about the importance of passion and perseverance, as well as effective writing.

Fast-forwarding to the present, I am thankful for the support I have received from my two daughters, Jordan and Brooke Carrier. Throughout the duration of this project, five-year-old Jordan has written numerous "books." I will always remember the untold hours of her sitting by my side studiously doing her "work." And I fear I may also bear some responsibility for three-year-old Brooke's infatuation with colored tape flags, whose many purposes I never fathomed.

My highest gratitude is reserved for my wife, Sharri Horowitz. Sharri has shown more patience and understanding than anyone could reasonably (or unreasonably) ask. I could never have written a book of this scope in 12 months without her unflagging support and tolerance of nights and weekends at the keyboard. In allowing me to pursue my dream, I am eternally grateful to Sharri.

INTRODUCTION

Innovation 2
Innovation's Laws 3
Innovation's Conflict 4
Innovation's Urgency 5
Innovation's Solution: Primer 5
Innovation's Solution: Copyrights 6
Innovation's Solution: Patents 7
Innovation's Solution: Antitrust 9
Innovation's Solution: Innovation 10
Global Application 11
The Road Map 12

Innovation is crucial to us. It is our iPods. Our YouTubes. Our prescription drugs. Our LPs becoming CDs becoming MP3 files. We may not always focus on innovation's importance. But we cannot imagine life without it. Nor is it just us, consumers in American society. Economists, who do not often see eye to eye, have consistently emphasized the significant role that innovation plays in economic growth.

Innovation, however, has been threatened in recent years. Part of the blame, surprisingly enough, lies with the U.S. legal system. The antitrust laws have not sufficiently appreciated innovation. Nor have the intellectual property (IP) regimes—in particular, patent and copyright law. In certain cases, the laws have even stifled innovation.

This book aims to reverse this trend. It offers ten ambitious proposals to foster innovation. The proposals address generic drugs, BlackBerry devices, valid patents, peer-to-peer (P2P) software, and countless other cutting-edge challenges. They promise to improve our patent system. They show how copyright law can promote innovation and not quash fledgling technologies. And they illustrate how antitrust can incorporate innovation, particularly in the pharmaceutical industry.

Of the patent, copyright, and antitrust regimes, the patent system's effects on innovation have received the most attention. Countless books and editorials as well as congressional legislation have sought to remedy the adverse effects of patents. As I show in my proposals, there is still room for better patents, less dangerous patents, and recommendations for the biotechnology industry.

The effects of copyright law, in contrast, have been neglected. Courts have crafted elaborate tests to distinguish beneficial from infringing uses of technologies like P2P software. But such tests have created litigation land mines. I address these and other copyright hurdles to innovation.

Antitrust law also has not paid sufficient attention to innovation. But at least this regime—in contrast to copyright, which is moving in the wrong direction—has improved in recent years. A generation ago, the antitrust laws were hostile to IP and failed to consider innovation. Today the situation is far different. Nonetheless, there is still work to do, particularly in the pharmaceutical industry.

Why has innovation been neglected? One central reason is that it is difficult to measure.[1] The famous parable of the streetlight illustrates the point. A woman searches for her keys under a streetlight not because she dropped her keys there but because that is where the light is.

So too for innovation. Antitrust courts have shined the light on the more measurable indicator of price. Copyright courts have shined the light on the more observable effect of infringement.

But no one has systematically shined the light on innovation. That is the project of this book. The difficulty of measuring innovation does not mean it should be ignored. It only means, given its importance, that we need to redouble our efforts to account for it.

This book also embarks on a new era in the often-chilly IP-antitrust relationship. It recognizes, for the first time, that the IP and antitrust laws can have a positive influence on the other. Learning from each other can replace being at loggerheads. Collaboration, at least in certain areas, can replace conflict. Fresh from the 20th-century battles about which field should be superior, it offers a new, 21st-century road map for the laws.

INNOVATION

Given its central role in this book, the term *innovation* deserves elaboration. Chapter 1 is devoted to just this task, exploring its many facets. To quickly foreshadow, innovation refers to the process by which new and improved products are brought to the market. There are many types of innovation. Just to pick two, radical innovations represent technological breakthroughs, while incremental improvements involve modest changes to existing products. Each has a vital role to play. And as I show throughout the book, the law can have adverse effects on each of these (and other) types of innovation.

Having defined innovation, an even more basic question presents itself: Why devote an entire book to it?

The answer is easy. Innovation is vital to our economy and lives. As I show in Chapter 1, it is essential for economic growth, playing a more direct role than any other factor, such as capital or labor. Innovation also is central to our lives. New drugs improve our health. And new technologies improve our quality of

---

1. There are other reasons. The Chicago School of Economics, for example, has played an important role in promoting the price-based framework that antitrust courts often apply.

life in countless ways as our household devices, access to entertainment, and interactions with others reveal.

Because of its importance, innovation should be favored in the inevitable tradeoffs that confront IP and antitrust law. When copyright law is forced to choose between encouraging creative works of expression and fostering innovative technologies, it should choose the latter. And when antitrust law must select between striking down an agreement that would increase price and upholding it because it would encourage innovation, it should choose the latter.[2]

INNOVATION'S LAWS

Countless sources influence innovation. Education, government funding, firm culture, business climate, and tax incentives all play a role. So do the laws of contracts, torts, and corporate governance. Despite these numerous factors, some of the most direct effects come from the IP and antitrust laws.

The patent system has the most natural connection to innovation. Its goal is to encourage invention, the first step in creating marketable products. Its requirements that an invention be new and not obvious to someone in the field further this objective. And its right to exclude could allow owners to raise price, exclude rivals, or erect bottlenecks to future innovation.

By protecting original works of expression, copyright has encouraged creativity. But the law has also affected technological innovation. Copyright law determines whether dual-use technologies (which create new forms of interaction but also facilitate infringement) will flourish or be stifled in their infancy. It establishes whether exorbitant damages will prevent manufacturers from testing the legality of their activities. And it provides owners of functional devices with the ability to block competition and prevent innovation.[3]

Antitrust law also affects innovation. On the positive side, it can promote competition and remove entry barriers that block innovators.[4] On the negative side, it can (as it did in the mid-20th century) skeptically analyze licensing agreements and other business activity, thereby stifling innovation. In the first decade of the 21st century, it affects innovation in its treatment of standard-setting organizations, patent pools, innovation markets (markets for research and development), and settlements in the pharmaceutical industry.

---

2. A different result could be warranted where activity would significantly raise price but slightly increase innovation.

3. As I discuss in Chapter 2, the U.S. patent and copyright laws are consistent with a utilitarian framework in seeking to increase the number of inventions and creative works in society.

4. I explain the role that competition plays in promoting innovation in my discussion of innovation markets in Chapter 13.

The IP and antitrust laws share a natural overlap. Intellectual property laws operate through exclusion, which has tempted excluded rivals to file antitrust lawsuits and has led courts to lurch between condemning and deferring to such activity. The laws also promise market power, which tees up antitrust concern. As our society has come to rely on industries such as software, Internet-based business, and communications services, antitrust courts more frequently face IP issues.

INNOVATION'S CONFLICT

The traditional view has been that the IP and antitrust laws are in conflict. The reason for the conflict is plain to see. The foundation of the IP system is the right to exclude. This right allows inventors to recover their costs and obtain profits. Relatedly, it discourages "free riders" who imitate the invention and—because they have no costs to recover—undercut the price. The right to exclude, in short, is designed to increase invention.

But the very exclusion at the heart of IP might seem suspicious to antitrust, which focuses on harms to competition. The antitrust laws presume that competition leads to lower prices, higher output, and more innovation. They anticipate that certain agreements between rivals or conduct by monopolists prevents consumers from enjoying these benefits.

For much of the 20th century, courts lacked a justifiable framework for addressing these issues. They concluded that beneficial licensing agreements were likely to injure competition. And they assumed that IP not only intended to, but actually did, give its owner market power in every case. These harms were magnified as copyright's duration and rights expanded, and patents became more powerful and numerous.

At the end of the first decade of the 21st century, many of the most egregious errors have been rectified. Courts and the antitrust agencies have recognized the procompetitive effects of licensing and other IP-based activity. They have applied nuanced analyses to the activities of standard-setting organizations and the sharing of patents in patent pools. And they have come to appreciate that IP does not necessarily lead to market power.

Because of these improvements, there has been much less conflict between the laws. There are still rough spots, as I demonstrate in my proposals for innovation markets and drug settlement agreements.

And we would benefit from minimizing exposure to these issues. For there is no simple answer for antitrust courts considering IP. There is no compass to guide courts in analyzing harms to competition that arise from exclusion but are intended by the IP system. Until a framework for particular issues is hammered out, errors are inevitable and have profound consequences. This book provides an innovation-friendly blueprint that bridges some of the most egregious gaps in the antitrust-IP intersection.

INNOVATION'S URGENCY

The issues presented in this book are of the most pressing urgency. As this book goes to press in 2010, the law in nearly every chapter is in flux. Congress is considering patent reform legislation, statutory damages, and drug settlement agreements. Courts are grappling with dual-use technologies and patent infringement relief. Debates are raging about proposals for scientists to obtain access to patented research tools. The antitrust agencies are at odds with the courts over settlement agreements, and the Federal Trade Commission is split on the issue of innovation markets.

The need to act quickly is vital. Copyright laws on dual-use technologies and statutory damages are stifling new technologies. The Digital Millennium Copyright Act (DMCA) prevents users from improving products. Scientists are denied materials they need for research. And consumers spend billions of unnecessary dollars on prescription drugs because of agreements by which brand-name drug firms pay generics not to enter the market.

INNOVATION'S SOLUTION: PRIMER

The first part of this book provides an accessible introduction to readers interested in innovation, IP, or antitrust issues. A major challenge for a book addressing these topics is the specialized nature of the disciplines. Intellectual property often calls for technical knowledge. Antitrust sometimes requires a background in economics. The antitrust-IP intersection could demand both. My primer avoids any such prerequisites by discussing the issues as clearly as possible.

The primer offers generalist readers the tools needed to follow the breaking innovation stories of the day. And it allows policymakers, business people, lawyers, professors, students, and the interested public to learn one or both of these areas.

It also addresses the chasm that separates the inhabitants of the IP and antitrust universes. Even today, companies, lawyers, and policymakers often reveal fundamental misunderstandings of the other side of the divide.

Antitrust lawyers have been stumped by the patent universe. Just one example is provided by the Antitrust Modernization Commission, created by Congress to determine whether the antitrust laws needed to be modernized. This body, composed of some of the most respected antitrust attorneys in the country, issued a comprehensive report in 2007.

Although it did not call for modernization based on the "new economy," it laid most of the blame for the patent system's maladies at the feet of one doctrine. The Commission criticized the nonobviousness requirement of patentability, which asks whether an invention would have been obvious to a person having "ordinary skill" in the relevant field. This requirement in fact has been weakened in recent years, but the Commission did not even consider the required sacrifices or show how a change in this requirement would single-handedly have restored competition and innovation.

At the same time, many IP lawyers and IP-based companies treat antitrust as a mere speed bump on the path to unfettered protection. In recent years, they have viewed their patents and copyrights as absolute property, not subject to antitrust or any other limits. Just to pick one example, Jack Valenti, the former president of the Motion Picture Association, warned in 2002 that technological restrictions were needed "to protect private property from being pillaged."[5] But as IP gets stronger and lasts longer, antitrust becomes even more crucial. My book offers the two universes the tools they need to address the other half of the innovation divide.

The remainder of the book seeks to foster innovation by improving the copyright, patent, and antitrust laws.

INNOVATION'S SOLUTION: COPYRIGHTS

The typical observer and policymaker links copyright to creativity, not innovation. But in their exclusive focus on copyright infringement, courts have neglected innovation. To ensure that copyright law promotes innovation, the second part of the book offers new proposals for

- P2P software and other *dual-use technologies* used for copyright infringement and lawful purposes;
- *statutory damages*, which can dramatically increase the penalties obtained by copyright owners; and
- the *DMCA*, which prohibits the circumvention of technological measures protecting copyrighted works.

Each of these proposals individually fosters innovation. The first promotes radical and disruptive innovation offered by technologies such as the VCR, TiVo, YouTube, and P2P software. Even though these technologies offer new business models and promise to transform the way we interact, they are continually under assault in courts' analyses. I therefore call for a return to the most deferential test, articulated by the Supreme Court in *Sony Corporation of America v. Universal City Studios*, which protects technologies "capable of substantial non-infringing uses."[6] I show that such a rule is far more likely to promote innovation than any other analysis.

The second proposal addresses statutory damages. The copyright laws give owners, in the case of willful infringement, the ability to recover damages as high as $150,000 per infringing work. In the context of dual-use technologies, which could involve thousands of copyrighted works, potential damages could reach

---

5. Edmund Sanders & Jube Shiver, Jr., *Digital TV Copyright Concerns Tentatively Resolved by Group*, L.A. Times, Apr. 26, 2002, at C5.

6. 464 U.S. 417, 442 (1984).

into the *billions* of dollars. For that reason, I recommend eliminating the remedy for technology manufacturers. Such a proposal would remove the damages sword of Damocles that stifles new technologies and chills venture capitalists.

The third proposal improves the DMCA. The Act has expanded beyond its drafters' intentions in covering functional devices that contain small pieces of software. As a result, owners have prevented interoperability in alarming situations that involve printer toner cartridges and garage door openers. Anyone who has paid an exorbitant price for replacement inkjet printer cartridges (which cost more, per milliliter, than Dom Perignon champagne) knows the power of such control. I thus offer a proposal that limits the Act to the creative works the drafters envisioned.

The copyright proposals also herald a reduced burden for antitrust, as courts will less frequently confront difficult IP-antitrust issues and will not need to craft second-best solutions to IP problems. A limited DMCA that protects music and movies but not household devices would reduce antitrust scrutiny of complex issues. And an appreciation for disruptive new technologies could reduce the market power of entrenched companies. The copyright proposals, in other words, build on recent antitrust improvements in further reducing courts' exposure to the antitrust-IP conflict.

The linking of antitrust and copyright also provides new ideas for proposals to reform copyright. The concept of consumer demand, for example, is essential in antitrust law in determining a firm's market power. Drawing on this concept, this book offers pioneering insights that limit the scope of the DMCA by determining if consumer demand for a device is driven by its expressive copyrightable features or its functional elements.

This book also introduces antitrust's error-costs analysis—which minimizes the "false positive" costs that arise when courts erroneously punish lawful activity—into copyright. Such analysis crystallizes innovation asymmetries that have been neglected, thereby offering fresh insights for copyright law on P2P and other dual-use technologies. Courts' mistaken approval of technologies allowing copyright infringement may harm existing business models but often will not affect creativity. Erroneous condemnation, in contrast, directly harms innovation by permanently stifling technologies.

INNOVATION'S SOLUTION: PATENTS

The connection between the patent system and innovation has received more attention than the link between copyrights and innovation. To forge a tighter link between patents and innovation, the third part of the book introduces proposals offering

- *a post-grant opposition system,* an administrative procedure that allows parties to challenge patents after they are issued;
- a framework for determining *relief in patent infringement cases;*

- potential means to expand access to *patented research tools* in the biotechnology industry; and
- a new template for *material transfer agreements* that increases scientists' access to materials needed for research.

The post-grant opposition system promises better patents by allowing any party to challenge a patent after it is issued. Such a system would provide a quicker and cheaper determination of validity than litigation. And it would target the most valuable patents and reduce the number of invalid patents.

The second proposal curtails patentees' use of injunctions to shut down valuable products. For most of its first 25 years, the Federal Circuit, the appellate court with jurisdiction over patent cases, had ordered injunctive relief in all cases in which it had found patent infringement. But as four million BlackBerry users saw firsthand in 2006, the owner of any one of the hundreds or thousands of patents in a complex product possesses leverage to obtain an injunction shutting down a product. I therefore offer a proposal that fleshes out the framework for relief the Supreme Court articulated in *eBay v. MercExchange*, specifying when courts should deny injunctions.[7]

The third recommendation addresses scientists' access to patented research tools. This issue has been plagued by a significant disconnect between the "law on the books" (in which the Federal Circuit has restricted the most relevant defense, experimental use) and the "law on the ground" (in which industry and academia have crafted informal working solutions). Given the fragile success of such solutions, the three suggestions I offer can be held in reserve until the equilibrium breaks down.

The fourth proposal addresses scientists' needs for tangible materials (such as genes, cell lines, tissues, and organisms) in their research. In contrast to patented research tools, denial and delay of materials have hampered researchers. I thus offer recommendations on publication terms and adherence to model agreements.

Like the copyright section, the patent proposals borrow from antitrust. For example, the question of appropriate relief in patent infringement cases relies on consumer demand in determining whether consumers desire the product because of its infringing component.

The patent recommendations also reduce antitrust's burden. A post-grant opposition system would reduce the number of invalid patents, minimizing antitrust's exposure. And a more nuanced application of patent remedies reduces injunctive relief, relieving antitrust courts—and standard-setting organizations—of some instances of market power and holdup.

---

7. 547 U.S. 388 (2006).

INNOVATION'S SOLUTION: ANTITRUST

Antitrust law has improved its analysis of innovation issues in recent years. But several areas still can be improved. The fourth part of this book endeavors to advance the analysis of three areas:

- *Innovation markets,* in which merging firms are tempted to suppress innovation in research and development (R&D) when there are not yet products on the market;
- The rules of *standard-setting organizations (SSOs);* and
- *Settlement agreements* between brand and generic drug companies.

The first recommendation offers a more justifiable framework for merger challenges that incorporates the odds of drugs reaching the market and of the potential suppression of life-saving products. Should antitrust care when there is no drug on the market but the two firms closest to the market merge? Most commentators have said no. I argue, instead, that innovation-market enforcement is appropriate in the pharmaceutical industry. And I offer a new framework for such analysis.

The second proposal would facilitate the adoption of standards that allow products to work together. Consumers benefit from successful standards when an electrical plug fits into any outlet. Consumers suffer from fragmented standards when Blu-ray and HD-DVD offer incompatible formats for high-definition DVDs. Antitrust traditionally viewed the process of setting standards with suspicion as SSOs tend to be composed of industry rivals discussing sensitive information such as price. I describe the justifications for standard-setting activity in preventing "holdup" of a standard and call for deferential analysis of SSOs and their rules.

The third recommendation promises to bolster generic competition in the drug industry, increasing innovation and saving consumers billions of dollars. The Hatch-Waxman Act, enacted by Congress in 1984, sought to provide incentives for generic firms to challenge brand-name patents. But brand firms have recently paid generics millions of dollars, known as *reverse payments,* to drop their lawsuits and refrain from entering the market. Despite the concerns presented by these settlements, courts have recently blessed them. Building on the Supreme Court's decision in *Verizon Communications v. Trinko,* which underscored the importance in antitrust analysis of a regulatory regime, I explain why settlements with reverse payments should be presumptively illegal.[8]

Unlike the IP proposals, which modestly weaken the effect of patents and copyrights that have become excessively powerful in the past generation, the

---

8. 540 U.S. 398 (2004).

antitrust proposals are more mixed in nature. They call for antitrust's reinvigoration in the context of drug settlement agreements and a more context-specific approach for standards and innovation markets. This more nuanced assessment is the natural consequence of an antitrust regime that has shed its hostility to IP and an IP regime that has tilted strongly in favor of expansion.

In addition to improving antitrust, the proposals benefit IP. A more aggressive approach to drug settlements reduces the influence of weak patents. And a more nuanced approach to SSO rules reaffirms patents while not allowing them to amass excessive leverage.

The antitrust proposals also gain from a more thorough absorption of IP. The realities of drug innovation help determine the appropriate role for innovation-market analysis in the pharmaceutical industry. An appreciation for patent bottlenecks assists in analyzing SSO activity. And examining a proxy for patent validity (through the size of payments from brand firms to generics) provides critical evidence determining the antitrust legality of settlements.

INNOVATION'S SOLUTION: INNOVATION

The proposals offered throughout this book foster innovation at each of its stages. Innovation markets and access to patented research tools and materials apply before the product reaches the market. Recommendations on dual-use technologies and statutory damages enhance the survival of fledgling products. And proposals covering the DMCA, drug settlements, patent remedies, and SSOs prevent the quashing of marketplace rivals.

These proposals are fleshed out by assimilating insights offered by innovation scholars. While these insights have been influential in the business world, they have been largely ignored in the legal setting. This book is the most comprehensive attempt to incorporate the findings of innovation scholars into the law.

One prominent scholar whose ideas have not been considered in the law is Clayton Christensen, who has written several books emphasizing the benefits of disruptive innovation, which displaces existing business models. Christensen has found that disruptive innovators create new markets through simpler, cheaper, and more convenient products. In contrast, the most successful companies, employing the most respected business models, often fail because they are not rewarded for embracing disruptive innovations.

An example is offered by the recording industry. In 2000, the industry could have adapted to the new model that Napster provided. Such a model would have allowed it to meet a small but burgeoning demand for digital music. Instead, the industry sued Napster, only belatedly coming to recognize the potential of digital markets.

Two of my copyright proposals foster disruptive innovation. One bolsters dual-use technology, putting the thumb on the scale of innovation rather than crushing creators under the weight of complicated tests, legal threats, and litigation costs. The second abolishes mammoth statutory damages awards that stifle innovators and venture capital. In promoting disruptive innovation and confining the restrictive application of copyright laws, my proposals seek to cultivate the next iPod, TiVo, or BitTorrent file-sharing software, all the while creating new markets and business models.

Additional insights come from Eric von Hippel, who has written about user innovation, showing the benefits of innovation that originates with users, not manufacturers. I integrate the advantages of user innovation in two proposals. One modifies the DMCA to increase the variety of contributors to products. Copyright holders that have prevented users from improving video games and the activities of robotic pet dogs show the need for such a proposal.

The second recommendation crafts an experimental use defense for non-profit scientists that create research tools. These scientists present many of the characteristics of "lead users" that develop products at the leading edge of uncertain markets. Their research success depends on developing tools, and the "sticky information" they possess about their evolving needs cannot easily be transferred to manufacturers.

The prolific innovation literature has been influential outside the legal universe. But it has not yet been incorporated into (and barely even considered within) the confines of the law. By promoting disruptive and user innovation wherever possible, this book fleshes out the concept of innovation with some of its most exciting and documented variations.

GLOBAL APPLICATION

Although this book focuses most directly on the laws of the United States, many chapters consider other nations' treatments of the issues. Such references serve multiple purposes:

- I explore the different treatment provided by the European Union (EU) and U.S. in the Microsoft case.
- I confirm the growing problem of the DMCA by comparing similar legislation in Australia, China, the EU, and Japan.
- I verify the lack of a problem of access to patented research tools by analyzing empirical studies in Australia, Germany, and Japan.
- I draw lessons for post-grant oppositions from pre-grant systems in Japan and Korea and from the EU's experience with an opposition system.
- I gain ideas for the structure of an opposition system from maintenance fees levied in the EU and Japan.

- I build an experimental use defense by exploring the types of uses allowed by China, Germany, India, Japan, Korea, the Netherlands, and the United Kingdom.

This book should be of global interest even outside these examples. More than 100 countries have antitrust laws. Nearly double that number have signed onto IP treaties. Many nations, including Australia, Brazil, Canada, the EU, Israel, Japan, Singapore, South Africa, and South Korea, have enacted and applied antitrust laws that provide for varying treatment of IP activity. Countries also have moved in the direction of U.S. law by offering stronger IP protection. For nations that look to the U.S. for guidance on these issues, the book portends global appeal.

THE ROAD MAP

Chapters 1 through 5, making up the first part of the book, offer a primer on innovation, IP, and antitrust. Chapter 1 focuses on innovation. It describes its stages and subjects, and discusses several types. It highlights the difficulties of measuring innovation. And it surveys the literature exploring the connection between innovation and economic growth.

Chapter 2 presents IP. It begins by providing an overview of patents and copyrights. It asks whether IP is necessary and examines other incentives for innovation. And it traces dangers of IP protection such as monopoly loss, innovation bottlenecks, and harms to disruptive and user innovation.

Chapter 3 turns to antitrust. It begins with a primer explaining the most important of the regime's doctrines. It then places today's law in context by tracing the history of antitrust law. I conclude by surveying the evidence on the need for antitrust.

Chapter 4 examines the intersection of the IP and antitrust laws. It begins by discussing the conflict between the areas. I then trace the three stages of the intersection in the 20th century, in which courts first refused to impose liability for patent-based activity, then limited patentees' power, then moved toward a predominant IP. I conclude by examining important agency guidelines and courts' analyses of refusals to license.

Chapter 5 follows the intersection into the 21st century. It focuses on the antitrust case against Microsoft in the United States and EU. And it discusses the most important issues in the intersection today: innovation markets, SSOs, patent pools, and settlements and other questionable activity in the pharmaceutical industry.

Having set the stage for the innovation proposals, Chapters 6 through 15 introduce the proposals. The second part of the book focuses on copyright law. Of all the changes recommended, the copyright proposals promise to unleash the greatest amount of innovation.

Chapter 6 explores dual-use technologies. It shows the legal hurdles confronting such technologies, which are evaluated in their infancy and do not stand a chance against the widespread infringement offered by copyright holders. It demonstrates that the tradeoff between creativity and innovation is not as intractable as it first appears. Chapter 6 also explains how the deferential *Sony* rule is far more likely to promote radical, disruptive innovation than any other conceivable tests. And, to pick one example, it shows how P2P's decentralized architecture could offer an effective antidote to centralized cloud computing and Google's search engine predominance.

Chapter 7 analyzes the related issue of the danger posed by statutory damages. Copyright owners' ability to recover damages of $150,000 for each infringing work exerts a chilling effect on technology creators and venture capitalists. Given the silent effects of vanquished technologies and the gulf between Congress's intent in creating statutory damages and their use in this setting, this chapter recommends the elimination of the remedy for secondary infringers.

Chapter 8 addresses the DMCA, which prevents the circumvention of technological measures controlling access to copyrighted works. Because software is one such work, the Act has been stretched to cover functional products. But Congress sought to protect against movie and music piracy, not to shield functional devices. To implement the drafters' intent, I propose new limits to the DMCA.

The third part of the book addresses patents. These issues have received significant attention in recent years. I offer four proposals. Two apply generally to all patents. And two focus on the biotechnology industry, which has witnessed a plethora of proposals in recent years.

Chapter 9 seeks to create better patents by proposing a post-grant opposition system that would allow any party to challenge a patent after it has been issued. Many have called for such a change, but the specifics of an opposition process remain controversial. For that reason, I set forth numerous details of my proposed system.

Chapter 10 endeavors to create less dangerous patents by focusing on the framework for patent infringement relief. I flesh out the Supreme Court's *eBay* framework and explain when courts should award injunctions.

The book next turns to the biotechnology industry. Chapter 11 addresses the question of whether scientists are able to use patented research tools. I conclude that informal arrangements have, at least for now, prevented bottlenecks. But because this precarious equilibrium is subject to change, I offer several proposals if the situation deteriorates.

Chapter 12 addresses researchers' needs for tangible materials. Unlike the situation of patented research tools, scientists often cannot circumvent a refusal to license materials. I recount the evidence showing the problem of denial and delay of materials for scientific research. And I conclude with two recommendations.

The fourth part of the book addresses antitrust law. Improvements in antitrust's treatment of innovation have dispensed with the need for many proposals, leaving only three—one that confirms existing treatment and two that substantially revise it.

Chapter 13 examines innovation markets. It shows why the many criticisms of the concept can be rebutted in the pharmaceutical industry. And it creates a new framework to apply to innovation markets.

Chapter 14 addresses standards. It demonstrates the power bestowed on owners whose patents are incorporated into a standard. And it concludes that courts and the antitrust agencies should uphold standard-setting activity in the vast majority of cases.

Chapter 15 addresses patent settlements. Agreements by which brand-name drug companies have paid generic firms to delay entering the market have upset the delicate regulatory balance offered by the Hatch-Waxman Act. I demonstrate why presumptive illegality for these agreements is warranted.

The book's conclusion demonstrates the benefits of treating the IP and antitrust laws together. It recounts the wide swath of the economy and expanse of cutting-edge innovation topics covered by the proposals. It shows how the recommendations rescue Congress's intent. It recaps the nuance and practical nature of the proposals. And it underscores the global appeal of the topics and analysis of the laws of Australia, China, the EU, India, Japan, and Korea.

Measurement difficulties have kept innovation in the dark. Courts have shined their lights elsewhere—on price or copyright infringement. This book illuminates the light of innovation and shines it across an expansive range of business activity. The result: new proposals that show just how innovation has been neglected.

Like anyone losing a security blanket, it may make us apprehensive to abandon our crutches of price and creativity. But we must introduce innovation into copyright, patent, and antitrust law. We have no choice. Our livelihoods and our economy demand no less.

PART I

PRIMER

Innovation is everywhere. If there is any doubt, just check the newspaper headlines:

- "Supreme Court finds Grokster liable for copyright infringement."
- "Stem cell researchers hail breakthrough."
- "Microsoft liable for violating antitrust laws."
- "Bayer pays Barr $400 million to abandon generic Cipro."
- "Blackberry users face shutdown from patent ruling."

The reader may have an interest in these stories. But comprehension often lies behind a veil of secret code. This code is the law. Like any initiation, the laws affecting innovation do not make it easy for newcomers.

Patent law has its own language, of "claims," "patent prosecution," "interferences," and other specialized terms freely exchanged among members of the patent bar, if few others. This regime is often counterintuitive, with "final rejections" not final and "public use" not public.

Antitrust is no better, with its economics footing and inhospitable terminology. Courts bandy about "average variable cost" and "deadweight loss." And agencies discuss the "Herfindahl-Hirschman Index (HHI)" and "small but significant and nontransitory increases in price (SSNIP)."

Even copyright law—the regime with the least amount of secret code—grapples with challenging software issues, not to mention client-server and peer-to-peer (P2P) architectures.

These codes obscure comprehension. And the difficulties mount when the codes come together in the antitrust-intellectual property (IP) intersection.

Nor are the challenges unique to generalist readers. As I explain in the Introduction, antitrust and IP attorneys are often challenged by the other discipline.

In this book, I do not assume familiarity with any of the areas. Nor do I assume knowledge of economics, science, or technology.

Given the increasing convergence of the areas, the overview of the laws I offer in Chapters 1 through 5 promises to be helpful.

Chapter 1 introduces innovation. It discusses its various elements. And it introduces, as simply as possible, concepts such as the link between innovation and economic growth.

Chapter 2 tackles IP. It provides background on the patent and copyright systems by explaining what creators must do to obtain protection, what rights are provided by the laws, why we have the regimes, and whether we need them.

Chapter 3 turns to antitrust. It discusses the law's provisions as well as the reasons we have it and whether it achieves its goals.

Chapters 4 and 5 trace the history of the IP-antitrust intersection in the 20th and 21st centuries. They explore courts' varying treatments of business activity including patent pools, standard-setting organizations, settlement agreements, and refusals to license, as well as the Microsoft case.

In short, the first part of the book provides a tool kit for readers seeking to understand the pressing innovation stories of the day. For those ensconced in one of the fields, it offers a quick primer on the other. And for all, it offers a legal tour guide to accompany us on our journey to promote innovation in the 21st century.

1. INNOVATION

Definition 19
Stages 20
Subjects 20
Other Factors 22
Examples 24
    Early 20th-century Innovations 25
    Mid 20th-century Innovations 25
    Late 20th and Early 21st-century Innovations 25
Types of Innovation 26
    Discrete and Complex Innovation 26
    Radical and Incremental Innovation 26
    Disruptive and Sustaining Innovation 27
    User and Manufacturer Innovation 28
    My Proposals and Innovation 29
Measurement 30
Innovation and Economic Growth 31

The reader likely will be familiar with the term *innovation*. It is impossible to pick up a newspaper or financial report without coming across it. Given that innovation is the subject of this book, it is helpful to start by exploring its many facets.

This chapter begins by defining innovation and describing its stages and subjects. It then examines factors that affect innovation such as government funding, education, and tax policy. Next, it offers examples of innovation, reveals different types, and highlights the difficulties of measuring it. The chapter concludes by surveying the literature that explores the link between innovation and economic growth.

DEFINITION

I begin with a definition:

Innovation consists of the discovery, development, and commercialization of new and improved products and processes.

This definition can be fleshed out by exploring the various stages, subjects, and types of innovation.

STAGES

The first inquiry involves innovation's stages.[1] The initial stage consists of *invention* or *discovery*. Invention refers to the implementation of an idea, typically through prototypes or models.[2] Although inventions may appear inevitable in hindsight, this is far from the case ahead of time. The patent system is designed to award patents for inventions that are new and not obvious to persons in the field.

The second stage involves *development*, the array of activities by which a concept is modified and perfected until it becomes a marketable product. A company frequently engages in trial-and-error testing at this stage. In the pharmaceutical industry, for example, only one out of thousands of tested chemical compounds survives preclinical and clinical trials to reach the market.

The third stage, which in some cases precedes the second, includes *entrepreneurship* and *investment*. In this stage, the innovator decides to commercialize the invention, attain financial support, cultivate the market, and risk funds.

The final stage involves *diffusion*, by which a product spreads through the market. Licensing is vital in this stage, especially for universities, independent inventors, and small businesses that may not be able to commercialize the product themselves. In addition, competitors often follow the pioneering firm's lead, particularly where disruptive technologies uncover new markets and customers.

The proposals I offer in the book affect each of the stages. The opposition system I propose in Chapter 9 more tightly links patents with invention. I address development in Chapter 13 by incorporating the realities of drug innovation into antitrust analysis of mergers between firms with products not yet on the market. I aim to revive investment in disruptive technologies in Chapters 6 and 7, which address dual-use technologies and statutory damages. And I focus on diffusion in Chapter 4 (in evaluating courts' improved analysis of licensing) and Chapter 14 (in justifying antitrust deference to standard-setting organizations, which encourage the dissemination of products that can work together).

SUBJECTS

In addition to innovation's stages, my definition requires an analysis of its subjects. The innovations I consider in the book are protected by intellectual property (IP)—patented inventions and copyrighted works in particular. Many vital innovations that have contributed to economic growth have been protected by IP.

---

1. This structure is adapted from F.M. SCHERER & DAVID ROSS, INDUSTRIAL MARKET STRUCTURE AND ECONOMIC PERFORMANCE 616 (2d ed. 1980).

2. Robert P. Merges, *Commercial Success and Patent Standards: Economic Perspectives on Innovation*, 76 CAL. L. REV. 803, 808 (1988).

Patented inventions play significant roles in many industries. And copyrights have been important for innovation, especially since 1980, when Congress granted such protection to computer software.

The umbrella of IP typically embraces trademarks and trade secrets as well. Nonetheless, these subjects are not a direct focus of this book. The primary function of trademarks is to reduce customer confusion by preventing the imitation of well-known marks. To be sure, trademarks could affect innovation, as franchising agreements and pharmaceutical marketing reveal.[3] But such effects are less frequent and present less challenging issues than patent and copyright law.[4]

In addition, issues less often arise at the intersection of the trademark and antitrust laws. The market power that arises from a mark, for example, typically presents fewer concerns than the control over products that patents and copyrights can bestow.

The link between trade secrecy and innovation is more direct. A firm that holds, as a secret, information that is valuable and that it makes reasonable efforts to protect can sue anyone who misappropriates the information. Firms tend to elect trade secrecy rather than patents when they do not wish to disclose information. But unlike the patent, copyright, and antitrust laws, the law of trade secrets has not erected innovation roadblocks.

Trade secrets also do not typically implicate antitrust concerns. They are less likely than patents or copyrights to present market power.[5] In contrast to patents, which allow owners to prevent independent invention, trade secrets do not offer strong exclusionary rights.[6] They only prevent a party from acquiring a secret by improper means or using or disclosing it in breach of a confidential relationship. Rivals can always independently discover and protect information that is the subject of an existing trade secret.[7] As a result, trade secret owners are less likely to possess market power.[8]

---

3. *See* Herbert Hovenkamp et al., IP and Antitrust: An Analysis of Antitrust Principles Applied to Intellectual Property Law § 21.5a4, at 21–92 (2002) (franchisor could require franchisee who wishes to license trademarks also to buy its products); Nexium, http://www.purplepill.com/index.aspx (last visited August 28, 2008) (AstraZeneca markets heartburn medication through purple trademark).

4. *See also* U.S. Dep't of Justice & Fed. Trade Comm'n, Antitrust Guidelines for the Licensing of Intellectual Property § 1.0, at 1 n.1 (Apr. 9, 1995) (explaining that the Guidelines address "innovation-related issues" that arise with patent, copyright, and other agreements rather than "product differentiation issues" implicated by trademarks).

5. Courts have never presumed market power from trade secrets. *E.g., In re Data Gen. Corp. Antitrust Litig.*, 490 F. Supp. 1089, 1113–14 (N.D. Cal. 1980).

6. *See* 3 Roger M. Milgrim, Milgrim on Trade Secrets § 10.01[1][c][ii], at 10–53 (2008).

7. They can also reverse engineer (or work backward from) the product.

8. *See* Mark A. Lemley, *Trade Secrets and Antitrust*, 26 ALI—ABA Continuing Legal Educ. 285 (1996). Although refusals to share trade secrets could conceivably lead to

Trade secrets also do not present significant collusion concerns. Their owners have no desire to share their secrets with rivals. Antitrust concerns presented by patent pools or standard-setting organizations are absent.[9] Even licensees can compete with trade secret owners who license products containing the secret.[10]

OTHER FACTORS

The centerpiece of this book is the relationship between innovation and the patent, copyright, and antitrust laws. Courts, Congress, and scholars have not sufficiently appreciated this connection, and there are enough vital, complex issues presented to fill a book. But the reader should keep in mind that innovation is affected by many additional factors. Other important determinants include

- government funding for basic research
- the educational system
- science and engineering talent
- company atmosphere
- business climate
- tax policy
- other laws[11]

First, government funding for basic research plays a vital role in innovation. Scientists conduct basic research to achieve fundamental knowledge that eventually yields specific applications. Such research was crucial in creating transistors, computers, the Internet, communications technologies, and laser applications. In the past two decades, however, the United States has not followed other nations in significantly increasing the percentage of gross domestic product (GDP) it has

---

bottlenecks, owners in litigated cases have relied on other forms of IP, reducing the salience of determining an appropriate antitrust rule for trade secrets. *See* Katarzyna A. Czapracka, *Antitrust and Trade Secrets: The U.S. and the EU Approach*, 24 SANTA CLARA COMPUTER & HIGH TECH. L.J. 207, 244–48 (2008) (citing cases).

9. Antitrust issues nonetheless might arise when trade secret license provisions are used to extend patent protection beyond the end of the patent term. *See* HOVENKAMP ET AL., § 2.5a2, at 2–61. They also could occur when trade secret royalties extend beyond the life of the trade secret. MILGRIM, § 10.01[1][c][ii], at 10–55.

10. Czapracka, at 248. Licensing also is beneficial in disseminating the secret beyond the trade secret owner.

11. *See* THE ADVISORY COMMITTEE ON MEASURING INNOVATION IN THE 21ST CENTURY ECONOMY, INNOVATION MEASUREMENT: TRACKING THE STATE OF INNOVATION IN THE AMERICAN ECONOMY 12 (2008) [hereinafter INNOVATION MEASUREMENT].

spent on research and development (R&D).[12] As a result, the United States fell from second in the world in this measure (behind Japan) in 1991 to fifth (behind Israel, Finland, South Korea, and Japan) in 2004. Between 1970 and 2005, federal investment in physical sciences and engineering research fell by 50 percent.[13]

Second, the education system plays a significant role. Fewer U.S. students, particularly women and minorities, are pursuing science and engineering careers. As the *Innovate America* report of the Council on Competitiveness lamented: "U.S. high school students underperform most of the world on international math and science tests," with this performance declining as the students advance in school. The United States has fallen to seventeenth in the percentage of the college-age population earning science and engineering degrees, down from third a few decades ago. Two of many potential solutions to these problems include better education funding, particularly for science and engineering; and the revamping of curricula from kindergarten to graduate school to emphasize problem-based learning that crosses traditional discipline boundaries.[14]

A third factor affecting innovation is the pool of human talent. Although the United States has attracted science and engineering talent from abroad, immigration policies have hampered this ability. In particular, visa policies instituted after 9/11 have led to delays and difficulties that have reduced the influx of scientific talent. The *Innovate America* report reasonably suggested automatic work permits and residency status for foreign students with graduate degrees in science and engineering from American universities who "have been offered jobs by U.S.-based employers" and "have passed security screening tests."[15]

Fourth, company atmosphere and organizational structures matter. Firms display varying levels of toleration for risk and appreciation for a long-term perspective.[16] One noted example is Google, which has allowed employees to

---

12. GDP signifies gross domestic product and is a frequently used indicator of national output. PAUL A. SAMUELSON & WILLIAM D. NORDHAUS, ECONOMICS 568 (17th ed. 2001).

13. THE TASK FORCE ON THE FUTURE OF AMERICAN INNOVATION, MEASURING THE MOMENT: INNOVATION, NATIONAL SECURITY, AND ECONOMIC COMPETITIVENESS: BENCHMARKS OF OUR INNOVATION FUTURE II 4, 8, 9 (2006), http://www.futureofinnovation.org.

14. COUNCIL ON COMPETITIVENESS, INNOVATE AMERICA 19, 22, 49, 76 (2005), http://www.compete.org/images/uploads/File/PDF%20Files/NII_Innovate_America.pdf. *See also* CLAUDIA GOLDIN & LAWRENCE F. KATZ, THE RACE BETWEEN EDUCATION AND TECHNOLOGY 350–51 (2008) (recommending "greater access to quality pre-school education for children from disadvantaged families," improved K–12 schooling, and increased transparency and generosity of college financial aid).

15. *Id.* at 51.

16. ORGANISATION FOR ECONOMIC COOPERATION AND DEVELOPMENT, OSLO MANUAL: PROPOSED GUIDELINES FOR COLLECTING AND INTERPRETING Technological INNOVATION DATA, at 15, http://www.oecd.org/dataoecd/35/61/2367580.pdf (last visited June 30, 2008).

spend 20 percent of their time on projects not related to their daily jobs, fostering a culture that has spawned innovations such as Gmail.[17] As the numerous books discussing management techniques and organizational structures attest, these issues substantially affect a firm's efficiency and innovation.

Fifth, the state of the economy and business climate play a role. Access to financing and venture capital affects the ability to bring inventions to the market. Given that inventors, particularly small businesses, usually lack the ability to commercialize their inventions, such financing is crucial.

Tax policy is sixth. Tax credits can encourage R&D. Accelerated depreciation, which allows greater deductions—and thus less taxable income—in the early years of an asset's life,[18] can encourage investment in equipment. And tax changes giving preferential treatment to capital gains also can increase investment.[19]

Seventh, laws other than IP and antitrust are significant. Corporate governance laws affect managers' incentives to take the risks needed for innovation. Contract law shapes the enforceability of licenses, which determines whether a creator develops the invention itself or licenses it to others. And by exposing firms to liability, tort law also can affect innovation.

In short, innovation is affected by an expansive array of factors. Although I focus on the IP and antitrust laws in this book, the reader should keep in mind that the overall innovation framework involves many other elements.

Having sketched the factors affecting innovation, a quick survey of examples demonstrates what is at stake for our economy and society.

EXAMPLES

Even a listing of innovations in the past hundred years reminds us of their centrality to our lives.[20]

---

17. *Google Gets the Message, Launches Gmail*, GOOGLE, Apr. 1, 2004, http://www.google.com/press/pressrel/gmail.html.

18. *Accelerated Depreciation*, INVESTOPEDIA, http://www.investopedia.com/terms/a/accelerateddepreciation.asp (last visited June 28, 2008).

19. F.M. SCHERER, NEW PERSPECTIVES ON ECONOMIC GROWTH AND TECHNOLOGICAL INNOVATION 83–86 (1999).

20. The examples are taken from RODNEY CARLISLE, SCIENTIFIC AMERICAN INVENTIONS AND DISCOVERIES: ALL THE MILESTONES IN INGENUITY FROM THE DISCOVERY OF FIRE TO THE INVENTION OF THE MICROWAVE OVEN (2004); COLUMBIA ENCYCLOPEDIA (6th ed. 2001); THE NEW YORK PUBLIC LIBRARY DESK REFERENCE (Paul Fargis et al. eds., 1989); and WORLD OF INVENTION (Bridget Travers ed., 1994). Any such recitation is bound to elicit debate on the innovations included and dates selected. But the overall point of innovation's importance stands.

Early 20th-Century Innovations

- Air conditioner (1902)
- Radio amplifier (1906)
- Home vacuum cleaner (1907)
- Cellophane (1908)
- Zipper (1913)
- 35-millimeter photographic camera (1914)
- Television (1923)
- Penicillin (1928)
- Jet engine (1930)
- Radar (1934–35)

Mid 20th-Century Innovations

- Microwave oven (1945)
- Atomic bomb (1945)
- Radiocarbon dating (1947)
- Velcro (1948)
- DNA (1953)
- Transistor radio (1954)
- Lasers (1954)
- Electric guitar (1956)
- Communications satellites (1958)
- Integrated circuit (1959)
- Oral contraceptive (1960)

Late 20th and Early 21st-Century Innovations

- Digital camera (1972)
- Personal computer (1973)
- Genetic engineering (1973)
- Kevlar® brand fiber (1976)
- Cellular telephone (1978)
- Walkman (1979)
- Internet protocol (1983)
- World Wide Web (1989–90)
- Cloning of mammals (1996)
- Web TV (1996)
- MP3 player (1998)
- Electric artificial heart (2001)
- Genetic sequencing (2001)

TYPES OF INNOVATION

The breadth of innovations has led to distinctions between various categories. This section describes (1) discrete and complex, (2) radical and incremental, (3) disruptive and sustaining, and (4) user and manufacturer innovations. The overview does not explore every facet of the categories but introduces concepts that will be developed throughout the book.

Discrete and Complex Innovation

The first distinction is between discrete and complex technologies. Discrete inventions are well-defined, with a single patent typically covering a product. As examples from the pharmaceutical and chemical industries reveal, they stand on their own and do not incorporate a large number of components. In addition, they themselves are not components of a larger product or system. As a result, firms often can recover the costs of invention by exploiting the patent through licensing or commercialization.[21]

Complex technologies (in, say the software, electronics, and semiconductor industries) consist of numerous patents. Because firms do not have control over all the essential components of the technologies, they often enter into cross-licensing arrangements with other patent owners.[22] The technologies frequently are characterized by cumulative innovation, in which one generation's invention builds on those of previous generations. Cumulative innovation occurs in the automobile, aircraft, semiconductor, computer hardware, and software industries, and calls for nuanced analysis since strong patent rights help the initial innovator but hurt subsequent ones.[23]

Radical and Incremental Innovation

Innovations occur along a continuum ranging from incremental to radical. Incremental innovations involve modest changes to existing products that serve existing customer needs. Radical innovations represent technological breakthroughs that are completely different from existing products and often render

---

21. Robert P. Merges & Richard R. Nelson, *On the Complex Economics of Patent Scope*, 90 COLUM. L. REV. 839, 880–81 (1990) (describing discrete and cumulative inventions as well as chemical and science-based technologies).

22. Wesley M. Cohen et al., *Protecting Their Intellectual Assets: Appropriability Conditions and Why U.S. Manufacturing Firms Patent (or not)*, at 19 (Nat'l Bureau of Econ. Research, Working Paper No. 7552, 2000).

23. Michael A. Carrier, *Resolving the Patent-Antitrust Paradox Through Tripartite Innovation*, 56 VAND. L. REV. 1047, 1082 & n.158 (2003); *see generally* Suzanne Scotchmer, *Standing on the Shoulders of Giants: Cumulative Research and the Patent Law*, 5 J. ECON. PERSP. 29 (1991).

them obsolete.[24] These two types of innovations complement each other. Radical innovations introduce new systems but often are improved by incremental changes.[25]

The concept of radical innovation is often linked to disruptive innovation. While the two often overlap, they differ in their focus. *Radical* refers to the size of the innovation while *disruptive* refers to the size of the impact.[26]

Disruptive and Sustaining Innovation

Innovation scholar Clayton Christensen has influentially distinguished between *disruptive* and *sustaining* innovations. Disruptive innovations displace existing business models by creating simpler, more convenient, and cheaper products that appeal to new or less-demanding customers. Sustaining innovations, in contrast, improve existing products and involve incremental innovation.[27] Disruptive innovations often overlap with radical breakthroughs but sometimes represent advances in business models (as seen through Amazon.com's competition with Barnes & Noble) or companies "scaling up a niche market into a mass market."[28]

Leading companies have been successful at implementing sustaining innovations but have failed to keep pace with disruptive, radical innovations.[29] Why are established firms slow to respond? Because of their investments in employees, equipment, and materials linked to the existing technology.[30]

Leading firms also prefer sustaining innovations, which allow them to service their existing customers. In contrast to speculative future markets for disruptive technologies, sustaining innovations permit companies to raise their share price by increasing growth. And they are consistent with good management practices that include tracking rivals and investing in more profitable products.[31]

---

24. *Incremental vs. Radical Innovation*, INNOVATION ZEN, http://innovationzen.com/blog/2006/08/04/innovation-management-theory-part-2/ (last visited June 29, 2008); Robert Atkinson & Howard Wial, *Boosting Productivity, Innovation, and Growth Through a National Innovation Foundation*, at 5, Apr. 2008, http://www.itif.org/files/NIF.pdf.

25. Bart Verspagen, *Innovation and Economic Growth, in* THE OXFORD HANDBOOK OF INNOVATION 487, 494 (Jan Fagerberg et al. eds., 2005).

26. *See* Posting of Venkat to Innovate on Purpose blog, http://innovateonpurpose.blogspot.com/2008/03/incremental-and-disruptive-innovation.html (Mar. 6, 2008, 12:25 EST).

27. CLAYTON M. CHRISTENSEN & MICHAEL E. RAYNOR, THE INNOVATOR'S SOLUTION: CREATING AND SUSTAINING SUCCESSFUL GROWTH 32 (2003).

28. Constantinos Markides, *Disruptive Innovation: In Need of Better Theory*, 23 J. PRODUCT INNOVATION MGMT. 19, 19–24 (2006).

29. CLAYTON M. CHRISTENSEN, THE INNOVATOR'S DILEMMA: WHEN NEW TECHNOLOGIES CAUSE GREAT FIRMS TO FAIL 42 (1997).

30. JAMES M. UTTERBACK, MASTERING THE DYNAMICS OF INNOVATION: HOW COMPANIES CAN SEIZE OPPORTUNITIES IN THE FACE OF TECHNOLOGICAL CHANGE 163 (1994).

31. CHRISTENSEN, at 45, 98, 132–33, 147.

Firms entering a market, on the other hand, hold an advantage over established firms in pursuing disruptive innovations, which do not generate value in the existing network.[32] Entrants have more flexibility and are not burdened by "human and physical assets geared to highly specific production." Such firms, in short, have "every economic incentive to overturn the existing order" and "little to lose" in pursuing disruptive innovation.[33]

The list of disruptive innovators demonstrates the importance of this type of innovation. Christensen discusses more than 70 examples. A few include

- Amazon.com, a low-end disruption relative to bookstores
- Canon photocopiers, which partially replaced copy centers
- Charles Schwab, the online trading discount broker
- Community colleges, which enrolled nontraditional students
- eBay, which created auctions for low-budget collectible owners
- Henry Ford's Model T, which vastly increased the number of car owners
- Google, which disrupted directories such as the Yellow Pages
- Inkjet printers, which enabled students and others to become printer owners
- Intuit's TurboTax, which disrupted personal tax preparation service
- Online travel agencies such as Expedia and Travelocity, which disrupted full-service agencies[34]

Peer-to-peer (P2P) technology offers recent examples of disruptive innovation. Joost, for example, lets users watch TV while using chat and instant messaging tools. Skype offers free phone calls over the Internet. And BitTorrent allows the distribution of large files such as amateur movies.

User and Manufacturer Innovation

Professor Eric von Hippel has traced a different distinction in focusing on the identity of the innovator. He has explained that users tend to develop "functionally novel" innovations that incorporate information about their desires. Manufacturers, in contrast, develop "improvements on well-known needs."[35]

One of the promising consequences of user innovation is its ability to improve manufacturers' high market failure rates. Von Hippel concludes that manufacturers' "poor understanding of users' needs" explains why many of their

---

32. *Id.* at 55.

33. UTTERBACK, at 161, 164. *See also* Rebecca M. Henderson & Kim B. Clark, *Architectural Innovation: The Reconfiguration of Existing Product Technologies and the Failure of Established Firms*, 35 ADMINISTRATIVE SCI. Q. 9, 13 (1990) (describing architectural innovation, which emphasizes the use of "existing core design concepts in a new architecture" and results in established firms facing "a surprising degree of difficulty in adapting" to the innovation).

34. *See* CHRISTENSEN & RAYNOR, at 56–65.

35. ERIC VON HIPPEL, DEMOCRATIZING INNOVATION 8 (2005).

products do not succeed. User innovations offer better information. They also benefit consumers and the economy since most such innovations are developed by "lead users" who create new products "at the leading edge of markets where potential sales are small and uncertain."[36]

Examples of user innovation are all around us. Von Hippel discusses instances involving library search systems, sports communities, and hospital surgeons.[37] The Web site instructables.com allows users to document how-to projects such as cutting and folding box springs, demonstrating top kissing forms, and building PC cases out of Coca-Cola merchandise.[38] Users have employed inkjet printers to print images on birthday cakes and edible paper on sushi.[39] And open source software has allowed multiple users to create products such as the Linux operating system, Apache web server, and Firefox web browser.

My Proposals and Innovation

In this book, I do not impose a minimum threshold of innovation that products are required to meet. I rely, instead, on the subject matter of the patent and copyright regimes. To receive a patent, an applicant must show, among other things, that its creation is new and would not have been obvious to a person of "ordinary skill" in the relevant field. Relatedly, copyright protection requires originality. Because the IP laws protect incremental innovation, and because such innovation plays a vital role in improving breakthrough inventions and serving customer needs, borrowing the innovation threshold set by the IP laws makes more sense than arbitrarily seeking to protect only certain types of "worthy" innovations.

I also do not impose requirements that innovations be "beneficial." Some innovations—as asbestos, lead pipes, and nuclear power attest—may ultimately have harmful effects on society. But other regimes, such as environmental law and health regulation, are better able to draw these lines.[40] The IP systems, as well as my innovation proposals, do not offer the tools to make these distinctions.

Despite the expansive conception of innovation, several of my proposals foster the disruptive and user innovations discussed in this section. Radical, disruptive innovation is furthered by my proposals (1) to recognize the legality of nearly all "dual-use" technologies, which could be used for lawful purposes as well as copyright infringement and (2) to eliminate statutory damages that excessively

---

36. *Id.* at 107–08.

37. *Id.* at 25–30.

38. Instructables, http://www.instructables.com/ (last visited August 7, 2008).

39. David Bernstein, *When the Sous-Chef Is an Inkjet*, N.Y. Times, Feb. 3, 2005, http://www.nytimes.com/2005/02/03/technology/circuits/03chef.html?pagewanted=1&ei=5088&en=86bc342e2ce05d47&ex=1265086800&partner=rssnyt.

40. Michael A. Gollin, Driving Innovation: Intellectual Property Strategies for a Dynamic World 20–21 (2008).

punish technology manufacturers. User innovation would be encouraged by (1) modifications to the Digital Millennium Copyright Act (DMCA) that promote competition and (2) wider dissemination of research tools in the biotechnology industry.

MEASUREMENT

A central challenge confronting innovation is its measurement. The dimensions of price and quantity upon which economists have long focused do not wholly capture innovation's benefits.[41] Some results—for example, gains from the convenience of cell phones and the efficiency of e-mail and Internet shopping—improve quality of life in ways not easily measured.[42] Intangible items, such as IP used within a company or licensed to others, often are not quantified. And on an economy-wide level, new products are not easily encapsulated in U.S. income and productivity figures.[43]

For these reasons, antitrust courts and scholars have focused primarily on the effects of business activity on price. They have sought to promote *allocative efficiency* by emphasizing the relation between price and the marginal cost of producing an item.[44] Innovation has only recently appeared on the radar screen, and it still often takes a backseat to price.

The government's measurement tools offer scant assistance. Innovation measurement has been "piecemeal, incomplete, and accidental" and is "in its infancy." This is not much of a surprise given that the U.S. statistical agencies were created for other reasons.[45] The National Income and Product Accounts, for example, provide the framework for estimating output, income, expenditure, and wealth in the U.S. economy. The accounts "help[ed] policymakers deal with the severe economic fluctuations produced by the Great Depression and World War II" but have not measured innovation or ascertained the causes of long-term productivity growth.[46]

It is possible to improve the collection of data on innovation. A 2008 report to the Secretary of Commerce offered several proposals to address these issues. This report found that the government could combine the data collected from various agencies such as the Bureau of Labor Statistics and Bureau of Economic Analysis. It could create new accounts for measuring intangible assets. It could

---

41. Manuel Trajtenberg, Economic Analysis of Product Innovation 4, 12 (1990).

42. *See* Samuelson & Nordhaus, at 586.

43. Benn Steil et al., *Introduction and Overview, in* Technological Innovation and Economic Performance 45 (2002).

44. Marginal cost signifies the change in total cost from producing one additional unit.

45. Innovation Measurement, at 2, 5.

46. *Id.* at 7.

improve data from the service sector, which has lagged behind manufacturing data. And it could increase public access to data to facilitate more widespread innovation research.[47]

Difficulties in measuring innovation have led economists and antitrust courts to emphasize the more measurable unit of price. But in shining the spotlight on price, they have neglected innovation.

My goal in this book is to erect a sustained focus on innovation that ranges across IP and antitrust law. To be sure, my innovation spotlight often will not be as precise as the one shining on price. Innovation has too many characteristics to be reducible to a single metric. But at least the project shines a second light. Given the importance of innovation to economic growth, such action is vital.

INNOVATION AND ECONOMIC GROWTH

For the past half-century, economists have analyzed the connection between innovation and economic growth. More precisely, they have traced the role of technological change—new and improved products and processes—in explaining productivity growth. Such growth is typically measured by the increase in output per unit of input.[48]

Treatments of the connection in the modern era trace back to Nobel Prize winner Robert Solow.[49] Solow addressed the difficulties of measuring technological change by modeling a "growth accounting" approach. This approach isolated the contributions of various inputs—primarily labor (workers' education and training) and capital (equipment) to output growth. Any such growth not explained by an increase in inputs was attributed to technological change.[50] Solow found that this percentage was 87 percent.[51]

---

47. *Id.* at 7–13.

48. SCHERER, at 24.

49. Adam Smith, David Ricardo, and Thomas Malthus explored the issue in the 18th and 19th centuries. For 20th-century treatment preceding Solow, see SOLOMON FABRICANT, ECONOMIC PROGRESS AND ECONOMIC CHANGE, 34TH ANNUAL REPORT OF THE NATIONAL BUREAU OF ECONOMIC RESEARCH (1954) (90 percent of increase in output per capita between 1871 and 1951 was attributable to technical progress); Moses Abramovitz, *Resource and Output Trends in the United States Since 1870,* 46 AM. ECON. REV. 5, 8 (1956) (increase in productivity played important role in quadrupling of net national product per capita between 1869–78 and 1944–53); John W. Kendrick, *Productivity Trends: Capital and Labor,* 38 REV. ECON. STAT. 248, 251 (1956) (productivity gains accounted for 53 percent of growth). Solow's article may have had the impact it did because "his analysis was structured by a 'formal' theory whereas the earlier theories were . . . considered looser by the profession." Richard Nelson, *How New is New Growth Theory?,* 40 CHALLENGE 29, 40 (1997).

50. SAMUELSON & NORDHAUS, at 571, 582.

51. Robert M. Solow, *Technical Change and the Aggregate Production Function,* 39 REV. ECON. STAT. 312, 320 (1957).

Others built on Solow's framework. Economist Edward Denison concluded that 53 percent of the growth of potential output per worker between 1929 and 1969 could be attributed to advances in knowledge.[52] The Department of Labor concluded that total factor productivity growth (which includes R&D, education, and advances in knowledge) accounted for 37 percent of the increase in GDP between 1948 and 1997.[53] And Professors Michael Boskin and Lawrence Lau, synthesizing numerous studies conducted between 1956 and 1987, found that on average, technical progress accounted for 52 percent of economic growth.[54]

Later studies migrated away from treatments of technological change as an *exogenous* variable independent of other factors. They showed that technological change is affected by market incentives, interest rates, R&D spillovers, and other factors.[55] These studies continued to find that new ideas played an important role. Economist Charles Jones concluded that 70 percent of growth in the United States between 1950 and 1993 was attributable to a rise in the stock of ideas produced in the United States, France, West Germany, Japan, and the United Kingdom.[56] Given difficulties of measurement, the effects of new products likely are higher than they appear in the government's income and productivity statistics.[57]

Nor can there be any doubt about the importance of the economy's growth rate. As Professor Paul Romer explained, even a small increase in this figure would have a significant cumulative effect on living standards. Writing in 2000, Romer concluded that an increase of 0.5 percent per year in the growth rate would result in a 28 percent increase in GDP by 2050. Such growth could "resolve all the budget difficulties associated with the aging of the Baby Boomer generation" while still leaving ample resources to tackle other pressing social problems.[58]

---

52. EDWARD F. DENISON, ACCOUNTING FOR UNITED STATES ECONOMIC GROWTH 1929–1969, at 137 (1974).

53. SAMUELSON & NORDHAUS, at 583–84.

54. MICHAEL J. BOSKIN & LAWRENCE J. LAU, *Capital, Technology and Economic Growth*, in TECHNOLOGY AND THE WEALTH OF NATIONS 31 (N. Rosenberg et al. eds., 1992) (figure attributes changes in input quality to technical progress).

55. *See, e.g.,* Paul M. Romer, *Endogenous Technological Change*, 98 J. POLIT. ECON. S71 (1990).

56. Charles I. Jones, *Sources of U.S. Economic Growth in a World of Ideas*, 92 AM. ECON. REV. 220, 229 (2002).

57. Benn Steil et al., *Introduction and Overview,* in TECHNOLOGICAL INNOVATION AND ECONOMIC PERFORMANCE 45 (2002).

58. Paul M. Romer, *Should the Government Subsidize Supply or Demand in the Market for Scientists and Engineers?*, at 4, 11–12 (Nat'l Bureau of Econ. Research, Working Paper No. 7723, 2000), http://ssrn.com/abstract=230163.

In short, although the exact portion of economic growth attributable to innovation cannot be traced precisely, it is considerable. Studies demonstrate what our economy continues to reveal every day: innovation is paramount. To remain competitive in the 21st century, the United States must ensure that the antitrust and IP laws are marshaled most effectively to promote innovation. That is the project of this book.

2. INTELLECTUAL PROPERTY

Patents 36
    Requirements 36
    Application Process 36
    Infringement 37
    Defenses 38
    Remedies 39
Copyrights 39
    Requirements 39
    Rights 40
    Duration 40
    Infringement 41
    Limits and Defenses 41
    Remedies 43
Rationales 43
    Natural Rights 43
    Utilitarianism 45
Critique 46
    Patents 47
    Copyrights 49
Dangers 52
    Patents 52
    Copyrights 54

Of all the laws affecting innovation, IP has the most direct relation. Its goal is to encourage invention, the first step in creating marketable products.

Intellectual property is an umbrella concept that encompasses patents, copyrights, trademarks, and trade secrets. As discussed in Chapter 1, trademarks and trade secrets are not a direct focus of this book. Instead, my IP analysis centers on patents and copyrights.

These two regimes have been in the news in recent years, and not always for their roles in promoting innovation. Critics have lamented trivial patents on "inventions" such as crustless peanut butter and jelly sandwiches. They have bemoaned the hold-up potential of "patent trolls." They have criticized copyright duration that seems to extend without limit. And they have denounced the aggressive use of copyright rights to stifle creation.

This chapter provides an overview of patent and copyright law. To be sure, more than 200 years of law cannot easily be compressed into a single chapter. Instead, I offer a synthesis of the elements most important for innovation. Space constraints also restrict my chapter to U.S. law. But given the increasing convergence in recent years, especially after the enactment of the Trade-Related Aspects of Intellectual Property (TRIPs) agreement in 1994, similar frameworks appear around the world.[1]

Following the overview, this chapter explores justifications for IP. It then asks whether IP is necessary by examining other incentives for innovation. Finally, it traces dangers of IP protection such as monopoly loss, innovation bottlenecks, and harms to disruptive and user innovation.

PATENTS

The patent laws offer inventors a 20-year right to exclude others from making, using, selling, offering for sale, or importing their invention.[2] This right is uniquely powerful in IP law, enforceable even against inventors that independently create the same device.

Requirements

To receive a patent, an inventor must file an application with the U.S. Patent and Trademark Office (PTO) that satisfies five requirements:

- *Patentable subject matter.* The invention must be a "process, machine, manufacture, or composition of matter, or any new and useful improvement thereof."
- *Novelty.* It must be new—not previously known, used, patented, or described in a printed publication.
- *Utility.* It must work and serve some purpose.
- *Nonobviousness.* It cannot be obvious to "a person having ordinary skill in the [relevant] art" in light of what has previously been used or published.
- *Enablement.* It must be sufficiently described so that others can make it.[3]

Application Process

Trivial patents that have come to the public's attention in recent years have increased scrutiny of the application process. But as I describe more fully in Chapter 9, a quick look at the PTO reveals some of the challenges facing patent examiners.

Examiners have, on average, less than 20 hours to read applications; search for publications, patents, and inventions (*prior art*); evaluate patentability; and

---

1. The TRIPs Agreement was part of the Uruguay Round of the General Agreement on Tariffs and Trade (GATT) negotiations. It imposes minimum requirements for IP protection that World Trade Organization (WTO) members must satisfy.

2. 35 U.S.C. §§ 154(a)(1), 271(a) (2002).

3. 35 U.S.C. §§ 101 (subject matter, utility), 102(a) (novelty), 103 (nonobviousness), 112 (enablement).

write up conclusions. These challenges have become more difficult in recent years due to the expansion of patentable subject matter and the complexity of applications.[4]

Examiners' increased workloads are not helped by the *ex parte* nature of the process. Only the applicant communicates with the examiner. But the applicant is not required to search for the prior art that the examiner needs to reject an application.[5]

Added pressure comes from the system's pro-patent bias. Examiners receive credit only for actions such as allowing or abandoning applications. Incentives to grant applications are buttressed by examiners' backlogs and the nonfinal nature of appealable "final" rejections.

These difficulties are not theoretical. Courts that analyze patents often conclude that they should not have been granted, with some studies finding that nearly one of every two litigated patents is invalid.

To address these concerns, in Chapter 9 I recommend a post-grant opposition system that would allow any party to challenge a patent after it is issued. Such a recommendation would target the most valuable patents and provide a quicker and cheaper determination of validity than litigation. It also would reduce the number of important invalid patents.[6]

Infringement

Once a patent has been granted, a patentee can file suit against anyone who infringes any of its exclusive rights. In particular, patentees have the right to "make[ ], use[ ], offer[ ] to sell, or sell[ ] any patented invention, within the United States . . . during the term of the patent."[7]

A court determines whether infringement has occurred by examining the claims of the patent. The claims, which appear at the end of the patent, "point[ ] out and distinctly claim[ ]" the invention.[8]

Claims are important in determining a patent's *scope*. One setting in which the notion of scope arises is that of settlement agreements by which brand-name drug companies pay generic firms to delay entering the market. As discussed in Chapter 15, courts have determined the validity of these agreements by asking whether the activity falls within the scope of the patent.

Because it is difficult to describe an invention in words, the process of interpreting claims known as *claim construction* is a complicated task. It will often not

---

4. Full citations to the material in this section can be found in Chapter 9.

5. Pursuant to a duty of candor, the applicant must disclose information of which it is aware that is "material to patentability." 37 C.F.R. § 1.56.

6. The opposition system I propose builds on existing reexamination systems that, for reasons I discuss in Chapter 9, have not been significantly utilized.

7. 35 U.S.C. § 271(a).

8. 35 U.S.C. § 112.

be obvious if the accused device infringes the claim. In interpreting ambiguous claims, courts consult an array of sources. These sources include other claims in the patent, other parts of the patent (in particular, the *specification*, which describes the invention), the negotiation between the applicant and examiner (known as *prosecution history*), dictionaries, and experts.[9]

There are two types of infringement. *Literal infringement* occurs when a party makes, sells, or uses a device that is identical to every element in a patent claim.[10] The patentee also can sue under the *doctrine of equivalents*. Such a concept asks whether an accused product contains elements identical or equivalent to each element in a patent claim.[11] Despite the attention this doctrine has received, recent scholarship has questioned its importance, finding that patentees usually are unsuccessful in raising equivalents claims.[12]

A party can be liable for *contributory infringement* if it sells a component of a patented device for use in practicing a patented process, knowing that the component is "especially made or . . . adapted" for infringing uses. The component also must constitute a "material part" of the invention and cannot be a "staple" item "suitable for substantial noninfringing use."[13] A party also can be liable for more generally "induc[ing] infringement."[14]

Defenses

A defendant in an infringement suit typically challenges the validity of the patent and claims that it did not infringe the patent. It also can offer defenses such as:

- *Inequitable conduct*, which applies when a patentee engages in fraud in obtaining the patent;
- *Patent misuse*, which occurs when a patentee seeks to expand the boundaries of the patent;
- The *first-sale doctrine*, which provides that a patentee exhausts certain rights by selling the item to the public;
- The *repair defense*, which allows buyers of patented products to repair them;

---

9. *Phillips v. AWH Corp.*, 415 F.3d 1303 (Fed. Cir. 2005) (en banc).

10. *E.g., Larami Corp. v. Amron*, 27 U.S.P.Q.2d 1280 (E.D. Pa. 1993).

11. *Warner-Jenkinson Co. v. Hilton Davis Chem. Co.*, 520 U.S. 17 (1997). For another formulation, see *Graver Tank & Manufacturing Co. v. Linde Air Products Co.*, 339 U.S. 605 (1950) (analyzing whether the accused device "performs substantially the same function in substantially the same way to obtain the same result").

12. John R. Allison & Mark A. Lemley, *The (Unnoticed) Demise of the Doctrine of Equivalents*, 59 STAN. L. REV. 955 (2007).

13. 35 U.S.C. § 271(c).

14. 35 U.S.C. § 271(b).

- *The reverse doctrine of equivalents,* which excuses literal infringement if an invention is so dramatically changed that the claims no longer represent it;
- *The experimental use defense,* which allows a patented invention to be used for noncommercial, scientific inquiry;
- The *prior user right* for business methods, which permits those who used a method before the filing of a patent application to continue using it.[15]

Several of these defenses are more limited than they initially appear. For example, the Federal Circuit, the appellate court with jurisdiction over patent cases, has never applied the reverse doctrine of equivalents to excuse infringement. And as I discuss in Chapter 11, the court has drastically restricted the experimental use defense, limiting it to "amusement, . . . idle curiosity, or . . . strictly philosophical inquiry."[16]

Remedies
Remedies for infringement include injunctions; monetary damages; and, in cases of willful infringement or inequitable conduct, enhanced damages or attorneys' fees.

Until a few years ago, the Federal Circuit had, upon finding infringement, automatically granted injunctive relief. But the Supreme Court, in *eBay v. MercExchange,* reinvigorated the remedy of monetary damages.[17] As a result, courts today can select damages, typically lost profits or reasonable royalties, as an appropriate remedy. In Chapter 10, I offer a framework that provides guidance to courts on determining the appropriate remedy.

COPYRIGHTS

Requirements
Copyright protection covers "original works of authorship fixed in any tangible medium of expression."[18] The concept of originality is not particularly rigorous as it has allowed copyrights in compilations, recipes, and even dental insurance billing codes.[19] The Copyright Act protects literary, musical, dramatic, choreographic, pictorial, audiovisual, sound recording, architectural, and other

---

15. *See generally* ROBERT P. MERGES ET AL., INTELLECTUAL PROPERTY IN THE NEW TECHNOLOGICAL AGE 293–96, 308–30 (4th ed. 2006); JANICE M. MUELLER, AN INTRODUCTION TO PATENT LAW 327–64 (2d ed. 2006).

16. *Roche Prods., Inc. v. Bolar Pharm. Co.,* 733 F.2d 858, 863 (Fed. Cir. 1984), *superseded on other grounds by* 35 U.S.C. § 271(e).

17. 126 S. Ct. 1837 (2006).

18. 17 U.S.C. § 102.

19. *American Dental Ass'n v. Delta Dental Plans,* 126 F.3d 977 (7th Cir. 1997).

types of works.[20] In 1980, Congress expanded the definition of literary works to encompass computer software.[21]

Rights

The owner of a copyrighted work obtains exclusive rights to reproduce, distribute, publicly perform, publicly display, and prepare derivative works.[22] These rights have expanded over time. Copyright law initially protected only against copying, allowing uses such as translations, abridgments, and public performances.[23]

For the past two centuries, copyright owners have gained additional rights. Just to pick two examples, the Copyright Act of 1870 granted "the right to dramatize or translate," and the 1976 Act provided the exclusive right to prepare derivative works.[24] This expansion has greatly increased the power of copyright holders. Protection for derivative works, for example, reserves for copyright holders the ability to exploit their works in secondary markets.

The latest extension is provided by the Digital Millennium Copyright Act (DMCA).[25] As discussed in Chapter 8, the DMCA prevents the "circumvent[ion of] a technological measure that effectively controls access to a [protected] work."[26] To the extent works are increasingly accessed in digital form, copyright holders thus have greater control over the use of their works, blocking access to uncopyrightable works (or parts of them).[27]

Unlike patents, which are issued only after review by the PTO, copyright protection automatically begins when the work is created. To gain certain rights, however, such as the ability to file an infringement lawsuit, elect statutory damages, and receive attorneys' fees, owners must at least attempt to register their works with the Copyright Office.[28]

Duration

Mirroring copyright's expansion in scope over the past century has been an increase in duration. The extension of the copyright term has garnered the

---

20. 17 U.S.C. § 102(a).

21. Act of Dec. 12, 1980, Pub. L. No. 96-517, § 10(a), 94 Stat. 3015, *codified as amended at* 17 U.S.C. § 101.

22. 17 U.S.C. § 106.

23. Act of May 31, 1790, ch. 15, § 1, 1 Stat. 124, 124 (granting the exclusive right to "print, reprint, publish, or vend the [work]"). *See generally* Michael A. Carrier, *Cabining Intellectual Property Through a Property Paradigm*, 54 DUKE L.J. 1, 14 (2004).

24. Act of July 8, 1870, ch. 230, § 86, 16 Stat. 198, 212; Copyright Act of 1976, Pub. L. No. 94-553, ch. 1, § 101, 90 Stat. 2541, 2542 (*all codified at* 17 U.S.C. § 101 (2000)). Courts had recognized the right before Congress codified it in 1976.

25. Pub. L. No. 105-304, 112 Stat. 2860 (1998), *codified at* 17 U.S.C. § 1201.

26. 17 U.S.C. § 1201(a)(1)(A).

27. Carrier, at 15 n.33 (providing sources).

28. 17 U.S.C. §§ 411, 412.

most attention. The Copyright Act of 1790 provided for a term of 14 years with a potential 14-year renewal.[29] Duration expanded over the next two centuries until Congress, in the Copyright Act of 1976, provided for protection lasting the life of the author plus 50 years.[30] The controversial Sonny Bono Copyright Term Extension Act of 1998 added 20 years so that copyrights currently last for the life of the author plus 70 years.[31] For works made for hire or anonymous works, copyright extends, in most cases, 95 years from publication.[32]

Infringement

Authors can claim copyright infringement against anyone that infringes any of their exclusive rights. An owner can demonstrate infringement of its reproduction right by showing that the defendant copied its work and that the two works are "substantially similar."

In addition to suing direct infringers, copyright owners can sue any party that assists another in committing infringement. Traditionally there have been two theories of *secondary liability*. A party engages in *contributory infringement* by (1) knowing about the infringing activity and (2) causing or materially contributing to the infringement. One is *vicariously liable* if she (1) has the right and ability to control or supervise the infringing activity and (2) derives a financial benefit from the infringement.[33] Because Congress has not addressed these issues, courts have turned to patent law for guidance.

In Chapter 6, I discuss two of the most important decisions in the area of secondary liability. In *Sony Corporation of America v. Universal City Studios*, the Supreme Court found that Sony, the manufacturer of the Betamax home videocassette recorder (VCR), was not liable because the product—even if it contributed to copyright infringement—was capable of substantial noninfringing uses.[34] And in *MGM v. Grokster*, the Court found that P2P service Grokster was liable under a theory of inducement because "one who distributes a device with the object of promoting its use to infringe copyright, as shown by clear expression or other affirmative steps taken to foster infringement, is liable for the resulting acts of infringement by third parties."[35]

Limits and Defenses

In an infringement lawsuit, defendants can claim that the copyright is not valid. They can show that the two works are not substantially similar. They can

---

29. Act of May 31, 1790, ch. 15, § 1, 1 Stat. 124, 124.

30. Copyright Act of 1976, Pub. L. No. 94-553, 90 Stat. 2541.

31. Pub. L. No. 105-298, § 102, 112 Stat. 2827, *codified at* 17 U.S.C. § 302(a) (2000).

32. 17 U.S.C. § 302. If the work is in gestation more than 25 years, the copyright lasts 120 years from creation.

33. *Gershwin Publ'g Corp. v. Columbia Artists Mgmt.*, 443 F.2d 1159, 1162 (2d Cir. 1971).

34. 464 U.S. 417, 442 (1984).

35. 545 U.S. 913, 936–37 (2005).

show that they independently created the work. And they can demonstrate the applicability of copyright limits such as:

- The *idea-expression dichotomy*, which prevents copyright in any "idea, procedure, process, system, method of operation, concept, principle, or discovery";
- The *merger doctrine*, which precludes a copyright where there are only one or a few ways to express an idea;
- The *scenes-à-faire* doctrine, which bars copyright for standard plots, themes, or characters; and
- The *useful article doctrine*, which does not allow useful elements of pictorial, graphic, or sculptural works to be protected.[36]

Alleged infringers also can rely on defenses such as

- *Compulsory licenses* for public broadcasting, musical works, and cable and satellite retransmissions;
- *Exclusions from liability* for acts of libraries, certain activity in the public interest, and the making of ephemeral copies;
- The *first sale doctrine*, which limits copyright owners' rights to control distribution, allowing purchasers to dispose of lawful copies however they wish;
- *Copyright misuse*, which prevents owners who engage in certain types of misconduct from enforcing their copyrights;
- *Fraud on the Copyright Office*, which applies when a plaintiff makes materially false statements to the Office or omits essential facts from an application;
- *Copyright estoppel*, which prevents an owner from claiming a work is fictional after previously representing that the work was factual;
- *Equitable estoppel*, which applies when a defendant can prove that an owner's actions reasonably induced it to change position; and
- *Laches*, if a defendant proves that an owner's delay in filing an infringement suit results in prejudice.[37]

The most wide-ranging defense is *fair use*. Courts applying this defense consider four factors: (1) the purpose and character of the use, (2) the nature of the copyrighted work, (3) the amount of copying, and (4) the effect of the use on the market for the work.[38] Typical excused uses include news reporting, educational use, parody, criticism, and commentary. From the standpoint of innovation,

---

36. 17 U.S.C. § 102(b) (idea-expression dichotomy); *Morrissey v. Procter & Gamble*, 379 F.2d 675 (1st Cir. 1967) (merger); *Atari, Inc. v. North American Phillips Consumer Electronics*, 672 F.2d 607, 616 (7th Cir. 1982) (scenes-à-faire); 17 U.S.C. § 101 (useful article).

37. Carrier, at 90–95 (providing citations).

38. 17 U.S.C. § 107.

reverse engineering—working backward from a finished product to determine how it was created—is perhaps the most important application of the defense.[39]

Despite the breadth of the defense, its real-world effect does not always match its theoretical importance. Individuals who receive threatening cease-and-desist letters and do not wish to incur vast litigation costs and potential damages often decide not to use the copyrighted work.[40]

Remedies

Copyright owners can select from a range of potential remedies for copyright infringement. They can obtain an injunction preventing further infringement, impound infringing copies of the material, destroy infringing copies, recover actual damages and profits, obtain statutory damages, and recoup costs and attorneys' fees.[41]

Chapter 7 discusses how the statutory damages remedy has recently threatened innovation. Such damages range between $750 and $30,000 for each infringed work. In willful infringement cases, the court may increase the award to $150,000 for each work.[42] As applied to dual-use technologies (which can be used to create new forms of interaction or to facilitate infringement), such damages quickly reach into the *billions* of dollars.

RATIONALES

Why do we have IP? One set of explanations is based on natural rights. The other is centered on utilitarianism.

Natural Rights

Each of the two versions of the natural-rights theories focuses on rewarding the author. The *labor theory*, advanced by 17th-century philosopher John Locke, provides that individuals are entitled to the fruits of their labor. Locke explained that "every man has a property in his own person" and is entitled to whatever he

---

39. *Sega Enters. Ltd. v. Accolade, Inc.*, 977 F.2d 1510 (9th Cir. 1992).

40. *See, e.g.*, Chilling Effects Clearinghouse, http://chillingeffects.org/ (last visited August 5, 2008); Giselle Fahimian, *How the IP Guerrillas Won: (R) superTM Ark, Adbusters, Negativland, and the 'Bullying Back' of Creative Freedom and Social Commentary*, 2004 STAN. TECH. L. REV. 1, ¶¶ 62–64, http://stlr.stanford.edu/STLR/Articles/04_STLR_1/index.htm (withdrawal of "alternative Barbies" in response to cease-and-desist letter from Mattel).

41. 17 U.S.C. §§ 502–05 (2004). *See generally* JULIE E. COHEN ET AL., COPYRIGHT IN A GLOBAL INFORMATION ECONOMY 768–69 (2006). Destruction of infringing copies cannot occur until a court finds infringement, and the recovery of profits is limited to those not otherwise considered in the calculation of actual damages.

42. 17 U.S.C. § 504(c).

"removes out of the state [of] nature" and "mixe[s] his labour with."[43] Locke restricted the application of the theory to contexts in which "there is enough, and as good left in common for others."[44]

The *personhood* perspective asserts that individuals need property rights to control resources in their external environment. The 19th-century philosopher Georg Hegel explained that "[t]he person has for its substantive end the right of placing its will in any and every thing," which then belongs to that person.[45] Professor Margaret Radin developed this concept by distinguishing between fungible property, which is "wholly interchangeable with money," and objects that are so personal that "a government that must respect persons ought not to take it."[46]

The natural-rights theories do not explain most IP today. Expending significant labor does not lead to IP protection if the creation is not original.[47] Personhood justifications partially explain the Visual Artists Rights Act (VARA), which protects single or limited edition copies of paintings and photographs, and derivative rights, which allow authors to block unauthorized distortions or modifications of their work.[48] In contrast to the European Union, however, these justifications play only a minor role in the United States.

In addition, as compared to utilitarianism, the theories are far less consistent with the Constitution and much less recognized by courts. The natural-rights theories also suffer in providing tools that explain the granting, but not limiting, of rights. Because excessive protection threatens dangers, the absence of a mechanism to structure tradeoffs is costly.

---

43. John Locke, *Second Treatise of Government, in* Two Treatises of Government ¶ 27, at 305–06 (Peter Laslett ed., 2d ed. Cambridge Univ. Press 1967) (1690) (emphasis omitted).

44. *Id.* ¶ 27, at 288.

45. Georg Hegel, Philosophy of Right § 44 (T. Knox trans. 1942).

46. Margaret Jane Radin, *Property and Personhood*, 34 Stan. L. Rev. 957, 987, 1005 (1982). Related to the personhood theory is the notion of "moral rights," which protects authors' rights to the integrity, attribution, and disclosure of their works. The right of integrity blocks alterations of a work that destroy its character. The right of attribution prevents others from being acknowledged as the author. And the right of disclosure allows the author to determine when to publicly disclose the work. *See* Roberta Rosenthal Kwall, *Preserving Personality and Reputational Interests of Constructed Personas Through Moral Rights: A Blueprint for the Twenty-First Century*, 2001 U. Ill. L. Rev. 151, 152–53; Roberta Rosenthal Kwall, *Copyright and the Moral Right: Is an American Marriage Possible?*, 38 Vand. L. Rev. 1, 5–8 (1985).

47. Another challenge confronting the theory is that Locke's caveat that one leave enough and as good for others is not met when the IP has market power and buyers are not able to find a similar product elsewhere.

48. 17 U.S.C. §106A (VARA), § 106(2) (derivative rights).

Utilitarianism

The primary theory explaining U.S. IP law today is *utilitarianism*. Stated most simply, this theory, associated with the philosophers Jeremy Bentham and John Stuart Mill, judges actions by their effect on societal welfare. For our purposes, it refers to increasing the number of new and improved inventions and creations in society.[49]

The utilitarian theory is consistent with the language of the Constitution, which allows Congress to enact IP legislation "[t]o promote the Progress of Science and useful Arts." It also is the theory articulated most frequently by courts. The Supreme Court has stated that a patent is "an inducement to bring forth new knowledge"[50] and that copyrights "encourage the production of original literary, artistic, and musical expression for the good of the public."[51]

To be sure, it is difficult, if not impossible, to know what scope and duration of IP rights would maximize the number of inventions and creative works. But at least utilitarianism offers a framework by which these tradeoffs can be made. In fact, its efforts to provide incentives while minimizing monopoly and other losses is unique among the current applications of IP theories.

Two primary rationales have been advanced within the utilitarianism framework. The first focuses on the need for property rights to coordinate the commercialization of an invention. The earliest proponent of such a theory, Professor Edmund Kitch, analogized patents to "prospects" like the 19th-century mining claims for which the first to arrive received exclusive rights. Kitch advocated early, broad patents that allow a single owner to coordinate development.[52] More recent versions of the theory have treated patents as property rights that allow multiple parties to facilitate commercialization.[53] The theory's emphasis on fostering commercialization after invention, however, has not been as influential as the *incentive theory*, which focuses on providing incentives before invention and is the predominant justification in the United States today.

Why are exclusive rights necessary to foster new inventions and creative works? To answer this question, it is necessary to recount the traditional story supporting IP.

The story explains that innovators expend significant money and time in creating and developing inventions. Conducting research and development and bringing an innovation to market often are lengthy and expensive processes, with no guarantees of success at the end of the tunnel.

---

49. The systems also encourage public disclosure.

50. *Graham v. John Deere Co.*, 383 U.S. 1, 9 (1966).

51. *Fogerty v. Fantasy, Inc.*, 510 U.S. 517, 524 (1994).

52. Edmund W. Kitch, *The Nature and Function of the Patent System*, 20 J.L. & Econ. 265 (1977).

53. F. Scott Kieff, *Property Rights and Property Rules for Commercializing Inventions*, 85 Minn. L. Rev. 697 (2001).

And on those occasions when success is achieved, free riders who did not undertake such investments might be tempted to imitate the hard-earned innovation. Such opportunists could copy and sell the product more cheaply than the inventor. While innovators must price products at a level that allows them to recover their costs of creation, free riders only need to cover the much lower marginal costs of producing each item.[54] For obvious reasons, such behavior would tend to deter future innovators.

Intellectual property's unique characteristics increase the likelihood of free riders. Intellectual property is a public good. Such goods are, technically speaking, nonexclusive and nonrival. *Nonexclusivity* means that owners cannot exclude others from possession. A landowner can deny entry to outsiders by erecting a fence. An owner of an idea, in contrast, cannot exclude those who have been exposed to it.

Nonrivalrousness means that one person's use does not reduce the amount left for others. This condition does not apply to tangible property. If you take my book, there is less (that is, nothing) left for me. In contrast, if I share my idea with you, there is just as much left for others.

This characteristic magnifies the danger of nonexclusivity. Because one person's use does not reduce the amount left for others, and because owners cannot exclude others from ideas, many can use the information without depleting it. As a result, there generally is underproduction of public goods.

To prevent this result, the IP laws provide creators with a right to exclude. For a 20-year period, the inventor of a patented product can prevent all others from making, selling, or using the device.[55] And for a period lasting the author's life plus 70 years, the creator of a copyrighted work can prevent others from reproducing, distributing, or engaging in other activities related to the work.[56]

These rights allow creators to charge prices higher than their postinvention costs, thereby recovering their initial expenditures. In doing so, they are designed to increase innovation.

CRITIQUE

That is the traditional story of IP. It is a story that is powerful and often told. But is it correct?

The answer is complex. But in many settings, the connection between IP protection and innovation is attenuated. In analyzing this relation, one caveat is in order: No one knows the ideal duration and scope of IP rights. That is, no one knows the length or breadth of IP protection that would maximize innovation.

---

54. Marginal cost is the increase in total cost from producing one additional unit.

55. 35 U.S.C. § 154(a)(1, 2).

56. 17 U.S.C. §§ 106, 302.

Given the industry-specific nature of innovation, there may be as many answers as there are industries.

Nonetheless, it is possible to observe IP's general effectiveness in promoting innovation. Scholars have analyzed how innovation is achieved in various industries. In many contexts, IP protection does not appear to play a leading role in increasing innovation.

Patents

Firms seek patents for many reasons. Yet each of the major studies undertaken in the last 50 years has shown that they are the primary motivator for innovation in only a handful of industries—pharmaceuticals and biotechnology, and sometimes chemicals, medical products, and agricultural products.[57]

The pharmaceuticals and biotechnology industries are distinguished by high development costs.[58] Firms in these industries spend hundreds of millions of dollars and take 10 to 15 years to bring new drugs to the market.[59]

Before firms can bring a product to the market, they must (1) discover a target[60] for a particular condition; (2) find a molecule that can act on the target; (3) engage in preclinical testing in animals; (4) undertake three stages of clinical testing involving thousands of subjects; and (5) develop, manufacture, and market the drug.[61] Only one out of thousands of discovered compounds ever reaches the marketplace.[62]

---

57. See Richard C. Levin et al., *Appropriating the Returns from Industrial Research and Development*, in 1987 BROOKINGS PAPERS ON ECON. ACTIVITY, at 783, 802, 809; Wesley M. Cohen et al., *Protecting Their Intellectual Assets: Appropriability Conditions and Why U.S. Manufacturing Firms Patent (or not)*, at 9 (Nat'l Bureau of Econ. Research, Working Paper No. 7552, 2000); F.M. SCHERER ET AL., PATENTS AND THE CORPORATION 130–35 (2d ed. 1959); C.T. TAYLOR & Z.A. SILBERSTON, THE ECONOMIC IMPACT OF THE PATENT SYSTEM: A STUDY OF THE BRITISH EXPERIENCE 201–07 (1973); Edwin Mansfield, *Patents and Innovation: An Empirical Study*, 32 MGMT. SCI. 173, 174 (1986).

58. To the extent lines can be drawn, the conclusion for the biotechnology industry applies primarily to "downstream" commercialization (as opposed to "upstream" research).

59. *E.g.*, Pharmaceutical Research & Manufacturers of America (PhRMA), *Pharmaceutical Industry Profile 2004*, at 2 (2004), http://www.phrma.org/publications/publications/2004-03-31.937.pdf; Pub. Citizen, *Rx R&D Myths: The Case Against the Drug Industry's R&D "Scare Card,"* at 7 (2001), http://www.citizen.org/documents/acfdc.pdf; Tufts Center for the Study of Drug Development, *Outlook 2002*, at 1, http://csdd.tufts.edu/InfoServices/OutlookPDFs/Outlook2002.pdf.

60. A target is a molecule involved in a particular disease. PhRMA, *Drug Discovery and Development: Understanding the R&D Process*, at 3, http://www.phrma.org/files/RD%20Brochure%20022307.pdf.

61. *Id.*

62. Rosa M. Abrantes-Metz, *Pharmaceutical Development Phases: A Duration Analysis* (FTC Working Paper No. 274, at 9, tbl. B.2.A. (Oct. 2004)); FDA and the Drug Development

But in most other industries, patents are less vital for innovation. Instead, they are used more for strategic reasons. Some firms patent for defensive purposes such as gaining leverage in negotiations with competitors, preventing infringement lawsuits, or amassing patent portfolios.[63] Other firms use patents as a "signaling device" to consumers, competitors, or investors.[64] While some of these reasons affect innovation, the relationship is far less direct than the traditional theory suggests.

Patents, for example, play a relatively minor role in the creation of products in the automobile, Internet, office equipment, printing/publishing, rubber, steel, and textiles industries. Firms in these industries regard market-based incentives as more effective catalysts for innovation.[65]

A significant nonpatent incentive to innovate is the advantage from being the first to enter a market—in other words, a market pioneer. In some industries, such as cigarettes, investment banking, oil-drilling rigs, and pharmaceuticals, market pioneers have maintained significant market shares long after they entered the market. The computer and semiconductor industries also reward the first to arrive in a market. And in consumer goods businesses, pioneers tend to amass far more market share than late entrants.[66]

Such market dominance usually is explained by customer familiarity and brand loyalty. In addition, the first company to head down learning curves may obtain cost advantages that can be used to quickly recoup development costs and even to block entry.[67]

A type of market in which first-mover status is particularly important is a network effects market. Network effects occur in markets in which participants benefit from an expansion of the system. A telephone or e-mail system, for example, becomes more valuable as the number of people connected to it increases.

Process: How the Agency Ensures that Drugs are Safe and Effective, Dept. of Health & Human Servs., Publication No. FS 02-5, Feb. 2002.

63. Cohen et al., at 17; FED'L TRADE COMM'N, TO PROMOTE INNOVATION: THE PROPER BALANCE OF COMPETITION AND PATENT LAW AND POLICY, at 3–33 (2003) [hereinafter FTC INNOVATION REPORT]; Gideon Parchomovsky & R. Polk Wagner, Patent Portfolios, 154 U. PA. L. REV. 1, 36 (2005).

64. John Allison et al., Valuable Patents, 92 GEO. L.J. 435, 436 & n.6 (2004); Clarisa Long, Patent Signals, 69 U. CHI. L. REV. 625, 627–28 (2002).

65. See Cohen et al., tbl.1; Mansfield, at 174–75 & tbl.1; JOHN E. TILTON, INTERNATIONAL DIFFUSION OF TECHNOLOGY: THE CASE OF SEMICONDUCTORS 60–61 (1971).

66. William T. Robinson et al., First-Mover Advantages from Pioneering New Markets: A Survey of Empirical Evidence, 9 REV. INDUS. ORG. 1, 6, 9 (1994); 1 FED'L TRADE COMM'N, ANTICIPATING THE 21ST CENTURY: COMPETITION POLICY IN THE NEW HIGH-TECH, GLOBAL MARKETPLACE, ch. 6, at 15 (1996) [hereinafter FTC GLOBAL COMPETITION REPORT].

67. F.M. SCHERER & DAVID ROSS, INDUSTRIAL MARKET STRUCTURE AND ECONOMIC PERFORMANCE 627 (1990).

Relatedly, networks feature positive feedback. As the Microsoft case discussed in Chapter 5 shows, the more popular a computer operating system becomes, the more applications will be written for it. And as these additional applications become available, the system becomes even more popular, leading to more applications being written, and so on.[68]

Network effects markets provide a clear illustration of market-based incentives for innovation. The first to enter such markets receives significant rewards, such as (at least temporary) domination. Consequently, the fierce competition to arrive first and gain the critical mass of consumers to foster success encourages innovation. Any incentives provided by patents are less crucial.

In their recent book on the patent system, authors James Bessen and Michael Meurer offer additional evidence questioning the link between patents and innovation. They examine *historical evidence*, such as 19th-century World's Fairs, which showed that nations that had patent systems were not more innovative than those that did not. And they explore *cross-country studies*, which show that IP rights have had, at most, "only a weak and indirect relationship to economic growth."[69]

In short, in many cases patents are less critical for innovation than the traditional theory would posit. This conclusion, when combined with the dangers recounted later in this chapter, warrants potential modifications to the patent system, which I offer in Chapters 9 through 12.

Copyrights

The traditional incentive theory also is subject to question in copyright law.[70] Professors Dan Hunter and Greg Lastowka have demonstrated the vital role that amateurs have recently played in the creation, selection, production, dissemination, and promotion functions that had previously been subject to centralized control.[71] These five roles shed light on the diminished need for copyright today.

First, it has become easier to create products. Cheap, lightweight digital equipment and software have replaced more cumbersome analog technologies,

---

68. David S. Evans & Richard Schmalensee, *A Guide to the Antitrust Economics of Networks*, 1996 ANTITRUST 36, 36–37.

69. JAMES BESSEN & MICHAEL J. MEURER, PATENT FAILURE: HOW JUDGES, BUREAUCRATS, AND LAWYERS PUT INNOVATORS AT RISK 80, 84 (2008).

70. For an early discussion of this issue, see Stephen Breyer, *The Uneasy Case for Copyright: A Study of Copyright in Books, Photocopies, and Computer Programs*, 84 HARV. L. REV. 281 (1970) (questioning the need for copyright in creating books by pointing to publishers' lead-time advantages and threats of retaliation against copiers).

71. Dan Hunter & F. Gregory Lastowka, *Amateur-to-Amateur*, 46 WM. & MARY L. REV. 951, 977–78 (2004). The authors also discuss purchase and use. For a general discussion of "peer production" issues, see Yochai Benkler, *Coase's Penguin, or, Linux and the Nature of the Firm*, 112 YALE L.J. 369 (2002).

offering tools that had previously been available only to professionals.[72] Amateurs can now create music using software tools like Sony's Acid Pro and Apple's GarageBand, which inexpensively provide "high quality recording, looping, voice cleaning and audio effects."[73] They also can create movies. Jonathan Caouette's movie *Tarnation*, which was shown at the Sundance Film Festival, was edited on Apple's iMovie at a cost of $218.32 in videotape and materials.[74]

This observation is buttressed by numerous other incentives to create. Authors can take advantage of being the first to reach the market. They can employ price discrimination, charging different buyers different prices for the same item. They can utilize advertising models. They can use self-help technologies such as digital rights management, using measures such as encryption and watermarking to protect their product. And they can rely on non-monetary inducements such as fame, prestige, and personal goals.[75]

Many forms of expression—such as fashions, new words and slogans, jokes and magic tricks, and the food industry—have flourished without protection.[76] And most performers in the music industry make far more from live performances than from the sale of music.[77] Two of the most powerful examples of a reduced need for copyright are provided by the "open source" movement and Creative Commons licenses.

The open source model has employed a collaborative, decentralized process to create widely used products such as the Linux operating system and Apache web server. Because many programmers are able to fix bugs and improve software, the products are often of a higher quality than commercial products.[78] At the core of the open source movement are licenses that allow others to use the software but require that they maintain its open character. The popular

---

72. *Id.* at 982.

73. *ACID Pro 6: Professional Music Workstation*, Sony, http://www.sonycreativesoftware. com/acidpro (last visited August 10, 2008); *GarageBand*, iLife, http://www.apple.com/ ilife/garageband/ (last visited August 10, 2008); Lastowka & Hunter, at 982.

74. Jason Silverman, *Here's the Price of Fame: $218.32*, Wired, Jan. 20, 2004, http:// www.wired.com/entertainment/music/news/2004/01/61970.

75. *See generally* Mark S. Nadel, *How Current Copyright Law Discourages Creative Output: The Overlooked Impact of Marketing*, 19 Berkeley Tech. L.J. 785 (2004).

76. Emmanuelle Fauchart & Eric A. Von Hippel, *Norms-Based Intellectual Property Systems: The Case of French Chefs*, Jan. 2006, http://papers.ssrn.com/sol3/papers. cfm?abstract_id=881781; Tom G. Palmer, *Intellectual Property: A Non-Posnerian Law and Economics Approach*, 12 Hamline L. Rev. 261, 287 (1989); Kal Raustiala & Christopher Sprigman, *The Piracy Paradox: Innovation and Intellectual Property in Fashion Design*, 92 Va. L. Rev. 1687 (2006).

77. Raymond Shih Ray Ku, *The Creative Destruction of Copyright: Napster and the New Economics of Digital Technology*, 69 U. Chi. L. Rev. 263, 308, 311 (2002).

78. James Bessen, *Open Source Software: Free Provision of Complex Public Goods*, July 2005, http://papers.ssrn.com/sol3/papers.cfm?abstract_id=278148.

General Public License (GPL) allows licensees to use, modify, and distribute the software but requires them to distribute the software under the GPL's terms (keeping it open source) and to not charge royalties for published or distributed software.[79] The model thus uses copyright for inclusion, not exclusion.

The second example is provided by Creative Commons licenses. Creative Commons is a nonprofit organization that has developed model licenses that supplement the stark choice between full copyright (all rights) and the public domain (no rights) by allowing creators to retain some rights.[80] In particular, creators can choose among licenses that cover attribution, noncommercial use, "no derivative works," and "share alike."[81] Creative Commons licenses have been translated into more than 45 languages and used by millions of pages of web content.[82]

The second function of copyright is *selection*, which involves judgment as to which works should be reproduced and distributed. Selection agents have played an important role in high-risk industries like pop music and movies. In these fields, the stakes are high, with one successful hit covering the costs of many failures. But it is difficult to predict in advance which works will be successful. As discussed in Chapter 6, a reduction in production and distribution costs has reduced the need for such agents.[83]

The third stage is *production*, preparing a work for the market. Historically, large-scale commercial reproduction required investments in expensive machinery and physical media such as paper and film stock. Today, computers and the Internet allow an individual to undertake nearly all production tasks. As Hunter and Lastowka explain, the blogosphere and (more generally) Internet constitute

---

79. GNU General Public License, http://www.gnu.org/licenses/gpl.html; *see generally* Greg R. Vetter, *"Infectious" Open Source Software: Spreading Incentives or Promoting Resistance?*, 36 RUTGERS L.J. 53, 83–84 (2004).

80. *About*, CREATIVE COMMONS, http://creativecommons.org/about/ (last visited August 25, 2008).

81. *About: License Your Work*, CREATIVE COMMONS, http://creativecommons.org/about/license/ (last visited August 25, 2008). The "share alike" provision allows others "to distribute derivative works only under a license identical to the license that governs [the owner's] work."

82. *International*, CREATIVE COMMONS, http://creativecommons.org/international (last visited August 25, 2008) (46 nations have licenses, and 9 are in the process of developing them as of August 2008). *List of Projects Using Creative Commons Licenses*, WIKIPEDIA, July 8, 2008, http://en.wikipedia.org/wiki/List_of_projects_using_Creative_Commons_licenses. In addition to being translated into other languages, the substance of the legal code has been adapted to conform to local law in each of the countries. In August 2008, the Federal Circuit held that conditions in public licenses, like the open source and Creative Commons licenses, were enforceable under the copyright laws. *Jacobsen v. Katzer*, 2008 WL 3395772 (Fed. Cir. 2008).

83. Hunter & Lastowka, at 989–94.

"the greatest advance in self-expression and self-publishing . . . since the invention of the printing press."[84]

The fourth task is *dissemination.* Traditionally, content distributors have undertaken substantial investments in manufacturing, printing, packaging, and distribution. But the increasing digitization of creative works and rise of the Internet have reduced copyright's distribution function. The marginal cost of reproducing and distributing digital copies is zero. The public internalizes distribution costs by buying the components needed to connect to the Internet: a computer, Internet access, storage media, and electricity.[85] Dissemination has been facilitated by an expansion in hard disk size and bandwidth. As discussed in Chapter 6, P2P systems offer a decentralized means of distributing large files.

Promotion, the fifth stage, is needed to make consumers aware of a work's existence and interested in purchasing it. Singers, promoters, and record labels, for example, have used music videos, concert tours, live radio appearances, and magazine interviews to promote content.[86] Chapter 6 will also explain how user-created mechanisms such as eBay's rating system, YouTube's most-watched list, and Amazon.com's recommended items promise a new, more effective promotion regime.

In short, the five key stages of creation, selection, production, distribution, and promotion reveal a reduced need for copyright. In certain instances such as large-budget movies, copyright may be needed. But in others, it will be far less necessary.

DANGERS

In many cases, IP protection thus does not serve its intended purposes. Because of IP's dangers, this conclusion is ominous.

Patents

The right to exclude in patent law can result in monopoly loss and innovation bottlenecks. As already discussed, patentees can use the right to exclude to prevent others from selling or licensing their products for certain periods. Such a right may provide incentives by allowing patentees to recover their expenditures and obtain profits, but it does so by increasing price.

To be clear, in most instances, patents do not confer monopoly power.[87] Just because a patentee has the right to exclude others from its invention does not

---

84. *Id.* at 999–1001.
85. Ku, at 300–01.
86. Hunter & Lastowka, at 1006, 1009.
87. E.g., *Illinois Tool Works Inc. v. Independent Ink, Inc.,* 547 U.S. 28 (2006).

mean that there are no substitutes in the marketplace. In many cases, consumers can turn to an alternative technology if they believe the price of the patented product is excessive.

But in some instances, there are no effective substitutes. This leads to the dangers of deadweight loss and wealth transfers. As inventors raise price above marginal cost, some consumers, who would pay more than the competitive price but less than the monopoly price, will not buy the works. Because society loses these sales, economists call this a *deadweight loss*. Other consumers are willing to pay higher-than-competitive prices. In this case, society does not lose a sale, but wealth is transferred from consumers to IP owners.

Patents also threaten to create bottlenecks. In industries such as semiconductors and computer software, one product contains multiple patented components. If one of the owners refuses to license one such component, a bottleneck could arise. This danger is exacerbated when patents issue for products already on the market, as the patentee holds a commanding position over manufacturers in large-scale production who cannot easily redesign their products and are forced to comply with the patentee's demands.[88]

Another example occurs in industries marked by *cumulative innovation, in which each product generation builds on its predecessor*. Such innovation occurs in industries as diverse as automobiles, biotechnology, semiconductors, computer hardware, and software.[89] Across the range of industries marked by cumulative innovation, bottlenecks can block the path of innovation as the latest product generation is held hostage to its predecessor.[90]

One potential bottleneck that has received attention is the biotechnology anticommons, which arises from multiple owners having a right to exclude. Such a bottleneck has allegedly created obstacles to research and development (R&D) by requiring parties to gain "access to multiple patented inputs to create a single useful product."[91] Despite the number of proposals that have built on this theory, however, Chapter 11 shows that the empirical evidence does not currently support the existence of an anticommons.

---

88. Carl Shapiro, *Navigating the Patent Thicket: Cross Licenses, Patent Pools, and Standard Setting, in* 1 INNOVATION POLICY AND THE ECONOMY 119 (Adam B. Jaffe et al. eds., 2001).

89. SUZANNE SCOTCHMER, INNOVATION AND INCENTIVES (2005); Thomas M. Jorde & David J. Teece, *Innovation, Cooperation, and Antitrust, in* ANTITRUST, INNOVATION, AND COMPETITIVENESS 47, 48–49 (Thomas M. Jorde & David J. Teece eds., 1992); FTC INNOVATION REPORT, at 2–25 to 2–26.

90. Although licensing sometimes solves the problem, it often does not. *See* Mark A. Lemley, *The Economics of Improvement in Intellectual Property Law*, 75 TEX. L. REV. 989, 1052–61 (1997) (discussing transaction costs, strategic behavior, and uncertainty).

91. Michael A. Heller & Rebecca S. Eisenberg, *Can Patents Deter Innovation? The Anticommons in Biomedical Research*, 280 SCI. 698, 699 (1998). The anticommons stood in contrast to the "tragedy of the commons," by which resources held in common were depleted by overuse.

Copyrights

Copyright also can lead to dangers. The regime's expansion in recent years has threatened free speech and the decentralization and discourse that are crucial to democracy.[92] Although these harms lie outside the scope of this book, the protection of software leads to more direct effects on innovation.

As I explain in Chapter 8, the DMCA prohibits the circumvention of technological measures protecting copyrighted works. The danger is that functional, uncopyrighted devices such as garage door openers and printer toner cartridges often contain small pieces of software that allow owners to invoke the Act. Owners thus can prevent competition in *aftermarkets* for parts and service and can prevent innovation by users who wish to create customized products.

The law of secondary liability also threatens to stifle innovation. As illustrated in Chapters 6 and 7, dual-use technologies offer radical, disruptive innovations. They promise to transform the way we interact with each other and restructure our society. But they are continually under assault by the threat of mammoth statutory damages and the complicated tests promulgated by courts. They are evaluated in their infancy when their capabilities can barely be discerned. And they do not stand a chance against the widespread, concrete instances of infringement offered by the copyright holders.

In short, the IP system is characterized by significant dangers. These dangers accompany a system in which the traditional justifications are often subject to question. For these reasons, IP is not being used most effectively to promote innovation. The second and third parts of this book offer various proposals to address some of IP's dangers and to better promote innovation.

---

92. Carrier, at 49–51.

3. ANTITRUST

Primer 55
    Agreements 56
    Monopolization 58
    Mergers 59
Antitrust History 61
Evaluation: The Negative View 64
    Crandall & Winston 65
    Crandall-Winston Critique 66
Evaluation: The Positive View 67
Innovation Concerns 68

Antitrust is our legal system's forgotten middle child. It has never received the attention lavished on its older siblings, like constitutional law. It is not as electrifying as its younger siblings, like Internet law. Some have claimed it should not apply to the fast-moving, rule-changing new economy. And some whisper that its economic basis makes it impenetrable.

Just as the middle-child syndrome has effects on society, antitrust's neglect has effects on our economy. If the public does not understand and appreciate antitrust law, political support will be weak.[1] At the same time, the new-economy bogeyman (which taunts antitrust's slow pace) will bully the regime into a defensive crouch, in which it justifies its existence rather than affirmatively promoting competition and innovation.

This chapter sheds light on antitrust. It begins with a primer explaining the most important of the regime's doctrines. It then places today's law in context by tracing the history of antitrust law. It concludes by surveying the evidence on the need for antitrust.

PRIMER

Antitrust challenges an array of business activity. Three types of behavior are central. Agreements, monopolization, and mergers raise the most important antitrust issues today and are most likely to implicate IP. This chapter discusses antitrust law generally, with Chapters 4 and 5 addressing its treatment of IP issues. The chapter focuses on U.S. federal antitrust issues.

---

1. THE NEXT ANTITRUST AGENDA: THE AMERICAN ANTITRUST INSTITUTE'S TRANSITION REPORT ON COMPETITION POLICY TO THE 44TH PRESIDENT, ch. 1, at 24 (Albert A. Foer ed., 2008).

Agreements

The first area involves agreements. Such activity injures competition when rivals jointly increase price, reduce output, or stifle innovation. Certain agreements are so likely to lead to competitive harm and so unlikely to offer benefits that they are automatically condemned, or treated as per se illegal. Three types of horizontal agreements (between rivals) fall into this category:

- *Price fixing*, by which rivals raise, fix, or maintain the price of goods they sell
- *Bid rigging*, by which competitors agree in advance who will submit the winning bid on a contract
- *Market allocation*, by which firms divide markets and agree not to compete in rivals' territories[2]

Each of these kinds of agreements reduces or eliminates competition that would otherwise have lowered price or increased innovation. At the same time, such agreements almost always fail to offer redeeming benefits for consumers.[3] As a result, the mere fact of agreement is sufficient to impose liability without proof of adverse competitive effects.

Most agreements do not present these concerns. Parties enter into contracts and licenses all the time. Courts uphold many horizontal collaborations and joint ventures under the Rule of Reason. And they apply minimal scrutiny to *vertical agreements* (which occur between firms at different levels of the distribution chain, such as manufacturers and dealers).

In the past decade, the Supreme Court has accelerated its quest, begun in the late 1970s, to wipe away all vestiges of per se treatment for vertical agreements. Vertical nonprice restraints—which occur when a manufacturer instructs a dealer to operate in a certain territory or sell to certain customers—were the first to disappear. In *Continental T.V. v. GTE Sylvania*, the Court applied Rule-of-Reason analysis to these agreements, which, even if they limit *intrabrand* competition (between a manufacturer's distributors), promote *interbrand* competition (between different manufacturers).[4] Two decades later, the Court applied the Rule of Reason to manufacturers' agreements to set the *maximum* prices at which dealers could resell products.[5] And in 2007, the Court overturned its century-old prescription of per se analysis for *minimum* resale price restrictions.[6] In short, courts now apply the Rule of Reason to all vertical agreements.

---

2. U.S. Dept. of Justice Antitrust Division, An Antitrust Primer for Federal Law Enforcement Personnel, at 4–11 (rev. 2005).

3. One example of an arrangement offering beneficial results involves price fixing that accompanies the creation of a new product that would not otherwise be available. *See BMI Music v. Columbia Broad.*, 441 U.S. 1 (1979). Courts evaluate such a situation under the Rule of Reason.

4. 433 U.S. 36 (1977).

5. *State Oil Co. v. Khan*, 522 U.S. 3 (1997).

6. *Leegin Creative Leather Prods., Inc. v. PSKS, Inc.*, 127 S. Ct. 2705 (2007).

What exactly *is* the Rule of Reason? Most courts asking this question begin by turning to its most-cited precedent, *Board of Trade of Chicago v. United States*, which calls for a comprehensive analysis that considers

> the facts peculiar to the business to which the restraint is applied; its condition before and after the restraint was imposed; the nature of the restraint and its effect, actual or probable[, as well as] [t]he history of the restraint, the evil believed to exist, the reason for adopting the particular remedy, [and] the purpose or end sought to be attained.[7]

Even more frequently, courts explain that when applying the Rule of Reason, they balance an agreement's anticompetitive and procompetitive effects. In contrast to the discussion of balancing and the *Chicago Board of Trade* kitchen-sink approach, the reality is different. A decade ago, I examined the roughly 500 Rule-of-Reason cases decided since *Sylvania*. I found that courts engaged in a burden-shifting analysis, dismissing 84 percent of the cases because the plaintiff could not show that the restraint had a significant anticompetitive effect. Courts disposed of other cases on the grounds that the restraint was not necessary or the defendant could not offer a valid justification. In only 4 percent of the cases did courts balance the restraint's anticompetitive and procompetitive effects.[8]

This burden-shifting approach is not as beneficial for plaintiffs as it might initially appear. The first stage—addressing harms to competition—typically requires evidence that the defendant has market power. A plaintiff can make this showing only after defining the relevant market, a task characterized by dueling experts and extensive document productions. Rule-of-Reason litigation, in other words, is expensive and lengthy, raising the burdens confronting plaintiffs.[9]

In part because of these burdens, some courts have employed a *quick look* analysis. Where a restraint, on its face, presents evidence of reduced output or increased price, the plaintiff need not demonstrate market power. Rather, its showing of anticompetitive effects shifts the burden to the defendant to justify the restraint.[10] As the Supreme Court recognized in *California Dental Ass'n v. FTC*, there is no clear line distinguishing quick-look from Rule-of-Reason cases.[11]

---

7. 246 U.S. 231, 238 (1918).

8. Michael A. Carrier, *The Real Rule of Reason: Bridging the Disconnect*, 1999 B.Y.U. L. REV. 1265, 1268–69.

9. *See Bell Atl. Corp. v. Twombly*, 127 S. Ct. 1955, 1967 (2007) (discussing the "unusually high" discovery costs in antitrust cases).

10. *E.g.*, *FTC v. Indiana Fed'n of Dentists*, 476 U.S. 447 (1986); *NCAA v. Bd. of Regents*, 468 U.S. 85 (1984).

11. 526 U.S. 756 (1999). Two other types of quick-look analysis have not received as much attention. The first condemns conduct where the efficiencies that would save an arrangement from per se treatment are not substantial. The second exonerates conduct without analysis of effects or efficiencies if the parties collectively lack market power. ANDREW I. GAVIL ET AL., ANTITRUST LAW IN PERSPECTIVE: CASES, CONCEPTS AND PROBLEMS IN COMPETITION POLICY 206 (2d ed. 2008).

In short, in Sherman Act Section 1 litigation today, courts treat the most concerning categories of horizontal agreements as per se illegal, but uphold the vast majority of vertical agreements under the Rule of Reason.

Monopolization

The second area of antitrust enforcement targets monopolization. This offense has two elements: (1) monopoly power and (2) predatory or exclusionary activity.

First, a plaintiff needs to show that a defendant has monopoly power. Monopoly power has been defined as "the power to control prices or exclude competition."[12] Courts often examine a defendant's market share and informally set a minimum threshold of at least 70 percent to demonstrate monopoly power.[13]

High market share alone, however, is not sufficient for the offense. The defendant also must engage in forbidden behavior. What exactly is prohibited? Courts typically address the question by citing the distinction drawn in *United States v. Grinnell Corp.* between the "willful acquisition or maintenance of [monopoly] power" and "growth or development as a consequence of a superior product, business acumen, or historic accident."[14]

It is more difficult to apply this standard than to state it. Certain cases nonetheless have served as landmarks that have guided analysis. In *Aspen Skiing Co. v. Aspen Highlands Skiing Corp.*, the owner of three downhill skiing facilities in Aspen, Colorado failed to offer a justification for withdrawing from a joint ticketing arrangement with the owner of the only other facility. The Supreme Court found that the monopolist was willing to forgo ticket sales and consumer goodwill in order to harm its smaller competitor.[15] The *Aspen Skiing* guidepost thus could penalize a monopolist who withdraws from an existing arrangement without a valid justification.[16]

Another theme of increasing significance is the presence of a regulatory regime. Where such a regime covers the challenged activity, the Supreme Court has reduced antitrust's role. In *Verizon Communications v. Trinko*, the Court held that the Telecommunications Act of 1996 promoted competition by breaking up local phone service monopolies and effectively did so by imposing a regulatory regime that included penalties and reporting requirements. As a result, "the additional benefit to competition provided by antitrust enforcement" was minimal.[17]

---

12. *United States v. E.I duPont de Nemours & Co.*, 351 U.S. 377, 391 (1956).

13. 3A PHILLIP E. AREEDA & HERBERT HOVENKAMP, ANTITRUST ¶ 801a (2d ed. 2002) (presuming monopoly power from a market share that "has exceeded 70 or 75 percent for the five years preceding the complaint").

14. 384 U.S. 563, 570–71 (1966).

15. 472 U.S. 585, 608 (1985).

16. In *Verizon Communications v. Trinko*, the Supreme Court referred to *Aspen Skiing* as "at or near the outer boundary of § 2 liability." 540 U.S. 398, 409 (2004).

17. 540 U.S. 398, 411 (2004). *See also Credit Suisse Securities v. Billing* (concluding that the securities law regime "implicitly precluded" the application of the antitrust laws

Finally, courts have articulated tests for specific behavior, such as *predatory pricing* (in which a monopolist lowers its price below cost to drive a rival out of the market and then raises it), *tying* (in which a monopolist sells a product only on the condition that the buyer purchases a second product from it), and *refusals to deal* (in which a monopolist refuses to deal with a competitor). I will address refusals to license IP in Chapter 4 and tying in Chapter 5.

Mergers

The third category involves mergers between competitors, or horizontal mergers.[18] The antitrust enforcement agencies play the primary role in shaping merger law today. With most merger challenges settled rather than litigated and the Supreme Court not considering a substantive merger case since the mid-1970s, courts in recent years have played a secondary role.[19]

The most important benchmark is provided by agency guidelines. The Department of Justice and Federal Trade Commission issued Horizontal Merger Guidelines in 1992 (and revised them in 1997). The overriding inquiry in these Guidelines asks whether a merger is "likely to create or enhance market power or to facilitate its exercise." It answers the question through a five-step process:

- Determine whether the merger would significantly increase concentration and result in a concentrated market.
- Evaluate potential adverse competitive effects.
- Assess whether entry would deter or counteract adverse effects.
- Evaluate procompetitive efficiencies.
- Determine whether either of the merging firms would otherwise have failed and been forced to exit the market.[20]

The agencies make these determinations before the merger occurs.[21] As a result of Congress's enactment of the Hart-Scott-Rodino Antitrust Improvements Act in 1976, firms above a certain size must provide the agencies with information about planned transactions before they merge. It is much easier for the agencies

---

because the challenged conduct fell "squarely within the heartland of securities regulations" and the Securities and Exchange Commission had authority to supervise the activity and "continuously exercised" such authority). 127 S. Ct. 2383, 2387, 2393, 2397 (2007). The breadth of *Trinko* is an open question, with expansive interpretations treating it as a limit on antitrust enforcement in regulated industries or even on general Section 2 liability.

18. Two other types of mergers have been less frequently challenged: *vertical* mergers (between firms at different levels of the supply chain) and *conglomerate* mergers (which involve firms selling neither substitutes nor complements).

19. GAVIL ET AL., at 431, 472–73.

20. U.S. DEP'T OF JUSTICE & FED. TRADE COMM'N, HORIZONTAL MERGER GUIDELINES § 0.2 (1997).

21. *See generally* GAVIL ET AL., at 472–78.

to challenge mergers before they occur than to "unscramble the assets" after the transaction. The vast majority of mergers today are allowed without challenge. In the first decade of the 21st century, merger challenges, as a percentage of filings, were lower than at any point since the second Reagan administration.[22]

Of the horizontal mergers that are challenged, most occur where firms compete in product markets.[23] The traditional concern is that such mergers could make it easier for all the firms in the market to collude and raise prices. This theory of *coordinated effects* has been supplemented in the past two decades with the concern of *unilateral effects*, by which firms with similar products could raise price after the merger regardless of the actions of other firms in the market.[24]

In addition to mergers in goods markets, two other types of markets have garnered attention. *Technology markets* consist of IP that is licensed, and *innovation markets* consist of the research and development (R&D) directed toward new products.[25] The theory behind innovation markets is that a merger between the only two (or two of a few) firms conducting R&D might increase the incentive to suppress at least one of the research paths. With no other firms ready to enter the market, the merging firms might not wish to introduce a second product that would reduce sales of the first.

The theory, however, has received significant criticism. Opponents have claimed that (1) the participants in such "markets" cannot be reliably identified; (2) conduct can be challenged at a later time, negating the need for the concept; (3) the relationship between R&D and innovation is unclear; and (4) the market structure most conducive to innovation is unknown. I address these claims in

---

22. Jonathan B. Baker & Carl Shapiro, *Reinvigorating Horizontal Merger Enforcement*, at 17 (June 2007), http://faculty.haas.berkeley.edu/shapiro/mergerpolicy.pdf. Baker and Shapiro detail courts and agencies' decreasing attention to market concentration and increasing openness to parties' arguments about concentration, entry, and efficiencies. *Id.* at 41. David Meyer, the former Deputy Assistant Attorney General for Antitrust, downplayed the reduction in challenges, asserting that the number fails to account for increased agency guidance, fewer transactions that raise concern, and more mergers in the quickly changing services and technology industries. David L. Meyer, *Merger Enforcement Is Alive and Well at the Department of Justice*, Nov. 15, 2007, http://www.usdoj.gov/atr/public/speeches/227713.htm.

23. The full details of merger enforcement are beyond the scope of this chapter. For additional analysis, see Baker & Shapiro; Malcolm B. Coate & Shawn W. Ulrick, FTC Bur. of Econ., *Transparency at the Federal Trade Commission: The Horizontal Merger Review Process 1996–2003*, Feb. 2005, http://www.ftc.gov/os/2005/02/0502economicissues.pdf; William Kolasky, *U.S. Merger Review: A 'Goldilocksian Perspective'* (July 2005), http://law.bepress.com/wilmer/papers/art14.

24. GAVIL ET AL., at 434.

25. U.S. DEP'T OF JUSTICE & FED. TRADE COMM'N, ANTITRUST GUIDELINES FOR THE LICENSING OF INTELLECTUAL PROPERTY §§ 3.2.2, 3.2.3 (1995).

Chapter 13 by explaining how features of the pharmaceutical industry rebut these critiques and justify the application of innovation markets.

There are numerous other antitrust doctrines. But the most relevant to IP are agreements, monopolization, and mergers. The current law in these areas can best be understood in the context of antitrust's shifting analysis through the past century.

ANTITRUST HISTORY

Federal antitrust law is traced to the passage of the Sherman Antitrust Act in 1890.[26] The period after the Civil War had witnessed business consolidation and the rise of organizations such as trusts, which allowed companies to combine their power to dominate the sugar, railroad, oil, whiskey, and other industries.[27] This accumulation of power engendered public hostility, which led Congress to address the "tyrannies" and "commercial monsters" by enacting the Sherman Act.[28]

The Sherman Act has two primary provisions. Section 1 targets agreements, outlawing "every contract, combination . . ., or conspiracy, in restraint of trade."[29] Section 2 focuses on unilateral acts, making it illegal for a company to "monopolize, or attempt to monopolize" any part of interstate or foreign commerce.[30]

The vague nature of the Act's text is not clarified by its legislative history.[31] The drafters discussed several goals for antitrust: consumer welfare, the protection of small businesses, the process of competition, and economic fairness.[32] In contrast to this mélange, however, stood one issue on which the legislative history was crystal clear: the courts' role in developing antitrust law. The drafters uniformly recognized that the courts were to turn to the "old and well recognized principles of the common law" in fleshing out gaps in the Sherman Act.[33]

---

26. Several states had enacted antitrust laws before the Sherman Act. States still play a role in enforcing the antitrust laws, as witnessed by claims against Microsoft that went beyond the federal government's case. Lawsuits also are initiated by private plaintiffs, who can recover treble damages and attorneys fees under the Clayton Act. 15 U.S.C. § 15(a).

27. American Antitrust Institute, *About Antitrust*, http://www.fairfightfilm.org/about-antitrust.html (last visited July 10, 2008).

28. 20 Cong. Rec. 2726 (1890); 20 Cong. Rec. at 1457 (1889). *See generally* Carrier, at 1294–96 (providing sources).

29. 15 U.S.C. § 1 (2004).

30. 15 U.S.C. § 2.

31. *See generally* Michael A. Carrier, *Resolving the Patent-Antitrust Paradox Through Tripartite Innovation*, 56 Vand. L. Rev. 1047 (2003).

32. *E.g.*, Robert H. Bork, *The Role of Courts in Applying Economics*, 54 Antitrust L.J. 21, 24 (1985); Robert H. Lande, *Wealth Transfers as the Original and Primary Concern of Antitrust: The Efficiency Interpretation Challenged*, 34 Hastings L.J. 65, 93–106 (1982).

33. 21 Cong. Rec. 2456, 2460 (1890).

This open-ended delegation to courts has resulted in analysis that has swung markedly in the past century.[34] In the first two decades after the Act's passage, courts grappled with its meaning. They pared it back so it did not apply to "every contract," which would have encompassed harmless licensing agreements. Instead, they limited the Act's scope to *unreasonable* agreements.[35] Similarly, they drew distinctions between *naked* restraints that had no purpose except harming competition and agreements that were *ancillary* to a legitimate objective.[36]

Congress was concerned with the courts' weakening of the law. As a result, in 1914 it enacted the Clayton Act and Federal Trade Commission (FTC) Act. The Clayton Act prohibited tying arrangements (in which a buyer who wishes to purchase one product is forced to take a second), exclusive dealing agreements (in which a buyer agrees to buy products from a certain seller), and mergers and acquisitions that "substantially . . . lessen competition or . . . tend to create a monopoly."[37] The FTC Act created the Federal Trade Commission and gave it authority to challenge "[u]nfair methods of competition."[38]

From 1915 until the mid-1930s, courts permissively treated most business activity.[39] The onset of the Great Depression played a role. Courts were more tolerant of collusion, as witnessed in the case of *Appalachian Coals, Inc. v. United States*, in which the Supreme Court upheld a joint marketing arrangement that allowed coal producers to fix prices.[40]

Beginning in the late 1930s, however, antitrust enforcement increased. In *United States v. Socony-Vacuum Oil Co.*, the Court concluded that price-fixing agreements among competitors should automatically be condemned as per se illegal.[41] For the next three decades, the Court imposed per se rules in many other areas including tying, vertical nonprice restraints, group boycotts, market allocation agreements, and exclusive sales territories accompanying joint ventures.[42]

---

34. For an excellent overview of these shifts, see William E. Kovacic & Carl Shapiro, *Antitrust Policy: A Century of Economic and Legal Thinking*, 14 J. Econ. Persp. 43 (2000).

35. *Standard Oil Co. v. United States*, 221 U.S. 1 (1911).

36. *United States v. Addyston Pipe & Steel Co.*, 85 Fed. 271, 281–82 (6th Cir. 1898) (upholding noncompetition agreements related to partners, employees, and property owners).

37. 15 U.S.C. §§ 14, 18.

38. 15 U.S.C. § 45; *see generally* Kovacic & Shapiro, at 46.

39. 246 U.S. 231 (1918).

40. 288 U.S. 344 (1933).

41. 310 U.S. 150 (1940).

42. *Northern Pacific Ry. Co. v. United States*, 356 U.S. 1 (1958) (tying arrangements); *United States v. Arnold, Schwinn & Co.*, 388 U.S. 365 (1967) (vertical nonprice restraints); *Klor's, Inc. v. Broadway-Hale Stores, Inc.*, 359 U.S. 207 (1959) (group boycotts); *Timken Roller Bearing Co. v. United States*, 341 U.S. 593 (1951) (market allocation); *United States v. Topco Assocs., Inc.*, 405 U.S. 596 (1972) (exclusive territories). *See generally* Kovacic & Shapiro, at 50.

The Court also skeptically examined the activity of dominant firms. In one case, it condemned Alcoa's practice of anticipating new demand for aluminum by adding capacity.[43] And in another, it condemned the practice of United Shoe's leasing of machines even after praising the defendant's R&D and noting its customers' approval of the policy.[44]

During this period, courts emphasized goals for antitrust such as protecting small businesses and addressing the effects of concentration. This was most prominent in the area of mergers. In the markets for beer, shoes, and grocery stores, for example, courts struck down mergers that would have resulted in market shares of 4.5, 5, and 7.5 percent, respectively, relying on the trend toward concentration.[45]

The pendulum swung back in the 1970s. The Chicago School of Economics, actively advanced by Robert Bork and Richard Posner, shifted the focus to *neoclassical microeconomics*.[46] This framework assumes that individuals and firms act rationally in their self-interest. Individuals as consumers seek to maximize utility by buying products until the costs of doing so outweigh the gains. Firms seek to maximize profits as producers by manufacturing goods until the marginal cost of producing an additional unit outweighs the revenue it would generate.[47] In other words, the framework emphasizes *allocative efficiency*, or the optimal allocation of goods and services to consumers, typically through equating price with marginal cost.

Court decisions incorporated the microeconomic framework, and the Supreme Court began to offer an approach that reflected Chicago School reasoning. In *Continental TV v. GTE Sylvania*, the Court replaced per se treatment with a more deferential Rule-of-Reason analysis for nonprice vertical restrictions.[48] And merger decisions made it easier for defendants to rebut high market shares and introduce evidence that it was easy to enter the market, and that the merger promised efficiencies.[49]

---

43. *United States v. Aluminum Co. of America*, 148 F.2d 416, 430–31 (2d Cir. 1945).

44. *United States v. United Shoe Mach. Corp.*, 110 F. Supp. 295, 323, 330–32, 336 (D. Mass. 1953). *See generally* Kovacic & Shapiro, at 52.

45. *United States v. Pabst Brewing Co.*, 384 U.S. 546, 551 (1966) (4.5 percent); *Brown Shoe Co. v. United States*, 370 U.S. 294, 315, 343–44 (1962) (5 percent); *United States v. Von's Grocery Co.*, 384 U.S. 270, 272 (1966) (7.5 percent).

46. The Chicago School originated in the work of Aaron Director in the 1940s and 1950s. *See* Kovacic & Shapiro, at 53. For a history of neoclassical microeconomics, see Herbert J. Hovenkamp, *The Neoclassical Crisis in U.S. Competition Policy, 1890–1955*, July 2008, http://ssrn.com/abstract=1156927.

47. E. Roy Weintraub, *Neoclassical Economics, in* THE CONCISE ENCYCLOPEDIA OF ECONOMICS, http://www.econlib.org/Library/Enc/NeoclassicalEconomics.html (last visited August 20, 2008).

48. 433 U.S. 36 (1977).

49. *United States v. Gen. Dynamics Corp.*, 415 U.S. 486 (1974) (market share rebuttal); *Fed. Trade Comm'n v. Univ. Health, Inc.*, 938 F.2d 1206 (11th Cir. 1991) (efficiencies);

The Chicago School did not have a monopoly on economic reasoning, however. In the 1990s, the Post-Chicago School introduced more elaborate conceptions of competitive harm. Scholars applied game theory, by which firms consider their rivals' anticipated reactions in deciding to engage in particular behavior.

The most prominent judicial adoption of the theory occurred in *Eastman Kodak Co. v. Image Technical Services, Inc.* In that case, Kodak manufactured photocopiers in a competitive *primary* market of copiers but restricted access to replacement parts in the *secondary* market of Kodak copiers. The Court concluded that Kodak had monopoly power in this aftermarket and relied on game-theory concepts in pointing to the potential harm from information and switching costs that "locked in" customers to the copiers.[50] The notion of aftermarkets as potential monopolies has been a controversial one, however, and post-*Kodak* courts have "bent over backwards" to construe the case "as narrowly as possible."[51]

In the first decade of the 21st century, the Supreme Court showed an active interest in reforming antitrust law. It consistently came down on the side of the defendant.[52] And as seen in areas such as vertical price fixing and a market power presumption from patents, it replaced decisions that had applied per se analysis with more deferential Rule-of-Reason treatment.[53]

EVALUATION: THE NEGATIVE VIEW

Have the antitrust laws been successful in achieving their goals? This is a difficult question to answer precisely.

In contrast to the mid-20th century, when noneconomic goals were advanced, antitrust courts and commentators today take as their starting point

---

United States v. Baker Hughes, Inc., 908 F.2d 981 (D.C. Cir. 1990) (market share rebuttal); *United States v. Waste Mgmt., Inc.*, 743 F.2d 976 (2d Cir. 1984) (ease of entry). *See generally* Kovacic & Shapiro, at 54.

50. *Eastman Kodak Co. v. Image Tech. Servs., Inc.*, 504 U.S. 451, 473–77 (1992).

51. Herbert Hovenkamp, *Post-Chicago Antitrust: A Review and Critique*, 2001 COLUM. BUS. L. REV. 257, 286.

52. *E.g., Texaco, Inc. v. Dagher*, 547 U.S. 1 (2006) (joint ventures); *Illinois Tool Works, Inc. v. Independent Ink, Inc.*, 547 U.S. 28 (2006) (market power presumption); *Weyerhaeuser Co. v. Ross-Simmons Hardwood Lumber Co.*, 127 S. Ct 1069 (2007) (predatory bidding); *Bell Atlantic Corp. v. Twombly*, 127 S. Ct. 1955 (2007) (pleading standards); *Leegin Creative Leather Prods. v. PSKS, Inc.*, 127 S. Ct. 2705 (2007) (minimum resale price maintenance); *Credit Suisse Securities v. Billing*, 127 S. Ct. 2383 (2007) (effect of securities laws).

53. *State Oil Co. v. Khan*, 522 U.S. 3 (1997) (vertical maximum price fixing); *Illinois Tool Works, Inc. v. Indep. Ink, Inc.*, 547 U.S. 28 (2006) (patent does not automatically demonstrate market power); *Leegin Creative Leather Prods., Inc. v. PSKS, Inc.*, 127 S. Ct. 2705 (2007) (vertical minimum price fixing).

an economics-based framework. But that does not resolve the challenges confronting an assessment of antitrust's success.

For starters, there are many versions of economics. Just to pick one example, the neoclassical economist's rational actor competes with the behavioral economist's often-irrational actor.

In addition, courts and commentators have focused on several types of efficiencies. As discussed earlier, *allocative efficiency* refers to the allocation of goods and services to buyers who value them most. *Productive efficiency* denotes the production of goods in the most cost-effective manner. And *innovative efficiency* signifies gains through the invention, development, and diffusion of new products and processes that increase social wealth.[54]

Nor do the difficulties end there. Even assuming that a primary goal of antitrust is innovative efficiency, there is no simple way to trace the effect of antitrust on economic growth. One cannot confidently predict how events would have played out in the absence of antitrust. None of these difficulties, however, has prevented commentators from advancing arguments about the need for antitrust.

Crandall & Winston

Robert Crandall and Clifford Winston have offered the most prominent pessimistic assessment of antitrust. They have concluded that there is "little empirical evidence" that antitrust enforcement has "provided much direct benefit to consumers or significantly deterred anticompetitive behavior."[55]

Crandall and Winston examined the effectiveness of antitrust policy in three areas: monopolization, collusion, and mergers. First, they analyzed six landmark monopolization cases, concluding that the cases failed to benefit consumers because the remedies had a "negligible practical impact" and the cases' "protracted length" prevented them from effectively addressing the market.[56] Second, the authors relied on three studies in finding that there was not "much direct benefit" from "curbing alleged instances of collusion." Third, they conducted empirical research and concluded that "the mergers blocked by antitrust authorities ha[d] no significant effect."[57] In addition to these deficiencies, the

---

54. Joseph F. Brodley, *The Economic Goals of Antitrust: Efficiency, Consumer Welfare, and Technological Progress*, 62 N.Y.U. L. Rev. 1020, 1025 (1987); *see also* Albert A. Foer, *The Goals of Antitrust: Thoughts on Consumer Welfare in the U.S.*, in Handbook of Research in Trans-Atlantic Antitrust 566 (Philip Marsden ed., 2006). An efficiency is "a decision or event that increases the total value of all economically measurable assets in the society." Brodley, *id.*

55. Robert W. Crandall & Clifford Winston, *Does Antitrust Policy Improve Consumer Welfare? Assessing the Evidence*, 17 J. Econ. Persp. 3, 4 (2003).

56. The cases involved Standard Oil, American Tobacco, Alcoa, Paramount, United Shoe Machinery, and AT&T. *Id.* at 7–14.

57. *Id.* at 13, 14, 18–19.

authors blame the "apparent ineffectiveness of antitrust policy" on challenges presented by new-economy issues, political forces influencing antitrust cases, and the market's ability to spur competition and curb anticompetitive abuses.[58]

Crandall-Winston Critique

The Crandall-Winston argument, if true, would be devastating. It would show that antitrust offers little benefit. This would be particularly harmful when combined with antitrust's costs, as seen in expensive and lengthy litigation and complex jury issues. Nor would the error costs of wrong decisions be tolerable. Chicago School commentators—and recently the Supreme Court—have been concerned with false positives, or the costs of decisions that wrongly impose liability on innocent firms.[59] A legitimate antitrust regime would weigh the error costs of false positives against false negatives in which wrongdoers are mistakenly not penalized. In contrast, Crandall and Winston's argument against antitrust would not need to tolerate false positives and would retreat to, at most, "only the most egregious anticompetitive violations."[60]

Luckily for antitrust, the argument advanced by Crandall and Winston does not withstand scrutiny. As several commentators have shown, it is riddled with fundamental flaws; I will only mention three. First, the authors rely on a "startlingly selective use of the evidence."[61] They cite only one study on the effect of price fixing on collusion, failing to mention the numerous other studies that found that bid rigging had increased prices as much as 36 percent in the construction, food, used car, and real estate auction industries and that price fixing had raised prices as much as 34 percent in the lysine, citric acid, and vitamins cartels.[62] Second, the empirical analysis they conduct for mergers uses industry classifications that are far too general to bear any resemblance to markets affected by the mergers.[63] Third, Crandall and Winston's analysis of monopolization law relies on cases "at least a half-century old" and "lumps together all possible objections" to the cases to draw conclusions about future antitrust policy.[64]

---

58. *Id.* at 23.

59. *Verizon Communications, Inc. v. Law Offices of Curtis V. Trinko LLP*, 540 U.S. 398, 414 (2004); Frank H. Easterbrook, *The Limits of Antitrust*, 63 Tex. L. Rev. 1, 2–3 (1984).

60. Crandall & Winston, at 4.

61. John E. Kwoka, Jr., *The Attack on Antitrust Policy and Consumer Welfare: A Response to Crandall and Winston*, at 3 (Northeastern University, Department of Economics Working Paper 03-005, Mar. 2003).

62. Gregory J. Werden, *The Effect of Antitrust Policy on Consumer Welfare: What Crandall and Winston Overlook*, at 1–2 (Economic Analysis Group Discussion Paper, EAG 03-2, Jan. 2003) (citing studies).

63. *Id.* at 3.

64. Kwoka, at 2–3.

EVALUATION: THE POSITIVE VIEW

Professor Jonathan Baker has most exhaustively articulated the benefits of antitrust enforcement. He relies primarily on four "informal experiments" that examine the performance of markets in periods in which antitrust enforcement was weak or nonexistent.[65]

The first experiment involved industry performance in the United States before the passage of the Sherman Act in 1890. Studies revealed coordination in the steel, bromine, railroad, and petroleum refining industries. In addition, exclusionary behavior was prominent in the activities of Standard Oil (which acquired nearly all of the nation's oil refining capacity through anticompetitive means) and American Tobacco (which forced rivals to be acquired on unfavorable terms).[66]

The second experiment occurred in the 1930s when Congress enacted the National Industrial Recovery Act, which allowed industries to develop "Codes of Fair Competition." Many industries used their codes to fix prices by setting minimum prices, prohibiting sales below cost, and outlawing secret or selective price-cutting. Steel producers and other industries took advantage of the elimination of antitrust to collude and increase prices.[67]

The third experiment built on the 1918 repeal of antitrust laws for export cartels, by which firms agreed to charge certain export prices.[68] A study of cartels in nearly 100 industries in the 20th century uncovered many examples of durable export agreements based on price fixing, with one-fourth of the cartels lasting at least 15 years.[69]

The last experiment occurred in the mid-1980s at a time when the Department of Transportation was responsible for reviewing airline mergers. During this period, mergers involving Northwest and Trans World Airlines (TWA) proceeded despite opposition by the Department of Justice. Studies found that fares in certain markets increased as a result of the mergers.[70]

The four experiments thus provide evidence of reduced competition and increased prices when antitrust is not enforced. In particular, they offer examples of firms using the absence of antitrust to exercise market power and harm consumers.[71]

---

65. Jonathan B. Baker, *The Case for Antitrust Enforcement*, 17 J. ECON. PERSP. 27, 36 (2003).

66. *Id.* at 36–37.

67. *Id.* at 37.

68. *Id.*; OECD, *Glossary of Statistical Terms*, 2003, http://stats.oecd.org/glossary/detail.asp?ID=3213.

69. Baker, at 37–38.

70. *Id.* at 38.

71. *Id.*

The anecdotal nature of these experiments points to the difficulties in offering a net calculation of antitrust's effect on welfare. There is no magic formula available. Baker nonetheless estimated (in 2003) that the annual cost of the U.S. antitrust laws was roughly $2 billion.[72] On the other hand, he believed that the benefits, in preventing collusion and price fixing, challenging monopolies, and blocking anticompetitive mergers, could exceed 1 percent of the U.S. Gross National Product (GNP), which would equal more than $100 billion each year.[73]

One example of antitrust's benefits can be seen in its punishment of price overcharges imposed by cartels. Professors John Connor and Robert Lande, after conducting the most exhaustive survey of the issue, concluded that the median cartel overcharge was 25 percent.[74] One prominent example is offered by the vitamins industry, which peaked in the 1990s with 16 cartels. The average vitamins cartel lasted six to ten years and increased price between 20 and 90 percent.[75] The deadweight loss from purchasers not buying vitamins they would have bought at lower, competitive prices has been estimated at between $50 million and $100 million per year.[76]

In conclusion, the numbers for antitrust's costs and benefits cannot be offered with precision. But it seems safe to conclude that antitrust's benefits outweigh its costs.

INNOVATION CONCERNS

Antitrust can foster innovation, as it does when it removes entry barriers or promotes competition. But specific harms to IP and innovation could arise from imprudent antitrust enforcement. As Chapter 4 will show, courts and agencies in the mid-to-late 20th century demonstrated just these concerns. Licensing activity needed for innovation was viewed hostilely, and patents were automatically assumed to create market power.

---

72. *Id.* at 42–43 (including $150 million in direct governmental enforcement costs, $500 million in costs to firms to comply with merger review, $400 million in private costs, and a maximum $1 billion in indirect costs).

73. *Id.* at 45.

74. John M. Connor & Robert H. Lande, *How High Do Cartels Raise Prices? Implications for Optimal Cartel Fines*, 80 TUL. L. REV. 513, 535, 543 (2005). Their finding was based on 845 estimates of cartel overcharges or undercharges in 234 markets. The authors supported their conclusion by examining final verdicts in collusion cases and finding a median overcharge of 21 percent. *Id.* at 556. They use median figures because of the distorting effect of "a few very high overcharges" on mean figures. *Id.* at 540.

75. John M. Connor, *The Great Global Vitamins Conspiracy: Sanctions and Deterrence*, at 26, 28, Feb. 24, 2006, http://www.agecon.purdue.edu/staff/connor/papers/The%20Great%20Global%20Vitamins%20Conspiracy%20Sanctions%20and%20Deterrence.pdf.

76. Baker, at 43.

These mistakes threatened false positives, which were concerning in this context because of their effects not only on innocent parties but also on the IP system. They also threatened false negatives when they deferred completely to IP. Many of these concerns have been addressed as the law and economics of antitrust has evolved. But antitrust still must be cognizant of its effect on innovation. To elaborate on these issues, the next two chapters address the intersection of antitrust and IP in the 20th and 21st centuries.

4. ANTITRUST AND IP: 20TH CENTURY

Conflict 71
Early IP Dominance 73
The Decline of Patent Immunity 74
The Apex of Antitrust 76
The Loosening of the Antitrust Reins 78
    Courts 78
    Congress 79
IP Guidelines 81
    Market Power Presumption 81
Refusals to License 82
    Rebuttable Presumption of Legality 82
    Intent-based Rebuttal 83
    Near-per se Legality 84

The marriage between IP and antitrust has suffered stormy periods. This chapter explores the underpinnings of their mutual distrust and the various stages of their relationship.

It begins by discussing the conflict between the areas of IP and antitrust. It then traces the history of the relationship in the 20th century, in which IP's position lurched from immunity to hostility and back to predominance.

The framework for Chapters 4 and 5 bears a caveat. I address the relationship in two chapters. But there is no clean break between the 20th and 21st centuries. The agencies' IP Guidelines and courts' treatments of refusals to license, discussed at the end of this chapter, are still important in the 21st century.

In addition, the subjects I address in the next chapter—the *Microsoft* case, innovation markets (markets for research and development), patent pools, standard-setting activity, and settlement agreements—witnessed important developments in the late 20th century. The divide nonetheless is useful in tracing the history of the relationship and in assembling, in the next chapter, the most important current issues in the intersection.

CONFLICT

The foundation of the IP system is the right to exclude. As discussed in Chapter 2, such a right allows innovators to charge prices higher than their postinvention costs.[1] As a result, innovators can recoup their investment costs and gain profits, thereby encouraging future innovation.

---

1. Because IP does not always provide market power, innovators are not always able to increase price for a sustained period.

The concern is that the very exclusion that forms the foundation of the patent and copyright systems may be punished under the antitrust laws. The antitrust laws scrutinize activity that restricts competition because competition generally leads to lower prices, higher output, and (often) more innovation. Monopolists, for example, typically lack the constraints provided by competitive markets. As a consequence, they may be free to reduce output, raise prices, or limit innovation.

Similarly, agreements between IP holders and licensees restrict competition by their very operation. Patentees may impose restrictions on licensees such as

- *quantity restrictions*, which limit the amount of products that can be sold
- *royalty payments*, which determine the royalties that can be received
- *grantbacks*, by which licensors reserve rights in licensees' improvements
- *territorial restrictions*, which restrict licensees to certain areas
- *field-of-use restrictions*, which limit licensees' uses of inventions to certain fields.[2]

On a larger scale, owners could combine their IP. Patentees could jointly set royalties for multiple patents in a *patent pool*. Copyright holders could offer *blanket licenses* that provide access to numerous (even millions of) copyrighted works. And IP owners could enter into joint ventures and mergers.

This broad range of activity may make perfect sense from the standpoint of dispersing or exploiting the protected innovation. Cross-licensing and patent pools avoid bottlenecks. Blanket licenses reduce transaction costs. Licensing allows owners to maximize use of an innovation. But the greater need for cooperation from IP's perspective could trigger antitrust's suspicion.

In short, the IP and antitrust systems operate in different ways. Can this conflict be remedied? Some have sought to do so by pointing to broad objectives. The Federal Circuit stated that the patent and antitrust laws are "complementary" because "both are aimed at encouraging innovation, industry and competition."[3] And a leading commentator on the intersection, Ward Bowman, explained that the two regimes "have a common central economic goal" of "maximiz[ing] wealth by producing what consumers want at the lowest cost."[4]

These broad objectives, however, operate on a plane too abstract to resolve particular questions. How, for example, would these objectives provide guidance on the proper treatment of patent pools? Standard-setting activity? Refusals to license? While a common objective for the laws would be beneficial, it does not offer specific guidance that would resolve the conflict in particular settings.

---

2. *See generally* Michael A. Carrier, *Resolving the Patent-Antitrust Paradox Through Tripartite Innovation*, 56 Vand. L. Rev. 1047, 1048–53 (2003).

3. *Atari Games Corp. v. Nintendo of America, Inc.*, 897 F.2d 1572, 1576 (Fed. Cir. 1990).

4. Ward S. Bowman, Jr., Patent and Antitrust Law: A Legal and Economic Appraisal 1 (1973).

The IP-antitrust conflict thus cannot be remedied by pointing to the regimes' goals. Courts' treatment of the issue nonetheless provides some clues as to how it can be minimized. In the period immediately following the enactment of the Sherman Act in 1890, courts treated IP as paramount. By the middle of the 20th century, they had adopted an approach hostile to IP. By the 1980s, the pendulum had swung back, with courts deferring once again to IP.

From our vantage point in the early 21st century, much of antitrust's deference to IP is beneficial and—most important—has reduced the saliency of the IP-antitrust conflict. But as the history of the intersection in the 20th century reveals, this has been a rocky road.

EARLY IP DOMINANCE

The period from 1890 to 1912 marked the first stage. In this period, courts refused to impose antitrust liability for patent-based activity. They treated IP as owners' private property and licensing arrangements as activity within their discretion.[5] Three representative cases demonstrate this view.

In *Heaton-Pennisular Button-Fastener Co. v. Eureka Specialty Co.*, the patentee invented a machine that stapled buttons onto shoes. In selling the machines, the patentee required buyers to purchase fasteners to use with the machines. The Sixth Circuit upheld the arrangement. It concluded that "[t]he monopoly in the unpatented staple results . . . from the monopoly in the use of [the] invention" and thus was "a legitimate result of the patentee's control over the use of his invention."[6]

The Supreme Court articulated an even more expansive notion of immunity in *E. Bement & Sons v. National Harrow Co.*[7] This case involved a patent pool that included float-spring tooth harrows (toothed combs attached to tractors that help maintain farmland).[8] Twenty-two firms, representing more than 90 percent of float-spring tooth harrows in the United States, licensed patents relating to the manufacture, use, and sale of the harrows to National Harrow Company.[9]

National Harrow, in turn, licensed the patents to the contributing firms on the condition that they follow agreed-upon price schedules and sell only the type of harrows they had contributed to the pool. In upholding the arrangement, the Supreme Court stated that "[t]he very object of the [patent] laws is monopoly" and explained that "any conditions which are not in their very nature illegal . . . will

---

5. *See* Willard K. Tom & Joshua A. Newberg, *Antitrust and Intellectual Property: From Separate Spheres to Unified Field*, 66 ANTITRUST L.J. 167, 169 (1997).

6. 77 F. 288, 288–89, 296 (6th Cir. 1896).

7. 186 U.S. 70 (1902).

8. Harrow, *Free Dictionary*, http://columbia.thefreedictionary.com/Harrow.

9. *National Harrow Co. v. Hench*, 76 F. 667, 668 (E.D. Pa. 1896).

be upheld by the courts." Price fixing among competitors, in other words, was an incidental, lawful, by-product of the patent monopoly.[10]

Ten years later, in *A.B. Dick v. Henry*, the Court again construed the rights of a patent holder expansively. A.B. Dick patented and manufactured a mimeograph machine, which made copies by pressing ink through stencil openings. It licensed its machines on the condition that users only use the company's stencil, paper, ink, and other supplies. The Supreme Court concluded that the arrangement was a "reasonable stipulation, not inherently violative of some substantive law, imposed by a patentee as part of a sale of a patented machine."[11]

THE DECLINE OF PATENT IMMUNITY

Congress responded to the Court's decision in *A.B. Dick* two years later by enacting the Clayton Act, which prohibited the tying of patented and unpatented products.[12] At around the same time, courts began to limit the power of patentees. In *Standard Sanitary Manufacturing Co. v. United States*, the Court recognized that IP rights were subject to the "positive prohibitions" of the Sherman Act.[13] And in *Motion Picture Patents Co. v. Universal Film Manufacturing Co.*, the Court asserted that the rights of patent owners flowed not from patent law but from the "general law [of] the ownership of . . . property."[14]

The *Motion Picture Patents* case, in particular, signaled a new approach. The Motion Picture Patent Company had tied its patented movie projectors to films it produced. The Court held that such a restriction was invalid because the film was not part of the patented invention and the tie sought to expand the patent monopoly beyond the scope of the projector. The Court overruled its earlier decision in *A.B. Dick* and remarked that the Clayton Act "confirmed" its analysis under the patent laws.[15]

This trend continued in *Morton Salt Co. v. G.S. Suppiger Co.* Morton Salt had invented and patented a machine that deposited salt tablets in canned goods. It also licensed its patented machine to firms in the canning industry on the condition that they bought salt from it. The defendant had built a machine that was similar to Morton Salt's patented machine, and Morton Salt brought an infringement suit against it.[16]

---

10. 186 U.S. at 72–73, 91.

11. 224 U.S. 1, 11, 31 (1912).

12. 15 U.S.C. §§ 12–27 (1914); *see generally* Herbert Hovenkamp, *IP and Antitrust Policy: A Brief Historical Overview*, at 11 (University of Iowa Legal Studies Research Paper, No. 05-31, 2005).

13. 226 U.S. 20, 49 (1912).

14. 243 U.S. 502, 513 (1917).

15. *Id.* at 505–07, 517–18.

16. 314 U.S. 488, 489, 491 (1942); *see also G.S. Suppiger Co. v. Morton Salt Co.*, 117 F.2d 968, 970 (7th Cir. 1941).

The Court stated that Morton Salt used "its patent monopoly to restrain competition in the marketing of unpatented articles . . . and is aiding in the creation of a limited monopoly in the tablets not within that granted by the patent." Because Morton Salt had improperly tied its salt tablets to the machines, it could not successfully pursue an infringement suit. The Court did not find it necessary to rely on the antitrust laws because, under patent law, "to restrain . . . manufacture or sale of the alleged infringing machine[ ] [was] contrary to public policy."[17]

As the *Motion Picture Patents* and *Morton Salt* cases demonstrated, courts during this period refused to enjoin infringement when a patentee acted outside the scope of its patent. One exception occurred in the case of *United States v. General Electric,* in which the Court upheld a price-fixing arrangement. General Electric and its licensees had agreed on prices to be charged for lightbulbs. The Court explained that the price of a patented article "ha[s] a more direct relation . . . to the rights of the patentee than the unpatented material with which the patented article may be used." In fact, the Court continued, "price fixing is usually the essence of that which secures proper reward to the patentee."[18] Subsequent courts have interpreted the case narrowly.[19]

The Court began to recognize antitrust limits on patentees in *Carbice Corp. of America v. American Patents Development Corp.* In this case, the Court confronted a patent for a refrigerating transportation package consisting of solid carbon dioxide (dry ice) that "revolutionized the transportation of ice cream." The patent's exclusive licensee required purchasers to buy its dry ice to use along with the package. The patentee and licensee claimed that the defendant had committed contributory infringement by selling dry ice. The Court barred recovery because a patent could not be used to "secure a limited monopoly of unpatented material used in applying the invention." While the Court relied primarily on principles of patent misuse, it also remarked that "the attempt to use the patent unreasonably to restrain commerce is . . . a direct violation of the Anti-Trust Acts."[20]

The trend toward antitrust limits continued in *Mercoid Corp. v. Mid-Continent Investment Co.* In *Mercoid*, the exclusive licensee under a combination patent required that buyers use unpatented components along with its patented heating system. In the first of two decisions, the Court held that a patentee and its exclusive licensee could not claim contributory infringement against one of the sellers of the unpatented components.[21]

Although the Court did not specify whether it relied on patent misuse or antitrust, a second *Mercoid* decision a year later explicitly relied on antitrust.

---

17. *Id.* at 491, 494.
18. 272 U.S. 476, 493 (1926).
19. *See* Hovenkamp, at 24–25 (listing cases).
20. 283 U.S. 27, 29–30, 33–34, 34 n.4 (1931).
21. 320 U.S. 661, 663, 669 (1944).

The Court stated that "[t]he legality of any attempt to bring unpatented goods within the protection of the patent is measured by the anti-trust laws, not [ ] the patent law" and that "the effort . . . made to control competition in this unpatented device plainly violates the anti-trust laws."[22] For the first time, the Court had relied on antitrust in penalizing a patentee that had tied patented and unpatented components.

Congress was concerned by the courts' narrowing of the doctrine of contributory infringement and broad application of patent misuse. As a result, it amended the Patent Act in 1952, limiting the patent misuse doctrine, overruling the *Mercoid* cases, and declaring that the sale of a product "made or especially adapted for use in an infringement of such patent" constituted contributory infringement.[23]

THE APEX OF ANTITRUST

At the same time, the Court was adopting an even more aggressive stance toward IP. It invalidated as per se illegal patent tying measures, cross-licensing agreements, territorial restraints, and other IP-based arrangements.[24]

The first case demonstrating this approach was *International Salt Co. v. United States.* In this case, a patentee owned patents on industrial salt-processing machines that dissolved rock salt and injected salt tablets into canned products. The company leased the patented machines on the condition that licensees also bought unpatented salt and salt tablets. The Court did not analyze the issue of market power since "the tendency of the arrangement to accomplishment of monopoly seems obvious." It also found that the tying arrangement was per se unlawful because "the patents confer no right to restrain use of, or trade in, unpatented salt."[25]

Fifteen years later, in *United States v. Loew's,* the Court addressed "block booking," by which a party conditions the license or sale of desired movies on the buyer's acceptance of a package containing unwanted films. In striking down such a practice, the Court explained that "[t]he requisite economic power is presumed when the tying product is patented or copyrighted."[26] For more than 40 years, the Court followed this presumption.

On a slightly different front, the Court was attacking cross-licensing arrangements. In *United States v. Line Material Co.,* the Court found that such an arrangement constituted price fixing. Southern States Equipment held a patent

---

22. *Mercoid Corp. v. Minneapolis-Honeywell Regulator Co.,* 320 U.S. 680, 684 (1944).

23. 35 U.S.C. § 271(c) (2005); *see* Daniel J. Gifford, *The Antitrust/Intellectual Property Interface: An Emerging Solution to an Intractable Problem,* 31 HOFSTRA L. REV. 363, 377–78 (2002).

24. Gifford, *id.*

25. 332 U.S. 392, 394–96 (1947).

26. 371 U.S. 38, 45 (1962).

for an electrical fuse. Line Material developed a simpler and cheaper version of the fuse. Because Line Material could not produce its fuse without infringing Southern's patent, the two firms entered into a cross-licensing agreement that set minimum price levels for the fuses produced under the arrangement. Even though the public could "obtain the full benefit of the efficiency and economy of the inventions" only by using both fuses, the Court found that the arrangement constituted unlawful price fixing, noting that "a contract to fix or maintain prices in interstate commerce has long been recognized as illegal per se under the Sherman Act."[27]

Aligned with the Court's increasingly hostile approach to patent tying and cross-licensing arrangements were the "Nine No-No's," which were announced by the Department of Justice Antitrust Division in 1970 and followed from 1968 to 1981.[28] The Nine No-No's encompassed IP licensing activities that the agency regarded as suspect under the antitrust laws. The list included nine activities:

(1) The tying of patented and unpatented products
(2) Mandatory grantbacks, by which licensors reserve rights in licensees' improvements[29]
(3) Postsale restrictions on resale by buyers of patented goods
(4) Tie-outs—agreements that a seller will sell a product only if the buyer does not buy it from another party
(5) Licensee veto power over grants of additional licenses
(6) Mandatory package licensing
(7) Compulsory payment of royalties not reasonably related to sales of the patented product
(8) Restrictions on sales of unpatented products made by a patented process
(9) Specification of the prices licensees could charge in reselling licensed products[30]

This list, which encompassed many arrangements having no economically harmful aspects, seemingly added to the logic of *International Salt*, *Loew's*, and *Line Material* by assuming that many IP arrangements automatically violated the antitrust laws. In finding competitive concern with activities falling within the scope of the patent, it went even further than the courts.[31]

---

27. 333 U.S. 287, 290–91, 297, 307 (1948).

28. Bruce B. Wilson, *Patent and Know-How License Agreements: Field of Use, Territorial, Price and Quantity Restrictions*, Address Before the Fourth New England Antitrust Conference (Nov. 6, 1970); Tom & Newberg, at 178–79 n.67.

29. U.S. Dep't of Justice & Fed. Trade Comm'n, Antitrust Guidelines for the Licensing of Intellectual Property § 5.6 (Apr. 9, 1995) [1995 Guidelines].

30. Tom & Newberg, at 179–81.

31. For example, veto power over additional licenses resembles an exclusive license within a patent's scope.

THE LOOSENING OF THE ANTITRUST REINS

Beginning in the 1970s, the courts retreated from the overtly hostile approach to various IP arrangements. They began to follow a more economics-based approach, analyzing the competitive effects of arrangements. Scholars affiliated with the Chicago School of Economics played a pivotal role in the transformation. Also critical was the passage of legislation such as the Federal Courts Improvement Act of 1982, the National Cooperative Research Act of 1984, and the Patent Misuse Reform Act of 1988.

Courts

One of the pivotal cases of the era was *Continental T.V., Inc. v. GTE Sylvania, Inc.* As discussed in Chapter 3, the Supreme Court in *Sylvania* examined whether a territorial restraint violated Section 1 of the Sherman Act. Sylvania manufactured television sets and sold them through franchisees that were limited to selling the sets in certain designated areas.[32]

The Court began by discarding a formalistic approach that had depended on whether title to the object had changed hands. In *United States v. Arnold, Schwinn & Co.*, the Court had deemed vertical territorial restraints to be per se illegal after a manufacturer had parted with title to the item.[33] The *Sylvania* Court, in contrast, analyzed the market effect of the restrictions—in particular, "their potential for a simultaneous reduction of intrabrand competition and stimulation of interbrand competition." The Court noted that intrabrand restraints often induced retailers to invest in products, engage in promotional activities, and provide service and repair facilities. It concluded that the restraints should be considered under the Rule of Reason.[34] This holding had a significant effect on IP licensing arrangements, which often take the form of nonprice vertical restraints and which are nearly always upheld today.

Another case strengthening IP's position was *BMI Music, Inc. v. Columbia Broadcasting, Inc.* In this case, the Court analyzed blanket licenses, which allowed licensees to perform any of the millions of copyrighted musical works in the package. Although there was an element of price fixing in the arrangement, the Court held that Rule-of-Reason analysis applied given the license's benefits in creating a product that would not otherwise have been available.[35]

Finally, several cases upheld parties' activities in introducing new products. In *Berkey Photo, Inc. v. Eastman Kodak Co.*, the Second Circuit refused to punish Kodak's failure to "predisclose" its products to competitors. It explained that

---

32. 433 U.S. 36, 38–39 (1977).
33. 388 U.S. 365, 379 (1967).
34. 433 U.S. at 51, 55, 59.
35. 441 U.S. 1, 5, 19, 21–22 (1979).

"withholding . . . advance knowledge of one's new products . . . ordinarily constitutes valid competitive conduct." The court recognized that a contrary rule that compelled a firm to share the benefits of "risky and expensive R&D" would "vitiate[ ]" innovation incentives.[36]

Courts also refused to punish firms that introduced new products that had the effect of injuring competitors. They found that

- Kodak could design a new film that provided better results than previous film, even if the change reduced compatibility with complementary products[37];
- IBM could redesign its products "to make them more attractive to buyers" rather than "constrict[ing] its product development so as to facilitate sales of rival products"[38];
- IBM could adopt a design for the interface between a computer and storage device "primarily to preclude . . . competition" as long as the design was superior.[39]

These cases reflect the law today. Unless the innovation truly is a "sham" that does not offer an improvement but is introduced only to injure a rival, courts will uphold the activity.[40]

Congress

In addition to the courts, Congress played a role in the rehabilitation of IP. The first example is provided by the National Cooperative Research Act of 1984.[41] This Act required that antitrust courts consider joint ventures engaging in R&D under the Rule of Reason. Such analysis would prevent automatic condemnation of such activities and thereby encourage collaborations.[42]

Another example is the Patent Misuse Reform Act of 1988.[43] The Act limited the range of activities that led to a finding of patent misuse. The doctrine of patent misuse prohibits a patentee from enforcing its patent against or recovering damages from an infringer. This doctrine historically applied to a broader

---

36. 603 F.2d 263, 281 (2d Cir. 1979).

37. *Id.* at 286.

38. *Cal. Computer Prods., Inc. v. IBM Corp.*, 613 F.2d 727, 744 (9th Cir. 1979).

39. *In re IBM Peripheral EDP Devices Antitrust Litig.*, 481 F. Supp. 965, 1005 (N.D. Cal. 1979).

40. In *C.R. Bard, Inc. v. M3 Sys., Inc.*, 157 F.3d 1340, 1382 (Fed. Cir. 1998), the court found liability where the "real reasons" a monopolist modified its product were to harm competitors.

41. Pub. L. No. 98-462, 98 Stat. 1815 (1984).

42. *Id.* § 3. In the National Cooperative Research and Production Act (NCRPA), Congress extended the provisions of the NCRA to joint ventures for production. *See* 15 U.S.C. §§ 4301–4306 (1993).

43. Pub. L. No. 100-703, 102 Stat. 4676 (1988), *codified at* 35 U.S.C. § 271(d) (1994).

range of activity than antitrust, in large part due to its origins in equity and absence of requirements such as market power.[44] Thus, while patent-related violations of the antitrust laws often constituted patent misuse, the converse was not necessarily true.

The Patent Misuse Reform Act declared that two types of activity would no longer be considered misuse: (1) a refusal to license a patented item and (2) tying of a patented good to a second product where the inventor lacked market power in the tying product. The first category did not significantly change existing case law, but the second closed the door to a potentially expansive conception of patent misuse by adopting the antitrust requirement of market power.

Finally, Congress passed the Federal Courts Improvement Act of 1982.[45] This legislation created the Federal Circuit, which had exclusive jurisdiction over appeals from final decisions of district courts on claims of patent infringement. Congress intended the court to provide uniformity, enhance predictability, and eliminate "the expensive, time-consuming and unseemly forum-shopping" characterizing patent litigation.[46] Many of these goals have come to pass as the Federal Circuit has crafted a more predictable and uniform patent law. But, as the *Xerox* case discussed below shows, the court also has favored patents in cases arising at the patent-antitrust intersection.

This patent-friendly trend has an even more pronounced effect given the court's attempts to enlarge its influence through an expansive interpretation of its jurisdiction. In *Nobelpharma AB v. Implant Innovations, Inc.,* the Court overruled prior Federal Circuit case law that had applied the antitrust law of the regional circuit from which a case arose and held that a patentee's immunity under the antitrust laws was to be decided as a matter of the court's exclusive jurisdiction.[47]

The court noted that the claim of antitrust immunity is typically raised as a counterclaim in a patent infringement lawsuit. It explained that "most cases involving these issues will . . . be appealed to this court" in concluding that it would decide the issues "as a matter of Federal Circuit law." The court claimed to be in "the best position to create a uniform body of federal law" and promised that it would not decide other antitrust issues, such as market power.[48] This ruling ensures that much of the patent-antitrust intersection will be interpreted not by the 12 generalist courts of appeals but by the patent-focused Federal Circuit.

Two developments in the 1990s reflected IP's increasing dominance: the IP Guidelines and courts' treatment of IP refusals to license.

---

44. *See Morton Salt Co. v. G.S. Suppiger Co.,* 314 U.S. 488 (1942).
45. H. REP. No. 97-312, 97th Cong., 1st Sess. 18 (1981).
46. *Id.* at 20.
47. 141 F.3d 1059, 1067 (1998).
48. *Id.* at 1068.

IP GUIDELINES

A seminal event in the rise of IP occurred in 1995 when the Department of Justice and Federal Trade Commission jointly published the *Antitrust Guidelines for the Licensing of Intellectual Property.* The Guidelines embodied three principles:

- IP is "essentially comparable" to any other form of property.
- IP does not automatically create market power in the antitrust context.
- IP licensing is generally procompetitive.[49]

These three principles slammed the door on a half-century of hostility to IP. First, they made clear that IP should not be treated more harshly than real property, concluding that even if IP is not "particularly free from scrutiny under the antitrust laws," it also is not "particularly suspect under them."[50]

Second, the Guidelines confirmed the long-ignored reality that even though the IP right "confers the power to exclude with respect to the *specific* product, process, or work in question, there will often be sufficient actual or potential close substitutes for such product, process, or work to prevent the exercise of market power."[51]

Third, the Guidelines explained that IP "typically is one component among many in a production process" that "derives value from its combination with complementary factors." In most cases, the patentee is only able to realize the patent's value by collaborating with others. Licensing "can lead to more efficient exploitation" of IP, "benefiting consumers through the reduction of costs and introduction of new products." And by increasing IP's expected returns, licensing can "promote greater investment in research and development."[52]

The Guidelines also provided that, in "the vast majority" of cases, IP licensing agreements should be analyzed under the Rule of Reason.[53] Finally, they applied general principles to categories of activity such as horizontal restraints, tying arrangements, cross-licensing, patent pools, and acquisition of IP.[54]

Market Power Presumption

The Supreme Court confirmed one of the general principles of the Guidelines—the lack of a presumption of market power from the existence of IP—in 2006 in *Illinois Tool Works, Inc. v. Independent Ink, Inc.*[55] Although commentators had

---

49. *1995 Guidelines* § 2.0.
50. *Id.* § 2.1.
51. *Id.* § 2.2.
52. *Id.* § 2.3.
53. *Id.* § 3.4.
54. *Id.* §§ 5.1, 5.3, 5.5, 5.7.
55. 126 S. Ct. 1281 (2006).

long recognized that patents did not automatically demonstrate market power, the governing Supreme Court precedent on the issue was to the contrary. In *United States v. Loew's*, as discussed above, the Court explained that "[t]he requisite economic power [for purposes of a tying arrangement] is presumed when the tying product is patented or copyrighted."[56]

The *Independent Ink* case overturned that presumption, which arose in the context of patent misuse, and thus was entitled to less deference after Congress enacted the Patent Misuse Reform Act, which refused to assume market power from patents in tying arrangements. It would not make sense, the Court believed, to remove the market power presumption in determining whether a patentee could enjoin infringement while retaining it for the severe sanctions of antitrust.[57]

REFUSALS TO LICENSE

The other example of IP's rise is revealed by courts' treatment of refusals to license. Does a monopolist's refusal to license IP violate Section 2 of the Sherman Act? Three courts at the end of the 20th century came to different conclusions, with the most IP-friendly decision seemingly generating the longest coattails.

Rebuttable Presumption of Legality

In the first case, *Data General v. Grumman Systems Support Corp.*, Data General created a computer program that diagnosed problems in its computers. Data General (which had approximately 5 percent of the *primary market* for minicomputers) occupied about 90 percent of the *aftermarket* for the service of its computers; Grumman had approximately 3 percent.

Data General had initially pursued liberal policies that allowed third parties to use the diagnostic software. But it subsequently altered these policies, restricting the licensing of the software to its own technicians and equipment owners who performed their own service. As a result, Grumman was not able to use the software. Data General sued Grumman for copyright infringement and trade secret misappropriation, and Grumman filed an antitrust counterclaim challenging Data General's refusal to license the diagnostic software.[58]

The First Circuit articulated the legislative assumption underlying the copyright laws that the right to exclude "creates a system of incentives that promotes consumer welfare . . . by encouraging investment in the creation of desirable artistic [ ] works of expression." Antitrust defendants thus should not

---

56. 371 U.S. 38, 45 (1962).
57. 126 S. Ct. at 1291.
58. 36 F.3d 1147, 1152–56 (1st Cir. 1994).

be required "to prove and reprove the merits of [the] legislative assumption in every case where a refusal to license a copyrighted work comes under attack."[59]

The court therefore concluded that a party's "desire to exclude others from [use of] its [protected] work is a presumptively valid business justification." But it never explained how the presumption could be rebutted, stating only that "there may be rare cases in which imposing antitrust liability is unlikely to frustrate the objectives of the Copyright Act." Applied to the facts of the case, the court found that Data General's exercise of its right to exclude was "a presumptively valid business justification" that Grumman could not rebut.[60]

Intent-Based Rebuttal

In the second case, *Image Technical Services, Inc. v. Eastman Kodak Co.*, Kodak manufactured high volume photocopiers in a competitive market. Kodak also sold and installed replacement parts for its equipment. In this activity, it competed with independent service organizations (ISOs). The company repaired at least 80 percent of the machines it manufactured.

Although Kodak had, at one time, sold parts for repair service to ISOs, it began to restrict this practice as competition from the ISOs increased. As a result of the limited access, ISOs lacked a reliable supply of parts and thus were not able to compete with Kodak in providing multiyear service contracts. Several ISOs alleged that the parts shortage forced them out of business. The ISOs sued Kodak, claiming that its restrictive parts policy violated Sections 1 and 2 of the Sherman Act. A jury entered a verdict against Kodak.[61]

The Ninth Circuit affirmed the verdict. To ensure that the jury would account for the "procompetitive effects and statutory rights extended by the intellectual property laws," the court adopted the *Data General* presumption but held that it could be rebutted by evidence of pretext. The court explained: "Neither the aims of intellectual property law, nor the antitrust laws justify allowing a monopolist to rely upon a pretextual business justification to mask anticompetitive conduct."[62]

In applying its rebuttable presumption, the court found that "the proffered business justification played no part in the [defendant's] decision to act."[63] It explained that "Kodak photocopy and micrographics equipment requires thousands of parts, of which only [sixty-five] were patented" and that Kodak's parts manager testified that patents "did not cross [his] mind" when the company instituted its parts policy. As a result, the court concluded that "it is more

---

59. *Id.* at 1186–87.

60. *Id.* at 1187–88.

61. 125 F.3d 1195, 1200–01 (9th Cir. 1997); No. C-87-1686-AWT, 1996 U.S. Dist. LEXIS 2386, at *2 (N.D. Cal. Feb 28, 1996).

62. 125 F.3d 1195, 1219 (9th Cir. 1997).

63. *Id.* at 1218–20.

probable than not that the jury would have found Kodak's presumptively valid business justification rebutted on the grounds of pretext." Even though the district court's instructions to the jury "fail[ed] to give any weight" to Kodak's IP rights, the court concluded that such error was harmless.[64]

Near-per se Legality

The Federal Circuit provided the final example in *In re Independent Service Organizations Antitrust Litigation (Xerox)*. Xerox manufactured, sold, and serviced high-volume photocopiers. It instituted a policy of not selling parts for one (and later, all) of its lines of copiers to ISOs unless they also were end-users of the copiers. At one point, Xerox cut off certain ISOs' abilities to directly purchase such restricted parts.

A class of ISOs filed an antitrust lawsuit, and Xerox settled the suit by agreeing to suspend its parts policy and licensing its diagnostic software for a period of time. One ISO opted out of the settlement and sued, alleging that Xerox violated the antitrust laws by setting the prices on its patented parts higher for ISOs than for end-users in an attempt to force ISOs to raise their prices.[65] Such conduct ostensibly was designed to eliminate ISOs as competitors in service markets for Xerox copiers.

The Federal Circuit held that Xerox did not violate Section 2. It emphasized the centrality of the right to exclude in the patent system before carving out three limited categories in which a patentee would not be immune from antitrust liability: (1) tying patented and unpatented products, (2) obtaining a patent through knowing and willful fraud, and (3) engaging in sham litigation. The Federal Circuit also refused to examine the patentee's subjective intent in refusing to deal with a competitor. And it confirmed that action "within the scope" of the patent could not violate the antitrust laws. Because the court concluded that Xerox's refusal to sell its patented parts did not exceed the scope of the patent and did not fall within any of the three exceptions, it concluded that Xerox did not violate the antitrust laws.[66]

The *Xerox* case has been cited in support of antitrust immunity for refusals to license. The court in *Townshend v. Rockwell International Corporation* found that

---

64. *Id.* at 1218. For a critique of analysis based on a party's subjective intent, see Michael A. Carrier, *Unraveling the Patent-Antitrust Paradox*, 150 U. Pa. L. Rev. 761, 793–94 (2002) (contending that intent tests prove too much in antitrust law since the purpose of competition is to defeat one's competitors, that this result is particularly dangerous in penalizing a defendant for its intention in refusing to deal when the purpose of the patent laws is to exclude others from the patented product, and that numerous obstacles lie in the path of determining a company's intent).

65. 203 F.3d 1322, 1324 (Fed. Cir. 2000); *see also* 989 F. Supp. 1131, 1133 (D. Kan. 1997).

66. 203 F.3d at 1326–28.

a patentee "has the legal right to refuse to license his or her patent on any terms" and thus "a predicate condition to a license agreement cannot state an antitrust violation."[67] The *Xerox* case also is consistent with a line of cases that grants immunity as long as the challenged activity lies within the "scope" of the patent.[68] The extreme deference to IP articulated in the opinion nonetheless could limit liability to the narrow categories of tying, fraud, and sham litigation.[69]

In short, the IP Guidelines and refusals to license, building on *Sylvania*, the National Cooperative Research Act, and the Patent Misuse Reform Act, reflect a tilting of the scales toward IP.

The conflict between antitrust and IP has led to a wildly swinging pendulum that has favored IP, then antitrust, and now IP again. Throughout the 20th century, courts fastened their gaze on unhelpful characteristics. An emphasis on economic analysis has solved many of the problems. But the challenges presented by the IP-antitrust intersection have followed us into the 21st century.

---

67. No. C99-0400, 2000 U.S. Dist. LEXIS 5070, at *26 (N.D. Cal. Mar. 28, 2000).

68. *E.g., Zenith Radio Corp. v. Hazeltine Research, Inc.*, 395 U.S. 100, 136 (1969); *Ethyl Gasoline Corp. v. United States*, 309 U.S. 436, 456 (1940); *Motion Picture Patents Co. v. Universal Film Mfg. Co.*, 243 U.S. 502, 510 (1917); *United States v. Studiengesellschaft Kohle, m.b.H.*, 670 F.2d 1122, 1135 (D.C. Cir. 1981); *United States v. Westinghouse Elec. Corp.*, 648 F.2d 642, 647 (9th Cir. 1981); *SCM Corp. v. Xerox Corp.*, 645 F.2d 1195, 1206 (2d Cir. 1981).

69. *See* Herbert Hovenkamp, Mark D. Janis, & Mark A. Lemley, *Unilateral Refusals to License*, 2 J. COMPETITION L. & ECON. 1, 34–42 (2006) (concluding that the court did not intend such an expansive holding).

5. ANTITRUST AND IP: 21ST CENTURY

Microsoft: United States 87
Microsoft: European Union 89
Innovation Markets 92
Standard-Setting Activity 93
Patent Pools 95
Drug Settlement Agreements 97
Other Anticompetitive Drug Conduct 98

In the first decade of the 21st century, IP maintained its predominance over antitrust. For the most controversial issue—settlement agreements in the pharmaceutical industry—courts bent over backward to defer to patents. And drug firms used other measures to extend their monopoly at the end of the patent term.

Most of the other categories reflect more nuance. This chapter begins with Microsoft, the most prominent antitrust case in recent years, exploring the IP aspects of the U.S. and European Union cases. It then examines innovation markets, standard-setting organizations, and patent pools before concluding with settlements and other activity in the pharmaceutical industry.

MICROSOFT: UNITED STATES

The *Microsoft* case has garnered widespread attention as a pivotal case of the application of antitrust to IP and the "new economy." The lawsuit, filed in 1998, challenged the company's activities in protecting its Windows operating system monopoly. It covered numerous practices:

- Exclusive dealing agreements by which Internet access providers agreed to promote Microsoft's Internet browser in return for certain inducements
- Threatening to cancel Mac Office, used by 90 percent of Apple Macintosh users who ran suites of office applications
- Deceiving developers and coercing Intel regarding its Microsoft-specific version of Sun's Java programming language and Java Virtual Machine[1]

Two additional activities are of most direct interest for our purposes. The first involved Microsoft's integration of its Internet Explorer (IE) browser into its

---

1. *United States v. Microsoft Corp.*, 253 F.3d 34, 67–78 (D.C. Cir. 2001). Java Virtual Machine translates bytecode (machine language) into instructions to multiple operating systems.

Windows operating system in a way that made IE difficult to remove. In its 2001 decision, the D.C. Circuit concluded that this technological bundling constituted monopolization.[2] It also reversed the district court, which had found an illegal tie based on Microsoft (1) requiring Windows licensees to license IE, (2) refusing to allow computer manufacturers to remove IE from the Windows desktop, (3) preventing users from removing IE through the Add/Remove Programs utility, and (4) overriding the user's choice of default web browser.[3]

One of tying's central requirements is the presence of two separate products. A leading Supreme Court case had required separate consumer demand for the two items.[4] But the D.C. Circuit found that the consumer demand inquiry, as applied to "new and innovative integration," was "backward-looking."[5] Because there appeared to be a "robust 'distinct' market for the tied product" before the integration, the requirement punished the first firm to merge the two functionalities. The court also concluded that per se illegality was inappropriate based on the "pervasively innovative character of platform software markets."[6]

The second activity involved license restrictions by which Microsoft prohibited computer manufacturers from (1) removing desktop icons, folders, and "Start" menu entries; (2) modifying the initial boot sequence (which occurs when users turn on the computer for the first time); and (3) otherwise altering the appearance of the Windows desktop. The company explained that the restrictions guaranteed that "all Windows users experience the product the way Microsoft intended it the first time they turn on their . . . systems."[7] And it relied on its exercise of rights as "the holder of valid copyrights."[8]

The D.C. Circuit dismissed Microsoft's broad copyright argument as "border[ing] upon the frivolous." It refused to accept Microsoft's claim that the exercise of lawfully acquired IP rights "cannot give rise to antitrust liability." Such an assertion is "no more correct," the court colorfully wrote, than the claim that "use of one's personal property, such as a baseball bat, cannot give rise to tort liability." The court instead retreated to the opposite assertion that IP rights "do not confer a privilege to violate the antitrust laws."[9]

Microsoft also claimed, more narrowly, that a copyright holder can limit a licensee's ability to engage in significant and deleterious alterations of

---

2. The monopolization conclusion was based on Microsoft's (1) commingling of browser and operating system code and (2) exclusion of its browser from the utility by which users could add or remove programs. *Id.* at 64–67.

3. *Id.* at 84–85. The issue was remanded to the district court, but the Justice Department did not pursue the claim on remand.

4. *Jefferson Parish Hosp. Dist. No. 2 v. Hyde,* 466 U.S. 2 (1984).

5. For similar reasons, the court rejected inquiries into industry custom.

6. *Microsoft,* 253 F.3d at 89, 93.

7. *United States v. Microsoft Corp.,* 84 F. Supp. 2d 9, 61, 64–65 (D.D.C. 1999).

8. *Microsoft,* 253 F.3d at 61–63.

9. *Id.* at 63.

a copyrighted work. The court accepted this argument for Microsoft's prohibition on automatically launching a substitute interface after completion of the boot process, finding that "a shell that automatically prevents the Windows desktop from ever being seen by the user is a drastic alteration of Microsoft's copyrighted work" that outweighs any anticompetitive effects. But it found that the prohibitions on the removal of icons and modification of the initial boot sequence represented "uses of Microsoft's market power to protect its monopoly, unredeemed by any legitimate justification."[10]

MICROSOFT: EUROPEAN UNION

The European Union also challenged Microsoft's conduct. In March 2004, the European Commission adopted a decision that found that Microsoft had infringed Article 82 of the Treaty Establishing the European Community (EC Treaty), which prohibits "abuse of a dominant position."

In reaching its conclusion, the Commission focused on two types of activity. First, it addressed the firm's tying of Windows Media Player to the Windows operating system. Second, it targeted Microsoft's refusal to supply rivals with information necessary to interoperate with its work group server operating systems. The Commission concluded that Microsoft "leverag[ed] its near monopoly in the market for PC operating systems onto the markets for work group server operating systems and . . . media players" and that the conduct "hindered innovation . . . to the detriment of consumers."[11]

In September 2007, the Court of First Instance upheld the Commission's decision.[12] For the first claim, it concluded that Microsoft had illegally tied its media player to its operating system. It found that (1) Microsoft had a dominant position on the operating system market, (2) there was separate consumer demand for media players, (3) consumers could not acquire the Windows operating system without acquiring Windows Media Player, and (4) the tie altered the balance of competition in favor of Microsoft.[13]

The second type of behavior implicated the IP-antitrust intersection more directly. The factual setting is complicated. Microsoft's activity targeted *work*

---

10. *Id.* at 63–64.

11. Press Release No. 63/07, Judgment of the Court of First Instance in Case T-201/04, *Microsoft Corp. v. Comm'n of the European Cmtys.*, Sept. 17, 2007, at 1 [hereinafter Sept. 17 press release].

12. The Court of First Instance is a court of the European Union that consists of at least one judge from each Member State and that issues rulings that can be appealed to the European Court of Justice. *Court of First Instance*, http://curia.europa.eu/en/instit/presentationfr/index_tpi.htm (last visited July 31, 2008).

13. Sept. 17 press release, at 3.

group servers, which provide services used by office workers such as file and print sharing, as well as security and user identity management. Microsoft denied rivals information needed to connect non-Microsoft work group servers with Windows computers and servers.[14]

In particular, Microsoft denied the "specifications for the protocols" implemented in the server operating systems. The protocols provide the rules of interconnection. And the specifications are the technical documentation showing how to format and interpret messages, when to originate them, and how to address incorrect ones.[15]

The Court analogized the protocols to a language and the specifications to the syntax and vocabulary. Those who know a language's syntax and vocabulary can understand each other. And just like those not privy to syntax and vocabulary cannot understand the language, rivals without access to the specifications would not be able to develop interoperable work group server operating systems.[16]

The Court found that the lack of interoperability hurt users. Some, for example, were required to log on twice to access Windows-based resources and resources offered by rivals' work group servers. Others were denied access to rivals' work group server operating systems, which offered better reliability and security. Even though Microsoft "lag[ged] behind its competitors" on these qualities, consumers chose its products because of "the interoperability barrier" facing rivals. Relatedly, the lack of interoperability "discouraged . . . competitors from developing and marketing work group server operating systems with innovative features."[17]

Microsoft claimed an IP defense, alleging that its protocols and specifications were protected by patents, copyrights, and trade secrets. For purposes of its decision, the Court assumed such coverage but still found that this did not protect Microsoft from an Article 82 violation.[18]

By way of background, the law in the European Union is more amenable than U.S. law to punishing firms that refuse to share IP with rivals. In *RTE & ITP v. Commission (Magill)*, the court found that three Irish television stations violated Article 82 by refusing to license their copyrighted daily program listings. The European Court of Justice found that a refusal to deal can constitute an abuse of dominance in "exceptional circumstances," which were met since (1) the

---

14. Case T-201/04, *Microsoft v. Comm'n*, Judgment of the Court of First Instance (Grand Chamber) of 17 Sept. 2007, O.J. 2007 C269/45, ¶¶ 160, 162 [hereinafter CFI Decision]; *Antitrust: Commission Welcomes CFI Ruling Upholding Commission's Decision on Microsoft's Abuse of Dominant Market Position*, Europa, Sept. 17, 2007, http://europa.eu/rapid/pressReleasesAction.do?reference=MEMO/07/359.

15. CFI Decision ¶¶ 137, 196, 198.

16. *Id.* ¶¶ 103, 137.

17. *Id.* ¶¶ 415, 635, 652, 653.

18. *Id.* ¶¶ 270–73, 690.

information was indispensable in creating a comprehensive weekly TV guide, (2) the refusal prevented the appearance of a new product, (3) there was no justification for the refusal, and (4) the stations "reserved to themselves the secondary market of weekly television guides by excluding all competition on that market."[19]

In another important case, *IMS Health GmbH & Co. OHG v. NDC Health GmbH & Co. KG*, IMS refused to supply information on sales of drug products in a large number of small areas called "bricks." Such a system allowed IMS to offer data without identifying sales by individual pharmacies. After finding that the criteria identified in *Magill* needed to be satisfied, the European Court of Justice found an abuse of dominance.[20]

The *Microsoft* court synthesized these cases, stating that exceptional circumstances would be met when a refusal

- relates to a product indispensable to behavior on a neighboring market,
- excludes effective competition on that market, and
- prevents the appearance of a new product for which there is potential consumer demand.[21]

The Court found such circumstances in the *Microsoft* case since the refusal (1) covered indispensable interoperability information, (2) threatened to eliminate competition in the market for work group server operating systems, and (3) limited technical development.[22] The Court's recitation expanded liability from the *Magill* and *IMS* cases. It indicated that it could find liability even in the absence of one of the exceptional circumstances. And it extended the third factor from preventing a new product to limiting technical development.[23]

Nor did the Court find that Microsoft could offer a justification based on IP rights. The company only offered "vague, general, and theoretical arguments" to support its claim that disclosure would adversely affect innovation incentives. In fact, there was even evidence that Microsoft had a policy of "adopting preexisting protocols" and "making minor and pointless changes to them" to prevent interoperability.[24] Finally, the Court stated that providing interoperability information would not allow competitors to clone Microsoft's products.[25]

---

19. Case C-241/91P, [1995] ECR I-743 ¶¶ 49–50, 54–56.

20. In particular, the Court required proof of the new-product, lack-of-objective-justification, and secondary-market criteria. Case C-418/01, [2004] ECR I-5039 ¶¶ 38, 52.

21. CFI Decision ¶ 332.

22. Id. ¶¶ 436, 620, 647–49.

23. Id. ¶¶ 336, 649–58; *see generally* Renata B. Hesse, *Counseling Clients on Refusal to Supply Issues in the Wake of the EC Microsoft Case*, 22 ANTITRUST 32, 33–34 (2008).

24. CFI Decision ¶¶ 282, 698.

25. Id. ¶ 657. For a contrary view, see William H. Page & Sheldon J. Childers, *Bargaining in the Shadow of the European* Microsoft *Decision: The Microsoft-Samba Protocol License* (2008), http://ssrn.com/abstract=1117641.

In the end, the Court found that Microsoft's refusal to supply such information violated Section 82. As a remedy for each of the two illegal activities, the Court upheld the Commission's levy of a 497 million euro (roughly $613 million) fine.[26]

INNOVATION MARKETS

The second development in the 21st century is provided by *innovation markets*, or the research and development (R&D) directed toward new products.[27] As discussed in Chapter 3, opponents have leveled numerous criticisms against the concept. Nonetheless, in the past two decades, the agencies have brought (and settled) ten cases challenging mergers in innovation markets. Eight of the ten cases involved the pharmaceutical industry.[28] In particular, the Federal Trade Commission (FTC) challenged

- the Roche-Genentech merger affecting certain drugs to treat HIV/AIDS,
- the American Home Products-American Cyanamid merger for the vaccine for rotavirus (a form of diarrhea causing children's deaths),
- the Glaxo-Wellcome merger for noninjectable treatment for migraines,
- the Upjohn-Pharmacia merger for chemotherapy drugs targeting colon cancer,
- the Baxter-Immuno merger for fibrin sealants, which stop bleeding and heal wounds,
- the Ciba-Geigy–Sandoz merger for gene therapy products,
- the Pfizer–Warner-Lambert merger for inhibitors for solid cancerous tumors, and
- the Glaxo Wellcome–Smith Kline Beecham merger for a prophylactic herpes vaccine.[29]

---

26. The $613 million figure reflected the exchange rate at the time of the March 2004 order. *Microsoft Hit by Record EU Fine*, Mar. 25, 2004, http://www.cnn.com/2004/BUSINESS/03/24/microsoft.eu/. For its failure to comply with the European Commission's remedy order, the Commission fined Microsoft an additional 280.5 million euro in July 2006 and 899 million euro in February 2008. European Commission, *Antitrust: Cases—Microsoft Case* (last visited August 29, 2008). Microsoft appealed the February 2008 order. *Microsoft Appeals Against Record Anti-trust Fine*, EU BUSINESS, May 11, 2008, http://www.eubusiness.com/news-eu/1210349873.14/.

27. U.S. DEP'T OF JUSTICE & FED. TRADE COMM'N, ANTITRUST GUIDELINES FOR THE LICENSING OF INTELLECTUAL PROPERTY §§ 3.2.2, 3.2.3 (1995).

28. In six of the eight mergers, the FTC challenged activity in markets other than innovation markets. In the Glaxo-Wellcome and Upjohn-Pharmacia mergers, the agency focused only on the activity in the innovation market. *In re Glaxo PLC*, 119 F.T.C. 815 (1995); *In the Matter of Upjohn Co.*, 121 F.T.C. 44 (1996).

29. *See* Michael A. Carrier, *Two Puzzles Resolved: Of the Schumpeter-Arrow Stalemate and Pharmaceutical Innovation Markets*, 93 IOWA L. REV. 393, 448 (2008).

The theory behind innovation markets is that a merger between the only two firms in R&D might increase the incentive to suppress at least one of the research paths. With no other firms ready to enter the market, the merging firms might not wish to introduce a second product that would reduce sales of the first.

Although the agencies have not brought any innovation market cases since 2000, this could change with an increase in antitrust enforcement. The danger, however, is that an ad hoc analysis of the concept could accompany any such revival. In Chapter 13, I remedy this situation by offering a new test that builds on the Horizontal Merger Guidelines and incorporates a realistic assessment of the hurdles of drug development.

STANDARD-SETTING ACTIVITY

In the past 25 years, the antitrust agencies have challenged activity of standard-setting organizations (SSOs) when participants engaged in deception or manipulation of the process.

Some cases involved manipulation. In *Allied Tube & Conduit Corp. v. Indian Head, Inc.*, manufacturers packed an SSO meeting to defeat a rival's attempt to certify its product for the standard.[30] In *American Society of Mechanical Engineers v. Hydrolevel Corp.*, a vice president of the firm dominating the market, in his capacity as vice chairman of the relevant SSO subcommittee, interpreted a code so that a rival's product was deemed unsafe.[31] And in *In re American Society of Sanitary Engineering*, the SSO protected existing manufacturers by refusing to approve a new toilet tank fill valve that was safer, cheaper, and more durable.[32] Courts or the FTC found an antitrust violation in each of the three cases.

Other cases involved a participant's deceptive conduct. In *In re Dell*, an SSO adopted a standard based on a Dell representative's promise that a proposal did not infringe its IP. But after the standard became widely adopted, Dell sought payment for the use of its IP.[33] The FTC also challenged the misrepresentation of the Union Oil Company of California (Unocal), which failed to disclose relevant patents and applications. After manufacturers had spent billions of dollars to comply with the new standards, Unocal sought to collect royalties that would have cost consumers more than $500 million annually.[34] The FTC obtained a consent decree halting the behavior in both cases.

---

30. 486 U.S. 492, 496–97 (1988).
31. 456 U.S. 556, 559-63, 577–78 (1982).
32. 106 F.T.C. 324 (1985).
33. *In re Dell*, 121 F.T.C. 616, 617, 623–24 (1996).
34. *In re Union Oil Co. of California*, No. 9305, ¶¶ 9, 10, 26, 31, 61, 63 (F.T.C. Nov. 25, 2003), http://www.ftc.gov/os/2003/11/031126unionoil.pdf, *rev'd*, No. 9305 (F.T.C. July 7, 2004); FTC Statement, *In re Union Oil Co. of California*, Docket No. 9305 (June 10, 2005), www.ftc.gov/os/adjpro/d9305/050802statement.pdf.

Finally, in *In re Rambus*, the FTC found that Rambus had "engaged in representations, omissions, and practices likely to mislead JEDEC members," which "significantly contributed to its acquisition of monopoly power."[35] In 2008, the D.C. Circuit, focusing on causation, reversed this conclusion, finding that JEDEC might have adopted Rambus's technology even absent any deception. As a result, any "loss of an opportunity to seek favorable licensing terms" did not, without more, constitute "antitrust harm."[36]

In seeking to prevent deception, many SSOs have adopted rules that require members to disclose relevant patents and agree to licensing terms before the standard is selected. The SSO VITA, which developed computer architecture standards, required members to announce their most restrictive licensing terms (including maximum royalty rates) before the standard's adoption.[37] VITA sought approval in the form of a business review letter, by which a party asks the Department of Justice's Antitrust Division to review proposed conduct and state its enforcement intentions.[38] Thomas Barnett, the head of the Division, upheld VITA's policy, concluding that it helped to prevent holdup and allowed the group to evaluate technologies on not only technical merit but also licensing terms.[39]

The final development constitutes the agencies' most aggressive prosecution of SSO activity to date. In January 2008, the FTC filed a complaint against Negotiated Data Solutions (N-Data). N-Data licensed patents used in equipment employing Ethernet, a ubiquitous networking standard. N-Data's predecessor had committed to license its technology for a one-time royalty of $1,000 per licensee, but N-Data later demanded royalties "far in excess of that commitment."[40]

---

35. *In re Rambus*, No. 9302, 2006 WL 2330117, at 5–6, 8, 50, 67, 104, 118 (Aug. 2, 2006).

36. *Rambus Inc. v. F.T.C.*, 522 F.3d 456, 466–67 (D.C. Cir. 2008).

37. Letter from Thomas O. Barnett, Assistant Att'y Gen'l, Dep't of Justice, to Robert A. Skitol (Oct. 30, 2006), at 5–6, http://www.usdoj.gov/atr/public/busreview/219380.pdf [hereinafter VITA letter]. Other VITA policies required members to make a "good faith and reasonable inquiry" into patents and disclose any patents or applications that they believed could become essential to the specification being developed.

38. 28 C.F.R. § 50.6. The letter addressed VITA and its standards development subcommittee, VSO.

39. Technically, he stated that the Division "has no present intention to take antitrust enforcement action" against VITA's policies. VITA letter, at 8–10. For another important and deferential approach to SSO licensing, see Deborah Platt Majoras, Chairman, Fed. Trade Comm'n, Recognizing the Procompetitive Potential of Royalty Discussions in Standard Setting, Sept. 23, 2005, at 6–7, http://www.ftc.gov/speeches/majoras/050923stanford.pdf.

40. FTC, *FTC Challenges Patent Holder's Refusal to Meet Commitment to License Patents Covering 'Ethernet' Standard Used in Virtually All Personal Computers in U.S.*, Jan. 23, 2008, http://www.ftc.gov/opa/2008/01/ethernet.shtm; FTC, Statement, *In re Negotiated Data Solutions LLC*, File No. 0510094, http://www.ftc.gov/os/caselist/0510094/080122statement.pdf.

By a vote of 3-2, the Federal Trade Commission challenged N-Data's action. It did not allege a violation of the Sherman Act but instead claimed an unfair method of competition and unfair act or practice under Section 5 of the Federal Trade Commission Act. The majority asserted that N-Data's behavior harmed consumers and businesses and explained that its exercise of its "unique" authority was needed to "preserv[e] a free and dynamic marketplace."[41] Two dissents were filed. Deborah Majoras, the former Chairman,[42] bemoaned a lack of meaningful guideposts for liability, and then-Commissioner (and current Chairman) William Kovacic lamented a failure to distinguish between unfair methods of competition and unfair acts or practices.[43]

In Chapter 14, I explain why the concerns about standard-setting are almost always outweighed by the significant procompetitive benefits that SSOs (and their IP rules) offer. I conclude that courts and the antitrust enforcement agencies should apply Rule-of-Reason analysis to SSOs and uphold standard-setting activity in the vast majority of cases.

PATENT POOLS

Business review letters also have played an important role in patent pools. In the past decade, the agencies have examined pools relating to

- MPEG-2, a video compression technology underlying the transmission, storage, and display of digitized moving images and sound tracks;
- DVD-ROM and DVD-video formats describing "the physical and technical parameters for DVDs for read-only-memory and video applications";

---

41. *Id.*

42. The FTC Act adopts the term "Chairman," and this title has been used in connection with all such officials. 15 U.S.C. § 41.

43. Dissenting Statement of Chairman Majoras, *In re Negotiated Data Solutions LLC*, File No. 0510094, http://www.ftc.gov/os/caselist/0510094/080122majoras.pdf (lack of guideposts); Dissenting Statement of Commissioner Kovacic, *In re Negotiated Data Solutions LLC*, File No. 0510094, http://www.ftc.gov/os/caselist/0510094/080122kovacic.pdf (lack of distinction).

As this book went to press, the FTC was considering a challenge to Rembrandt, which acquired patents related to digital television and then repudiated its predecessor's commitment to license on a reasonable and nondiscriminatory basis. The American Antitrust Institute called on the FTC to investigate Rembrandt, which "brought 14 patent infringement suits against the four major television networks, . . . five major cable systems, and television and equipment manufacturers seeking licensing royalties that [would] increase the costs of digital television by tens of millions of dollars." American Antitrust Institute, *American Antitrust Institute Calls on FTC To Investigate Rembrandt for Anticompetitive Conduct that Threatens Digital Television Conversion*, Mar. 26, 2008, http://www.antitrustinstitute.org/archives/files/AAI%20petition%20re%20rembrandt%20press%20release3.26.08_032520082005.pdf.

- third generation (3G) wireless communication systems; and
- lasers used in photorefractive keratectomy (PRK), a form of eye surgery used to correct vision disorders.

The Department of Justice sanctioned the first three pools, but the Federal Trade Commission filed a complaint against the fourth.[44]

Critical to the agencies' analysis of the pools was the distinction between essential and substitute patents. Patents are essential if the product or standard at issue in the pool cannot be produced without infringing the patent. Essential patents do not have substitutes and typically are complementary, possessing a greater value if the licensee can use other essential patents. Substitute patents, in contrast, are not necessary for the use of a technology in the pool but present alternate ways of creating products that otherwise would compete with each other.[45]

The MPEG-2, 3G, and DVD pools sanctioned by the agencies were composed solely of essential patents. Strengthening these conclusions was the determination by an independent expert that the technology was essential at and after the pool's formation.[46]

The Summit-VISX pool, on the other hand, was composed of competing patents. In its Complaint, the FTC explained that, if not for the pool, the two firms would have competed against each other "by using their respective patents, licensing them, or both."[47]

To be sure, it is not always obvious whether patents are substitutes or complements.[48] Nonetheless, the concept is valuable to focus the analysis on the

---

44. Letter from Joel I. Klein to Gerrard R. Beeney (June 26, 1997), http://www.usdoj. gov/atr/public/busreview/1170.htm [hereinafter MPEG letter]; Letter from Joel I. Klein to Gerrard R. Beeney (Dec. 16, 1998), http://www.usdoj.gov/atr/public/busreview/2121.htm [hereinafter DVD letter]; Letter from Charles A. James to Ky P. Ewing (Nov. 12, 2002), http://www.usdoj.gov/atr/public/busreview/200455.htm [hereinafter 3G letter]; *In re* Summit Technology, Inc., FTC Dkt. No. 9286, http://www.ftc.gov/os/1998/9803/ summit.cmp.htm. *See generally* Michael A. Carrier, *Resolving the Patent-Antitrust Paradox Through Tripartite Innovation*, 56 VAND. L. REV. 1047, 1093–96 (2003).

45. An example of a substitute patent involves the inclusion in a pool for DVD standards of one of several alternative patented methods for placing DVD-ROMs into packaging. DVD letter, at 5–6.

46. In the MPEG and 3G pools, the patents were limited to those that were technically essential. In the DVD pool, the patents were restricted to those necessary "as a practical matter" for compliance with the DVD standard specifications. MPEG letter, at 3, 6, 9; 3G letter, at 6; DVD letter, at 2.

47. *In re Summit Tech., Inc.*, FTC Dkt. No. 9286, ¶ 8, http://www.ftc.gov/os/1998/9803/ summit.cmp.htm. The VISX complaint was ultimately settled, with the parties agreeing to dissolve the pool and make pricing and licensing decisions independently.

48. HERBERT HOVENKAMP ET AL., IP AND ANTITRUST: AN ANALYSIS OF ANTITRUST PRINCIPLES APPLIED TO INTELLECTUAL PROPERTY LAW § 34.2, at 34-8 to 34-10 (2002). It is not the case that

relationship among the patents. And it is more nuanced than most other frameworks that have been used to analyze antitrust and IP issues.

DRUG SETTLEMENT AGREEMENTS

Such nuance has been missing in courts' analysis of settlement agreements in the pharmaceutical industry. In the past few years, brand-name drug manufacturers and generic firms have entered into questionable agreements settling patent litigation.

The framework for such agreements has been the Hatch-Waxman Act, which Congress enacted in 1984. One of the Act's goals was to encourage generics to challenge brand-name patents. But brand firms have recently paid generics millions of dollars to drop their lawsuits and refrain from entering the market.

These *reverse payments,* which differ from typical licensing payments that flow from challengers to patentees, may even exceed what the generic could have earned by entering the market. Despite the concerns presented by these settlements, courts have recently blessed them.

They have explained that the agreements reduce costs and increase innovation. They have referred to settlements as "natural by-products" of the Act. And they have pointed to patents' presumption of validity in demonstrating the agreements' reasonableness. Although the FTC (which enforces the antitrust laws in the drug industry) and scholars have voiced strong arguments against courts' leniency, these have fallen on judicial deaf ears.

In the first case to examine the issue, the Sixth Circuit in *In re Cardizem CD Antitrust Litigation* found "a classic example of a per se illegal restraint of trade" when a firm agreed not to market any generic version of a brand drug, including those not covered by the patent.[49]

Courts, however, quickly retreated from such analysis. The Eleventh Circuit in *Schering-Plough Corp. v. FTC* upheld settlements that fell "within the protections of the . . . patent" and stated that it "cannot be the sole basis for a violation

---

every patent in the pool needs to be essential for the pool to promote innovation. *See U.S. Philips Corp. v. Int'l Trade Comm'n*, 424 F.3d 1179, 1190–93 (Fed. Cir. 2005) (inclusion of nonessential patents does not foreclose competition); A. Douglas Melamed, *Patents and Standards: The Unimportance of Being Essential*, Feb. 11, 2008, at 7 (licensors that include nonessential patents in a pool offer licensees "insurance against the risk they will later be faced with infringement claims based on patents they did not initially believe to be essential"). In addition, the question of the essential nature of patents could divert attention from the larger issue of whether the technologies specified in a standard are essential. *See id.* at 12 (explaining that patent pools "merely reduce[] incentives to use alternative technologies" while standards "can effectively prohibit their use altogether").

49. *Cardizem*, 332 F.3d 896, 907–08 (6th Cir. 2003).

of antitrust law" for a brand firm with a patent to pay a generic competitor.[50] And the Second Circuit in *In re Tamoxifen Citrate Antitrust Litigation* concluded that as long as "the patent litigation is neither a sham nor otherwise baseless" or beyond the patent's scope, the patentee can enter into a settlement "to protect that to which it is presumably entitled: a lawful monopoly over the manufacture and distribution of the patented product."[51]

In the *Schering-Plough* case, the FTC sought Supreme Court review of the Eleventh Circuit decision, and was backed by 34 states, the AARP, and a patent policy think tank.[52] Reflecting a rare disagreement between the agencies, the Justice Department recommended against granting certiorari. The Supreme Court denied certiorari.

In Chapter 15, I explain why reverse-payment settlements should be presumptively illegal. I rely on the Supreme Court's decision in *Verizon v. Trinko*, which underscored the importance of the relevant regulatory framework.[53] I show how the Hatch-Waxman Act's competition-promoting framework has been rendered ineffective by the agreements. And I describe the concerning aspects and anticompetitive harm presented by reverse payments.

OTHER ANTICOMPETITIVE DRUG CONDUCT

In addition to settlement agreements, drug companies have engaged in an array of other activity that raises antitrust concern. Much of this behavior occurs near the end of the patent term. The activity has included

- *fraud* in obtaining a patent, including false representations to the U.S. Patent and Trademark Office
- *sham litigation* that discourages entry through frivolous patent claims against generic firms
- *authorized generics*, which are identical to brand-name drugs but which brand firms market as generics to discourage entry[54]
- *evergreening*, or extending the period of patent protection by obtaining patents on trivial modifications of a drug

---

50. 402 F.3d 1056, 1076 (11th Cir. 2005).

51. 466 F.3d 187, 208–09, 213 (2d Cir. 2006).

52. Christopher M. Holman, *Do Reverse Payment Settlements Violate the Antitrust Laws?*, 23 SANTA CLARA COMPUTER & HIGH TECH. L.J. 489, 491 (2007).

53. 540 U.S. 398 (2004).

54. Notice of Authorized Generic Drug Study, 71 Fed. Reg. 16,779, 16,780 (Apr. 4, 2006).

- *improper listings of patents in the "Orange Book"* (which lists drugs and related patents) to block generic substitutes
- filing *citizen petitions* with the U.S. Food & Drug Administration (FDA) to delay the approval of generic drugs[55]

To pick one example, citizen petitions allow the public to express concerns about a drug's safety. Brand firms, however, have used this process to delay generic entry, filing petitions on the eve of FDA approval after the agency has found the generic to be safe and effective.

Between 2003 and 2006, the FDA denied 20 of the 21 petitions it decided. Ten of these were identified as "eleventh hour petitions" (filed within six months of the generic's anticipated entry). Although none of the ten had merit, the petitions caused an average delay of ten months. In one case, each day of delayed generic drug entry resulted in an estimated gain to the brand firm of $7 million.[56]

In conclusion, a snapshot of the 21st century reveals IP in a predominant position. This causes the greatest concern in the pharmaceutical industry, especially as brand firms pay generics not to enter the market. Other activity—in particular, patent pools and SSOs—reveals more nuance. But the complexity of the issues presented in this chapter shows just how difficult the intersection of the IP and antitrust laws can be.

In the remainder of the book, I offer ten proposals that address many of these problems. From an antitrust vantage point, I address settlements, SSOs, and innovation markets. And from the IP angle, I offer seven proposals that improve copyright and patent law to foster innovation. The remainder of the book introduces and develops these proposals.

---

55. *See generally* David Balto, *Roadblocks on the Pharmaceutical Competition Highway: Strategies to Delay Generic Competition*, 2009 DUKE L. & TECH. REV. __ (forthcoming 2009).

56. *Kohl, Leahy Introduce Bill To Stop Frivolous Citizen Petitions, Speed Generic Drug Approval*, Sept. 28, 2006, http://leahy.senate.gov/press/200609/092806a.html; *The Generic Drug Maze: Speeding Access to Affordable, Life Saving Drugs: Hearing Before the S. Special Comm. on Aging*, July 20, 2006 (statement of Heather Bresch), http://media.mylan.com/index.php?s=press_releases&item=237.

PART II

COPYRIGHT

Quick. Think of the law that has the most direct effect on innovation.

Got it?

What did you pick? Chances are, like most observers, you chose the patent system. That makes sense. The regime is set up to encourage new inventions. And patents have received no shortage of attention and criticism in recent years. I address these issues in Part III.

My guess, however, is that precious few of you chose the copyright regime. The typical observer links copyright to creativity, not innovation. Contributing to the narrative is the image of an author writing books, movies, or music while reaping rewards through copyright protection.

This scenario, however, misses a crucial part of the analysis. New technologies present opportunities for copyright infringement. But they also promise to transform the way we consume entertainment, interact with each other, and possibly even restructure our society. Although we may not be able to measure the precise effects of the patent and copyright systems on innovation, we must bolster the neglected relationship between copyright and innovation.

By shining the spotlight on innovation, this section uncovers the acute threats posed by our copyright laws. Of all the innovation-promoting changes I recommend in this book, the most far-reaching are the copyright proposals to (1) return the law of secondary liability to the test offered in *Sony Corporation of America v. Universal City Studios*, (2) eliminate statutory damages for dual-use technology manufacturers, and (3) amend the Digital Millennium Copyright Act (DMCA) to foster competition and interoperability. These three changes would help remove shackles that have chilled venture capital in the 21st century and stanched the flow of new technologies.

Even more exciting, the changes would encourage disruptive innovation. Technologies such as iPods, digital video recorders, and peer-to-peer (P2P) file-sharing software will (as long as they are not stifled by copyright law) create new markets. They also promise to unleash—as Austrian economist Joseph Schumpeter put it—a "gale of creative destruction" that replaces the old business models.

Disruptive innovation is essential for consumers and for our economy. But it tends not to be appreciated by firms with large market shares and established ways of doing business. The recording industry, for example, failed to appreciate Napster's early potential to meet a fledgling but burgeoning demand for digital music. Instead of adapting to the new model, the industry tried to sue it into oblivion. And even more worrisome than effects on the music industry are effects on the next wave of disruptive innovation, which is being buried under the oppressive weight of complicated tests, legal threats, and litigation costs.

Disruptive innovation also is threatened by statutory damages. Such a remedy was originally intended to offer modest deterrence and to allow copyright owners to recover when damages were difficult to prove. It was not designed to apply in the context of secondary liability, where manufacturers could be penalized

$150,000 for each act of willful infringement. With widespread use and a loose definition of willfulness, damages could quickly reach into the *billions* of dollars. Such awards make no sense other than chilling investment and new technologies.

Nor is disruptive innovation the only harm threatened by copyright today. The duration of copyright has expanded dramatically so that it currently lasts the life of the author plus 70 years. Scope also has burgeoned as revealed through derivative rights protection that allows copyright owners to exploit their works in secondary markets. Many scholars have lamented the harmful effects of copyright's expansion on creativity, expression, the public domain, and democracy. As concerning as these effects are, their indirect effect on innovation takes them outside the scope of this book.

One expansion, however, that does directly affect innovation is the DMCA. This statute was enacted to prevent the piracy of digital music and movies. But it has been stretched far beyond this realm. Because the DMCA covers software that controls even uncopyrighted devices, manufacturers have invoked the statute to block competition and interoperability. Such activity restricts innovation by users who customize advances in new markets. In the DMCA context, users have been blocked from improving video game experiences and the activities of robotic pet dogs.

In short, the link between copyright and innovation is crucial to our growth as a society. But this link has been lost in the glare of the creativity spotlight that courts and scholars have shined on copyright law. These three chapters endeavor to change that. We must revise the laws of secondary liability and statutory damages to unleash the disruptive innovation promised by new technologies. And we must amend the DMCA to promote competition and user innovation.

6. PIONEERING PEER-TO-PEER AND OTHER DISRUPTIVE DUAL-USE TECHNOLOGIES

Dual-use Technologies 106
Secondary Liability 108
Sony 109
P2P Technology 111
    Client-Server Model 111
    P2P 112
    Hybrid P2P 114
    Superpeer P2P 114
P2P Legal Trilogy 115
Creativity-Innovation Tradeoff 119
    Reasons for Declining Sales 121
    Other Remedies 122
    Artist Creativity 124
    New Markets and Disruptive Innovation 126
Innovation Asymmetry 128
Error-Costs Asymmetry 131
Litigation Asymmetry 131
Evaluation of Judicial Tests 133
    Sony 133
    Napster/Grokster 135
    Aimster 136
P2P Benefits 139
    Distribution 139
    The Long Tail 141
    Promotion 141
Tip of Innovation Iceberg 142
Recommendation 144

Question: What do the VCR, computer, CD burner, iPod, TiVo, and peer-to-peer (P2P) file-sharing software have in common?

Answer: They can be utilized (1) to create revolutionary new forms of interaction and entertainment or (2) to facilitate widespread copyright infringement.

How, then, should copyright law treat these *dual-use technologies*? Should it consider the technology's primary use? Determine whether it has a substantial noninfringing use? Examine its creator's intent?

Courts have considered these tests, among others, in applying copyright law to dual-use technologies. But most of the tests threaten to stifle innovation. And the sheer number of analyses have made this one of the most elusive areas in IP law, further endangering innovation. Given the potentially revolutionary nature of dual-use devices, particularly in the digital era, and their importance to our economy and livelihoods, the consequences are monumental.

This chapter begins by offering several examples of dual-use technologies from the past century. Next, it discusses the crucial case of *Sony Corporation of America v. Universal City Studios*, in which the Supreme Court held that the manufacturer of the Betamax VCR was not liable for contributory copyright infringement.[1] Given the importance of P2P software to dual-use debates today, the chapter then introduces the technology and three judicial treatments of it.

The focus then shifts from a description to a critique of dual-use issues. It shows that the tradeoff between innovation and creativity is not as intractable as most courts and scholars have thought. The reason is that (at least in the context of P2P technology and CD sales) innovation, but not creativity, is drastically threatened by the selected test. In particular, disruptive innovation is threatened. At the same time, copyright holders have remedies other than suing dual-use manufacturers, including lawsuits against direct infringers, legislation addressing specific technologies, and technological protection measures.

Next, this chapter introduces three dangers facing innovation. First, an *innovation asymmetry* downplays new technologies' future benefits and overemphasizes copyright owners' present losses. Second, an *error-costs asymmetry* reveals that a technology's abandonment has a far more drastic effect than its wrongful continuation. Third, a *litigation asymmetry* ensnares small technology makers in a web of complex tests and unaffordable lawsuits.

After analyzing the P2P court decisions and exploring the technology's benefits, this chapter concludes by recommending a return to the *Sony* test. Such a proposal would maximize innovation. In particular, it would promote the radical, disruptive variety that consumers relish, that challenges the entrenched copyright industries, and that is barely visible in the tip of the innovation iceberg.

DUAL-USE TECHNOLOGIES

Dual-use technologies are not new. Many of the innovations that consumers have enjoyed throughout the past century fall into this category: the telephone, camera, jukebox, radio, television, photocopier, VCR, computer, Internet, iPod, and P2P file-sharing software, to name just a few.

Each of these technologies has offered the public new modes of entertainment and communication. Each has promised to generate new profit opportunities and markets for creative works. But each also has introduced new prospects for the unauthorized reproduction and distribution of those works. It is this threat that consistently has caused copyright holders to be wary of dual-use technologies and to issue predictions of doom upon their introduction.

---

1. 464 U.S. 417 (1984).

At the turn of the 20th century, sheet music publishers viewed the player piano, which used copyrighted sheet music in the pianos (and threatened to reduce revenue) with great alarm.[2] Composer John Philip Sousa bemoaned the introduction of the technology, predicting "a marked deterioration in American music and musical taste, an interruption in the musical development of the country, and a host of other injuries to music in its artistic manifestation."[3]

Eight decades later, Jack Valenti, the then-head of the Motion Picture Association of America (MPAA), the trade group representing the U.S. motion picture industry, warned that the market for copyrighted movies would be "decimated, shrunken [and] collapsed" by the VCR and that "the VCR is to the American film producer and the American public as the Boston strangler is to the woman home alone."[4] The year after the *Sony* decision, with box office revenues at their lowest levels in nearly a decade, the industry lamented that "VCR dates" were replacing the teenage ritual of going to the movies.[5]

Just a few other examples demonstrate the point. Copyright owners in the late 1980s "declared war" on recordable CDs.[6] They later attacked broadband networks, claiming that "Verizon and SBC have little or no economic incentive to combat piracy . . . [because] music downloading is driving the [DSL] business."[7] And they charged that "[t]he killer app for the computer industry is piracy" and accused Apple of "telling people 'that they can create a theft if they buy this computer.'"[8]

---

2. *Sony v. Universal Symposium (Panel 3): A New World Order?*, 34 Sw. U. L. Rev. 211, 218 (2004).

3. John Philip Sousa, *The Menace of Mechanical Music*, 8 Appleton's Mag., 278–84 (1906).

4. *Home Recording Of Copyrighted Works: Hearings on H.R. 4783 et al. before Subcomm. on Courts, Civil Liberties and the Admin. of Justice of the H. Comm. on the Judiciary*, 97th Cong. 4, 8 (1982), http://cryptome.org/hrcw-hear.htm.

5. Jennifer Holt, *In Deregulation We Trust: The Synergy of Politics and Industry in Reagan-Era Hollywood*, 55 Film Q. 22, 23, http://caliber.ucpress.net/doi/pdf/10.1525/fq.2001.55.2.22. To be clear, the entertainment industry was primarily concerned with the VCR's "record" (not "play") button, though a market for VCRs without the record function likely would have been far less robust.

6. Comm. Daily (Nov. 10, 1988).

7. *Consumer Privacy and Gov't Tech. Mandates in the Digital Media Marketplace: Hearing Before the Sen. Comm. on Commerce*, 108th Cong. (2003) (testimony of Cary Sherman, President and Counsel, RIAA), *available at* http://commerce.senate.gov/hearings/testimony.cfm?id=919&wit_id=2584.

8. Brooks Boliek, *Mouse Grouse: Dis Boss Lays into Computer Biz*, The Hollywood Rptr., Mar. 1, 2002, http://www.larta.org/pl/NewsArticles/02Mar01_HR_Eisner.htm (comments of Michael Eisner, then-CEO of Disney). *See generally* http://www.eff.org/IP/P2P/MGM_v_Grokster/20050301_internet_industry.pdf (providing examples of copyright owners' "ominous rhetoric").

Copyright owners, however, have frequently exaggerated the harm threatened by new technologies. Notwithstanding the protests against the VCR, home video had become the industry's chief revenue source within two years of the *Sony* decision, providing distributors with almost half a billion more dollars than box office revenues.[9] By 2003, home entertainment was responsible for more than 80 percent of movie studios' revenues, with box office receipts making up less than 20 percent.[10] Nor are the incorrect predictions harmless. For in each case, copyright owners, facing threats to their business models, attempt to change the law to block the technologies. The copyright law of secondary liability presents the setting in which these debates have most frequently taken place.

SECONDARY LIABILITY

The copyright laws give creators exclusive rights to reproduce, distribute, publicly perform and display, and prepare derivative works.[11] Any person that engages in any of these activities without permission directly infringes the copyright.

In addition to suing direct infringers, copyright owners can sue any party that assists another in committing infringement. The two primary theories of such *secondary liability* are contributory infringement and vicarious liability. Though often described separately, the courts sometimes blur the theories in application.[12]

Contributory infringement stems from the tort concept of enterprise liability, which penalizes someone marginally involved in illegal activity as much as partners playing a more central role.[13] A party commits this offense by (1) knowing about the infringing activity and (2) causing or materially contributing to the infringement.[14]

Vicarious liability grew out of agency principles, by which a principal was held liable for the acts of its agent.[15] One is vicariously liable if he or she (1) has the right and ability to control or supervise the infringing activity and (2) derives a financial benefit from the infringement.[16]

---

9. Boliek, *Mouse Grouse*.

10. Edward Jay Epstein, *Gross Misunderstanding: Forget About the Box Office*, SLATE, May 16, 2005, http://slate.com/id/2118819/.

11. 17 U.S.C. § 106.

12. In contrast to patent law (which has been codified by Congress), copyright secondary liability is entirely judge-made law.

13. *Demetriades v. Kaufmann*, 690 F. Supp. 289, 292 (S.D.N.Y. 1988).

14. *Gershwin Publ'g Corp. v. Columbia Artists Mgmt.*, 443 F.2d 1159, 1162 (2d Cir. 1971).

15. E.g., *Fonovisa v. Cherry Auction*, 76 F.3d 259, 262 (9th Cir. 1996).

16. *Gershwin Publ'g*, 443 F.2d at 1162.

Early cases applying indirect liability concepts involved the owners of facilities. Courts punished record store owners who sold customers blank tapes and loaned them sound recordings that they copied on store-provided systems.[17] They also found liable a dance hall owner who hired an orchestra that played copyrighted compositions without authorization.[18]

A particularly expansive case applying these theories is *Fonovisa v. Cherry Auction*. In this case, the defendant ran a swap meet (or flea market) and rented booths to vendors, some of whom sold counterfeit recordings of copyrighted music. The Ninth Circuit reversed the lower court's dismissal of the case, finding that the plaintiff presented a claim of vicarious liability. First, because it could terminate vendors for selling counterfeit records (or any other reason), it had control. And second, because it benefited from rental and admission fees, as well as parking and concession stand revenues paid by those coming to buy counterfeit records, it had (an admittedly indirect) financial interest.[19] The defendant also was guilty of contributory infringement because it knew about the activity and materially contributed to it by providing "space, utilities, parking, advertising, plumbing, and customers."[20]

SONY

How would these theories of secondary liability apply in the context of dual-use devices? The first test came in *Sony Corporation of America v. Universal City Studios.*[21]

Universal City Studios and Walt Disney Productions sued Sony, the manufacturer of the Betamax home videocassette recorder (VCR), the first compact and affordable such device on the market. The studios claimed that Sony had committed contributory infringement by providing a device that allowed consumers to record copyrighted movies and television shows. The district court denied relief to the movie studios, but the Ninth Circuit reversed, finding that Sony had committed contributory infringement.[22]

In offering a test to apply to dual-use technologies, the Supreme Court reached into patent law to import the *staple article of commerce* doctrine. This doctrine

---

17. *Elektra Records v. Gem Elec. Distribs.*, 360 F. Supp. 821 (E.D.N.Y. 1973).

18. *Sony*, 464 U.S. at 438 n.18 (describing cases).

19. For a narrower conception of financial interest, see *Ellison v. Robertson*, 357 F.3d 1072, 1079 (9th Cir. 2004) (holding that a plaintiff must show that a defendant received "a direct financial benefit" from the infringing activity).

20. 76 F.3d 259, 260–64 (9th Cir. 1996).

21. 464 U.S. 417 (1984)

22. 464 U.S. at 419–20; *see* Steve Lohr, *Hard-Hit Sony Girds for a Fight in the American Market*, N.Y. TIMES, Aug. 14, 1983, § 3 at 8.

finds parties liable for contributory patent infringement if they sell a component that can only be used in a patented invention, as opposed to one that is a "staple article . . . suitable for substantial noninfringing use."[23]

In what was to become one of the most quoted sentences in all of copyright law, the Court asserted that

> the sale of copying equipment, like the sale of other articles of commerce, does not constitute contributory infringement of a copyright if the product is widely used for legitimate, unobjectionable purposes, or even if merely *capable of substantial non-infringing uses*.[24]

The Court also understood that "when major technological innovations alter the market for copyrighted materials," it was the role of Congress—not the courts—to "fashion[] the new rules." Only the legislature "has the constitutional authority and . . . institutional ability to accommodate fully the varied permutations of competing interests that are inevitably implicated by such new technology."[25]

The Court concluded that the consumers' recordings did not constitute direct infringement. Some copyright owners had granted permission to record their shows. And even for those who did not, the use of "time-shifting," or taping of a show to watch later, would tend to increase the potential audience. In addition, the plaintiffs had not been able to prove harm to the value of their copyrights from the practice.[26]

Because time-shifting constituted fair use, the Court found that the technology had a substantial noninfringing use. It thus reversed the Ninth Circuit and found that Sony was not liable for contributory infringement.[27]

In recent years, the exact contours of the *Sony* test have been subject to debate. The entertainment industry has focused on the language "widely used for legitimate, unobjectionable purposes" and has explained that consumers had used the VCR primarily for noninfringing uses.[28] But the more common, broader, reading—advanced by technology manufacturers—requires only that the device is "capable of substantial noninfringing uses" to escape liability.

The reverence in which *Sony* is held by technology makers is matched only by the razor-thin margin by which the test became law. For starters, the Court was only able to obtain the four votes needed to grant certiorari to overturn the Ninth Circuit's holding for the movie studios with a vote from Justice Harry Blackmun.

---

23. 35 U.S.C. § 271(c). Other requirements for the offense are knowledge and the presence of a material component.

24. 464 U.S. at 442 (emphasis added).

25. *Id.* at 431.

26. *Id.* at 443–56.

27. *Id.* at 456.

28. Brief for Motion Picture Studio and Recording Company Petitioners at 30, 36, *MGM v. Grokster*, 125 S. Ct. 2764 (2003).

Given that Justice Blackmun wished to reaffirm the ruling, and that Justices in such a position often do not vote to grant certiorari, the merits of the case could very well have never reached the Court.[29]

On the merits themselves, the outcome was far from ordained. The Court initially voted to affirm the finding of liability. Justice Blackmun was assigned the task of drafting the majority opinion.[30] But there were vigorous debates among the Justices on numerous issues relating to private copying, fair use, and the test for secondary liability. Justice Sandra Day O'Connor, in particular, appeared to be the swing vote. Justice Blackmun accepted some of her suggestions, but the course of copyright history was forever changed when he refused to accept all, declaring that "[f]ive votes are not that important to me when I feel that proper legal principles are involved."[31]

Still not able to reach a decision by the end of the term, the Court reheard argument during the following term. It ultimately found for Sony, with Justice John Paul Stevens writing the majority opinion reversing infringement and Justice Blackmun dissenting.

How would *Sony* fare when applied to the very different technology of, and activity unleashed by, P2P file-sharing software? Before examining the courts' treatment of this issue, a brief background on the technology is warranted.

P2P TECHNOLOGY

Client-Server Model

The Internet is, among other things, a vast repository of information, similar to a library. As with any large library, a user performs two steps to get the data she wants. First, the user queries an index (such as a search engine) to locate the address of the data she desires. Second, the user goes to that address to retrieve the data.

For much of the Internet's history, these two exchanges occurred in a *client-server* model. The user loads *client* software—a web browser like Internet Explorer or Mozilla Firefox—and contacts a search engine such as Google that runs *server* software. In response to a query, Google returns an address that the user can click. That click initiates the second transaction in which the browser contacts a server that delivers the desired data. The World Wide Web is an example of this model.[32]

---

29. Jonathan Band & Andrew J. McLaughlin, *The Marshall Papers: A Peek Behind the Scenes at the Making of* Sony v. Universal, 17 COLUM.-VLA J.L. & ARTS 427, 432 (1993).

30. *Id.* at 432–33.

31. Letter from Associate Justice Harry A. Blackmun to Associate Justice Sandra Day O'Connor at 1 (June 28, 1983).

32. Tim Wu, *When Code Isn't Law*, 89 VA. L. REV. 679, 719–20 (2003).

The data flow in the client-server model is overwhelmingly from server to client.[33] This asymmetry is reflected in the computing resources required. A client machine, which sends messages to the server, does not need to be powerful. A server, in contrast, could be required to find and present the desired data for thousands of requests at the same time.[34]

Two drawbacks plague the client-server model. First, it is not scalable (able to self-adjust to different levels of demand[35]); with each additional user or file, the server must add scarce resources to accommodate the higher usage. Relatedly, the increase in bandwidth costs for widely distributed large files can be prohibitive for many users.[36] Second, it is not robust; a crash at the central server takes down the entire system.[37]

Many copyright owners nonetheless prefer the client-server architecture, which presents little threat to their business models. Servers are few and well-funded, and they decisively control data flow. Owners thus are able to exert pressure to stop infringement at a few discrete points. If they find infringing content on a server, they can ask the operator to remove the material or find a court to order the server shut down.[38]

But the very control that copyright owners appreciate in the client-server model reveals its weakness. For this control mirrors vulnerability. With just a few points that can bring down the network, client-server architectures are more vulnerable to glitches, crashes, and even terrorist attacks, earthquakes, and wars.[39]

As the price of computing resources fell in the 1990s, the client-server model would become subject to challenge. More and more Internet users, running programs like Instant Messenger or Napster, would become servers in their own right.

P2P

By 2000, the price of advanced computing resources had dropped low enough to be within the average household's budget. The price of one megabyte of hard

---

33. James D. McCabe, Network Analysis, Design and Architecture 181 (2007).

34. Wolfgang Gruener, *Google Now Controls More than 50% of Search Requests from Americans*, TG Daily (June 23, 2007), http://www.tgdaily.com/content/view/32603/118/ (noting that Google processed approximately 4 billion search requests in one recent month).

35. Brief for Respondents, at 7, *MGM v. Grokster*, 125 S. Ct. 2764 (2003).

36. Brief for Creative Commons as Amicus Curiae in Support of Respondents at 7, *MGM v. Grokster*, 125 S. Ct. 2764 (2003) [hereinafter Creative Commons Brief].

37. Brief for Respondents, at 7.

38. Wu, at 719.

39. Simson Garfinkel, *Pushing Peer-to-Peer*, Tech. Rev., Oct. 2003, http://www.technologyreview.com/Infotech/13334/?a=f.

disk drive storage (which holds approximately 100 pages of single-spaced text) fell from $100 in 1985 to $1 in 1995 to 3/100 of 1¢ in 2008.[40] Accordingly, the price to store 1 gigabyte (1000 megabytes) of material—the typical size of a movie—fell from $100,000 to 30¢. And the price of persistent broadband Internet connections dropped from thousands of dollars a month to less than $100. Consumers could now afford such a connection to the Internet through cable modem or digital subscriber line (DSL). Once server-class resources became available to many, the client-server model was no longer inevitable. Thus began the era of P2P information-sharing networks.

The defining characteristic of a P2P network is that the second data acquisition step—the transfer of the file—is performed directly between users without any intervening server. On a P2P network, every user is both a client and a server. P2P thus does not suffer from the client-server model's lack of scalability and redundancy.

Peer-to-peer scales more quickly and cheaply because all users bring to the table their broadband connection, drive space, and files. Instead of clients queuing up at the gates of the server, the users simply ask each other for the data they want. On the lower end, the network also provides an opportunity for smaller, niche databases.

Peer-to-peer also provides a more robust system. One peer's crash does not affect the other peers on the system. And rather than residing on one central server, multiple redundant copies of data are dispersed throughout the network. In contrast to the typical client-server architecture, a P2P model improves with each additional user.

In addition to benefits for scalability and redundancy, P2P also has offered a more participatory experience. Users have created compilations and modified popular works, thus "assert[ing] a more active, self-defining role in the enjoyment, use, and creation of cultural expression."[41] In addition, every owner of a home movie or other large file is, for the first time, able to distribute it.

To be sure, there are drawbacks to P2P networks. It is more difficult to perform upgrades on the systems. Files on the networks are often of low quality

---

40. G. Kent Webb, *A Rule-Based Forecast of Computer Hard Drive Costs*, at 341 (2003), www.iacis.org/iis/2003_iis/PDFfiles/Webb.pdf (providing figures for 1985 and 1995); www.pcconnection.com (last visited August 31, 2008) (providing figure based on Lacie 500-gigabyte external hard drive offered for $149.95 (equivalent to.02999 pennies per megabyte)).

41. Neil W. Netanel, *Impose a Noncommercial Use Levy to Allow Free Peer-to-Peer File Sharing*, 17 HARV. J.L. & TECH. 2, 3 (2003).

or even spoof files inserted by record companies.[42] And some networks have installed intrusive "spyware" onto users' machines.[43]

In the short history of P2P networks, two types have been particularly influential: hybrid and superpeer. The two vary in how they perform the first data acquisition step of searching an index to get the address of desired data.

Hybrid P2P

In *hybrid* networks, the first data acquisition step is performed under a client-server model. Each peer indexes the files on his or her machine and deposits that index with the central server, which aggregates the files into one giant index. The peers then consult a central server to locate desired information. The P2P aspect occurs when the peers conduct the data transfer between themselves.[44]

The rapidly adopted Napster was a hybrid network that introduced the world at large to the potential of P2P.[45] Napster scaled with astounding ease and swiftness. Only a year after its launch in 1999, the network was swapping three billion MP3 music files a month, a feat that could not have been duplicated with client-server architecture.[46]

Another example of hybrid P2P is provided by instant messaging (IM). Instant messaging servers facilitate communication by maintaining a dynamic list of who is online at any given time and searching for (and presenting a list of) a user's "friends." The communication between friends is done directly through P2P rather than the IM server.

As discussed more fully below, litigation over the Napster system encouraged a movement away from hybrid P2P networks to an architecture set up to prevent an owner's knowledge of, or control over, peers' activities.

Superpeer P2P

This architecture, the second P2P model, is a *superpeer* (also known as supernode, ultrapeer, or decentralized) network.[47]

In such a network, the creator does not designate specific machines to serve as index servers. Instead, the software running on all the peers takes stock of

---

42. Spoof files are "cleverly concealed fakes" that have included silence, a song's chorus repeated endlessly, or bands speaking about a song. Gil Kaufman, *Music Industry Uses 'Spoofs' To Throw Off Illegal File Traders*, THE ENQUIRER, May 18, 2003, http://www.enquirer.com/editions/2003/05/18/tem_download18.html.

43. Bill Rosenblatt, *Learning from P2P: Evolution of Business Models for Online Content*, INDICARE, Oct. 12, 2004, http://www.indicare.org/tiki-read_article.php?articleId=61.

44. *See generally* Wu, at 720.

45. Benny Evangelista, *Napster Names CEO, Secures New Financing*, SAN FRAN. CHRON., May 23, 2000, at C1.

46. Wu, at 710. Peer-to-peer file-sharing is facilitated by the compression of music into a digital file format known as MPEG Layer-3 (MP3), which speeds up transfers between computers.

47. *Id.* at 734.

each other's available resources, including bandwidth, drive space, and processing power. If a peer is well-endowed and the software determines that a new index server is needed, the P2P software will automatically elevate that machine to superpeer status. The superpeer then becomes the index server for a group of nearby "children" peers. Superpeers communicate amongst themselves, creating a secondary network of high-performance, self-managing index servers that can dynamically scale and operate hidden from the network owner.[48]

Superpeer networks, while less centralized than hybrid models, solved the problems confronting even more decentralized systems, known as *pure* networks. In these systems (such as early versions of Gnutella), users maintain an index only of the contents of their own machines, and search queries proceed in an expanding fashion from immediate neighbors outward.[49] But because they lack centralized indexes or supernodes, pure P2P networks are inefficient. Every search must traverse a large number of tiny, individual indexes, with a request for an obscure file or a large set of query results clogging the network with thousands of requests and reply messages. Pure networks thus have not played as important a role as the other two systems.

The most famous superpeer network is FastTrack, which debuted in 2000. Multiple programs, including KaZaA and Grokster, have built on this network. When Napster shut down operations in 2000, millions of file-sharers migrated to FastTrack. The network scaled admirably and soon was supporting more users and swapping more files than Napster at its height.[50]

The overriding legal question with dual-use technologies is whether they are used for infringing or noninfringing purposes. With superpeer networks, however, the software's owner cannot answer this question. Once a user downloads the P2P software, the owner does not know how it is being used. Nor can the owner terminate peers or alter their activity.

The differences among the hybrid and superpeer architectures are crucial in explaining how courts have analyzed these issues.

P2P LEGAL TRILOGY

Courts in three cases have considered the application of secondary liability theories to P2P software: *A&M Records, Inc. v. Napster, Inc.*,[51] *In re Aimster Copyright Litigation*,[52] and *MGM v. Grokster*.[53]

In the *Napster* case, the court addressed Napster's MusicShare software, which, at the time of the district court decision, was responsible for the sharing

---

48. *See generally Peer Architectures*, http://www.leuf.com/books/p2p-html/p2p-02.htm.
49. Wu, at 731.
50. *Id.* at 734.
51. 239 F.3d 1004 (9th Cir. 2001).
52. 334 F.3d 643 (7th Cir. 2003).
53. 545 U.S. 913 (2005).

of approximately 10,000 music files per second.[54] Since most of these files were copyrighted, the recording industry sued Napster for facilitating copyright infringement.

Napster worked as follows. First, a user downloaded from the company's Web site its MusicShare software, which allowed it to access the network. Second, the user specified files to be shared with others, and when the user was online the list of files was supplied to Napster. Third, the user searched for other users' files. Finally, to transfer a copy of the file, the user received the Internet address of the "host user" (who had the files) from the Napster servers, connected to the host user, and downloaded a copy of the file directly from the other computer in a "peer-to-peer" fashion.[55]

The district court issued a preliminary injunction against Napster.[56] The Ninth Circuit affirmed, concluding that Napster would likely be held liable for contributory infringement.[57] The company's actual knowledge was revealed through its notice of more than 12,000 infringing files as well as a document asserting "the need to remain ignorant of users' real names and IP addresses 'since they are exchanging pirated music.'" The court sidestepped the *Sony* question, finding that, even if Napster were capable of a substantial noninfringing use, its actual knowledge was sufficient to impose liability.

In addition to actual knowledge, the company had constructive knowledge because its executives, who had recording industry experience and had enforced IP rights, downloaded copyrighted songs and "promoted the site with 'screen shots listing infringing files.'" In addition, Napster materially contributed to the infringing activity since its services were crucial to finding and downloading desired music.

The Ninth Circuit also found it likely that Napster would be vicariously liable. The company benefited from the increase in users that resulted from the availability of copyrighted works. And it had the right to terminate users' access to the system. Vital to this control was the architecture of hybrid P2P systems. Because it managed the centralized search indexes, Napster could observe the peers' activities and eject users from the system.

The second case, *In re Aimster Copyright Litigation*, involved largely similar facts. But there were a few differences: the system operated over the America Online Instant Messaging System, it included tutorials teaching users how to use the software for swapping computer files, and it encrypted communications.[58]

---

54. *A&M Records, Inc. v. Napster, Inc.*, 114 F. Supp. 2d 896, 902 (N.D. Cal. 2000).

55. The description of the Napster technology is taken from the Ninth Circuit decision. *See* 239 F.3d at 1011–12.

56. In the context of a preliminary injunction, courts predict the likelihood of success as opposed to making conclusive determinations.

57. The court's legal analysis appears at 239 F.3d at 1020–24.

58. 334 F.3d at 646.

The Seventh Circuit affirmed an injunction against the file-sharing service on the grounds of contributory infringement.[59] In cases of substantial noninfringing uses, the court called for an "estimate of the respective magnitudes of these uses." And it added its own gloss to *Sony* by stating that an actual (as opposed to a potential) noninfringing use was needed to avoid liability. Applying its test, the court concluded that Aimster had "failed to produce any evidence that its service has ever been used for a noninfringing use."

The court rejected Aimster's argument that encryption prevented it from learning about infringement, concluding that "[w]illful blindness is knowledge." And it found knowledge in company tutorials that used only copyrighted works.

Finally, the court raised the bar against technology providers even higher when it required them to show, in cases of substantial infringing uses, that "it would have been disproportionately costly . . . to eliminate or at least reduce substantially the infringing uses." Aimster's inability to make this showing contributed to the court's imposition of liability against the file-sharing service.

The hybrid P2P architecture at issue in the *Napster* and *Aimster* cases thus did not bode well for future P2P operators. It is not surprising, then, that P2P networks moved in the direction of decentralized systems.

Just such a network was at issue in the third case, *MGM v. Grokster.* Grokster's software used the FastTrack technology that routed user requests to computers (supernodes) that collected temporary indexes of files and disclosed the file location for downloading purposes. StreamCast's Morpheus software used Gnutella technology, which was similar but in some versions replaced supernodes with peer computers that communicated directly with each other.[60]

A group of copyright holders, including movie studios, recording companies, songwriters, and music publishers, sued Grokster and StreamCast for contributory infringement. The district court granted summary judgment for Grokster and StreamCast, and the Ninth Circuit affirmed. The appellate court refused to find contributory infringement because there were no central servers that could intercept search requests or mediate the users' file transfers.[61] In short, the software did not allow control over index files or provide the "site and facilities" for infringement. The court denied vicarious liability because the defendants could not prevent users from obtaining access.

The Supreme Court granted certiorari. The copyright community eagerly awaited the Court's resolution of the issue. How would it apply the crucial dual-use technology case, *Sony*? How would the doctrines of contributory infringement and vicarious liability apply in the P2P context?

These questions would go unanswered. The Court highlighted the defendants' evidence of intent and explained that "the [*Sony*] case was never meant to foreclose

---

59. The court's legal analysis appears at 334 F.3d at 649–53.
60. 545 U.S. at 921–22.
61. *MGM Studios, Inc. v. Grokster Ltd.*, 380 F.3d 1154, 1163, 1165 (9th Cir. 2004).

rules of fault-based liability derived from the common law."[62] It also downplayed the traditional notions of contributory infringement and vicarious liability in relying on a theory of inducement.[63] It held that

> one who distributes a device with the object of promoting its use to infringe copyright, as shown by clear expression or other affirmative steps taken to foster infringement, is liable for the resulting acts of infringement by third parties.

The Court promised that liability would not attach to "mere knowledge" of potential or actual infringing uses or "ordinary acts incident to product distribution, such as offering customers technical support or product updates."

The Court overturned summary judgment for the defendants, finding that they could be held liable for inducement. It found that the defendants advertised a message designed to stimulate others to commit infringement. StreamCast urged the adoption of an OpenNap program for Napster patrons, Grokster distributed an electronic newsletter with links to articles promoting its software's ability to access popular copyrighted music, and both defendants responded to requests for help in locating and playing copyrighted materials.

The Court focused on three pieces of evidence in particular. First, the defendants targeted the market of former Napster users through advertisements, software functions similar to Napster, and (in the case of Grokster) a name derived from Napster and diversions of Napster queries to its own Web site. Second, neither company attempted to reduce infringement by using filtering tools or other similar mechanisms. Third, the companies' business models demonstrated a financial benefit from infringement, as the sharing of copyrighted works increased the user base, which boosted advertisements and revenue. The Court indicated that the second and third factors standing alone would not constitute infringement, but never explained exactly what activity would suffice.

Although the Court did not apply *Sony* to the facts of the case, two concurrences addressed the issue. Speaking for three Justices, Justice Ruth Bader Ginsburg found that the case "differ[ed] markedly from *Sony*" since "there has been no finding of any fair use and little beyond anecdotal evidence of noninfringing uses." Instead, the software was "overwhelmingly used to infringe."[64]

In contrast, Justice Stephen Breyer, also speaking for three Justices, found that the technology was "capable of substantial noninfringing use" and that defendants' 10 percent noninfringing uses were similar to the Sony

---

62. The Court's analysis appears at 545 U.S. at 934–40.

63. As the *Sony* Court did in borrowing the staple-article doctrine, the *Grokster* Court turned to patent law in borrowing the concept of inducement. Such importation is partially explained by the absence of statutory standards for secondary liability in copyright law.

64. *Id.* at 945, 948 (Ginsburg, J., concurring).

VCR's 9 percent authorized uses. He also supported the *Sony* rule as clear, forward-looking, and protective of new technologies.[65]

After the decision, Grokster settled with the copyright industry, agreeing to not give away its software or participate in the theft of copyrighted works and to pay $50 million.[66] StreamCast continued to litigate but lost at the summary judgment stage. The district court found that the solicitation of former Napster users, assistance to infringing users, advertisement-based business model, and failure to implement filtering technology demonstrated an intent to induce infringement. It explained that the "ultimate question" involved the defendant's intent. And it concluded that a court could find "an inference of intent to encourage infringement . . . [e]ven if filtering technology does not work perfectly and contains negative side effects on usability."[67]

Shortly after the *Grokster* decision, the Recording Industry Association of America (RIAA), the trade group representing the U.S. recording industry, launched suits against other popular P2P programs such as BearShare and LimeWire. These companies and others settled with the RIAA, bringing to a halt nearly all commercial development of P2P software.

The *Napster*, *Aimster*, and *Grokster* courts presented three different views of *Sony* and secondary liability doctrines. Which, if any, got it right?

CREATIVITY-INNOVATION TRADEOFF

To answer this question, we must wrestle with the fundamental challenge in dual-use technology cases: how to encourage creativity while not stifling innovation. Creativity could be promoted by strong copyright rights but threatened by the reproduction and rapid, widespread distribution of perfect digital copies of works. Aggressive tests for indirect copyright infringement, however, come at the price of innovative dual-use technologies. The more that such technologies are restricted, the fewer revolutionary innovations will be offered.

At first glance, the tradeoff between creativity and innovation may seem intractable. How do we compare the apples of creativity to the oranges of innovation? At least in the context of P2P technology and CD sales, a closer look dispels any struggle. For innovation is far more directly affected by the test selected than creativity.

---

65. *Id.* at 952, 957–58 (Breyer, J., concurring). For a view that the concurrences focused on whether a substantial portion of the device's uses were actually noninfringing, see R. Anthony Reese, *The Temporal Dynamics of "Capable of Substantial Noninfringing Uses,"* 13 MICH. TELECOMM. & TECH. L. REV. 197, 218 (2006) [hereinafter Reese, *Temporal Dynamics*].

66. Associated Press, *Grokster Agrees To Shut Down for Good*, Nov. 7, 2005, http://www.msnbc.msn.com/id/9959133/.

67. *MGM Studios, Inc. v. Grokster, Ltd.*, 454 F. Supp. 2d 966, 985–90 (C.D. Cal. 2006).

Four findings demonstrate this point:

(1) There are numerous reasons why CD sales have declined in recent years.
(2) Copyright holders have many potential remedies other than targeting P2P networks.
(3) Individual artists play a crucial role in creativity.
(4) Innovation can create new markets and models for copyrighted works.

In relying on these findings, I do not challenge the conclusion that file sharing has reduced CD sales. Some studies in fact have found such an effect:

- A survey of college students in 2003 concluded that downloading reduced students' purchases of hit albums by approximately 10 percent.[68]
- Downloading "could have caused a 20 percent reduction in music sales worldwide" between 1998 and 2002.[69]
- "Countries with higher internet and broadband penetration have experienced higher reductions in music sales."[70]

But others, in contrast, have concluded that

- because of music sampling, "file sharing has only had a limited effect on record sales . . . statistically indistinguishable from zero"[71];
- file sharing reduced the purchases of 15-to-24-year olds while increasing the purchases of those over 25[72];
- among Canadians engaging in file-sharing, "one additional P2P download per month . . . increased music purchasing by 0.44 CDs per year."[73]

---

68. Rafael Rob & Joel Waldfogel, *Piracy on the High C's: Music Downloading, Sales Displacement, and Social Welfare in a Sample of College Students*, at 1, Nov. 2004, http://papers.ssrn.com/sol3/papers.cfm?abstract_id=612076.

69. Martin Peitz & Patrick Waelbroeck, *The Effect of Internet Piracy on Music Sales: Cross-Section Evidence*, 1 REV. ECON. RES. ON COPYRIGHT ISSUES 71, 78 (2004) (examining country-level figures).

70. Alejandro Zentner, *File Sharing and International Sales of Copyrighted Music: An Empirical Analysis with a Panel of Countries*, 5 TOPICS ECON. ANALYSIS & POL'Y, at 13–14 (2005) (relying on country-level data).

71. Felix Oberholzer & Koleman Strumpf, *The Effect of File Sharing on Record Sales: An Empirical Analysis*, at 3 (2004), http://www.unc.edu/~cigar/papers/FileSharing_March2004.pdf (using download and sales data).

72. Eric S. Boorstin, *Music Sales in the Age of File Sharing*, at 2, http://www.cs.princeton.edu/~felten/boorstin-thesis.pdf (analyzing the relationship between Internet access and CD sales).

73. Birgitte Andersen & Marion Frenz, *The Impact of Music Downloads and P2P File-Sharing on the Purchase of Music: A Study for Industry Canada*, at 33 (2007), http://www.ic.gc.ca/epic/site/ippd-dppi.nsf/vwapj/IndustryCanadaPaperMay4_2007_en.pdf/$FILE/IndustryCanadaPaperMay4_2007_en.pdf.

In offering a conservative approach that gives the benefit of the doubt to creativity in the innovation-creativity tradeoff, I credit the evidence that file-sharing has reduced sales. But even with this approach, four other factors demonstrate the selected test's more direct effect on innovation.

Reasons for Declining Sales

First, even if CD sales have decreased, there are many possible causes other than file-sharing:

- Higher CD prices
- An unwillingness to offer singles to customers
- Smaller FM radio playlists from consolidation among radio owners and record labels
- The increasing importance of mass market retailers (like Wal-Mart) that carry far fewer titles
- Reduced quality
- Increased offline sharing in the form of burned CDs and DVDs, swapped hard drives, and shared USB drives
- A high sales benchmark in the late 1990s from new acts such as Britney Spears, 'NSync, and Christina Aguilera as well as the conversion of LP and cassette collections to CDs
- A downturn in the global economy
- Increasing competition for consumers' entertainment dollars from DVDs and video games.[74]

Even an internal study done by a recording company showed that "between two-thirds and three-quarters of the drop in sales in America had nothing to do with internet piracy."[75] The RIAA itself conceded, in announcing shipment figures for the first half of 2006, that "[c]ompetition for spending on entertainment, especially in a tough economy, likely played a factor" in reduced sales of CDs and DVDs.[76]

In addition, declines in CD sales have been matched by increases in legal digital downloads. In a 2006 press release, the Chairman and CEO of the RIAA

---

74. Digital Connections Council of the Comm. for Econ. Development, *Promoting Innovation and Economic Growth: The Special Problem of Digital Intellectual Property*, at 20–21 (2004), *available at* http://www.ced.org/docs/report/report_dcc.pdf; Letter from Electronic Frontier Foundation to Commissioner Deborah Platt Majoras et al., Jan. 18, 2005, at 3–5, http://www.eff.org/deeplinks/archives/EFF%20FTC%20P2P%20comments%20Jan05.pdf; Electronic Frontier Foundation, *Campus Lawsuits Against P2P = Stopping File Sharing*, May 30, 2007, http://www.eff.org/deeplinks/archives/005280.php.

75. *Music's Brighter Future*, THE ECONOMIST, Oct. 30, 2004.

76. *RIAA Announces First Half 2006 Music Shipment Numbers II*, Oct. 12, 2006, http://www.riaa.com/newsitem.php?news_year_filter=&resultpage=7&id=10D868A5-AAD7-6142-4307-2207FE6D7B53.

proclaimed that "[t]he appetite for music is as strong as ever" and that "a digital marketplace now worth nearly $2 billion has emerged virtually overnight." He supported this enthusiasm by pointing to digital music formats, with 586 million downloaded singles representing a 60 percent increase over the previous year, and 28 million downloaded albums representing a 103 percent increase. In short, he claimed, even if "[t]oday's music marketplace has challenges . . . it also offers reason for hope and optimism."[77]

Other Remedies

Second, even if there were a reduction in sales that could be linked to P2P file sharing, secondary liability is only one potential avenue available to copyright owners. For example, owners could sue direct infringers. And they have: as of July 2006, the RIAA had sued more than 20,000 individuals for file sharing.[78]

Copyright owners also could go to Congress to address particular technologies, which the legislature has done on numerous occasions. It has enacted special provisions for computer programs and rentals of software and sound recordings.[79] It has crafted compulsory license rules for musical works, jukeboxes, public broadcasting, and cable television and satellite systems.[80] It passed the Audio Home Recording Act of 1992 (AHRA), which imposed royalties on digital recording equipment and blank recording media, dividing the revenue among music copyright owners and performers.[81] And it enacted the Digital Millennium Copyright Act (DMCA) to punish the circumvention of technological measures controlling access to copyrighted works.[82] This statute revealed another tool in Congress's arsenal in its safe harbor for Internet service providers that implemented termination procedures for repeat infringers and honored "standard technical measure[s]" for preventing infringement.[83]

In the file-sharing context, Congress could choose from an array of proposals that scholars have recently offered. Professors William Fisher and Neil Netanel

---

77. *RIAA Releases 2006 Shipment Report*, Apr. 17, 2007, http://www.riaa.com/newsitem.php?news_year_filter=&resultpage=3&id=D98F4958-EBBE-56A7-4B05-FE354C991826. Growth continued the following year, with 810 million downloaded singles representing a 38 percent increase from 2006, and 42 million downloaded albums representing a 54 percent increase. Recording Industry Association of America, *2007 Year-End Shipment Statistics*, http://76.74.24.142/81128FFD-028F-282E-1CE5-FDBF16A46388.pdf (last visited June 1, 2008).

78. Electronic Frontier Foundation, *How To Not Get Sued for File Sharing*, http://www.eff.org/IP/P2P/howto-notgetsued.php.

79. 17 U.S.C. §§ 109(b), 117.

80. 17 U.S.C. §§ 111, 115, 116, 118.

81. 17 U.S.C. §§ 1001–10.

82. 17 U.S.C. §§ 1201–05.

83. 17 U.S.C. § 512(i).

have separately called for levy regimes by which products used for file sharing are taxed, with the revenue distributed to copyright owners.[84] Another proposal would create a dispute resolution system that would allow copyright owners to obtain quick relief against abusers of P2P networks.[85]

At least in theory, Congress is better able to address the issue than courts.[86] The legislature can craft solutions for particular technologies. It can draw on a wide array of remedies that includes compulsory licenses, exemptions, and specific technological prescriptions. And it can hold hearings, undertake studies, and engage in other in-depth fact-finding and consensus building. Courts, in contrast, cannot operate with such precision. They issue rules that affect all technologies, including new ones of which they may not even be aware. Their range of remedies is much narrower. They lack broad fact-finding capabilities.

Another avenue for copyright owners involves technological protection measures. Encryption allows only those with special knowledge (a "key") to read protected information.[87] Electronic digital watermarks are identification tags built into digital files that are invisible to humans but that can be tracked by computers.[88] And digital fingerprinting technology converts the content of a work into a unique digital identification mark.[89] These, and other forms of digital rights management (DRM) technologies, allow copyright owners to impose limits on how their works are used.

Owners also could offer improved legal options for offering music and movies online. Apple's iTunes store, which features songs, movies, TV shows, audiobooks, and podcasts, is one obvious example. In April 2008, less than five years after its introduction, Apple became the number one music retailer in the country, with 50 million customers purchasing more than

---

84. WILLIAM W. FISHER, III, PROMISES TO KEEP: TECHNOLOGY, LAW, AND THE FUTURE OF ENTERTAINMENT, ch. 6 (2004); Neil W. Netanel, *Impose a Noncommercial Use Levy to Allow Free Peer-to-Peer File Sharing*, 17 HARV. J.L. & TECH. 2 (2003).

85. Mark A. Lemley & R. Anthony Reese, *Reducing Digital Copyright Infringement Without Restricting Innovation*, 56 STAN. L. REV. 1345, 1351 (2004).

86. Congress's institutional superiority does not automatically mean its attempts will be successful. For example, in the proposed Inducing Infringement of Copyrights Act (Induce Act), Congress would have expansively punished anyone who "intentionally aids, abets, induces, or procures" infringement. S.2560, 108th Cong. (2004).

87. *Encryption*, WIKIPEDIA, http://en.wikipedia.org/wiki/Encryption.

88. Timothy K. Andrews, *Control Content, Not Innovation: Why Hollywood Should Embrace Peer-to-Peer Technology Despite the MGM v. Grokster Battle*, 25 LOY. L.A. ENT. L. REV. 383, 416 (2005).

89. Lionel S. Sobel, *DRM as an Enabler of Business Models: ISPs as Digital Retailers*, 18 BERKELEY TECH. L.J. 667, 681 (2003).

four billion songs.[90] Other examples are CinemaNow, which offers, and Movielink, which used to offer, movies and TV shows for rental or sale.[91]

This array of options is even more palatable because it is far from clear that rulings banning particular file-sharing systems would have a measurable effect. Peer-to-peer downloading has skyrocketed even after the decisions against Napster, Aimster, and Grokster. By 2007, more than 9 million users in the United States were simultaneously connected to the P2P networks at any given time.[92]

Moreover, off-shore companies such as KaZaA lie outside the reach of U.S. copyright law. Private networks known as "darknets" are difficult to detect. And the decentralization and widespread distribution of P2P software ensures that, even after an adverse court decision, the file-sharing genie cannot be put back in the bottle.

Artist Creativity

Third, even if the "big four" major recording labels—Sony BMG, Universal, EMI, and Warner Brothers—have suffered losses, this does not equate with reduced creativity.[93] The Copyright Clause of the Constitution endeavors to promote the progress of "Science and the useful Arts," not to maximize the profitability of the entertainment industry.

One of the most useful functions provided by the recording industry is discovering the next superstar.[94] But, as discussed later in this chapter, P2P can serve such a function in a different (and more inclusive) fashion by drawing on the strength of a broad universe of users. The industry has also played a role in producing and promoting albums. Significant declines in the cost of recording equipment, however, have allowed musicians to set up their own recording studios. And the roles of the industry and radio stations in promoting music are being displaced by social networking websites such as MySpace and Facebook.[95]

Even reduced CD sales flowing from P2P would not affect the creators themselves as artists nearly always receive most, if not all, of their income from

---

90. Apple, *iTunes Store Top Music Retailer in the US*, Apr. 3, 2008, http://www.apple.com/pr/library/2008/04/03itunes.html.

91. www.cinemanow.com.

92. Eric Bangeman, *P2P Traffic Shifts Away from Music, Towards Movies*, ARSTECHNICA, July 5, 2007, http://arstechnica.com/news.ars/post/20070705-p2p-traffic-shifts-away-from-music-towards-movies.html.

93. Because the record industry has fewer revenue sources than the music industry, it relies more on CD sales.

94. Theo Papadopoulos, *Are Music Recording Contracts Equitable? An Economic Analysis of the Practice of Recoupment*, 4 MEIEA J. 83 (2004), http://www.meiea.org/Journal/html_ver/Vol04_No01/Vol_4_No_1_A5.html.

95. FISHER, PROMISES TO KEEP, at 21–23.

live performances. The Grateful Dead, for example, encouraged free copying and distribution of their live performances but still earned $50 million per year in the early 1990s.[96] Record companies charge artists for production, marketing, and promotion costs, and an artist typically must sell more than one million copies of a CD before receiving royalties. Artists thus are far more likely to be in debt to the recording industry than to receive royalties from CD sales.[97] It is not a surprise, then, that a majority of 2,500 surveyed artists and musicians were not concerned about file-sharing and that two-thirds indicated that the practice poses "a minor threat or no threat" to the movie and music industries.[98] At a minimum, lesser-known artists prefer the sampling and increased exposure that accompanies file-sharing.[99]

Artists have explored ways of distributing their music through P2P channels. A few examples include

- Steve Winwood's release of a free song on a P2P network, followed by a 700 percent increase in album sales in certain regions
- Heart's release of an album on a "try it before you buy it" basis that sold more copies through P2P networks than through Apple's iTunes store
- The model and singer Tila Tequila, who landed a record deal through her active involvement in MySpace, where she accumulated 2 million friends
- Sananda Maitreya (formerly Terence Trent D'Arby), who exclusively released songs on his own customized version of P2P software
- The Dave Matthews Band, which uses BitTorrent to share files and seeks to "foster greater interaction within the fan community" through the trading of taped performances
- Wilco, which responded to AOL Time Warner's Reprise Records' refusal to release its album by distributing it for free over a P2P network, receiving interest from several labels, and garnering a gold album[100]

---

96. Ted Drozdowski, *Jam Nation: The Dead Return to a Diversifying Field of Like-Minded Bands*, THE PROVIDENCE PHOENIX, June 20, 2003, http://www.providencephoenix.com/music/other_stories/documents/02965382.asp; Urs Gasser et al., *Content and Control: Assessing the Impact of Policy Choices on Potential Online Business Models in the Music and Film Industries*, at AV-2, Jan. 7, 2005, http://papers.ssrn.com/sol3/papers.cfm?abstract_id=654602.

97. Charles C. Mann, *The Heavenly Jukebox*, ATLANTIC MONTHLY, at 39, 50 (Sept. 2000).

98. Mary Madden, *Pew Internet & American Life Project, Artists, Musicians and the Internet*, at 21, Dec. 5, 2004, http://www.pewinternet.org/PPF/r/142/report_display.asp.

99. Ram D. Gopal et al., *Do Artists Benefit From Online Music Sharing?*, at 38, Feb. 2004, http://papers.ssrn.com/sol3/papers.cfm?abstract_id=527324.

100. Katie Dean, *Winwood: Roll with P2P, Baby*, WIRED.COM, July 9, 2004, http://www.wired.com/entertainment/music/news/2004/07/64128; Tony Smith, *P2Pers: We Can Make File-Sharing Secure and Outsell iTunes*, July 22, 2004, http://www.theregister.co.uk/2004/07/22/p2p_vs_itunes/ (Heart); *Multi-Platinum Grammy-Award Winning Artist Sananda Maitreya Becomes the First Major Artist To Fully Embrace File Sharing with his Own*

New Markets and Disruptive Innovation

Fourth, innovation can enhance creativity. Even if new technologies threaten an existing business model in the short term, they promise to make copyrights more valuable by creating new markets and models in the long run.[101] And because innovation is crucial to economic growth, stifled technologies threaten to hamper the nation's economy. Thwarting innovation could be particularly dangerous because of the revolutionary nature of many of the dual-use technologies, which—as the camera, photocopier, TV, iPod, and others reveal—have a profound effect on our lives.

Of course, copyright owners fear changes that would upset established business models with which they are familiar and from which they have gained significant profits. Their crusades against the player piano, VCR, broadband networks, and other technologies reveal the depth of their concern with any effects on their business models. But "history has shown," as the Ninth Circuit in *Grokster* explained, "that time and market forces often provide equilibrium in balancing interests, whether the new technology be a player piano, a copier, a tape recorder, a video recorder, a personal computer, a karaoke machine, or an MP3 player." This court thus correctly promised "to exercise caution before restructuring liability theories for the purpose of addressing specific market abuses, despite their apparent present magnitude."[102]

In fearing the potential of the new business models, the recording labels offer a classic example of market leaders that fail to appreciate disruptive innovation. Clayton Christensen famously showed that, when faced with a new technology that threatens to upset a profitable business model, the market leader tends not to appreciate the full potential of the new paradigm, instead implementing sustaining innovations.[103] These improvements appear less risky because managers serve customers with known needs and increase their market share.[104] But the very reason they are effective with sustaining innovations explains why they cannot analyze markets that do not exist and cannot appreciate the paradigm shift of disruptive technologies.[105]

Branded P2P File Sharing Software, http://trustyfiles.com/corp-press-sananda.php (last visited June 2, 2008); *Dave Matthews Band Fansite Starts Using BitTorrent To Share Songs*, ZEROPAID, http://www.zeropaid.com/news/8230/Dave%B1Matthews%B1B and%B1fansite %B1starts%B1 (last visited May 21, 2008); *The Official Dave Matthews Band Website*, http://www.davematthewsband.com/legal/index.html (last visited May 21, 2008); Andrews, at 411 (Wilco).

101 Fred von Lohmann, *Betamax Was a Steppingstone*, http://www.eff.org/IP/P2P/ MGM_v_Grokster/?f=betamax_20th.html.

102. *Grokster*, 380 F.3d at 1167.

103. CLAYTON M. CHRISTENSEN, THE INNOVATOR'S DILEMMA: WHEN NEW TECHNOLOGIES CAUSE GREAT FIRMS TO FAIL 42 (1997).

104. *Id.* at 45.

105. *Id.* at 147.

The recording industry's response to Napster's arrival provides evidence of this blindness. The top executives of the music industry held secret talks in 2000 with Napster. Napster's vice president of product development, Don Dodge, explained that the company's goal was to be "the online distribution channel for the record labels, much like iTunes and the 'new' Napster is today." Napster held out the promise of a new revenue stream that could target niche markets, quickly and cheaply introducing new artists to specific markets while saving the record labels manufacturing and promotion expenses. Although the recording industry initially indicated a willingness to enter licenses with Napster and the company made an offer of $1 billion, the two sides never reached an agreement.[106]

As Dodge explained, the labels "wanted us dead because they felt Napster's digital distribution business would kill the CD business." And as Hillary Rosen, the then-CEO of the RIAA explained, "The record companies needed to jump off a cliff, and they couldn't bring themselves to jump." Unwittingly reading from the script of disruptive innovation, Rosen explained that retailers were telling the industry that they could not "sell anything online cheaper than in a store" and that artists were urging them not to "screw up [their] Wal-Mart sales."[107]

So instead of striking a deal with Napster, the sole dominant P2P service, that would have seamlessly transported the recording industry into the digital era, the industry went on the attack, suing Napster for secondary copyright infringement. And while it may have won the battle in shutting down the service, it began to lose the war as former Napster users migrated to other P2P networks and refused to wait two years until the arrival of the first user-friendly legal alternative to file-sharing, Apple's iTunes Music Store.[108]

Although they missed the critical window in the early part of this decade, the recording industry has belatedly come to appreciate its ability to benefit from new business models. In the past few years, the RIAA has welcomed the "spur to innovation" resulting from new music formats.[109] As it has trumpeted:

We have transformed the way we do business and deliver music to consumers. The ways fans can enjoy music—and the ways the industry can recognize a

---

106. Don Dodge, *Napster—The Inside Story and Lessons for Entrepreneurs, Don Dodge on the Next Big Thing*, Oct. 3, 2005, http://dondodge.typepad.com/the_next_big_thing/2005/10/napster_the_ins.html; Brian Hiatt & Evan Serpick, *The Record Industry's Decline*, ROLLING STONE, June 28, 2007, http://www.rollingstone.com/news/story/15137581/the_record_industrys_decline.

107. Hiatt & Serpick, *The Record Industry's Decline*.

108. The subscription services started by the labels, PressPlay and MusicNet, were not successful due to their cost, inability to allow CD burning, and failure to work with existing MP3 players.

109. *RIAA Issues 2004 Year-End Shipment Numbers*, Mar. 21, 2006, http://www.riaa.com/newsitem.php?news_year_filter=&resultpage=23&id=15F0FBEE-62A2-DB32-AADF-708D6145E675.

return on its investment—have never been greater: download and subscription services, mobile phone content, enhanced value CDs, burn-on-demand kiosks, digital radio services.[110]

In short, as the RIAA has slowly come to recognize, innovation can have a positive effect on creativity. We thus do not need to choose sides in the tradeoff between creativity and innovation. Copyright owners' predictions of short-term doom notwithstanding, new technologies promise to create new markets and business models. They do not threaten creativity. And the revolutionary innovation they unleash is essential to consumers' livelihoods and the growth of the U.S. economy.

Given the importance of innovation, it is disturbing that courts have been reducing their solicitude for it. A central reason for this development is what I call the *innovation asymmetry*, by which courts downplay new technologies' future benefits and overemphasize copyright owners' present losses. This danger is exacerbated by an *error-costs asymmetry*, which reveals that a technology's abandonment has a far more drastic effect than its wrongful continuation. And dual-use technology makers suffer even more from a *litigation asymmetry*, as a thicket of complex tests providing multiple routes of challenge could push them into bankruptcy.

INNOVATION ASYMMETRY

Courts in dual-use cases consider a technology's infringing and noninfringing uses. But their comparison will systematically overemphasize the infringing uses and underappreciate the noninfringing uses. Why?

Because infringing uses are immediately apparent, quantifiable, and advanced by motivated, well-financed copyright holders. Noninfringing uses, in contrast, are less tangible and less apparent at the onset of a technology. I call this the *innovation asymmetry*.

The costs of infringing uses can be quantified. A market exists to assign a value to copyrighted works. And the costs are accentuated by the abundant evidence: because infringement has already occurred, plaintiffs need not speculate about future potential infringement. Surveys of downloaded works present tangible evidence of (often massive) copyright infringement to the court on a silver platter.[111]

---

110. *RIAA Issues 2005 Year-End Shipment Numbers*, Mar. 31, 2006, http://www.riaa.com/newsitem.php?news_year_filter=&resultpage=11&id=B30462E2-ACC9-5EDE-1827-B45EBCAC729A.

111. R. Anthony Reese, *The Problems of Judging Young Technologies: A Comment on Sony, Tort Doctrines, and the Puzzle of Peer-to-Peer*, 55 CASE W. RES. L. REV. 877, 890–91 (2005).

Moreover, the costs are vivid in threatening the copyright industries' business models. As the Ninth Circuit explained in *Grokster*, "[t]he introduction of new technology is always disruptive to old markets, and particularly to those copyright owners whose works are sold through well-established distribution mechanisms."[112] Copyright owners' panic upon the introduction of numerous technologies in the past century provides concrete illustrations of this threat.

Finally, all of the tasks needed to demonstrate harms from copyright infringement can easily be undertaken by the recording and motion picture industries, which have no shortage of resources.

In contrast, noninfringing uses are less tangible, less obvious at the onset of a technology, and not advanced by an army of motivated advocates.

First, they are less tangible. Noninfringing uses are difficult to quantify. How do we put a dollar figure on the benefits of enhanced communication and interaction? Estimates of future noninfringing uses will be less convincing than the actual, hard-dollar figures presented by copyright owners.

Second, they are more fully developed over time. When a new technology is introduced, no one, including the inventor, knows all of the beneficial uses to which it will eventually be put.[113] The path of history is replete with inventions for which nobody foresaw the eventual popular and revolutionary use:

- Alexander Graham Bell thought the telephone would be used primarily to broadcast the daily news.
- Thomas Edison thought the phonograph would be used "to record the wishes of old men on their death beds."
- Railroads were originally considered to be feeders to canals.
- Radio technology (which eventually resulted in radar, cell phones, microprocessors, and wireless telecommunications) initially would be used in isolated locations or for ships at sea, where wire communications were not possible.
- Electricity and lasers were not used for decades after their discovery since they did not represent "an obvious substitute for anything that already existed."
- IBM envisioned only 10 to 15 orders for the computer in 1949.
- The VCR (which eventually created the market for the sale and rental of movies) was initially intended only to be used by TV stations, and even after being introduced to households, was employed primarily for time-shifting.
- The iPod (which is used to listen to books, for the distribution of educational lectures, and for time-shifted internet radio broadcasts (podcasting)) initially was used only to listen to music.[114]

---

112. *MGM Studios, Inc. v. Grokster Ltd.*, 380 F.3d 1154, 1167 (9th Cir. 2004).
113. *See* Reese, at 889.
114. *See* Dave Finley, *The Radio Century*, ALBUQUERQUE J., Nov. 26, 1999, *available at* http://www.aoc.nrao.edu/~dfinley/radcent.html (radio); Carol Haber, *Electronic Breakthroughs: Big*

There are many reasons it is difficult to accurately forecast the importance of new technologies, including (1) "[t]he initial primitive understanding of innovations," (2) "competitive relationships among technologies," and (3) "[t]he limited capacity . . . to envision entirely new technological systems, rather than simply improvements to existing systems."[115]

Given the uncertainty surrounding a technology's future benefits, it is not surprising that courts tend to discount them. The *Aimster* court, for example, refused to credit five potential noninfringing uses of the P2P system. It downplayed uses that involved uncopyrighted music, increased a recording's value, allowed groups to exchange information, encrypted uncopyrighted works, and permitted a user to copy an already-purchased CD.[116] The court quickly brushed aside these uses in focusing on the widespread infringing uses.

Additionally, the interplay between short-term infringement and long-term development of noninfringing uses has been all but ignored. Infringing uses of digital music have significantly increased awareness of "the advantages and potential of digital music." In fact, such uses have forced copyright owners to create legitimate digital music markets. Digital music thus bears some similarity to the VCR, which consumers bought to record TV programs but then used for prerecorded videotapes and DVDs.[117] It should not be a surprise that uses change as content providers "probe the best ways to exploit new technologies and markets."[118]

Finally, future noninfringing uses are less likely to be raised by a coordinated and motivated group of advocates. The disappearance of those uses (along with the new technology) also will not be lamented as it would be less likely to disrupt settled expectations.[119]

In the end, even if the future benefits of a new technology ultimately outweigh copyright owners' current losses, uncertainty and intangibility lead to insufficient appreciation. That is the innovation asymmetry.

Picture Eludes Many, ELECTRONIC NEWS, June 13, 1994, at 46, http://findarticles.com/p/articles/mi_moEKF/is_n2018_v40/ai_15516743 (radio, electricity and lasers, computer, and VCR); Mika Pantzar, *Domestication of Everyday Life Technology: Dynamic Views on the Social Histories of Artifacts*, 13 DESIGN ISSUES 52, 52 (1997) (telephone); Nathan Rosenberg, *Factors Affecting the Diffusion of Technology*, 10 EXPLORATIONS IN ECON. HIST. 3, 13–14 (1972) (radio, phonograph, railroads); Brief Amici Curiae Of Innovation Scholars And Economists In Support Of Affirmance at 17, *MGM v. Grokster*, 125 S. Ct. 2764 (2003) [hereinafter Innovation Scholars Brief] (iPod).

115. Haber, *Electronic Breakthroughs*.

116. *In re Aimster Copyright Litigation*, 334 F.3d 643, 652–53 (7th Cir. 2003); Reese, at 887–88.

117. Reese, at 891, 893.

118. Brief of Amici Curiae, The Consumer Electronics Ass'n et al., at 24, *MGM v. Grokster*, 125 S. Ct. 2764 (2003).

119. Lemley & Reese, at 1389.

ERROR-COSTS ASYMMETRY

The innovation asymmetry explains why a court would discount a technology's future benefits. The error-costs asymmetry exacerbates this effect. Error costs signify the costs of erroneous judicial decisions. Error costs have played an important role in antitrust law. Courts have pointed to *false positives*, or the costs of wrongly punishing benign activity, to justify a more deferential antitrust regime.

In the P2P context, one type of error, a false positive or Type I error, occurs when a court erroneously shuts down the technology. The other type, a *false negative* or Type II error, occurs when a court mistakenly upholds the technology even though it should have imposed liability. Are the two errors equivalent?

They are not. For in the second (Type II error) case, society can witness the effects of the technology. And Congress can always step in to compensate copyright holders. But in the first (Type I error) case, consumers will never know what they are missing.[120] We can only see the tip of the innovation iceberg, and a technology's abandonment will forever deny consumers its possibilities. The error-costs asymmetry is another reason for erring on the side of not quashing the technology.

LITIGATION ASYMMETRY

The innovation and error-costs asymmetries apply directly to the technology. But a *litigation asymmetry* arises from the effect of the test on technology manufacturers.

Protracted litigation is expensive and favors those with deep pockets. Copyright owners tend to be large media corporations such as the recording and movie studios. Vertical integration and consolidation have only increased these companies' resource advantages. And the industries often join forces in litigation. Thirty entertainment companies brought suit against Grokster, while 28 sued ReplayTV, a digital VCR that allowed users to automatically skip commercials.[121]

In contrast, upstart dual-use manufacturers often lack the financial resources to wage lengthy legal battles. One dual-use maker that needed to raise $60 million in convertible debt to stay afloat found itself face-to-face in litigation over its digital video recorder with a united $100 billion entertainment industry.[122]

---

120. Raymond Shih Ray Ku, *Grokking Grokster*, 2005 WIS. L. REV. 1217, 1282; Lemley & Reese, at 1389.

121. Innovation Scholars Brief, at 19.

122. Claire Tristram, *Hollywood's War on Innovation*, SALON.COM, Sept. 9, 2002, http://dir.salon.com/story/tech/feature/2002/09/09/sonicblue/index.html.

Another technology executive explained the catch-22 the company faced: "We couldn't raise funding because of the legal issues. . . but we couldn't also fight the lawsuit without raising funding."[123] And given that some of the most revolutionary innovation comes from small inventors—such as the "upstarts who developed the first MP3 players" in the 1990s, which paved the way for the iPod—such consequences are severe.[124] A legal standard that does not resolve the issue of secondary liability at an early stage of the proceedings will lead to "debilitating uncertainty" and exert a chilling effect on innovation.[125]

The danger of the litigation asymmetry is that the copyright industry does not even need to win on the merits. All it needs to do is throw up roadblocks in the form of expensive, complicated litigation.

The carcasses strewn on the side of the technology highway speak volumes:

- Napster filed for bankruptcy after the unfavorable Ninth Circuit decision.[126]
- Aimster's CEO and his two operating companies filed for bankruptcy after the unfavorable Seventh Circuit decision.[127]
- 321 Studios, whose software allowed users to make backup DVD copies, shut down after being subject to seven lawsuits and injunctions that prevented it from selling its products.[128]
- RecordTV.com, which allowed users to record television shows and replay them on their computers, sold its assets after settling a lawsuit brought by the movie industry.[129]
- Scour.com, which allowed Internet users to share music and video files, laid off most of its workforce and filed for bankruptcy shortly after being sued by the music and movie industries.[130]

---

123. Gwendolyn Mariano, *RecordTV.com To Sell Assets*, CNETNews.com, May 23, 2001, http://news.com.com/RecordTV.com±to±sell±assets/2100-1023_3-258187.html.

124. Heather Green, *Are The Copyright Wars Chilling Innovation?*, Bus. Wk. Online, Oct. 11, 2004, http://www.businessweek.com/magazine/content/04_41/b3903473.htm.

125. Innovation Scholars Brief, at 15.

126. Benny Evangelista, *Napster Files for Bankruptcy*, San Fran. Chron., June 4, 2002, at B1.

127. Brian Garrity, *Victory Eludes Legal Fight Over File Swapping: The Music Industry May Win a Few Battles While Losing Multiple Logistical Wars*, Billboard, Apr. 13, 2002, at 86.

128. Katie Dean, *321 Studios Shuts Its Doors*, Wired.com, Aug. 3, 2004, http://www.wired.com/news/digiwood/0,1412,64453,00.html.

129. Gwendolyn Mariano, *RecordTV.com To Sell Assets*.

130. Dick Kelsey, *Listen.com Buys Assets of Bankrupt Scour*, Newsbytes News Network, Nov. 1, 2000, http://findarticles.com/p/articles/mi_moNEW/is_2000_Nov_1/ai_66532929.

- SonicBlue, which created ReplayTV, a digital video recorder with automatic commercial skipping and Internet video sharing features, spent $3 million per quarter on legal fees before being forced into bankruptcy.[131]

Venture capital firms, which provide the funding necessary for technology start-ups to grow, naturally have been less likely to invest as a result of these events. By 2002, "[m]ost investment in peer-to-peer technology . . . dried up . . . partly as a result of the threat of litigation."[132] Investors also have been justifiably fearful about vicarious liability, which has put at risk the personal wealth of a start-up's investors. Lawsuits against Napster's investors proved that this was not a theoretical concern.[133]

In short, the innovation, error-costs, and litigation asymmetries exert a strong, though often hidden, pull in the evaluation of infringing and noninfringing uses. Given the unique importance of innovative new technologies for our economy and livelihoods, any appropriate analysis must take into account such characteristics. It is in this vein that I turn to the specific tests that courts have applied to dual-use technologies.

EVALUATION OF JUDICIAL TESTS

Sony

The Supreme Court in *Sony* asked if a dual-use technology was "capable of substantial non-infringing uses." Of all the tests offered, this is the most deferential to innovation. As long as there is at least a *potential* substantial noninfringing use, the technology escapes liability. The Court thus offered a solution that squarely addressed the innovation asymmetry.[134]

Of course, the Court also found that most VCRs were being used for lawful purposes. A narrower version of *Sony*, akin to a test determining primary use, would, as discussed below in the context of the *Aimster* test, run into problems.

---

131. Benny Evangelista, *SonicBlue Goes into Chapter 11*, S.F. CHRON., Mar. 22, 2003, at B1.

132. Garrity, *Victory Eludes Legal Fight*, at 86.

133. *In re Napster, Inc. Copyright Litig.*, 2005 WL 273178, at *1 (N.D. Cal. Feb. 03, 2005) (venture capital firm Hummer Winblad Venture Partners); *UMG Recordings, Inc. v. Bertelsmann AG*, 222 F.R.D. 408, 413–14 (N.D. Cal. 2004) (investor Bertelsmann); *see generally* Brief of the National Venture Capital Association as Amicus Curiae in Support of Respondents at 17 n.14, *MGM v. Grokster*, 125 S. Ct. 2764 (2003) [hereinafter NVCA Brief].

134. Another potential reading, consistent with the two concurring opinions in *Grokster*, asks if the device is *actually* used for noninfringing purposes. Reese, *Temporal Dynamics*, at 215–19.

But the more widespread reading of *Sony* offers a relatively bright-line rule. At a minimum, the rule is easier to apply than other articulated tests that explore primary uses, subjective intent, or sufficient filtering measures. The test also focuses attention on the technology itself as opposed to engaging in endless hunts for subjective intent.[135]

An important advantage of this clarity is that it allows courts to dismiss disputes at a preliminary stage of litigation, allowing technology makers to avoid getting embroiled in the deepest recesses of complex, lengthy litigation. Receiving a quick summary judgment addresses the litigation asymmetry, increasing the likelihood that innovators can manage risk. Fact-intensive investigations into intent or primary use, in contrast, could spell bankruptcy for small defendants.

Another advantage of *Sony* is that it allows inventors to innovate without needing to receive permission from copyright holders. More aggressive tests, by threatening costly litigation, tempt the innovator to alter its technology to satisfy copyright owners. But as Professors Mark Lemley and Tony Reese remind us, "[t]he history of technologies over which copyright owners obtain early control is not promising—ask (if you can find them) owners of digital audio tape decks, dual-deck VCRs, laserdiscs and D[IVX] machines."[136]

Just one example of the effects of obtaining permission is provided by the "broadcast flag," a proposed Federal Communications Commission (FCC) rule that would have required digital TV tuners to recognize a signal embedded in broadcasts that would allow copyright owners to limit consumers' use of the shows. The D.C. Circuit struck down the rule as beyond the FCC's authority.[137] But before doing so, the agency allowed the MPAA to examine the technologies under development. It should not be a surprise that the movie industry "coerced companies including RealNetworks, Thomson, and Microsoft to cut innovative features out of their latest media software programs" that would have "allowed users to make legal copies of TV programs and transmit them over the [Internet] to a limited number of personal devices in, say, a car or a vacation home."[138]

Final support for *Sony* is provided by the robust flourishing of new technologies that has accompanied the regime. In the two decades after the decision, an explosion of dual-use devices rolled off the world's manufacturing lines: VCRs, computer hard drives, Walkmans, digital cameras, CD/DVD burners, iPods, and DVRs, to name just a few. Consumers have received wave after wave of ever

---

135. The test also seemed to constrict liability beyond the requirements of traditional contributory infringement as Sony had knowledge that the Betamax was being used for infringing purposes. *See* Jonathan Band, *So What Does Inducement Mean?*, at 2 (Nov. 2005), http://www.policybandwidth.com/doc/inducement.pdf.

136. Lemley & Reese, at 1387 n.161.

137. Declan McCullagh, *Court Yanks Down FCC's Broadcast Flag*, May 6, 2005, http://news.com.com/2100-1030_3-5697719.html.

138. Green, *Are The Copyright Wars Chilling Innovation?*

cheaper, ever more feature-rich devices that can copy and store ever-larger collections of files. This revolution has created millions of jobs and contributed billions of dollars to the nation's economy.[139]

While counterfactual hypotheticals should be greeted with a dose of salt, it appears that if the Court had decided *Sony* the other way, the pace and scope of innovation would have been reduced. In such a world, the electronics industry, instead of simply giving the public what they wanted, would have had to thread a needle between the desires of consumers and those of the copyright industry. This would be a monumental task; consumers' desire for all types of content in all settings at all times would not have been easily reconciled with the copyright industry's impulse to restrict consumer options to the few consistent with their existing business models. New products might have had to wait years until the movie or music industry could reach consensus on a particular encoding format or encryption scheme. In short, the consumer electronics industry's incentive to innovate would have been curtailed.

But even if *Sony* has stood guard to a deluge of innovation, is the test still appropriate given the widespread copyright infringement facilitated by P2P networks?

Napster/Grokster

Certainly the courts considering the P2P cases have emphasized the differences between the technologies. The various P2P architectures nonetheless demonstrate the difficulties of applying knowledge-based tests in this context.

Under a typical application of secondary liability analysis, Napster would be guilty and Grokster would go free. Why? Because, by having access to the central index, Napster would be guilty of contributory infringement on account of its knowledge of and material contribution to infringing activity. And it would be vicariously liable (assuming a financial benefit) because of its control over users.

But because of the decentralized nature of the software used by Grokster, that company would lack knowledge and control, and thus not be secondarily liable under either theory. What sort of incentives does such a regime provide? Incentives to design the architecture to reduce knowledge.

In addition, the application of the concepts rests on an appropriate determination of "knowledge" or "control." But the binary nature of such conclusions—one either has knowledge or control or one does not—fails to account for the nuanced characteristics of the activity.[140]

Fleshing this out a bit more, what exactly must defendants know about? That their software could be used for infringing activity? That such activity is likely?

---

139. NVCA Brief, at 29.

140. Alfred C. Yen, *Sony, Tort Doctrines, and the Puzzle of Peer-to-Peer*, 55 CASE W. RES. L. REV. 815, 851 (2005).

That specific users will commit specific acts of infringement? The first two inquiries would ensnare most technologies—including the VCR—in their grasp. The last would not.

These questions reveal a major difficulty with applying the contributory infringement and vicarious liability theories in the P2P context. A store owner who gave customers blank and prerecorded tapes, or a dance hall owner who watched a musical group perform, had a closer relationship to the infringer, evidencing greater knowledge and control. In contrast, the creator of decentralized P2P software relinquishes all control over that technology at the point of sale and thus lacks knowledge of how the technology is used or how to prevent infringing uses.

Nor is the answer to the dual-use technology issue to be found in Grokster's *active inducement* test. For starters, while the contributory infringement and vicarious liability analyses can be situated in the context of *Sony*, active inducement cannot. It thus adds another layer of potential liability for dual-use manufacturers. Having a technology capable of substantial noninfringing uses no longer is enough to escape liability. The innovator now must worry about how a court interprets its intent. Early disposal of a case thus becomes less likely.

In addition, the Court found active inducement based on evidence such as a name and software similar to Napster, an advertising-based model, and a failure to design filtering tools.[141] These bases for punishment are questionable. In particular, liability for using an advertising model could threaten a vast array of Internet-based and other businesses. And a filtering requirement significantly complicates the analysis and opens the door to unending claims about insufficient remedial measures.

A final irony to this development is that Sony itself would not have escaped liability under the *Grokster* rule. The company did not try to implement a technology that would have reduced the copying of infringing materials, even though such a mechanism was feasible.[142] And with its advertisements exhorting customers to "build a library" and record "favorite shows," the company likely would have lost even under a narrow version of active inducement limited to clear expressions and affirmative steps.[143]

Aimster

Perhaps Judge Richard Posner, the esteemed and prolific jurist and author sitting on the Seventh Circuit and penning the *Aimster* opinion, would offer the solution. In fact, the *Aimster* court introduced new analyses that endeavored to

---

141. *MGM v. Grokster*, 545 U.S. 913, 939–40 (2005).

142. In 1985, the movie studios began encoding their prerecorded VHS tapes with Macrovision, a technology that prevents duplication to another videocassette. *Macrovision*, WIKIPEDIA, http://en.wikipedia.org/wiki/Macrovision.

143. *Sony*, 464 U.S. at 459 (Blackmun, J., dissenting).

steer a middle ground between creativity and innovation. The court's focus on a technology's primary use and a defendant's remedial measures promised to forge a happy medium. Or did it?

First, the court endeavored to determine the primary use of the technology.[144] But even though it sounds simple in theory, such a determination would prove exceedingly difficult in application.

For reasons mentioned above, the infringing uses would be presented to the court on a silver platter as concrete, already-suffered harms. The noninfringing uses, in contrast, would be less tangible and more likely to arise in the future. In addition, a primary-use test would require courts to trace exactly how many copyright owners permit or oppose use of their works. Finally, any attempts to recognize the evolving nature of uses would face significant predictability hurdles. If inventors do not know how their product will eventually be used, how could they possibly forecast the use that will be predominant?

The *Aimster* court's second novelty required dual-use manufacturers to show that "it would have been disproportionately costly . . . to eliminate or at least reduce substantially the infringing uses."[145] Again sounding reasonable in theory, a practical application reveals considerable dangers.

No technology can block all infringement. It is always possible to do more.[146] Because of this, copyright owners could always claim that technology makers could have done more to reduce infringing uses. Plaintiffs could continually suggest more restrictive fingerprinting, watermarking, encryption, or other technologies.

Of practical significance, such a determination introduces complexity and eliminates early disposition of the case. Litigation over which fingerprinting system to adopt presents a nuanced factual question and forces judges to grapple with intractable issues about the sufficiency of various solutions. In the *Grokster* case, computer scientists explained that Grokster and Streamcast could not force users to install and update filtering software and that filters were so easy to defeat that they would set off an "open-ended arms race between the filter designers and noncompliant users."[147] In *Napster*, even though the company examined dozens of audio fingerprinting systems and installed one that "was able to

---

144. Because the court required an actual noninfringing use and did not find any, there was very little for the court to "balance." *In re Aimster Copyright Litig.*, 334 F.3d 643, 653 (7th Cir. 2003).

145. *Id.*

146. Perfect enforcement of the copyright laws has never been the goal. Lemley & Reese, at 1432.

147. Brief Amici Curiae of Computer Science Professors Harold Abelson et al., at 14–16, *MGM Studios, Inc. v. Grokster, Ltd.*, No. 04-480 (Feb. 28, 2005).

prevent sharing of much of plaintiffs' noticed copyrighted works," the court demanded "zero tolerance" and shut down Napster.[148]

As a more general concern, feasibility questions could "enmesh courts in disputes comparable to those that have bedeviled design defect litigation in products liability."[149] In cases involving manufacturing flaws, courts can compare a product to the manufacturer's standards. In contrast, there is no objective standard of comparison for design defects since the product is used in its intended condition. The courts thus must "weigh various engineering, marketing, and financial factors" in providing their own standard of defectiveness.[150] Similarly with P2P remedial measures, courts lack a benchmark and could be tempted to find that defendants failed to do enough. Given the cost of such measures and lack of guarantee that they would stop infringement, innovation is threatened.

Adopting a test focusing on whether a technology maker employed sufficient remedial measures would threaten innovation, as the manufacturer would need to consider (1) each of the ways a technology could be used for infringement, (2) how much a court would expect it to spend on modifications, and (3) whether it would need to make these improvements if they would only be partially effective or would depend on users' actions.[151] The manufacturer would also need to continually monitor the technology and how it was used.

Think back, as Professor Tony Reese has, to the onset of the World Wide Web in the mid-1990s. And imagine if the creators of browsers and servers were required, before posting content on a publicly available website, to quarantine that content "for 48 or 72 hours at a special Web site accessible only to copyright owners, who could screen the content before it went online . . . and object to content that they alleged to be infringing." Such a requirement might have been viewed as a reasonable precaution to limit infringement. But it would have led to a far less useful and innovative technology than the Internet we have known and cherished.[152]

Similarly, imagine if courts had required photocopiers to be modified to prevent the copying, absent a copyright owner's approval, of "any document displaying a ©." And imagine if, absent authorization on a webpage, Microsoft were forced to "deactivate the 'print' function from its Internet Explorer browser."[153]

---

148. *Sony v. Universal Symposium (Panel 2): The Revolution Arrives*, 34 Sw. U. L. Rev. 179, 193 (2004); *A&M Records, Inc. v. Napster, Inc.*, 284 F.3d 1091, 1096–97 (9th Cir. 2002).

149. Diane Leenheer Zimmerman, *Daddy, Are We There Yet? Lost in Grokster-Land*, 9 N.Y.U. J. Legis. & Pub. Pol'y 75, 92 (2005–06).

150. Michael J. Toke, *Note, Restatement (Third) of Torts and Design Defectiveness in American Products Liability Law*, 5 Cornell J.L. & Pub. Pol'y 239, 241 (1996).

151. Innovation Scholars Brief, at 15–16.

152. Reese, at 894.

153. Innovation Scholars Brief, at 16.

In the end, giving copyright owners the ability to design dual-use devices might allow them to exploit their business models but would threaten innovation.

* * *

P2P BENEFITS

After *Grokster*, widespread commercial development of P2P technology independent of the copyright industry has been restricted to a few, supporting roles. Even though it is secure, cheap, and offers unique distribution possibilities, it has had a much more modest effect than is warranted by its promise, appearing mostly in academia, government, and the open-source community. Some examples include:

- Penn State University's LionShare, which has been used to share large digital video files and to allow professors from different universities to collaborate on presentations
- Bibster, which allows researchers to share bibliographic data
- The Internet Archive—a public, nonprofit Internet library that offers permanent digital access to historical collections and that uses five P2P systems, allowing it to distribute files "without going broke on bandwidth fees"
- Soulseek, a site designed to promote underground music by helping unsigned and independent artists
- Skype, a free internet-telephony service that uses P2P architecture to route voice calls between computers
- Joost, an online TV service that includes features such as search, chat, and instant messaging
- Groove Networks, which provides shared workspaces for online collaboration, such as multiple users editing a document at the same time[154]

Distribution

One of P2P's most significant benefits is its ability to distribute large files. BitTorrent, for example, has solved the file-sharing problem of quick downloading but slow uploading.[155] It does so by requiring downloaders to upload pieces

---

154. Jamie Oberdick, *Best Uses for LionShare, Penn State's Peer-to-Peer Academic Collaboration Tool*, http://css.psu.edu/news/nlfao6/lionshare.html (LionShare); http://bibster.semanticweb.org/objectives.htm (Bibster); http://www.archive.org/about/about.php (Internet Archive); *In Praise of P2P*, THE ECONOMIST, Dec. 4, 2004 (Internet Archive, Skype, Groove); http://slsknet.org/ (Soulseek); http://www.joost.com/ (Joost).

155. Clive Thompson, *The BitTorrent Effect*, Jan. 2006, WIRED.COM, http://www.wired.com/wired/archive/13.01/bittorrent.html.

of the file to others, thereby allowing uploading to occur as quickly as downloading. And it spreads the cost and bandwidth of uploading files among all users rather than just the host server.[156]

An obvious illustration of such large files involves home movies. One example is provided by the amateur videos that showed the devastation of the 2004 Indian Ocean tsunami and were shared across the globe. The worldwide demand for videos of the event "brought down even the largest traditional hosting providers."[157] But by pooling the bandwidth of many sites, BitTorrent avoided these problems. One site, for example, was able to serve more than 150 gigabytes of bandwidth at a cost of only 1.26 gigabytes.[158]

Another example is provided by *Outfoxed*, a documentary critical of Fox News. One user put part of it on his Web site as a 500-megabyte torrent (a small file containing data about the files to be shared). Almost 1,500 people had downloaded the torrent within two months, resulting in almost 750 gigabytes of traffic. But the site only needed to transmit 5 gigabytes, leading to a bandwidth bill of merely $4.[159]

Other examples include

- Blizzard Entertainment, which uses the network to distribute its online multiplayer game *World of Warcraft*
- NASA, which uses it to distribute high-resolution photos of the Earth
- eTree, which allows fans to distribute authorized live recorded performances of bands
- Software updates that can be downloaded and distributed 20 times faster than a client-server model allows
- Video content that can be distributed by speakers—such as community colleges, religious leaders, and school boards—that could not otherwise afford to do so[160]

---

156. Bram Cohen, *Incentives Build Robustness in BitTorrent*, May 22, 2003, http://www.bittorrent.org/bittorrentecon.pdf. Web hosting companies typically impose bandwidth limits that prescribe how much data can be transferred to or from the Web site or server in a specified time period. *Bandwidth*, WIKIPEDIA, http://en.wikipedia.org/wiki/Bandwidth.

157. Torrentocracy Blog, Feb. 18, 2005, http://www.torrentocracy.com/blog/archives/2005/02/getting_to_99_b.shtml.

158. *Id.*; Creative Commons Brief, at 11.

159. Clive Thompson, *The BitTorrent Effect*.

160. http://www.blizzard.co.uk/wow/faq/bittorrent.shtml (World of Warcraft); http://visibleearth.nasa.gov (NASA); Joe Stewart, *BitTorrent and the Legitimate Use of P2P*, Feb. 24, 2004, http://www.joestewart.org/p2p.html#foot27 (eTree); Iljitsch van Beijnum, *Dropping 22TB of Patches on 6,500 PCs in 4 Hours: BitTorrent*, Mar. 9, 2008, http://arstechnica.com/news.ars/post/20080309-dropping-22tb-of-patches-on-6500-pcs-in-4-hours-bittorrentdropping-22tb-of-patches-on-6500-pcs-in-4-hours-bittorrent.html (software updates); Creative Commons Brief, at 12 (speakers).

The Long Tail

Peer-to-peer offers a distribution benefit not only in disseminating large files but also in increasing exposure to little-known works. Chris Anderson, editor-in-chief of Wired magazine, introduced the concept of the Long Tail, which emphasizes the decline of the "small number of 'hits' . . . at the head of the demand curve" and rise of the "huge number of niches in the tail." Even though consumers covet such variety, it was not available until advances in technology lowered production and distribution costs. Bricks-and-mortar retailers with limited shelf space could only stock anticipated hits. Online retailers and P2P networks are not so constrained.[161]

Peer-to-peer fosters the Long Tail by allowing artists to easily and cheaply distribute their works. Such low-cost marketing not only helps the artists increase their visibility but also provides consumers with more options.[162] Peer-to-peer offers "B sides," live recordings, and foreign music never before available. An architecture that allows millions of users to collect works promises to unearth far more than a centralized, top-down approach.

Relatedly, P2P allows users to select the quality of the distribution they receive. For example, iTunes has, to date, only offered a single quality version of its MP3s. Peer-to-peer, in contrast, lets users shop for different, higher (or lower) quality versions of works they desire.

Promotion

The promotion of copyrighted works reveals P2P's third benefit. Until recently, scarce bandwidth, capital, shelf space, and movie screens have constrained copyright owners. As a result, the owners have relied on tastemakers such as Hollywood studio executives, store purchasing managers, and artist and repertoire (A&R) talent scouts for record labels.[163]

In the 20th century, these selection agents played the primary role in attempting to predict which works would be successful. This was difficult, however, as new artists and products could fail to resonate with the public. In a formula that has been widely cited, 80 percent of products in various industries have lost money, with the remaining 20 percent generating all the profits.[164] Such a model explains tastemakers' fixation on marketing "hits" that pay for all the "misses."

In the 21st century, times are changing. Reduced production and distribution costs often allow all content to be produced and delivered, displacing the need

---

161. *About Me*, http://www.longtail.com/about.html (last visited August 9, 2008); Chris Anderson, The Long Tail: Why the Future of Business is Selling Less of More 253 (2008).

162. Anderson, at 74.

163. *Id.* at 122.

164. *E.g.*, Papadopoulos, *Are Music Recording Contracts Equitable?* (recording industry). For elaboration of the 80/20 concept, see Anderson, at 130–35.

for tastemakers.[165] The challenge then becomes sifting through vast quantities of information. Aggregators such as Rhapsody (music), Netflix (movies), and eBay (goods) collect products and make them easy to find.[166] But consumers still need guidance in wading through the morass.

One such tool, collaborative filtering, uses similarities between customers to make recommendations.[167] Google ranks the relevance of Web sites by determining the number of other sites linked to it. In doing so, it "filter[s] out the vast panoply of irrelevant material" by collecting users' relevance assessments. Other examples incorporate what "customers like you" have purchased among Amazon's books and Netflix's movies.[168] The broader concept of collective intelligence pools the input of crowds, as seen through eBay's rating system, YouTube's most-watched list, and news sites' "top 10 most emailed" articles.

These filters are superior to tastemakers because they do not need to predict in advance which products will be successful. Instead, they cull through products that have already reached the market. And they provide more customized information and transcend the "generalities, inconsistencies, and information deficits" that have plagued tastemakers.[169]

Peer-to-peer can play an effective role in this context. The sheer number of users with diverse, eclectic interests ensures that a vast array of works will be rated. The unfiltered nature of the recommendations provides another benefit. The threat with more centralized collaborative filters is that the server could influence the feedback. Amazon.com, for example, could recommend products in which it owns a stake. Peer-to-peer is far less subject to such constraints, with millions of users offering reactions absent influence by the intermediary.

Peer-to-peer networks offer additional benefits. Their architecture is able to accommodate an influx of users. And, with thousands of peers (as opposed to one company) assisting, it is easier for users to find what they are looking for.[170]

TIP OF INNOVATION ICEBERG

Finally, if history is any guide, we can barely see the tip of the P2P innovation iceberg. The technology offers benefits that we cannot even contemplate.

165. Dan Hunter & F. Gregory Lastowka, *Amateur-to-Amateur*, 46 Wm. & Mary L. Rev. 951, 993 (2004).

166. Anderson, at 88.

167. *What's the Difference Between "Collective Intelligence" and Collaborative Filtering?*, O'Reilly Media, http://getsatisfaction.com/oreilly/topics/whats_the_difference_between_collective_intelligence_and_collaborative_filtering (last visited August 10, 2008).

168. Hunter & Lastowka, at 994–95.

169. Anderson, at 122; Hunter & Lastowka, at 995.

170. As discussed earlier in the chapter, the centralized indices of hybrid P2P would be more effective at facilitating users' searches than pure P2P models.

As discussed earlier, no one foresaw the widespread uses of inventions such as telephones, phonographs, and lasers. In addition, P2P concepts are being applied elsewhere. For example, YouTube, MySpace, Pandora, last.fm, Apple's iTunes, and Yahoo! Music Jukebox have borrowed P2P concepts in allowing users to share playlists with others.

Peering into the future, P2P could offer the technology to challenge Google's search engine predominance.[171] Companies must invest billions of dollars in server farms (clusters of servers) to offer competitive search engines. But by harnessing the capacity of users, P2P technologies do not confront these costs. Faroo's search engine relies on an algorithm that indexes users' Web page visits. The simple act of visiting Web pages (with no need even to link to them) provides all the information necessary for page ranking.[172]

Peer-to-peer also could offer protection against cloud computing. Cloud computing refers to Web-based applications and data storage in the "cloud" of the Internet.[173] Examples include Google applications, remote storage, and "software as a service."[174] Cloud computing allows users to move their software applications and data from their desktop computers to remote servers accessible through any Internet connection.[175]

Despite its promise, cloud computing poses threats. Centralized outages threaten access to data. In the summer of 2008, Amazon's online storage service was not available for a 6-hour period and users could not access Google's Gmail service for 2 hours.[176] As another example, it is notoriously difficult for users to

---

171. See Bernard Lunn, *Could P2P Networks Enable a Google Killer?*, READWRITEWEB, Jan. 9, 2008, http://www.readwriteweb.com/archives/p2p_networks_search.php.

172. Faroo, *P2P Web Search*, http://www.faroo.com/english/technology/architecture. html (last visited August 31, 2008).

173. Erica Naone, *Computer in the Cloud: Online Desktop Systems Could Bridge the Digital Divide*, MIT TECH. REV., Sept. 18, 2007, http://www.technologyreview.com/Infotech/ 19397/.

174. One example of software as a service is Salesforce.com, which offers customer relationship management. *See generally* Galen Gruman & Eric Knorr, *What Cloud Computing Really Means*, INFOWORLD, April 7, 2008, http://www.infoworld.com/article/ 08/04/07/15FE-cloud-computing-reality_1.html.

175. See M. Scott Boone, *The Past, Present, and Future of Computing and its Impact on Digital Rights Management*, 2008 MICH. ST. L. REV. 413, 431.

176. Richard MacManus, *More Amazon S3 Downtime: How Much is too Much?*, READWRITEWEB, July 20, 2008, http://www.readwriteweb.com/archives/more_amazon_ s3_downtime.php (Amazon); Juan Carlos Perez, *Gmail Users Hit by Outage Again*, NETWORK WORLD, Aug. 12, 2008, http://www.networkworld.com/news/2008/081208- gmail-users-hit-by-outage.html (Google). *See generally* Bernard Lunn, *Cloud Failures Are Serious—Time To Revisit P2P?*, READWRITEWEB, Aug. 14, 2008, http://www.readwriteweb. com/archives/google_failures_serious_time_t.php.

---

remove data from the social networking Web site Facebook.[177] Finally, the continual updating of cloud-based services prevents users from retaining older versions of an application and the security features built into them.[178]

Peer-to-peer addresses many of these concerns by keeping users' data on their desktop computers. At the same time, the technology offers benefits flowing from the power of a network of peers. To illustrate, P2P can offer storage that harnesses peers' capacity and allows users to store backup copies of their data, reducing the likelihood of catastrophic data loss.[179] For future users seeking an alternative to centralized cloud computing, P2P's decentralized architecture offers an effective antidote.

In short, like any new technology, we can only discern the tip of the P2P innovation iceberg. Although the technology's uses for copyright infringement have received significant attention, we cannot fathom all the benefits P2P could eventually offer. Presenting alternatives to the Google search engine and the coming cloud computing system are just two of many potential benefits.

RECOMMENDATION

The innovations promised by dual-use technologies are revolutionary. They promise to transform the way we consume entertainment and interact with each other, and possibly even restructure our society. But such technologies are continually under assault in courts' P2P analyses. They are evaluated in their infancy when their capabilities can barely be discerned. And they do not stand a chance against the widespread, concrete instances of infringement offered by the copyright holders. Given the silent consequences of a vanquished technology and the carcasses of innovators strewn on the side of the technology highway, courts must alter their analysis to better appreciate innovation.

Sony offered just this deference. It understood the various asymmetries that challenge innovation. It left the door open for Congress to narrowly address particular technologies. It has accompanied an explosion of dual-use devices.

---

177. Maria Aspan, *How Sticky is Membership on Facebook? Just Try Breaking Free*, N.Y. TIMES, Feb. 11, 2008.

178. Ephraim Schwartz, *The Dangers of Cloud Computing*, INFOWORLD, July 7, 2008, http://www.infoworld.com/article/08/07/07/28NF-cloud-computing-security_1.html.

179. Amir Javidan et al., *VanDisk: An Exploration in Peer-To-Peer Collaborative Back-Up Storage*, 22 ELECTRICAL & COMPUTER ENGINEERING 219 (2007), http://ieeexplore.ieee.org/Xplore/login.jsp?url=/iel5/4232658/4232659/04232719.pdf?tp=&isnumber=&arnumber=4232719 (describing proposal to alleviate "data backup problems" through "a virtual array of network disks that . . . replicates a user's data over multiple remote machines to increase data availability and durability").

And it even assisted antitrust law in favoring disruptive technologies that could reduce the market power of entrenched companies.

Even if music copyright owners' existing business models are significantly threatened by P2P technologies, creativity is not. Most artists do not receive any royalties from the recording industry. In any event, copyright owners can always sue direct infringers or urge Congress to act.

Sony also is consistent with an error-costs analysis. Courts' mistaken approval of technologies allowing copyright infringement may harm existing business models but often will not affect creativity. Erroneous condemnation, in contrast, directly harms innovation by permanently stifling technologies.

In the end, the case for innovation is at least as strong today as it was at the time of *Sony*. In particular, disruptive innovation plays a starring role in the story of P2P. It explains the recording industry's failure to recognize the potential offered by Napster in 2000. And it is threatened by the complicated tests that courts have promulgated in the area of secondary liability. Although we may never realize what we are missing, the future of innovation—and thus our economy and livelihoods—depends on a return to *Sony*.

7. DAMAGING COPYRIGHT DAMAGES

Statutory Damages: Law 148
Statutory Damages: Legislative History 149
MP3.com 153
XM Radio 155
Personal Investor Liability 156
Statutory Damages/Secondary Liability Disconnect 158
Proposal 160

Threats to innovation come not only from copyright's substantive law but also from its remedies for infringement. Of particular concern is the law of damages. Among other remedies, the copyright laws allow owners to recover *statutory damages* regardless of the amount of harm they suffer. These damages can reach $150,000 for infringement of each individual work.

Such relief does not appear in any other IP regime. Nor has its recent use promoted Congress's intent. As discussed in the last chapter, dual-use devices such as peer-to-peer (P2P) software, digital video recorders, and portable satellite radio receivers can be used not only for lawful purposes but also to commit copyright infringement. Subjecting the manufacturers of such devices to statutory damages does not advance the legislature's purposes of (1) awarding damages that cannot be proven and (2) offering modest, but not excessive, deterrence.

Instead, copyright owners have wielded the remedy as a sword of Damocles, decapitating dual-use technologies not because of the merits of their infringement cases but because of the sheer size of the potential award. The statutory damages regime allows copyright owners to seek $150,000 for each act of willful infringement. With widespread use and a loose definition of willfulness, such damages quickly reach into the *billions* of dollars. Just one recent example involves Viacom, which sued YouTube and Google for copyright infringement based on 160,000 unauthorized clips available on YouTube.[1] Multiplied by a potential $150,000 per clip, YouTube could be liable for *$24 billion,* nearly 15 times the $1.65 billion Google spent to buy the entire company.

This threat is exacerbated by two related issues. First, the size of the award often will prevent technology companies from posting the bond necessary for appellate review. As a result, the firms will not be able to appeal adverse rulings and may be forced into bankruptcy. Second, contrary to the general rule of

---

1. *Viacom Files Federal Copyright Infringement Complaint Against YouTube and Google,* Mar. 13, 2007, VIACOM, http://www.viacom.com/news/News_Docs/Viacom%20Press%20 Release.pdf. The district court granted Google's summary judgment motion, which Viacom promised to appeal to the Second Circuit.

corporate law, courts in statutory damages cases have held investors personally liable for a company's debts, which has chilled the flow of venture capital.[2]

Despite these roadblocks to innovation, the momentum, believe it or not, is in favor of *increasing* damages. In May 2008, the U.S. House of Representatives passed the Prioritizing Resources and Organization for Intellectual Property (PRO IP) Act of 2008, which was designed to increase IP enforcement.[3] One provision in an earlier version of the legislation would have increased damages, allowing copyright owners to obtain "multiple awards of statutory damages" for the infringement of compilations.[4] In other words, owners could have sought statutory damages for each song on a CD or each article and photograph in a magazine. This provision was ultimately removed from the bill due to opposition and copyright owners' inability to offer any examples of inadequate compensation.[5] The incident nonetheless demonstrates the live and precarious nature of the issue.

This chapter begins by providing an overview of the law of statutory damages. Next, it examines Congress's intent, describing the purposes of assuring adequate compensation and deterring infringement. It then discusses two cases that demonstrate the perils posed by bond requirements and the application of statutory damages in the context of indirect infringement. The chapter concludes with a proposal to prohibit the application of statutory damages to secondary infringers, limiting the remedy to actual damages and profits. Such a recommendation promises to increase radical, disruptive innovation.

STATUTORY DAMAGES: LAW

Copyright owners can select from a range of potential remedies for copyright infringement:

- Obtain an injunction preventing further infringement
- Impound infringing copies of the material
- Destroy infringing copies

---

2. *E.g., UMG Recordings, Inc. v. Bertelsmann AG*, 222 F.R.D. 408 (N.D. Cal. 2004); *Capitol Records, Inc. v. Wings Digital Corp.*, 218 F. Supp. 2d 280, 285 (E.D.N.Y. 2002).

3. Final Vote Results for Roll Call 300, H.R. 4279, May 8, 2008, http://clerk.house.gov/evs/2008/roll300.xml.

4. Prioritizing Resources and Organization for Intellectual Property Act of 2007, H.R. 4279, 110th Cong., 1st Sess. §104 (2007).

5. *See* Richard Esguerra, *'PRO IP Act' Aims To Increase Infringement Penalties and Expand Government Enforcement*, Dec. 7, 2007, http://www.eff.org/deeplinks/2007/12/pro-ip-act-increase-infringement-penalties-and-drastically-expand-government-enfor; Sherwin Siy, *Roundtable on Copyright Damages: "What Are We Doing Here?,"* Jan. 28, 2008, http://www.publicknowledge.org/node/1369.

- Recover actual damages and profits
- Obtain statutory damages
- Recover costs and attorneys' fees[6]

Chapter 7 focuses on the remedy of statutory damages. At any time before the court enters a final judgment, a copyright owner, as long as its work is registered with the Copyright Office, can choose between receiving statutory damages, on the one hand, and actual damages and profits, on the other.[7] The current version of the statute provides that copyright owners can obtain

an award of statutory damages for all infringements . . . with respect to any one work . . . in a sum of not less than $750 or more than $30,000.

The court may increase the award to $150,000 when a copyright owner demonstrates willful infringement. It can reduce the award to $200 when the infringer shows that it "was not aware and had no reason to believe" that its activity constituted infringement.[8]

STATUTORY DAMAGES: LEGISLATIVE HISTORY

The first comprehensive scheme for statutory damages appeared in the 1909 Copyright Act.[9] The Act provided that "in lieu of actual damages and profits," the court could award "such damages as . . . appear to be just." Such statutory damages generally ranged between $250 and $5,000. But specific categories of works were subject to different ranges:

- $50 to $200 for newspaper reproductions of photographs
- $10 for each infringing copy of paintings, statues, and sculptures

---

6. 17 U.S.C. §§ 502, 503, 504, 505 (2004). *See generally* Julie E. Cohen et al., Copyright in a Global Information Economy 768–69 (2006). Destruction of infringing copies cannot occur until a court finds infringement, and the recovery of profits is limited to those not otherwise considered in the calculation of actual damages.

7. 17 U.S.C. § 412. A copyright owner can receive statutory damages only for (1) unpublished works it registers with the Copyright Office before infringement and (2) published works it registers within three months of publication.

8. 17 U.S.C. §§ 504(c)(1), (c)(2).

9. The first version of statutory damages appeared in the Copyright Act of 1790, which imposed damages of 50 cents for each infringing sheet of maps, charts, or books "found in [the infringer's] possession." Act of May 31, 1790, ch. 15, § 2, 1 Stat. 124 (1790). Subsequently, the Copyright Act of 1856 provided damages of at least $100 for any person giving an unauthorized performance of a dramatic work. William S. Strauss, *The Damages Provisions of the Copyright Law*, Copyright Revision Study No. 22, 86th Cong., 2d Sess. 3 (1960).

- $1 for each infringing copy of books, periodicals, maps, drawings, photographs, and prints
- $50 for each infringing delivery of a lecture, sermon, or address
- $10 for each infringing performance of a musical composition[10]

In addition to its complexity, the 1909 Act did not specify the role for statutory damages when the copyright owner could prove actual damages or profits. As a result, courts split on the issue, with some not permitting statutory damages and others allowing it in their discretion.[11] This "confusion and uncertainty" encouraged Congress to provide courts with "specific unambiguous directions concerning monetary awards" in the 1976 Copyright Act.[12] Dissatisfaction with the 1909 Act also stemmed from plaintiffs' frequent inability—despite the "substantial expense and inconvenience" of case preparation and trial—to recover more than nominal damages.[13]

This scheme would be simplified in the 1976 Copyright Act, which allowed courts to set statutory damages of $250 to $10,000. Courts could adjust the award up to $50,000 for willful infringement and down to $100 for innocent infringement.[14] The Act clarified that copyright owners could obtain either "actual damages and any additional profits of the infringer" or statutory damages, but not both.[15] The legislative history of the Act stretches over two decades as the Copyright Office authorized a series of studies in preparation for a comprehensive revision of the law.[16]

The two central purposes of statutory damages were presented most succinctly in the 1961 Report of the Register of Copyrights:

(1) "Assur[ing] adequate compensation to the copyright owner for his injury"
(2) "Deter[ring] infringement"[17]

These rationales trace back at least to the early 20th century. In its consideration of the 1909 Copyright Act, Congress highlighted the primary purpose in

---

10. Act of Mar. 4, 1909, ch. 320, § 25, 35 Stat. 1081 (1909). The award was $100 for the first infringement of dramatic, choral, or orchestral compositions and $50 for each subsequent performance.

11. Strauss, at 7–8 (providing examples of courts on both sides of the issue).

12. S. Rep. No. 94-473, at 143 (1975).

13. Strauss, at 9.

14. Pub. L. No. 94-553, 90 Stat 2541, *codified at* 17 U.S.C. § 504(c)(1), (2) (1976).

15. 17 U.S.C. § 504(a) (1976).

16. Staff of House Comm. on the Judiciary, 87th Cong., 1st Sess., *Report of the Register of Copyrights on the General Revision of the U.S. Copyright Law* iii (Comm. Print 1961), *reprinted in* 3 Omnibus Copyright Revision Legislative History (George S. Grossman ed., 1976) [hereinafter 1961 Report].

17. *Id.* at 103.

recognizing the difficulty of proving actual damages and profits. Representatives declared that damages "not easily proven . . . should be recovered" and that the "object of th[e] clause" was "a specific remedy to reimburse [a copyright owner] where he is unable to prove the exact amount of injury."[18] Copyright owners also testified to the difficulties in calculating profits when an illustration was inserted in a magazine or a "pirated article" included in a newspaper.[19]

The 1961 Report reiterated that "actual damages are often conjectural, and may be impossible or prohibitively expensive to prove" because of the uncertain value of copyrights and losses caused by infringement. Relatedly, "[a]n award of the infringer's profits" would be inadequate in many cases because "there may have been little or no profit, or it may be impossible to compute the amount of profits attributable to infringement."[20]

Congress's second reason for implementing statutory damages was to deter potential infringers. The remedy played a role in the early and middle 20th century in reducing infringement in music performance rights, motion pictures, and sheet music. Exhibitors in the 1930s, for example, had displayed movies at unauthorized times and places. But after owners raised copyright awareness, "every exhibitor knew and understood that the copyright law provided minimum statutory damages of $250 per copyright infringed." As a result, the tens of thousands of unauthorized showings were "virtually . . . stamped out."[21]

A generation later, the Register of Copyrights explained that statutory damages were necessary "for the copyright law to operate as an effective deterrent against numerous small, erosive violations of a copyright owner's rights."[22] And the most recent congressional amendment in 1999 increased damages "to provide more stringent deterrents to copyright infringement."[23] Congress explained

---

18. 3 LEGISLATIVE HISTORY OF THE 1909 COPYRIGHT ACT 229, 236 (E. Fulton Brylawski & Abe Goldman eds., 1976).

19. *Id.* at 230, 235.

20. 1961 Report, at 102–03. *See also* George E. Frost, *Comments and Views Submitted to the Copyright Office on the Damage Provisions of the Copyright Law*, COPYRIGHT REVISION STUDY No. 22, 86th Cong., 2d Sess. 38 (1960) (noting that actual damages and profits are often uncertain or "too small to be meaningful").

21. Ralph S. Brown, Jr., *The Operation of the Damage Provisions of the Copyright Law: An Exploratory Study*, COPYRIGHT REVISION STUDY No. 23, 86th Cong., 2d Sess. 76 (1960); Harry G. Henn, *Comments and Views Submitted to the Copyright Office on the Operation of the Damage Provisions of the Copyright Law*, COPYRIGHT REVISION STUDY No. 23, 86th Cong., 2d Sess. 101 (1960).

22. House Comm. on the Judiciary, 89th Cong., 1st Sess., *Copyright Law Revision, Part 6: Supplementary Report of the Register of Copyrights on the General Revision of the U.S. Copyright Law: 1965 Revision Bill* 137 (Comm. Print 1965), *reprinted in* 4 OMNIBUS COPYRIGHT REVISION LEGISLATIVE HISTORY (George S. Grossman ed., 1976).

23. Congress increased the damages range to $750 to $30,000, with an adjustment up to $150,000 for willful infringement. In 1988, the legislature had increased the damages range to $500 to $20,000, with an adjustment up to $100,000 for willful infringement

that statutory damage levels had not taken into account "inflation . . ., increased utilization of certain types of [IP], or current trends in global distribution and electronic commerce." In particular, the legislature lamented software piracy, which caused nearly $3 billion in theft that led to "lost U.S. jobs, lost wages, lower tax revenue, and higher prices for honest purchasers of copyrighted software."[24] And it targeted computer users who "believe[d] that they [would] not be caught or prosecuted for their conduct" and infringers that "continue infringing, even after a copyright owner puts them on notice."[25]

Despite the importance of deterrence, Congress has recognized the role of an upper limit on statutory damages. The legislative history of the 1909 Act includes discussion of keeping the damages "small enough to enable the jury to [award] a verdict" and less than the "hundreds of thousands of dollars" that a court would be "very doubtful" to enforce.[26] Courts and Congress have also acknowledged the importance of judicial discretion in limiting excessive awards. Courts have "exercise[d] their discretion in arriving at an equitable result" when application of the 1909 Act schedules would have led to "exorbitant statutory damages in comparison with actual damages."[27] And one of the legislature's primary goals in its revisions to the 1976 Act was to allow courts to "adjust recovery to the circumstances of the case, thus avoiding some of the artificial or overly technical awards resulting from the language of the existing statute."[28]

The drafters were aware of the draconian effects of statutory damages on innocent infringers. They thus included a provision that "protected against unwarranted liability in cases of occasional or isolated innocent infringement."[29] They also crafted an exception to damages awards for employees of nonprofit educational institutions, libraries, archives, and public broadcasting entities that reasonably believed their activity was protected by the "fair use" defense.[30]

The legislative history includes a recognition of the dangers of secondary liability, as the imposition of statutory damages against theaters and radio stations would result in "a staggering problem unrelated to the reality of the

---

and down to $200 for innocent infringement. These changes roughly track inflation. Berne Convention Implementation Act of 1988, Pub. L. No. 100-568, § 10, 102 Stat. 2853; Digital Theft Deterrence and Copyright Damages Improvement Act of 1999, Pub. L. No. 106-160, § 2, 113 Stat. 1774; U.S. Dept. of Labor, Bureau of Labor Statistics, Consumer Price Index Inflation Calculator, http://data.bls.gov/cgi-bin/cpicalc.pl (last visited Apr. 23, 2008).

24. H.R. REP. 106-216, at 2, 3, 6 (1999).

25. *Id.* at 3.

26. 3 LEGISLATIVE HISTORY OF THE 1909 COPYRIGHT ACT 235, 241.

27. Strauss, at 11.

28. S. REP. No. 94-473, 94th Cong., 1st Sess. 143 (1975).

29. H.R. REP. No. 94-1476, 94th Cong., 2d Sess. 163 (1976); S. REP. No. 94-473, at 145.

30. 17 U.S.C. § 504(c)(2).

damage sustained."[31] And the drafters recognized that "the line between innocent . . . and willful infringement" may have been clear in 1909—when "[a]ll the known methods of infringement involved using a published copy of the copyrighted work" and "the mere fact of infringement demonstrated automatically that it had been willful"—but that advances in technology muddied the issue.[32] In short, for both direct infringement and secondary liability, the drafters recognized the need for limits on statutory damages. The MP3.com and XM cases demonstrate the dangers that flow from the neglect of these limits.

MP3.COM

MP3.com created a service that enabled subscribers to build an online library permitting them to listen to their music at any location with access to the Internet. Before using the service, a subscriber needed to buy a CD of the desired recording or prove that she already owned it.[33]

The Recording Industry Association of America (RIAA), the trade group representing the U.S. recording industry, sued the company for copyright infringement, claiming the unauthorized copying and storage of music files. The district court rejected MP3.com's fair use defense, finding that the defendant had a commercial purpose, that the entirety of creative works was copied, and that the activity "usurp[ed]" a market. As a result, it granted the RIAA's partial motion for summary judgment, finding MP3.com liable for infringement.[34]

Four months later, the judge considered the remedy of statutory damages. He concluded that MP3.com "had actual knowledge that it was infringing plaintiffs' copyright" and thus was a willful infringer. Based in part on the plaintiffs' failure to demonstrate any actual damages, the judge decided not to grant the maximum award of $150,000 per infringed CD. Instead, he concluded that "the appropriate measure of damages [wa]s $25,000 per CD." Such an award would result in damages of either $118 million (according to the defendant's claims of 4,700 potentially infringed CDs) or $250 million (according to the plaintiffs' claims of 10,000 CDs).[35]

---

31. Henn, at 53.
32. Strauss, at 26.
33. *UMG Recordings, Inc. v. MP3.Com, Inc.*, 92 F. Supp. 2d 349, 350 (S.D.N.Y. 2000).
34. *Id.* at 350–53.
35. *UMG Recordings, Inc. v. MP3.Com, Inc.*, No.00 CIV.472 (JSR), 2000 WL 1262568, at *4, *6 (Sept. 6, 2000); Jim Hu & Evan Hansen, *Ruling Against MP3.com Could Cost $118 Million*, NEWS.COM, Sept. 6, 2000, http://www.news.com/Ruling-against-MP3.com-could-cost-118-million/2100-1023_3-245377.html.

Rather than appealing, MP3.com paid more than $53 million to settle the case.[36] Why? As its founder, Michael Robertson, explained:

> We didn't want to settle. I wanted to take it the appellate court for examination of our issues. However, we weren't able to do this. This is because the media companies can elect statutory damages. So although they could not prove they were harmed even $1 (and we had ample evidence that they actually profited from our technology), they were able to elect statutory damages which meant potentially tens of billions of dollars in damages.
>
> The problem arises in that to appeal you have to first bond the judgment assuming you lose at any step. Well, there's no way a small company can bond even a hundred million dollar award much less a multi-billion one. This means that the media companies can find just one judge to rule in their favor, elect statutory [damages] and the legal battle is over.[37]

In other words, even if MP3.com had legitimate arguments that its activity constituted fair use (because users were required to purchase the CDs and the service could have increased demand), it never had the chance to present those arguments to an appellate court. The reason can be traced to the requirement of posting bond.

A party can stay (in other words, delay) a damages award while its appeal is pending by posting a *supersedeas bond*.[38] Such a bond is "required of one who petitions to set aside a judgment or execution" and allows "the other party [to] be made whole if the action is unsuccessful."[39] Its purpose is to maintain the status quo during the pendency of the appeal, thereby protecting the interest of the nonappealing party.[40] A company that is not able to post bond typically will not be able to stay the enforcement of the judgment.[41] When a district court awards astronomical statutory damages, the firm's inability to post bond effectively precludes appeal.

---

36. *UMG Recordings, Inc. v. MP3.com, Inc.*, 2000 U.S. Dist. LEXIS 17907 (S.D.N.Y. Nov. 14, 2000).

37. Tim Lee, *Why the MP3.Com Decision Was Never Appealed*, TECHNOLOGY LIBERATION FRONT, http://www.techliberation.com/archives/038260.php (last visited Apr. 15, 2008).

38. FED. R. CIV. P. 62(d).

39. BLACK'S LAW DICTIONARY 1438 (6th ed. 1990).

40. *E.g.*, *Wilmer v. Board of County Commissioners*, 844 F. Supp. 1414, 1417 (D. Kan. 1993); *Poplar Grove Planting & Refining Co. v. Bache Halsey Stuart, Inc.*, 600 F.2d 1189, 1190–91 (5th Cir. 1979).

41. In certain cases, the district court judge could exercise an "inherent, discretionary power" to reduce the amount of the bond below a full supersedeas bond. *Alexander v. Chesapeake, Potomac & Tidewater Books, Inc.*, 190 F.R.D. 190, 192 (E.D. Va. 1999). For present purposes, however, courts that award statutory damages to secondary infringers are likely to adopt the deterrence rationale and unlikely to reduce bond significantly.

In the *MP3.com* case, the company settled but ultimately entered bankruptcy.[42] Even higher statutory damages were threatened in the case of XM radio.

XM RADIO

XM radio offers another example of the statutory damages roadblocks on the path of innovation. Satellite radio offered "commercial-free digital audio transmissions broadcast from satellites."[43] XM broadcast music, sports, and entertainment on 170 channels.[44] It also created the Pioneer Inno, which allowed subscribers to record and store up to 50 hours of broadcasts and combined "[t]he first live portable satellite radio and MP3 player."[45] The Inno offered radio, storage, and recording functions.

On behalf of the major record labels, the RIAA sued XM. It recognized that XM was a subscription transmission, which was "limited to particular recipients and for which consideration [wa]s required to be paid . . . to receive the transmission."[46] As a result, XM had the right to publicly perform copyrighted works pursuant to a compulsory license.[47] But the RIAA claimed that XM had developed a subscription service that "transform[ed its] satellite transmission from a radio broadcast into a digital download delivery service" allowing the creation of sound recording libraries.[48] Even though XM had limited storage (1 gigabyte, or 50 hours of recording) and did not allow users to transfer recorded music to other listening devices, the RIAA's CEO, Mitch Bainwol, complained that XM offered listeners "a free version of iTunes without paying the music companies for the right to sell their songs."[49] The RIAA also lamented XM's

---

42. Vivendi Universal acquired MP3.com, but, because of difficulties in growing the service, eventually dismantled the original site. *MP3.com*, WIKIPEDIA, http://en.wikipedia.org/wiki/Mp3.com (last visited May 4, 2008).

43. Jason A. Auerbach, *Recording Satellite Radio: Adapting to Modern Technology or Infringing Copyright?*, 29 CARDOZO L. REV. 331, 348 (2007).

44. XM, http://www.xmradio.com/whatisxm/index.xmc (last visited May 1, 2008).

45. Pioneer Inno, http://www.xmradio.com/pioneerinno/index.xmc (last visited May 1, 2008).

46. 17 U.S.C. § 114(j)(14).

47. 17 U.S.C. § 114. Different rules apply to (1) nonsubscription broadcast transmissions (such as AM/FM radio broadcasts), which do not receive any copyright protection, and (2) interactive transmissions, which enable recipients to receive specially created programs or to select particular recordings. 17 U.S.C. §§ 114(d)(1)(a), (j)(7).

48. Complaint, *Atlantic Recording Corp. v. XM Satellite Radio, Inc.*, Civ. Action No. 06-CV-3733, ¶ 6 (S.D.N.Y. 2006), http://www.publicknowledge.org/pdf/plaintiff-complaint-20060516.pdf.

49. Eric Bangeman, *Universal, XM Settle Suit Over Receiver's Ability To Record*, ARS TECHNICA, Dec. 17, 2007, http://arstechnica.com/news.ars/post/20071217-universal-xm-settle-suit-over-receivers-ability-to-record.html; Robert Strohmeyer, *Opinion: RIAA Sues XM, Deserves Squat*, WIRED.COM, May 22, 2006, http://blog.wired.com/gadgets/2006/05/opinion_riaa_su.html.

10-minute buffer, which permitted users to record songs after they had started and "facilitat[ed] the storage and librarying of permanent unlawful copies."[50]

The RIAA alleged nine counts against XM. (In 2007 and 2008, XM settled with the four major record labels, with the undisclosed settlement terms likely granting the recording industry a more active role in managing XM's innovation.[51]) In its complaint, the RIAA claimed that XM directly infringed its exclusive distribution and reproduction rights and that it was liable for inducement, contributory copyright infringement, and vicarious liability. The latter three claims most vividly underscore the statutory damages threat. For each one, the RIAA sought, among other remedies, "the maximum statutory damages" of "$150,000 with respect to each infringing copy made by each subscriber."[52]

XM's buffering allegedly infringed "every song on every channel to which an Inno user is tuned." As a result, the $150,000 figure would be multiplied by roughly (and as detailed in the footnotes) 250,000 different songs each year.[53] The result: *$37.5 billion in statutory damages.* Such an award would be multiples of the gross revenues of the *entire recording industry.*[54] Nor would it be remotely needed to effectuate Congress's intent to "assure adequate compensation" or "deter infringement."

PERSONAL INVESTOR LIABILITY

The threats revealed in the *MP3.com* and *Inno* cases are exacerbated by courts' willingness to impose personal liability on a firm's officers and shareholders. A fundamental principle of corporate law is that shareholders are not responsible for a company's liabilities. Their maximum loss is the amount they invest in

---

50. Complaint ¶ 35.

51. Tyler Savery, *XM, Sony Settle Portable Receiver Lawsuit*, SEEKING ALPHA, Feb. 4, 2008, http://seekingalpha.com/article/62918-xm-sony-settle-portable-receiver-lawsuit; Joseph Weisenthal, *XM Settles with Warner Music Group Over Pioneer Inno; Second Settlement This Week*, PAIDCONTENT.ORG, Dec. 21, 2007, http://www.paidcontent.org/entry/419-xm-settles-with-warner-music-group-over-pioneer-inno-second-settlement-/; *EMI, XM Settle in Pioneer Inno Lawsuit*, ELECTRONISTA, June 10, 2008, http://www.electronista.com/articles/08/06/10/emi.xm.settle.inno.suit/.

52. Complaint ¶¶ 85, 96, 107.

53. Fred von Lohmann at the Electronic Frontier Foundation arrives at this figure by calculating that (1) "XM broadcasts 160,000 different songs each month"; (2) "20% of the songs each month are different from the last"; and (3) "Inno users are tuned into at least half of those songs." Fred von Lohmann, *Record Labels Sue XM Radio*, ELECTRONIC FRONTIER FOUNDATION, May 17, 2006, http://www.eff.org/deeplinks/2006/05/record-labels-sue-xm-radio.

54. *Id.*

the corporation. Nearly all states have enacted laws limiting shareholder liability on the grounds that such limits encourage beneficial, but risky, activity that shareholders would avoid if they bore personal responsibility.[55]

Limited liability encourages efficient investment levels in two ways. First, it reduces information costs, allowing individuals "with money but neither the skill nor information needed for business management" to invest in others' enterprises without losing their entire portfolio. The investor is spared the task of "acquir[ing] detailed information on corporate operations, potential corporate liability, and potential individual exposure," which might otherwise persuade them to forgo the investment. Second, limited liability corrects excessive risk aversion, which follows from an investor's unreasonable fear of "the risk of losing all her assets."[56] As a result of these benefits, limited liability allows more efficient diversification and optimal investment decisions.[57]

At times, however, courts have *pierced the corporate veil* to impose personal liability on shareholders. Such cases have involved close corporations (such as family-owned businesses), parent-subsidiary relations, and instances of fraud or misrepresentation.[58] Veil piercing has been common in copyright cases.

One court rejected a motion to dismiss against Hummer Winblad, a venture capital firm charged with vicarious and contributory copyright infringement for investing in and controlling the operations of Napster.[59] Another held a president and sole shareholder of a company replicating CDs liable for contributory infringement and vicarious liability.[60]

When the personal assets of a corporation's officers, directors, and shareholders are on the table, venture capitalists will think twice before becoming involved in technology firms. As a result, small firms with disruptive new ideas often will not be able to bring the ideas to the market. In fact, such a chilling effect at least partially explains why funding for these firms has fallen in recent years.[61]

---

55. *E.g.*, Nina A. Mendelson, A *Control-Based Approach to Shareholder Liability for Corporate Torts*, 102 COLUM. L. REV. 1203, 1204, 1211 (2002).

56. *Id.* at 1217–18.

57. Frank H. Easterbrook & Daniel R. Fischel, *Limited Liability and the Corporation*, 52 U. CHI. L. REV. 89, 96–97 (1985); Joshua M. Siegel, Comment, *Reconciling Shareholder Limited Liability with Vicarious Copyright Liability: Holding Parent Corporations Liable for the Copyright Infringement of Subsidiaries*, 41 U. RICH. L. REV. 535, 538–40 (2007).

58. Easterbrook & Fischel, at 109–12.

59. *UMG Recordings, Inc. v. Bertelsmann AG*, 222 F.R.D. 408 (N.D. Cal. 2004). The court later dismissed the suit because of the running of the statute of limitations.

60. *Capitol Records, Inc. v. Wings Digital Corp.*, 218 F. Supp. 2d 280, 285 (E.D.N.Y. 2002).

61. Dawn Kawamoto, *Lawsuits Dampen VCs' File-sharing Enthusiasm*, CNET NEWS, Sept. 4, 2000, http://www.news.com/2100-1023-245275.html.

STATUTORY DAMAGES/SECONDARY LIABILITY DISCONNECT

Congress never intended for the remedy of statutory damages to be a "corporate death penalty" plunging technology manufacturers into bankruptcy.[62] It primarily intended to provide relief when a copyright owner was not able to prove damages. It secondarily, and relatedly, sought to deter infringement. As I show below, neither of those two goals is needed for secondary infringers. Nor are statutory damages appropriate for secondary infringers because of the uncertainty of liability, as exacerbated by bond requirements and personal liability.

First, the purpose of providing adequate compensation is not needed since the amount of damages generally can be ascertained. The amount of damages for which technology manufacturers could be held responsible equals the market value of the infringed copyrighted works.[63] This can be calculated by multiplying (1) the revenues a plaintiff would have gained from each work absent infringement by (2) the number of infringed works.[64] This figure can be estimated, especially as compared to the situations that motivated the drafters (such as where a plaintiff's losses were uncertain, a defendant's profit could not be calculated, or a defendant gained little or no profit).

For the first factor, a plaintiff can introduce evidence of its anticipated revenues per work. Even if an exact number cannot be ascertained, a rough estimate (certainly within an order of magnitude) is possible. And for the second, the statutory damage determination provides no added benefit since it requires the *exact same* computation that actual damages calls for: the number of infringed works. In other words, if the number of infringing copies is unclear for actual-damage determinations, it is unclear for statutory damages.

Statutory damages thus would assist in providing adequate compensation only if a plaintiff's revenues were incalculable and the statutory damage award was in the ballpark of the injury suffered. Neither of these conditions, however, is likely to be true. In fact, the only guarantee of a statutory damages award of $750, $30,000, or $150,000 for each musical work against a secondary infringer is that it will bear no resemblance to actual compensation. A monkey throwing darts at a dartboard of potential lost value would be more likely to award adequate compensation than a jury granting statutory damages. Even more impressively (or disturbingly), the monkey would come orders of magnitude closer to the actual damages.

---

62. Fred von Lohmann, *Remedying Grokster*, ELECTRONIC FRONTIER FOUNDATION, July 25, 2005, http://www.eff.org/deeplinks/archives/003833.php.

63. 4 MELVILLE B. NIMMER & DAVID NIMMER, NIMMER ON COPYRIGHT § 14.02, at 14–14 (2006).

64. The number of infringed works reflects the injury suffered given that the sales of the plaintiff and defendant likely would occur in the same market and that the plaintiff would be able to show that infringement caused its losses. *Id.*

Further demonstrating that statutory damages are not needed for compensation purposes, plaintiffs in many cases will not suffer *any* damages or will even *benefit* from the manufacturer's activity. Most of the technologies offer new opportunities to experience the works—in different locations, at different times, and in different forms. In other words, they tend to increase the value of copyrighted works. This is especially true where, as in the *MP3.com* case, listeners were required to buy CDs before being able to listen to them.

It thus is not a surprise that in *MP3.com* the plaintiffs never sought to introduce evidence of their actual damages. This is consistent with other cases. In 2007, the RIAA recovered $222,000 in statutory damages from an individual who uploaded 24 copyrighted songs even though a Sony BMG official admitted that "We haven't stopped to calculate the amount of damages we've suffered due to downloading."[65] Of course, where copyright owners have suffered, at most, a trivial amount of damages, statutory damages are not needed for adequate compensation.

The second rationale for statutory damages, deterring infringement, also is not needed. Part of this goal overlaps with the primary objective: if the copyright owner is not able to calculate damages, it may not be able to recover. As a result, the infringer would be unlikely to be deterred. This problem, again, is not present here. In addition, statutory damages are not needed for more general deterrence. Actual damages provide a powerful tool against technology manufacturers. Copyright owners are able to recover their lost damages as well as any additional profits the defendant gained. The owners have never shown, in the context of secondary liability, that actual damages are insufficient to provide deterrence.

In addition to not being needed for the two primary purposes, statutory damages threaten three unique, related difficulties as applied to technology manufacturers.

First, they are not appropriate given the uncertainty of the activity's validity. Liability is clear for pirates directly infringing copyrighted works. Technology manufacturers, in contrast, are far less likely to know if their activity is legal. As discussed in Chapter 6, secondary liability is one of the murkiest areas of copyright law. In the *Grokster* case, the Supreme Court could not decide how the *Sony* noninfringing use test applied to P2P software, mustering only dueling concurrences on the issue. Given the potpourri of tests—based on, among other issues, the defendant's intent, the technology's primary use, the presence of a substantial noninfringing use, and the use of filtering measures—manufacturers typically will not be able to forecast whether a court will find them secondarily liable.

---

65. Eric Bangeman, *Judge Tells Record Labels to Cough up Download Expenses*, ARS TECHNICA, Nov. 27, 2007, http://arstechnica.com/news.ars/post/20071127-judge-tells-record-labels-to-cough-up-download-expenses.html; Eric Bangeman, *RIAA Trial Verdict Is In: Jury Finds Thomas Liable for Infringement*, ARS TECHNICA, Oct. 4, 2007, http://arstechnica.com/news.ars/post/20071004-verdict-is-in.html.

The "line between innocent . . . and willful infringement" may have been clear in 1909, and may still be apparent to pirates directly infringing copyrighted works. But it is not clear to secondary infringers today. Advances in technology and the indirect nature of infringement make secondary infringers a poor target for statutory damages.

Second, the magnitude of statutory damages has prevented firms even from determining the murky secondary liability issues discussed above. Copyright owners seeking settlements have brandished statutory damages as a sword of Damocles. The remedy also has prevented manufacturers from appealing their cases. Damage awards are so high that secondary infringers ordered to pay such damages in district court often cannot post the required bond while the case is on appeal. As a result, as the *MP3.com* case revealed, they are not able to appeal.

Third, all of these land mines strike close to home through courts' willingness to pierce the corporate veil and impose sizeable personal costs on individuals. Given astronomical risks and unclear liability, few shareholders and officers will resist the temptation to settle. As Mark Lemley explained: "If an innovator is at risk of losing her whole company (and her house and her children's education), even a very small chance of liability will be enough to deter valuable innovation."[66]

In short, applying statutory damages to secondary infringers has startling, unjustifiable consequences, which are not needed to carry out Congress's purposes and which pose great peril for innovation.

PROPOSAL

I propose amending the copyright laws to limit statutory damages to cases of direct infringement. Such an approach would strike a more reasonable balance between promoting the creation of new technologies capable of noninfringing uses and deterring willful direct infringers. It would not have adverse effects on Congress's goals of providing adequate compensation and offering deterrence. It would remove the sword of Damocles hanging over innovators and investors. And it would promote innovation.

Copyright owners could still seek to recover significant actual damages from or impose injunctive relief against secondary infringers. But the proposal would allow technology innovators to make reasonable business decisions based on manageable levels of legal risk. No longer would they face a corporate death penalty at the hands of unpredictable and unjustified legal standards and remedies.[67]

---

66. Mark A. Lemley, *Should a Licensing Market Require Licensing?*, 70 LAW & CONTEMP. PROBS. 185, 199 n.81 (2007).

67. Fred von Lohmann, *Remedying Grokster*.

As the threat of statutory damages for secondary copyright infringement recedes, innovation—disruptive innovation, in particular—would flourish. The next generation of DVR, portable radio receiver, and iPod would not be stifled in its infancy.

It is difficult to envision, of course, the hypothetical world of products we would have enjoyed if not for the existence of statutory damages. We cannot know how many inventors and investors have pulled their innovation punches because of the threat of statutory damages. But the *MP3.com* case offers a glimpse of the entrepreneur carcasses lying on the side of the innovation highway. And the *Inno* case hints at the perils of innovation managed by the copyright industry. An amendment to the Copyright Act that eliminates statutory damages in secondary liability cases would play a significant role in fostering innovation.

8. THE DIGITAL MILLENNIUM COPYRIGHT ACT: FROM PIRATES TO USER INNOVATORS

Software Overview 167
Reverse Engineering 168
Aftermarkets 170
Software and Copyright 171
 Copyright Law and Reverse Engineering 174
Early Copy Protection Efforts 177
The Entertainment Industry and Digital Rights Management 177
The Digital Millennium Copyright Act 179
 Introduction 179
 Text 179
 Global Treatment 181
 Legislative History 182
 Accidental Aftermarket Protection 184
Lexmark v. Static Control Components 185
Chamberlain v. Skylink 186
Davidson Associates v. Jung 187
The Aibo Incident 190
The Triennial Exemption Review 190
Proposal 193
Conclusion 197

The ink in printer toner cartridges is one of the most expensive materials on the planet, costing as much as $5 per milliliter.[1] In contrast, Dom Perignon champagne (vintage 1998) costs $0.17 per milliliter, and gasoline costs less than $0.01 per milliliter. Between 1999 and 2007, while the average price of ink increased less than 13 percent, inkjet ink prices skyrocketed more than 350 percent.[2] How can manufacturers charge such exorbitant prices for such simple materials? The answer is to be found in the Digital Millennium Copyright Act (DMCA).

Congress enacted the DMCA in 1998 to protect copyrighted works from "pirates" who could easily reproduce and distribute digital copies of the works. But the statute has amassed considerable power because the copyrighted works

---

1. *See* HP 75 Tri-color Inkjet Print Cartridge (CB337WN), http://h10010.www1.hp.com/wwpc/us/en/sm/WF06c/A10-12771-64199-69422-69422-3266753-3266754-3266759.html (3.5-milliliter cartridge priced at $17.99) (last visited August 29, 2008).

2. Larry F. Darby & Stephen B. Pociask, *Inkjet Prices, Printing Costs, and Consumer Welfare*, Am. Consumer Inst., Nov. 19, 2007, at 18-21, http://www.aci-citizenresearch.org/Inkjet%20Final.pdf.

it protects include computer software. And unexpectedly, software appears in ubiquitous everyday objects such as garage door openers, iPods, and cell phones.

This concern is exacerbated because firms often must use competitors' software. Software must interoperate, or work together, with computer hardware or other software. Users, however, cannot make their products interoperable without engaging in copyright infringement. Unlike other copyrighted works, such as music or movies, users can understand software only by making a copy of it, thereby infringing the copyright owner's exclusive right of reproduction.

Courts have long upheld the process of *reverse engineering*, or working backward from a product to determine how it was created.[3] Pursuant to trade secret laws, courts have treated reverse engineering as a lawful means of disclosure rather than as misappropriation. Applying copyright laws, courts have viewed reverse engineering as a privileged fair use.

In the 1990s, however, reverse engineering came under attack. The entertainment industry worried about digital piracy as programmers evaded its encryption and other protection systems. So the industry convinced Congress to enact the DMCA, which prohibited the reverse engineering of measures protecting copyrighted works and banned the distribution of such tools.

The DMCA vastly increased the anticompetitive use of software by allowing vendors to exert control over *aftermarket* goods, which are supplied for a durable product after its initial sale.[4] Competition in aftermarkets lowers price and encourages producers to develop new, innovative products. For example, the aftermarket for automobile parts is a $250 billion industry that includes independent repair shops, replacement parts manufacturers and retailers, and producers of interoperable car accessories.[5] Before the introduction of aftermarket parts, auto makers had increased the price of replacement parts as much as 800 percent.[6]

Under cover of the DMCA, manufacturers have embedded software that has allowed

- printer manufacturers to control toner cartridges;
- garage door opener manufacturers to control remote controls;

---

3. *Kewanee Oil v. Bicron*, 416 U.S. 470 (1974); *see* REST. TORTS § 757, cmt. (f).

4. ROBERT P. MERGES ET AL., INTELLECTUAL PROPERTY IN THE NEW TECHNOLOGICAL AGE 572 (4th ed. 2006).

5. *Auto Aftermarket M&A Industry Update*, GLOBALAUTOINDUSTRY.COM, Oct. 2006, http://www.globalautoindustry.com/article.php?id=1070&jaar=2006&maand=10&target=Ameri; Brief of Amicus Curiae Consumers Union Supporting Skylink Technologies, Inc.'s Opposition to the Chamberlain Group, Inc.'s Motion for Summary Judgment, *The Chamberlain Group, Inc. v. Skylink Technologies, Inc.*, No. 02 C 6376, at 6 (N.D. Ill. May 8, 2003).

6. *Competitive Auto Replacement Parts*, 2001 OHIO INSURANCE FACTS, at 2, http://www.ohioinsurance.org/factbook2001/chapter1/chapter_1m.htm.

- online music stores to control portable music players; and
- digital camera makers to control the development of "raw" (unprocessed) image files.

Nor is the danger limited to these instances. Future uses could allow

- automakers to control tires, wiper blades, and oil filters;
- television manufacturers to control remote control devices;
- computer manufacturers to control keyboards, monitors, and other peripherals; and
- mobile phone makers to control replacement batteries, ring tones, and other products.[7]

Because of a fundamental flaw in the DMCA, these uses extend far beyond what Congress envisioned. The legislature sought to prevent the piracy of digital music and movies. It did not seek to protect software that played a peripheral role in a functional product. But because the DMCA covers software that controls even uncopyrighted devices, it has been invoked in this context. This was not Congress's intent.[8]

Such an expansive conception of the DMCA threatens user innovation. In contrast to manufacturers, who develop "improvements on well-known needs," users tend to develop "functionally novel" innovations that employ contextual data and incorporate information about their desires.[9] By incorporating information about users' needs, such innovation promises to lower manufacturers' high market failure rates. Unfortunately, however, manufacturers have employed the DMCA to block users from offering improvements in settings such as video games and robotic pet dogs.

This conception also complicates antitrust law. After the Supreme Court in 1992 held that a manufacturer in a competitive primary market could have monopoly power in the aftermarket for the service or parts of its own equipment, the floodgates opened to numerous antitrust claims.[10] Because of the typically robust competition in primary markets such as those for printers or copiers, however, these claims have been controversial. As a result, courts have "bent over backwards" to avoid findings of monopolization in these cases.[11] Given this

---

7. Brief of Amicus Curiae Consumers Union Supporting Static Control Component, Inc.'s Appeal To Vacate the District Court's Grant of Preliminary Injunction, *Static Control Components, Inc. v. Lexmark International, Inc.*, No. 03 5400, at 6–7 (6th Cir. June 30, 2003) [hereinafter Consumers Union Brief].

8. For a discussion of the expansive use of the DMCA, see Dan L. Burk, *Anticircumvention Misuse*, 50 UCLA L. REV. 1095, 1110–14 (2003).

9. ERIC VON HIPPEL, DEMOCRATIZING INNOVATION 8 (2005).

10. *Eastman Kodak Co. v. Image Technical Services, Inc.*, 504 U.S. 451 (1992).

11. Herbert Hovenkamp, *Post-Chicago Antitrust: A Review and Critique*, 2001 COLUM. BUS. L. REV. 257, 286.

history and the contentious nature of the claims, vendors' use of the DMCA to control aftermarkets (and thereby tempt competitors to file antitrust claims) leads to unnecessary difficulties for antitrust. Paring back the DMCA's expansive interpretation reduces antitrust courts' exposure to aftermarket claims.

This issue is of global significance today. In implementing treaty obligations, Europe, China, and Japan have enacted variations on the DMCA. The United States has included anti-circumvention obligations in free trade agreements with Jordan, Singapore, Chile, Morocco, Australia, Bahrain, Oman, Peru, Costa Rica, the Dominican Republic, El Salvador, Guatemala, Honduras, and Nicaragua, and has signed agreements with Colombia, Panama, and South Korea that are pending congressional approval. Nor has the United States shown any signs of retreating from this strategy, as confirmed by negotiations with 33 countries for the Free Trade Area of the Americas (FTAA).[12]

This chapter begins by tracing the role that reverse engineering has played in the software industry as a matter of technology and law. It then introduces the DMCA's text and legislative history. It explores the most important cases that have applied the statute to competition-related issues. And it examines the review process that the Copyright Office has conducted in granting new exemptions from liability.

The chapter concludes with a proposal that promises to remedy the anticompetitive use of the DMCA. Given the statute's direct effects on competition, the proposal draws on market-based ideas developed in antitrust and copyright law. It requires a plaintiff alleging a DMCA violation to show that (1) the expressive copyrightable features of a product covered by a technological protection measure play an essential role in consumer demand for the item and (2) it would suffer a direct negative market effect from the challenged circumvention or distribution.

Since its passage in 1998, the DMCA has fostered numerous profound concerns, including the weakening of fair use and the chilling of scientific research and free expression, that lie outside the direct scope of this book. But the proposal offered in this chapter at least would address the most pressing competition and innovation concerns. And it would return the DMCA to the scope envisioned by its drafters—one that covers digitized music, books, and movies, but not program code that plays a trivial role in uncopyrighted products.

The chapter begins with an overview of software, which is at the heart of the DMCA.

---

12. Office of the United States Trade Representative, *Bilateral Trade Agreements*, http://www.ustr.gov/Trade_Agreements/Bilateral/Section_Index.html (last visited June 1, 2008); Electronic Frontier Foundation, *FTAA and Bilateral FTA Resources*, http://w2.eff.org/IP/FTAA/ (last visited June 1, 2008).

SOFTWARE OVERVIEW

A computer system includes hardware (physical computer equipment) and software (computer programs).[13] The process of writing software begins when a software designer creates a specification that includes a program's ideas and algorithms. A programmer then uses the specification to create *source code*, a high-level language that can be understood by anyone with knowledge of the language. Programmers embed in the source code explanatory comments that do not affect the program's operation but that offer essential information to those who modify or fix errors in the program.[14]

Computers do not run programs in source code. Instead, compilers or assemblers convert the source code to *object code*. Object code is composed of zeroes and ones and is unintelligible even to trained software programmers. It specifies the instructions for the computer to execute but does not include the higher-level comments explaining the instructions.[15]

Software companies distribute their programs in object code. Such distribution permits them to maintain the source code as a trade secret. Distribution of object code also allows software firms to prevent *interoperability*, or the ability of hardware and software components to interact. In particular, firms can block compatibility by not sharing their *interface specifications*, or rules governing interaction with hardware or other software.[16] One type of interface specification is the *application programming interface* (API). The API tells application developers how a program receives and sends information, allowing applications to be compatible with programs.[17] One of the central challenges of the European Commission's case against Microsoft focused on the firm's refusal to share its APIs, which made it difficult for rivals to offer their own work group servers that could interoperate with the Windows operating system.[18]

Application programming interfaces enable a crucial principle of software design known as *modularity*. Modularity divides a project into its smallest

---

13. JONATHAN BAND & MASANOBU KATOH, INTERFACES ON TRIAL: INTELLECTUAL PROPERTY AND INTEROPERABILITY IN THE GLOBAL SOFTWARE INDUSTRY 2–3 (1995).

14. *Id.* at 13; Andrew Johnson-Laird, *Software Reverse Engineering in the Real World*, 19 U. DAYTON L. REV. 843, 856–57 (1994).

15. S. Carran Daughtrey, *Reverse Engineering of Software for Interoperability and Analysis*, 47 VAND. L. REV. 145, 151 (1994).

16. BAND & KATOH, at 5, 7.

17. Pamela Samuelson and Suzanne Scotchmer, *The Law and Economics of Reverse Engineering*, 111 YALE L.J. 1575, 1615–16 (2002).

18. *The Court of First Instance Essentially Upholds the Commission's Decision Finding that Microsoft Abused its Dominant Position*, Sept. 17, 2007, http://curia.europa.eu/en/actu/communiques/cp07/aff/cp070063en.pdf. The Commission also challenged Microsoft's refusal to supply protocols, or tools for communicating with Windows.

component tasks, with software written for those tasks and reused whenever possible.[19] Most programs consist of hundreds of modules that communicate and interact with each other. A major desktop word-processing or web-browser program could consist of thousands of these modules, which programmers could not easily assemble without access to the API.

REVERSE ENGINEERING

As important as the APIs and interface specifications are, however, developers often will not have access to them. For modern, complex software programs, the only way to reconstruct an API is to re-create the software's source code.[20] But the starting point for this project, decompiled object code, resembles "a novel that has been stripped of all adjectives, adverbs, articles, and other explanatory words [and] reorganized to be completely chronological with no chapters or paragraphs."

The programmer begins to re-create the source code by disassembling object code into *assembly code,* a level between object and source code that offers a "bare-bones interpretation" of a program's operation.[21] She then adds her own explanations in reconstructing the source code. This entire process is time-consuming, often lasting longer than the initial creation of the software. The process also does not reveal a program's "inner secrets," as the original source code cannot be precisely reconstructed.[22]

Why would a company engage in such difficult and time-consuming reverse engineering? A few of the many possible reasons include

- observing software to see how it works;
- finding, assessing, and fixing bugs;
- determining how to add extra features;
- making certain that a competitor has not infringed the company's source code;
- ensuring that a music CD is not installing virus-like software on a hard drive;

---

19. MERGES ET AL., INTELLECTUAL PROPERTY IN THE NEW TECHNOLOGICAL AGE, 2006 STATUTORY SUPPLEMENT [hereinafter MERGES ET AL., STATUTORY SUPPLEMENT] at 527; LESLEY ANNE ROBERTSON, SIMPLE PROGRAM DESIGN: A STEP-BY-STEP APPROACH 104 (3d ed. 2000).

20. Another option, *black box testing* (by which a programmer sends messages to the software and records what it does in response) is feasible with small, primitive programs that have limited vocabularies. MERGES ET AL., at 1021.

21. Daughtrey, at 151–52.

22. BAND & KATOH, at 15; Johnson-Laird, at 896.

- making modifications to a critical piece of old, custom software that is no longer supported (as occurred during the Year 2000 scare);
- ensuring that installed software is not illegally collecting and reporting back private personal data.[23]

Most important for our purposes, reverse engineering allows a competitor to reconstruct a withheld interface specification, thereby gaining compatibility with hardware or other software.[24] Such activity fosters interoperability that allows developers to improve programs rather than reinventing the wheel to avoid copyright infringement.[25] It offers consumers additional features as well as products that have different uses.[26]

If radical innovation played a more vital role in the industry, interoperability could potentially have a negative effect by making it less likely that consumers would switch to a new (and possibly superior) standard.[27] But this concern is not pressing in this context because the software industry is characterized by cumulative, or incremental, innovation. Programmers implement software design elements by "looking around for examples or remembering what worked in other programs." The automation of known tasks at the heart of much software development "by definition involves . . . incremental innovation."[28]

Even the most innovative software programs have built on others' creations.[29] One commentator, writing in 1990, explained that "[i]t is impossible to point to a single element of any current mass-market program's interface that did not have a progenitor in one or more prior programs."[30] In short, interoperability

---

23. Brief of IEEE-USA as Amicus Curiae in Support of Appellants and Reversal, *Davidson & Assocs., Inc. v. Internet Gateway, Inc.*, at 7–8 (Jan. 24, 2005) [hereinafter IEEE Brief] (observing software); Samuelson & Scotchmer, at 1642 (fixing bugs, adding features); Jeffrey D. Sullivan & Thomas M. Morrow, *Practicing Reverse Engineering in an Era of Growing Constraints under the Digital Millennium Copyright Act and Other Provisions*, 14 ALB. L.J. SCI. & TECH. 1, 7, 10 (2003) (detecting infringement, modifying old software); Recommendation of the Register of Copyrights in RM 2005-11, at 53, www.copyright. gov/1201/docs/1201_recommendation.pdf (blocking virus installation); 17 U.S.C. § 1201(i) (preventing data collection).

24. Daughtrey, at 172.

25. Gary R. Ignatin, *Let the Hackers Hack: Allowing the Reverse Engineering of Copyrighted Computer Programs To Achieve Compatibility*, 140 U. PA. L. REV. 1999, 2030 (1992).

26. Brief Amicus Curiae of Computer & Communications Industry Ass'n in Support of Skylink Technologies, Inc. and Urging Affirmance, No. 02-CV-6376, at 7 (Fed. Cir. Apr. 1, 2004).

27. Ignatin, at 2030.

28. Pamela Samuelson et al., *A Manifesto Concerning the Legal Protection of Computer Programs*, 94 COLUM. L. REV. 2308, 2330–31 (1994).

29. Ignatin, at 2031.

30. Thomas M.S. Hemnes, *Three Common Fallacies in the User Interface Copyright Debate*, 6 COMPUTER L. & PRAC. 163, 167 (1990).

leads to "a larger variety of software applications from a wider array of software developers with fewer wasted application development costs."[31] The primary beneficiary of this interoperability is consumers.

AFTERMARKETS

The key to the interoperability discussed in the previous section is the API. But there is no guarantee that an API exists for a particular program. And even if one does exist, developers often do not provide it.[32]

Vendors also can prevent interoperability by using a *lock-out code*, or security system barring the use of unauthorized components. To unlock the primary device, the component must correctly provide a code sequence or respond to an authentication process. A vendor thus has the ability to control which (if any) software will interoperate with its own software.[33]

Do companies disclose their APIs? The answer often depends on the level of competition they face. Firms with market power tend to withhold or condition the release of their API, while those without market power tend to distribute it freely.[34] The maker of a new operating system, for example, is likely to make its API freely available to attract more developers and programs. The maker of a dominant operating system, in contrast, typically demands a licensing fee from those writing programs for the system or refuses to license the API, offering a "closed" system.

The anticompetitive uses of closed software extend far beyond the world of the PC. Software today is at the heart of even the most humble devices that interact with accessories or supplies. Examples include TV set-top boxes and remotes, security systems and keypads, and inkjet printers and toner cartridges. It is a trivial matter for a manufacturer to write software for the primary product to accept only those accessories or supplies whose software speaks the recognized language. If the language is a well-kept secret, the net effect is complete control of the aftermarket.

Given that aftermarkets often provide more profits and revenues than the markets for primary products, such a strategy is alluring. The aftermarket strategy is traced to King Gillette's idea, conceived in 1906, to "give razors away, but charge whatever traffic will bear for the blades." The strategy is successful

---

31. Samuelson & Scotchmer, at 1625.

32. Julie E. Cohen, *Reverse Engineering and the Rise of Electronic Vigilantism: Intellectual Property Implications of "Lock-out" Programs*, 68 S. CAL. L. REV. 1091, 1094 (1995); Samuelson & Scotchmer, at 1615–20.

33. *Lexmark Int'l Inc. v. Static Control Components, Inc.*, 387 F.3d 522, 536 (6th Cir. 2004).

34. Samuelson & Scotchmer, at 1615–20.

because aftermarket products and services are "sold repeatedly to the entire installed base of primary product customers."[35] Even if sales of the primary product decrease (or even cease), customers that are locked in will continue to buy the manufacturer's products.

One commentator estimated that leading manufacturers derive 40 to 60 percent of their revenues and 50 to 90 percent of their gross margin from aftermarkets.[36] Inkjet printer makers, for example, sell the printers for "little or no profit" and "derive most of their profits from ink."[37] Ink cartridges are primarily responsible for the most popular printer manufacturer, Hewlett-Packard, deriving most (up to 75 percent) of its profit from its imaging and printing business.[38]

Manufacturers have used tools such as patents, copyrights, contracts, and technological protection measures to prevent rivals from competing in aftermarkets. Rivals, however, could circumvent many of these mechanisms, such as those based on copyrighted software, through reverse engineering. And courts long upheld the legality of this circumvention, even if manufacturers' aftermarket business models were threatened. Before analyzing courts' treatment of reverse engineering of copyrighted works, this chapter explores the relationship between software and copyright.

SOFTWARE AND COPYRIGHT

Software began as a free value-added service to the mainframe hardware leasing business. With the development of microcomputers in the 1970s, software became a major business in its own right.[39] That new status was accompanied by calls for stronger patent, copyright, or other IP protection.

Before the 1980s, software had received protection only under the law of trade secrecy. This regime protects information that derives value from being not known to (and typically not ascertainable by) others, as long as its owner undertakes reasonable efforts to maintain its secrecy.[40] Competitors who use improper means or breach a confidential relationship in acquiring or using such a secret

---

35. Michael Bean, *Developing an Aftermarket Strategy*, Forio, http://forio.com/resources/developing-an-aftermarket-strategy/.

36. James Ilaria, *Avoid Turning Your Aftermarket Into An Afterthought*, IndustryWeek.com, Mar. 1, 2006, http://www.businessweek.com/adsections/2003/ptc/ptc_11.htm.

37. William M. Bulkeley, *Kodak's Strategy for First Printer—Cheaper Cartridges*, Wall St. J., Feb. 6, 2007, at B1.

38. *Monks Praise the Inkjet Deal*, Wired.com, June 15, 2003, http://www.wired.com/techbiz/media/news/2003/06/59256.

39. Merges et al., Statutory Supplement, at 515–16.

40. Uniform Trade Secrets Act § (4).

are liable for misappropriation.[41] Courts have consistently held that reverse engineering does not constitute misappropriation.[42]

The protected status of reverse engineering would not be guaranteed, however, as software came to be encompassed in patentable and copyrightable subject matter. The Supreme Court in 1981 provided the first indication that software could be patented in upholding a patent for a rubber-curing process that included software and explaining that a claim does not become unpatentable "simply because it uses a mathematical formula, computer program, or digital computer."[43] Thirteen years later, the Federal Circuit upheld "a computer operating pursuant to software."[44] In 2008, the Federal Circuit required patentable software to be "tied to a particular machine or apparatus" or to "transform[] a particular article into a different state or thing."[45]

In certain industries, a patentee's obligation to disclose its inventions will minimize the need for reverse engineering. But in the software industry, applicants only need to disclose a functional description—not the source code—to receive a patent.[46] A programmer thus typically must engage in decompilation to re-create the source code. And in undertaking this activity, the programmer "makes [or] uses" the invention, thus infringing the patent.[47] Patents have played an important role in protecting software. But in this chapter, I focus on the copyrighted elements of software, which have produced even more surprising effects under the DMCA.

In 1974, Congress established the National Commission on New Technological Uses of Copyrighted Works (CONTU) to propose revisions to the IP laws based on new technologies.[48] A majority of the Commission concluded that software should be protected under copyright law, and Congress amended the Copyright Act in 1980 to implement this recommendation.[49] Significant difficulties have flowed from this amendment.

---

41. *Id.* § (2).

42. *E.g.*, RESTATEMENT (THIRD) OF UNFAIR COMPETITION § 43 (1995); *Kewanee Oil Co. v. Bicron Corp.*, 416 U.S. 470, 476 (1974).

43. *Diamond v. Diehr*, 450 U.S. 175, 187–91 (1981).

44. *In re Alappat*, 33 F.3d 1526, 1543–45 (Fed. Cir. 1994) (en banc).

45. *In re Bilski*, 545 F.3d 943, 954 (Fed. Cir. 2008) (finding method for hedging risk in commodities trading unpatentable).

46. *See Fonar Corp. v. General Electric Co.*, 107 F.3d 1543, 1549 (Fed. Cir. 1997); Julie E. Cohen & Mark A. Lemley, *Patent Scope and Innovation in the Software Industry*, 89 CAL. L. REV. 1, 24–25 (2001).

47. 35 U.S.C. § 271(a); *see* Cohen & Lemley, at 19–21.

48. Act of Dec. 31, 1974, Pub. L. No. 93-573, § 201, 88 Stat. 1873; National Commission on New Technological Uses of Copyrighted Works, *Final Report* (1978) [hereinafter CONTU *Report*].

49. Act of Dec. 12, 1980, Pub. L. No. 96-517, § 10(a), 94 Stat. 3015, *codified as amended at* 17 U.S.C. § 101; *see generally* Peter S. Menell, *An Analysis of the Scope of Copyright Protection for Application Programs*, 41 STAN. L. REV. 1045, 1047 (1989).

The first challenge stems from software's utilitarian nature. Perhaps the most important distinction in determining copyright protection is the idea-expression dichotomy. Expression can be protected. But because of the dangers of stifled competition and communication, ideas cannot.[50] This dichotomy does not easily apply to computer software, which is utilitarian in nature.[51] In contrast to the words used in books and movies, those appearing in source code are not written to amuse or entertain. Instead, they are written to perform a task. Computer programs are shaped by factors such as function, efficiency, compatibility, and industry demand.[52]

Second, interoperability is vitally important to software. Unlike other copyrightable works such as movies or books, which can stand on their own, software "can function only in conjunction with hardware and other software." Two computer products can interoperate, or work together, only if they conform to the same set of rules known as interface specifications.[53]

Software's unique status is made clear by examining those who seek to access a work's elements that are uncopyrightable or protected by fair use. A reviewer who wishes to quote from a book can read the book. A writer who desires to build on a theme from a play can watch the performance. A programmer, in contrast, who wishes to use software cannot simply look at the object code. Rather, she must reverse engineer it, thereby making a copy and committing a prima facie case of infringement.

Third, copyright law historically had not needed to deal with competition and aftermarket issues. As desirable as copyrightable material has been, it has not been necessary to engage in functional activities. Moreover, books, music, and movies do not control the operation of devices or render them incompatible. Software, in contrast, often plays an essential, functional role. And a manufacturer can use it to force consumers to purchase additional products.

The patent system, which targets useful articles, had long dealt with such competition-related issues. It had recognized defenses of misuse and exhaustion that prevented patentees from stifling competition and extending control beyond the scope of their patent. Copyright law, in more recently entering the competition realm, did not have the benefit of such developed doctrines.

The copyrightability of software also created a potential conflict between copyright and antitrust principles. As the most functional type of copyrightable subject matter, software threatens the most dangerous market effects. Reverse engineering is the primary antidote to software's anticompetitive potential. But the copy made by a programmer in the decompilation process could be treated

---

50. 17 U.S.C. § 102(b).
51. *Sega Enterprises Ltd. v. Accolade, Inc.*, 977 F.2d 1510, 1524 (9th Cir. 1992).
52. *Id.*
53. IEEE Brief, at 5.

as infringing activity. How would courts treat reverse engineering? Into this unexamined issue stepped the *Sega* and *Connectix* courts.

Copyright Law and Reverse Engineering

The case of *Sega Enterprises Ltd. v. Accolade, Inc.* involved video game systems. Unlike software writers for personal computers, who write for others' hardware and operating systems, many video game firms use closed systems. They make the hardware platform, program the operating system, and write (or license to developers) the game software.[54]

In the 1990s, Sega introduced the Genesis system and sold licenses to game developers on the condition that the games would not be available on other platforms (such as Nintendo). Accolade, an independent developer, objected to this exclusivity provision and refused to sign a licensing agreement.

In seeking to make video games compatible with the Sega Genesis console, Accolade reverse engineered Sega's game programs. It bought a console and three Sega game cartridges, and used a decompiler to generate a version of the source code. It then identified common elements in the programs and determined the interface specifications for the console. Armed with this information, it was able to create its own games for the Sega system.

To engage in this activity, Accolade needed to get around protection that Sega had built into its system. Concerned about piracy, Sega had introduced a console that inspected each game cartridge for characters in certain locations in the cartridge's code—in other words, a password or lock-out code. In reverse engineering the Sega system, Accolade discovered the lock-out code. Sega sued.

The Ninth Circuit analyzed whether Accolade's reverse engineering constituted copyright infringement. The court found that the defendant's creation of files and printouts of disassembled code constituted a type of intermediate copying that infringed Sega's exclusive right of reproduction.[55] The court then analyzed whether the fair use defense applied to this activity. It relied on the standard fair-use factors in analyzing this question:

(1) The purpose and character of the use, including whether such use is of a commercial nature or is for nonprofit educational purposes
(2) The nature of the copyrighted work
(3) The amount and substantiality of the portion used in relation to the copyrighted work as a whole
(4) The effect of the use upon the potential market for or value of the copyrighted work.[56]

---

54. 977 F.2d 1510, 1514 (9th Cir. 1992); *see generally* Samuelson & Scotchmer, at 1618. The facts are taken from the *Sega* opinion. *See* 977 F.2d at 1514–16.

55. *Id.* at 1518.

56. 17 U.S.C. § 107.

Applying the first factor, the court found that even though Accolade's ultimate purpose was commercial, it copied the software only to discern unprotected, functional elements and only because it could not otherwise connect with the console. Moreover, in increasing the array of independently designed video game programs, Accolade contributed to the "growth in creative expression . . . that the Copyright Act was intended to promote."[57]

The second factor, the nature of the copyrighted work, also favored Accolade because Sega's games "contain unprotected aspects that cannot be examined without copying."

The only factor favoring Sega was the third, the portion of the copyrighted work used. Accolade disassembled the entire program.

The fourth factor, the effect on the market, favored Accolade because customers typically purchased more than one game. The court also explained that "an attempt to monopolize the market by making it impossible for others to compete" contravened copyright's goal of promoting creative expression and could not form the basis for denying fair use.

The court concluded that Accolade's reverse engineering constituted fair use that absolved it from liability for copying Sega's programs. When software protection had migrated from trade secret to copyright, the question was whether reverse engineering would follow. *Sega* emphatically answered that question in the affirmative by finding a new home in the fair use defense. The court not only located support in most of the fair use factors but also linked the activity to essential policy goals of the copyright system.

Sega had a significant effect on subsequent cases.[58] Perhaps the most important such case was *Sony Computer Entertainment v. Connectix Corporation*, in which the Ninth Circuit again upheld reverse engineering.[59]

Sony produced a PlayStation console, a small computer with hand controls that connected to a television and played games inserted into the PlayStation. Sony owned a copyright on the basic input-output system (BIOS), the software program that operated its PlayStation.

Connectix made and sold a software program called Virtual Game Station. The purpose of the software was "to emulate on a regular computer the functioning of the Sony PlayStation console." By doing so, computer owners could play Sony PlayStation games on PC and Macintosh computers. In creating the Virtual Game Station, Connectix engaged in reverse engineering and "repeatedly copied Sony's copyrighted BIOS" to ascertain the operation of Sony PlayStation.

Connectix's activity threatened a more significant market effect than Accolade's copying of Sega's games. Accolade's games competed with, but did

---

57. The court's fair-use analysis appears at 977 F.2d at 1522–28.

58. Samuelson & Scotchmer, at 1612.

59. 203 F.3d 596 (9th Cir. 2000). The facts are taken from the *Connectix* opinion. See *id.* at 598.

not displace, Sega's games. Connectix's emulator, in contrast, had no purpose other than to mimic a PlayStation.

The Ninth Circuit nonetheless found for Connectix. In doing so, it relaxed the first and fourth fair use factors even more than *Sega* had. The court was assisted in this endeavor by the Supreme Court's intervening 1994 decision in *Campbell v. Acuff-Rose Music, Inc.* that offered broad fair use protection to commercial uses as long as the resulting product was transformative.[60]

The court found that Connectix's Virtual Game Station was transformative in creating a "wholly new product" that allowed Sony PlayStation games to be played in the different setting of personal computers. The court discerned an "expressive element" in Connectix's software in the "organization and structure of the object code that runs the computer."

Even more striking, the court found that Sony's loss of console sales and profits did not demonstrate an adverse market effect under the fourth fair use factor. It reached this result by emphasizing the transformative nature of Connectix's product and concluding that because it "does not merely supplant the PlayStation console," Virtual Game Station is "a legitimate competitor in the market for platforms on which Sony and Sony-licensed games can be played." The court thus dismissed Sony's economic loss and denied its attempt to "seek[ ] control over the market for devices" that play Sony games.[61]

The overall effect of *Sega* and *Connectix* was to uphold the continuing legitimacy and need for reverse engineering in a world in which software was copyrighted. Moreover, the opinions mirrored treatment outside the United States. Reverse engineering had received a specific exemption in the 1991 European Union Software Directive, which has been implemented in most of the member states of the European Union.[62] In addition, nations including Australia, Hong Kong, India, Singapore, and the Philippines amended their copyright systems in the 1990s to allow software reverse engineering.[63]

After *Sega* and *Connectix*, software developers could not prohibit reverse engineering, so they shifted their focus from legal to technological measures protecting their works.

---

60. 510 U.S. 569 (1994). The court's conclusions appear at 203 F.3d at 606–07.

61. *See also* James Surowiecki, *Games People Play*, THE NEW YORKER, at 36, May 7, 2001 ("Sony loses money on every PlayStation 2 it makes.").

62. Council Directive 91/250/EEC, *On the Legal Protection of Computer Programs*, arts. 5 and 6, 1991 O.J. (L 122) 42; JONATHAN BAND & MASANOBU KATOH, INTERFACES ON TRIAL 258–62 (1995).

63. Copyright Amendment (Computer Programs) Bill, 1999 (Austl.); Ord. No. 92 (1997) (H.K.); Act 49 (1999) (India); Republic Act 8293 (1996) (Phil.); Copyright (Amendment) Bill (1998) (Sing.).

EARLY COPY PROTECTION EFFORTS

In the 1980s, the software industry began to experiment with forms of copy protection such as those (1) preventing users from copying from the installation floppy disks more than once by using hidden files and (2) requiring users to supply evidence that they had bought the software, for example, by supplying a passphrase appearing in the owner's manual. These measures were eventually hacked as utilities unhid files, and bulletin boards collected passphrases.[64]

By the mid-1980s, the personal computer software industry had abandoned copy protection. Not only was the technology easily defeated and the legal remedies insufficient, but even worse, consumers hated it.[65] Telling paying customers that they could not reinstall their software does not make a good business plan, especially after the customer has just suffered a hard drive failure. Software makers thus enticed consumers to buy their products by including additional materials with the software that were less easily reproduced such as large, detailed user manuals.

THE ENTERTAINMENT INDUSTRY AND DIGITAL RIGHTS MANAGEMENT

The inability of the software and videogame industries to stop reverse engineering and the illicit copying of software was a cautionary tale to another industry that was becoming more involved with digital distribution: the entertainment industry.

This industry saw that the future of entertainment was digital and online. The compact disc (CD), first manufactured in 1982, had become a household staple, demonstrating the superiority of digital music.[66] By the mid-1990s, nearly 100 million IBM-compatible personal computers had been sold in the

---

64. Roger Nichols, *Copy Protection*, June 2001, www.rogernichols.com/EQ/EQ_2001_05. html; Power Technology, *Software and Media Copy Protection Backgrounder*, http://www. power-t.com/copy_protect.html; Alan Zisman, *Copy Protection Still a Hot Topic* (Feb. 2000), www.zisman.ca/Articles/2000/Copy_protect.html.

65. *See* Barbara Cohen, *A Proposed Regime for Copyright Protection on the Internet*, 22 BROOKLYN J. INT'L L. 401, 411 (1996) (users believed that protection measures "interfered with legitimate use of the software" and "complained of the time and complexity" involved in dealing with the measures); Julie E. Cohen, *Lochner in Cyberspace: The New Economic Orthodoxy of "Rights Management,"* 97 MICH. L. REV. 462, 523–24 (1998) (noting the "inconvenience and sheer frustration" suffered by consumers, especially corporate and governmental consumers of software products).

66. Philips, *Philips Celebrates 25th Anniversary of the Compact Disc*, Aug. 16, 2007, http://origin.newscenter.philips.com/about/news/press/20070816_25th_anniversary_ cd.page.

United States.[67] At the same time, more consumers were navigating their way online through Internet service providers such as America Online (which, due to a 15-fold increase in 3 years, reached 3 million subscribers in 1995).[68]

Before the Napster tidal wave that began in 1999, content companies were considering online distribution business models. The profit potential was enormous, but as the software industry had witnessed, so was the potential for rampant illegal copying. Any of millions of computers was capable of committing significant copyright infringement by generating an unlimited number of perfect copies of any song or movie. Although the great "digital convergence" was coming, no content owner would put its wares on the Web unless it had effective legal and technological tools to deter this infringement.

But those tools, again, did not exist. Sega and Connectix provided legal protection for reverse engineering. The Supreme Court's 1984 decision in Sony Corporation of America v. Universal City Studios that a defendant could avoid liability for contributory infringement by offering a substantial noninfringing use protected the reverse engineers themselves (who created backup copies of legitimately acquired programs).[69] And every copy protection measure used by the software industry had been circumvented.

What the entertainment industry needed before charging headlong onto the Internet were revolutionary changes in both technology and the law. Indeed, a revolution was occurring in the world of protection technology. Crude passwords, hidden files, and key disks gave way to sophisticated encryption software using complex mathematical processes and long numbers or *keys* to scramble files. To play these files, users needed special software that possessed the complementary equations and keys to unscramble the files. Moreover, owners could dynamically update these systems over the Internet.

On paper, then, systems protected by *technological protection measures* (TPMs) looked like they would succeed where copy protection had failed, providing copyright owners with the holy grail of a technological self-help measure offering complete protection.[70] The entertainment industry nonetheless was not content to rely on technology alone. It wanted airtight legal protection for its TPMs. As Sony and Sega had showed, the courts were unwilling to provide this protection. So the industry lobbied for legislation that prohibited reverse engineering. In 1998, it got its wish as Congress made the anticircumvention of TPMs a crime.

---

67. Computer Industry Almanac, Inc., *25-Year PC Anniversary Statistics*, Aug. 14, 2006, http://www.c-i-a.com/pr0806.htm.

68. *America Online!*, WIRED.COM, Sept. 1995, http://www.wired.com/wired/archive/3.09/aol.html. Five years later, by the year 2000, AOL would reach 23 million subscribers. AOL Time Warner, Inc., *History of America Online*, http://ecommerce.hostip.info/pages/48/Aol-Time-Warner-Inc-HISTORY-AMERICA-ONLINE.html.

69. 464 U.S. 417 (1984).

70. TPMs are often used in digital rights management (DRM) schemes.

THE DIGITAL MILLENNIUM COPYRIGHT ACT

Introduction

The Digital Millennium Copyright Act (DMCA), enacted in 1998, consists of five titles addressing topics as wide-ranging as boat hull designs, copyright management information, and online service provider liability.[71] As discussed above, the entertainment industry was instrumental in the enactment of the DMCA.

The Act also was justified as bringing the United States into compliance with the World Intellectual Property Organization (WIPO) Copyright Treaty, which establishes global norms for applying copyright law in the digital environment.[72] U.S. law, however, already was in compliance with nearly all the treaty provisions. In particular, the doctrine of contributory infringement offered "adequate legal protection and effective legal remedies" against the circumvention of technological controls.[73] Because of the overlap between the treaty obligations and U.S. law, the Clinton administration initially considered sending the treaty to the Senate without implementing legislation.[74] Nonetheless, on October 28, 1998, the DMCA became law.

Text

The section of the statute that is most relevant for our purposes is Section 1201, which prohibits the circumvention of technological measures. The statute's importance, unfortunately, is not matched by its readability.

The first provision covers *acts* of circumvention.[75] Section 1201(a)(1)(A), known as the *access ban*, prohibits the "circumvent[ion of] a technological measure that effectively controls access to a work protected under this title."[76]

---

71. Pub. L. No. 105-304, 112 Stat. 2860 (1998), *codified at* 17 U.S.C. § 1201.

72. World Intellectual Property Organization: Copyright Treaty, Dec. 20, 1996, 36 I.L.M. 65 (1997) [hereinafter WIPO Copyright Treaty]; *see generally* Pamela Samuelson, *Intellectual Property and the Digital Economy: Why the Anti-Circumvention Regulations Need To Be Revised*, 14 BERKELEY TECH. L.J. 519, 521 (1999) [hereinafter Samuelson, *Anti-Circumvention*]. The Act also implemented the WIPO Performances and Phonograms Treaty of 1996.

73. WIPO Copyright Treaty, art. 11; *see generally* Burk, at 1103. For a discussion of how the selected standard was weaker than an earlier version that had specifically prohibited the "importation, manufacture, or distribution of protection-defeating devices," see Pamela Samuelson, *The U.S. Digital Agenda at WIPO*, 37 VA. J. INT'L L. 369, 409–15 (1997).

74. Samuelson, *Anti-Circumvention*, at 530; *Clinton Administration is Undecided on Implementing Steps for WIPO Treaties*, 53 PAT. TRADEMARK & COPYRIGHT J. 241, 242 (1997).

75. *See generally* EFF, *Unintended Consequences*; Samuelson, *Anti-Circumvention*, at 534–35.

76. 17 U.S.C. § 1201(a)(1)(A).

To circumvent means to "descramble a scrambled work, . . . decrypt an encrypted work, or otherwise . . . avoid, bypass, remove, deactivate, or impair a techno-logical measure, without the authority of the copyright owner."[77] And while the statute prohibits the circumvention of measures controlling *access* to a work, it does not punish the circumvention of measures controlling *use* of a work. Such a prohibition was not needed, according to the Act's drafters, since "[t]he copyright law has long forbidden copyright infringements."[78]

The second set of provisions covers the *distribution of tools* used for circum-vention. The first of these provisions, Section 1201(a)(2), prohibits the trafficking in circumvention tools that can be used to access protected works. The section provides that "[n]o person shall manufacture, import, offer to the public, provide, or otherwise traffic in any technology, product, service, device, component, or part thereof" if it

(1) is primarily designed or produced for the purpose of circumventing,

(2) has only limited commercially significant purpose or use other than to circumvent, or

(3) is marketed by that person or another acting in concert with that person with that person's knowledge for use in circumventing the technological measure.[79]

The other trafficking measure, Section 1201(b)(1), prohibits the same range of activity but in the context of use of a work rather than access to the work. In other words, one cannot distribute tools that would allow others to circumvent measures controlling use of a work. A user who herself is able to circumvent a measure controlling use of a lawfully obtained work does not violate the Act, but trafficking tools that allow others to avoid such measures violates Section 1201(b)(1).

The DMCA offers exceptions. Section 1201(c) states that the Act will not affect "rights, remedies, limitations, or defenses to copyright infringement, including fair use."[80] It also creates exemptions to the access ban for encryption research, nonprofit institutions, law enforcement and government, the protection of personal information, and security testing.[81] In general, the access ban is subject to a greater range of exceptions than the trafficking bans.

---

77. 17 U.S.C. § 1201(a)(3)(A).

78. S. REP. No. 105-190, at 12 (1998).

79. 17 U.S.C. § 1201(a)(2).

80. 17 U.S.C. § 1201(c).

81. 17 U.S.C. § 1201(d) (nonprofit institutions), § 1201(e) (law enforcement and govern-ment), § 1201(g) (encryption research), § 1201(i) (protection of personal information), § 1201(j) (security testing).

Section 1201(f)(1) provides the most relevant exemption, covering interoperability. It allows the circumvention of a technological measure where

- the program being reverse engineered was lawfully acquired,
- there is no other way to obtain access to the information,
- the reverse engineering process itself does not constitute copyright infringement, and
- the reverse engineering is undertaken "for the sole purpose of identifying and analyzing those elements of the program that are necessary to achieve interoperability of an independently created computer program with other programs."[82]

The statute defines interoperability as "the ability of computer programs to exchange information, and of such programs mutually to use the information which has been exchanged."[83]

Global Treatment

Given the global interest in complying with the WIPO treaty, it is not surprising that other nations have implemented anticircumvention legislation similar to the DMCA.[84] The EU Copyright Directive, like the DMCA's access control measures, requires Member States to "provide adequate legal protection against the circumvention of any effective technological measures."[85] And similar to the DMCA's trafficking measures, the Directive urges Member States to "provide adequate legal protection" for devices, products, and services that are "marketed for the purpose of circumvention of," have "only a limited commercially significant . . . use other than to circumvent," or "are primarily designed [or] produced" to "enable or facilitate the circumvention of . . . technological measures."[86]

China's copyright statute also mirrors the DMCA. One section bans the "disarm[ing], destroy[ing], or . . . circumvent[ing]" of TPMs used "to prohibit or restrict others from accessing works."[87] Another prohibits the "manufacture[ ], import[ing], [or] offer[ing] to the public" of devices for "disarming, destroying,

---

82 17 U.S.C. § 1201(f)(1).

83. 17 U.S.C. § 1201(f)(4).

84. *See generally* Digital Media Project, The Berkman Center for Internet & Society at Harvard Law School, *iTunes: How Copyright, Contract, and Technology Shape the Business of Digital Media—A Case Study*, at 37–39 (2004), http://cyber.law.harvard.edu/media/uploads/81/iTunesWhitePaper0604.pdf.

85. Council Directive 2001/29/EC, art. 6(1), 2001 O.J. (L 167) 10, 17, http://eur-lex.europa.eu/pri/en/oj/dat/2001/l_167/l_16720010622en00100019.pdf.

86. *Id.* art. 6(2).

87. Copyright Act of China, art. 80, *available at* http://www.tipo.gov.tw/eng/laws/e1-4-1an93.asp.

or circumventing" TPMs.[88] The statute provides an exemption for reverse engineering.[89]

Japan also has adopted anticircumvention legislation that punishes the sale or manufacture of devices whose "principal function" is to circumvent TPMs.[90] Unlike the DMCA, the Japanese statute does not punish the simple circumvention of a TPM but instead requires manufacture or distribution for liability.[91]

A final example that illustrates safeguards absent in the DMCA is provided by legislation that Australia enacted in 2006 after signing a free trade agreement with the United States. The legislation prohibited a party from circumventing access control TPMs. But it excluded from this ban devices that bypassed embedded computer programs—such as those in printer cartridges and garage door openers—that "restrict[ed] the use of goods (other than the work) or services in relation to the machine or device."[92]

Legislative History

In enacting the DMCA, Congress was concerned that copyright owners would not "make their works . . . available on the Internet" because of the "massive piracy" resulting from the "ease with which digital works [could] be copied and distributed worldwide virtually instantaneously."[93] The legislature thus supported owners' efforts to protect their works by making it a crime to circumvent TPMs or to distribute such technologies.[94]

In strengthening the tools possessed by copyright owners, Congress sought to promote "a thriving electronic marketplace for copyrighted works on the Internet."[95] The DMCA would encourage the availability of the "movies, music,

---

88. *Id.*

89. *Id.* ¶ 8.

90. Copyright Law of Japan, art. 120bis (i, ii), *available at* http://www.cric.or.jp/cric_e/clj/cl8.html.

91. Brian Bolinger, *Focusing on Infringement: Why Limitations on Decryption Technology Are Not the Solution to Policing Copyright*, 52 CASE W. RES. L. REV. 1091, 1108 (2002). Each of the regimes is more complicated than the version described in the text. For example, the range of activity protected includes categories such as (in the case of the EU Copyright Directive) "manufacture, import, distribution, sale, rental, advertisement . . ., or possession for commercial purposes." Council Directive 2001/29/EC, art. 6(2).

92. Copyright Amendment Act of 2006, No. 158, Schedule 12, Part 1, sections 1, 3, 5, http://www.comlaw.gov.au/ComLaw/Legislation/Act1.nsf/0/E53C3691BD9BAA0ACA2 57307001B2EC7/$file/1582006.pdf; Gwen Hinze, *Brave New World Ten Years Later: Reviewing the Impact of Policy Choices in the Implementation of the WIPO Internet Treaties' Technological Protection Measure Provisions*, 59 CASE W. RES. L. REV. __ (forthcoming 2009).

93. S. REP. NO. 105-190, at 8 (1998).

94. *Universal Studios, Inc. v. Corley*, 273 F.3d 429, 435 (2d Cir. 2001).

95. H.R. REP. NO. 105-551, pt. 1, at 9–10 (1998). For a general discussion of the legislative history, see Consumers Union Brief, at 14–19.

software, and literary works that are the fruit of American creative genius."[96] It also would preserve the growth of the copyright industries, which "contribute more to the U.S. economy and employ more workers than any single manufacturing sector."[97]

The legislature nonetheless worried about potential abuse of the anticircumvention and antitrafficking provisions. The House Commerce Committee chairman, Tom Bliley (D-Va.), made clear that, because of "the unfortunate proclivity of some in our society to file spurious lawsuits," the provisions had "very limited scope."[98]

Both the House and Senate Judiciary Committees sought to ensure that the interoperability exception would foster "competition and innovation" in the software industry.[99] The Conference Committee, in reconciling differences between the House and Senate bills, anticipated that "makers of computers, consumer electronics, and telecommunications devices" would help content owners develop protection measures.[100]

Further demonstrating support for the interoperability exception, the Senate Judiciary Committee explained that it "allow[ed] legitimate software developers to continue engaging in certain activities for the purpose of achieving interoperability to the extent [previously] permitted by law."[101] "[M]anufacturers, consumers, retailers, and professional servicers," Rep. Bliley stated, "should not be prevented from correcting an interoperability problem . . . resulting from a technological measure. . . ."[102] In fact, the Register of Copyrights rejected a request for a specific exemption to the DMCA on the grounds that the statute's interoperability exception was "a far more robust remedy for insuring competitive activity in the marketplace."[103]

Despite the legislature's intent not to modify the case law, the DMCA interoperability exception narrowed the prevailing conception of reverse engineering. In contrast to *Sega* and *Connectix*, which had treated reverse engineering as presumptively lawful, the DMCA treated the activity as presumptively illegal. It authorized reverse engineering for the purpose of producing only interoperable

---

96. S. REP. No. 105-190, at 8 (1998).

97. *Id.* at 10.

98. 144 CONG. REC. E2136 (1998).

99. S. REP. No. 105-190, at 13; H. COMM. ON THE JUDICIARY, 105TH CONG., SECTION-BY-SECTION ANALYSIS OF H.R. 2281, at 14 (Comm. Print 1998).

100. H. R. REP. No. 105-796, at 64–65 (1998).

101. S. REP. No. 105-190, at 13.

102. 144 CONG. REC. E2138

103. Marybeth Peters, *Register of Copyrights, Recommendation of the Register of Copyrights in RM 2002-4,* at 178 (Oct. 27, 2003), http://www.copyright.gov/1201/docs/registers-recommendation.pdf.

software, not hardware devices, network protocols, or data.[104] And even the island provided by the interoperability exception appeared in a sea of prohibitions banning reverse engineering.

Nearly a decade after the DMCA's enactment, Bruce Lehman, an architect of the Act and former Commissioner of Patents and Trademarks, acknowledged that Clinton administration policies related to the DMCA "didn't work out very well" and that its "attempts at copyright control" were not successful.[105] Lehman also explained that the DMCA "was crafted to protect copyright owners' rights, not people that make machines or . . . the machine itself."[106]

Accidental Aftermarket Protection

Congress was aware that, in granting such strong legal protections to technological measures, the DMCA would encourage software writers to use the measures not only to defend their code against pirates but also to defend their markets against competitors. Unfortunately, however, the interoperability exception it envisioned providing relief was far too limited to do so.

The problem is that the DMCA's language covers more than just online movies and music. The statute encompasses any measure that protects any work "protected by this title"—in other words, any copyrighted work. Books, movies, and music are copyrightable, but so is software. And the software protected might not even be the product desired by the consumer. Instead, it could be a peripheral appendage to a desired, functional product. Despite its oblique relationship to the works Congress sought to protect, such software provides the hook allowing manufacturers to employ the DMCA.

And such a hook allows device makers to exercise a vise-like grip on their markets and aftermarkets, forcing consumers to purchase supplemental products. This power could be applied to the universe of household items that include software.

For a manufacturer with market power and a desire to control its aftermarket, the DMCA was a dream come true. Before the statute, any attempt to create an aftermarket monopoly via incompatible software and security measures would be defeated by competitors' lawful reverse engineering. But now the tables were turned. Even competitors believing they had a legitimate defense would likely be deterred by protracted litigation and disputed issues of circumvention and interoperability.

The DMCA's dangers were revealed in the first cases interpreting the statute, which involved makers of devices with embedded peripheral software.

---

104. Burk, at 1139; Tim Lee, *Reverse Engineering and Innovation: Some Examples*, at 3, June 21, 2006, http://www.techliberation.com/archives/039730.php#more.

105. Michael Geist, *DMCA Architect Acknowledges Need For A New Approach*, Mar. 23, 2007, http://www.michaelgeist.ca/content/view/1826/125/.

106. Eriq Gardner, *Original Intent*, LAW.COM, at 2, Oct. 25, 2004.

Because litigated disputes represent the tip of the iceberg, there most likely have been numerous other instances expanding the statute in similar contexts.[107] But the litigated cases themselves present significant cause for concern. And even if courts in several of the cases ultimately rejected a plaintiff's overreaching DMCA claim, much of the courts' reasoning would allow modestly revised claims to survive.

LEXMARK V. STATIC CONTROL COMPONENTS

The first case was *Lexmark International, Inc. v. Static Control Components, Inc.*[108] Lexmark made laser and inkjet printers and toner cartridges for the printers. At the time of the litigation, Lexmark was the second largest manufacturer of laser printers.

Two computer programs were at issue in the case. Lexmark's Toner Loading Program (TLP), located on a microchip in the toner cartridges, measured the amount of toner remaining in the cartridge. And its Printer Engine Program (PEP), located in the printer, controlled functions such as paper feed and movement.

On each Lexmark toner cartridge was a microchip that contained the TLP and secret cryptographic keys and equations. When the printer was turned on or the printer door was opened or closed, the PEP established communication with the cartridge microchip and performed several routines. The failure of any of these routines caused the PEP to block printing.

Lexmark asserted that these routines were necessary to enforce the company's "prebate" toner cartridge program. Customers who bought discounted prebate cartridges from Lexmark agreed not to refill the cartridge with third-party vendors, but to return the empty cartridges to Lexmark for refilling. A third-party refiller that received a cartridge would not know the secret changes that Lexmark performed to the software upon refilling and thus could not offer a cartridge that would comply with the three routines.

Defendant Static Control Components (SCC) made a cartridge microchip that bypassed each of these measures and sold that chip to third-party cartridge refillers. Static Control Components was able to do this only by copying Lexmark's TLP.

Lexmark sued SCC, claiming that its bypassing of the authentication sequence circumvented technological measures that protected access to two copyrighted works—the PEP and TLP programs—and thus violated Section 1201(a)(1)(A) of the DMCA. The district court granted Lexmark's request for a preliminary injunction, finding that SCC circumvented measures controlling access to the

---

107. *See* Burk, at 1113 ("court action is always the exception, rather than the rule, in legal disputes").

108. 387 F.3d 522, 529 (6th Cir. 2004). The facts of the case are taken from the *Lexmark* opinion. *See id.* at 529–31.

PEP and TLP programs and that the reverse engineering exception did not apply.[109] The Sixth Circuit reversed.

On the PEP claim, the appellate court found that the Lexmark authentication sequence did not control access to the PEP because the PEP code was not encrypted. Therefore, anyone who purchased a Lexmark printer could easily read the PEP code from the printer's memory.

On the TLP claim, the court concluded that because the TLP was not copyrightable, the DMCA did not apply. In the alternative, it found that SCC's chip did not provide access to the TLP but replaced it entirely.[110]

Although the DMCA claim did not succeed in *Lexmark*, the decision rested precariously on the specific facts of the case. In a concurring opinion, Judge Gilbert Merritt lamented the narrow reach of the majority opinion. He asserted that future DMCA plaintiffs could achieve success simply by "tweaking the facts," for example, by creating a more complex and creative TLP or cutting off other access to the PEP.[111]

Judge Merritt also contrasted Lexmark's activity with the DMCA's purpose "to prohibit the pirating of copyright-protected works such as movies, music, and computer programs." He noted that Lexmark's interpretation of the statute could allow manufacturers to "create monopolies for replacement parts simply by using similar, but more creative, lock-out codes." And he emphasized that Congress "did not intend to allow the DMCA to be used offensively" but sought only "to reach those who circumvented protective measures 'for the purpose' of pirating works protected by the copyright statute."[112]

CHAMBERLAIN V. SKYLINK

Software embedded in functional objects also appeared in the second case, *Chamberlain Group, Inc. v. Skylink Technologies, Inc.* Chamberlain made garage-door opener (GDO) systems, which consisted of a garage door opening device inside a garage and a handheld portable transmitter. The opening device consisted of a receiver with signal processing software and a motor to open or close the garage door. To open or close the door, a user needed to activate the transmitter, which sent a radio frequency signal to the receiver on the opening device. Once the opener received a recognized signal, the signal processing software instructed the motor to open or close the door.[113]

---

109. *Lexmark Int'l, Inc. v. Static Control Components, Inc.*, 253 F. Supp. 2d 943, 966–71 (E.D. Ky. 2003), *rev'd*, 387 F.3d 522, 529 (6th Cir. 2004).

110. *Lexmark*, 387 F.3d at 544, 546, 549–50.

111. *Id.* at 551–52.

112. *Id.* at 552.

113. 381 F.3d 1178 (Fed. Cir. 2004). The facts are taken from the opinion. *See id.* at 1183.

Homeowners who desired replacement transmitters historically could purchase universal transmitters in the aftermarket that could be programmed to inter-operate with any GDO system. Although Chamberlain and Skylink had distributed such universal transmitters, Chamberlain decided to create a new line, the "Security+" GDO, that utilized a new "rolling code" computer program that continuously changed the code that opened the door. Competitor Skylink reverse engineered the rolling code system and introduced the Model 39 remote opener that worked with the Security+ GDO.

Chamberlain sued Skylink on multiple theories, including a section 1201(a)(2) trafficking claim. It claimed that the defendant circumvented rolling codes, which were "technological measures" that "control[led] access" to computer programs.[114] The district court, however, granted Skylink's motion for summary judgment on the DMCA claim, and the Federal Circuit affirmed.

The appellate court held that the DMCA required a plaintiff to demonstrate the unauthorized nature of a defendant's access. But because of longstanding industry expectations and because the copyright laws authorized Chamberlain's customers to use the software in the GDOs they had purchased, this element was not satisfied. Since Chamberlain had authorized its users, its Section 1201(a)(2) trafficking claim failed.[115]

The court addressed the dangers threatened by the DMCA. It noted that the plaintiff's interpretation of the Act "would allow any manufacturer of any product to add a single copyrighted sentence or software fragment to its product, wrap the copyrighted material in a trivial 'encryption' scheme, and thereby gain the right to restrict consumers' rights to use its products in conjunction with competing products." Such a construction "would allow virtually any company to attempt to leverage its sales into aftermarket monopolies—a practice that both the antitrust laws and the doctrine of copyright misuse normally prohibit."[116]

Despite this strong language, the *Chamberlain* holding was based on circumstances that could easily have varied. Different expectations about authorized access, for example, could have led to a far different outcome.

DAVIDSON ASSOCIATES V. JUNG

The final example is offered by *Davidson Associates v. Jung*, in which the courts applied the DMCA's interoperability defense in the context of Internet multi-player video games. The district and appellate courts issued decisions that fundamentally narrowed the defense.[117]

---

114. *Id.* at 1185.

115. *Id.* at 1193, 1204.

116. *Id.* at 1201.

117. *Davidson & Assocs. v. Internet Gateway*, 334 F. Supp. 2d 1164 (E.D. Mo. 2004). The facts are taken from the opinion. *See id.* at 1168–74.

Davidson Associates, commonly known as Blizzard Entertainment, was the maker of popular computer-based video games such as Diablo, StarCraft, and WarCraft. Every copy of each of its games (except Diablo) came with a CD Key, or unique combination of letters and numbers that a user entered when installing the software.

Customers who desired to play against others could do so via modems or local area networks, but those methods were limited. To make multiperson play easier, Blizzard introduced Battle.net, an online service available to purchasers of its computer games. The service allowed game owners to play against each other, set up private chat channels, keep records of wins and losses, and participate in tournament play.

Every Battle.net session began with an encrypted secret handshake in which the user's Blizzard game software transmitted to Battle.net the CD Key used during installation. If that CD Key was invalid or in use by another player logged onto the service, the session would terminate.

By 2004, Battle.net had 12 million users who were spending more than 2 million hours a day online. The service, however, suffered drawbacks including frequent crashes, server slowdowns, cheating players, and frequent profanity.[118]

A group of volunteers sought to address these challenges by writing their own version of Battle.net called BnetD. To do so, they needed to reverse engineer Blizzard's proprietary communications protocol (or set of rules for communicating) so BnetD could work with Blizzard games. In doing so, they breached Battle.net's Terms of Use, which prohibited reverse engineering. Because the defendants could not ascertain Blizzard's CD Key algorithm, they offered to enact a version of the CD Key, but Blizzard rejected this overture.[119] The defendants therefore programmed the service to accept all CD Keys supplied by users.

The BnetD team posted its software on the Internet where anyone could download it for free and set up their own game server. The software was available under the GNU[120] General Public License (GPL), which allows users to modify the source code.[121]

The district court found that BnetD violated the DMCA by circumventing the secret handshake between Blizzard games and Battle.net that "effectively controlled access to Battle.net mode."[122] It rejected the interoperability defense on

---

118. Howard Wen, *Battle.net Goes to War*, at 4, Apr. 18, 2002, http://www.salon.com/tech/feature/2002/04/18/bnetd/print.html.

119. David Becker, *Group Backs ISP in Online Gaming Dispute*, CNETNEWS.COM, Apr. 5, 2002, http://www.news.com/2100-1040-858414.html.

120. GNU is an acronym for "GNU's Not [the operating system] Unix." *GNU Operating System*, 2008, http://www.gnu.org/.

121. Kenneth Hwang, *Blizzard Versus Bnetd: A Looming Ice Age for Free Software Development?*, 92 CORNELL L. REV. 1043, 1053 (2007).

122. The court's analysis appears at *Davidson*, 334 F. Supp.2d at 1184–86.

several questionable grounds.[123] It found that the defense "only exempts those who obtained permission to circumvent the technological measure." This reasoning, however, limits the defense to settings in which, because a defendant with permission does not violate the Act, it is not even needed. And it held that the defendants' actions in allowing users to circumvent Blizzard's security measure "constituted more than enabling interoperability" and were not entitled to the defense. This analysis would effectively eliminate the defense since any program achieving interoperability would need to bypass the protection measure.[124]

The court also found that the defendants violated the trafficking provision of Section 1201(a)(2). Similar to its reasoning on the access restrictions, the court held that the BnetD emulator did not have a "sole purpose" of "enabl[ing] interoperability" because the defendants sought to "avoid the anticircumvention restrictions of the game and . . . the restricted access to Battle.net."

The Eighth Circuit affirmed the district court's decision in an even more opaque decision. The appellate court found a violation of the DMCA's access provisions by comparing the facts to those in *Lexmark* and holding that Battle.net codes "were not accessible by simply purchasing a Blizzard game or logging onto Battle.net."[125]

The court also concluded that the BnetD.org emulator "had limited commercial purpose because its sole purpose was to avoid the limitations of Battle.net." The defendants, however, wished to bypass Battle.net for a reason. They endeavored to improve users' gaming experience by avoiding the crashes, profanity, and cheating that plagued Battle.net. In fact, the defendants offered a model that promised to *enhance* Blizzard's profits. Blizzard made money from the games it sold, whether they were used on Battle.net or any other Web site.[126] The *improved* setting BnetD offered for online multiplayer games would tend to encourage additional sales of Blizzard games.[127]

---

123. For a persuasive critique of the opinion, see Paul J. Neufeld, *Circumventing the Competition: The Reverse Engineering Exemption in DMCA § 1201*, 26 REV. LITIG. 525, 537–40, 549–50 (2007).

124. The court also found that BnetD was a functional alternative to Battle.net, and thus did not satisfy the exception's requirement of an "independently created program" (thus preventing the exception from covering any competitive products). And without ever defining the copyrighted work protected by Blizzard's security measure, the court concluded that the defendants' activities "extended into the realm of copyright infringement."

125. *Davidson & Assocs. v. Jung*, 422 F.3d 630, 641–42 (8th Cir. 2005).

126. Wen, at 4.

127. Of course, this assumes that the games were not pirated. Use of a version of the CD key (as BnetD offered Blizzard) would reduce this concern by allowing only those who had purchased Blizzard games to use the BnetD servers.

THE AIBO INCIDENT

Nor was *Davidson* the only setting in which the DMCA was invoked to challenge the activity of programmers who sought to improve a product. Sony's programmable robotic dog known as "Aibo" (which means "companion" or "partner" in Japanese) provided an analogous example.[128] These dogs engaged in various activities, expressed emotion, and had unique personalities that were shaped by interactions with their owners. Such characteristics originated in preprogrammed sets of instructions and memory sticks that Aibo owners could purchase from Sony.[129] A hobbyist known as Aibopet made numerous enhancements to his dog, allowing a user "to see . . . what Aibo sees," develop custom dance moves, and discern its "vital signs, emotions, mood, [and] voice recognition."[130]

The hobbyist distributed tools that allowed Aibo owners to make similar modifications to their dogs, but only on the condition that they had already purchased the relevant memory stick from Sony. So, for example, if an owner wanted to implement Aibopet's dancing dog routine, she would first need to purchase Sony's dancing program.

Even though Sony designed the dogs so they could be programmed, and the tools could only be used by those who had lawfully purchased the dog, Sony claimed a violation of the DMCA because Aibopet circumvented the software's technical protections.[131] The Aibo community rebelled against Sony, with hundreds "vowing to never again buy Sony."[132] In response to this uproar, Sony permitted the hobbyist to repost programs and released a development kit designed to "actively promote [open] architecture for entertainment robots by highlighting its ability to modify the robots' functionality."[133] The incident nonetheless offers another example of the use of the DMCA to block improvements.[134]

THE TRIENNIAL EXEMPTION REVIEW

The drafters of the DMCA built in a review process that allowed the Register of Copyrights to issue temporary exemptions to the Act's coverage every three years. The House Commerce Committee explained that such a process was

---

128. David Labrador, *Teaching Robot Dogs New Tricks*, SCI. AM., at 3, Jan. 21, 2002, http://www.sciam.com/article.cfm?articleID=0005510C-EABD-1CD6-B4A8809 EC588EEDF.

129. James Middleton, *Sony Plays Ball with Aibo Hackers*, May 7, 2002, http://www.vnunet.com/news/1131538.

130. Farhad Manjoo, *Aibo Owners Biting Mad at Sony*, WIRED NEWS, Nov. 2, 2001, http://www.wired.com/news/business/0,1367,48088,00.html.

131. Burk, at 1113.

132. Manjoo, *Aibo Owners Biting Mad*.

133. Middleton, *Sony Plays Ball with Aibo Hackers*.

134. EFF, *Unintended Consequences*.

needed as a "fail-safe" mechanism because "marketplace realities" could "result[ ] in less access, rather than more, to copyrighted materials that are important to education, scholarship, and other socially vital endeavors."[135]

The DMCA thus exempts from the ban "persons who are users of a copyrighted work which is in a particular class of works, if such persons are or are likely to be . . . adversely affected" by the access ban in "their ability to make noninfringing uses" of the class of works.[136] Every three years, the Register of Copyrights holds hearings in which the public can seek exemptions for certain classes of works.[137] The Register then makes her recommendations to the Librarian of Congress, who implements them. The exemptions are valid until the next triennial meeting at which time, if not restated, they lapse.

Such a review, while sounding advantageous in theory, has actually weakened the effect of exemptions. For starters, it has come at the expense of courts, which could apply a broad-ranging fair use defense after a defendant has engaged in the infringing activity. The Register of Copyrights, in contrast, can only make exemptions prospectively. In addition, the Register can consider exemptions only to the access ban, not the antitrafficking bans. As a result, the exemptions are "effectively useless" for those who cannot themselves circumvent the restrictions.[138]

This is a critical deficiency. An exemption was granted in the 2006 proceedings, for example, for programs allowing wireless phone handsets to connect to wireless phone communication networks. New Jersey teenager George Hotz received brief national fame when he unlocked Apple's iPhone, which would allow him to use any wireless network. But even if Hotz's circumvention were allowed, his distribution of the solution would not be covered by the exemption.[139]

The exemption process also has raised concern because of the Copyright Office's apparent bias in favor of copyright owners. The Office has viewed this group as "its real constituency" and, in the 1990s, began "moving firmly into the content industry's pocket." Such a position can be explained by the Office's limited budget and reliance on clients and copyright attorneys (from the "revolving door" between staff and law firms representing copyright owners). As a result of these characteristics, the Register of Copyrights "has routinely given positions advanced by the content industry her enthusiastic endorsement."[140]

---

135. H.R. Rep. No. 105-551, pt. 2, at 36 (1998).

136. 17 U.S.C. § 1201(a)(1)(B).

137. 17 U.S.C. § 1201(a)(1)(C).

138. Bill D. Herman and Oscar H. Gandy, Jr., *Catch 1201: A Legislative History and Content Analysis of the DMCA Exemption Proceedings*, 24 Cardozo Arts & Ent. L.J. 121, 124, 143–44 (2006).

139. Jennifer Granick, *Legal or Not, IPhone Hacks Might Spur Revolution*, Wired News, Aug. 28, 2007, http://www.wired.com/politics/onlinerights/commentary/circuitcourt/2007/08/circuitcourt_0829.

140. Jessica Litman, Digital Copyright 74 (2006).

In the context of the triennial review provisions, the Register, for the most part, has not vigorously implemented exemptions for consumers. She has explained that "[t]he fears of copyright owner abuse of Section 1201 have not become a reality in any significant respect."[141] The Electronic Frontier Foundation (EFF), an organization that has intervened in numerous digital rights battles and that participated in the 2000 and 2003 rulemakings, did not even participate in the 2006 proceedings, explaining that "[w]here consumer interests are concerned, the rulemaking process is simply too broken."[142]

In light of the foregoing, it should not be a surprise that the triennial review exemptions have tended to be narrow. As of 2009, a total of six classes of works are exempted from the circumvention ban[143]:

(1) The use of short portions of motion pictures on DVDs for purposes of criticism or comment

(2) Computer programs enabling wireless phone handset owners to "jailbreak," or download unapproved software applications

(3) Computer programs that allow wireless phone handsets to connect to wireless phone communication networks

(4) The good faith testing, investigation, or correction of security flaws or vulnerabilities that compromise the security of personal computers and that are created by technological protection measures controlling access to video games

(5) Computer programs protected by hardware locks (known as dongles) that are designed to prevent unauthorized software access but that, due to malfunction or damage (or becoming obsolete), prevent authorized access

(6) E-books with access controls that block the read·aloud function

None of these six categories would have an effect on the DMCA cases discussed above. Any significant and lasting changes to the statute are unlikely to come from the triennial review process. Instead, an amendment to the DMCA would have a more dramatic effect.

---

141. *Operations of the U.S. Copyright Office: Hearing Before the Subcomm. on Courts, the Internet, and Intellectual Property of the H. Comm. on the Judiciary*, 108th Cong. 9 (June 3, 2004) (statement of Marybeth Peters, Register of Copyrights), http://frwebgate.access. gpo.gov/cgi-bin/getdoc.cgi?dbname108_house_hearings&docid=f:94033.wais.pdf.

142. Fred von Lohmann, *DMCA Triennial Rulemaking: Failing Consumers Completely*, Nov. 30, 2005, http://www.eff.org/deeplinks/2005/11/dmca-triennial-rulemaking-failing-consumers-completely.

143. Letter from Marybeth Peters, Register of Copyrights, to James H. Billington, Librarian of Congress re: "*Recommendation of the Register of Copyrights in RM 2008-8*," at 1–2, June 11, 2010, http://www.copyright.gov/1201/2010/initialed-registers-recommendation-june-11-2010.pdf. At the time this book went to press, the Register had not yet implemented the 2009 exemptions.

PROPOSAL

Balance is at the core of IP. Patents and copyrights are limited in breadth and duration. Within these confines, exclusive rights are designed to encourage innovation. Outside these boundaries, competition contributes to innovation. The DMCA, in prohibiting access to elements of works not protected by IP, intrudes onto the competition baseline underlying the U.S. economy.

From the standpoint of competition and innovation, the fundamental problem with the DMCA is its overinclusive nature. Congress sought to promote "a thriving electronic marketplace for copyrighted works on the Internet" by encouraging the availability of the "movies, music, software, and literary works that are the fruit of American creative genius." In particular, the drafters aimed to target the "large-scale, unauthorized commercial reproduction and distribution of copyrighted works in competition with the legitimate copyright owner."[144]

But the statute's text applies to measures protecting *any copyrighted work*, which includes software. More specifically, it covers not only software that constitutes a consumer's desired end product (such as a video game), but also software that plays a peripheral role in a functional, unprotected end product. As a result, the statute has been stretched to cover cases such as *Lexmark*, which "none of [the drafters] had in mind."[145] Companies have seized on this accident of drafting to embed software into routine devices to eliminate competition and control aftermarkets. Further demonstrating the incongruity, the protection of copyright owners' access to embedded software might force consumers to buy aftermarket parts from it but would not "promote the development of an online market for the embedded software or any other copyrighted work."[146]

The DMCA needs to be fixed. To more faithfully implement the drafters' intent, I propose an amendment to the statute that would require a plaintiff bringing a DMCA anticircumvention claim to show that

(1) the expressive copyrightable features of a product protected by a TPM play an essential role in consumer demand for the item, and

(2) it would suffer a direct negative market effect from the challenged circumvention or distribution.

If either of these conditions is not met, DMCA liability should not apply. In other words, there should be no liability if the product that the consumer desires lacks expressive copyrightable elements or if there is no market harm from

144. Burk, at 1135.

145. Rep. Zoe Lofgren, *Edited Transcript of the David Nelson Memorial Keynote Address: A Voice from Congress on DRM*, 18 BERKELEY TECH. L.J. 495, 497 (2003).

146. Computer & Communications Industry Ass'n, *Exemption to Prohibition of Copyright Protection Systems For Access Control Technologies*, Copyright Office RM Dkt. No. 2002-4A, Mar. 10, 2003.

access or the distribution of circumvention tools. The most effective forum for the proposal is an amendment to the DMCA, which would have a more universal and consistent effect than courts' implementation on a case-by-case basis.

Competition is at the core of the DMCA. The purpose of the Act was to prohibit pirates from unlawfully accessing protected works and thereby displacing copyright owners' sales. But the drafters also recognized that the statute could be used to suppress competition in a manner harming consumers. Given the importance of competition, market-based principles could help determine the appropriate scope of the Act. I rely on these principles, as they appear in antitrust law and the fair use defense in copyright law, to flesh out my proposal.

The first insight comes from antitrust law. Market power is vital to antitrust. Firms that have market power (as indicated by an ability to increase price for a sustained period) are more likely to threaten anticompetitive harm. For that reason, a plaintiff will often need to show market power before an antitrust court imposes liability.[147]

Determining market power typically requires a court to ascertain the relevant market.[148] To do this, the court must determine the items that consumers would view as close substitutes. The presence of items to which consumers would turn within a reasonable period in response to a sustained price increase reduces the likelihood of market power.

Because it is not always apparent which items will be viewed as sufficiently close substitutes or how quickly consumption patterns will change, these determinations are complex in antitrust law. But the notion of consumer demand would be easier to apply in the context of the DMCA. For rather than determining the relationship between multiple products, it examines consumer demand for a single product. Even more promising, it could be used to cabin the Act's current overbroad reach, thereby effectuating the drafters' intentions.

In enacting the DMCA, Congress did not intend to protect works in which IP did not play a central role. Even if software technically could be found in such works, the legislature's primary concern was protecting the entertainment industry's music and movies. In fact, Congress did not wish to significantly expand the scope of copyright liability. It encouraged software developers to foster interoperability, which would promote competition and innovation in the industry. And it made numerous references to not hurting consumers by limiting competition.

---

147. A plaintiff need not demonstrate market power for offenses that courts view as per se illegal, such as price fixing or market division.

148. Market power can also be determined through more direct evidence, such as *cross-price elasticity of demand* (which measures how much demand changes in response to changes in the price of a different item) or evidence of exclusion on grounds other than efficiency. ANDREW I. GAVIL ET AL., ANTITRUST LAW IN PERSPECTIVE: CASES, CONCEPTS AND PROBLEMS IN COMPETITION POLICY 479, 490 (2d ed. 2008).

It will be obvious in most situations what the typical consumer ultimately desires.[149] The cases make this clear, with consumers seeking to obtain access to copyrighted movies or video games, on the one hand, or unprotected functional devices such as inkjet printers or garage door openers, on the other. A consumer demand test thus offers a simple mechanism to determine the desired object. Where the expressive copyrightable features play a central role in demand, the first element would be satisfied. Where they do not, DMCA protection would not apply.

Consumers generally do not care (or even know) about the software in their printer that communicates with the printer toner software.[150] They only wish to use the printer. Similarly, consumers do not care about the software allowing their garage door opener to open their garage. Devices into which software could be peripherally embedded, including microwave ovens, cameras, vacuum cleaners, and automobiles, would fall outside the reach of the DMCA.

A consumer demand test also is helpful in focusing on the object's ultimate use. The distinction it traces between expressive copyrightable works on the one hand and functional, uncopyrightable works on the other is faithful to the legislative history and does not bog down in complications about the presence of tangential (but copyrightable) software.[151] Instead, its emphasis on consumer demand ensures a commonsense analysis of whether the drafters intended to protect the object under the DMCA.

As technology evolves, these distinctions may become more nuanced. For example, consumers desire Apple's iPhone for both its hardware (phone) and software (music). In that case, the significant interest in expressive software elements should be sufficient to satisfy the test. Only where there are no significant expressive elements and the consumer desires solely the unprotected functional device would the first factor not be satisfied.

The second limitation comes from the fair use defense in copyright law. In determining whether a use is fair, and thus privileged from a finding of copyright infringement, one of the crucial factors is the effect of the challenged use on the market for the copyrighted work. If the use displaces sales of the original work, a court is more likely to find that the defense does not apply. If, on the other hand, the use does not displace sales, the defense will more likely be satisfied.

---

149. The test focuses on a typical, or reasonable, consumer as opposed to one with eclectic interests.

150. See Jacqueline Lipton, *The Law of Unintended Consequences: The Digital Millennium Copyright Act and Interoperability*, 62 WASH. & LEE L. REV. 487, 524 (2005).

151. Relatedly, in focusing the analysis and emphasizing the device's use, the proposal improves on the *Chamberlain* test that restricted the DMCA to "forms of access that bear a reasonable relationship to the protections that the Copyright Act otherwise afford[ed] copyright owners." 381 F.3d at 1202.

Such an inquiry serves as the second pillar of support in establishing the harm targeted by the drafters. Piracy concerns related to rampant copying in the digital environment assume harm to the copyright owner in the market for the protected work. Absent such harm, there would not be a need for the Act.

So where the copyright holder does not suffer a direct market effect from the circumvention of access, its DMCA claim should fail. In the *Blizzard* case, the BnetD creators improved the gaming experience for *those who had already bought a copy of the Blizzard software*. As a result, Blizzard did not lose sales from the circumvention. In fact, it may have even *gained* sales. The developers offered a better gaming experience, improving a server that had suffered from slowdowns, cheating players, and profanity. And in offering an open source platform, the developers did not even financially benefit from their actions.

Sony provides another example in its threats to sue a hobbyist who circumvented access to create enhancements to Aibo, the robotic pet dog. The hobbyist allowed his tools to be used only by Aibo owners who had already purchased Sony's relevant memory stick. Sony nonetheless challenged the activity until backing down in response to numerous protests.

In each of these cases, users who had already purchased the product sought to circumvent access to improve its operation. Such activity benefits copyright owners, who did not suffer reduced sales and might even have gained profits through a better product. The drafters never envisioned that the DMCA would be used to punish improvements.

Nor should copyright owners be able to point to harm suffered in other markets. Even if the BnetD server caused Blizzard to lose revenues from a future business model based on subscription service (in which users paid a monthly fee to play on the Battle.net server), such an effect would occur only outside the video game market covered by the TPM. The drafters never meant for the DMCA to control such markets. Nor did they intend to upset the existing case law, in which (pursuant to *Connectix*) a video game manufacturer could not show market harm by alleging a loss of ability to control a secondary market.[152]

The second factor is modest in nature. Plaintiffs who claim lost profits in aftermarkets would satisfy it. But where a plaintiff cannot demonstrate any negative market effect, the divergence from the legislative intent is conspicuous.

A plaintiff must demonstrate both the first and second factors of the test. The drafters' concerns with protecting copyrighted works only make sense when consumers demand an object for its copyrighted features. And the drafters' solicitude for the effects of unchecked piracy only applies when the plaintiffs suffer financial harm in the form of lost profits or sales.

The DMCA, in short, has been stretched beyond its intended purposes in covering unprotected functional works and punishing activity that does not have

---

152. 203 F.3d at 607.

a harmful effect on copyright owners. The incorporation of market-based antitrust principles and the copyright fair use doctrine can restore the DMCA to its intended role.

CONCLUSION

Reverse engineering has long played a central role in limiting IP. Trade secrecy law recognizes the activity as appropriate. And the *Sega* and *Connectix* cases carved out a defense to copyright infringement because of its acknowledged importance for competition and innovation.

An overbroad application of the DMCA has undone much of that legacy, threatening to remove the most powerful tool addressing the anticompetitive uses of software. The two market-based elements I incorporate into the DMCA test would pare back the statute to its drafters' intentions. And they would restore competition where it is in danger of suppression but where it would be vital to the economy.

A limited DMCA also would confine antitrust courts' exposure to thorny aftermarket issues. Such claims resulted from the Supreme Court's decision that a company that lacked market power in a primary market could have monopoly power in the servicing or parts aftermarket for its product. In the past two decades, courts and commentators have sought to limit the scope of the decision. But vendors' use of the DMCA to control aftermarkets has forced antitrust courts to more frequently confront these contentious claims. The *Chamberlain* court, for example, recognized that the DMCA could allow firms to "leverage [their] sales into aftermarket monopolies," which it claimed (in oversimplifying the issue) "the antitrust laws . . . normally prohibit."[153]

My proposal would reverse this development. By removing from copyright owners' tool kits the most anticompetitive elements of the DMCA, the proposal would reduce antitrust courts' exposure to a problematic universe of cases.

Finally, it would foster innovation. Users would be able to customize products to satisfy individual needs. Owners could no longer block improvements for online gaming or robotic pet dogs. And by allowing competitors to offer interoperable products, the proposal would benefit consumers.

---

153. 381 F.3d at 1201.

PART III

PATENT

In the 21st century, discussions of law and innovation usually begin and end with patents. In the past decade alone, several books and countless articles have explored this relationship. The harmful consequences of patents have been splashed across the newsstands. And Congress has repeatedly considered patent reform, with the House of Representatives approving such legislation in 2007.

Why has there been such an uproar? Part of the problem can be traced to the U.S. Patent and Trademark Office (PTO), which does not have the resources to comprehensively examine each of the 3,500 patents issued each week. Frivolous patents—like a method of exercising a cat and a crustless peanut butter and jelly sandwich—have riveted the public's attention.

Another concern is presented by companies that obtain patents for reasons having little to do with innovation. Firms in certain industries obtain patents to have leverage in negotiations with competitors or to prevent lawsuits. In addition, nonpracticing entities, often called *patent trolls*, do not manufacture products and thus do not face patent infringement counterclaims, emboldening them to file lawsuits.

Also bearing some of the blame is the U.S. Court of Appeals for the Federal Circuit. This court, created in 1982 to solve problems of forum-shopping and hostility to patent claims, has pivoted strongly in the other direction for most of its existence. In fact, many have criticized its formalistic rules on injunctive relief, obviousness, experimental use, and other doctrines.[1]

Despite the dire picture of patents painted by the above story, the past few years have witnessed a modestly improved setting. For starters, the Supreme Court has reined in the Federal Circuit. Just by reinserting itself into patent cases after a long period on the sidelines, it has limited the court.

The Supreme Court also has decided important cases. In *KSR v. Teleflex*, the Court made it easier to prove that a patent was obvious when it struck down the Federal Circuit's requirement that an alleged infringer show a specific "teaching, suggestion, or motivation" to combine pieces of prior art.[2] In *eBay v. MercExchange*, the Court reminded the Federal Circuit that certain instances of infringement do not require injunctions.[3]

And in *Medimmune v. Genentech*, the Court allowed licensees to challenge patent validity without repudiating their licenses. One beneficial result of this change can be seen in the context of the Hatch-Waxman Act. Brand-name drug firms had been able to delay generic entry and immunize such behavior by not

---

1. *MercExchange v. eBay*, 401 F.3d 1323 (Fed. Cir. 2005) (injunctive relief); *Teleflex, Inc. v. KSR Int'l Co.*, 119 Fed. Appx. 282 (Fed. Cir. 2005) (obviousness); *Madey v. Duke Univ.*, 307 F.3d 1351 (Fed. Cir. 2002) (experimental use).

2. *KSR Int'l Co. v. Teleflex, Inc.*, 127 S. Ct. 1727 (2007).

3. *eBay, Inc. v. MercExchange, LLC*, 547 U.S. 388 (2006).

filing a lawsuit. But *Medimmune* facilitated lawsuits by generics, reducing the likelihood of bottlenecks.[4]

The Federal Circuit has also pared back some of its most concerning rulings. One of the most ominous involved willful infringement. For nearly its entire existence, the court had allowed patentees to make such claims (and receive up to treble damages) by showing that infringers had failed to exercise due care in determining whether they had engaged in infringement. Such a standard obliged potential infringers to seek opinion letters from their counsel and led to patentees alleging willful infringement in 92 percent of cases.[5] It also discouraged the reading of rivals' patents, thus undermining the essential role played by disclosure in innovation.

The Federal Circuit addressed this deficiency in *In re Seagate* by raising the standard for willful infringement claims. It required a patentee to show that (1) the infringer acted "despite an objectively high likelihood that its actions constituted infringement" and (2) the risk was "known or so obvious that it should have been known" to the accused infringer.[6] By cabining willful infringement to the cases in which the infringer actually engaged in such behavior, such a change promises to promote disclosure and innovation.

In short, proposals that I might have offered a few years ago are no longer needed. Even my proposal dealing with injunctive relief is more modest than it would have been before *eBay*.

Further confining the breadth of action are unavoidable difficulties built into the patent system. The PTO, for example, cannot spend the resources it would need to ensure that it issues only valid patents. Patent examiners have spent, on average, less than 20 hours to read an application, search for prior art, evaluate patentability, and reach and write up conclusions. In 2009, the PTO suffered under a backlog of more than 735,000 applications.[7]

While this state of affairs is concerning, any attempt to remedy it would entail exorbitant costs. To increase average examiner time per application could cost $13 to $15 million per hour. At the same time, because most of the issued patents lack commercial significance, it does not make sense to aim for perfection in the initial review of applications.

---

4. *Teva Pharmaceuticals USA, Inc. v. Novartis Pharmaceuticals Corp.*, 482 F.3d 1330 (Fed. Cir. 2007).

5. Kimberly A. Moore, *Empirical Statistics on Willful Patent Infringement*, 14 Fed. Cir. B.J. 227 (2004) (reviewing filings between 1999 and 2000).

6. 497 F.3d 1360, 1371 (Fed. Cir. 2007).

7. Citations for the material in this and the following paragraph are presented in Chapter 9.

Another fundamental problem plaguing the regime is its uncertainty. Patent claims do not have clear boundaries.[8] Unlike tangible property, for which someone can stand in the middle of a clearly marked parcel of land and locate the borders, inventions lack physical equivalents and boundaries. Relatedly, the process of interpreting claims known as claim construction is notoriously difficult. The inventive step forming the basis for a patent often cannot be expressed in words, which helps to explain the Federal Circuit's reversal of roughly one-third of district court claim construction determinations.[9]

Despite the recent changes and fundamental challenges of patent law, there is still room for improvement. I thus offer four proposals. Two apply generally to all patents. And two focus on the biotechnology industry, which has received significant attention in recent years.

The first recommends a post-grant opposition system that would allow any party to challenge a patent after it is issued. Such a recommendation would target the most valuable patents and provide a quicker and cheaper determination of validity than litigation. Many have called for such a change, but the specifics of an opposition process remain controversial. For that reason, I set forth numerous details of my proposed system, including the timing of the process, features of the proceeding, and other factors.

My second proposal fleshes out a framework for patent infringement relief that builds on *eBay*. While the Supreme Court reminded the Federal Circuit of the propriety of monetary damages in certain cases, its lack of additional guidance has led some courts to focus on unhelpful issues. I thus offer a framework that emphasizes the most significant factors and places them in a predictable model.

The third proposal turns to the biotechnology industry. In particular, it explores whether scientists are able to access patented research tools. This issue is plagued by a significant disconnect between the "law on the books" (in which the Federal Circuit has restricted the defense of experimental use) and the "law on the ground" (in which industry and academia have crafted informal working solutions).

I conclude that the law on the ground has, at least for now, prevented bottlenecks. But because this precarious equilibrium is subject to change, I offer three proposals if the situation deteriorates. The proposals (1) specify permissible uses of the patent, (2) create an exception to the Bayh-Dole Act (which encourages the commercialization of federally funded inventions) directed to universities and

---

8. *See generally* Michael A. Carrier, *Why Modularity Does Not (and Should Not) Explain Intellectual Property*, 117 YALE L.J. POCKET PART 95 (2007).

9. David L. Schwartz, *Practice Makes Perfect? An Empirical Study of Claim Construction Reversal Rates in Patent Cases*, 107 MICH. L. REV. 223 (2008); Kimberly A. Moore, *Markman Eight Years Later: Is Claim Construction More Predictable?*, 9 LEWIS & CLARK L. REV. 231, 239 (2005).

nonprofit institutions, and (3) incorporate notions of user innovation based on the conduct of researchers.

The fourth proposal addresses scientists' needs for tangible materials (such as genes, cell lines, tissues, and organisms) in their research. In contrast to patented research tools, the empirical evidence reveals a problem with owners denying materials and forcing recipients to enter into "material transfer agreements." I therefore suggest publication terms for transfers between academia and industry, and propose that federal funding recipients abide by a model agreement.

In short, my proposals address two issues of general significance that could apply to every issued patent and every litigated patent. And they address the industry that has witnessed the greatest chasm between the empirical evidence and academic proposals. Even if some concerns with the patent system lie beyond our reach, these proposals should modestly foster innovation.

9. BETTER PATENTS: A POST-GRANT OPPOSITION PROCEDURE

Patent Application Process 206
Initial Review 209
Litigation 209
Reexamination 211
Post-Grant Opposition 213
Threshold Showing 218
Timing 219
Reviewable Subject Matter 223
Nature of Evidentiary Showing 224
Judges and Appeals 225
Proceeding 225
Real Party in Interest 227
Estoppel Effect 228
Conclusion 229

The patent system is designed to promote innovation. Patents give their owners a right to exclude others from making, selling, or using an invention for a period of 20 years. Inventions covered by valid patents often foster innovation. In contrast, invalid patents threaten to increase price and limit competition without any countervailing benefits.

For that reason, the process by which patents are granted is particularly important. But this mechanism is far from perfect. This chapter begins by detailing difficulties with the application process that explain the issuance of invalid patents. It then shows why this problem is not effectively addressed by other means. Litigation is not an ideal alternative because of its costs and the parties' unequal incentives. And two types of patent office reexamination are plagued by characteristics that have minimized their use.

Given the inadequacy of these alternatives, this chapter demonstrates the benefits of a *post-grant opposition system.* Such a system would allow any party to challenge a patent after it is issued. It would provide a quicker and cheaper determination of validity than litigation. It would target the most valuable patents. It would allow the U.S. Patent and Trademark Office (PTO) to access important information held by competitors. It would reduce uncertainty, thereby encouraging investment and commercialization. And it would reduce the number of invalid patents. In short, it would promote innovation.

In addition to its benefits for the patent system, a post-grant opposition system would improve antitrust law. The presence of invalid patents increases the frequency with which courts must address the challenging intersection of IP and antitrust. As described in Chapters 4 and 5, courts have encountered difficulty in this sphere. Reducing the number of invalid patents, especially important ones likely to be challenged and to lead to market power, promises benefits for antitrust.

Many in recent years have advocated a post-grant opposition system. Congress has considered it, as have government agencies, commissions, attorneys, and scholars. But the unity on the big picture has not extended to the specifics of an opposition process. These differences are vital as they determine whether the process will be used and whether it will be fair to patentees and challengers.

I thus set forth numerous details of my proposed opposition system, including (1) the threshold a challenger must clear to commence an opposition, (2) the timing of the process, (3) the grounds on which a patent can be challenged, (4) the nature of the required evidentiary showing, (5) the procedure's judges and appeals, (6) the materials that can be introduced in the proceeding, (7) the disclosure of the requester's identity, and (8) the preclusive effect of an opposition.

PATENT APPLICATION PROCESS

To receive a patent, an inventor files an application with the U.S. Patent & Trademark Office (PTO). The application is assigned to an examiner who specializes in the field of invention.[1] The examiner then searches for printed publications, previously issued patents, patent applications, and related inventions (together known as *prior art*) that help her determine whether the application meets the requirements of patentability. In particular, the examiner determines if the invention is novel, useful, and not obvious to a person in the relevant field and if it would enable others to create the invention.

These tasks have become more difficult in recent years. In the 1980s and 1990s, courts dramatically expanded the range of patentable subject matter by holding that inventions related to biotechnology, computer software, and methods for doing business were all potentially patentable.[2] This development has at least partially explained the increase in patent applications.[3] In 2009,

---

1. 4 DONALD S. CHISUM, CHISUM ON PATENTS § 11.01 (2005).

2. *Diamond v. Chakrabarty*, 447 U.S. 303 (1980) (biotechnology); *Diamond v. Diehr*, 450 U.S. 175 (1981) (software); *State Street Bank & Trust Co. v. Signature Fin. Group, Inc.*, 149 F.3d 1368 (Fed. Cir. 1998) (business methods). Before receiving a patent, an applicant must also show that its invention satisfies the other patentability requirements.

3. USPTO, *U.S. Patent Activity: Calendar Years 1790 to the Present* (Apr. 23, 2008), http://www.uspto.gov/go/taf/h_counts.pdf.

1.2 million patent applications were pending examination, with 735,000 not having received a preliminary examination.[4]

In addition, the length and complexity of patent applications has increased in the past quarter-century.[5] Despite this development, production quotas were not updated between 1976 and 2010.[6] On average, each patent examiner was expected to process 87 applications per year at a rate of 19 hours per application.[7] Within this period, examiners had to read the application, search for prior art, communicate with the applicant, evaluate patentability, and reach and write up conclusions.[8]

Increases in workloads are not helped by the *ex parte* nature of the process, with only the applicant communicating with the examiner. To reject an application, the examiner must discover prior art. Although the applicant has a duty to disclose information that is known and material to patentability, it is not required to search for prior art.[9]

This challenge is particularly acute in areas in which it is difficult to locate prior art. For software, for example, prior art tends to be integrated into marketed products or discussed in textbooks that examiners cannot readily access.[10] PTO examiners are required to rely on the agency's three computer systems— the Examiner's Automated Search Tool (EAST), Web-Based Examiner Search Tool (WEST), and Foreign Patent Access System (FPAS). These systems provide

---

4. United States Patent and Trademark Office, Performance and Accountability Report Fiscal Year 2009, at 114 tbl. 3, http://inventivestep.files.wordpress.com/2009/12/2009annualreport1.pdf [USPTO 2009 Report]; *Unreasonable Patent Applicant Delay and the USPTO Backlog*, PATENTLYO, July 9, 2010, http://www.patentlyo.com/patent/2010/07/unreasonable-patent-applicant-delay-and-the-uspto-backlog.html.

5. The average number of claims at filing increased from 18 in 1999 to 24 in 2002. U.S. Department of Commerce, Office of Inspector General, *USPTO Should Reassess How Examiner Goals, Performance Appraisal Plans, and The Award System Stimulate and Reward Examiner Production, Final Inspection Report No. IPE-15722*, at 17 (Sept. 2004), http://www.oig.doc.gov/oig/reports/2004/USPTO-IPE-15722-09-04.pdf [hereinafter OIG Report].

6. United States Government Accountability Office Report to Congressional Committees, *Intellectual Property: USPTO Has Made Progress in Hiring Examiners, but Challenges to Retention Remain*, GAO-05-720, at 29 (June 2005), http://www.gao.gov/new.items/d05720.pdf.

7. *Id.* at 28.

8. FED. TRADE COMM'N, TO PROMOTE INNOVATION: THE PROPER BALANCE OF COMPETITION AND PATENT LAW AND POLICY, Exec. Summary, at 9-10 (2003) [hereinafter TO PROMOTE INNOVATION].

9. 37 C.F.R. § 1.56(a) (2008). Pursuant to a duty of candor, the applicant must disclose information of which it is aware that is "material to patentability." 37 C.F.R. § 1.56.

10. Julie Cohen, *Reverse Engineering and the Rise of Electronic Vigilantism: Intellectual Property Implications of "Lock-out" Programs*, 68 S. CAL. L. REV. 1091, 1178 (1995).

access to U.S. patents, certain patent applications, and foreign patent abstracts.[11] But they do not offer comprehensive databases of product sales or nonpatent published materials. And in most cases, due to security concerns, examiners cannot use the Internet for research.[12] Difficulties in prior art searching are confirmed by a study that concluded that examiners were at a "strong comparative disadvantage" in searching for prior art that appeared in nonpatent prior art or foreign patents.[13] Examiners accounted for 41 percent of citations to U.S. patents but only 10 percent of citations to nonpatent prior art.[14]

Until recently, the objective of issuing valid patents came under additional pressure from the system's pro-patent bias. Examiners received credit for only certain actions, such as the allowance or abandonment of applications, as well as the examination of new applications known as "first office actions on the merits."[15] They did not receive credit for other activities such as advisory actions, examiner interviews, or actions on the merits after the first action. In February 2010, the PTO implemented changes to its "count" system that addressed many of these deficiencies.[16]

Courts that analyze patents often conclude that they should not have been granted. According to one oft-cited study, courts have found that 46 percent of patents litigated to judgment are invalid.[17]

In short, patents are important to innovation. But the PTO grants many invalid patents every day. What can be done? We have four choices: (1) fix the initial review of patent applications, (2) rely on patent validity litigation, (3) use the current forms of reexamination, or (4) institute a new post-grant opposition

---

11. United States Patent and Trademark Office, Manual of Patent Examining Procedures § 902.03(e) (8th ed. 5th rev. 2006) [hereinafter MPEP].

12. *Id.* § 904.02(c). Examiners must "restrict search queries to the general state of the art" unless the PTO has established "a secure link over the Internet with a specific vendor to maintain the confidentiality of the unpublished patent application."

13. Bhaven N. Sampat, *Determinants of Patent Quality: An Empirical Analysis*, at 2–3, 11, Sept. 2005, http://siepr.stanford.edu/programs/SST_Seminars/patentquality_new.pdf_1. pdf.

14. *Id.* at 8.

15. Examiners also receive credit for writing an Examiner's Answer in response to an appealed application.

16. USPTO, *Recently Announced Changes to USPTO's Examiner Count System Go Into Effect*, Feb. 18, 2010, http://www.uspto.gov/news/pr/2010/10_08.jsp; Robert P. Merges, *As Many As Six Impossible Patents Before Breakfast*, 14 BERKELEY TECH. L.J. 577, 607 (1999); OIG Report, at 24–28; Randolph A. Smith, *USPTO Examiners Performance System*, at 8–10, Nov. 22, 2005, http://www.miyoshipat.co.jp/seminar/pdf/seminar051122.pdf.

17. John R. Allison & Mark A. Lemley, *Empirical Evidence on the Validity of Litigated Patents*, 26 AIPLA Q.J. 185, 205 (1998). To be sure, figures on litigated patents do not include cases in which the parties settle, which could involve a higher frequency of valid patents.

procedure. In this chapter, I demonstrate the difficulties with the first three options and promise of the fourth.

INITIAL REVIEW

One way to reduce the number of invalid patents would be to ensure that they are not granted in the first place. While that is a tall order, resources would go a long way toward solving the problem. If Congress provided the PTO with more resources, examiners could devote more time to each application, increasing the likelihood of reaching the correct outcome. If patents are so powerful but often invalid, wouldn't the economy benefit from eliminating many of the bad patents?

It might seem so. But the first problem with such a solution is its exorbitant cost. More than 3,500 patents are issued every week.[18] To increase average examiner time per application could cost as much as $13 to $15 million per hour.[19] Even if a more rigorous examination process would reduce the number of applications, the vastly increased cost of the process would outweigh any savings in litigation expenses.[20]

Nor does it make sense to aim for perfection in the initial review of applications. Most of the issued patents lack commercial significance. Patents that sit on a shelf often do not have a direct effect on innovation or competition. It thus is not efficient to spend substantial resources to achieve an ideal initial review.[21]

Perhaps litigation could serve as the tool to remedy invalid patents. The most important patents are the ones that are brought to market and that are likely to be infringed. So why not just wait for lawsuits?

LITIGATION

Litigation certainly is a targeted method to address invalid patents. It focuses directly on the most important patents rather than patents that will never be

---

18. USPTO 2009 Report, at 112 tbl. 1 (more than 190,000 patents were issued in 2009).

19. Transcript of Federal Trade Commission Public Hearing on Competition and Intellectual Property Law and Policy in the Knowledge-Based Economy, at 78 (Oct. 25, 2002) (statement of former PTO Commissioner Q. Todd Dickinson), http://www.ftc.gov/opp/intellect/021025trans.pdf.

20. Mark A. Lemley, *Rational Ignorance at the Patent Office*, 95 Nw. U. L. Rev. 1495, 1509 (2001).

21. *Id.* For evidence that the PTO may be doing a better job than it typically gets credit for, see Mark A. Lemley & Bhaven Sampat, *Is the Patent Office a Rubber Stamp?*, July 7, 2007, at 42, http://papers.ssrn.com/sol3/papers.cfm?abstract_id=999098 (concluding, based on a review of applications filed in January 2001, that the PTO rejects 15–20 percent of applications and amends approximately 40 percent of patents that issue).

used. And it utilizes the considerable tools and antagonistic clash of two warring sides to reach an accurate validity determination. Or does it?

Perhaps not. High costs and skewed incentives are to blame. Litigation is costly and expensive. The typical patent litigation occurs seven to ten years after a patent is issued and is not resolved for an additional two to three years.[22] As of 2009, for patent infringement litigation in which there was more than $25 million at risk, the median cost for each party was $5.5 million.[23] For cases in which there was $1 to $25 million at risk, the cost was $2.5 million.[24] Such costs reasonably dissuade many (in particular small) companies.

In many cases of dispute, therefore, the parties prefer licensing to litigation. Licensing allows potential infringers with a product on the market to remain on the market. In contrast, filing a lawsuit to demonstrate a patent's invalidity often leads to a counterclaim that would prevent alleged infringers from selling their products or require them to pay substantial damages. At a minimum, licensing fees tend to be cheaper than litigation. Nor is the expense of litigation borne by two parties with equal incentives.

Patentees, with the most at stake, typically spend more than infringers.[25] Much of this flows from a *public goods* problem. As a result of a 1971 Supreme Court decision, a party that successfully challenges a patent cannot block competitors from relying on the court's ruling.[26] A free-riding problem thus develops. A successful validity challenge benefits all potential infringers, who subsequently can make the product, while uniquely burdening the challenging infringer, the sole party paying litigation costs. The challenging infringer, in other words, incurs all the costs of challenging the patent but can enjoy only a fraction of the invalid patent's benefits.[27] As a result of this asymmetry, infringers wait for others to sue.[28] In contrast, the patentee enjoys 100 percent of the gain from a validity finding. It is not hard to see why the patentee would have a greater incentive to do what it takes to win.

Of course, spending money matters. Hiring more lawyers and better experts, trying out more theories, and engaging in more extensive trial preparation

---

22. Nat'l Research Council of the Nat'l Acads., A Patent System for the 21st Century 95–96 (Stephen A. Merrill et al. eds., 2004) [hereinafter Patent System for 21st Century].

23. AIPLA, *Report of the Economic Survey 2009*, at 29 (2009).

24. *Id.*

25. Joseph Farrell & Robert P. Merges, *Incentives to Challenge and Defend Patents: Why Litigation Won't Reliably Fix Patent Office Errors and Why Administrative Patent Review Might Help*, 19 Berkeley Tech. L.J. 943, 950 (2004).

26. *Blonder-Tongue Labs., Inc. v. Univ. of Ill. Found.*, 402 U.S. 313, 350 (1971).

27. Farrell & Merges, at 952; Joseph Scott Miller, *Building a Better Bounty: Litigation-Stage Rewards for Defeating Patents*, 19 Berkeley Tech. L.J. 667, 687–88 (2004).

28. Alternatively, they enter into licenses with patentees.

increases the odds of victory.[29] Success in patent litigation thus often boils down to resources as opposed to a neutral determination of validity.

Further illustrating litigation's skewed incentives, multiple infringers that compete in a product market can "pass through" any higher royalties they are required to pay to consumers.[30] This activity makes it even less likely that invalid patents will be challenged. Other problems plaguing litigation include the unpredictability of jury trials, the assertion of entire patent portfolios against defendants, and the availability of treble damages.[31]

Because of these difficulties, litigation is not a fail-safe mechanism to eliminate important invalid patents. Not only are there insufficiently few challenges, but infringers' validity challenges tend to be less aggressively litigated than patentees' validity defenses. And the cost and expense of litigation is unavoidable.

REEXAMINATION

Another option for remedying invalid patents involves the PTO's reexamination of issued patents. Two such systems exist in the United States. But each is marked by flaws that have limited its use.

In 1980, Congress enacted an *ex parte reexamination* system, by which a third party could seek reexamination of a patent.[32] At the time, the legislature, as part of an effort to revive the nation's competitiveness, sought to restore confidence in U.S. patents.[33] One way of doing so was to address the high cost of patent litigation by creating a system by which patent owners could test validity in an "efficient and relatively inexpensive manner."[34]

Pursuant to the procedure, any individual can request reexamination at any time during the patent term.[35] Reexamination will be ordered if the PTO Director finds that the challenger has raised "a substantial new question of patentability."[36] The examiner evaluates materials not considered in the initial examination in the form of patents and printed publications (but not public uses or sales).[37]

---

29. Farrell & Merges, at 949.

30. *Id.* at 953.

31. Carl Shapiro, *Patent System Reform: Economic Analysis and Critique*, 19 BERKELEY TECH. L.J. 1017, 1034 (2004).

32. Pub. L. No. 96-517, § 1, 94 Stat. 3016 (1980).

33. Gerald J. Mossinghoff & Vivian S. Kuo, *Post-Grant Review of Patents: Enhancing the Quality of the Fuel of Interest*, 85 J. PAT. & TRADEMARK OFF. SOC'Y 231, 235 (2003).

34. H.R. REP. No. 96-1307, pt. 1, at 4, *reprinted in* 1980 U.S.C.C.A.N. 6460, 6463. *See generally* Farrell & Merges, at 965.

35. 35 U.S.C. §§ 303, 312.

36. 35 U.S.C. § 304.

37. 35 U.S.C. §§ 302, 303. A useful summary of the process appears in Mossinghoff & Kuo, at 236–38.

Between 1981 and 2009, using approximate figures, the PTO granted 9,200 and denied 800 of the 10,000 requests for *ex parte* reexamination on which it ruled.[38] Of the requests that were finally decided, 24 percent resulted in the confirmation of all the claims in the patent, 11 percent led to cancellation of all the claims, and 65 percent resulted in amendments to the claims.[39] The reexaminations thus had a significant effect, with more than 75 percent of decided requests leading to at least a narrowing of the patent. But the procedure was not invoked frequently as it applied, on average, to approximately 350 patents per year.[40]

In creating the reexamination system, Congress was concerned about challengers' potential harassment of patentees.[41] For that reason, it limited third parties' rights to participate to an initial filing and a response to a patentee's (optional) reply to the filing. But the *ex parte* nature of the process, marked by only the patentee's involvement, has limited use by challengers.[42] Patentees, in fact, have filed many of the reexaminations to provide newly discovered prior art to the PTO and preempt competitors' validity challenges.[43] In the end, challengers' inability to participate in *ex parte* reexamination has dampened use of the procedure.

Congress responded to this situation by creating an *inter partes reexamination* system in the American Inventors Protection Act in 1999.[44] Such a regime has allowed the requester to respond to each patentee filing and to appeal to the USPTO's administrative Board of Patent Appeals and Interferences.[45] Three years after the passage of the Act, Congress granted the requester the right to appeal to the Federal Circuit and allowed challenges based on patents or printed publications that the PTO had previously considered.[46]

But even with these amendments, *inter partes* reexamination has been plagued by deficiencies that have limited its use. First, it has allowed challenges only on grounds of novelty or nonobviousness. Other requirements, such as subject matter, utility, and enablement, cannot be raised. Second, it has not allowed the

---

38. USPTO, Ex Parte *Reexamination Filing Data*, Dec. 30, 2009, http://www.uspto.gov/patents/stats/ep_quarterly_report_december_31_2009.pdf.

39. *Id.; see generally* Mossinghoff & Kuo, at 238. The figures apply to 6,000 *ex parte* reexamination certificates (which are issued after an appeal has concluded or the period for appeal expires). U.S. Patent & Trademark Office, *Manual of Patent Examining Procedure* § 2288, at 2200-150 (8th ed., 5th rev. 2006).

40. In the past few years, there have been roughly 700 requests filed per year.

41. H.R. REP. No. 96-1307, pt. 1, at 3–4, *reprinted in* 1980 U.S.C.C.A.N. at 6463. *See generally* Farrell & Merges, at 965.

42. 35 U.S.C. § 305.

43. Qin Shi, *Reexamination, Opposition, or Litigation? Legislative Efforts to Create a Post-Grant Patent Quality Control System*, 31 AIPLA Q.J. 433, 440–41 (2003).

44. Pub. L. No. 106-113, 113 Stat. 1501.

45. 35 U.S.C. § 315.

46. Pub. L. No. 107-273, §§ 13105, 13106, 116 Stat. 1758–59 (2002).

requester to participate beyond a single response to a patentee's filing. The requester cannot, for example, cross-examine the assertions of the patentee or its witnesses.

Third, and most important, it has created two strong estoppel provisions. One has prevented a requester from challenging the validity of any fact determined in the examination.[47] The other has prohibited a requester from later asserting the invalidity of a patent on any ground that it "raised or could have raised."[48] The latter part of this definition has proven particularly elusive. It is not clear how extensively a requester must conduct a prior art search to avoid estoppel. The PTO determines whether an issue could have been raised on a "case-by-case basis" by "evaluating all the facts and circumstances of each individual situation."[49]

The effect of these three failings in combination is particularly pronounced. A requester who cannot raise fundamental validity challenges and cannot engage in cross-examination would be especially wary of being bound by such strong estoppel provisions. It thus should not be a surprise that the *inter partes* reexamination has not been used frequently. Between 1999 and June 2009, the PTO received only 671 requests for *inter partes* reexamination.[50] Using approximate figures, the Office granted 550 and denied 30 of the 580 requests on which it ruled. Of the 77 requests that were finally decided, 4 resulted in the confirmation of all the claims in the patent, 46 led to cancellation of all the claims, and 27 resulted in amendments to the claims.[51]

POST-GRANT OPPOSITION

The first three options for reducing the incidence of invalid patents are not ideal. Perfecting the application process is not the best use of limited government resources. Litigation addresses some of the most important invalid patents, but

---

47. Intellectual Property and Communications Omnibus Reform Act of 1999, Pub. L. No. 106-113, § 4607, 113 Stat. 1501 (1999). The estoppel does not apply to facts later proven false based on evidence unavailable at the time of reexamination. *See generally Patent Quality Improvement—Post-Grant Opposition: Hearing Before Subcomm. on Courts, the Internet, & Intellectual Property of the H. Comm. on Judiciary*, 108th Cong. 16 (2004) (statement of Jeffrey P. Kushan) [hereinafter *Hearing*].

48. 35 U.S.C. § 315(c)

49. USPTO Report to Congress on Inter Partes Reexamination, *Analysis of Comments*, http://www.uspto.gov/web/offices/dcom/olia/reports/reexam_report.htm [hereinafter Analysis of Comments].

50. Inter Partes *Reexamination Filing Data*, June 30, 2009, http://www.uspto.gov/web/patents/documents/inter_partes.pdf. As this book went to press, use of the procedure had recently increased.

51. *Id.* The figures apply to *inter partes* reexamination certificates (which are issued after an appeal has concluded or the period for appeal expires). U.S. Patent & Trademark Office, *Manual of Patent Examining Procedure* § 2688, at 2600-171 (8th ed., 5th rev. 2006).

cost and other factors reduce its effectiveness. And the limited participation for requesters as well as estoppel provisions have prevented the reexamination systems from being fully utilized. In order to fix invalid patents that can stifle innovation and harm consumers, we need a new opposition system.

Such an opposition could occur before or after the patent grant. A minority of scholars has advocated a pre-grant opposition system, by which a competitor could oppose a patent before its issuance. But two fundamental disadvantages accompany such a process.

First, it requires early disclosure of patent applications, which could provide secret information to competitors.[52] Second, large firms are more likely to use pre-grant opposition to delay the issuance of patents to small inventors.[53] Japan and South Korea, which had pre-grant opposition systems, witnessed such behavior. Inventors in Japan lamented holdups as long as 11 years and complained about the targeting of applications with "high technological and commercial value."[54] As a result of these problems, the two countries switched to post-grant opposition systems.[55]

These two impediments help explain why nearly all commentators have reasonably recommended a post-grant opposition system. Such a system offers a quick and cheap alternative to litigation that solves the problems that have plagued reexamination. It also offers at least seven additional benefits.

First, it promises to improve *patent quality* by bringing more information into the process. In particular, it taps competitors, who often are aware of the most relevant prior art and can "probe beneath the surface" of an applicant's declarations and affidavits.[56] Relatedly, the system could help educate examiners in issues presented by emerging technologies.[57] Because third parties are likely to have more knowledge of prior art in new fields, opposition proceedings could uncover areas unknown to examiners.[58] Even for established technologies,

---

52. Jay P. Kesan & Andres A. Gallo, *Why "Bad" Patents Survive in the Market and How Should We Change?—The Private and Social Costs of Patents*, 55 EMORY L.J. 61, 110 (2006). Such disclosure would occur before it would have under the current patent system, either because it would take place within the 18-month period before applications are published or because the patent falls in a category that is not published.

53. Jay P. Kesan, *Carrots and Sticks to Create a Better Patent System*, 17 BERKELEY TECH. L.J. 763, 783 (2002).

54. Robert J. Girouard, *U.S. Trade Policy and the Japanese Patent System*, at 5 (BRIE Working Paper 89, Aug. 1996), http://brie.berkeley.edu/publications/WP%2089.pdf.

55. Kesan, at 778.

56. To PROMOTE INNOVATION, at 215 n.19.

57. Jonathan Levin & Richard Levin, *Benefits and Costs of an Opposition Process*, in PATENTS IN THE KNOWLEDGE-BASED ECONOMY 120, 140 (Wesley M. Cohen & Stephen A. Merrill eds., 2003).

58. *Id.*

examiners would receive earlier guidance through oppositions than litigation.[59] In increasing the amount of information available to examiners, the process would buttress the recent valuable effort of the Peer-to-Patent Community Patent Review, a pilot program that has allowed the public to provide the PTO with far more prior art than it typically receives from third parties.[60]

Second, it focuses on the *most valuable* patents. The patents that are most likely to have an effect on the marketplace are most likely to be opposed. One study comparing European oppositions and U.S. reexaminations concluded that "more 'valuable' or technologically important patents . . . are more likely to trigger challenges."[61] Another that examined European oppositions in the biotechnology and pharmaceutical industries concluded that patent value is a "relevant predictor[] of the likelihood of opposition."[62]

Third, reducing the number of invalid patents would *lower prices.* Invalid patents reduce the number of noninfringing substitutes that consumers can purchase in the marketplace. They increase defensive patenting, in which firms seek patents in order to gain bargaining chips against rivals.[63] They threaten incumbents that have sunk investments.[64] They raise competitors' costs, which are typically passed on to consumers.[65] And they require rivals to pay licensing royalties.[66]

---

59. Patent System for 21st Century, at 103.

60. *The Peer to Patent Project: Community Review of Patents, Public Successfully Participates in U.S. Patent Examination Process,* Apr. 28, 2008, http://cairns.typepad.com/peertopatent/2008/04/public-successf.html (noting that the PTO received one third-party prior art submission for every 500 patent applications published in 2007 and that in the Peer-to-Patent pilot program, "volunteer reviewers supplied nearly four prior art references for each pilot application"). As this book went to press, the program covered 400 applications in computer architecture, software, information security, and computer-implemented business methods, and allowed the public to search for, submit, and evaluate prior art. Peer to Patent, *Community Patent Review,* http://www.peertopatent.org/ (last visited August 29, 2008).

61. Stuart J.H. Graham et al., *Patent Quality Control: A Comparison of U.S. Patent Reexaminations and European Patent Oppositions, in* Patents in the Knowledge-Based Economy 74, 114.

62. Dietmar Harhoff & Markus Reitzig, *Determinants of Opposition against EPO Patent Grants—The Case of Biotechnology and Pharmaceuticals,* 22 Int'l J. Indus. Org. 443, 478 (2004). Any harassment effects that would result from the focus on valuable patents could be addressed through the procedure's details, as I discuss later in the chapter.

63. Eric Williams, *Remembering the Public's Interest in the Patent System—A Post-Grant Opposition Designed to Benefit the Public,* 2006 B.C. Intell. Prop. & Tech. F. 110702.

64. Bronwyn H. Hall & Dietmar Harhoff, *Post-Grant Reviews in the U.S. Patent System—Design Choices and Expected Impact,* 19 Berkeley Tech. L.J. 989, 993 (2004).

65. Farrell & Merges, at 945.

66. Shapiro, at 1019.

Fourth, the system offers *increased flexibility*. Unlike courts, which can only uphold or invalidate a patent, the PTO can compel an applicant to narrow its claim. In most cases, in fact, the applicant amends its claims in response to an examiner's initial rejection of all or some of the claims.

Fifth, the procedure could encourage firms to review patents shortly after they are issued. Such activity would tend to increase *technology spillovers*, by which other firms benefit from a patentee's improvements. And it would build on the recent Federal Circuit decision in *In re Seagate Technology, LLC*, which raised the threshold for willful infringement claims, thereby removing the disincentive under prior case law of reading rivals' patents.[67]

Sixth, the system could address the *uncertainty* that hampers innovation. Inventors and potential infringers may not be certain that a patent is valid for years after its issuance. The typical patent litigation occurs seven to ten years after a patent is issued.[68] And more than two years elapse, on average, between the filing of a complaint and trial.[69] Nor is predictability bolstered when courts reverse PTO validity findings in least one-third of the cases.[70]

This uncertainty could reduce investment and commercialization. A patentee uncertain of validity would be less likely to secure investments that facilitate the invention's development.[71] Uncertainty also makes licensing more difficult. And competitors are hurt, as they are less likely to enter the market or offer improvements by designing around the patent. The practice of circumventing a patent claim's boundaries to create a noninfringing alternative increases competition and benefits consumers.[72] But designing around a patent claim becomes more difficult as the claim's uncertainty increases.

Seventh, by offering a quicker and cheaper method of resolving validity, the system offers *small companies* a new avenue to challenge patents. Small firms have no simple and effective way to determine a patent's validity. The cost of litigation and unending discovery often renders litigation infeasible for small companies. In fact, smaller firms, with relatively higher litigation costs, are more

---

67. 497 F.3d 1360 (Fed. Cir. 2007).

68. PATENT SYSTEM FOR 21ST CENTURY, at 95–96.

69. PricewaterhouseCoopers, *2008 Patent Litigation Study: Damages Awards, Success Rates and Time-to-Trial*, at 11-12, http://www.pwc.com/extweb/pwcpublications.nsf/docid/EBC144CF6220C1E785257424005F9A2B/$file/2008_patent_litigation_study.pdf.

70. Kimberly A. Moore, Markman *Eight Years Later: Is Claim Construction More Predictable?*, 9 LEWIS & CLARK L. REV. 231, 239 (2005); John R. Allison & Mark A. Lemley, *Empirical Evidence on the Validity of Litigated Patents*, 26 AIPLA Q.J. 185, 205 (1998).

71. Craig Allen Nard, *Certainty, Fence Building, and the Useful Arts*, 74 IND. L.J. 759, 759 (1999). Markets implicitly discount the value of patents untested in court. Roundtable Discussion at the Federal Trade Commission, Hearings on Competition and IP Law and Policy in the Knowledge-Based Economy, at 204–05 (Feb. 26, 2002), http://www.ftc.gov/opp/intellect/020226trans.pdf (comments of David Teece).

72. Nard, at 791.

likely to avoid areas in which incumbents have many patents.[73] The high costs also lead to the free-rider problem plaguing patent challenges.

In addition to all these benefits, a reduced-cost opposition allows small companies to challenge a patent without being countersued for infringement.[74] Nor, as evidence from European oppositions reveals, have independent inventors and smaller entities more frequently been subject to validity challenges.[75]

The U.S. and European patent systems admittedly are dissimilar, with resultant differences in incentives to use opposition systems. Nonetheless, the use of oppositions in Europe provides important lessons for a proposed U.S. system. In the European system, third parties can file an opposition within nine months of the grant of a patent.[76] They can challenge a patent's subject matter, novelty, inventive step (similar to nonobviousness), and enablement.[77] The examination is conducted by three examiners, at least two of whom did not participate in the initial grant of the patent.[78] The proceedings may include an oral hearing.[79] There are no estoppel provisions.

Between 1980 and 1995, approximately 8 percent of European patents were opposed.[80] The median duration of the opposition was almost two years, with an appeal lasting another two years. Combined with the more than four years taken by initial examination, the process lasted approximately eight years. But it had a significant effect. More than one-third of patents were revoked and roughly another third were narrowed through amendment. Less than 28 percent of patents survived the opposition process unscathed.[81]

Patent reform legislation that the U.S. Congress has considered in the past several years has included a post-grant opposition process. Many other organizations,

---

73. Josh Lerner, *Patenting in the Shadow of Competitors*, 38 J.L. & Econ. 463, 465 (1995).

74. To the extent a public good problem still affects oppositions, the process might need to be revised. For example, Professor John Thomas has offered the idea of a cash prize, or "bounty," to encourage citizens to provide the PTO with information relevant to patentability. John R. Thomas, *Collusion and Collective Action in the Patent System: A Proposal for Patent Bounties*, 2001 U. Ill. L. Rev. 305, 342.

75. Stuart J.H. Graham & Dietmar Harhoff, *Can Post-Grant Reviews Improve Patent System Design? A Twin Study of U.S. and European Patents*, at 23 (Centre for Economic Policy Research (CEPR), Discussion Paper No. 5680, 2006); Harhoff & Reitzig, at 476.

76. Convention on the Grant of European Patents, Oct. 5, 1973, art. 99, http://www.epo.org/patents/law/legal-texts/html/epc/1973/e/ma1.html [hereinafter European Patent Convention]. A patent granted under the European Patent Convention is effective in each of the member states. *Id.* art. 2.

77. European Patent Convention, art. 100.

78. *Id.* art. 19(2); *see generally* Hall & Harhoff, at 1002–03.

79. European Patent Convention, art. 117.

80. Hall & Harhoff, at 1003; *see also* Harhoff & Reitzig, at 445 (noting that, between 1978 and 1992, 8.2 percent of patents were subject to opposition).

81. Hall & Harhoff, at 1003–04.

including the Federal Trade Commission, National Academies of Science, American Intellectual Property Lawyers Association (AIPLA), and PTO, have also proposed an opposition procedure.

While the concept of a post-grant opposition process may not be overly controversial, the details are. Major questions need to be answered:

- What threshold must a requester clear to commence an opposition?
- When can such a process be invoked?
- On what grounds can a patent be challenged?
- What is the nature of the required evidentiary showing?
- Who will hear the challenge (and its appeal)?
- What materials can be introduced in the proceeding?
- Must the requester's identity be disclosed? and
- What is the preclusive effect of the opposition?

The remainder of this chapter will address these questions.

THRESHOLD SHOWING

The first question involves the threshold a requester must satisfy to initiate an opposition. To begin an *ex parte* or *inter partes* reexamination, a requester must demonstrate "a substantial new question of patentability" for the claims for which it seeks reexamination.[82] Although such a showing sounds reasonable in theory, the ambiguity of such a standard has led to reexaminations being granted in nearly every case.[83] The PTO granted 92 percent of the *ex parte* reexamination requests between 1981 and 2009 and 95 percent of the *inter partes* reexamination requests between 1999 and 2009.[84] Some have claimed that examiners "routinely rubber-stamp requests for reexamination" and can "parrot back the requester's language" to demonstrate a substantial new question of patentability.[85]

One potential more-rigorous threshold would require a requester to establish a prima facie case of unpatentability. Such a showing would set a higher threshold than the current reexamination standards. But in certain cases, it would call for the requester to make showings that would not be possible without discovery,

---

82. 35 U.S.C. §§ 303(a), 312(a).

83. Mark D. Janis, *Rethinking Reexamination: Toward a Viable Administrative Revocation System for U.S. Patent Law*, 11 Harv. J.L. & Tech. 1, 47 n.202 (1997).

84. USPTO, Ex Parte *Reexamination Filing Data*, Dec. 30, 2009, http://www.uspto.gov/patents/stats/ep_quarterly_report_december_31_2009.pdf; Inter Partes *Reexamination Filing Data*, June 30, 2009, http://www.uspto.gov/web/patents/documents/inter_partes.pdf.

85. Janis, at 48.

and in all cases it would require the PTO to engage in an extensive additional step of analysis.[86]

A middle ground appears in the proposed Patents Depend on Quality Act of 2006.[87] This legislation would allow the PTO director to "dismiss an opposition request that. . . lacks substantial merit."[88] It would not require overly burdensome showings, while still allowing the PTO to dismiss claims that are harassing and without substantial merit. And while the test bears some similarity to the current reexamination threshold, it is offered on a fresh slate, devoid of a rubber-stamp history.

In fleshing out such a threshold, the standard for preliminary injunctions could prove helpful. A patentee seeking to enjoin infringement must demonstrate, among other factors, a likelihood of success on the merits. It will not receive the injunction, however, if the alleged infringer asserts a validity or infringement defense that the patentee cannot prove "lacks substantial merit."[89] Courts have held that this standard only requires the challenging party to demonstrate a patent's vulnerability (rather than a higher standard of invalidity).[90] In the context of post-grant hearings, the PTO can dismiss a challenger's request that lacks substantial merit.

TIMING

Perhaps the most controversial issue is the time frame within which an opposition must be filed. Several possibilities have been offered. Some proponents have advocated a single window lasting 9 to 12 months after the grant of the patent. Others have included a second window of four to six months after a party receives notification that it is infringing the patent. A smaller minority has advocated an open window throughout the patent term.

The timing decision implicates a tradeoff between certainty and fairness. A patentee desires the certainty of knowing, within a single window after receiving the patent, that its patent is no longer subject to challenge.[91] On the other

---

86. USPTO, *Post-Grant Review of Patent Claims*, at 5, http://www.uspto.gov/web/offices/com/strat21/action/sr2.htm.

87. Patents Depend on Quality Act of 2006, *available at* http://nip.blogs.com/patent/files/17672_patenttext.pdf.

88. 35 U.S.C. § 325(a)(1) (proposed). AIPLA has proposed the same standard. Hearing, at 31 (statement of Michael K. Kirk, Executive Director, American Intellectual Property Law Association (AIPLA)); *id.* at 35 (proposed statute).

89. *Genentech, Inc. v. Novo Nordisk, A/S*, 108 F.3d 1361, 1364 (Fed. Cir. 1997).

90. *E.g., Amazon.com v. Barnesandnoble.com, Inc.*, 239 F.3d 1343, 1359 (Fed. Cir. 2001).

91. *See, e.g., Perspectives on Patents: Post-Grant Review Procedures and Other Litigation Reforms: Hearing Before the S. Comm. on the Judiciary*, at 5, May 23, 2006 (statement of Philip S. Johnson), http://judiciary.senate.gov/print_testimony.cfm?id=1911&wit_id=5367

hand, parties often cannot examine every patent issued and, long before any commercial application is apparent, determine which patents to challenge.

For that reason, many have relied on a fairness argument in advocating a second window that typically lasts four to six months after receiving notification of infringement. By that point, it is clear which patents are commercially viable and (obviously) which patents are allegedly infringing. Proponents of a single window contend that patents subject to challenge years after issuance suffer reduced certainty. But businesses cannot, within one year of issuance, reasonably review all patents, determine all possible claim interpretations, and challenge all that may be applicable and suspect.[92]

Certain industries are particularly likely to need a second window. Pharmaceutical firms will not know at the time a patent is issued whether it will survive lengthy and uncertain clinical trials. Medical device companies do not obtain marketing approval until years after a patent's issuance.[93] Computers, cell phones, airplanes, cars, and communications networks, among other technology products, consist of hundreds or thousands of components against which a patentee could assert a claim. Such companies will not know within a year of a patent's issuance whether the patent might be relevant in the future. In many cases, this problem is exacerbated because infringement claims often do not have much relation to the invention described in the patent.[94]

I propose an opposition procedure with two windows and, tentatively, a third window lasting the life of the patent.

The first window should last for one year after the patent's issuance. Twelve months is a reasonable period of time and is consistent with the PTO's suggested plan.[95] Any party could challenge a patent within the first window.

The second window should last six months after a party receives notification of infringement. Six months gives sufficient, but not excessive, time for an alleged infringer to challenge a patent.[96] The second window would be limited

---

("Were it possible to bring an opposition throughout the life of a patent, competitors knowing of invalidating art or some other validity defect would have no incentive to bring an opposition during the initial period of doing so.").

92. *Perspectives on Patents: Post-Grant Review Procedures and Other Litigation Reforms: Hearing before the S. Comm. on the Judiciary*, at 2, May 23, 2006 (statement of Andrew Cadel), http://judiciary.senate.gov/print_testimony.cfm?id=1911&wit_id=5370.

93. *Hearing on The Patent Reform Act of 2007, before the H. Rep. Subcomm. on Courts, the Internet, and Intellectual Property*, at 11, Apr. 26, 2007 (statement of John R. Thomas).

94. *Perspectives on Patents: Post-Grant Review Procedures and Other Litigation Reforms: Hearing before the S. Comm. on the Judiciary*, at 4, May 23, 2006 (statement of Mark Chandler), http://judiciary.senate.gov/print_testimony.cfm?id=1911&wit_id=5366.

95. USPTO, *Post-Grant Review of Patent Claims*, at 4. *See also* PATENT SYSTEM FOR 21ST CENTURY, at 101 (recommending one-year window).

96. *See* Patents Depend on Quality Act of 2006, at 4 (recommending second window of six months).

to parties that receive notification of infringement. Any concern that PTO oppositions would significantly delay parallel court proceedings could be addressed, as I explain below, by tightly controlling the proceeding and discovery and requiring completion of the opposition within one year.

The most difficult question is whether the opposition procedure should be available outside these two windows. Certainty could be reduced if oppositions were available throughout the patent term. On the other hand, such a position would be fair to requesters, who would not need to quickly challenge a patent before its commercial application is known. In addition, the removal of time limitations could help small companies, which are less likely to have the resources to monitor patents as they are issued.[97]

An open time frame might even have the counterintuitive effect of *reducing* patent challenges. Evidence from early 20th-century Germany provides the first example of this effect. Initially, challengers could bring a nullity proceeding (allowing them to challenge validity) only within five years of the patent grant. But after 30 years of debate between various industries on issues of certainty and abuse, the five-year period was abolished. *After the restrictions on the time period were removed, fewer nullity actions were filed.*[98]

Oppositions in Europe today provide similar evidence. One study found that more than 97 percent of European Patent Office opposition cases are filed within five days of the nine-month opposition deadline.[99] Removal of the deadline would eliminate an artificial limit motivating challenges.

What about the critique that such an open regime would reduce certainty? The patentee, after all, could not be confident, throughout the term of the patent, that it would not be subject to challenge. One response would rely on the importance of challenging invalid patents. Courts have found as many as 46 percent of patents litigated to judgment to be invalid.[100] Because of the harms of invalid patents, opportunities to ascertain validity should be promoted even at the cost of modestly reduced certainty.

In addition, potential validity challenges would not be a wholly new development. Throughout the life of the patent, reexamination systems allow for challenges, and any person may cite "prior art consisting of patents or printed publications" that has "a bearing on the patentability of any claim."[101] Patentees today, in seeking to strengthen their patents, file almost 50 percent of

---

97. Patent System for 21st Century, at 101.

98. N. Thane Bauz, *Reanimating U.S. Patent Reexamination: Recommendations for Change Based Upon a Comparative Study of German Law*, 27 Creighton L. Rev. 945, 975 (1994); Janis, at 119 n.518.

99. Hall & Harhoff, at 1008.

100. Allison & Lemley, at 205.

101. 35 U.S.C. § 301.

ex parte reexaminations.[102] One result of an open time period for post-grant oppositions would be an increased incentive for the patentee to search for and disclose prior art.

But given that the opposition system is designed to be used more frequently by challengers, what adjustments could be made to address the concern of reduced certainty? Two additional modifications could cabin the harassment potential of an open challenge period.

The first would impose a one-way fee shifting mechanism for unsuccessful challenges outside the first and second windows.[103] Challenges made outside the first two windows bear a greater potential for harassment. Therefore, requiring the challenger to pay the patentees' costs and attorneys' fees if the patent is judged valid could reduce meritless challenges. The challenger would not be required to pay fees where any patent claim is held invalid or amended. The fee-shifting proposal, at a minimum, would raise the cost to challengers who rely on questionable evidence in filing oppositions outside the two windows.[104]

The second modification would impose a fee system for opposition challenges similar to the PTO's current structure for patent maintenance fees. The PTO requires patentees to pay maintenance fees 3½ years, 7½ years, and 11½ years after the issuance of the patent.[105] Failure to make such payments on the due date (or within a six-month grace period) leads to the expiration of the patent.[106]

The fee structure was adopted to make the PTO self-financing. A central element of the system was the provision for patent fees to be paid in installments over the life of the patent. Such a structure, which has been adopted by the European Patent Office, Japan, and many developing countries, was designed to "soften the impact on inventors." If the invention ultimately does not have commercial value, the inventor can let the patent expire, avoiding the need to pay additional fees. If, in contrast, the invention has achieved market success, fees would not present a significant burden.[107]

Another key element is the 50 percent reduction for small entities in maintenance fees and the original application fee.[108] As of July 2010, the maintenance fee for a patent in force more than eight years was $2,360 for typical inventors and $1,180 for small entities.[109] The category of small entities includes

---

102. PATENT SYSTEM FOR 21ST CENTURY, at 96.

103. For an example of fee shifting, see President's Commission on the Patent System, *To Promote the Progress of . . . Useful Arts*, S. Doc. No. 5, at 37 (1967) (proposing that parties unsuccessful in canceling claims pay the patentee's costs and attorneys' fees).

104. Janis, at 120.

105. 35 U.S.C. § 41(b) (2002); 37 C.F.R. § 1.20 (e)–(g) (2008); 37 C.F.R. § 1.362 (2008).

106. 35 U.S.C. § 41(b).

107. Todd Dickinson, "Study of Alternative Fee Structures," 65 Fed. Reg. 58746, 58747 (Oct. 2, 2000), http://www.uspto.gov/web/offices/com/sol/notices/staltfeestr.html.

108. 35 U.S.C. § 41(h)(1).

109. 37 C.F.R. § 1.20(f).

individuals, small business concerns (with fewer than 500 employees), and nonprofit organizations such as universities, 501(c)(3) organizations, and non-profit scientific or educational institutions. To be covered, these entities cannot convey or license rights in the invention to parties that are not small entities themselves.[110]

The PTO's fee structure provides a useful framework for oppositions. A requester offers the most justifiable challenges in the first two windows, immediately after the patent is issued and after it is sued for infringement. Challenges outside these two windows should be subject to fees.

Like patent maintenance fees, opposition fees could follow an increased schedule. One possible schedule would require fees of $1,000 per year. For example, a challenger filing in year 10 would pay a $10,000 fee, and one filing in year 16 would pay a $16,000 fee. The fees would only apply to challenges outside the first two windows. The increased fees over time would impose a modest deterrent effect against later challenges.

Another element of the maintenance fee system that could be imported involves reduced fees for small entities. Inventors, small businesses, and nonprofit organizations should pay lower fees. A 50 percent reduction seems reasonable.

The open period for challenges and fee-shifting provisions should be monitored. If fee shifting and opposition fees do not prevent excessive improper challenges, then it would be appropriate to limit challenges to the two windows (or even to impose fees escalating over time within the two windows). If few challenges occur outside the two windows, but there is evidence that many important invalid patents are not being challenged, then perhaps less-deterrent (e.g., partial) fee shifting would be appropriate.

In short, the open period should be subject to reassessment and empirical review. But at a minimum, the first and second windows are needed.

REVIEWABLE SUBJECT MATTER

Current reexamination procedures allow requesters to challenge only a patent's novelty or nonobviousness. They can do so by introducing only prior patents or publications.[111]

My proposed opposition would cover more grounds for challenging a patent's validity. In particular, a requester could challenge a patent's novelty, nonobviousness, utility, subject matter, enablement, and written description. The utility requirement ensures that the invention is useful. Subject matter makes certain

---

110. 37 C.F.R. § 1.27(a)–(b) (2008); 13 C.F.R. § 121.802 (2008).
111. 37 C.F.R. § 1.510(b).

that the invention falls in a proper category. Enablement and written description ensure that an owner is entitled to the breadth of its patent and is in possession of the invention at the time of filing.[112] Finally, I would allow challenges based on evidence other than patents and printed publications, such as an invention's prior use or sale.

Two validity requirements should not be examined because they would require examiners to delve into a patentee's mental state. The best mode of carrying out the invention and the priority race (by which the PTO decides which of two claimants is the first inventor) require subjective determinations that threaten to introduce delay and complication into the process. These issues depend on an inventor's state of mind and cannot be resolved without extensive discovery that would lengthen the proceeding and significantly increase its cost.[113] Issues of patent enforcement such as fraud and inequitable conduct also should not be considered because they threaten to bog down the opposition in nuanced, fact-intensive inquiries and because the PTO less frequently considers these subjects.[114]

At a minimum, expanding the grounds for validity challenges would allow most such challenges to occur in one forum. It would take advantage of the agency's expertise, as the PTO is familiar with validity issues. But it would not venture outside the agency's strengths and introduce burdensome inquiries.

NATURE OF EVIDENTIARY SHOWING

The requester would need to establish facts, by a preponderance of the evidence, that demonstrate the patent's invalidity. This is the traditional standard that the PTO requires proponents to satisfy in administrative proceedings such as patent examinations and reexaminations, reissue proceedings, and most interference proceedings.[115] In its proposal for a post-grant opposition system, the PTO recommended the preponderance standard.[116]

An alleged infringer challenging a patent's validity in court must demonstrate invalidity by the higher standard of clear and convincing evidence. The lower preponderance standard thus encourages validity challenges in post-grant opposition proceedings.[117] This lower standard, combined with a relatively

---

112. Hearing, at 14 (statement of Jeffrey P. Kushan).

113. Hearing, at 31 (testimony of Michael K. Kirk, Executive Director, American Intellectual Property Law Association (AIPLA)); id. at 35 (proposed statute).

114. USPTO, *Post-Grant Review of Patent Claims*, at 5.

115. *Id.* at 10.

116. *Id.*

117. Hearing, at 28 (Kirk testimony).

inexpensive forum and judges knowledgeable about patent law, should encourage use of the procedure.

JUDGES AND APPEALS

Which judges will hear oppositions? Not the examiners who initially granted the patent, as they might be hesitant to overturn their initial decision. The PTO, in its proposed plan, reasonably called for the proceedings to be conducted by Administrative Patent Judges (APJs) of the Board of Patent Appeals and Interferences.[118] A panel of three judges could consider the opposition.

The opposition should be completed within one year. The PTO advocated such a time frame in its proposed system, pointing to its experience in meeting one-year deadlines in other contexts.[119] And the European opposition, with drawn-out proceedings and no limits, serves as a reminder of the dangers of an excessively open-ended approach.

The panel could issue a written decision on the patentability of the contested claims by confirming the patent, cancelling it, or requiring it to be amended.[120] A party could file a request for reconsideration of the decision. And the final determination could be appealed to the Federal Circuit.[121]

Institution of an opposition procedure would reduce the need for *inter partes* reexaminations. In fact, an opposition procedure would allow parties to proceed on all grounds available under *inter partes* reexamination.[122] Given that the PTO is most aware of its resource constraints, its recommendation to eliminate *inter partes* reexamination should be entitled to deference.[123]

PROCEEDING

What form would the opposition take? It should allow greater involvement for the requester and a broader range of validity challenges than the current reexamination systems. But it should not expand to the point that it imitates the cost and breadth of litigation.

---

118. USPTO, *Post-Grant Review of Patent Claims*, at 1.

119. *Id.* at 13.

120. PATENT SYSTEM FOR 21ST CENTURY, at 101. This new responsibility may require an increase in APJs. Hearing, at 33 (Kirk testimony).

121. USPTO, *Post-Grant Review of Patent Claims*, at 17; Patents Depend on Quality Act of 2006, at 10–11.

122. USPTO, *Post-Grant Review of Patent Claims*, at 13.

123. *Id.* at 13–15.

One effective way to reduce expense is to call for the requester to present its case through affidavit and deposition, thereby eliminating live direct testimony.[124] This technique was effective in the sprawling Microsoft antitrust case as the judge required all direct witness testimony to be submitted in writing, which dramatically reduced the length of the proceedings.[125]

The patentee could then challenge the requester's case by cross-examining any of the parties who submitted an affidavit or deposition. Cross-examination is essential for testing a declarant's assertions, especially for issues other than the application of printed prior art.[126] It is needed to make credibility determinations and to encourage requesters (who may be prevented from raising particular issues again) to use the process. And it should ensure the appellate court's deference, as the panel can observe witnesses' demeanor.[127] Similarly, the requester should be able, in the opposition proceeding, to cross-examine any party that submits an affidavit or deposition for the patentee.[128]

Most of the expense of district court litigation stems from expansive document requests, interrogatories, and other forms of discovery. Post-grant opposition proceedings will offer an advantage over litigation only by streamlining discovery. One simple means to control discovery is to not require document productions.[129] Another is provided by the PTO plan, which calls for *mandatory limited disclosures* but allows discovery only for good cause.[130]

Disclosures should cover only information related to the potential grounds of an opposition. Because I propose opposition challenges on the basis of novelty, nonobviousness, utility, subject matter, enablement, and written description, the parties can introduce information relevant to these grounds. In contrast, issues dealing with, for example, infringement, inequitable conduct, and inventive activity would not be disclosed.

One example of mandatory disclosures is provided by the local patent rules of the district court of the Northern District of California. The rules, which other courts have adopted, require alleged infringers to disclose (1) the grounds on which they rely in claiming invalidity and (2) the prior art supporting their claims of anticipation or obviousness.[131] Such disclosures have made it easier for judges to determine validity.

---

124. *Id.* at 11.

125. Andrew I. Gavil, *The End of Antitrust Trench Warfare?: An Analysis of Some Procedural Aspects of the Microsoft Trial*, 13 ANTITRUST 7, 8–9 (1999).

126. To PROMOTE INNOVATION, at 215.

127. *Id.*

128. Hearing, at 32 (Kirk testimony).

129. Hearing, at 18 (statement of Jeffrey P. Kushan).

130. USPTO, *Post-Grant Review of Patent Claims*, at 9–10.

131. N.D.CAL. PATENT L.R. 3-3. The grounds include anticipation, obviousness, indefiniteness, enablement, and written description.

Another potential framework is provided by trademark registration disputes. Parties to *inter partes* proceedings before the Trademark Trial and Appeal Board must make initial disclosures within 30 days of the opening of discovery and cannot seek discovery until providing the disclosures.[132]

The challenger in a post-grant opposition could engage in further discovery only after demonstrating "good cause," such as when third parties hold information not available through the initial disclosure.[133] A rigorous interpretation of good cause would, as the PTO Plan explained, "restrict [the] nature and volume" of discovery, ensuring lower expenses than litigation.[134]

Finally, the PTO can take advantage of its expertise. The judges' technical backgrounds and experience in particular fields reduce the need for experts and offer an advantage over litigation.[135]

REAL PARTY IN INTEREST

Another contentious issue is whether the requester must disclose its identity. Disclosure could limit patentee harassment and reduce conflicts of interest. A conflict could arise if a requester relies on factual evidence or expert opinions in the form of affidavits or declarations.[136] In that case, the PTO would not be able to ascertain the relationship between the requester and the party supporting its position.

On the other hand, disclosure could discourage challenges by parties fearing "large infringement targets being painted on their backs."[137] Such fear would have a pronounced effect on smaller competitors or rivals that have substantially invested in a product or have products on the market. The latter two categories would be especially likely to accept royalty payments rather than taking the risk of reducing the value of their investments from an adverse court ruling.[138]

In its patent reform "white paper," the American Bar Association Section of IP Law offered a reasonable compromise. It proposed that the requester disclose its identity to the PTO but not to the patent owner unless it relies on affidavit or

---

132. 37 CFR § 2.120 (2007). The Trademark Trial and Appeal Board is an administrative tribunal of the PTO that determines the registration of marks and has jurisdiction over oppositions, cancellations, interferences, and concurrent use proceedings. USPTO, Trademark Trial and Appeal Board Manual of Procedure (TBMP), §§ 102.01 to 102.02, at 100-6 to 100-8 (2d ed. 2003, 1st rev. 2004), http://www.uspto.gov/web/offices/dcom/ttab/tbmp/100.pdf.

133. USPTO, *Post-Grant Review of Patent Claims*, at 10.

134. *Id.* at 9.

135. Hearing, at 18 (statement of Jeffrey P. Kushan).

136. Patents Depend on Quality Act of 2006, at 4.

137. Williams, *Remembering the Public's Interest in the Patent System*.

138. *Id.*

declaration evidence.[139] Such a proposal would protect the requester from becoming a target for infringement litigation while allowing the patentee to determine the relationship between the real party in interest and any party submitting a declaration or affidavit.

ESTOPPEL EFFECT

One of the primary failings of the *inter partes* reexamination statute has been its overbroad estoppel provisions. In preventing parties from subsequently raising any fact at issue in the proceeding as well as any ground that could have been raised, the estoppel provisions have greatly discouraged reexaminations.

Estoppel should apply only to grounds that were raised and addressed in the reexamination. Requesters should not be prohibited from later advancing arguments that they could have raised, but did not, during reexamination. Congress incorporated estoppel provisions in the reexamination statute to "prevent harassment" of patentees and to serve as "the insulation that effectively protects patent holders."[140] This purpose is directly implicated when a party gets two bites at the invalidity apple.

But issues not raised by the requester do not implicate such policy. The requester does not get two bites at the apple because it does not actually raise the issue during opposition. Limiting estoppel to grounds that are raised also allows parties and courts to avoid determining the elusive issue of the grounds the requesters *could* have raised.

The second element of estoppel is that the PTO addresses the argument. Even if a requester raises an issue, she should not be barred from later relying on it if the PTO does not address it. There is no guarantee that the PTO will address all arguments against patentability. If unaddressed issues could lead to estoppel in later proceedings, requesters would be less likely to use the process.

Finally, if the requester could not, at the time of the reexamination, reasonably have discovered new evidence that is material to an issue, then it should not be precluded from later raising the evidence and the issue affected by it.[141] Such a rule is fair to the requester. And because the evidence could not have been raised, such a rule also does not implicate patentee harassment.

---

139. ABA Section of Intellectual Property Law, *A Section White Paper: Agenda for 21st Century Patent Reform*, at 31, http://www.abanet.org/intelprop/home/PatentReformWP. pdf. Disclosure also would be required if the requestor became a party to a Federal Circuit appeal so the judges could determine whether to recuse themselves.

140. 145 Cong. Rec. E1788, E1790 (daily ed. Aug. 3, 1999) (statement of Rep. Coble) (harassment); 145 Cong. Rec. H6929, H6944 (daily ed. Aug. 3, 1999) (statement of Rep. Rohrabacher) (insulation).

141. Patents Depend on Quality Act of 2006, at 12.

CONCLUSION

The patent system plays a crucial role in fostering innovation. But the existence of invalid patents threatens to hamper innovation.

The initial patent examination will not, and should not, be perfect. Litigation is expensive and offers skewed incentives to the parties. And the flaws plaguing the current reexamination systems have minimized their role. A new opposition system is needed.

The opposition system described in this chapter offers a cheaper and more effective means to promote certainty. It would focus on the most valuable patents, increase the information available to patent examiners, and reduce the number of invalid patents. In short, it would promote innovation.

An added bonus of the proposal would be its effect on antitrust. By providing a low-cost avenue to remove invalid patents, it would reduce the incidence of market power. Market power allows parties to increase the price paid by consumers and to reduce innovation. Not all patents, to be sure, give their holders market power. And not all market power provided by patents is unwanted. In fact, it is the anticipated consequence of providing patent protection.

But market power resulting from invalid patents is undesirable and bogs antitrust courts down in unnecessary cases. Antitrust cases in general are complex and expensive. They are even more complicated when patents are involved. As discussed in Chapters 4 and 5, antitrust courts confront real challenges in addressing patent-related issues. Reducing such cases would have desirable effects.

10. LESS DANGEROUS PATENTS: A FRAMEWORK FOR RELIEF

The Problem 233
Patent Remedies 235
Federal Circuit Injunctions 236
eBay 237
Post-eBay Landscape 238
Cases Granting Injunctions 239
    Irreparable Harm 239
    Inadequate Legal Remedy 240
    Balance of Hardships 241
    Public Interest 241
Cases Denying Injunctions 242
    Irreparable Harm 242
    Inadequate Remedy 242
    Balance of Hardships 243
    Public Interest 243
Synthesis 244
Proposed Framework 244
    Competition and Irreparable Harm 244
    Core Component and Inadequate Legal Remedy 246
    Balance of Hardships 248
    Public Interest 249
Operation of Test 250
Conclusion 251

As a nation, we have become addicted to our BlackBerrys. They are our browsers, our e-mail, our phones, our GPS systems. But imagine our BlackBerrys being shut off. All across the country. All at once. A wireless nation gone dark. Just a short time ago, this nearly happened.

New Technologies Products (NTP) was a patent-holding company that administered patents developed by its founder, Thomas Campana, Jr.[1] It claimed that several of its patents were infringed by the BlackBerry devices manufactured by Research in Motion (RIM). New Technologies Products sued RIM and won a jury verdict. The judge issued (and then stayed) an order barring the sale of BlackBerrys in the United States.[2]

---

1. George H. Pike, *Blackberry: Lawsuit and Patent Reform*, INFO. TODAY, May 2006, http://www.infotoday.com/IT/mayo6/Pike.shtml.

2. Barrie McKenna et al., *Patently Absurd: The Inside Story of RIM's Wireless War*, THE GLOBE & MAIL, Feb. 21, 2006, http://www.theglobeandmail.com/servlet/story/RTGAM.20060221. wpatentlyabsured-rim21/BNStory/RIM2006/home.

Research in Motion appealed. While the lawsuit was on appeal, the U.S. Patent and Trademark Office (PTO) issued final rejections for two of the five disputed patents and continued to review three patents that had already received preliminary rejections.[3] The parties then entered into a settlement agreement by which RIM paid $612.5 million to NTP. Nor was RIM the only firm subject to NTP pressure, as licensing agreements with Nokia and Good Technology revealed.[4]

To be sure, NTP's Campana—in contrast to entities that acquire patents without playing any role in their creation or commercialization—was an inventor who developed nationwide paging systems and other technologies.[5] But the potential effect of shutting down four million users' BlackBerrys demonstrates the dangers of reflexively granting injunctive relief.

Until the Supreme Court's decision in 2006 in *eBay, Inc. v. MercExchange, LLC*, the Federal Circuit had granted injunctive relief in every case in which it had found patent infringement.[6] Patentees appreciated this framework, which offered a strong remedy for infringement. But even property law—through doctrines of trespass, easements, and encroachments—reveals that owners sometimes are limited to damages remedies in enforcing their right to exclude.[7]

In this chapter, I first describe the problems posed by automatic injunctive relief. I then discuss the array of potential remedies for infringement. Next, I summarize the Court's decision in *eBay*. Finally, I examine the post-*eBay* landscape, synthesizing the cases and offering a framework that provides guidance to courts in determining the form of relief in patent infringement cases.

I conclude that injunctive relief is appropriate where

(1) the patentee competes with the infringer in the marketplace,
(2) the patented technology is a core component of the defendant's product, or
(3) (in most cases) a party willfully infringes the patent.

When these elements are not satisfied, courts should examine other factors, which include the effect of injunctive relief on the public. Damages will be appropriate in certain cases such as where a manufacturer inadvertently infringes a patented component making up a small part of a product and the public would suffer substantial harm from injunctive relief. Despite these scenarios, courts

---

3. Andrew R. Hickey, *BlackBerry Dodges Blackout Bullet for Now*, MobileComputing.com, Feb. 24, 2006, http://searchmobilecomputing.techtarget.com/news/article/0,289142,sid40_gci1168761,00.html. The "final rejections" were less final than they might initially appear, as NTP could appeal them to the PTO's Board of Patent Appeals and Interferences and, eventually, the Federal Circuit.

4. David Radack, *Patent Trolls*, IP Frontline, Apr. 11, 2006, http://www.ipfrontline.com/depts/article.asp?id=10306&deptid=3.

5. McKenna et al., *Patently Absurd*.

6. 547 U.S. 388 (2006).

7. Michael A. Carrier, *Cabining Intellectual Property Through a Property Paradigm*, 54 Duke L.J. 1, 52–81 (2004).

should still apply a default rule that injunctive relief is the appropriate remedy for patent infringement.

THE PROBLEM

The problem with automatic injunctive relief can be traced to the evolving relationship between patents and the products in which they appear. For much of the nation's history, an invention tended to be covered by a single patent.[8] But in the late 20th century, devices more frequently incorporated numerous components, each of which could be patented. This shift is mirrored in the decline of mechanical inventions (which are often covered by a single patent) and rise in software, Internet, and semiconductor inventions (which could be covered by hundreds or thousands of patented components).[9]

One illustration of the growth in multiple patented inputs appears in the burgeoning field known as *convergent medical technologies*, which lies at the intersection of biopharmaceuticals, information technology, and nanotechnology.[10] Drug-eluting stents, for example, combine a stent (metal scaffold) with a drug that inhibits artery reblocking after an angioplasty procedure. Because separate parties could own the stent, the polymer[11] harboring the drug, and the drug, an injunction on any of the components could remove the life-saving technology from the market.[12]

For most of the past quarter-century, until the *eBay* case, any patentee could receive an injunction that removed the product from the market. Such relief gave commanding leverage to the patentee to obtain settlements that greatly exceeded a reasonable royalty and reflected the significant costs of switching technologies.[13] Manufacturers might be required to spend millions of dollars to redesign their products after designing, testing, packaging, and

---

8. Mark A. Lemley & Philip J. Weiser, *Should Property or Liability Rules Govern Information?*, 85 TEX. L. REV. 783, 797 (2007).

9. John R. Allison & Mark A. Lemley, *The Growing Complexity of the United States Patent System*, 82 B.U. L. REV. 77, 93 tbl.1 (2002).

10. Nanotechnology refers to "the engineering of functional systems at the molecular scale." Center for Responsible Nanotechnology, *What is Nanotechnology?*, http://www.crnano.org/whatis.htm (last visited August 29, 2008).

11. A polymer is a high-molecular-weight material composed of repeating subunits. *Polymer*, ANSWERS.COM, http://www.answers.com/topic/polymer?cat=technology (last visited May 26, 2008).

12. *Drug-Eluting Stent Overview*, ANGIOPLASTY.ORG, http://www.ptca.org/des.html (last visited May 26, 2008); Ogan Gurel, *Innovation Increases Patent Law Turmoil*, WALL ST. J., Apr. 17, 2006.

13 Testimony of Mark A. Lemley before Sen. Comm. on Judiciary, June 14, 2005, at 7, http://judiciary.senate.gov/print_testimony.cfm?id=1535&wit_id=4352 [Lemley testimony].

marketing them.[14] They also could be forced to retrain workforces, retool assembly lines, renegotiate licenses, or even shut down product lines.[15]

Some of the patentees seeking settlements have been referred to as *patent trolls.* Such a term comes from fairy tales in which a troll hiding under a bridge leaps out to demand a toll before letting anyone cross. Certain patentees, so the analogy goes, wait until products incorporating the patented technology are marketed, at which point they surface to charge a toll of licensing fees.

Peter Detkin, then-assistant general counsel at Intel, coined the term, asserting that a patent troll is "somebody who tries to make a lot of money off a patent that they are not practicing and have no intention of practicing and in most cases never practiced."[16] No single definition of the term is accepted today, but the general concept applies to entities that do not manufacture products but acquire patents to obtain settlement payments.

The term *troll*, of course, elicits condemnation. Not all trolls are worthy of such treatment. For example, universities and individual inventors often license, but lack the capability to manufacture, products. Because of the negative connotations (which are not useful in determining appropriate relief), I instead use the term *nonpracticing entity.*[17]

Nonpracticing entities have characteristics that distinguish them from practicing patent owners and make them less hesitant to file lawsuits. First, they typically are not concerned with liability exposure. Because they do not manufacture products, they need not worry about patent infringement counterclaims. As a result, they may be emboldened to file lawsuits. Second, nonpracticing entities usually do not confront customers exerting pressure to settle litigation or shareholders skeptical of patent enforcement.[18]

As a result, nonpracticing entities may be emboldened to threaten lawsuits and injunctions. One example was provided by NTP in the BlackBerry case. Two other examples reveal nonpracticing entities offering even less evidence of inventive activity.

The first involved Intel. In 2001, TechSearch, a patent-holding company, sued Intel for infringing its patent on a method for transmitting data between computers. TechSearch did not invent the technology or manufacture products

---

14. CCIA brief, at 7.

15. Gavin D. George, *What Is Hiding in the Bushes? eBay's Effect on Holdout Behavior in Patent Thickets*, 13 MICH. TELECOMM. & TECH. L. REV. 557, 570 (2007); Brief for Amicus Curiae Computer & Comms. Industry Ass'n in Support of Petitioners, *eBay Inc. v. MercExchange*, LLC, No. 05-130, at 2-3 (U.S. Jan. 26, 2006) [hereinafter CCIA brief].

16. Brenda Sandburg, *Trolling for Dollars*, THE RECORDER, July 30, 2001, at 1, http://www.law.com/regionals/ca/stories/edt0730a.shtml.

17. FED. TRADE COMM'N, TO PROMOTE INNOVATION: THE PROPER BALANCE OF COMPETITION AND PATENT LAW AND POLICY 147 (2003), http://www.ftc.gov/os/2003/10/innovationrpt.pdf.

18. Danielle Williams & Steven Gardner, *Basic Framework for Effective Responses to Patent Trolls*, NORTH CAROLINA BAR ASS'N, at 1, Apr. 2006, *available at* http://www.kilpatrickstockton.com/publications/downloads/IPLinksApril2006.pdf.

based on it.[19] But it spent $50,000 to buy the patent in bankruptcy proceedings and waited for a company to infringe its patent. Intel infringed the patent, one of thousands of patented components in its microprocessor, and TechSearch sought $5 billion for patent infringement.[20] Although Intel won the case, roughly 100 companies (including Sears and Hyatt) have paid millions of dollars to license TechSearch's technology.[21]

A second example is provided by Acacia. This company's attorneys claimed that its patents covered "virtually all on-demand transmissions of compressed audio and video over the Internet, cable TV lines, satellite and wireless services."[22] In 2003, Acadia sent letters to colleges and universities demanding licensing fees for audio or video files transferred for distance-education purposes. In 2004, it expanded its claims, seeking compensation for each transmission of audio or video files (including for purposes other than distance education) and a minimum annual royalty of $5,000.[23] In addition to these demands, Acacia sued Direct TV, Comcast, Echostar, and others for patent infringement and entered into more than 300 licensing agreements with companies providing online entertainment, cable TV, hotel on-demand TV services, and corporate advertising and promotion.[24]

Questions concerning the existence of nonpracticing entities and the magnitude of the problem they pose arouse spirited debate today. For our purposes, these issues do not need to be resolved. For the remedy determination does not depend on the answers. As the facts of the z4 v. Microsoft and Toyota v. Paice cases described later in this chapter reveal, patentee commercialization activity is less important than (1) the competitive relationship between the patentee and infringer, (2) whether the patented technology is a core component of the infringer's invention, and (3) the effect of an injunction on the public.

PATENT REMEDIES

Once a court finds a defendant liable for patent infringement, it can choose from an array of remedies. One set of remedies aims to prevent or deter future infringement.

---

19. Ifran A. Lateef & Joshua Stowell, A Supreme End to Patent Trolls, 49 ORANGE COUNTY LAW. 18, 19 (Aug. 2007).

20. Brenda Sandburg, A Modest Proposal, THE RECORDER, May 9, 2005, at 1, http://www.law.com/jsp/article.jsp?id=1115370308794.

21. Sandburg, Trolling for Dollars, at 1.

22. John Borland, Streaming Patent Claims Go to Court, CNET NEWS, Feb. 14, 2003, http://www.news.com/2100-1023-984698.html.

23. Wesley D. Blakeslee, The Acacia Patent Claims and Options for Educational Institutions, 2004, at 1–2, http://www.nacua.org/documents/Blakeslee-Acacia3.pdf#search='The%20Acacia%20Patent%CC20Claims%CC20and%CC20Options%CC20.

24. Acacia Unit Sues DirecTV, Others, LOS ANGELES BUS., June 16, 2004, http://www.bizjournals.com/losangeles/stories/2004/06/14/daily22.html; Terrence P. McMahon et al., Who Is a Troll? Not a Simple Answer, 7 SEDONA CONF. J. 159, 162 (2006).

Courts can issue injunctions ordering defendants to stop using, manufacturing, selling, or distributing infringing products.[25] They can award punitive damages of up to three times the amount of compensatory damages.[26] And in exceptional cases, they can award reasonable attorneys' fees.[27]

The second set of remedies compensates the patentee for infringement. The traditional measure of damages, available when the patentee and infringer compete in the same market, is the patentee's lost profits. In other cases, when the parties do not compete or the patentee cannot prove lost profits, courts have awarded reasonable royalties.[28] Courts also can award interest for prejudgment infringement and for postjudgment delay in paying damages.[29]

For most of the 20th century, courts issued injunctions in nearly all of the cases in which they found infringement. The sole exception involved the few cases affecting public health. In one of these cases, a court refused to issue an injunction that would have prohibited Milwaukee from operating its sewage plant, thereby forcing it to dump raw sewage into Lake Michigan.[30] In another, a court denied an injunction that would have led to an increased incidence of rickets.[31]

FEDERAL CIRCUIT INJUNCTIONS

For the first 25 years of its existence, the Federal Circuit automatically issued injunctive relief in cases in which it found patent infringement. Three years after the court's creation, in 1985, it stated that "injunctive relief against an infringer is the norm."[32] A year later, the Federal Circuit affirmed an injunction even though the infringer likely would have been put out of business.[33]

Subsequent cases adhered to this pattern, emphasizing that injunctions should be granted as a matter of course.[34] The court in 2005, for example, overturned

---

25. Courts can award permanent injunctions after, and preliminary injunctions before, final judgments of infringement. DONALD S. CHISUM ET AL., PRINCIPLES OF PATENT LAW 1340 (3d ed. 2004).

26. 35 U.S.C. § 284.

27. 35 U.S.C. § 285.

28. CHISUM ET AL., at 1286.

29. *Id.* at 1334–35. The statute provides that patentees can receive "damages adequate to compensate for the infringement, but in no event less than a reasonable royalty." 35 U.S.C. § 284.

30. *City of Milwaukee v. Activated Sludge, Inc.*, 69 F.2d 577, 593 (7th Cir. 1934).

31. *Vitamin Technologists, Inc. v. Wisconsin Alumni Research Found.*, 146 F.2d 941, 942, 945 (9th Cir. 1944).

32. *KSM Fastening Sys's, Inc. v. H.A. Jones Co.*, 776 F.2d 1522, 1524 (Fed. Cir. 1985).

33. *Windsurfing Int'l v. AMF, Inc.*, 782 F.2d 995, 1003 n.12 (Fed. Cir. 1986).

34. *See, e.g.*, *W.L. Gore & Assoc. v. Garlock, Inc.*, 842 F.2d 1275, 1281 (Fed. Cir. 1988); *Richardson v. Suzuki Motor Co.*, 868 F.2d 1226, 1247 (Fed. Cir. 1989).

a district court's denial of an injunction, finding "no reason to depart from the general rule that courts will issue permanent injunctions against patent infringement absent exceptional circumstances."[35]

The issue of remedies would be dramatically altered in the case of *eBay v. MercExchange*.

eBay

MercExchange owned a business method patent for online auction technology. eBay operated the well-known Web site that allowed users to buy products by participating in live auctions. The system at issue in the litigation allowed users to avoid the auction process and purchase products at a fixed price.[36] MercExchange offered to license this technology to eBay. The parties, however, were unable to reach agreement, which led to MercExchange filing suit. A jury found that eBay and its subsidiary willfully infringed the patent, and that the damages totaled $35 million.[37]

After trial, MercExchange sought a permanent injunction.[38] The district court denied this relief, holding that

(1) MercExchange had not suffered irreparable harm since it "d[id] not practice its inventions and exist[ed] merely to license its patented technology to others,"
(2) an adequate legal remedy existed since MercExchange had previously licensed its patents,
(3) the balance of hardships favored eBay, and
(4) the widespread concern about business method patents confirmed that the denial of injunctive relief was in the public interest.[39]

MercExchange appealed. The Federal Circuit reversed on the grounds that the district court had failed to "provide any persuasive reason to believe th[e] case [wa]s sufficiently exceptional to justify the denial of a permanent injunction." The court rejected each of the grounds advanced by the district court to justify the denial of injunctive relief. And it restated its general rule that "a permanent injunction will issue once infringement and validity have been adjudged."[40]

---

35. *MercExchange v. eBay*, 401 F.3d 1323, 1339 (Fed. Cir. 2005), *vacated, eBay, Inc. v. MercExchange, LLC*, 547 U.S. 388 (2006).

36. *Id.* at 1325.

37. *Id.* at 1326.

38. *MercExchange LLC v. eBay, Inc.*, 275 F. Supp.2d 695, 710 (E.D. Va. 2003), *rev'd*, 401 F.3d 1323, 1339 (Fed. Cir. 2005), *vacated, eBay, Inc. v. MercExchange, LLC*, 547 U.S. 388 (2006).

39. *Id.* at 711–15.

40. *MercExchange*, 401 F.3d at 1338, 1339.

eBay appealed, and the Supreme Court granted certiorari. The Court reversed, reminding the Federal Circuit that well-established equity principles require courts to apply the traditional four-factor test in determining whether to grant injunctive relief. In particular, a plaintiff must demonstrate that

(1) it has suffered irreparable injury;

(2) remedies available at law, such as monetary damages, are inadequate to compensate for that injury;

(3) considering the balance of hardships between the plaintiff and defendant, a remedy in equity is warranted; and

(4) the public interest would not be disserved by a permanent injunction.[41]

The Court explained that the Patent Act provides that injunctions "may" issue in accordance with principles of equity.[42] And it made clear that such discretion is not limited by the property attributes of patents, as "the creation of a right is distinct from the provision of remedies for violations of that right."[43]

The Court then found that both the district court and Federal Circuit had incorrectly applied the test. The district court had erred by relying on the plaintiff's lack of commercial activity and willingness to license to demonstrate irreparable harm. The Federal Circuit, on the other hand, had erred in creating an automatic presumption for injunctive relief. The Court concluded that lower courts should decide whether to grant or deny injunctive relief in their discretion and consistent with principles of equity.[44]

There were two concurrences in the case. In one, Chief Justice Roberts (joined by Justices Scalia and Ginsburg) urged the court to limit its discretion by looking to precedent, which demonstrated the longstanding propriety of injunctive relief.[45] In the other, Justice Kennedy (joined by Justices Stevens, Souter, and Breyer) explained that the historical practice reflected a different type of innovation and advised courts to deny injunctive relief when "the patented invention is but a small component of the product the companies seek to produce and the threat of an injunction is employed simply for undue leverage in negotiations."[46]

POST-*eBay* LANDSCAPE

As a result of the Supreme Court's *eBay* decision, courts no longer automatically grant permanent injunctions in patent infringement cases. How have courts

---

41. *eBay, Inc. v. MercExchange, LLC*, 547 U.S. 388, 391 (2006).

42. *Id.* at 392; *see* 35 U.S.C. § 283.

43. *eBay*, 547 U.S. at 392.

44. *Id.* at 394.

45. *Id.* at 394–95 (Roberts, J., concurring).

46. *Id.* at 395–97 (Kennedy, J., concurring).

applied the four-factor test in the wake of *eBay*? I next explore the post-*eBay* cases, analyzing each of the factors, first in the cases granting injunctions and then in the cases denying injunctions. Nearly all of the cases are district court decisions. In the several years since the *eBay* decision, the Federal Circuit has played a limited role in the area.

CASES GRANTING INJUNCTIONS

Irreparable Harm

The first factor asks whether the plaintiff will suffer irreparable harm in the absence of an injunction. The most crucial element of irreparable harm is the presence of competition between the parties. When the parties compete in the same market (especially an emerging or small market), the plaintiff is more likely to suffer irreparable harm in the form of losses to market share, profits, or reputation.

Five cases are illustrative. In the first, *TiVo Inc. v. Echostar Communications Corp.*, defendant EchoStar sold digital video recorders (DVRs) that infringed plaintiff TiVo's patent. The two parties competed to sell their products in the DVR market, with EchoStar "specifically target[ing] potential TiVo customers." As a result of EchoStar's infringing activity, TiVo, "a relatively new company with only one primary product," lost market share. Even worse, it did so in a market that was just developing and that consisted of consumers exhibiting brand loyalty.[47]

In the second case, *Transocean Offshore Deepwater Drilling, Inc. v. GlobalSantaFe Corp.*, GlobalSantaFe's deep water drilling rigs, used to extract oil, infringed Transocean's patents. GlobalSantaFe used its rigs "to win contracts over competing bids from Transocean," which was particularly harmful in a developing market with a small customer base.[48]

In *MGM Well Services, Inc. v. Mega Lift Systems, LLC*, defendant Mega Lift sold a product that infringed MGM's two-piece plunger lift system, used in gas wells to remove liquids and increase gas flow. The companies competed in several markets and were the only ones marketing the device covered by the patent.[49]

In *Smith & Nephew, Inc. v. Synthes*, the defendant used the plaintiff's patent to treat hip fractures. The two parties competed in the market. The defendant had suffered "stagnant growth" until producing the infringing products, at which point it gained significant sales. Its sales had a "direct negative impact" on plaintiff's sales, hurting its ability to create customer relationships and making it less likely to develop new products.[50]

---

47. 446 F. Supp. 2d 664, 666, 669–70 (E.D. Tex. 2006).
48. 2006 WL 3813778, at *3, *4 (S.D. Tex. Dec. 27, 2006).
49. 2007 WL 1231682, at *1, *13 (S.D. Tex. Apr. 25, 2007).
50. 466 F. Supp. 2d 978, 981, 983 (W.D. Tenn. 2006).

Finally, *Commonwealth Scientific and Industrial Research Organisation v. Buffalo Technology Inc.* shows that, in certain cases, injunctive relief may be appropriate even in the absence of competition. Commonwealth Scientific and Industrial Research Organisation (CSIRO) was the principal scientific research organization of the Australian federal government. It did not compete with the defendant in the marketplace for products incorporating its wireless local area network (WLAN) technology, but the court found that it lost irrecoverable research opportunities and that its reputation suffered in the global market for resources and ideas.[51]

Inadequate Legal Remedy

Courts have considered several factors in determining whether a plaintiff is able to prove the second factor, the lack of an adequate legal remedy.

In the *Transocean* case, the court analyzed the relationship between the patents and the defendant's products. It found that the infringing elements were not "small components" of the drilling rigs but were "structures . . . related to the rigs' core functionality."[52]

In other cases, courts held that harms to the plaintiff's reputation showed the inadequacy of a damages remedy. In *Smith & Nephew*, the court found that the defendant's sales in competition with the plaintiff "damag[ed its] goodwill and brand name recognition." Moreover, because "intangible losses such as the loss of goodwill" could not be accurately ascertained, there was no adequate legal remedy.[53]

Similarly, in *Black & Decker, Inc. v. Robert Bosch Tool Corporation*, plaintiff Black & Decker sued defendant Bosch for selling infringing Power Box radio chargers (used with radios on job sites) in the same market. Not only did such competition result in lost sales, but it also resulted in reputation harms from product confusion.[54]

In *Brooktrout, Inc. v. Eicon Networks Corp.*, the defendant induced infringement of a patent in the market for fax server boards. The court found that a damages remedy was inadequate because of an "inability to calculate the plaintiff's future loss with reasonable precision."[55]

And in *Buffalo Technology*, the court found that the infringement "relate[d] to the essence of the technology," and that the patentee's "reputation as a research institution [w]as impugned."[56]

---

51. 492 F. Supp. 2d 600, 604 (E.D. Tex. 2007).
52. *Transocean*, 2006 WL 3813778, at *5.
53. 466 F. Supp. 2d at 984.
54. 2006 WL 3446144, at *4 (N.D. Ill. Nov. 29, 2006).
55. 2007 WL 1730112, at *2 (E.D. Tex. June 14, 2007).
56. 492 F. Supp. 2d at 606.

Balance of Hardships

To prove the third factor, a plaintiff must demonstrate that the hardships it would suffer from the denial of an injunction would outweigh those that the defendant would suffer from the grant of an injunction. Two factors favoring the plaintiff are

(1) a showing that the core of its business is related to the infringed patent while the defendant's business is not based on the infringing product, and

(2) the defendant's ability to easily modify its product to avoid infringement.

The court considered both factors in *TiVo*, in which the defendant's infringing DVR competed with the plaintiff's product. As a "new and small company," TiVo was harmed every day the infringing product was on the market. In contrast, the defendant would not suffer as directly since the core of its business, satellite transmission, would not be affected by an injunction. In addition, the defendant did not dispute that it could have transmitted software updates to its products that would have disabled the infringing features.[57]

Such a potential for modification also played a role in *Transocean*. The senior vice president of GlobalSantaFe conceded that the company had several options to avoid infringement, one of which would have been "minimally disruptive."[58]

Public Interest

In most cases, the factor relating to public interest does not play an important role. Many courts explain that injunctive relief promotes the public's interest in "a strong patent system"[59] and that "public policy favors the enforcement of patent rights."[60] Courts also have granted injunctive relief when the infringing products have not involved the public's health and safety.[61]

In *Telequip Corp. v. Change Exchange*, the defendant infringed plaintiff's patent with its coin/token changer products. The court reasoned that an injunction served society's interests by maintaining incentives for innovation and the value of patents.[62]

And in *Buffalo Technology*, the court supported its decision to award injunctive relief because of the role of research institutions in making "substantial scientific advances" and producing "enormous benefits to society in the form of new products and processes."[63]

---

57. *TiVo*, 446 F. Supp. 2d at 670.
58. *Transocean*, 2006 WL 3813778, at *6.
59. *TiVo*, 446 F. Supp. 2d at 670.
60. *Black & Decker*, 2006 WL 3446144, at *5; *see also Transocean*, 2006 WL 3813778, at *7.
61. *TiVo*, 446 F. Supp. 2d at 670.
62. 2006 WL 2385425, at *2 (N.D.N.Y. Aug. 15, 2006).
63. 492 F. Supp. 2d at 607.

CASES DENYING INJUNCTIONS

Irreparable Harm

Courts that deny injunctive relief typically find that a plaintiff will not suffer irreparable harm because it does not compete with the defendant.

In *Paice LLC v. Toyota Motor Corp.*, defendant Toyota's hybrid vehicles infringed plaintiff Paice's patents. But the parties did not compete, as the plaintiff licensed its technology rather than making competing vehicles. In addition, the plaintiff was not able to trace any reduction in licensing activity it suffered to Toyota's infringement.[64]

Similarly, in *z4 Technologies, Inc. v. Microsoft Corp.*, Microsoft infringed z4's product activation software, which reduced the unauthorized use of software. But the two companies did not compete. Because Microsoft did not separately distribute product activation software, z4 was free to market, sell, or license its technology to any software developer other than Microsoft.[65]

And in *MercExchange, LLC v. eBay, Inc.*, the district court, on remand from the Supreme Court, found that MercExchange did not compete with eBay and was not able to identify market share lost to the defendant. The court noted that injunctive relief was not needed to protect MercExchange's "brand name, market share, reputation, goodwill, or future research and development opportunities." The court also distinguished MercExchange from "the typical small inventor or researcher" that uses licensees to develop its patents.[66]

Other courts have focused on the plaintiffs' failure to offer sufficient evidence of irreparable harm. The case of *Praxair, Inc. v. ATMI, Inc.* involved infringement of a technology allowing the safe discharge of toxic gas from pressurized containers. Even though the parties were in "direct and head-to-head competition," the court found that the plaintiff failed to offer "specific sales or market data" or identify the "market share, revenues, and customers" it lost as a result of infringement.[67]

Inadequate Remedy

Courts have denied injunctive relief when the infringed claims made up a small part of the defendant's product. In *z4*, the infringing product activation software was a "very small component" of Microsoft's Windows and Office software. In addition, the product activation software was "in no way related to the core functionality" for which consumers purchased Microsoft software products.[68]

---

64. 2006 WL 2385139, at *2 (E.D. Tex. Aug. 16, 2006), *vacated in part on other grounds, Paice LLC v. Toyota Motor Corp.*, 504 F.3d 1293, 1315 (Fed. Cir. 2007).

65. 434 F. Supp. 2d 437, 438, 440 (E.D. Tex. 2006).

66. 500 F. Supp. 2d 556, 570, 572, 578 (E.D. Va. 2007).

67. 479 F. Supp. 2d 440, 441, 442, 444 (D. Del. 2007).

68. *z4 v. Microsoft Corp.*, 434 F. Supp.2d at 441.

For similar reasons, the court in *Paice* denied injunctive relief. Of the tens of thousands of parts making up an automotive vehicle, the infringed claims implicated only a part of the hybrid transmission. When this book went to press, the Federal Circuit had remanded the case for a more complete documentation of the value of the infringed patents.[69] But even an increase in the jury verdict of 700 percent would result in the plaintiff's patents equaling only 1 percent of the vehicle's value.[70]

Balance of Hardships

When a defendant would suffer greater hardship from the grant of an injunction than a plaintiff would suffer from its denial, the scale tips in favor of denial.

In the z4 case, injunctive relief would have required defendant Microsoft to release new versions of its Office software in 450 variations in 37 languages and its Windows software in 600 variations in more than 40 languages. The company would have needed to expend resources testing, repackaging, and distributing the products. In addition, new versions of its software would have been delayed because of the transfer of personnel from Microsoft's development team. Finally, because Microsoft would have been required to turn off its product activation system, pirated software would have flooded the market, making it more difficult to offer product updates. These factors outweighed any harms suffered by the plaintiff, particularly since z4 could have distributed its software to any purchaser other than Microsoft.[71]

Courts have also considered harm to third parties that would result from the grant of injunctive relief. In *Paice*, third party dealers and suppliers could have suffered if defendant Toyota were forced to stop selling its hybrid vehicles. In addition, the "burgeoning" hybrid market itself could have been harmed by "frustrat[ing] . . . the research and expense of bringing its product line to market."[72]

Public Interest

Finally, a focus on third parties has played a role in the factor relating to the public interest. The court in z4 concluded that this factor would not support an injunction because the public had an "undisputed and enormous reliance" on Microsoft products that would be upset where product distribution was disrupted. The public also would have been harmed by a significant increase in pirated copies of the software.[73]

---

69. *Paice*, 504 F.3d at 1315.
70. *Paice*, 2006 WL 2385139, at *3, *6.
71. z4, 434 F. Supp. 2d at 442–43.
72. *Paice*, 2006 WL 2385139, at *6.
73. z4, 434 F. Supp. 2d at 443–44.

SYNTHESIS

Since *eBay*, district courts have applied the four-factor test in determining appropriate relief. Some courts have presumed that injunctive relief is necessary to protect a patentee's right to exclude. But most courts have focused on more relevant factors such as the relationship between patent and product, the balance of hardships, the effect on the public, and (especially) competition between the parties. The precise role played by these factors nonetheless is unclear. Faced with individual cases, courts cannot synthesize the elements or offer a broadly applicable structure of analysis.

This chapter proposes a fleshed-out framework that situates the most important elements within the four-factor test. The framework promises to increase predictability by clarifying the most important elements of each of the factors. It also promises to foster innovation by making certain that patentees can receive injunctive relief when their profits, market share, or reputation are most at risk. At the same time, the framework recognizes that a damages award is sometimes sufficient to maintain incentives while preventing patentees from amassing disproportionate rewards, significantly injuring the public, and stifling innovation.

PROPOSED FRAMEWORK

Competition and Irreparable Harm

The existence of competition between the parties should play a central role in determining whether there is irreparable harm.

Competition makes sense in this role. Patent law is utilitarian in nature.[74] The Constitution grants Congress the power "[t]o promote the Progress of Science and useful Arts."[75] The exclusionary rights at the heart of the patent system allow inventors to raise price above cost, thereby recovering their initial investment. This system is directly implicated when the patentee competes in the marketplace. Of course, patentees are not *required* to bring their inventions to the market. But innovation is most directly furthered when inventions do reach it.

For these reasons, a patentee that reaches the market but suffers lost sales because of infringement is the most deserving recipient of injunctive relief. The infringer's continued presence in the market threatens to reduce the patentee's profits and thus constitutes the most direct impediment to innovation. Future inventors would be hesitant to commit resources knowing they would have to share the market with infringers.

---

74. Michael Carroll, *Patent Injunctions and the Problem of Uniformity Cost*, 13 MICH. TELECOMM. & TECH. L.J. 421, 433–34 (2007).

75. U.S. CONST. art. I, § 8, cl. 8.

It should be clear in particular cases whether there is ~~direct competition~~ between the parties. ~~A plaintiff can demonstrate this~~ ~~by offering proof of sales in~~ ~~the same market or to the same customers.~~ It also can illustrate direct competition by showing that it ~~lost market share, profits, or reputation as a result of the~~ ~~infringing activity.~~

The cases in which courts found irreparable harm and granted injunctive relief align with this framework:

- In *TiVo*, the plaintiff lost market share in the early development of a market in which it was unlikely to subsequently recover losses.[76]
- In *Transocean*, a competitor won contracts from the plaintiff in a developing market with a small customer base.[77]
- In *MGM*, the companies competed in several markets and were the only firms marketing the device covered by the patent.[78]
- In *Smith & Nephew*, the defendant's sales, which significantly increased after it began selling infringing products, had a "direct negative impact" on the plaintiff's sales.[79]

The factor ~~also would incorporate reputation harms~~ that courts granting injunctive relief have considered in determining the second factor, the legal remedy's adequacy. For example,

- in *Smith & Nephew*, defendant's sales damaged plaintiff's "goodwill and brand name recognition"[80];
- in *Black & Decker*, competition with the infringing product resulted in reputation harms from product confusion.[81]

Rather than straddling the first and second factors, ~~the revised framework~~ ~~would consider the market effects together in determining whether the plaintiff~~ ~~had suffered irreparable harm.~~ Because reputation harms naturally lead to market losses, such a convergence makes sense.

The framework also would explain courts' denials of injunctive relief where the lack of competition showed the absence of irreparable harm. For example,

- in *z4*, the plaintiff was free to market, sell, or license its technology since the defendant did not separately distribute the patented item[82];

---

76. 446 F. Supp. 2d at 670.
77. 2006 WL 3813778, at *4.
78. 2007 WL 1231682, at *13.
79. 466 F. Supp. 2d at 983.
80. *Id.* at 984.
81. 2006 WL 3446144, at *4.
82. 434 F. Supp. 2d at 440, 441.

- in *Paice*, the parties did not compete, as the plaintiff licensed its technology rather than making competing vehicles (and as it was not able to link its reduction in licensing activity to Toyota's infringement).[83]

Most important, the test would remedy mistakes that result when courts impose an artificially high threshold on plaintiffs. In *Praxair*, for example, the parties were in "direct and head-to-head competition," offering "the only two mechanical-based systems for the controlled delivery of industrial gases on the market." The defendant sold more than $6 million of the infringing product in four years, with sales increasing over time.[84]

The court nonetheless denied an injunction because it found that the plaintiff failed to offer "specific sales or market data" or identify the "market share, revenues, and customers" it lost as a result of infringement. The court also contended that sales of the plaintiff's product were "not critical" to its "overall corporate success" and that its "desire to become a monopoly supplier . . . [wa]s not conclusive evidence of any factor."[85]

Despite the *Praxair* court's conclusion, however, the presence of direct competition between the parties should be sufficient for finding irreparable harm. A framework that focuses on this factor would prevent courts from setting an excessively high threshold that would harm patentees waiting to amass sufficient proof of market losses.

Core Component and Inadequate Legal Remedy
A patentee lacks an adequate legal remedy when it will not be sufficiently compensated by monetary damages and an injunction is necessary to prevent further injury. This factor should be satisfied when damages are particularly difficult to ascertain, such as when the harms from infringement are hard to calculate. In many cases, the factor will be linked to irreparable harm. If there is irreparable harm, a damages remedy will not adequately protect the patentee. If there is no sufficient legal remedy, irreparable harm is likely.

For that reason, courts have blurred the two factors in analyzing the test. They have found that competition between the parties demonstrates not only irreparable harm but also the lack of an adequate legal remedy. Such blurring, however, has double counted the same issue. In other words, the existence of competition is considered under two factors.

Such treatment is not fatal. As this chapter proposes, the presence of competition between the parties should convince courts to grant injunctive relief. But the blurring renders analysis less predictable. And it could reduce the effect of competition, as some courts have separately treated losses to market share

---

83. 2006 WL 2385139, at *2, *5.
84. 479 F. Supp. 2d at 442–43.
85. *Id.* at 444.

(which show irreparable harm) and losses to reputation (which show an inadequate remedy).

Moreover, in cases in which the parties do not compete, the blurring of the factors could minimize the importance of a related, but separate, factor: the relationship between the infringing claims and the defendant's product. Where the patent is a core component of the defendant's product, the analysis will often overlap with the competition analysis. Damages will be inadequate as consumers buy the infringing product (rather than the patentee's) because of the core component.[86]

The analysis, however, will play a more prominent role when the patented component is not central to the defendant's product. When consumers do not buy the defendant's product because of the infringing component, damages would be more likely to suffice.

Courts can determine whether the patent is a central component by examining whether the infringing component is related to the core functionality of the defendant's product. Where the infringing component plays a central role in the operation of the defendant's product, damages will not be appropriate. This central role can be ascertained by analyzing consumer demand. Do consumers demand the product because of its infringing component? If not, the patent is not related to the core functionality of the defendant's product.

In *Transocean*, the defendant sold a structure on deep water rigs that was "related to the rigs' core functionality."[87] Customers desired the defendant's product because of its infringing component. In fact, some of the plaintiff's potential customers switched to the defendant because of the infringing element. And in *Buffalo Technology*, the patentee's invention was not a "small component" but rather the "core technology" of the defendant's product.[88] In these cases, monetary damages are not adequate.

In contrast, where the infringing component is not related to the core functionality of the defendant's product, damages will typically suffice. In *z4*, the product activation software was "a very small component" of Microsoft's products that was "in no way related to the core functionality" for which consumers purchased Microsoft software products.[89] Because it played such a peripheral role, Microsoft did not acquire customers by employing the technology. An award of damages would have been sufficient to compensate z4 for Microsoft's use of its technology.

---

86. The analysis of the patent's effect on the defendant's product depends on the patented claims. Where patentees draft multiple claims for the same invention, the core-component analysis applies to each of the claims.

87. 2006 WL 3813778, at *5.

88. 492 F. Supp. 2d at 606.

89. *z4*, 434 F. Supp. 2d at 441.

Similarly, of the tens of thousands of parts making up an automotive vehicle, the infringed claims in *Paice* implicated only a part of the hybrid transmission.[90] The value of the plaintiff's technology thus was minor in comparison to the value of the defendant's product. Nor did consumers buy Toyota vehicles for the particular infringing element of the transmission. The patent did not play a central role in the defendant's product.

Focusing on the relationship between the patent and the defendant's product also promises to minimize any holdup threatened by nonpracticing entities. The issuance of an injunction when the infringement does not affect a core component of the defendant's product would allow nonpracticing entities to remove useful products from the market. Injunctions would give these parties leverage in negotiations and could force a manufacturer to spend millions of dollars to redesign its product.[91] In contrast, a damages award would reduce such leverage while still compensating the patentee.

An emphasis on the relation between patent and product also would ensure that courts remain focused on the central issues. Two examples reveal courts veering off course. In *Telequip Corp. v. Change Exchange*, the court found that damages were not adequate because "the principal value of a patent is its statutory right to exclude."[92] And in *3M Innovative Properties Co. v. Avery Denison Corp.*, the court found that monetary damages were insufficient for a plaintiff whose patent was infringed by defendant's marketing film because it was "barred from exercising its right to exclude."[93] The Supreme Court in *eBay*, however, correctly explained that intrusion onto the right to exclude is not sufficient to demonstrate the inadequacy of legal damages.

Balance of Hardships

Courts apply equitable notions in balancing the hardships suffered by the plaintiff (if the injunction is denied) with those of the defendant (if the injunction is granted). This factor is not as critical as the first two. In fact, the balance of hardships will be affected by the presence of competition between the parties as well as the relationship between the patent and the defendant's product. The inquiry nonetheless can embrace two relevant issues that might not otherwise be considered: (1) whether the patent is a core component of the *plaintiff's* product and (2) whether the defendant can modify its product to avoid infringement.

In determining the adequacy of damages, we examined the relationship between the infringed patent and the *defendant's* product. This relationship will also be relevant in determining the hardship that the parties would suffer as a result of the court's decision. A patent that is a core component of the

---

90. *Paice*, 2006 WL 2385139, at *6.
91. CCIA brief at 2–3.
92. 2006 WL 2385425, at *2 (N.D.N.Y. Aug. 15, 2006).
93. 2006 WL 2735499, at *1 (D. Minn. Sept. 25, 2006).

defendant's product would tend to substantially harm the plaintiff if the infringement were not enjoined. In contrast, an injunction against a patent that is not a core component of the defendant's product would not lead the plaintiff to suffer as directly but would be more likely to cause the defendant, which offers a product with many other inputs, to suffer hardship.

The balance-of-hardships factor also examines the relationship of the patent to the *plaintiff's* product. If the patent is central, then the plaintiff would more likely suffer hardship upon the denial of an injunction. For instance, in *TiVo*, the patents were central to TiVo's DVRs. Given that TiVo was "a relatively new company with only one primary product," it would suffer grave harm if the court did not grant injunctive relief.[94] Conversely, Echostar's business model revolved around the different product of satellite transmissions.

In general, nonpracticing entities would not satisfy this test. These entities typically acquire patents without any intention of bringing a product to market. As a result, the patents are not central to products on the market.

Courts considering the balance of harms also should analyze a defendant's ability to modify its product to remove the infringing features. Such a capability reduces the hardship suffered by an enjoined defendant. In *Transocean*, for example, GlobalSantaFe could have altered its rigs, thereby avoiding infringement while still providing its customers with service.[95]

Public Interest

The final factor involves the public interest. Courts awarding injunctive relief have typically applied this factor to affirm that "public policy favors the enforcement of patent rights."[96] Until the *eBay* case, courts had denied injunctions only where such relief would have adversely affected the public's health and safety.[97]

There is an important role for this factor to play, however, in two additional settings. In the first, the patent plays a peripheral role in the demand for the defendant's product and the public would be significantly and adversely affected by an injunction.[98] In the second, the defendant has willfully infringed the patent.

In the first setting, the public interest suggests the denial of injunctive relief. In *z4*, the public would have been harmed if Microsoft had removed Windows from the market for even a short period of time. Moreover, the public did not buy Microsoft's products because of the presence of infringing product activation software. An injunction thus would have harmed the public while not providing indispensable relief to the plaintiff.

---

94. *TiVo*, 446 F. Supp. 2d at 670.
95. 2006 WL 3813778, at *6.
96. *Black & Decker*, 2006 WL 3446144, at *5; *see also Transocean*, 2006 WL 3813778, at *7.
97. *TiVo*, 446 F. Supp. 2d at 670.
98. Of course, an injunction often will allow the patentee to increase price, but that is not the unique adverse effect contemplated here.

Similarly, in *Paice*, third-party dealers and suppliers could have suffered if defendant Toyota were forced to stop selling its hybrid vehicles. In addition, the "burgeoning" hybrid market could have been harmed by "frustrat[ing] . . . the research and expense of bringing its product line to market."[99]

In the second setting, a defendant's willful infringement of a patent will often necessitate injunctive relief. Even if none of the other factors are met, a defendant in most cases should not be able to willfully infringe a patent knowing that its only penalty will be to pay a reasonable royalty. Such a remedy would encourage defendants to engage in infringing activity.

Until recently, the Federal Circuit expansively applied the doctrine of willful infringement, imposing a duty of due care that penalized parties for reading rivals' patents and that did not provide a useful indication of punishable intent.[100] But in 2007, the court, in *In re Seagate Technology, LLC*, elevated the willfulness threshold to objective recklessness, requiring patentees to show that

(1) the infringer acted despite an objectively high likelihood that its actions constituted infringement of a valid patent, and

(2) the risk was known or should have been known to the accused infringer.[101]

As a result of this important case, willful infringement findings now reflect an infringer's recklessness or intent to infringe. Granting injunctive relief for such conduct should discourage the activity and ensure that the bargaining power of small firms provided by patents is preserved.

The only instances in which willful infringement might not result in an injunction would involve cases such as *z4* and *NTP* (the BlackBerry case), in which third parties rely on a product of which the patented component is a small part and would suffer significant harm from an injunction. Courts in these cases can weigh the harm a patentee would suffer from a denial of an injunction against the harm the public would suffer from products being pulled from the market. Such inquiries admittedly are nuanced. But they should not occur in many cases. And the presence of legitimate interests on both sides of the ledger requires such balancing.

OPERATION OF TEST

The four-part framework offers several opportunities for the patentee to definitively demonstrate its entitlement to injunctive relief. Such relief is appropriate if it can show

---

99. *Paice*, 2006 WL 2385139, at *6.

100. For that reason, the findings of willful infringement in the *NTP* (BlackBerry), *eBay*, and *Microsoft* cases should not have a material effect on the remedy.

101. 497 F.3d 1360, 1371 (Fed. Cir. 2007).

under the first factor that it competes with the infringing defendant, or under the second factor that the patent is a core component of the defendant's product.

A patentee's demonstration of either of these factors should automatically result in injunctive relief. The harms threatened to innovation incentives by a patentee losing sales to competing infringers or having its technology used as a core component of the defendant's product are severe enough to warrant injunctive relief.

Similarly, as discussed in the last section, a patentee that can show under the fourth factor that a defendant willfully infringed its patent should, in most cases, be entitled to injunctive relief.

If the patentee cannot make these showings, courts will face more nuanced determinations. They cannot resolve these settings by reciting, as the Federal Circuit often did before *eBay*, that infringement of a right to exclude automatically demonstrates irreparable harm. Rather, they must engage in more complex analyses. Damages may be appropriate where

- under the first factor the parties do not compete,
- under the second factor the patent is not a core component of the defendant's product, or
- under the fourth factor, the public would be significantly and adversely affected by injunctive relief.

Making these determinations does not automatically show the propriety of damages. The *Buffalo Technology* case showed that research institutions may require injunctive relief even where the above factors are present.

Nonetheless, the confluence of several of the factors should point strongly in the direction of damages. Damages typically will be appropriate where (1) the public would be adversely affected by injunctive relief and (2) the infringer does not compete with the patentee and offers a product for which the patent is not a core component. Yet other cases would require more nuanced determinations that could include issues such as the relationship between the patent and the plaintiff's product and a defendant's ability to modify its product to avoid infringement.

In short, the remedies framework is more complicated than the Federal Circuit's law before *eBay*. But the need for damages in certain cases makes this a welcome development.

CONCLUSION

The *eBay* case correctly restored balance to the determination of relief in patent infringement cases. Courts should award injunctive relief in most patent infringement cases, but not all.

By reminding the Federal Circuit that the remedy determination is equitable in nature, the Supreme Court began to construct a framework conducive to innovation. District courts have applied this structure to focus on many of the most important factors. But without additional guidance, the framework's lack of predictability has led some courts to focus on unhelpful factors and has threatened additional incorrect decisions.

This chapter offers a framework that emphasizes the most significant factors and places them in a predictable model. Patentees in many cases, particularly when they compete with infringing defendants or possess a patent that is a core component in the infringing product, will be entitled to injunctive relief. My focus on these factors could even increase courts' awarding of injunctive relief by eliminating cases such as *Praxair*, in which the court set an excessively high threshold of proving market loss.

Injunctive relief might be appropriate when these factors are not met, as the research entity in the *Buffalo Technology* case demonstrated. But damages will frequently be the proper remedy when the parties do not compete, the patented element is a minor part of the defendant's product, or third parties would be significantly and adversely affected by injunctive relief.

In short, the new framework is consistent with the Supreme Court's mandate to apply the four-factor test. But it fleshes out the test to provide guidance to courts and parties. Its more developed scaffolding focuses on the most crucial issues while still recognizing the importance of injunctive relief in the majority of cases. Given its importance in reducing holdup, it also promises benefits for antitrust courts, which would less frequently confront bottlenecks imposed by firms with market power. In short, my proposal offers a more nuanced and justifiable remedies framework that promises to foster innovation.

11. BIOTECHNOLOGY DILEMMA 1: PATENTED RESEARCH TOOLS AND EXPERIMENTAL USE

Biotechnology Research Tools 254
Anticommons 255
Patent Infringement and Experimentation 256
The Common-law Defense 257
Statutory Exemption 260
Empirical Studies 261
    Explanation 1: Biotechnology 263
    Explanation 2: Licensing 264
    Explanation 3: University-Industry Relations 264
No Present Proposal 267
Three Future Proposals 268
Experimentation on Patented Invention 269
    Global Treatment 270
Bayh-Dole Act 271
    NIH Guidelines 274
    University Practice 275
User Innovation and Research Tools 275
Conclusion 277

Research tools used by scientists are essential for innovation in the biotechnology industry. In recent years, the patenting of such tools has skyrocketed. Many scholars and organizations have lamented this development. They have focused, in particular, on reduced access to research tools and an *anticommons* characterized by multiple patentees exercising rights to exclude.

These concerns are exacerbated by the disappearance of the most relevant defense to infringement. Noncommercial and academic researchers historically relied on a defense of *experimental use*. These researchers were able, at a minimum, to experiment on a patented invention to discover its properties.

But in the past two decades, the Federal Circuit has scaled back the defense. It has made clear that the "narrow" defense is limited to "amusement, . . . idle curiosity, or . . . strictly philosophical inquiry" and does not automatically apply to universities.

Given the combination of increased patents and decreased defenses, scholars have offered a plethora of solutions. At the same time, however, empirical studies have demonstrated an absence of bottlenecks. Admittedly, the state of the law is far from ideal. And many nations offer a more robust experimental use defense than the United States. But I conclude in this chapter that industry and academia have forged a relationship that, at least at the present time, has displaced the need for changes to the law.

To be sure, this is a precarious equilibrium. And there is no guarantee it will continue. For that reason, I offer three proposals that could be implemented if the situation changes. First, I would protect *experimentation on* the invention, which uses the invention to study its technology or design around the patent. Second, I offer an amendment to the Bayh-Dole Act (which encouraged the commercialization of nonprofit inventions) that would require universities and nonprofit institutions to reserve the right to use the invention for noncommercial research. Third, I recommend empirical study of *user innovation* among research tool innovators. Such study could lay the framework for a defense exempting research use by (1) nonprofit entities and (2) anyone seeking to use inventions patented by nonprofit entities.

If lawsuits, anticommons, or restrictive licensing becomes a problem, these proposals should be seriously considered. In the meantime, today's fragile equilibrium is adequate.

BIOTECHNOLOGY RESEARCH TOOLS

The field of biotechnology covers proteins (the building blocks of organisms) and genes (DNA sequences on chromosomes coding for proteins). After a researcher isolates a gene for a particular protein, she can clone the gene by inserting it into a cell. The researcher then can produce large quantities of the protein.[1]

Research tools are essential for innovation in the industry. These tools encompass "the full range of resources that scientists use in the laboratory," such as cell lines, drug targets, cloning tools, equipment, databases, and computer software.[2] Some of the most important tools in the biotechnology industry have included

- Harvard's tumor-prone "oncomouse," useful as a model in cancer research;
- DuPont's cre-loxP mouse, in which genes of interest can be activated or de-activated[3];
- Cohen-Boyer's patents for the basic method of gene cloning;
- PCR (polymerase chain reaction) technology, which amplifies DNA sequences;

---

1. Arti K. Rai, *Intellectual Property Rights in Biotechnology: Addressing New Technology*, 34 WAKE FOREST L. REV. 827, 832 (1999).

2. Report of the National Institutes of Health (NIH) Working Group on Research Tools, at 3 (June 4, 1998), http://www.nih.gov/news/researchtools/index.htm [hereinafter NIH Research Tools Report].

3. http://jaxmice.jax.org/models/cre_intro.html.

- the enzyme Taq DNA polymerase, the key reagent in PCR that is used when forensic scientists analyze blood from crime scenes or laboratory technicians test AIDS patients' HIV levels;
- expressed sequence tags (ESTs) that are identified in the decoding of the human genome;
- human embryonic stem cells, which can develop into any type of human tissue.[4]

Perhaps the case most frequently cited to demonstrate the dangers of patented research tools is that of Myriad Pharmaceuticals. Myriad owns patent rights on a test that identifies mutations in the genes BRCA 1 and BRCA 2, associated with breast cancer. It utilized its patent (recently invalidated by a district court) to prevent researchers from improving diagnostic tests on the genes.

The sequencing technology on which Myriad relied, however, was not able to detect 10 to 20 percent of mutations. Although it could detect small-scale deletions and rearrangements of nucleotides in BRCA genes, it was not able to detect large deletions and rearrangements.[5] Only after "considerable pressure from the scientific community" did Myriad, in 2006 (more than 10 years after introducing clinical genetic testing) add methods to test for these deletions and re-arrangements.[6]

The company also required all samples for BRCA diagnostic testing to be sent to its Utah laboratory, preventing researchers from using their own labs. Although it now charges reduced royalties for certain researchers, the firestorm it generated prompted multiple law reform efforts.[7] Other proposals for change can be traced to the discovery of the next concept.

ANTICOMMONS

In 1998, Professors Michael Heller and Rebecca Eisenberg highlighted the dangers of patented research tools by describing an *anticommons in which multiple*

---

4. Janice Mueller, *"No Dilettante Affair": Rethinking the Experimental Use Exception to Patent Infringement for Biomedical Research Tools*, 76 WASH. L. REV. 1, 2, 12–14 (2001) (citing multiple sources).

5. Bryn Williams-Jones, *History of a Gene Patent: Tracing the Development and Application of Commercial BRCA Testing*, 10 HEALTH L.J. 123, 127, 139 (2002).

6. *Stifling or Stimulating—The Role of Gene Patents in Research and Genetic Testing: Hearing Before the H. Jud. Subcomm. on Courts, the Internet, and IP*, at 3 (2007) (statement of Dr. Wendy Chung).

7. Jordan Paradise, *European Opposition to Exclusive Control over Predictive Breast Cancer Testing and the Inherent Implications for U.S. Patent Law and Public Policy: A Case Study of the Myriad Genetics' BRCA Patent Controversy*, 59 FOOD & DRUG L.J. 133, 147, 149–50 (2004); Shanshan Zhang, *Proposing Resolutions to the Insufficient Gene Patent System*, 20 SANTA CLARA COMPUTER & HIGH TECH. L.J. 1139, 1159 (2004).

owners have a right to exclude. Such a framework created obstacles to research and development (R&D) by requiring downstream developers to gain "access to multiple patented inputs to create a single useful product."[8]

Heller and Eisenberg contended that the biomedical anticommons arose in two ways. First was through the creation of too many concurrent fragments of IP rights, as occurred when gene fragments were patented before the corresponding gene, protein, or commercial product was identified.[9] Second, reach-through license agreements on patented research tools gave rights in subsequent downstream (commercialized) discoveries to the owner of inventions utilized in upstream (basic) research. The anticommons was created "as upstream owners stack[ed] overlapping and inconsistent claims on potential downstream products."[10]

Compounding these difficulties, participants were not able to negotiate around these obstacles. First, the field was composed of a diverse array of participants that included universities, government agencies, and biotechnology and pharmaceutical firms. Second, owners of upstream patents tended to overvalue their discoveries and disparage claims of their opponents. Third, significant transaction costs arose from the involvement of public institutions, the difficulty of valuation, and the need for licensing at an early stage when the outcome of a project was uncertain.[11]

The anticommons has played a significant role in motivating proposals that would expand the experimental use defense. Nonetheless, as shown later in the chapter, the empirical evidence does not demonstrate its existence.

PATENT INFRINGEMENT AND EXPERIMENTATION

Patented research tools and anticommons could present challenges by increasing the likelihood of infringement. The patent statute provides that anyone who

makes, uses, offers to sell, or sells any patented invention, within the United States . . . during the term of the patent . . . infringes the patent.[12]

---

8. Michael A. Heller & Rebecca S. Eisenberg, *Can Patents Deter Innovation? The Anticommons in Biomedical Research*, 280 Sci. 698, 699 (1998). The anticommons stood in contrast to the "tragedy of the commons," by which resources held in common were depleted by overuse.

9. This problem was ameliorated by the PTO's Utility Guidelines, issued in 2000, which provide a more rigorous threshold of utility that requires a "specific" and "substantial" utility before a patent is issued. Utility Examination Guidelines, 66 Fed. Reg. 1092, 1098 (Dep't of Commerce Jan. 5, 2001). *See In re Fisher*, 421 F.3d 1365, 1372 (Fed. Cir. 2005) (upholding Guidelines).

10. Heller & Eisenberg, at 699.

11. *Id.* at 700; *see generally* Michael A. Carrier, *Resolving the Patent-Antitrust Paradox Through Tripartite Innovation*, 56 Vand. L. Rev. 1047, 1085–86 (2003).

12. 35 U.S.C. § 271(a).

Scientists will often need to use patented research tools in conducting their research. Several developments in the past generation have increased the role of patents.

First, advances in drug discovery shifted from trial and error to knowledge of genes and proteins that are more likely to be patented.[13] Second, court decisions expanded the scope of patentable subject matter to cover live, human-made microorganisms.[14] Third, in 1980 Congress enacted the Patent and Trademark Law Amendments Act (known as the Bayh-Dole Act), which has encouraged scientists at universities and nonprofit organizations to patent their discoveries.[15]

Taken together, these developments reduced the sharing and "relatively unfettered access to fundamental knowledge" that used to characterize biomedical research.[16] Scientists had historically followed a "Mertonian ethos," or system of open science that fostered the sharing and criticism of results.[17] This system, however, has waned with the rise of commercial, profit-centered relationships. Although this development has positive consequences (as revealed by increased licensing and commercialization in the wake of Bayh-Dole), it also could raise concerns of reduced basic research and stifled innovation.

THE COMMON-LAW DEFENSE[18]

The long-standing experimental use defense has traditionally applied when patented inventions were used for scientific inquiry.

The first case to recognize the defense, *Whittemore v. Cutter*, involved the infringement of a plaintiff's patented design to build a machine that manufactured playing cards. The court rejected the claim of infringement. In his instructions to the jury, Justice Joseph Story stated that "[I]t could never have been the intention of the legislature to punish a man, who constructed such a machine merely for philosophical experiments, or for the purpose of ascertaining the sufficiency of the machine to produce its described effects."[19]

---

13. Arti K. Rai & Rebecca S. Eisenberg, *Bayh-Dole Reform and the Progress of Biomedicine*, 66 L. & CONTEMP. PROBS. 289, 289 (2003).

14. *Diamond v. Chakrabarty*, 447 U.S. 303 (1980).

15. Pub. L. No. 96-517, *codified as amended at* 35 U.S.C. §§ 200–12 (1994).

16. Rai & Eisenberg, at 289.

17. Rochelle Dreyfuss, *Protecting Public Domain of Science: Has the Time for an Experimental Use Defense Arrived?*, 46 ARIZ. L. REV. 457, 463–64 (2004).

18. The judiciary's role in developing the experimental use defense explains why it is generally referred to as a common-law defense. The defense also can be viewed as a statutory interpretation of the limits of the patent right. Henrik Holzapfel & Joshua D. Sarnoff, *A Cross-Atlantic Dialog on Experimental Use and Research Tools*, 48 IDEA 123, 136 (2008).

19. 29 F. Cas. 1120, 1121 (C.C.D. Mass. 1813) (No. 17,600).

Justice Story applied the defense again in *Sawin v. Guild*. In that case, an inventor claimed that a sheriff was liable for infringement for seizing and selling his patented nail-cutting machine to settle the inventor's debt. Justice Story explained that infringement occurs only when a patented invention is used, made, or sold "with an intent to . . . profit" and to "deprive the owner of the lawful rewards of his discovery."[20]

For the remainder of the 19th century, few cases addressed the experimental use defense. Its emphasis would be shaped, however, in 1890 when it was included in Professor William Robinson's influential treatise. Robinson asserted that an act constitutes infringement only when it "[a]ffects the [p]ecuniary [i]nterests" of the patentee.[21] This focus soon led to a distinction between commercial and noncommercial users that displaced other factors in experimental use analysis.[22]

In three cases in the mid-20th century, for example, courts found that the defense applied where the defendant engaged in noncommercial use of patented technology. In *Dugan v. Lear Avia, Inc.*, the defendant "built [the patented] device only experimentally" and did not manufacture it for sale or make any sales.[23] In *Ruth v. Stearns-Roger Manufacturing Co.*, the court refused to impose liability for "[t]he making or using of a patented invention merely for experimental purposes, without any intent to derive profits or practical advantage."[24] And in *Chesterfield v. United States*, because the defendant used the patent "only for testing and . . . experimental purposes," the court concluded that it did not engage in "an infringing use."[25]

The most dramatic changes to the experimental use defense resulted from the creation of the Federal Circuit in 1982. In the first case, *Roche Products, Inc. v. Bolar Pharmaceutical Co.*, the holder of a patent on the active ingredient in a sleeping medication sued Bolar for infringement. Bolar had planned to offer a generic equivalent of the drug when Roche's patent expired. Accordingly, it conducted pre-market testing and applied to the Food and Drug Administration (FDA) for approval to market a generic version of Roche's drug.[26]

Even though Bolar did not intend to engage in commercial use during the two years that remained in Roche's patent term, the Federal Circuit found that the

---

20. 21 F. Cas. 554, 555 (C.C.D. Mass. 1813) (No. 12,391).

21. 3 WILLIAM C. ROBINSON, THE LAW OF PATENTS FOR USEFUL INVENTIONS § 898 (1890).

22. Katherine J. Strandburg, *What Does the Public Get? Experimental Use and the Patent Bargain*, 2004 WIS. L. REV. 81, 96 [hereinafter Strandburg, *Patent Bargain*].

23. 55 F. Supp. 223, 229 (S.D.N.Y. 1944).

24. 13 F. Supp. 697, 713 (D. Colo. 1935), *rev'd on other grounds*, 87 F.2d 35 (10th Cir. 1936).

25. 159 F. Supp. 371, 375–76 (Ct. Cl. 1958). *See generally* David G. Sewell, *Rescuing Science from the Courts: An Appeal for Amending the Patent Code To Protect Academic Research in the Wake of Madey v. Duke University*, 93 GEO. L.J. 759, 763 (2005).

26. 733 F.2d 858, 860 (Fed. Cir. 1984), *superseded on other grounds by* 35 U.S.C. § 271(e).

defense did not apply. It stated that the defense could only be employed for "dilettante affair[s]" in which a patented invention is used "for amusement, to satisfy idle curiosity, or for strictly philosophical inquiry."[27] Given that the use was an "unlicensed experiment" conducted to adapt "the patented invention to the experimentor's business," the defense did not apply. The court refused to adopt a broad interpretation of the defense "in the guise of 'scientific inquiry'" when such inquiry had "definite, cognizable, and not insubstantial commercial purposes."[28]

Sixteen years later, in *Embrex, Inc. v. Service Engineering Corp.*, the Federal Circuit further narrowed the defense. Embrex was the exclusive licensee of a patent for a method of inoculating chickens against disease by injecting a vaccine into a specified region of the egg before hatching. Service Engineering sought to design around the patent by injecting the vaccine into a different region than was covered in the patent.[29]

The court applied *Roche*'s holding that the defense did not apply when a party infringed while designing around a patent for "definite, cognizable, and not insubstantial commercial purposes." The defendant's attempt to develop new drugs and delivery machines for chicken inoculation thus prevented the application of the defense. Judge Rader's concurring opinion went even further, stating that the defense did not apply if the researcher's use had even "the slightest commercial implication."[30] The *Embrex* case is especially noteworthy because the scientists were attempting to avoid infringement of Embrex's patent. If the defendants had succeeded, there would not even have been patent infringement.[31]

The Federal Circuit confined the "very narrow and strictly limited" exception one last time in *Madey v. Duke University*. Professor Madey invented the free electron laser (FEL), which "use[d] moving electrons to produce high-intensity beams of infrared light" and could be employed in applications including brain surgery and the detection of chemical and biological weapons. In 1988, Madey left Stanford University to join Duke University. The Duke laboratory soon became a large and influential FEL laboratory.[32]

Ten years later, in 1998, Madey left Duke to go to the University of Hawaii. Duke continued to operate the laboratory. Madey sued Duke, claiming infringement of patents he owned on FEL components.[33]

---

27. *Id.* at 863.

28. *Id.*

29. *Embrex, Inc. v. Service Engineering Corp.*, 216 F.3d 1343, 1346 (Fed. Cir. 2000); *see* Strandburg, *Patent Bargain*, at 86.

30. 216 F.3d at 1349, 1353; *see* Sewell, at 765.

31. 216 F.3d at 1346–47. The experiments were not successful since the injections leaked into areas covered by the patent.

32. *Madey v. Duke Univ.*, 307 F.3d 1351, 1361–62 (Fed. Cir. 2002); *see* Sewell, at 766.

33. Sewell, at 766 n.44.

Duke claimed that its work "was fundamental scientific research . . . not designed for commercial purposes" and thus should be covered by the experimental use defense. The court held that even though Duke was not a commercial institution, its research "unmistakably further[ed] the institution's legitimate business objectives" by "educating and enlightening students and faculty participating in the[] projects." As a result, Duke did not satisfy the "very narrow and strictly limited experimental use defense."[34]

In short, courts have whittled down the experimental use defense to the point that it does not cover university researchers or those attempting to avoid infringement by using a patent to design around it. For all intents and purposes, researchers cannot lawfully rely on the defense.

STATUTORY EXEMPTION

A more potent defense than the common-law exception is the statutory experimental use exemption. In response to the Federal Circuit's 1984 *Bolar* decision, Congress enacted 35 U.S.C. § 271(e), which exempts from infringement "uses reasonably related to the development and submission of information" under the Federal Food, Drug, and Cosmetic Act (FDA Act).[35] This statute allows generic firms to conduct tests in preparation for FDA regulatory approval. In 2005, the Supreme Court, in *Merck KGaA v. Integra Lifesciences I, Ltd.*, expansively interpreted the statute.[36]

In *Merck*, a university researcher had partnered with Merck to explore the applications of various peptides (amino acid compounds) for a drug that would inhibit new blood vessels from sprouting from existing ones. This, it was thought, might slow the advance of diseases such as cancer, arthritis, and retinopathy.[37]

Integra owned patents covering one of these peptides, which it claimed were infringed in Merck's research. The defendants countered that their research was covered by the statutory safe harbor of 35 U.S.C. § 271(e). A jury found Merck liable for infringement.[38]

The Federal Circuit affirmed, holding that the activity fell outside the safe harbor because it was not "clinical testing to supply information to the FDA, but only general biomedical research to identify new pharmaceutical compounds."[39]

---

34. 307 F.3d at 1362–63; *see also Pitcairn v. United States*, 547 F.2d 1106, 1125–26 (Ct. Cl. 1976) (rejecting the defense when "[t]ests, demonstrations, and experiments . . . are in keeping with the . . . [defendant's] business"); Dreyfuss, at 460–61.

35. 35 U.S.C. § 271(e).

36. *Merck KGaA v. Integra Lifesciences I, Ltd.*, 545 U.S. 193 (2005).

37. *Id.* at 197.

38. *Id.* at 200–01.

39. *Id.* at 201 (citations and internal quotations omitted).

The Supreme Court reversed, broadly interpreting the scope of the defense. It stated that the exemption "extends to all uses of patented inventions that are reasonably related to the development and submission of any information under the [FDA Act]." This language includes the use of patented compounds in preclinical studies related to the FDA regulatory process. The Court, however, did not address the applicability of the exemption to research tools, explaining that Integra did not claim that the peptide was such a tool.[40] Consequently, on remand, the district court granted Merck judgment as a matter of law.[41]

EMPIRICAL STUDIES

The Supreme Court's robust version of the statutory experimental defense stands in marked contrast to the Federal Circuit's constricted interpretation of the common-law defense. Perhaps the most important question in this chapter is whether innovation has suffered as a result of the narrow defense. The answer, as shown by the empirical evidence, is that it has not, at least to a level that warrants expansion of the defense. The most influential studies have been conducted by Professor John Walsh and his co-authors.

The most recent and comprehensive Walsh study, published in 2007, sampled 1125 biomedical researchers in universities, government labs, and nonprofit institutions and received 414 responses. It found that an increase in patenting did not determine researchers' choice of projects. Respondents chose projects based on scientific importance, interest, feasibility, and access to funding (all of which were cited by at least 80 percent). In contrast, only 7 percent of respondents mentioned the patentability of research results and number of involved patents as factors influencing project selection. Moreover, for projects seriously considered but not pursued, an excess of patented inputs explained the researchers' decisions in only 3 percent of the cases, with factors such as a lack of funding and feasibility being far more important.[42]

---

40. *Id.* at 202, 205 n.7. On remand to the Federal Circuit, Judge Rader, in dissent, stated that the majority's decision "eliminate[s] protection for research tool inventions." *Id.* at 1349 (Rader, J., dissenting and concurring). The Federal Circuit subsequently limited the application of Section 271(e)(1) to research tools by requiring an alleged infringer's device to be subject to a de facto patent term extension (which results from an inability to begin the regulatory approval process during the patent term). *Proveris Scientific Corp. v. Innovasystems, Inc.*, 2008 WL 2967100 (Fed. Cir. Aug. 5, 2008) (rejecting defense for device that was "not subject to FDA premarket approval" and thus did not "face[] regulatory barriers to market entry upon patent expiration").

41. *Merck KGaA v. Integra Lifesciences I, Ltd.*, 496 F.3d 1334 (Fed. Cir. 2007).

42. John P. Walsh et al., *Where Excludability Matters: Material versus Intellectual Property in Academic Biomedical Research*, 36 RES. POL'Y 1184, 1188 (2007) [hereinafter Walsh, *Excludability*].

One reason for patents' minimal effects involved researchers' lack of awareness. A mere 5 percent of respondents regularly checked for patents related to their research. Nor did the *Madey* decision substantially increase notification letters, which were received by 3 percent of researchers in 2002 and 5 percent in 2007.[43]

Of greatest significance, no respondents reported that they had abandoned a line of research because of a patent.[44] In addition, only 1 percent claimed that they were forced to modify or delay (for more than a month) a project as a result of a patent. The authors concluded that "access to patents on knowledge or information inputs into biomedical research . . . rarely imposes a significant burden for academic biomedical researchers."[45]

The National Research Council of the National Academies issued a comprehensive report in 2006 that confirmed the results of an earlier, less exhaustive Walsh study. The report concluded that "the number of projects abandoned or delayed as a result of difficulties in technology access is reported to be small." And while it warned that the results could change if firms demanded more restrictive licensing terms, it mirrored the Walsh study in concluding that "access to patented inventions . . . rarely imposes a significant burden for biomedical researchers."[46]

Relatedly, a comprehensive study of biotechnology patents granted between 1990 and 2004 found that the field was characterized by a "low ownership density." No single entity owned more than a small percentage of patents, and the largest firms received fewer than 30 each year. The study also found evidence inconsistent with an anticommons: a rising number of entrants, small patent portfolios, and a low number of required patents. Finally, it underscored the emphasis, among those observing an anticommons, on the number of patents to the exclusion of the "scope of the relevant scientific commons and the distribution of patents within it."[47]

---

43. *Id.* at 1190.

44. Another study (AAAS, *The Effects of Patenting in the AAAS Scientific Community* (2006)), which showed a greater effect (10 percent of researchers abandoned a project because of IP), did not distinguish between the acquisition of patented research tools and patented materials. *See* Katherine J. Strandburg, *Sharing Research Tools and Materials: Homo Scientificus and User Innovator Community Norms*, at 6–7 (2008), http://ssrn.com/abstract=1136606. I discuss the dangers presented by the denial of materials in Chapter 12.

45. To be sure, self-reporting might not be fully accurate (with busy scientists engaged in multiple research projects not recalling each delay) or unbiased (with participants tempted to understate the role of patent incentives and commercial motivations). Walsh, *Excludability*, at 1189. These critiques, however, have lost much of their force as studies in other nations using different methodologies have confirmed the Walsh study's conclusions.

46. National Research Council, *Reaping the Benefits of Genomic and Proteomic Research: Intellectual Property Rights, Innovation, and Public Health*, at 2–3 (2006).

47. David E. Adelman & Kathryn L. DeAngelis, *Patent Metrics: The Mismeasure of Innovation in the Biotech Patent Debate*, 85 TEX. L. REV. 1677, 1679, 1681, 1697 (2007).

Studies from other countries support the findings of the Walsh surveys. A study of the Australian biotechnology industry concluded that there is "little . . . empirical evidence" of an anticommons. The study found "hardly any evidence of research tool patents having an adverse impact on research and development." Participants avoided blockages by ignoring patents, inventing around patented technology, and entering into collaborations and licenses. At the same time, firms did not enforce patents against research institutions because they would only have been able to recover minimal damages and would have suffered harms to their reputation.[48]

A survey of pharmaceutical and biotechnology firms in Japan found that companies confronting patented research tools were far more likely to enter into licensing agreements, use alternative research methods, or ignore the patents than abandon the research. It also found that even when patentees offered "unreasonable" terms, licensing occurred in the vast majority of cases.[49]

Finally, a survey of pharmaceutical and biotechnology firms, research institutions, and clinical genetic test centers in Germany found "no accumulation of law suits," with the parties instead resolving their disputes informally. The survey also concluded that there was no evidence of licensing breakdowns and that the use of research tools "was not seen as problematic."[50] Mirroring the rationales offered in the United States, the authors explained the absence of a problem by noting the availability of research tools, difficulty of uncovering infringement "behind locked laboratory doors," ignorance among employees of the implications of using patented tools, and minimal incentives to sue research institutes that "generated no revenue through patent infringement."[51]

In short, there is a significant disconnect between the absence of empirical evidence of harm, on the one hand, and the restricted state of the experimental use defense and numerous remedial proposals, on the other. Such a divide can be explained by three reasons: (1) the nature of biotechnology, (2) the prevalence of licensing, and (3) the symbiotic relationship between universities and industry.

Explanation 1: Biotechnology

The first explanation is provided by the field of biotechnology. There is a vast disparity between the ability of biotechnology tools to generate data such as

---

48. Dianne Nicol & Jane Nielsen, *Patents and Medical Biotechnology: An Empirical Analysis of Issues Facing the Australian Industry*, Occasional Paper No. 6, at 92, 175, 256–57 (2003).

49. Sadao Nagaoka, An *Empirical Analysis of Patenting and Licensing Practices of Research Tools from Three Perspectives*, Presentation to OECD Conference on Research Use of Patented Inventions, at 18–20 (2006), http://www.oecd.org/dataoecd/20/54/36816178.pdf.

50. Joseph Straus, *Genetic Inventions and Patents—A German Empirical Survey*, Presentation to the BMBG & OECD Workshop on Genetic Inventions, IP Rights, and Licensing Practices, at 5–6 (2002), http://www.oecd.org/dataoecd/36/22/1817995.pdf.

51. JOSEPH STRAUS ET AL., GENETIC INVENTIONS AND PATENT LAW: AN EMPIRICAL SURVEY OF SELECTED GERMAN R&D INSTITUTIONS 26 (2004).

genome sequences and to produce drugs.[52] Less than 2 percent of the human genome codes for proteins, with more than 50 percent consisting of repetitive sequences with undefined functions.[53] In addition, environmental and other factors weaken the causal relationship between genes and a person's susceptibility to disease. As a result, most diseases can be treated through multiple approaches. This makes it harder to link genes to diseases and treatment options. And it reduces the likelihood of bottlenecks.[54]

Explanation 2: Licensing

The second reason stems from the ubiquity of licensing. Walsh and his co-authors reported that "general purpose" tools with numerous applications are made widely available through nonexclusive licensing. Between 1990 and 1997, there was an average of nearly 380 licenses each year in the pharmaceutical and chemical industries, nearly 40 percent more than the electronics industry (in which cross-licensing is common).[55] Bottlenecks are also reduced because researchers—even if they initially consider hundreds of patents—seriously address fewer than a dozen. In the typical setting, the researcher need not license any patents.[56]

In addition to licensing, Walsh pointed to other "working solutions" that allowed research to proceed such as inventing around patents, going offshore, challenging patent validity, and developing and using public databases.[57]

Explanation 3: University-Industry Relations

The final explanation is provided by the symbiotic relationship between universities and industry. Researchers have ignored patents and companies have not sued them for infringement.

There are many reasons why companies have refrained from suing researchers who infringe patents. For starters, not all infringement is known to patentees. Even if it were, the amount of damages that could be recovered for basic research tends to be minimal, especially when compared to the high costs of litigation.[58]

---

52. David E. Adelman, *A Fallacy of the Commons in Biotech Patent Policy*, 20 Berkeley Tech. L.J. 985, 987 (2005).

53. Alan E. Guttmacher & Francis S. Collins, *Genomic Medicine—A Primer*, 347 New Eng. J. Med. 1512, 1514 (2002).

54. Adelman, at 1014.

55. John P. Walsh et al., *Effects of Research Tool Patents and Licensing on Biomedical Innovation*, 285, 322–23, *in* Patents in the Knowledge-Based Economy (Wesley M. Cohen & Stephen A. Merrill eds., 2003) [hereinafter Walsh, *Effects*].

56. *Id.* at 294, 323–24. This conclusion may depend on researchers' lack of knowledge of patents.

57. *Id.* at 331.

58. In addition, state universities are protected from suit under the doctrine of *sovereign immunity*. *See* U.S. Const. amend. XI ("The Judicial power of the United States shall

By filing suit, patentees also could risk a court's narrowing or invalidation of its patent.[59] Patentees might even benefit from infringing noncommercial research, which could develop knowledge or lead to new uses of patented technology.[60]

Firms also have not sued universities because of the reputation harms they would suffer. As one technology transfer officer explained:

> Asserting against a university doesn't make sense. First, there are no damages . . . What have you gained? You've just made people mad. Also, these firms are consumers of technology as well. No one will talk to you if you sue. We all scratch each others' backs. *You will become an instant pariah if you sue a university.*[61]

The mention of firms' role as consumers reveals another reason for forbearance: the increasing alliances between private companies and universities. Firms rely on universities to "expand their internal research capabilities, stay abreast of new developments, provide access to the highest quality scientists, and gain access to cutting-edge technologies."[62]

Universities can exploit their leverage. They can use it as a stick to punish firms that enforce patents against researchers. And they can use it as a carrot by entering into alliances with firms that have forged reputations as collaborators. One example of such power is revealed by DuPont, which began to assert its rights against universities after it stopped conducting molecular biology research. Because DuPont no longer had to cooperate with university researchers, it had "little to lose and revenue to gain" when it "sacrifice[d] the goodwill of that community."[63]

Relationships between universities and industry persist over time. As the field of game theory explains, parties' optimal actions incorporate the anticipated reactions of their collaborators. Numerous repeated dealings between firms and universities discourage the filing of lawsuits. Even if it would make sense in an individual case for a company to sue, the risk of backlash that would block future collaborations would discourage suit.[64]

In other words, a regime of informal *norms*, or socially enforced rules, has, at least for now, replaced the formal law of the experimental use defense. Norms

---

not be construed to extend to any suit in law or equity, commenced or prosecuted against one of the United States by Citizens of another State, or by Citizens or Subjects of any Foreign State."); *Hans v. Louisiana*, 134 U.S. 1, 15–16 (1890) (sovereign immunity prevents suits by citizens against their state in federal court).

59. John P. Walsh et al, *Working Through the Patent Problem*, 299 Sci. 1021 (2003).

60. Walsh, *Effects*, at 317.

61. *Id.* at 325 (emphasis added).

62. Cristina Weschler, *The Informal Experimental Use Exception: University Research After Madey v. Duke University*, 79 N.Y.U. L. Rev. 1536, 1555 (2004).

63. Walsh, *Effects*, at 326; Weschler, at 1561.

64. Walsh, *Effects*, at 326.

exercise a powerful influence across many segments of society. Small close-knit communities, for example, have developed norms that help govern the use of scarce resources. Professor Robert Ellickson famously traced these rituals in the cattle industry in Shasta County, California, uncovering norms that held livestock owners responsible for their animals' actions and that trumped formal laws.[65] Other communities have followed internal rules to govern the management of resources held in common.[66]

The norms in university-industry collaborations have protected noncommercial research. Such research is typically characterized by low damages and likelihood of detection as well as high reputation costs from suit. In contrast, firms are more likely to sue when universities use research tools with commercial applications, as the amount of damages increases and harm to reputation decreases.[67]

This assessment is borne out by the single area in which gene patents have been shown to restrict access: clinical diagnostic testing. Such testing has commercial purposes as labs charge patients or insurers for conducting diagnostic tests.[68] A survey of laboratory directors that performed DNA-based genetic tests for clinical purposes found that 65 percent of the respondents indicated that their labs had been contacted by a patentee concerning infringement. It also found that 25 percent of respondents had stopped performing a clinical test they had been offering because of a patent. And the presence of a patent resulted in 53 percent not developing a new clinical test. The authors of the survey, conducted in 2003, noted that previous studies were consistent with their results.[69]

In addition to not filing lawsuits, many companies allow universities to license their patented materials at significantly reduced rates. The genomics[70] firm Celera charged companies as much as $15 million for access to its collection of

---

65. ROBERT C. ELLICKSON, ORDER WITHOUT LAW: HOW NEIGHBORS SETTLE DISPUTES 52–64 (1991).

66. The leading scholar investigating such communities, Professor Elinor Ostrom, has offered a number of examples, including the Alanya fishery, the Törbel mountain village, several Japanese villages, and Huerta irrigation institutions. ELINOR OSTROM, GOVERNING THE COMMONS: THE EVOLUTION OF INSTITUTIONS FOR COLLECTIVE ACTION 18–21, 61–82 (1990).

67. Weschler, at 1564.

68. COMM. ON IP RIGHTS IN THE KNOWLEDGE-BASED ECON., NAT'L RESEARCH COUNCIL OF THE NAT'L ACAD., A PATENT SYSTEM FOR THE 21ST CENTURY 73 (Stephen A. Merrill et al. eds., 2004).

69. Mildred K. Cho et al., *Effects of Patents and Licenses on the Provision of Clinical Genetic Testing Services*, 5 J. MOLECULAR DIAGNOSTICS 3 (2003).

70. Genomics is the study of the functions and interactions of genes. Guttmacher & Collins, at 1514

data and software tools but allowed universities to access it for less than $15,000.[71] Even Myriad, which created the firestorm on its patented breast cancer gene, reduces its fee more than 50 percent for researchers funded by the National Institutes of Health (NIH).[72]

Relatedly, public and private entities have created public databases that have made genomic information widely available. And scientific journals have sought to increase access to research materials. Biology journals "have long made it a condition of publication that authors deposit sequences in public databases such as GenBank or Protein Data Bank."[73]

In short, the symbiotic relationship between universities and industry has prevented the bottlenecks that could have stifled innovation. This relationship, together with the nature of biotechnology and frequent licensing, explains the absence of an anticommons and restricted access. Given this status, I do not propose a current expansion of the experimental use defense.

NO PRESENT PROPOSAL

The Federal Circuit's restriction of the experimental use defense went too far. Every use of a patented invention by a researcher in a laboratory should not be infringement. Nonetheless, informal norms between academia and industry have addressed these concerns. There is no guarantee, of course, that this equilibrium will continue. But for the present, there is no urgent need for proposals that would expand the experimental use defense.

A devil's advocate might ask what the harm would be from a narrow defense protecting, say, noncommercial researchers. And in many cases, there would not be significant harm. But the blurring boundaries between academia and industry make such an exception more nuanced than it initially appears. If we do not need to draw these lines (which could have effects on incentives) at this time, then we should not.

On the other hand, if companies begin to sue universities, the dangers of stifled innovation would rise, and the informal norms would be stripped away, laying bare the constricted state of the case law. In such a setting, close calls on the border between commercial and noncommercial uses could be tolerated. The adverse effects of blocked innovation would be paramount.

---

71. Weschler, at 1553–54; Tabitha M. Powledge, *Changing the Rules*, 2 EUROPEAN MOLECULAR BIOLOGY ORG. 171 (2001), http://www.pubmedcentral.nih.gov/articlerender.fcgi?artid=1083851.

72. Tom Reynolds, *NCI-Myriad Agreement Offers BRCA Testing at Reduced Cost*, 92 J. NAT'L CANCER INST. 596, 596 (2000), http://jncicancerspectrum.oupjournals.org/cgi/content/full/jnci;92/8/596.

73. Walsh, *Effects*, at 329.

THREE FUTURE PROPOSALS

If evidence of an anticommons develops or industry begins to enforce its patents by suing universities, proposals to fix the law must be considered. No magic formula will determine when this threshold is triggered. But the filing of two or three lawsuits on important patents would raise concern that could cross this boundary. Restricted access to a tool critical to a broad range of research, such as Cohen-Boyer (gene cloning) or PCR (gene sequence amplification), could harm innovation.[74] Similarly, evidence of limited access to tools that mirrors the bottlenecks plaguing materials, as discussed in the next chapter, would rise to that level. And if researchers begin to abandon or modify projects because of patent concerns, the proposals could be invoked.

In such a case, what should be done? I offer three proposals:

(1) Apply the defense to experimentation on the patented invention.
(2) Amend the Bayh-Dole Act to require universities and other nonprofit research institutions to reserve rights for themselves and other similar entities to use the invention for noncommercial research.
(3) Undertake empirical study of user innovation among research tool innovators in laying the framework for a defense exempting research use by (a) nonprofit entities and (b) anyone seeking to use inventions patented by nonprofit entities.

The third proposal is the most ambitious and would have the greatest effect on incentives. It is promising in incorporating a type of innovation—by users—that the law does not typically consider. As I discuss below, further empirical study is necessary before such a proposal is implemented.

Each of the first two proposals could more quickly be implemented to ameliorate restrictions on biotechnology patents that arise. The first would permit certain uses that explore the patent itself. It would allow the user to determine how the tool worked. And it would harmonize U.S. law with that of many other jurisdictions.

The second proposal is more ambitious in requiring university and nonprofit patentees to permit use of the tool in research by others. But it is limited to use by certain actors and to inventions created with federal funding. Given its tailoring to research tools, it likely would be the first choice if firms begin to sue universities or anticommons appear to develop.

There is a role for both proposals as the second only applies to tools created with federal funding and the first only covers a subset of potential uses. Even the combination of the two proposals would not cover the full range of experimentation

---

74. Adelman, at 1020–21 (distinguishing tools, such as ESTs and drug targets, that are specific to certain problems and for which restricted licensing is unlikely to threaten innovation).

with patented tools created or used by nonprofit entities, thus leaving room for the third recommendation to operate.

EXPERIMENTATION ON PATENTED INVENTION

The first proposal would protect experimentation on the patented invention. Any expansion of the experimental use defense could reasonably begin with the type of activity that has historically been recognized and is less likely to affect innovation incentives.

Experimentation *on* the patented invention uses the invention to study its technology or verify, design around, or improve the patent. Experimentation *with* an invention, in contrast, uses the invention as a research tool "to study something else." This activity more directly implicates innovation incentives, as researchers could use such a defense to avoid paying royalties on research tools.[75]

Experimentation on the invention implements the disclosure function of patents. As part of the bargain at the heart of the patent system, patentees obtain exclusive rights in return for enabling others to make the device. A patent will not be issued if it does not explain "the manner and process of making and using [the invention] in such full, clear, concise, and exact terms as to enable any person skilled in the art . . . to make and use [it]."[76]

On certain occasions one must make an invention to test whether the patent is valid. And in many cases, understanding is "a hands-on experience" that requires experimentation.[77] A defense for experimentation on the patented invention thus would promote the disclosure function of patents.

Disclosure also plays a crucial role in the dissemination of inventive concepts. Upon completion of the patent term, others can copy the method described in the patent. Even during the term, rivals can use the claims as a template for improving on and *designing around* the invention.[78] This circumvention of patent claims increases competition by creating alternative products.[79] It also allows others to benefit from the concept and race to be the first to the market with

---

75. NIH Research Tools Report, app. D; Strandburg, *Patent Bargain*, at 89. Any recognition of a defense for experimenting on the patented invention must distinguish between the two types of experimentation. Such an inquiry will not be clear in every case, but should be in many settings.

76. 35 U.S.C. § 112.

77. Strandburg, *Patent Bargain*, at 103.

78. *Id.* at 101 n.94. Improvements also may be related to "blocking patent" inventions, which add to (and can block) the patented claims.

79. Craig Allen Nard, *Certainty, Fence Building, and the Useful Arts*, 74 IND. L.J. 759, 791 (1999).

inventions building on the idea. It is often impossible to design around broad claims without using the invention.

Relatedly, the statute itself contemplates the patenting of "improvement[s]."[80] And as Federal Circuit Judge Pauline Newman pointed out, firms' experimentation is revealed by "the routine appearance of improvements on patented subject matter."[81]

One potential version of such a defense could protect experimentation

for the purpose of evaluating a patent's validity or scope, or improving or designing around the invention.[82]

Global Treatment

An exception for experimentation on the patented invention would be consistent with most other nations' treatments of the issue. Several European nations have recognized such an exception. United Kingdom (U.K.) patent law provides an exception for "private" activity that does not have commercial purposes but has "experimental purposes relating to the subject-matter of the invention." Germany offers a nearly identical version, and the Netherlands protects acts "solely serving for research on the patented subject matter."[83]

Other countries offer statutes that could be interpreted even more expansively. The Japanese Patent Act allows the use of patents "for the purposes of experiment or research." The Korean Patent Law offers a similar defense. India protects uses "for the purpose merely of experiment or research." And China allows use of a patent "solely for the purposes of scientific research and experimentations."[84] These versions could conceivably protect experimentation with the invention.

---

80. 35 U.S.C. § 101.

81. See Integra Lifesciences I, Ltd. v. Merck KGaA, 331 F.3d 860, 875 (Fed. Cir. 2003) (Newman, J., concurring in part and dissenting in part).

82. For other similar proposals, see Strandburg, *Patent Bargain*, at 103; Rebecca S. Eisenberg, *Patents and the Progress of Science: Exclusive Rights and Experimental Use*, 56 U. CHI. L. REV. 1017, 1078 (1989).

83. Patents Act 1977, ch. 37, § 60(5), http://www.wipo.int/clea/en/text_html. jsp?lang=en&id=1623 (UK); German Patent Law, § 11, 1980, http://www.wipo.int/clea/ en/text_html.jsp?lang=en&id=1035#JD_DE081_S1; Patent Act 1995 Netherlands, Art. 53(3) (exception for "acts solely serving for research on the patented subject matter"). The overlapping treatment is explained by the Convention for the European Patent for the Common Market (Community Patent Convention) art. 31(A)–(B) 76/76/EEC (1975), *superseded by* Agreement Relating to Community Patents art. 27(a)–(b) 89/695/EEC (1989). The Act was not ratified but has served as the basis for the countries' exceptions.

84. Japanese Patent Law § 69(1) (1959, *amended* 1999), http://www.wipo.int/clea/en/ text_html.jsp?lang=en&id=2652; Korean Patent Act § 96(1)(i) (1961, *amended* 1998), http://www.wipo.int/clea/en/text_pdf.jsp?lang=EN&id=2751; The Patents Act 1970,

In short, recognition of activity experimenting on the patented invention would bring U.S. law closer to the laws of other jurisdictions. Allowing experimentation on the invention also would be a logical first step in resuscitating the experimental use defense. Recognition of such a defense could have benefits across other industries. But I do not propose its adoption in this chapter because my focus is biotechnology research tools, which presently do not need the defense.

BAYH-DOLE ACT

A second proposal would amend the Bayh-Dole Act to promote the noncommercial use of federally funded inventions.[85] Such a proposal would have a significant effect given that the federal government provides roughly 60 percent of R&D funding performed in universities.[86]

Congress enacted the Bayh-Dole Act in 1980 to increase the commercialization of federally funded inventions. At the time, there was no single government policy for ownership of such inventions. Less than 5 percent of the 28,000 patents to which the government held title were licensed to industry to develop products.[87]

---

§ 47(3) (1970, *amended* 1999), http://www.ipindia.nic.in/ipr/patent/patAct1970-3-99.html; Maritime Procedure Law of the People's Republic of China, art. 63.

Each of the foreign statutes complies with the World Trade Organization (WTO)'s TRIPS Agreement, which provides that members "may provide limited exceptions" to patent rights that "do not unreasonably conflict with a normal exploitation of the patent and do not unreasonably prejudice the legitimate interest of the patent owner, taking account of the legitimate interests of third parties." Agreement on Trade-Related Aspects of Intellectual Property Rights, Apr. 15, 1994, Marrakesh Agreement Establishing the World Trade Organization, Annex 1C, art. 30 (1994).

85. For other proposals to amend the Bayh-Dole Act, see Dreyfuss, at 471 (universities and nonprofit research institutions can use material without permission if they publish the results of their work and do not seek patents); Rai & Eisenberg, at 310–11 (federal funding agencies can restrict patentee's right to retain title or can "march in" to receive rights).

86. NSF, Science and Engineering Indicators 2006, ch. 5, at 5-11 to 5-12, http://www.nsf.gov/statistics/seind06/c5/c5h.htm (last visited June 19, 2008) (63 percent in 2003). Federal funding comes primarily from the NIH, National Science Foundation (NSF), and Department of Defense (DOD).

87. Council on Government Relations (COGR), *The Bayh-Dole Act: A Guide to the Law and Implementing Regulations*, Oct. 1999, at 2, http://www.cogr.edu/docs/Bayh_Dole.pdf; *see also* Rebecca S. Eisenberg, *Public Research and Private Development: Patents and Technology Transfer in Government-Sponsored Research*, 82 VA. L. REV. 1663, 1702–05 (1996) (criticizing figure of 5 percent).

This state of affairs arose because the government retained title to inventions and did not market them. At the same time, the nonexclusive licenses it issued discouraged firms from making investments in creations that could be copied.[88]

The Bayh-Dole Act addressed this problem by allowing universities and small businesses to elect title to patentable inventions arising from the use of federal funding.[89] If recipients elect title, they must file patent applications, seek commercialization opportunities, and inform the funding agency of efforts to obtain utilization.[90]

The Act imposed several limits on this right. The government automatically gained a nonexclusive license to practice the invention.[91] It could eliminate a recipient's ability to patent the invention in "exceptional circumstances" when such action would "better promote the [Act's] policy and objectives."[92] And its ability to exercise "march-in" rights could compel the patentee to grant a license to third parties if the patentee did not "alleviate health or safety needs" or "take . . . effective steps to achieve practical application of the . . . invention."[93] The "exceptional circumstances" exception has rarely been invoked, and the march-in power has never been used.

Bayh-Dole has vastly increased university patenting. Although causation is difficult to trace precisely given contemporaneous developments such as courts' allowance of biotechnology patents, the Act has played an important role in commercializing patents. In 2002, the *Economist* magazine referred to the Act as "[p]ossibly the most inspired piece of legislation to be enacted in America over the past half-century." "More than anything," the article continued, "this single policy measure helped to reverse America's precipitous slide into industrial irrelevance."[94]

The Act, however, has not been without its detractors. Professors Rebecca Eisenberg and Arti Rai have lamented that the Act "may hinder rather than accelerate biomedical research" and have contended that funding agencies, not patentees, should determine when publicly funded research discoveries should be dedicated to the public.[95] In addition, while the Act's primary goal is to foster patenting and commercialization, it also seeks to ensure that the government "obtains sufficient rights in federally supported inventions" to meet its needs and "protect the public against nonuse or unreasonable use of inventions."[96]

---

88. *See generally* COGR, at 2.

89. The Act covered universities, small businesses, and nonprofit organizations. I generally refer to universities in my discussion, which present the most frequent setting.

90. NIH Research Tools Report, App. B.

91. 35 U.S.C. § 202(c)(4). The government also has the right to direct research by others "on [its] behalf." 35 U.S.C. § 209(d)(1).

92. 35 U.S.C. § 202(a)(ii).

93. 35 U.S.C. § 203(a)(1, 2).

94. *Innovation's Golden Goose*, ECONOMIST, Dec. 14, 2002, at 3.

95. Rai & Eisenberg, at 291.

96. 35 U.S.C. § 200.

Even more relevant, Congress amended the Act's preamble in 2000 to add an additional purpose: ensuring that inventions do not "unduly encumber[] future research and discovery." Another amendment required an exclusive license's scope to be "no[] greater than reasonably necessary" to provide incentives to commercialize or promote public use of the invention.[97]

The Act's drafters did not debate these amendments. But if universities' exclusive licensing of research tools begins to markedly reduce access, these two changes provide a foundation for an amendment to the Act. Not "unduly encumbering" R&D and limiting the scope of exclusive licenses provide strong support for an exception.

The amendment could require universities and nonprofit research institutions that create federally funded, patented inventions, in granting exclusive licenses to firms, to

> reserve rights for themselves and other academic or nonprofit institutions to use the invention for noncommercial research.[98]

This exception thus imposes three limits: (1) application to federally funded research, (2) invocation by academic or nonprofit research institutions, and (3) use for noncommercial research. The first condition would be met as long as any part of the invention was funded with federal funds. The second element, academic or nonprofit status, should be clear. And in most cases, the third also will be apparent, based on the distinction between individual researcher use and commercial distribution.[99]

The exception would promote the goals of the Bayh-Dole Act by increasing distribution of federally funded inventions among researchers engaging in noncommercial use. Widespread distribution is consistent with the goals of Bayh-Dole as well as the NIH Guidelines and university licensing principles discussed below.

At the same time, it would apply only to use, not sale, of the invention, and thus not materially reduce commercialization and patenting. It also should not substantially affect incentives. For research tools that do not need further development after invention in the lab, federal funding displaces the need for patent incentives.[100] Incentives also would not be affected where the later-developed

---

97. Technology Transfer Commercialization Act of 2000, Pub. L. No. 106-404, 114 Stat. 1742, 1745, *codified at* 35 U.S.C. § 200 (2000).

98. For related proposals, see Sara Boettiger & Alan B. Bennett, *Bayh-Dole: If We Knew Then What We Know Now*, 24 NATURE BIOTECHNOLOGY 320, 321 (2006); Gary Pulsinelli, *Share and Share Alike: Increasing Access to Government-Funded Inventions Under the Bayh-Dole Act*, 7 MINN. J.L. SCI. & TECH. 393, 442 (2006).

99. Close calls may arise. But at least the judgments are limited to cases in which the inventions were created with federal funding.

100. The discussion in the text conservatively assumes that patent incentives are needed for research tools.

product is patentable, as the commercial developer, who typically does not receive federal funding, is not subject to the exception.[101]

Incentives could be affected for inventions that need commercializing activity after invention. But even in this case, firms often are protected by non-license means of appropriation such as sales of kits that researchers purchase rather than creating themselves. The exception would not affect incentives in the vast majority of cases since most research tools will be simple enough to not need further development or complex enough to be patentable or benefit from sales of services such as kits.[102]

NIH Guidelines
The proposal also would build on two sets of guidelines promulgated by the NIH, the largest entity providing federal funding. The guidelines have encouraged the dissemination of biomedical research tools. While they have not had the force of law, they have increased sharing of NIH-funded inventions.

In 1999, the NIH issued guidelines for sharing biomedical research resources. It stated that institutions that receive NIH funding "have an obligation to preserve research freedom." Consistent with the Bayh-Dole Act, funding recipients "are expected to maximize the use of their research findings" not only through commercialization but also "by making them available to the research community and the public."[103]

The guidelines explained that for research tools, licensing practices may "thwart rather than promote" utilization, commercialization, and public availability. For that reason, recipients were expected to disseminate the fruits of their research through publication or nonexclusive licensing. The guidelines discouraged exclusive licenses, except where the research tool is made widely available, and concluded that restrictive licensing "is antithetical to the goals of the Bayh-Dole Act."[104]

Similarly, in its 2005 guidelines for the licensing of genomic inventions, the NIH stated that "non-exclusive licensing should be pursued as a best practice . . . [w]henever possible" because it "facilitates making broad enabling technologies and research uses of inventions widely available." Where exclusive

---

101. Pulsinelli, at 450. This may not hold true for small businesses, which are covered by the Act.

102. *Id.* at 446–53. The kits contain reagents, substances or compounds consumed during chemical reactions. *Reagant*, WIKIPEDIA, http://en.wikipedia.org/wiki/Reagent (last visited June 17, 2008). Incentives could be affected to the extent that patentees recover through means other than kits, such as reach-through royalties.

103. Principles and Guidelines for Recipients of NIH Grants and Contracts on Obtaining and Disseminating Biomedical Research Resources, 64 Fed. Reg. 72090, 72092–93 (Dec. 23, 1999).

104. *Id.* at 72093, 72095.

licensing is necessary, it should be "appropriately tailored to ensure expeditious development of as many aspects of the technology as possible."[105]

The agency also encouraged licensing policies that "maximize[d] access, as well as commercial and research utilization of the technology to benefit the public health." For that reason, it encouraged funding recipients to "reserve in their license agreements the right to use the licensed technologies for their own research and educational uses, and to allow other institutions to do the same."[106]

University Practice

The proposal also is consistent with the recent practice of universities in retaining rights to their inventions. In 2007, a group of research universities promulgated the *Nine Points to Consider in Licensing University Technology*. The universities contended that they "should consider reserving rights . . . even if the invention is licensed exclusively to a commercial entity, for themselves and other non-profit and governmental organizations . . . to practice inventions and use associated information and data for research and educational purposes." They also suggested structuring exclusive licenses "in a manner that encourages technology development and use," offering the example of a license exclusive for sale, but not use, of the product. Finally, they sought to ensure that universities "make research tools as broadly available as possible."[107] More than 74 institutions, to date, have endorsed the principles.[108]

In short, Congress could address future problems of access to research tools by amending the Bayh-Dole Act to require universities and nonprofit institutions licensing patented, federally-funded inventions to reserve rights to use the invention for noncommercial research.[109]

USER INNOVATION AND RESEARCH TOOLS

The final proposal is the most ambitious. It incorporates notions of *user innovation* in determining why researchers develop research tools. Professor Eric von Hippel

---

105. Best Practices for the Licensing of Genomic Inventions, 70 Fed. Reg. 18413, 18415 (Apr. 11, 2005).

106. *Id.*

107. *In the Public Interest: Nine Points to Consider in Licensing University Technology*, Mar. 6, 2007, at 2–5, http://news-service.stanford.edu/news/2007/march7/gifs/white paper.pdf.

108. The Association of University Technology Managers, *Endorse the Nine Points to Consider*, http://www.autm.net/ninepoints_endorsement.cfm (last visited July 15, 2010).

109. My proposal requires (rather than permits) the reservation of rights to advance beyond the NIH Guidelines and recent university practice and to protect universities and nonprofits that are not party to the exclusive license.

has shown that users play a vital role in creating new products. Users often develop revolutionary innovations that employ specific information about their needs. Manufacturers, in contrast, tend to develop more incremental improvements on existing needs.[110]

The field of research tools would seem to provide a fruitful setting for application of the theory. Research tools are produced by nonprofit researchers and commercial research innovators, tool suppliers, and tool licensing firms.[111] Nonprofit researchers resemble user innovators in inventing and using research tools. They also present many of the characteristics of "lead users" that develop products at the leading edge of uncertain markets[112]:

- The success of their research depends on devising "cutting edge" research methods.
- They have heterogeneous needs for individualized tools for their experiments.
- They have "sticky information" about their needs that evolves and cannot easily be transferred to manufacturers.
- They have expertise in inventing tools and can access sophisticated equipment.[113]

In addition to reflecting traits of user innovators, nonprofit researchers are motivated to invent for many reasons other than gaining patent protection. Faculty, postdoctoral researchers, and graduate students benefit directly from creating research tools. Such tools play a crucial role in obtaining and publishing results. This, in turn, enhances their reputation, intellectual satisfaction, ability to obtain funding, and participation in social discourse. And these incentives are bolstered by the first-mover nature of publication, which bestows on the first to publish advantages vital to career advancement.[114]

Because university researchers exhibit characteristics of user innovators, and because patents do not appear to play a central role in their creation of tools, a new experimental use defense could be considered. Professor Katherine Strandburg has offered a proposal that would exempt (1) research use by nonprofit entities and (2) research use by anyone of inventions patented by nonprofit entities.[115]

Such a proposal would operate symmetrically to remove nonprofit entities from the receiving end of infringement suits but also prevent them from

---

110. Eric von Hippel, Democratizing Innovation 8 (2005).

111. Katherine J. Strandburg, *Users as Innovators: Implications for Patent Doctrine*, at 23 (2007), http://ssrn.com/abstract=969399 [hereinafter Strandburg, *Users as Innovators*].

112. Hippel, at 108.

113. Strandburg, *Users as Innovators*, at 23–24.

114. *Id.* at 24–26.

115. *Id.* at 42.

enforcing their patented tools. Commercial tool suppliers and licensing firms might benefit from the arrangement. They would be able to sue competitors for infringement. And even though they would lose the ability to license their tools to nonprofit researchers, they would gain the ability to use pioneering tools created by these entities without paying royalties.

Because this is such an ambitious proposal and because it could reduce incentives, further study needs to be undertaken before it is implemented. Questions that would need to be addressed include the following: What would be the effect of the proposal on the parties? Would firms suffer reduced incentives to develop such tools? Can we draw meaningful lines between nonprofit and commercial researchers in the university setting?

Evidence on these questions exists. In 1988, Eric von Hippel found that for four types of significant scientific instruments, users developed 77 percent of innovations.[116] Five years after conducting this study, von Hippel (together with William Riggs) found that users developed 44 percent of innovations on two types of instruments used to study the chemical composition of surfaces.[117] Updating these surveys and applying them to different research tools would be invaluable.

To be clear, I do not think such a proposal should be employed until, and unless, access to research tools deteriorates. In addition, more recent evidence on the above questions would be helpful. But if those conditions are met, a proposal that incorporates innovation's real-world effects would be welcome.

CONCLUSION

The law on the experimental use doctrine is cramped and does not reflect what is actually occurring in the biotechnology field. Nonetheless, informal norms and working solutions have, at least as of the time this book was published, effectively substituted for a more expansive doctrine. If it were costless to bolster the experimental use defense, none could justifiably withhold their consent. But because the boundaries between many of the proffered categories—such as commercial and noncommercial—are unclear and the doctrine's expansion could potentially affect innovation incentives, I conclude that the informal norms need not be supplemented at this time.

This conclusion, of course, is subject to change at any time. A few high-profile lawsuits against researchers would knock out the scaffolding currently supporting

---

116. The instruments, which scientists use to collect and analyze data, were the gas chromatograph, nuclear magnetic resonance spectrometer, ultraviolet spectrophotometer, and transmission electron microscope. ERIC VON HIPPEL, THE SOURCES OF INNOVATION 11 (1988).

117. William Riggs & Eric von Hippel, *Incentives to Innovate and the Sources of Innovation: The Case of Scientific Instruments*, 23 RES. POL'Y 459, 459 (1994).

this precarious state of affairs. But there are significant reasons that firms have not sued universities. Because the situation is fragile and because this book cannot be revised at the instant the equilibrium breaks down, I have offered three proposals that could, if needed, bolster the experimental use defense.

The first protects experimentation on the patented invention, which would have little impact on incentives to invent but would implement the purpose of patent disclosure and promise a return to the open access that characterized the scientific community until recently.

The second would amend the Bayh-Dole Act to require universities and nonprofit institutions to reserve rights for themselves and other academic or nonprofits to use the invention for noncommercial research. This would be consistent with the Act's goals and ensure the dissemination of vital federally funded research.

The third would recommend empirical study of user innovation among research tool innovators. Such study could lay the framework for a defense exempting research use by (1) nonprofit entities and (2) anyone seeking to use inventions patented by nonprofit entities.

There is a temptation, in conclusion, to expand the cramped experimental use defense. And there has been no shortage of proposals to do just that. But given the lack of evidence of anticommons and restricted access to research tools, the costs of adopting such proposals currently outweigh the benefits. If this changes, with an increase in withheld research tools, anticommons, and lawsuits, the proposals would offer a lifeline. But for now, those life preservers can remain on board, ready to be thrown to researchers when the waters of stifled biotech innovation rise.

12. BIOTECHNOLOGY DILEMMA 2: MATERIAL TRANSFER AGREEMENTS

MTAs 279
General Dangers 281
    Withheld Materials 281
    Abandoned Research Lines 282
    Delays in Receiving Materials 282
    Publication Restrictions 283
    Additional Harms 283
IP-related Dangers 283
Example: Stem Cells 284
A Partial Solution 286
A Proposal 287
    Federally Funded Entities 287
    University-Industry Transfers 288
Conclusion 290

The previous chapter demonstrated the present lack of concern with access to patented research tools. More concern is presented when scientists need tangible materials for their research. Unlike the situation of patented research tools, scientists often cannot circumvent a refusal to license materials. In providing materials, owners frequently require recipients to enter into *material transfer agreements* (MTAs). Given their high transaction costs and role in forcing scientists to abandon research paths, these agreements have threatened innovation.

MTAs

Scientists frequently need and request materials owned by others. Such requests occur in many settings including universities, federal laboratories, pharmaceutical and biotechnology firms, and nonprofit institutions.[1] The most common request involves biological materials. Researchers use genes, cell lines, tissues, and organisms to create new products. They also request proteins, unpublished information, databases, and software.[2] Each of these materials is an input in the

---

1. Univ. of Cal., *Technology Transfer*, at 2 (2006), http://www.ucop.edu/ott/faculty/overacad.html [Technology Transfer].

2. J.P. Walsh et al., *Where Excludability Matters: Material Versus Intellectual Property in Academic Biomedical Research*, 36 RES. POL'Y 1184, 1192 (2007).

R&D process, allowing scientists to create new products that eventually could be used by the public.

In many cases, the recipient must sign an MTA. Such an agreement can be defined as

> a contract between the owner of a material and a party that wishes to use the material for research purposes.[3]

Why must scientists obtain material from other parties? Because they are unable to create it themselves. In most cases, they cannot spare the time and cost to create the materials.[4] In addition, they generally lack the equipment, information, and expertise necessary to do so.

MTAs cover a range of activity. They specify how the material can be used.[5] They may ensure compliance with government regulations, addressing the recipient's handling, use, and distribution of materials.[6] And they often include publication restrictions, confidentiality requirements, indemnification clauses, and restrictions on the use of research tools.[7] One clause, for example, might prevent publication until approved by the materials provider. Another could require recipients to indemnify the provider against liability from the use of the material. A third could prohibit a recipient from sharing the materials with other researchers or utilizing them for commercial purposes.[8]

One clause that appears in many MTAs is a *reach-through* license that grants providers rights in new materials or IP created by the recipient.[9] Such rights take the form of ownership of, licenses for, or royalties from future discoveries made with the materials.[10]

In addition to transferring physical materials, MTAs also frequently include patent licenses.[11] As discussed in the previous chapter, several developments have increased the importance of patents in the past generation:

- Advances in drug discovery shifted from trial and error to knowledge of genes and proteins more likely to be patented.[12]

---

3. *See* Nat'l Inst. of Health, *Report of the National Institute of Health (NIH) Working Group on Research Tools*, app. B (1998), http://www.nih.gov/news/researchtools/ [hereinafter *Research Tools Report*].

4. Walsh, at 1192.

5. *Research Tools Report*, app. B.

6. Sean O'Connor, *The Use of MTAs To Control Commercialization of Stem Cell Diagnostics and Therapeutics*, 21 BERKELEY TECH. L.J. 1017, 1018 (2006).

7. *Research Tools Report*, at 8–11.

8. *See generally id.*

9. Technology Transfer, at 3.

10. *Research Tools Report*, at 17.

11. O'Connor, at 1018.

12. Arti K. Rai & Rebecca S. Eisenberg, *Bayh-Dole Reform and the Progress of Biomedicine*, 66 L. & CONTEMP. PROBS. 289, 289 (2003).

- Court decisions expanded the scope of patentable subject matter to cover live, human-made microorganisms.[13]
- The Bayh-Dole Act promoted the utilization of federally funded inventions and increased collaboration between private firms and universities.[14]

Providers have strengthened their control over materials by leasing the material.[15] A lease allows the owner to avoid the *first sale* doctrine, which reduces an IP owner's control over the buyer's use of the product. As a result, the owner could impose a wider range of restrictions on the recipient, such as prohibitions on reverse engineering or on the transfer of physical property.[16]

Owners also increase control by bundling patent licenses and physical material. Recipients who need a patent license could be forced to take the materials, and those who need the materials could be forced to take a patent license. Such activity could potentially violate the antitrust laws, which prohibit certain tying arrangements that force the buyer to purchase a second (unwanted) product along with the first (desired) product.

GENERAL DANGERS

MTAs present at least five threats to innovation in the biotechnology industry: (1) withheld materials, (2) abandoned research lines, (3) delays in receiving material, (4) publication restrictions, and (5) other harms.

Withheld Materials

Two significant empirical studies in the past decade have revealed the danger of materials withheld from recipients. The first study, conducted by Eric Campbell and others, and covering 2,000 academic genetics researchers, found that 47 percent of respondents did not receive requested materials, data, or information.[17] The second, conducted by John Walsh and others (and described in the previous chapter), found that 18 percent of materials requests to academics and

---

13. *Diamond v. Chakrabarty*, 447 U.S. 303 (1980).

14. Pub. L. No. 96-517, *codified as amended at* 35 U.S.C. §§ 200–12 (1994).

15. O'Connor, at 1019. *E.g.*, Memorandum of Understanding between WiCell Research Institute, Inc. and Public Health Service, § 2(a), http://ott.od.nih.gov/pdfs/WiCell MOUnonhuman.pdf [WiCell Memorandum] (provider maintains ownership of materials).

16. O'Connor, at 1021.

17. Eric Campbell et al., *Data Withholding in Academic Genetics*, 287 JAMA 473, 477 (2002) (covering period between 1997 and 2000).

33 percent of requests to industry researchers were not fulfilled. Like the Campbell study, Walsh concluded that denials increased over time.[18]

The studies explored reasons for the rise in denials. The Campbell study noted a higher incidence when owners participated in commercial activities and when they received a high number of requests. The Walsh study found that the likelihood of sharing was reduced by scientific competition and a history of business activity.[19]

Abandoned Research Lines

The most pronounced effect of withheld materials occurred when scientists were forced to abandon research lines. The Campbell study found that 21 percent of researchers abandoned a promising line of research. And the Walsh study concluded that each year "one in nine researchers report abandoning a promising line of research" because they did not receive requested materials.[20]

Delays in Receiving Materials

Material withholding also led to delays. The studies concluded that MTAs required complex negotiations that often prevented scientists from conducting research for lengthy periods. The Walsh study found that 26 percent of MTAs resulted in negotiations lasting more than one month, and that 8 percent of all requests suffered research stoppages of more than one month. The Campbell study concluded that MTAs "have become so complex and demanding that they inhibit sharing."[21] The delays affected each of the stakeholders:

- Scientists "wait months or even years to carry out experiments."
- University technology transfer offices complain of limited resources being overwhelmed by "the burden of reviewing and renegotiating each of a rapidly growing number of agreements" for what previously were "routine exchanges."
- Large pharmaceutical and small biotech firms report "growing frustration" with the burden of and delay accompanying agreement negotiations.[22]

---

18. Walsh, at 1200. For additional studies reflecting similar results, see David Blumenthal et al., *Data Withholding in Genetics and the Other Life Sciences: Prevalences and Predictors*, 81 ACAD. MED. 137, 140 (2006) (2000 survey of 1,800 faculty showed that 44 percent of geneticists and 32 percent of other life scientists withheld data); Christine Vogeli et al., *Data Withholding and the Next Generation of Scientists: Results of a National Survey*, 81 ACAD. MED. 128, 131 (2006) (2003 survey of 1,000 second-year doctoral students and postdoctoral fellows revealed that 23 percent reported denials of materials associated with published research and 51 percent reported negative effects on their research from withholding).

19. Campbell, at 478; Walsh, at 1195–96.

20. Campbell, at 478; Walsh, at 1200.

21. Walsh, at 1193; Campbell, at 479.

22. Rebecca S. Eisenberg, *Bargaining over the Transfer of Proprietary Research Tools: Is this Market Failing or Emerging?*, in EXPANDING THE BOUNDARIES OF INTELLECTUAL

Publication Restrictions

Fourth, MTAs often impose restrictions on publication. The Walsh study found that publication restrictions appeared in 30 percent of MTAs and 70 percent of MTAs involving drugs. Some clauses require the provider's approval before the recipient can submit a manuscript for publication. Others utilize confidentiality provisions that "are so far-reaching in their coverage as to interfere with effective publication of research results, presentations at conferences, or validation of results by other investigators." The Campbell study found that 24 percent of respondents suffered "significantly delayed" publications.[23]

Additional Harms

The Campbell study revealed additional dangers. Twenty-eight percent of respondents were unable to replicate published research and 28 percent ended a collaboration as a result of the withholding. More generally, 73 percent thought that denials slowed the rate of scientific progress. Fifty-eight percent reported harmful effects of withholding on their own research, and 77 percent thought that denials had "detracted somewhat or greatly" from communication in their field.[24]

IP-RELATED DANGERS

Intellectual property rights exacerbate these problems. Recipients lament reach-through provisions, which allow materials owners to retain rights in products made with the requested materials. The Walsh study found that reach-through provisions appeared in 38 percent of MTAs.[25]

One concern with these clauses is their tendency to reduce scientists' incentives to conduct research. The provisions could limit scientists' freedom to pursue lines of inquiry because they no longer own their research results. They also could inadequately compensate scientists for their efforts.[26] Finally, they could offer windfalls for materials providers, who could wind up with greater rights than the sponsors that provided funding for the entire project.[27]

Reach-through rights, by divesting scientists of control over their discoveries, also reduce the likelihood of future research funding. This situation is especially concerning where the license encompasses inventions that do not directly incorporate the transferred materials. In such a case, the user cannot work with firms

---

PROPERTY: INNOVATION POLICY FOR THE KNOWLEDGE SOCIETY 223, 225 (R. Dreyfuss et al. eds., 2001).

23. Walsh, at 1193; *Research Tools Report*, at 8; Campbell, at 478.
24. Campbell, at 478.
25. Walsh, at 1193.
26. Technology Transfer, at 3.
27. *Research Tools Report*, at 9.

that would provide significant assistance "because they have mortgaged their future [IP] to gain access to a research tool."[28]

Relatedly, reach-through rights could lead to conflicts between funding sponsors and materials providers. Promises of derivative creations could violate previous commitments to research sponsors. Where, for example, a recipient has received federal funding, the assignment of ownership could violate the Bayh-Dole Act, which reserves rights for the federal government.[29]

Finally, the combination of IP provisions and physical property rights further reduces sharing. An MTA that prohibits a recipient from engaging in reverse engineering or using material for certain purposes strengthens the embedded patents. A recipient may unwittingly strengthen a rival's patent when, as a condition of taking the material, it agrees to use it for research and not commercial purposes. At the same time, a recipient who seeks a patent license could be forced to take the provider's material. This combination strengthens the provider's ability to control not only the use of the material but also downstream development derived from it.[30]

EXAMPLE: STEM CELLS

The field of stem cell research has offered an example of the powerful combination of IP licenses and physical material leases. In 1998, Dr. James Thomson, a developmental biologist at the University of Wisconsin, isolated and cultured human embryonic stem cells. Embryonic stem cells are undifferentiated cells that can develop into nearly any cell in the human body, including bone, muscle, liver, or blood cells. In contrast to adult stem cells, which are specialized and not always able to reproduce easily, embryonic stem cells can reproduce indefinitely and grow into any type of human tissue.[31]

The study of embryonic stem cells promises momentous gains in medical research. The ability to generate many types of human cells allows scientists to understand and treat cell-based diseases by replacing faulty cells with healthy cells. Stem cells also could repair damaged cells in the heart, spinal cord, and other organs not capable of repairing themselves. The list of conditions and diseases potentially treatable or curable as a result of stem cell research is breathtaking: Parkinson's, diabetes, Alzheimer's, heart disease, stroke, spinal cord injuries, and burns.[32]

---

28. *Id.*

29. *Id.* at 8.

30. O'Connor, at 1020–23.

31. Embryonic Stem Cells: Research at the University of Wisconsin-Madison, http://www.news.wisc.edu/packages/stemcells/facts.html#1 (2007).

32. *Id.*; WiCell Research Institute, *Stem Cell Basics*, http://www.wicell.org/index.php?option=com_content&task=category&id=161&Itemid=155&sectionid=8.

After his breakthrough, Thomson assigned to the Wisconsin Alumni Research Foundation (WARF), the University of Wisconsin's technology transfer office, both the patent rights to the stem cells and the physical property rights to the cells themselves. Wisconsin Alumni Research Foundation created the WiCell Research Institute to distribute the stem cells.[33]

In August 2001, President George W. Bush announced that federal funding would no longer be available for new stem cell lines.[34] As of August 2008, there were only six sources of stem cells in the world, with three of the six in the United States.[35] Consequently, as one of the few providers of stem cells and the owner of three broad patents, WARF/WiCell had considerable influence over stem cell research. This control was bolstered by its packaging of patents and stem cells.

Professor Sean O'Connor demonstrated how researchers who desired either the stem cells or patent licenses were required to take both. As of the time O'Connor wrote in 2006, researchers seeking access to the Thomson patent could not enter into a stand-alone patent license. The only available licenses required researchers to accept WiCell's stem cells.[36] From the other direction, all licensees that had received WiCell's stem cells also had obtained a sublicense to the patents. WARF/WiCell did not appear to have offered any stand-alone MTAs.[37] WARF/WiCell recently untied this combination, allowing researchers to obtain stem cells elsewhere.[38]

Wisconsin Alumni Research Foundation further loosened restrictions in January 2007, allowing companies to sponsor research at academic or nonprofit institutions without a license and permitting researchers to transfer cells to others without a license.[39] In short, WARF/WiCell has recently improved access to stem cells. But its prior position demonstrates the dangers of control over patents and materials.

---

33. Commission on Intellectual Property Rights, *Workshop 10: Research Tools, Public-Private Partnerships, and Gene Patenting*, Jan. 22, 2002, at 2, http://www.iprcommission.org/papers/text/workshops/workshop10.txt.

34. Press Release, President Discusses Stem Cell Research (Aug. 9, 2001), http://www.whitehouse.gov/news/releases/2001/08/20010809-2.html.

35. Nat'l Inst. of Health, NIH Human Embryonic Stem Cell Registry, http://stemcells.nih.gov/research/registry/.

36. O'Connor, at 1042.

37. *Id.*

38. WiCell Research Institute, *Industry FAQs*, http://www.wicell.org/index.php?option=com_content&task=blogcategory&id=123&Itemid=177 (last visited August 18, 2008).

39. Wisconsin Alumni Research Foundation, *Wisconsin Alumni Research Foundation Changes Stem Cell Policies To Encourage Greater Academic, Industry Collaboration*, Jan. 23, 2007, http://www.warf.org/news/news.jsp?news_id=209. WARF also increased its commercial licenses from 7 in 2005 to 30 in June 2008. Meredith Wadman, *Licensing Fees Slow Advance of Stem Cells*, 435 NATURE 272, 273 (2005); *U.S. Patent Office Issues Certificates to Uphold WARF Stem Cell Patents*, WARF, June 26, 2008, http://www.warf.org/news/news.jsp?news_id=234.

A PARTIAL SOLUTION

Significant transaction costs accompany MTAs. These costs could be lowered by the implementation of model agreements that streamline the parties' options. This was the reason the Public Health Service (acting through the National Institutes of Health (NIH)), together with representatives of academia and industry, developed a proposed uniform biological MTA (UBMTA) in 1995.[40]

While private industry could "choose to adopt th[e] agreement," the UBMTA was geared to public and nonprofit organizations. As researchers came to "rely on common acceptance of its terms," the agreement "could reduce the administrative burden of sharing materials." In particular, transfers could occur as the parties referred to the UBMTA "without the need for separate negotiation of an individual document to cover each transfer."[41]

The most relevant clauses in the agreement provide that

- the provider owns the material,
- the recipient owns modifications,
- the material will be used "solely for teaching and academic research purposes,"
- the provider has no obligation to license the material for commercial purposes,
- the recipient can file patent applications claiming inventions it made as a result of using the material,
- the recipient assumes liability for damages from the material's use,
- the agreement "shall not be interpreted to prevent or delay publication of research findings resulting from the use of the material,"
- the material is provided "at no cost, or with an optional transmittal fee solely to reimburse the provider for its preparation and distribution costs."[42]

Although more than 400 institutions have signed onto the UBMTA, it has not had its intended effect as many signatories have substituted their own agreements for the UBMTA.[43] Because university technology transfer officials "see their primary job as bringing licensing revenue into the university," they are "tempt[ed] . . . to depart from the [UBMTA] whenever they think a particular material may have commercial value."[44] Even the public and nonprofit institutions

---

40. O'Connor, at 1026.

41. Uniform Biological Material Transfer Agreement: Discussion of Public Comments Received; Publication of the Final Format of the Agreement, 60 Fed. Reg. 12,771, 12,771 (Mar. 8, 1995) [UBMTA].

42. Id. ¶¶ 1, 2(a), 3(a), 7, 8, 10, 11, 15.

43. Association of University Technology Managers, *Signatories to the March 8, 1995 Master UBMTA Agreement*, http://www.autm.net/aboutTT/aboutTT_umbtaSigs.cfm.

44. Rai & Eisenberg, at 306.

that were the focus of the agreement could "handle specific material with unusual commercial or research value on a customized basis."[45]

A PROPOSAL

Material transfer agreements present complicated issues. Materials owners seek to extract any value they can from research tools. Private firms view certain tools as crucial to maintaining their competitive advantage.[46] While industry has historically guarded its valuable assets in maximizing value for shareholders, university technology transfer offices now are seeking commercialization as well. Nonetheless, the delays and potentially stifled innovation brought about by MTAs require a more widespread adoption of a model agreement.

The UBMTA was an agreement that offered promise. Its terms appeared reasonable for the vast majority of transactions. But it was insufficiently utilized. I offer two modest proposals that build on the UBMTA: (1) requiring nearly all recipients of federal funding to enter into the UBMTA and (2) suggesting publication terms for transfers between academia and industry.

Federally Funded Entities

First, government agencies could require recipients of funding to agree to the provisions of the UBMTA.[47] As a condition of providing funding, agencies such as the NIH and National Science Foundation (NSF) can set the terms with which recipients must comply.

In most of the cases, institutions receiving federal funding should adopt the UBMTA. As the Report of the NIH Working Group on Research Tools explained, "nonprofit institutions . . . have no duty to return value to shareholders, and their principal obligation under the Bayh-Dole Act is to promote utilization, not maximize financial returns." Restrictions on broad research tools used for noncommercial purposes are not consistent with the Act.[48]

In the many cases in which the recipients of federal funding do not seek to commercialize their research tools, reach-through licenses would not be necessary. Most nonprofit institutions receiving NIH funding, for example, have only a "remote . . . prospect of financial gain." Nonetheless, as the NIH Working Group suggested, a reach-through license exception from the UBMTA could be warranted when entities develop resources *"for the express purpose of manufacture and sale to the research community."*

---

45. UBMTA, at 12,771–72.
46. *Research Tools Report*, at 13.
47. *Id.* at 19.
48. *Id.* at 21.

Such an exception implicates the Bayh-Dole Act's goal of encouraging commercialization. It recognizes that the UBMTA was intended to cover "most, . . . not all" transfers.[49] And it acknowledges that academics have different incentives when they use materials for their research than when they license them to industry. Refusing to recognize an exception for researchers' most valued materials would encourage universities to continue to ignore the UBMTA. It makes more sense to acknowledge researchers' need for customized licensing terms in such a setting.

To be sure, ascertaining whether there is an "express purpose of manufacture and sale" may not be clear in certain cases. But at least a default rule of adherence to the UBMTA, with an exception for commercializable materials, addresses the problems with MTAs better than the existing framework in which universities routinely ignore the UBMTA and substitute their own form agreements. The default position would require departure from the agreement to be justified, not typical.[50]

University-Industry Transfers

Creating a model agreement between university and industry confronts significant hurdles. Despite the increasing commercialization of academia, the two spheres still follow different models. A cautionary tale is offered by the effort that NIH began in 1995 to devise a model contract for transfers between firms and nonprofit institutions. The agency created a "three-level scheme of increasingly complex legal formats" based on the degree of clinical testing completed for the material. In the end, however, the industry group did not accept the agreement, as its members were "not comfortable working with language . . . prepared by an external organization."[51]

Perhaps the two most difficult issues in MTAs are reach-through licenses and publication restrictions.[52] The issue of reach-through licenses is too case-specific to be addressed with a model provision. On the other hand, I propose model publication terms for transfers between academia and industry.

Materials providers often require recipients to agree to reach-through licenses. It would be possible, based on the ability of these clauses to reduce innovation, to offer a proposal urging firms to limit the use of such licenses. But any exhortation to do so would not be realistic. When firms believe their "crown

---

49. *Id.* at 21.

50. The funding agency could determine whether the provider makes this showing. Such showings should not be onerous, but if they become a significant drain on agency resources, the proposal could be reevaluated.

51. Eliot Marshall, *Need a Reagent? Just Sign Here . . .* , 278 SCI. 212 (1997).

52. *See Research Tools Report*, at 22 ("Negotiations between providers and users of research tools are repeatedly stalled over a small number of contract terms governing publication, disclosure, and future [IP] rights.").

jewels" are at stake, they will aggressively seek to obtain rights in discoveries attained by using the materials. Companies should be able to protect materials they view as essential to their competitive advantage.[53] In the end, if firms assert that reach-through provisions are needed because of a specific material's importance, it would be counterproductive to second-guess the decision and demonstrate the superiority of adherence to the UBMTA.[54]

On the other hand, model publication terms are more plausible.[55] Publication need not be instantaneous with material distribution. Providers are entitled to a window of time before the publication of papers discussing the materials. They should have time to file patent applications before disclosure. And they should be able to make certain that confidential information is not disclosed.

But this period of restriction on publication is finite. Materials providers should not have an effective veto power over the publication of results with which they disagree. They should not be able to utilize expansive confidentiality provisions that interfere with publication or the validation of investigators' results. And they cannot offer plausible justifications based on confidentiality or patent novelty when blocking the prepublication review of materials discussed in a published paper.

The UBMTA prohibited the "prevent[ion] or delay" of the publication of research findings.[56] Such guidance should be made more specific. A period of 60 days should be sufficient to file a patent application and ensure that confidential information is not disclosed.[57] By allowing publication after 60 days, a model agreement would reduce transaction costs and increase dissemination.

Such a model agreement also could include clauses that

- bar automatic coauthorship rights for providers,
- ensure that recipients can publish conclusions that differ from those published by the materials provider,
- prevent limits on a recipient's ability to discuss research results with laboratory members before publication, and

---

53. *Id.* at 13.

54. In addition, universities may use reach-through licenses so their scientists can continue their research and not be blocked by licensed firms that create patentable inventions from the materials. E-mail from Sean O'Connor to Michael A. Carrier, August 15, 2008.

55. *Research Tools Report*, at 22. My proposal is consistent with the NIH's Public Access Policy, implemented in May 2008, which requires scientists to submit "final peer-reviewed journal manuscripts that arise from NIH funds" to a digital archive accessible to the public. *Public Access: Frequently Asked Questions*, NIH PUB. ACCESS, May 2, 2008, http://publicaccess.nih.gov/FAQ.htm#a1.

56. UBMTA ¶ 11.

57. *Id.*, app. A, at 1.

- bar prepublication review when the transfer involves materials related to a published paper.[58]

Materials providers do not need these clauses for patent or confidentiality purposes. Rather, each imposes a cost on the dissemination of research findings. As a result, the clauses, together with the 60-day limit on publication restriction, would remove one significant hurdle to materials negotiations confronting universities and industry.

CONCLUSION

As a result of the two proposals, scientists would be able to spend more time conducting research and less time negotiating MTAs. Transaction costs would decrease as would potential blockages and stifled projects. My proposals recognize that the UBMTA cannot apply in every case. Allowing firms to protect their crown jewels prevents such adherence. But a tighter tethering to the model agreement for institutions receiving federal funding and a use of model publication terms in negotiations between academia and industry promises to foster research and innovation in the biotechnology industry.

---

58. Board on Life Sci., Nat'l Res. Council, Nat'l Acad. of Sciences, *Sharing Publication-Related Data and Materials: Responsibilities of Authorship in the Life Sciences*, at 55–56 (2003), http://books.nap.edu/openbook.php?isbn=0309088593.

PART IV

ANTITRUST

Promoting innovation has not traditionally been one of antitrust's top priorities. In the mid-20th century, courts adopted a rigid stance toward IP, automatically condemning tying and licensing arrangements. In the 1970s, the Justice Department followed a "Nine No-No's" policy that assumed that an array of harmless licensing activities violated the antitrust laws.

By the 1980s, the tide had turned. Courts applied the more lenient Rule of Reason to licensing arrangements and upheld blanket licenses containing price fixing.[1] Congress passed laws creating a federal court to hear patent appeals, requiring Rule-of-Reason analysis for joint ventures engaging in research and development, and limiting the range of activities that demonstrated patent misuse.[2]

By the 1990s, innovation was even more explicitly recognized. The antitrust agencies jointly issued Guidelines for the Licensing of Intellectual Property that appreciated the procompetitive benefits of licensing and recognized that IP does not necessarily indicate market power. More enlightened analysis of business activity, including patent pools, standard setting organizations, and new product introductions, conformed to this approach.

Because of this advance, the breadth of my antitrust proposals is far less than it would have been a generation ago. There is no urgent need, for example, to address licensing or patent pools. I conclude that antitrust only needs three recommendations to improve its treatment of innovation. And one of those proposals encourages the agencies and courts to continue on their path of not punishing the activities of standard-setting organizations.

The other two proposals apply in an industry vital to our economy and lives. The pharmaceutical industry is marked by high development costs and steep odds of reaching the market. If any industry needs patent protection, it is pharmaceuticals. If commercialization presents challenges anywhere, it is pharmaceuticals. But the realities of innovation in this industry have not been incorporated into antitrust analysis.

That is what I do in this section. In my proposal for innovation markets, I urge the agencies, when evaluating the likelihood that merging firms would suppress research lines, to consider how close the products are to market. There is a difference between drug compounds in preclinical studies that have a 1 in 4,000 chance of reaching the market and products in Stage III of clinical trials that have a 57 percent chance of reaching the market. The framework also imports the structure of the Merger Guidelines, increasing predictability.

---

1. *Continental T.V. v. GTE Sylvania*, 433 U.S. 36 (1977); *BMI Music v. Columbia Broadcasting*, 441 U.S. 1 (1979).

2. Federal Courts Improvement Act, Pub L. No. 97-164, 96 Stat. 25 (1981); National Cooperative Research Act, Pub. L. No. 98-462, 98 Stat. 1815 (1984); Patent Misuse Reform Act of 1988, Pub. L. No. 100-703, 102 Stat. 4674 (1988).

My second proposal is even more pressing. For the disconnect between courts and commentators is nowhere as pronounced as it is in the area of patent settlements. Courts have deferred to these agreements, citing a preference for settlements and a presumption of patent validity. In contrast, commentators and the Federal Trade Commission have vigorously criticized the agreements, lamenting their negative effects on competition and the billions of dollars they take from consumers' pockets. But the proposals that commentators have offered, such as those highlighting the "probabilistic," or uncertain, nature of patents, have run headlong into courts that presume patent validity.

I introduce a new framework to allow the agencies to challenge these agreements. The framework builds on *Verizon Communications v. Trinko*, in which the Supreme Court held that the presence of an effective regulatory regime that promoted competition reduced antitrust's role.[3] The Court in that case found such a regime as the Telecommunications Act of 1996 effectively employed penalties and reporting requirements against firms that discriminated in providing access to local phone markets.

I find that, like the Telecommunications Act, the Hatch-Waxman Act presents a regulatory regime. But this regime has not been effective in its competition-promoting goals of encouraging generics and challenging patents. Settlements by which brand-name firms pay generics to stay off the market and not challenge patents contravene the drafters' intent to promote competition. I therefore carve out a role for antitrust.

In short, antitrust courts and agencies have dramatically improved their appreciation of innovation issues in the past century. As a result, I can limit my recommendations. But the proposals I offer are vital, particularly as they apply to the life-and-death issues raised by the pharmaceutical industry.

---

3. 540 U.S. 398 (2004).

13. INNOVATION MARKETS: SAVING LIVES AND MONEY IN THE PHARMACEUTICAL INDUSTRY

Theory 297
Critiques 297
Rebuttal 299
    Product and Process Innovation 300
    Drastic and Nondrastic Innovation 301
    Technological Opportunity 301
    Appropriability 302
New Framework 303
Step 1: Evaluate Market Concentration 304
    FDA Review Process 304
    Concentration 305
Step 2: Assess Competitive Harm 306
Step 3: Evaluate Entry 308
Step 4: Evaluate Efficiencies 309
Step 5: Evaluate Schumpeterian Defense 311
Empirical Studies 312
    Roche-Genentech 313
    Glaxo-Wellcome 314
    Baxter-Immuno 316
    Pfizer–Warner-Lambert 318
    Genzyme-Novazyme 319
Conclusion 321

Pompe disease is a fatal disorder affecting infants and young children.[1] In 2001, Genzyme and Novazyme, the two leading companies researching the disease, merged.

Three years later, the Federal Trade Commission (FTC) split 3-1-1 on the question of whether to challenge the merger. In a statement accompanying the majority decision not to challenge, Chairman Timothy Muris emphasized the importance of bringing a treatment for Pompe disease to the market as

---

1. National Institute of Health, National Institute of Neurological Disorders and Stroke, *NINDS Pompe Disease Information Page*, http://www.ninds.nih.gov/disorders/pompe/pompe.htm (last visited July 25, 2008). For a more expansive version of the argument presented in this chapter, see Michael A. Carrier, *Two Puzzles Resolved: Of the Schumpeter-Arrow Stalemate and Pharmaceutical Innovation Markets*, 93 IOWA L. REV. 393 (2008)

soon as possible.[2] In contrast, Commissioner Mozelle Thompson's dissent highlighted the dangers of a merger that leads to monopoly.[3]

The commonsense concern about a merger between the two most advanced firms in a market explains not only the dissent in the *Genzyme* case but also the FTC's eight challenges to mergers in innovation markets in the pharmaceutical industry.

Common sense, however, is not economic foundation. Not when the relationship between market structure and innovation is as disputed as it is. This chapter offers the foundation that has been missing from innovation-market analysis.

It begins by defining innovation markets. It then sets forth the critiques that have been leveled against the markets. And it rebuts the criticisms by emphasizing the realities of the pharmaceutical industry.

The chapter then proposes a new five-part test for the antitrust enforcement agencies—the U.S. Department of Justice (DOJ) and FTC—to apply to innovation markets. First, the agencies must show that the merger would lead to significant concentration among firms reasonably likely to reach the market. Second, the agencies must offer a theory that the merging firms will suppress innovation. Third, the firms can rebut the agencies' case by showing that another firm is likely to reach the market. Fourth, the merging firms can proffer an efficiencies defense. Fifth, a "Schumpeterian" defense can be offered by small firms that would not otherwise be able to navigate the regulatory process.

The test improves the current analysis in several ways. It replaces the seemingly ad hoc approach with a comprehensive framework based on the Merger Guidelines. And it breaks new ground in considering not just the number of firms in research and development (R&D) but also their respective stages of U.S. Food and Drug Administration (FDA) review. Given the wildly varying odds of success in reaching the market from the preclinical stage and each of the clinical stages, it is indefensible to continue to neglect this factor.

This chapter concludes by presenting the results of five case studies from the past two decades—four mergers that the FTC challenged and one that it did not. The studies are important because there is so little public information about the mergers. Because the matters have been settled by consent decree, courts have not analyzed these issues and discussion has been limited to the facts alleged in agency complaints.

---

2. Statement of Chairman Timothy J. Muris, In the Matter of Genzyme Corporation/ Novazyme Pharmaceuticals, Inc., at 18, 25, Jan. 13, 2004 [hereinafter Muris Statement], http://www.ftc.gov/os/2004/01/murisgenzymestmt.pdf.

3. Dissenting Statement of Commissioner Mozelle W. Thompson, In the Matter of Genzyme Corporation/Novazyme Pharmaceuticals, Inc., at 1, Jan. 13, 2004 [hereinafter Thompson Statement], http://www.ftc.gov/os/2004/01/thompsongenzymestmt.pdf.

THEORY

The concept of innovation markets burst into attention (at least of scholars and the agencies) in 1995. In that year, the DOJ and FTC promulgated the Antitrust Guidelines for the Licensing of Intellectual Property. The most controversial aspect of the Guidelines was the creation of an innovation market, which was defined as

> A[ ] . . . market [that] consists of the research and development directed to particular new or improved goods or processes, and the close substitutes for that research and development.[4]

The agencies promised that they would target innovation markets "only when the capabilities to engage in the relevant research and development [could] be associated with specialized assets or characteristics of specific firms."[5]

The theory behind innovation markets is that a merger between the only two, or two of a few, firms in R&D might increase the incentive to suppress at least one of the research paths. With no other firms ready to enter the market, the merging firms might not wish to introduce a second product that would reduce sales of the first.

This concern is heightened given the importance of innovation to economic growth. Given the difficulty of measuring innovation, allegations of harm must be considered cautiously. But because innovation is so crucial, we cannot ignore activity that can only be addressed in R&D markets.

Innovation markets have not played a role in most of the cases brought by the agencies. Despite the small number of challenges, however, critics have vociferously disparaged the concept.

CRITIQUES

Critics have leveled four central attacks against innovation markets:

(1) Innovation is speculative and includes unidentifiable market participants.
(2) The relationship between R&D and innovation is unclear.
(3) Innovation markets are not needed because conduct can be challenged at a later time.
(4) The market structure most conducive to innovation is unclear.

---

4. U.S. Dep't of Justice & Fed. Trade Comm'n, Antitrust Guidelines for the Licensing of Intellectual Property ¶ 3.2.3, at 13 (Apr. 9, 1995), http://www.usdoj.gov/atr/public/guidelines/0558.pdf.

5. Id.

First, innovation is speculative. It is "intangible, uncertain, unmeasurable, and often even unobservable, except in retrospect."[6] As a result, it may be impossible to identify all the firms in a particular innovation market. As two commentators explain, "[B]ecause the results of R&D are so difficult to predict, the analyst may be unable to determine all, or even most, of the relevant firms who might produce competitive products in the future."[7]

Second, "the optimal amount of R&D is unknown."[8] More R&D does not necessarily result in more innovation. A merger could allow for more efficient R&D by reducing duplicative expenditures.[9]

Third, innovation-market analysis is unnecessary because the relevant conduct can be challenged at a later stage. It can be addressed at the product-market stage, when the products can be identified. Or it can be challenged at the *potential competition* stage, when at least one firm is on the market and another is about to enter.[10] As a result, some have called innovation markets "superfluous."[11]

Fourth, we do not know the market structure most conducive to innovation. Economists have fiercely debated whether monopoly or competition best promotes innovation. After a half-century of debate and innumerable studies, the consensus is that there is no clear answer to the question. The opposing positions of economists Joseph Schumpeter (favoring concentration) and Kenneth Arrow (favoring competition) both garner support in unending bouts of hand-wringing.[12]

Schumpeter famously highlighted the role played by concentration in promoting innovation. He explained that perfect competition (in which firms lack market power) is always suspended "whenever anything new is . . . introduced." In contrast, monopoly allows long-range planning and is "the most powerful engine of [economic] progress."[13]

Arrow, on the other hand, contended that "the incentive to invent is less under monopolistic than . . . competitive conditions." Unlike the monopolist, for which some of the profits from the new invention come at the expense of the old technology, the competitor receives all of the returns from a new invention.[14]

---

6. Richard T. Rapp, *The Misapplication of the Innovation Market Approach to Merger Analysis*, 64 ANTITRUST L.J. 19, 27 (1995).

7. Dennis Carlton & Robert Gertner, *Intellectual Property, Antitrust and Strategic Behavior*, *in* 3 INNOVATION POLICY AND THE ECONOMY 29, 42 (Adam B. Jaffe et al. eds., 2003).

8. Rapp, at 46.

9. Carlton & Gertner, at 38.

10. PHILLIP AREEDA ET AL., ANTITRUST ANALYSIS: PROBLEMS, TEXT, AND CASES ¶ 545, at 782 (6th ed. 2004).

11. Rapp, at 20.

12. For a more complete discussion on market structure and innovation, see Carrier, at 403–14.

13. JOSEPH A. SCHUMPETER, CAPITALISM, SOCIALISM AND DEMOCRACY 88, 103, 105, 106 (1942).

14. Kenneth J. Arrow, *Economic Welfare and the Allocation of Resources for Invention, in* ESSAYS IN THE THEORY OF RISK-BEARING 144, 157–58 (3d ed. 1976); *see generally* Richard Gilbert,

REBUTTAL

There is an element of truth to each of the critiques. In many cases we do not know all the potential innovators or the optimal relationship between R&D and innovation. For that reason, an expansive notion of the innovation-market concept is not appropriate. But a narrow version, applied to the pharmaceutical industry, withstands the critiques.

First, innovation in the industry is not carried out by unknown innovators. The barriers to entry provided by patents and a lengthy regulatory process restrict the universe of potential innovators. Unlike other industries, there are no garage inventors springing up to create a drug product. Because the regulatory process requires a lengthy and costly period of discovery, preclinical testing, and clinical trials, an entrant is not able to "leapfrog" into the market. Rather, it must engage in years of testing before catching up to current R&D efforts.[15]

Second, we know that higher amounts of R&D benefit innovation. Pharmaceutical R&D typically does not suffer from the duplication that afflicts other industries. It is not likely that multiple research tracks will be identical and equally effective. Even if ten companies test drugs for a particular cancer, the projects likely will involve "different research teams, different concepts, ideas, and directions, [and] different corporate cultures."[16]

Third, innovation-market analysis promises to target activity that could not be challenged at a later time. The inability to challenge at the R&D stage would be concerning because any restriction of innovation would appear only as a non-event.[17] In other words, it would not be apparent after the fact what was missing from the marketplace. We cannot observe the absence of innovation like we can observe higher prices. In addition, any harms to innovation cannot easily be remedied after the merger has occurred, the research line has been suppressed, and employees have taken on new projects.

Fourth, we can ascertain the market structure most conducive to innovation. To be sure, there is no single answer to this question. But we can begin to address the issue of whether monopoly or competition best promotes innovation by isolating four factors that determine the preferred structure in specific industries.

Looking for Mr. Schumpeter: Where Are We in the Competition-Innovation Debate?, in 6 INNOVATION POLICY AND THE ECONOMY 159, 165 (Adam B. Jaffe et al. eds., 2006).

15. Susan DeSanti & William Cohen, *Competition to Innovate: Strategies for Proper Antitrust Assessments*, in EXPANDING THE BOUNDARIES OF INTELLECTUAL PROPERTY: INNOVATION POLICY FOR THE KNOWLEDGE SOCIETY 317, 329 n.69, 335 (Rochelle Cooper Dreyfuss et al. eds., 2001) [hereinafter EXPANDING THE BOUNDARIES].

16. Dror Ben-Asher, *In Need of Treatment? Merger Control, Pharmaceutical Innovation, and Consumer Welfare*, 21 J. LEGAL MED. 271, 319–20 (2000).

17. DeSanti & Cohen, at 334.

Product and Process Innovation

The first factor involves the distinction between product and process innovation.[18] Product innovations refer to the creation of goods offering new or improved characteristics. Process innovations involve the use of new production methods to reduce the cost of making products.[19] Firms typically market product innovations externally and use process innovations internally.[20] Of the two, product-related R&D more often produces patentable innovations.[21]

In contrast, process innovations are not as likely to be patented. Generally speaking, these innovations are more difficult to define and enforce, are easier to invent around, and benefit more from secrecy.[22] But if processes are not patented, firms often must rely on other mechanisms, such as size, to appropriate their investments.[23] In many cases, monopoly power is just such a mechanism, allowing a firm to charge higher prices, thereby recovering the costs expended in creating the innovation.

Pharmaceutical companies devote approximately 75 percent of their R&D to product innovation.[24] Even more relevant, all the innovation-market drug

---

18. To be sure, the line between product and process innovations will not always be clear. *See* F. M. SCHERER, NEW PERSPECTIVES ON ECONOMIC GROWTH AND TECHNOLOGICAL INNOVATION 39 (1999) (showing relationship of products and processes in manufacturing and nonmanufacturing industries). Firms manufacturing machine tools, for example, sell them as products, while downstream buyers use the tools in their manufacturing processes. Product and process innovations also can be complements. A new surgical instrument, for example, is a product that a surgeon can use in inventing a new process. E-mail from Michael J. Meurer to Michael A. Carrier, dated August 18, 2008.

19. Section of Antitrust Law, American Bar Association, *The Economics of Innovation: A Survey*, at 4 (2002); Robert Atkinson & Howard Wial, *Boosting Productivity, Innovation, and Growth Through a National Innovation Foundation*, at 5, Apr. 2008, http://www.itif.org/files/NIF.pdf.

20. ORGANISATION FOR ECON. CO-OPERATION AND DEV. & STATISTICAL OFFICE OF THE EUR. CMTYS., OSLO MANUAL: PROPOSED GUIDELINES FOR COLLECTING AND INTERPRETING TECHNOLOGICAL INNOVATION DATA 47 (1997).

21. Albert N. Link & John Lunn, *Concentration and the Returns to R&D*, 1 REV. INDUS. ORG. 232, 233 (1984).

22. Wesley M. Cohen & Steven Klepper, *Firm Size and the Nature of Innovation within Industries: The Case of Process and Product R&D*, 78 REV. ECON. & STAT. 232, 233 (1996); Paul Geroski, *Markets for Technology: Knowledge, Innovation, and Appropriability*, in HANDBOOK OF THE ECONOMICS OF INNOVATION AND TECHNOLOGICAL CHANGE 90, 103 (Paul Stoneman ed., 1995).

23. In other cases, such as agriculture and the practice of medicine, universities play a role in creating process innovations.

24. Cohen & Klepper, at 232.

mergers challenged by the FTC involved products.[25] The importance of products results in the first factor favoring competition.

Drastic and Nondrastic Innovation

A second factor affecting the link between market structure and innovation is the presence of drastic or nondrastic innovation. Stated simply, a drastic product innovation is so superior that it displaces demand for the existing product.[26] A nondrastic innovation, in contrast, allows use of both the original and new products.[27]

For drastic innovations, competition is superior to monopoly. A monopolist is less likely to introduce a new product that will displace its control over the market. In contrast, a competitive firm will gain the full benefit of a drastic innovation without suffering any losses from reduced sales in the existing product.[28]

With nondrastic innovations, the old product will not be displaced. In this case, the monopolist will have at least as much incentive as the challenger to invest in R&D. In fact, it may even be more motivated because in contrast to entrants (who must share the market with the monopolist's old product), it can gain monopoly profits from the old and new products.

The distinction between drastic and nondrastic innovation will not apply in most innovation-market drug mergers. But two cases brought by the FTC illustrate the potential suppression of drastic innovations. In one, a noninjectable treatment for migraine headaches developed by merging firms Glaxo and Wellcome threatened to displace the need for Glaxo's injectable treatment. In the second, Glaxo Wellcome's drug that suppressed herpes was threatened by a prophylactic vaccine researched by Glaxo Wellcome and SmithKlineBeecham.[29]

Technological Opportunity

The third factor is technological opportunity, which is "the rate at which . . . advances in science and technology generate profitable new innovative

---

25. The nine mergers involved (1) a prophylactic herpes vaccine, (2) a rotavirus vaccine, (3) CD-4 based therapeutics used in treating HIV/AIDS, (4) EGFR inhibitors used to treat solid cancerous tumors, (5) enzyme replacement therapies for Pompe disease, (6) fibrin sealants, (7) gene therapy, (8) noninjectable migraine treatment, and (9) topoisomerase I inhibitors for colorectal cancer.

26. Richard J. Gilbert & Steven C. Sunshine, *Incorporating Dynamic Efficiency Concerns in Merger Analysis: The Use of Innovation Markets*, 63 ANTITRUST L.J. 569, 591 (1995). A drastic process innovation lowers the cost of production by such an extent that firms using an older process cannot compete with the innovator. Michael J. Meurer, *Business Method Patents and Patent Floods*, 8 WASH U. J.L. & POL'Y 309, 315 n.36 (2002).

27. Gilbert, at 166.

28. Einer Elhauge, *Defining Better Monopolization Standards*, 56 STAN. L. REV. 253, 299 n.141 (2003).

29. For additional detail, see Carrier, at 410–11.

possibilities."[30] Higher technological opportunity tends to be accompanied by greater incentives to engage in R&D and reap the benefits of innovation. Firms in industries with rapidly changing scientific knowledge face lower costs and are more likely to obtain patents, further reducing the need for concentration.[31]

Conversely, a slowly advancing and predictable science base could lead to excessive rivalry because of fewer opportunities to recover investments.[32] The process innovation and secrecy characterizing technologically unprogressive industries more often lead to concentration and monopoly.[33]

The drug industry is marked by high technological opportunity. It is one of the most closely linked industries to science. Institutions other than private drug companies—such as universities and government laboratories—contribute to technical knowledge. And there is positive feedback from technological advances as improving product performance spurs innovation in the industry.[34]

Appropriability

Appropriability signifies a firm's ability to recover its investment. This ability is threatened by rivals' imitation as well as *spillovers*, valuable information disclosed by the innovation that helps competitors devise their own creations.[35] A firm's incentive to invest in R&D increases as appropriability rises. In industries with high appropriability, monopoly is less needed to recover investment.[36]

Appropriability varies based on industry. An influential study found that certain industries, such as food processing and metal-working, were characterized by a lack of appropriability. In contrast, other industries relied on mechanisms such as patents, secrecy, lead time, quick movement down learning curves, and sales or service efforts to recover their investments.[37]

---

30. F.M. Scherer & David Ross, Industrial Market Structure and Economic Performance 645 (3d ed. 1990).

31. Alvin K. Klevorick et al., *On the Sources and Significance of Interindustry Differences in Technological Opportunities*, at 3 (Cowles Foundation, Discussion Paper No. 1052, 1993); John Lunn, *The Roles of Property Rights and Market Power in Appropriating Innovative Output*, 14 J. Legal Stud. 423, 427, 432 (1985).

32. Scherer & Ross, at 647.

33. For additional discussion of these issues, see Christopher S. Yoo, *Vertical Integration and Media Regulation in the New Economy*, 19 Yale J. Reg. 171, 277 (2002).

34. Klevorick et al., at 8–15, 22, 32, 40 tbl.2., 43 tbl.5.

35. F.M. Scherer, *Innovation and Technological Change, Economics of, in* 11 International Encyclopedia of the Social and Behavioral Sciences 7530, 7533 (2001).

36. This factor overlaps with the distinction between product and process innovation. Speaking most generally, appropriability tends to be higher for product innovations than process innovations.

37. Richard C. Levin et al., *Appropriating the Returns from Industrial Research and Development*, 1987 Brookings Papers on Econ. Activity 783, 794, 802. Appropriability is also affected by a company's structure. Pure (nonproducing) inventors are more likely to

This factor leads to mixed results for the drug industry. Before reaching the market, size is necessary to survive the FDA regulatory process. As described in more detail below, the process is lengthy, composed of preclinical testing and three stages of human clinical trials. Large firms are more likely to have the resources to survive this gauntlet.[38] But after the innovation reaches the market, the industry is marked by high appropriability. Numerous studies have shown that patents play a vital role in the industry.[39] Each of the products at issue in the merger challenges was protected by patents.

In short, most of the factors demonstrate that competition is important in the pharmaceutical industry. We thus can rebut the contention that only a concentrated market structure maximizes innovation. Competition's vital role confirms the propriety of enforcement in innovation markets for drugs. In fact, given the threats to competition from mergers between the two firms closest to the market, antitrust enforcement is essential for pharmaceutical innovation.

NEW FRAMEWORK

Despite the importance of innovation markets in the pharmaceutical industry, the agencies have engaged in an incomplete analysis. They have not considered many relevant factors, such as the likelihood the merging firms will reach the market. This truncated analysis is harmful as it justifies unnecessary merger challenges that drain finite resources. For that reason, I offer a new test for pharmaceutical innovation-market mergers.

My five-part analysis is based on the framework of the Horizontal Merger Guidelines. The Guidelines have provided a coherent, reasonable structure for merger evaluation. Of course, product and innovation markets are different. The Guidelines apply to actual products and justify challenges to mergers that would significantly increase concentration and lead to market power. Innovation markets nonetheless present analogous concerns.

---

appropriate value from patent licenses, as compared to vertically integrated firms (which engage in multiple stages of production), which can sell products.

38. Patricia M. Danzon, *The Pharmaceutical Industry, in* 3 THE ENCYCLOPEDIA OF LAW AND ECONOMICS 1055, 1083 (Boudewijn Bouckaert & Gerrit de Geest eds., 2000) (economies of scale and regulatory expertise); ALFONSO GAMBARDELLA, SCIENCE AND INNOVATION: THE U.S. PHARMACEUTICAL INDUSTRY DURING THE 1980s, at 76 (1995) (internal funding).

39. Levin et al., at 783, 797 tbl.2; Wesley M. Cohen et al., *Protecting Their Intellectual Assets: Appropriability Conditions and Why U.S. Manufacturing Firms Patent (or Not)*, at 32 tbl.1 (Nat'l Bureau of Econ. Research, Working Paper No. 7552, 2000); C.T. TAYLOR & Z.A. SILBERSTON, THE ECONOMIC IMPACT OF THE PATENT SYSTEM: A STUDY OF THE BRITISH EXPERIENCE 202 (1973); Edwin Mansfield, *Patents and Innovation: An Empirical Study*, 32 MGMT. SCI. 173, 174 (1986).

STEP 1: EVALUATE MARKET CONCENTRATION

The "unifying theme" of the Merger Guidelines is that "mergers should not be permitted to create or enhance market power or to facilitate its exercise."[40] Mergers cannot have this effect unless they "significantly increase[] concentration and result[] in a concentrated market."[41] A concentrated market increases the likelihood of collusion, by which competitors can increase price and reduce output.

There are no actual markets in innovation-markets analysis. It is not possible to ascertain consumer demand. Nonetheless, concentration similarly leads to concern. As the R&D markets become significantly concentrated, the odds of more than one firm reaching the market decrease. Consequently, the likelihood of product market competition decreases.

As discussed below, where the merging firms are the only ones close to the market, they have a greater ability and incentive to suppress one (and, in some cases, both) of their R&D paths. This tends to increase the likelihood of either product absence or monopoly. In short, the competition necessary for pharmaceutical innovation is thwarted.

The most important factor in determining the likelihood of reaching the market is the stage of FDA review. Firms in the pharmaceutical industry face daunting hurdles at each of the stages. A brief background of the review process demonstrates just how difficult it is to reach the market.

FDA Review Process

The FDA approval process is lengthy, proceeding through numerous stages. First, a company engages in discovery, selecting a target for a potential medicine and searching for a molecule that can act on the target.[42] When it finds such a molecule, the company enters preclinical testing, which utilizes tissue cell cultures, computer-based data analyses, and live animals to determine whether the chemical compound will be safe and effective for human use.[43]

The odds of success in the discovery and preclinical stages are low: only 1 out of 1000 tested compounds makes it to clinical studies.[44] And because only 1 out of

---

40. U.S. Dep't of Justice & Fed. Trade Comm'n, Horizontal Merger Guidelines § 0.1 (rev. Apr. 8, 1997), http://www.usdoj.gov/atr/public/guidelines/hmg.htm [hereinafter Merger Guidelines].

41. *Id.* § 1.0.

42. PhRMA, *Drug Discovery and Development: Understanding the R&D Process,* at 3, http://www.phrma.org/files/RD%20Brochure%20022307.pdf. A target is a molecule involved in a particular disease. *Id.*

43. John R. Thomas, Pharmaceutical Patent Law 303 (2005).

44. *See* Food & Drug Admin., Dep't of Health & Human Servs., Just the Facts Publication No. FS 02-5, *FDA and the Drug Development Process: How the Agency Ensures that Drugs Are Safe and Effective* (2002). In its complaints, the FTC does not distinguish

4 compounds in clinical trials makes it to the market, the odds of a compound in preclinical development reaching the market are less than 1 in 4,000. If the company manages to succeed in the preclinical stage, it files an application with the FDA. If accepted, the firm can begin three stages of clinical studies.[45]

Phase I investigations focus on the safety of the drug and involve closely monitored studies of 20 to 80 healthy individuals. Phase II trials evaluate safety and effectiveness for patients who have the disease and include up to several hundred participants. Phase III studies involve large-scale trials with thousands of patients and determine effectiveness and infrequent side effects.[46] Upon the completion of clinical testing, the firm prepares a New Drug Application (NDA) and submits it to the FDA for review.[47]

The likelihood that a drug will reach the market increases significantly with each stage of review. In previous research, I reviewed four of the most comprehensive studies that addressed the issue.[48] I found that the likelihood of reaching the market was 18 percent from Phase I, 30 percent from Phase II, and 57 percent from Phase III.[49]

Concentration

The astronomical odds confronting firms in preclinical development call for caution. If the odds are less than 1 in 4,000 that a firm will reach the market from preclinical development, there is less concern about the firm reducing its R&D paths in a way that would affect the likelihood of a product reaching the market.

With a 1,000-to-1 likelihood of reaching clinical studies from preclinical development, industry realities show not a race between competitors but a solitary quest to surmount the steep odds of making it to clinical trials. Drugs in

---

between discovery and preclinical testing. My use in this chapter of "preclinical development" and "preclinical studies" encompasses both stages.

45. *Id.*

46. 21 C.F.R. § 312.21(a), (b), (c) (2004); *see generally* Joseph A. DiMasi et al., *The Price of Innovation: New Estimates of Drug Development Costs*, 22 J. HEALTH ECON. 151, 156 (2003).

47. THOMAS, at 306.

48. Joseph A. DiMasi, *Risks in New Drug Development: Approval Success Rates for Investigational Drugs*, 69 CLIN. PHARMACOLOGY THERAPEUTICS 297, 303 (2001); Christopher P. Adams & Van V. Brantner, *New Drug Development: Estimating Entry from Human Clinical Trials*, at 20 tbl.4 (Fed. Trade Comm'n Bureau of Econ., Working Paper No. 262, 2003), http://papers.ssrn.com/sol3/papers.cfm?abstract_id=428040; Ismail Kola & John Landis, *Can the Pharmaceutical Industry Reduce Attrition Rates?*, 3 NATURE REVS. 711, 711–12 (2004); Rosa M. Abrantes-Metz et al., *Pharmaceutical Development Phases: A Duration Analysis*, at 9 tbl.B.2.A (Fed. Trade Comm'n Bureau of Econ., Working Paper No. 274, 2004), http://papers.ssrn.com/sol3/papers.cfm?abstract_id=607941.

49. *See* Carrier, at 417–18 (providing mean figures).

preclinical development are so unlikely to succeed that merger challenges do not effectively promote competition. I therefore part company with the agencies and commentators in concluding that the agencies should not consider firms with products in preclinical development in determining the concentration of the R&D market.[50]

Where, for example, the merging firms only have products in preclinical development, the staggering odds that either one would reach the market, let alone both, counsels the agencies not to challenge the merger. Nor does a merger between a firm with a product in advanced trials (say, Phase III) and one in preclinical development raise concern. Even if—as the FTC has alleged—those two firms are "closest" to the market, the improbability that the latter will ever reach the market reduces concern.

Once the market is limited to products in clinical trials, the most important factors in determining market concentration become (1) the number of firms with products in these stages and (2) the specific stage of FDA review. The greatest concern applies when the number of competitors is low and the parties are at an advanced stage of FDA review. This occurs when a merger is proposed between the only two firms in clinical studies, both of which are in Phase III. In this case, no potential entry is anticipated for the foreseeable future, and the firms are reasonably likely to reach the market. Because the firms are close to the market, they would have the greatest ability and incentive to suppress a research path.

To be sure, it is not certain that each of the merging firms in Phase III would have reached the market absent the merger. But there is a reasonable likelihood that they would have done so. And if the dangers of suppression apply anywhere, it is in this case.[51]

STEP 2: ASSESS COMPETITIVE HARM

Under the Merger Guidelines, the agencies must demonstrate potential adverse competitive effects from the merger.[52] Historically, the most important effect

---

50. Nor should agencies and commentators be concerned that firms in preclinical studies are more likely to have a significant share of future products that reach that stage. None of the challenged mergers discussed later in the chapter involved firms in preclinical studies that had a monopoly over—or even unique ability to develop—particular types of treatments.

51. Because it is unlikely that firms in Stage II and, especially, Stage I will reach the market, challenges should be limited to categories such as anticancer drugs and anti-HIV/AIDS drugs in which there is a greater likelihood of reaching the market or to other exceptional cases in which the anticompetitive harms seem particularly acute. *See* Carrier, at 418 (providing figures for these categories of drugs, as well as methods of administration more likely to reach the market).

52. MERGER GUIDELINES § 2.0.

has been the danger of collusion. As the number of firms in the market decreases, it becomes easier to reach an agreement to reduce supply and increase price.[53]

A second harm occurs even in the absence of collusion. According to the theory of *unilateral competitive effects*, the firms may—regardless of the actions of other market participants—raise price and reduce output.[54] This is a particular concern where the products of the merging firms are similar.

In innovation markets, the danger of collusion is markedly reduced. Reaching an agreement is difficult because in contrast to fixing a price on homogeneous products, it is hard to coordinate the multiple dimensions of R&D. And because innovation is typically "conducted in secret," it is easier to cheat on agreements.[55]

But there is an analogue in the innovation-market context to unilateral competitive effects. In certain cases, the merging firms might—regardless of the actions of other firms—not wish to introduce new products. The likelihood of suppression rises with product similarity.

The second requirement of my test is that the agencies allege a theory of competitive harm. That theory typically will involve the potential suppression of a research path. As concentration in the market increases and the products get closer to the market, the incentive and ability to suppress one of the research paths increases.

The *incentive* increases because it is more likely that a product will reach the market. Suppression matters most for probable future products as opposed to speculative research paths. Once success appears likely in the product market, firms naturally would recognize that suppression would have an effect. In contrast, in the early stages the incentive to suppress is more attenuated because it is not needed: the staggering odds of the regulatory process create the same result.

The *ability* to suppress also increases as the product gets closer to the market. The determination of the ability to suppress should incorporate the likelihood that suppression will have an effect. Of course, a firm technically can suppress a research path at any point. But suppression is more likely to have an effect as the likelihood of reaching the market rises.

Two additional factors increase the likelihood of suppression. First, if one of the merging firms has an existing treatment for a condition, its incentive to introduce a new product is reduced. For drastic innovations in particular, the monopolist has less incentive than the competitive firm to introduce new products because it would thereby displace its monopoly.

---

53. It also becomes easier to police the agreement.

54. *Id.* § 2.2.

55. Prepared Statement of M. Howard Morse Before the Antitrust Modernization Commission Hearing on Antitrust and the New Economy, at 11 (Nov. 8, 2005), http://www.amc.gov/commission_hearings/pdf/Statement_Morse_revd.pdf.

In most of the challenged mergers, this factor would not have applied since (1) there was no current treatment or (2) the treatment was offered by a nonmerging firm. But where one of the merging firms has market power in the existing product market and where the firm's R&D addresses a drastic innovation, it is more likely there will be competitive harm.[56]

The second factor involves the relationship between the two products. The closer the products, the greater the incentive is to suppress one of them. This conclusion overlaps with the Guidelines' recognition that the similarity of the merging firms' products increases the likelihood of unilateral competitive effects.[57] As the similarity of R&D paths increases, the need for both decreases. As a result, the merging firms have a greater incentive to suppress one of them.

STEP 3: EVALUATE ENTRY

In the third step, the merging firms can rebut the agencies' claim of concentration by showing that at least one other firm is likely to reach the market.

In the Merger Guidelines, entry negates the adverse effects of concentration. If entry into the market is easy, firms cannot sustain price increases, and it is less likely that the merger would lead to the creation of market power.[58]

In the innovation-market context, in contrast, there is no currently existing product market that an outside firm could enter. But the underlying policy of the Guidelines nonetheless applies. If another firm in addition to the merged firm makes it to the market, then by definition there will be competition. Competition is important for pharmaceutical innovation, and the presence of a competitor reduces suppression concerns.

To be sure, the analysis of entry is speculative in both the product and innovation-market contexts. The Guidelines require entry to be "timely, likely, and sufficient . . . to deter or counteract the competitive effects of concern."[59] Determining these characteristics is speculative. Similarly, in the innovation-market context, we do not know which companies eventually will make it to the market. But guidance is offered by the odds of success at each stage of FDA review.

---

56. One example occurred in the merger between Glaxo and Wellcome, in which Glaxo's monopoly in injectable migraine treatment was threatened by a noninjectable migraine treatment. A second occurred in the merger between Glaxo Wellcome and SmithKline Beecham, as the former's monopoly in suppressive herpes treatment was threatened by the firms' prophylactic herpes vaccine. *See* Carrier, at 432–33, 442.

57. *Merger Guidelines* § 2.211.

58. *Id.* § 3.0.

59. *Id.*

The merging firms, therefore, should be able to offer a defense based on the likelihood that another firm will enter the market. The identity of products in various stages is public information that is easily discoverable.[60] And the stage of review provides an instructive guide to the odds of reaching the market.

Firms in Phase III are the most likely to reach the market, with approximately a 57 percent likelihood of success. If two firms other than the merging companies are in Phase III, there is roughly an 81 percent chance that at least one of the nonmerging firms will reach the market (a 32 percent likelihood of success for both plus a 49 percent likelihood of success for one).[61] In this case, because the 81 percent chance demonstrates a significant likelihood that there will be competition in the market, the agencies should recognize entry as a powerful defense.

Where there is only one nonmerging firm in Phase III, the odds of that firm making it to the market, and thereby offering competition, are approximately 57 percent. In this case, although it is less certain that there will be competition, it is still a reasonable possibility. The agencies thus should accept a more qualified defense, which could make a difference in close cases.

This type of qualified defense also would apply in other cases with similar odds of success. For example, if two firms are in Phase II, the odds of success are 51 percent (a 9 percent likelihood of both and a 42 percent chance of one).[62] Different permutations determine the odds of entry.

STEP 4: EVALUATE EFFICIENCIES

An additional defense that the merging firms could offer is that the merger will lead to efficiencies. The Merger Guidelines recognize several types of efficiencies: an enhanced ability and incentive to compete, the introduction of new or improved products, and "a better utilization of existing assets" that allows the combined firm to lower its costs. The Guidelines explain that marginal cost reductions resulting from shifting production among facilities are the

---

60. For example, the National Institutes of Health "offers up-to-date information for locating federally and privately supported clinical trials for a wide range of diseases and conditions." ClinicalTrials.gov, *About ClinicalTrials.gov*, http://clinicaltrials.gov (last visited July 26, 2008).

61. The odds of both firms making it to the market are .57 *.57 =.3249. The odds of only one firm succeeding are 2 * (.57 *.43) =.4902. Therefore, the odds of at least one firm making it are .3249 +.4902 =.8151.

62. The odds of both firms making it to the market are.30 *.30 =.09. The odds of only one firm succeeding are 2 * (.30 *.70) =.42. Therefore, the odds of at least one firm making it are .09 +.42 =.51.

most substantial and verifiable type of efficiency. Research and development efficiencies "are potentially substantial" but "less susceptible to verification."[63]

In order to be considered, the efficiencies must be "merger-specific," achievable only through merger. The agencies consider whether cognizable efficiencies would be "sufficient to reverse the merger's potential to harm consumers in the relevant market." The efficiencies tend to achieve this result when the likely adverse competitive effects are "not great." In particular, they "almost never justify a merger to monopoly or near-monopoly."[64]

In the innovation-market context, there are no products for which marginal cost can be reduced. But the introduction of new products is the goal of pharmaceutical R&D. The relevant efficiency thus takes the form of an increased likelihood that the firms will reach the market. In certain cases, the merging firms may be able to combine complementary knowledge and expertise in a way that would increase the likelihood of success.

Pharmaceutical firms, of course, merge for numerous other reasons such as reducing costs and bolstering drug pipelines.[65] But sometimes the merger will help firms in the relevant R&D market.

One example is offered by the merger between Genzyme and Novazyme, two companies researching Pompe disease, a fatal and difficult-to-treat disease affecting infants and young children. The merger made comparative experiments possible as the companies could engage in a "comprehensive, blinded preclinical analysis" comparing the relevant enzymes. The merger also "provided information that enabled the Novazyme program to avoid drilling dry holes."[66] Finally, it allowed Novazyme to use Genzyme cell lines scalable for a Pompe enzyme, measure glycogen reduction, and learn patients' reactions to earlier Pompe products.[67] Because only Genzyme had this experience with Pompe disease, no other company could offer these benefits.

Where it is particularly difficult to reach the market and where there is no currently existing treatment, the agencies should most seriously consider efficiencies. In the Genzyme-Novazyme merger, for example, there was no available treatment for a fatal disease. Of equally significant concern, Pompe disease is 1 of 41 diseases known as lysosomal storage disorders (LSDs).[68] Developing drugs

---

63. MERGER GUIDELINES § 4.

64. Id.

65. Andrew Ross Sorkin, *Glaxo and SmithKline Agree to Form Largest Drugmaker*, N.Y. TIMES, Jan. 17, 2000, at A1; Patricia M. Danzon et al., *Mergers and Acquisitions in the Pharmaceutical and Biotech Industries*, at 32–33 (Nat'l Bureau of Econ. Research, Working Paper No. 10536, 2004), http://www.nber.org/papers/w10536.

66. Muris Statement, at 1, 17, 17 n. 42.

67. Douglas L. Wald & Deborah L. Feinstein, *Merger Enforcement in Innovation Markets: The Latest Chapter—Genzyme/Novazyme*, THE ANTITRUST SOURCE, July 2004, at 9, http://www.abanet.org/antitrust/at-source/04/07/Jul04-Feinstein7=23.pdf.

68. Id. at 2.

to treat LSDs is particularly challenging: As of 2008, there was a treatment for only 4 of the 41 diseases, with each developed by Genzyme.[69] The most important goal in these cases thus is not to ensure the presence of two products but to increase the likelihood that one product reaches the market.[70]

In short, the merging firms can proffer efficiencies that increase the likelihood that the product will reach the market. The agencies should most seriously consider these efficiencies as market concentration decreases and the difficulty of reaching the market increases.

STEP 5: EVALUATE SCHUMPETERIAN DEFENSE

The final defense bears some overlap with the current "failing firms" defense. The Guidelines state that "a merger is not likely to create or enhance market power or to facilitate its exercise, if imminent failure . . . of one of the merging firms would cause the assets of that firm to exit the relevant market." The rationale is simple: "In such circumstances, post-merger performance in the relevant market may be no worse than market performance had the merger been blocked and the assets left the market."[71]

Small firms in innovation markets may not be in danger of failing. But they face a related challenge in the towering hurdles of the regulatory process, which can block development. As discussed above, the process is lengthy, with Phase III trials requiring thousands of subjects. For this reason, a merger might allow a smaller firm to pursue expensive and complex clinical trials that otherwise would be impossible. Absent a merger or other collaboration, in other words, the firm would not be able to proceed through the development process.

Allowing a defense for such firms is a concrete manifestation of Joseph Schumpeter's framework, which emphasized the importance of size in fostering long-range planning and innovation.[72] The hurdles of the drug regulatory process demonstrate the need for size.

In many mergers this defense will not apply. Firms merge for many reasons such as cost pressures and emptying pipelines. Even in innovation-market cases, companies often focus on product markets, with their millions of dollars in sales. In addition, many of the cases involve large drug firms that could easily

---

69. Genzyme, *Genetic Diseases, in* Annual Report (2007), http://genzyme.com/2007_ann_rpt/genetic.asp.

70. The efficiencies defense also could apply to vaccines and to drugs subject to the Orphan Drug Act, 21 U.S.C. § 360bb(a)(2) (2000), which provides seven years of market exclusivity to products treating rare conditions.

71. Merger Guidelines § 5.0.

72. Joseph A. Schumpeter, Capitalism, Socialism and Democracy 41, 103 (1942).

conduct clinical studies. Merging firms in Phase III studies have already shown the ability to navigate the regulatory process.

But where a small firm with a promising compound could not otherwise pursue clinical trials, the agencies should consider such a defense. The firm could demonstrate an inability to proceed by introducing evidence of objective factors such as market capitalization, assets, and profits. Like the efficiency defense, the Schumpeterian defense would be most persuasive where there is only modest concentration among firms reasonably likely to reach the market.

In short, the proposed framework builds on the current merger analysis, adapting it to account for the realities and hurdles of the pharmaceutical regulatory process.

The most important factor is the first, by which the agencies must show that the merger would lead to significant concentration among firms reasonably likely to reach the market. Where this factor is met, the second factor, the theory of innovation suppression, likely is satisfied. And where it is absent, competitive harm is not a real concern.

The third, fourth, and fifth elements allow the merging parties to offer defenses to the agencies' claims. The third, by which the firms can demonstrate that at least one other entity is likely to reach the market, is important since a rival's entry promises to introduce competition into the market. The fourth (efficiencies) and fifth (Schumpeterian) factors will not apply in many cases. But when they do, the agencies will need to balance the threat from concentration against the proffered benefits. That they do not explicitly engage in such tradeoffs demonstrates what is missing in the analysis.

EMPIRICAL STUDIES

There have been ten challenges to (and one prominent refusal to challenge) mergers in innovation markets.[73] All except two occurred in the pharmaceutical industry.[74]

---

73. In 1993, the U.S. Department of Justice (in its only innovation-market case) challenged General Motors' attempt to sell one of its divisions to ZF Friedrichshafen AG on the basis that the two firms were the primary producers of heavy-duty automatic truck and bus transmissions. Complaint, *United States v. Gen. Motors Corp.*, No. 93-530 (D. Del. Nov. 16, 1993), 1993 WL 13610315. Two years later, the FTC challenged Sensormatic's acquisition of Knogo, claiming that the two firms were the only ones conducting R&D for the next generation of antishoplifting equipment. *Sensormatic Elec. Corp.*, 119 F.T.C. 520, 520 (1995).

74. In six of the eight pharmaceutical mergers, the FTC challenged activity in markets other than innovation markets. In the Glaxo-Wellcome and Upjohn-Pharmacia mergers, the agency focused only on the activity in the innovation market. *In re Glaxo PLC*, 119 F.T.C. 815 (1995); *In the Matter of Upjohn Co.*, 121 F.T.C. 44 (1996).

Until now, most of the discussion of these cases has been limited to the facts alleged in FTC complaints. Because these matters have been resolved by consent agreement, there has been little information available to the public. No court cases or scholarly analysis have examined the validity of the FTC's allegations. Nor have the merging firms questioned the determinations.

In short, there has been no comprehensive analysis of the FTC's pharmaceutical innovation-market challenges. In earlier work, I offered the first such assessment, analyzing the eight challenges and one refusal to challenge in pharmaceutical innovation markets. In this chapter, I explore five illustrative cases.

I conclude that the FTC correctly challenged two mergers—between (1) Glaxo and Wellcome and (2) Baxter and Immuno—and appropriately refused to challenge a third, between Genzyme and Novazyme. But the agency incorrectly challenged the mergers between (1) Roche and Genentech and (2) Pfizer and Warner-Lambert.[75]

Roche-Genentech

In November 1990, the FTC entered into a consent decree with Roche and Genentech. The relevant market covered "CD4-based therapeutics for the treatment of AIDS and HIV infection."[76] Human Immunodeficiency Virus (HIV) attacks a patient by attaching itself to the protein CD-4, a receptor on the surface of immune cells that helps the virus gain entry into the cells. Experimental drugs allowed an engineered CD-4 protein to circulate in the bloodstream, picking up the virus before it could affect living immune cells.[77]

The FTC alleged that Genentech was "the most advanced of a limited number of companies developing CD-4-based therapeutics for use in the treatment of AIDS/HIV infection." Roche was "also engaged in" similar R&D and "ha[d] patent applications pending on its products."[78]

At the time of the merger, Genentech was in Phase I studies. Roche was in preclinical studies.[79] A rival, Biogen, was in Phase I/II trials.[80] As a result of the

---

75. For a discussion of the remaining four mergers, in which I concluded that the agencies correctly challenged the Upjohn-Pharmacia and Glaxo Wellcome-Smith Kline Beecham mergers but incorrectly challenged the AHP-American Cyanamid and Ciba-Geigy-Sandoz mergers, see Carrier, at 427–45.

76. *In re Roche Holding Ltd.*, 113 F.T.C. 1086, 1086–87 (1990).

77. Joseph Palca, *New AIDS Drugs Take Careful Aim*, 246 SCI. 1559, 1559 (1989); Laura Jereski, *Biogen's New Moneymaking Genes*, BUSINESSWEEK, June 19, 1989, at 94.

78. *Roche*, 113 F.T.C. at 1088.

79. Laura Evenson, *Genentech Merger Gets FTC's OK*, S.F. CHRON., Sept. 1, 1990, at B1.

80. *See Biogen Inc. Signs Funding Agreement with New York Life Insurance Co.*, APPLIED GENETICS NEWS, Nov. 1, 1989, 1989 WLNR 1234342 (noting that Biogen conducted tests on its drug in Phase I/II clinical trials).

consent agreement, the FTC required Roche to grant nonexclusive patent licenses for its version of CD-4.

Because of unsuccessful studies and exorbitant costs, however, these companies abandoned their CD-4 efforts shortly after the merger.[81] Today, there are no first-generation CD-4 products on the market. The closest products are Hoffman La Roche's Fuzeon, which was approved by the FDA in 2003,[82] and Pfizer's Selzentry, which was approved in 2007.[83]

My test shows that the FTC should not have challenged this merger. In particular, the agency would not have been able to demonstrate the first step of a concentrated market. Genentech was in Phase I, and Roche was in preclinical studies. It was unlikely that either firm would have reached the market.

As it turns out, the compulsory licensing requirement imposed on Roche was not beneficial. In fact, because of unsuccessful studies and exorbitant costs, each of the merging firms abandoned their CD-4 efforts shortly after the merger. Although two related drugs have been approved, there are no drugs similar to those that Roche and Genentech developed on the market today.

Glaxo-Wellcome

In June 1995, the FTC entered into a consent decree with merging parties Glaxo and Wellcome. The parties each were developing noninjectable 5HT-1D agonists, which treat migraine attacks.[84] Migraine is "an often debilitating, biological disease characterized by severe pain, usually on one side of the head," with attacks that "occur periodically and . . . last from [4] to 72 hours."[85]

The FTC alleged that the merger would "[d]ecreas[e] the number of [R&D] tracks for non-injectable 5HT-1D agonists" and "[i]ncreas[e] Glaxo's ability to unilaterally reduce [R&D] of non-injectable 5HT-1D agonists."[86]

---

81. *See Progenics Developing CD4-IgG2 for HIV-Infection*, ANTIVIRAL AGENTS BULL., June 1995, 1995 WLNR 3761267.

82. *FDA Grants Traditional Approval for Fusion Inhibitor for HIV Treatment*, IMMUNOTHERAPY WKLY., Nov. 17, 2004, at 102, 2004 WLNR 7585320; *Timeline Set for Development of T-20 for HIV-Infection*, ANTIVIRAL AGENTS BULL., Oct. 2001, 2001 WLNR 7846734. In contrast to CD-4 products, which attach to the AIDS virus before reaching other cells, Fuzeon creates a barrier between the virus and healthy cells. Press Release, Roche Pharmaceuticals, *U.S. FDA Approves Fuzeon; First Drug to Block Entry of HIV into Immune Cells*, Mar. 14, 2003, http://www.roche.com/inv-update-2003-03-14.

83. *Entry Inhibitors*, AIDSMEDS & POZ, Oct. 19, 2007, http://www.aidsmeds.com/archive/EIs_1627.shtml.

84. *In re Glaxo PLC*, 119 F.T.C. 815, 815–16 (1995).

85. *FDA Approves Amerge for Migraine Treatment*, DOCTOR'S GUIDE, Feb. 11, 1998, http://www.docguide.com/dg.nsf/PrintPrint/2877C3E773686229852565A80060754A.

86. *Glaxo*, 119 F.T.C. at 817.

At the time of the merger, Glaxo had an injectable migraine treatment, Imitrex, but there were no noninjectable migraine drugs on the market.[87] Wellcome's 311C was in Phase III trials, and Glaxo's Naramig was in at least Phase II.[88] As a condition of the merger, the FTC required the companies to divest Wellcome's 311C.[89]

In 2006, Glaxo's Imitrex had 56 percent of the migraine drug market.[90] Products with at least 10 percent of the market included Merck's Maxalt, Pfizer's Relpax, and Zeneca's Zomig.[91] These figures show increasing competition as compared to figures from 2003 (when Imitrex had 60 percent, Zomig had 11 percent, and Maxalt had 8 percent) and especially 1999 (when Imitrex had 83 percent, Zomig had 7 percent, Glaxo Wellcome's Amerge had 3 percent, and Maxalt had 1 percent).[92]

The FTC correctly challenged this merger. Because Wellcome was in Phase III and Glaxo was in at least Phase II, the agency could have demonstrated the first step—significant concentration among firms reasonably likely to reach the market.

It also could have satisfied the second step by offering a theory of anticompetitive harm in the form of innovation suppression. Such a conclusion followed from the finding on market concentration. And it was bolstered by Glaxo's monopoly in injectable migraine treatment. Because most patients prefer oral to injectable treatment, the new product resembles a drastic innovation.[93]

---

87. *In re Glaxo PLC*, Agreement Containing Consent Order, File No. 951-0054, n.1 (F.T.C. Mar. 7, 1995), 1995 WL 140769.

88. Commission Regulation 4064/89, Case No. IV/M.555 (*Glaxo v. Wellcome*), 1995 O.J. (C 65) 3, ¶ 28 (EC), http://ec.europa.eu/comm/competition/mergers/cases/decisions/m555_en.pdf; Glaxo, Annual Report (Form 20-F), at 9 (Sept. 26, 1994).

89. *Glaxo*, 119 F.T.C. at 820–21.

90. Andy Stone, *No More Headaches?*, FORBES.COM, Apr. 17, 2006, http://www.forbes.com/2006/04/13/pozen-trexima-migraine-cz_as_0417pozen_print.html.

91. Stan Hull, Senior Vice President, U.S. Pharmaceuticals-RTP, PowerPoint Presentation, slide 41 (June 7, 2006), http://gsk.com/investors/presentations/2006/06072006roundtable-hull.pdf.

92. Al Branch, Jr., *A New Headache for Imitrex*, HIGHBEAM RESEARCH, June 1, 2003, http://www.highbeam.com/DocPrint.aspx?DocId=1G1:104577998; *The Fast Growing Migraine Drug Market*, 3 ASIA PAC. BIOTECH NEWS 62, 62 (1999). None of the market share figures distinguish between injectable and noninjectable treatments.

93. *See* Carl G.H. Dahlof, *Zolmitriptan Nasal Spray—An Important New Development in the Acute Treatment of Migraine*, Business Briefing, EUR. PHARMACOTHERAPY 80, 80 (2005) (oral formulations accounted for more than 90 percent of sales of migraine treatment in 2003 and 2004). Nor does the existence of nondrastic innovation (because of the need for injectable treatment for migraines with nausea or vomiting, "morning migraines," and "rapidly escalating migraines") negate the improvement offered by noninjectable treatment. *See Migraine—FDA Approves New Formulation of Imitrex (Sumatriptan*

Nor would the merging parties be able to offer defenses sufficient to reverse this outcome. No rivals were in clinical studies, let alone poised to enter the market. The efficiencies defense would not apply because there was already an injectable treatment on the market. And the size of the firms would prevent use of the Schumpeterian defense.

An ex post analysis confirms that the FTC correctly challenged the merger. There is currently a robust market for noninjectable migraine treatment as four companies (Glaxo, Merck, Pfizer, and Zeneca) each possess at least 10 percent of the market. Of particular significance, Wellcome's divestiture played a direct role in Zeneca's presence on the market today.

Baxter-Immuno

In March 1997, the FTC challenged Baxter's acquisition of Immuno. The agency alleged that the two companies were "two of only a small number of companies seeking FDA approval to market [f]ibrin [s]ealant in the United States."[94]

Fibrin sealant is "extracted from human plasma" and "used in surgical procedures to arrest bleeding and as an adjunct to wound healing."[95] At the time of the Baxter-Immuno merger, the products were used in Europe and Japan for these purposes.[96] In the United States, there were no commercial fibrin sealant products. Surgeons had prepared homemade fibrin sealants, but these products were not "standardized or consistent" and were "virally inactivated."[97]

At the time of the merger, Baxter's Sealagen was in Phase II/III.[98] Immuno's Tisseel appeared to be in either Phase II or Phase III.[99] A third company, Vitex,

---

Succinate) Injection, MED. NEWS TODAY, Feb. 6, 2006, http://www.medicalnewstoday.com/printerfiendlynews.php?newsid=37154.

94. *In re Baxter Int'l Inc.*, 123 F.T.C. 904, 906 (1997).

95. Haemacure Corp., 2000 Annual Information Form (Form 6-K), at 1 (Apr. 12, 2001), http://sec.edgar-online.com/2001/04/18/0000897069-01-500079/Section4.asp.

96. Press Release, Fed. Trade Comm'n, FTC Decision in Baxter/Immuno Acquisition to Preserve Competition in Two Markets for Plasma Products Ensuring Lower Prices for Consumers and Continued Research and Development (Dec. 19, 1996), http://www.ftc.gov/opa/1996/12/baxter.htm.

97. U.S. Food & Drug Admin., *FDA Talk Paper: New Fibrin Sealant Approved to Help Control Bleeding in Surgery*, May 1, 1998, http://www.fda.gov/bbs/topics/ANSWERS/ANS00865.html.

98. BAXTER INT'L, ANNUAL REPORT 4 (1996), http://www.baxter.com/about_baxter/investor_information/annual_report/1996/bax96ar_t.pdf. Phase II/III trials occur where "Phase II-like trial[s are] sufficient to produce statistically sufficient data for approval, removing the need for a Phase III trial." Ark Therapeutics, *Glossary*, http://www.arktherapeutics.com/main/glossary.php?content=glossary#P (last visited July 26, 2008).

99. Although the stage is not clearly documented, the strongest available evidence comes from a meeting of the Blood Products Advisory Committee of the Center for

had completed Phase II studies and was about to commence Phase III.[100] The FTC required Baxter to grant a nonexclusive, royalty-free license of Immuno's Tisseel to an approved licensee.[101]

The FDA approved Tisseel in May 1998.[102] One month later, Baxter marketed the product as Tisseel, and Haemacure (the licensee) marketed the identical product as Hemaseel.[103] Although Haemacure left the market in 2003, Baxter, Aventis, and Omrix currently manufacture fibrin sealants.[104]

The FTC correctly challenged the merger. Because Baxter had a product in Phase II/III and Immuno was in Phase II, the agency could have demonstrated significant concentration among firms reasonably likely to reach the market. Although there is modestly less concern because the merging firms were not quite in the final stages of review, that is not enough to prevent the conclusion of a significantly concentrated market. And a theory of innovation suppression, though slightly less persuasive because neither firm was in Phase III, would have followed from the showing of market concentration.

At the time of the merger, another firm, Vitex, was in Phase II. While this provides some solace, it does not rise to the level of likely entry by another firm. Nor would the efficiencies and Schumpeterian defenses have applied. Finally, the suitability of the FTC's licensing requirement is borne out by a robust market today.

Biologics Evaluation and Research, which approves biologic products. The minutes of one meeting describe the results of three clinical trials, each with more than 100 participants, and conclude that "[t]he sum of these studies is that the efficacy of . . . [Tisseel] has been demonstrated as a topical hemostatic agent, as an aid to surgeries involving the pancreas and as a tissue sealant in colostomy patients." U.S. Food & Drug Admin., Ctr. for Biologic Evaluation and Research, Blood Prods. Advisory Comm., 57th Meeting, Dec. 11, 1997, at 23, http://www.fda.gov/ohrms/dockets/ac/97/transcpt/3361t1.pdf.

100. V I Techs., Annual Report (Form 10-K), Ex. 10.20 at 3 (Mar. 31, 2000), http://sec. edgar-online.com/2000/03/31/16/0000927016-00-001138/Section29.asp.

101. *In re Baxter Int'l Inc.*, 123 F.T.C. 904, 920–21 (Mar. 24, 1997). Baxter retained exclusive rights to Tisseel outside the United States. *Baxter's Fibrin Sealant Ready*, MED. MATERIALS UPDATE, May 1, 1998, 1998 WLNR 3599648.

102. Haemacure Corp., Annual Report (Form 20-F), at 24 (Dec. 12, 2001), http://sec. edgar-online.com/2001/12/12/0000897069-01-500639/Section5.asp.

103. In 1999, Baxter had approximately 75 percent of fibrin sealant sales and Haemacure had 25 percent. HAEMACURE, ANNUAL INFORMATION FORM 3–4 (1999), http://www.haemacure. com/rtecontent/document/Rap99A.pdf.

104. *Initial Report: OMRIX Biopharmaceuticals, Inc. (NASDAQ: OMRI): Buy*, INVESTOLOGY RESEARCH, Aug. 11, 2006, at 9, http://www.herdonthestreet.com/protected/ Research%20Reports/OMRIX%20initial%2081106%20B.pdf; HAEMACURE CORP., 2006 ANNUAL REPORT, at 4, http://www.haemacure.com/rtecontent/document/Rapportannuel 2006.pdf; *U.S. Tissue Sealants Are Set to Boom*, BIOMEDICAL MATERIALS, May 1, 2002, 2002 WLNR 4969980; D. Paul Cohen, *Dirty Dozen Research: No Agenda*, at 29 (Oct. 12, 2001), http://www.cohenresearch.com/reports/kool_10-12-01.pdf.

Pfizer–Warner-Lambert

In June 2000, the FTC entered into a consent agreement with Pfizer and Warner-Lambert. The companies were developing "Epidermal Growth Factor receptor tyrosine kinase [EGFR] inhibitors for the treatment of solid cancerous tumors." Such tumors generally include "head and neck, non-small-cell lung, breast, ovarian, pancreatic and colorectal cancers." EGFR inhibitors "target the EGFR oncogene that regulates cancer cell growth" and seek to inhibit the "cell division signal transduction that results in cancer cell proliferation."[105]

The FTC alleged that Pfizer and Warner-Lambert "produce[d] two of the most advanced EGFr-tk inhibitors currently being developed, and [we]re among a relatively small number of companies working on these types of drugs." The agency claimed that as a result of the merger, "Pfizer could delay or simply fail to develop one of the two competing drugs, leading to less product innovation, fewer consumer choices, and higher prices in the marketplace."[106]

At the time of the merger, there were four companies with EGFR inhibitors in clinical studies. Pfizer's CP-358,774 compound was in Phase II trials. Warner-Lambert's CI-1033 was in Phase I. And AstraZeneca and Imclone each had products in Phase III. The consent order required Pfizer to divest its EGFR inhibitor to its development partner, OSI.[107]

Today, there are three firms on the market with an EGFR inhibitor.[108] The FDA approved Imclone's Erbitux in February 2004 for colorectal cancer and in March 2006 for cancer of the head and neck.[109] OSI's Tarceva was approved in November 2004 for advanced non-small cell lung cancer and in November 2005

---

105. Analysis of Proposed Consent Order to Aid Public Comment, Pfizer Inc., and Warner-Lambert Company, File No. 001 0059 (Fed. Trade Comm'n, June 19, 2000), http://www.ftc.gov/os/2000/06/pfizeranalysis.htm.

106. Press Release, Fed. Trade Comm'n, *FTC Order Clears Way for $90 Billion Merger of Pfizer Inc. and Warner-Lambert Company*, June 19, 2000, http://www.ftc.gov/opa/2000/06/pfizer.htm.

107. OSI Pharms., Inc., Current Report Pursuant to Section 13 or 15(d) of the Securities Exchange Act of 1934 (Form 8-K), at 2–3, June 19, 2000, http://www.sec.gov/Archives/edgar/data/729922/000095012300005877/0000950123-00-005877-0001.txt.

108. A fourth product, AstraZeneca's Iressa, came to the market in May 2003 but was pulled in December 2004 after a post-marketing clinical study failed to show a survival benefit. *See* Press Release, U.S. Food and Drug Admin., *FDA Statement on Iressa*, Dec. 17, 2004, http://www.fda.gov/bbs/topics/news/2004/new01145.html.

109. Press Release, U.S. Food and Drug Admin., *FDA Approves Erbitux for Colorectal Cancer*, Feb. 12, 2004, http://www.fda.gov/bbs/topics/news/2004/new01024.html; Press Release, U.S. Food and Drug Admin., *FDA Approves First Head & Neck Cancer Treatment in 45 Years; Data Shows Treatment with Erbitux Extends Survival*, Mar. 1, 2006, http://www.fda.gov/bbs/topics/news/2006/new01329.html.

for certain types of pancreatic cancer.[110] And the FDA approved Amgen's Vectibix in September 2006 for colorectal cancer.[111]

The FTC should not have challenged the merger, which did not threaten significant concentration among firms reasonably likely to reach the market. Neither of the merging firms had reached the final stage of FDA review: Pfizer was in Phase II, and Warner-Lambert was in Phase I. While Pfizer's development partner eventually was able to bring the divested product to market, the merged company did not encounter such success with Warner-Lambert's Phase I product.

In addition, the merging firms could have offered a powerful defense based on likely entry by competitors. Two firms, Astra-Zeneca and Imclone, each were in Phase III, making it likely that at least one of the firms would reach the market and offer competition. In fact, both products did reach the market. Although Astra-Zeneca's Iressa was pulled after a disappointing clinical trial, Imclone's Erbitux is still on the market.[112]

Genzyme-Novazyme

Genzyme acquired Novazyme in September 2001. At the time of the merger, both companies were engaged in preclinical studies to develop a treatment for Pompe disease, a rare and fatal genetic disorder affecting infants and children. Because there are few patients with the disease, therapies fall under the Orphan Drug Act, which provides seven years of market exclusivity to the first therapy to receive FDA approval.[113]

---

110. Press Release, U.S. Food & Drug Admin., *FDA Approves New Drug for the Most Common Type of Lung Cancer*, Nov. 19, 2004, http://www.fda.gov/bbs/topics/news/2004/ NEW01139.html; Press Release, Genentech, *FDA Approves Tarceva in Combination with Gemcitabine Chemotherapy for Treatment of Locally Advanced, Inoperable or Metastatic Pancreatic Cancer*, Nov. 2, 2005, http://www.gene.com/gene/news/press-releases/display. do?method=detail&id=9067.

111. CenterWatch, Drugs Approved by the FDA: Vectibix, http://www.centerwatch. com/patient/drugs/dru933.html (last visited July 26, 2008).

112. *See* Erbitux, http://www.erbitux.com/erbitux/erb/home/index.jsp?BV_UseBVCookie= Yes (last visited July 26, 2008). The challenge also was plagued by a questionable market definition. The FTC defined a market even though EGFR inhibitors targeted different cancers and worked in different ways. If the agency had defined the market according to the type of condition being treated, there likely would have been no challenge. For example, colorectal cancer could be treated through not only EGFR inhibitors but also other types of similarly effective treatment, which today are offered by Amgen, Genentech/Roche, Imclone/BMS, and others. *Market Report, Cancer Market: Overview, Strong Sales Growth Drives the Market*, PHARMACTIVS, Jul. 8, 2006, http://www.pharmactives. com/article.cfm?ref=577.

113. Muris Statement, at 1 n.1, 6 n.14; Press Release, Fed. Trade Comm'n, *FTC Closes its Investigation of Genzyme Corporation's 2001 Acquisition of Novazyme Pharmaceuticals, Inc.*, Jan. 13, 2004, http://ftc.gov/opa/2004/01/genzyme.htm.

The FTC began to investigate the matter shortly after the merger was completed. In January 2004, it voted 3-1-1 not to challenge the merger. There were three separate statements. Chairman Muris emphasized that "because there is currently no treatment for Pompe disease, the most important goal for patients is to get one effective treatment for Pompe disease on the market as soon as possible." He also warned that "[t]he adoption of presumptions without economic foundation would constitute a major step backward in antitrust law."[114]

Commissioner Thompson, in contrast, worried about the "consummated merger to monopoly" in the R&D of "a highly specialized drug" and lamented that "entry of a new market participant" would not "replace the innovation competition eliminated by the merger."[115] Commissioner Harbour abstained because she had joined the FTC in its final stages of review but emphasized the importance of innovation competition in the pharmaceutical industry.[116]

At the time of the merger in 2001 and at the time of the decision to close the investigation in 2004, there was no treatment for Pompe disease. Novazyme, which had been in preclinical studies at the time of the merger, was still in that stage in January 2004. Genzyme, which was in preclinical testing at the time of the merger, had reached Phase II/III clinical trials by 2004.[117] Genzyme had previously acquired two other companies researching the disease, but those products had both been abandoned by 2002.[118]

In April 2006, the FDA approved Genzyme's Myozyme, the first treatment for Pompe disease.[119]

The FTC correctly decided not to challenge the merger. This result is consistent with my analysis: even though Genzyme was in Phase II/III, Novazyme was only in preclinical studies. Because of the staggering odds that a firm in preclinical studies will reach the market, I would not include such firms in determining market concentration. The agency's refusal to challenge the merger

---

114. Muris Statement, at 18, 25.

115. Thompson Statement, at 1.

116. Statement of Commissioner Pamela Jones Harbour, Genzyme Corporation's Acquisition of Novazyme Pharmaceuticals Inc., at 2–3 (Jan. 14, 2004), http://www.ftc.gov/os/2004/01/harbourgenzymestmt.pdf.

117. Muris Statement, at 8–10, 18.

118. The Pharming product had been abandoned by the time of the merger, and the Synpac program was suspended in early 2002 because "manufacturing problems were preventing production on a scale sufficient for commercialization." Id. at 9.

119. Press Release, U.S. Food and Drug Admin., FDA Approves First Treatment for Pompe Disease, Apr. 28, 2006, http://www.fda.gov/bbs/topics/NEWS/2006/NEW01365.html. Amicus Therapeutics currently has a compound, AT2220, in Phase I trials for the treatment of the disease. Amicus Therapeutics, AT2220 for Pompe Disease, http://amicustherapeutics.com/pipeline/at2220.asp (last visited July 26, 2008).

thus is consistent with my conclusion that there was no significant concentration among firms reasonably likely to reach the market.

The merging firms also could have offered a strong efficiency defense under my test. The parties offered merger-specific benefits that made it more likely that one firm would reach the market, and reach it faster. This was particularly important because there was no treatment for a fatal disease, one that, as a type of lysosomal storage disorder (LSD), presented exceedingly difficult challenges.

The firms, additionally, could have offered a Schumpeterian defense. Novazyme was a small research company with approximately 80 employees, no sales revenue, and less than $10 million in assets.[120] It had no products in clinical trials and no large-scale manufacturing facilities.[121] The merger was necessary for Novazyme to survive the regulatory process.

Finally, an ex post analysis of the market shows that the lack of merger challenge did not prevent Genzyme's Myozyme from reaching the market in 2006.

Challenges to mergers in pharmaceutical innovation markets are most effective when the merging firms are the only companies in advanced clinical trials. This was the case in the FTC's challenges to the mergers between (1) Glaxo and Wellcome and (2) Baxter and Immuno. In a third correct decision, the FTC decided not to challenge the merger between Genzyme and Novazyme.

But the lack of an analysis similar to the Merger Guidelines and the neglect of the stage of FDA review led to unnecessary, counterproductive challenges in the mergers between (1) Roche and Genentech and (2) Pfizer and Warner-Lambert. By fleshing out the FTC's current incomplete analysis, my test offers a more justifiable and beneficial innovation-markets framework.

CONCLUSION

The concept of innovation markets has been much maligned. This chapter has shown that the characteristics of the pharmaceutical industry rebut most of the criticisms. In particular, the central role of competition in the industry confirms the propriety of enforcement in innovation markets.

On a practical level, the chapter has offered the first comprehensive framework that can be applied to innovation-market analysis. This framework improves the current analysis by considering not only the number of firms in R&D but also the stage of FDA review. Given the significant hurdles facing firms in drug development and the wildly varying odds of success at each of the stages, it is no

---

120. Muris Statement, at 8.
121. Wald & Feinstein, at 2.

longer appropriate to neglect this factor. Firms in preclinical development should not be considered part of the relevant market, and the most imminent harm is presented by merging firms in Phase III. The new test also creates new defenses based on entry, efficiencies, and lack of size.

Going forward, application of my test promises to make innovation-market analysis more predictable and to incorporate a more realistic assessment of pharmaceutical innovation. By preventing unnecessary challenges, it seeks to ensure the most effective use of limited government resources. And by increasing the odds that vital products will reach the market, it could foster innovation and even save lives.

14. SUPPORTING STANDARD-SETTING ORGANIZATIONS

Standard-Setting 325
    Types 325
      IP Rules 327
Patent Holdup 328
Manipulation 330
Deception 331
Potential Harms of Price Reduction 332
Announcement of Maximum Royalties 333
RAND Refusal 334
Anticompetitive Concerns 335
Monopsony 336
Procompetitive Justifications 339
    SSOs 339
      IP Rules 340
Proposal 342
Conclusion 343

A standard is a common platform that allows products to work together. Standards are ubiquitous in our economy. They allow us to speak to and understand one another. They let consumers access credit card and ATM machines. They offer phone, fax, and modem networks. They permit computer users to share videos and programs. They appear in countless other settings.[1]

In contrast, the absence of standards, from biblical times to the present, has had damaging effects. The multiplicity of languages at the Tower of Babel led to misunderstanding and conflict.[2] Before the standardization of time zones in the late 19th century, cities and towns used different forms of time, relying on clocks placed in town squares or jeweler's windows.[3] During the Great Baltimore Fire of 1904, which burned longer than 30 hours and destroyed more than 1,500 buildings, the city's hydrants did not fit the hoses of firefighters from nearby cities.[4] In the late 20th century, purchasers of Sony's Betamax VCRs

---

1. *See generally* Carl Shapiro, *Setting Compatibility Standards: Cooperation or Collusion?*, *in* EXPANDING THE BOUNDARIES OF INTELLECTUAL PROPERTY: INNOVATION POLICY FOR THE KNOWLEDGE SOCIETY 81, 83–84 (Rochelle Cooper Dreyfuss et al. eds., 2001).

2. *Id.* at 81.

3. U.S. Naval Observatory, Astronomical Applications Department, *U.S. Time Zones*, 2007, http://aa.usno.navy.mil/faq/docs/us_tzones.

4. Shapiro, at 81; *Great Baltimore Fire*, WIKIPEDIA, Jan. 2, 2008, http://en.wikipedia.org/wiki/Great_Baltimore_Fire.

were stranded as the market tipped to JVC's VHS format. And for nearly two years, consumers delayed buying high-definition DVD players and recorders until Toshiba abandoned its HD-DVD format, ceding the market to Sony's Blu-Ray technology.[5]

Standards, in short, are crucial to our economy. As is apparent from the examples, they are especially needed in *network effects markets*, in which users benefit from an increase in the number of other users in the system. A telephone or e-mail system, for example, becomes more valuable as more users connect to it. Networks also feature positive feedback. The more popular a computer operating system becomes, the more applications will be written for it.

Even though standards are vital, antitrust traditionally viewed the process of setting standards with suspicion. Standard-setting organizations (SSOs) tend to be composed of industry rivals discussing sensitive information such as price. As Adam Smith worried: "People of the same trade seldom meet together even for merriment or diversion, but the conversation ends in a conspiracy against the public, or in some contrivance to raise prices."[6]

Despite antitrust's concern, competitors have good reason to engage in such discussions. Before the selection of a standard, an SSO often can choose from an array of alternative technologies.[7] In contrast, after a standard is chosen and the industry has invested in a particular technology, flexibility is severely restricted. If the selected technology is patented, the owner could impose excessive licensing terms that reflect not just the value of the patent but also the significant costs of switching to a new technology. The patentee, in other words, could *hold up* the standard's implementation.

This threat of holdup explains why SSOs have required members to provide certain information before the standard's selection.[8] Some SSOs have mandated that participants disclose patents that could be implicated by the standard. Many have required members to agree to license their IP on reasonable and nondiscriminatory (RAND) terms. One SSO has compelled participants to specify the maximum royalties it would impose. Although the enforcement agencies have recently softened their position, antitrust law traditionally has been suspicious of such price-related activities. And this suspicion deters SSO members from sharing information that could prevent holdup.[9]

---

5. Maria Panaritis, *HD DVD Ready To Bow out of War with Blu-Ray*, Feb. 18, 2008, http://www.philly.com/philly/business/breaking/20080218_HD_DVD_ready_to_bow_out_of_war_with_Blu-ray.html.

6. ADAM SMITH, AN INQUIRY INTO THE NATURE AND CAUSES OF THE WEALTH OF THE NATIONS 145 (1776).

7. In certain settings, there may be only one superior technical option.

8. The threat also has encouraged the formation of patent pools, which I discuss in Chapter 5.

9. For example, firms in the computer hardware and software industries have explained that their standards-related discussions of licensing terms have been inhibited

In this chapter, I first describe the various types of standard-setting. I then offer a brief history of antitrust treatment of SSOs. Next, I set forth the anticompetitive concerns of standard-setting, including the harm posed by buyer power known as monopsony. I conclude that these concerns are almost always outweighed by the significant procompetitive benefits that SSOs and their IP rules offer. I conclude that courts and the agencies should apply Rule-of-Reason analysis to SSOs and uphold standard-setting activity in the vast majority of cases.

STANDARD-SETTING

Types

There are several types of standards and processes for setting them. Governments often enact *performance standards*, which address product quality, health, and safety.[10] Safety standards, for example, define features that products must possess to be sold on the market or to obtain approval from a standard-setting body.[11] Governments also have enacted other standards that they require market participants to adopt, such as standards for high-definition television (HDTV) and for interconnection between telephone networks.[12] Government-set standards have become less important in recent years and have suffered weaknesses such as failures to abandon inefficient standards and susceptibility to undue influence by entities with an interest in the outcome.[13]

A second type involves *de facto* standard-setting, which occurs when one firm dominates the market.[14] In such a case (exemplified by the QWERTY keyboard layout and Microsoft Windows operating system), the firm's position as market leader allows it to select the standard and (where the standard is protected by IP) force rivals to obtain licenses.[15] Because of the benefits of adopting the same

---

by antitrust concerns. Fed. Trade Comm'n, To Promote Innovation: The Proper Balance of Competition and Patent Law and Policy, ch. 3, at 3 (Oct. 2003).

10. Letter from Thomas O. Barnett, Assistant Att'y Gen'l, Dep't of Justice, to Robert A. Skitol, Oct. 30, 2006, at 7, http://www.usdoj.gov/atr/public/busreview/219380.pdf [VITA Letter].

11. James J. Anton & Dennis A. Yao, *Standard-Setting Consortia, Antitrust, and High-Technology Industries*, 64 Antitrust L.J. 247, 247 (1995).

12. 2 Herbert Hovenkamp, Mark D. Janis & Mark A. Lemley, IP and Antitrust: An Analysis of Antitrust Principles Applied to Intellectual Property Law, at 35–5 to 35–6 (2002).

13. *Id.* at 35–14 to 35–15; Mark A. Lemley, *Intellectual Property Rights and Standard-Setting Organizations*, 90 Cal. L. Rev. 1889, 1900 (2002) [hereinafter Lemley, *SSOs*].

14. Robert M. Webb, *There is a Better Way: It's Time To Overhaul the Model for Participation in Private Standard-Setting*, 12 J. Intell. Prop. L. 163, 168 (2004).

15. Janice M. Mueller, *Patent Misuse Through the Capture of Industry Standards*, 17 Berkeley Tech. L.J. 623, 633 (2002).

product as others, de facto standards are particularly likely in networks effects markets.[16]

This chapter focuses on the third type, standards voluntarily set by private industry groups known as SSOs. Hundreds of SSOs operate throughout the world in varying degrees of formality, size, and scope.[17] Formal SSOs include Underwriter's Laboratory, the Institute of Electric and Electronic Engineers, and the National Institute of Standards and Technology. In the United States, SSOs often fall under the umbrella of the American National Standards Institute, which requires due process principles and open participation.[18] Firms also have created informal consortia, such as the World Wide Web consortium, to exercise greater control and obtain faster implementation. While SSOs are voluntary in nature, they are sometimes incorporated into state laws or municipal ordinances that require compliance.[19]

Many companies participate in a range of SSOs. One of the central aspects of SSOs is their openness, with the standard available to all members and, often, outsiders as well. Standards are used throughout various industries and facilitate the interaction of users and providers.[20] They have typically been set by engineers, though lawyers have played a larger role in recent years. Because standards bodies do not have enforcement authority, disputes (including numerous antitrust claims) have been adjudicated by courts.[21]

An important category of standards set by SSOs, and the focus of this chapter, consists of *interface (or interoperability) standards.* These standards, vital to the economy, allow products made by different firms to work together.[22] The plethora of communications technologies today—such as laptop computers, personal digital assistants, cell phones, pagers, and other devices—would not be possible without interface standards.[23] In addition, nearly every aspect of using a computer or navigating the Internet is based on interface standards.[24] To illustrate, the application programming interfaces defining compatibility with

---

16. Lemley, *SSOs*, at 1899.

17. U.S. Dep't of Justice & Fed. Trade Comm'n, Antitrust Enforcement and Intellectual Property Rights: Promoting Innovation and Competition, ch. 2, at 33 n. 5 (2007), http://www.ftc.gov/os/2003/10/innovationrpt.pdf [hereinafter Antitrust Enforcement and IP Rights].

18. Shapiro, at 84.

19. Daniel J. Gifford, *Developing Models for a Coherent Treatment of Standard-Setting Issues under the Patent, Copyright, and Antitrust Laws*, 43 IDEA 331, 333 (2003).

20. *Id.*

21. Shapiro, at 85.

22. Lemley, *SSOs*, at 1892–93.

23. Mueller, at 633.

24. Larry Seltzer, *The Standards Industry: Corporate Consortia Are Supplanting Traditional Rule-Making Bodies*, Internet World, Apr. 15, 2001, at 50, *http://www.internetworld.com/magazine.php?inc=041501/04.15.01internettech1.html.*

the Windows operating system offer a standard that ensures that applications need not become their own "mini-operating systems."[25] Interface standards also are beneficial in clearing patent thickets and fostering cumulative innovation, with one generation's patented invention building on those of previous generations.[26]

Another benefit of interface standards is their ability to create new markets by avoiding *standards wars*, which occur when substitute products with incompatible designs are introduced in the marketplace.[27] In the period before one format emerges victorious, some consumers delay their purchases because they do not wish to be stuck with the losing format. Just to pick one example, 60 percent of consumers indicated they would not purchase HD DVD or Blu-ray technology "until there was just one format."[28] Standards wars are particularly likely in network effects markets, in which there are significant benefits to customers having compatible products.[29]

IP Rules

Standard setting organizations have adopted an array of IP-related rules designed to limit a patentee's imposition of licensing terms that could hold up the standard's implementation. *Disclosure rules* inform SSO members of IP held by participants.[30] The rules most typically cover patents and sometimes apply to patent applications and other IP rights. Disclosure rules allow members to make informed decisions but could increase costs for IP owners, even causing them to leave the organization.[31] Supplementing disclosure rules, some SSOs have adopted *search rules* that require members to search for relevant IP rights.[32]

Standard setting organizations also typically implement *licensing rules* that specify the terms under which the IP would be licensed. The most popular such rule requires members to license their patents on a *"reasonable and nondiscriminatory"* (RAND) basis.[33] The benefit of such a commitment, however, is reduced by its vagueness. "Reasonable" royalties do not specify an exact amount, leaving the parties to argue over the term's meaning. In particular, patentees whose patents have been incorporated into the standard tend to have higher conceptions

---

25. *Lemley, SSOs,* at 1896; Gifford, at 337.
26. Suzanne Scotchmer, *Standing on the Shoulders of Giants: Cumulative Research and the Patent Law,* 5 J. Econ. Persp. 29, 29 (1991).
27. Antitrust Enforcement and IP Rights, ch. 2, at 34 n.6.
28. Panaritis, *HD DVD Ready To Bow out of War with Blu-Ray.*
29. Antitrust Enforcement and IP Rights, ch. 2, at 34 n.6.
30. *Id.* at 42.
31. *Id.* at 43.
32. Lemley, *SSOs,* at 1905.
33. *Id.* at 1906.

of what constitutes a reasonable royalty than licensees.[34] Because of this uncertainty, some SSOs have required members to specify their most restrictive licensing terms, such as the maximum royalty they would charge.[35]

A few SSOs, such as those developing standards for the Internet, require members to commit to *royalty-free licensing*.[36] Such licensing dispenses with the difficulties of determining reasonable royalties and considers the views of open-source developers that might not otherwise use the standards. But the natural concern with such licensing is a potential reduction in innovation incentives.[37]

PATENT HOLDUP

One of the dangers facing standard setting is the likelihood of patent holdup. Before a standard's adoption, an SSO often can choose from an array of alternative technologies. At that time, a patentee has no more leverage than any other potential supplier and is unable to command more than a competitive price.[38]

After the SSO chooses a standard, however, the owner of the selected technology may gain significant power. If the technology is patented, the owner could impose royalties so high that members are effectively prevented from using the standard. In many cases, the royalties are passed on to consumers, who are forced to pay higher prices.[39]

Nor can SSO members, faced with demands for excessively high royalties, migrate easily to a different technology. After a standard is selected, industry

---

34. Philip J. Weiser, *Making the World Safe for Standard Setting*, at 26 (2007), http://ssrn.com/abstract=1003432 (citation omitted); *see also Nokia Corp. v. Qualcomm, Inc.*, No. CIV A 06-509-JJF, 2006 WL 2521328 (D. Del. Aug. 29, 2006); Mark A. Lemley, *Intellectual Property Rights and Standard-Setting Organizations*, 90 CAL. L. REV. 1889, 1965 (2002); Joseph Scott Miller, *Standard Setting, Patents, and Access Lock-in: RAND Licensing and the Theory of the Firm*, 40 IND. L. REV. 351, 358 (2007).

35. *See* VITA Letter. One response to the vagueness of RAND licensing is to enter into patent pools.

36. ANTITRUST ENFORCEMENT AND IP RIGHTS, ch. 2, at 47.

37. Daniel J. Weitzner, Testimony, U.S. Dept. of Justice & FTC, *Joint Hearings on Competition and Intellectual Property Law and Policy in the Knowledge-Based Economy: Standards and Intellectual Property—Licensing Terms*, Apr. 18, 2002, at 2, http://www.ftc.gov/opp/intellect/020418weitzner.shtm.

38. Deborah Platt Majoras, Chairman, Fed. Trade Comm'n, *Recognizing the Procompetitive Potential of Royalty Discussions in Standard Setting*, Sept. 23, 2005, at 2, http://www.ftc.gov/speeches/majoras/050923stanford.pdf.

The Supreme Court's decision in *eBay, Inc. v. MercExchange, LLC*, 547 U.S. 388 (2006), which is the focus of Chapter 10, would appear to reduce the likelihood of holdup, though the magnitude of the change is uncertain.

39. *Id.* at 3; Joseph Farrell et al., *Standard Setting, Patents, and Hold-Up*, 74 ANTITRUST L.J. 603, 645 (2007).

participants begin designing, testing, and producing goods that conform to the standard. That, as former FTC Chairman[40] Deborah Platt Majoras explained, is "the whole idea of engaging in standard setting."[41] But these efforts, in learning about a particular technology and investing in equipment and complementary products, typically do not have value if the user switches to an alternative technology.[42] In addition, the industry typically will incur the costs of selecting a new standard. As a result of all these costs, the industry will be locked into the chosen standard.

Holdup is not just a theoretical concern. Of many examples that could be offered, I will describe three. The first is provided by the Union Oil Company of California (Unocal). In the 1990s, the California Air Resources Board sought to reduce pollution by adopting a standard for reformulated gasoline.[43] After refiners invested $4 billion to comply with the standard, Unocal revealed a "clean fuels" patent covering the standard and demanded royalties.[44] Given their significant investments, the leading California refiners did not have a choice but to invest an additional $1.5 billion to comply with the standard.[45] Unocal's enforcement of its patents would have cost consumers roughly 5 cents per gallon, or more than $500 million annually.[46]

In the second example, computer memory developer Rambus refused to disclose patents and applications and engaged in other deceptive conduct in a semiconductor engineering SSO. As a result, manufacturers faced significant holdup. Abandoning the technology might have been easy early in the standard's development but, less than a decade later, became "near[ly] impossible." As the FTC's expert in the case explained, lock-in "grows over time," as manufacturers make sunk investments in complementary goods before "deploy[ing] the standardized product in volume."[47]

Lock-in arises from the accumulation of investments at each stage. For example, in the computer memory setting, it involves (1) designing chips and products conforming to the standard; (2) testing and verifying the designs; (3) building, testing, and qualifying prototypes; and (4) ramping up production on a commercial scale. As a result of these investments, manufacturers

---

40. The FTC Act adopts the term "Chairman," and this title has been used in connection with all such officials. 15 U.S.C. § 41.

41. Majoras, at 3.

42. Daniel G. Swanson & William J. Baumol, *Reasonable and Nondiscriminatory (RAND) Royalties, Standards Selection, and Control of Market Power*, 73 ANTITRUST L.J. 1, 9 (2005); Farrell et al., at 612 n.35.

43. Farrell et al., at 619.

44. Mueller, at 625.

45. Farrell et al., at 620–21.

46. *In re Union Oil Co. of California*, No. 9305, ¶ 63 (F.T.C. Nov. 25, 2003), http://www.ftc.gov/os/2003/11/031126unionoil.pdf, *rev'd* (F.T.C. July 7, 2004); Mueller, at 627.

47. *In re Rambus*, No. 9302, 2006 WL 2330117, at 100 (Aug. 2, 2006).

could spend hundreds of millions of dollars if forced to switch to a different technology. In the Rambus case, Cisco stated that the cost of redesigning and requalifying its products could have exceeded $1 billion.[48]

A third instance is provided by the World Wide Web Consortium, which develops technology standards for the Web, allowing users to link to and distribute documents across the world.[49] Holdup led this group to suffer significant delay, inefficient resource allocation, and excessive patentee control over design.[50] The head of the SSO's technology activities pointed to five design efforts, making up 10 percent of its activity, that suffered from patent holdup.[51] These efforts included standards for a Platform for Privacy Preferences (expressing Web sites' privacy preferences in a standard format) and Synchronized Multimedia Integration Language (allowing authors to write interactive multimedia presentations).[52]

Holdup and other concerning activities have surfaced in the SSO antitrust cases that the agencies have brought and the courts have considered. Many of the most important cases fall into two categories. The first involves SSO members manipulating the standard-setting process. In the second, participants engaged in deceptive conduct such as refusing to disclose patents. In addition to these categories, three recent actions are worthy of attention. One illustrated the danger of SSOs reducing the price paid to patentees. Another sanctioned an SSO rule requiring members to declare their most restrictive licensing terms before standard selection. And a third challenged an alleged refusal to comply with RAND obligations.

MANIPULATION

The first set of cases involves the manipulation of the standard-setting process. The case of *Allied Tube & Conduit Corp. v. Indian Head, Inc.* involved a fire protection association's code that specified the types of allowable electrical conduit (hollow tubing that carries electrical wires through a building's walls and floors) and was adopted by many state and local governments. Manufacturers of steel

---

48. *Id.* at 100, 108.

49. Weitzner testimony, at 1.

50. Daniel Weitzner, *Supplemental Comments* (Nov. 6, 2002), http://www.w3.org/2002/11/15-doj-ftc-ipr-weitzner-suppl.html.

51. *Id.* The five include Platform for Privacy Preferences (P3P), XML Linking (Xlink), Scalable Vector Graphics (SVG), Synchronized Multimedia Integration Language (SMIL), and Voice Extensible Markup Language (VoiceXML).

52. W3C, *The Platform for Privacy Preferences 1.0 (P3P1.0) Specification*, Apr. 16, 2002, http://www.w3.org/TR/P3P/; W3C, *Synchronized Multimedia Integration Language (SMIL 2.0)*, 2nd ed., Jan. 7, 2005, http://www.w3.org/TR/2005/REC-SMIL2-20050107/.

conduit packed an SSO meeting to defeat a rival's attempt to certify plastic conduit. The manufacturers recruited more than 200 persons to attend the meeting to vote against the proposal, telling them how to vote and communicating with them through walkie-talkies and hand signals. The steel manufacturers were successful in rejecting the proposal that would have allowed plastic conduit by four votes. The Supreme Court concluded that this activity violated the antitrust laws.[53]

At the heart of the second case, *American Society of Mechanical Engineers v. Hydrolevel Corp.*, was an SSO's Boiler and Pressure Vessel Code, adopted by 46 states. The code governed "low-water fuel cutoffs," which blocked the flow of fuel to water boilers when the water level fell so low that it could no longer moderate the boiler's temperature. The firm dominating the market for low-water fuel cutoffs benefited as its vice president, in his capacity as vice chairman of the relevant SSO subcommittee, interpreted the code so that its rival's product was deemed unsafe, thus discouraging customers from buying it. The Court sought to "ensure that standard-setting organizations will act with care when they permit their agents to speak for them" and concluded that the conduct presented an antitrust offense.[54]

DECEPTION

The second set of cases involves a participant's deceptive conduct. In *In re Dell*, the FTC examined the standard for VL-bus, which transferred instructions between a computer's central processing unit and its peripherals (such as hard disk drives and modems). The Video Electronics Standards Association required members to disclose IP they possessed that conflicted with the proposed standard. A Dell representative certified that the proposal did not infringe any of its trademarks, copyrights, or patents. Based on these assurances, the SSO adopted the standard. In the succeeding eight months, the standard was widely adopted, being included in more than 1.4 million computers. At that point, Dell informed SSO members that their implementation of the standard violated its "exclusive rights." The FTC entered into a consent agreement that prevented Dell from enforcing the patent against those implementing the standard.[55]

The FTC also challenged the misrepresentation of Unocal before the California Air Resources Board, which developed standards for low-emissions, reformulated gasoline. Unocal participated in the rulemaking proceedings, asserting that its research data (on which the agency relied) was "nonproprietary" and failing to disclose its relevant patents and applications. California refiners spent billions

---

53. 486 U.S. 492, 496–97 (1988).
54. 456 U.S. 556, 559–63, 577–78 (1982).
55. *In re Dell*, 121 F.T.C. 616, 617, 623–24 (1996).

of dollars modifying their refineries to comply with the new standards. Unocal then claimed that the standards infringed its patents and sought to collect royalties that would have cost consumers more than $500 million annually. The parties ultimately settled, with Unocal agreeing not to enforce patents related to the standards.[56]

A final FTC challenge occurred in *In re Rambus*. Rambus developed computer memory technologies known as DRAM (dynamic random access memory), which processes information and is used in computers, printers, and cameras. Rambus participated in the Joint Electron Device Engineering Council (JEDEC), a semiconductor engineering SSO made up of DRAM manufacturers and purchasers as well as producers of complementary products. The SSO's disclosure policy was not clear, leading the Federal Circuit to find that it suffered from "a staggering lack of defining details."[57]

The FTC nonetheless found that Rambus "engaged in representations, omissions, and practices likely to mislead JEDEC members," which "significantly contributed to its acquisition of monopoly power."[58] In 2008, the D.C. Circuit, focusing on causation, reversed this conclusion. It found that JEDEC might have adopted Rambus's technology even absent any deception. As a result, any "loss of an opportunity to seek favorable licensing terms" did not, without more, constitute "antitrust harm."[59]

POTENTIAL HARMS OF PRICE REDUCTION

A different type of concern is presented by a potential SSO conspiracy to depress the price paid to suppliers. The case of *Sony Electronics, Inc. v. Soundview Technologies, Inc.* involved standards for the "V-chip" technology in television sets that allows parents to block violent or sexually explicit programming.[60]

---

56. *In re Union Oil Co. of California*, No. 9305, ¶¶ 9, 10, 26, 31, 61, 63 (F.T.C. Nov. 25, 2003), http://www.ftc.gov/os/2003/11/031126unionoil.pdf, *rev'd*, No. 9305 (F.T.C. July 7, 2004); FTC Statement, *In re Union Oil Co. of California*, Docket No. 9305 (June 10, 2005), www.ftc.gov/os/adjpro/d9305/050802statement.pdf.

57. *Rambus, Inc. v. Infineon Technologies AG*, 318 F.3d 1081, 1102 (Fed. Cir. 2003).

58. *In re Rambus*, No. 9302, 2006 WL 2330117, at 5–6, 8, 50, 67, 104, 118 (Aug. 2, 2006).

59. *Rambus Inc. v. F.T.C.*, 522 F.3d 456, 466–67 (D.C. Cir. 2008). For a different analysis, see *Broadcom Corp. v. Qualcomm Inc.*, 501 F.3d 297, 314 (3d Cir. 2007) (denying a motion to dismiss since a false promise of RAND licensing could "harm[] the competitive process by obscuring the costs of including proprietary technology in a standard and increasing the likelihood that patent rights will confer monopoly power on the patent holder").

60. 157 F. Supp. 2d 180 (D. Conn. 2001).

The plaintiff, Soundview, alleged that members of an industry association agreed to reduce the price for licenses for a Soundview patent needed for the standard. An SSO subcommittee found that Soundview possessed the patent most likely to be infringed in the standard's operation. Although Soundview informed the SSO that it would license its patent "on a nonexclusive, nondiscriminatory basis," the organization allegedly did not respond to this offer.[61]

The SSO then apparently agreed on a uniform price for a license for Soundview's technology of 5 cents per television set. The court found that this adequately alleged *monopsony* harm, by which a powerful buyer reduces the price of goods it purchases. Although SSO members did not purchase fewer television sets as a result of the alleged conspiracy to reduce price, the price reductions could have harmed innovation. The court initially relied on the presence of these "complex questions" in refusing to dismiss Soundview's case.[62] Although the court later granted summary judgment against Soundview (because SSO members' technology did not infringe its patent), the case nonetheless provides the most direct illustration of potentially anticompetitive monopsony harms.[63]

ANNOUNCEMENT OF MAXIMUM ROYALTIES

A related development involved the announcement by SSO members, before a standard's adoption, of their most restrictive licensing terms. The SSO VMEbus International Trade Association (VITA) developed computer architecture standards enabling engineers to design systems used in ultrasound machines, semiconductor manufacturing equipment, and weapons systems radar. VITA's experiment with RAND licensing was unsuccessful, with members demanding excessively high royalties that delayed or blocked standards.[64] As a result, VITA revised its patent policy and sought approval in the form of a business review letter, by which a party asks the Department of Justice's Antitrust Division to review proposed conduct and state its enforcement intentions.[65]

One element of the VITA policy required members to make a "good faith and reasonable inquiry" into its patents and disclose any patents or applications that they believed could become essential to the specification being developed. Members also were required to specify the maximum royalty rate (in dollars or

---

61. *Id.* at 181–82.

62. *Id.* at 183–86, 190.

63. *Sony Electronics, Inc. v. Soundview Technologies, Inc.*, 281 F. Supp. 2d 399, 402 (D. Conn. 2003).

64. VITA Letter, at 1–4.

65. 28 C.F.R. § 50.6. The letter addressed VITA and its standards development subcommittee, VSO.

percentage of sales price) and the most restrictive nonprice licensing terms they would request.[66]

Thomas Barnett, the head of the Antitrust Division, began his analysis by explaining that the Division analyzes most standard-setting activities under the Rule of Reason.[67] He also pointed to the difficulties of holdup, explaining that SSO members "can choose among multiple substitute technological solutions" early in the process. In contrast, after a standard is developed, "it can be extremely expensive or even impossible" to substitute technologies, often requiring "the entire standard-setting process . . . to be repeated." Barnett applauded VITA's new policy, concluding that it would allow the group to evaluate technologies not only on technical merit but also on licensing terms. In addition, he did not worry about licensees forcing a price reduction since the policy prohibited the joint negotiation or discussion of licensing terms. Barnett concluded that the Division "has no present intention to take antitrust enforcement action" against VITA's new policies.[68]

RAND REFUSAL

The final development constitutes the most aggressive government prosecution of SSO activity to date. In January 2008, the FTC announced a complaint against and settlement with Negotiated Data Solutions (N-Data). Negotiated Data Solutions licensed patents used in equipment employing Ethernet, a networking standard "used by almost every American consumer who owns a computer." This technology enables devices in a local area network to "automatically configure themselves to optimize their communication." The company's predecessor had committed to license its technology for a one-time royalty of $1,000 per licensee. But N-Data later demanded royalties "far in excess of that commitment."[69]

By a vote of 3-2, the FTC challenged N-Data's action. It did not allege a violation of the Sherman Act but instead claimed an unfair method of competition and unfair act or practice under Section 5 of the Federal Trade Commission Act. The majority asserted that N-Data's behavior harmed consumers and businesses

---

66. VITA Letter, at 5–6.

67. The analysis would differ if the standard-setting process was "used as a sham to cloak naked price-fixing or bid rigging." *Id.* at 8.

68. *Id.* at 8–10.

69. FTC, *FTC Challenges Patent Holder's Refusal to Meet Commitment to License Patents Covering 'Ethernet' Standard Used in Virtually All Personal Computers in U.S.*, Jan. 23, 2008, http://www.ftc.gov/opa/2008/01/ethernet.shtm; FTC, Statement, *In re Negotiated Data Solutions LLC*, File No. 0510094, http://www.ftc.gov/os/caselist/0510094/080122statement.pdf.

and explained that its exercise of its "unique" authority was needed to "preserv[e] a free and dynamic marketplace."[70]

Deborah Platt Majoras, the former Chairman of the FTC, dissented, worrying that the majority did not "identif[y] a meaningful limiting principle" for determining an unfair method of competition. She also found no allegation of improper or exclusionary conduct and questioned whether N-Data had market power.[71] Then-Commissioner (and later Chairman) William Kovacic also dissented, stating that the FTC's challenge would have an unacknowledged effect on state enforcement and that the majority's failure to distinguish between its two theories of liability—unfair methods of competition and unfair acts or practices—masked weaknesses in its challenge.[72]

Having set forth the recent guideposts in standard-setting analysis, I next explore how such activity should be analyzed. Standard setting organizations potentially offer anticompetitive effects such as allowing firms to boycott rivals and reducing the price paid to suppliers. On the other hand, they provide significant procompetitive justifications in increasing consumer choice and preventing holdup.

ANTICOMPETITIVE CONCERNS

Though SSOs do not usually result in significant anticompetitive effects, there is a range of activity that could potentially cause antitrust concern. First, SSOs could restrict product diversity and consumer choice by creating an unnecessary standard and excluding certain products. As a leading treatise explains: "It is not clear . . . why the world would need consistent rules for steak knives, or coffee mugs, or couches."[73] Second, SSOs could increase prices. Such a result could flow from, for example, product safety restrictions or licensing board certifications.[74]

For our purposes, these two concerns are not central. In particular, the prevalence of interface standards that promote interoperability, and are the focus of this chapter, will almost always outweigh these concerns. The absence of interoperability standards will often lead to fewer products in the marketplace, diminishing any concerns of reduced diversity. In addition, unnecessary standardization does not appear to be a significant problem, and SSOs are far more likely to reduce price and make products available than increase price.

---

70. *Id.*

71. Dissenting Statement of Chairman Majoras, *In re Negotiated Data Solutions LLC*, File No. 0510094, http://www.ftc.gov/os/caselist/0510094/080122majoras.pdf.

72. Dissenting Statement of Commissioner Kovacic, *In re Negotiated Data Solutions LLC*, File No. 0510094, http://www.ftc.gov/os/caselist/0510094/080122kovacic.pdf.

73. HOVENKAMP, JANIS & LEMLEY, at 35–9.

74. *Id.* at 35–8 to 35–9.

A third concern is that SSOs could increase collusion in the downstream market for goods sold to consumers. By bringing together rivals and aggregating information, the organizations provide a ready-made setting for collusion. Standardized products also facilitate collusion by making it easier to monitor rivals' activity.[75] To be clear, just because SSOs agree on standards does not mean they will agree to set prices for the products they sell. But the antitrust agencies should be sensitive to this important concern and challenge any such behavior. As former Chairman Majoras correctly observed: "summary condemnation is almost certainly warranted" when "manufacturing rivals cross over the line from discussing the price of technology they will 'buy' if they choose a particular standard and start discussing—and fixing—the price of the products they sell."[76]

A fourth concern, arising in SSOs in which membership is restricted to a subset of an industry, involves a concerted refusal to deal with competitors, or boycott. Many of these *closed* SSOs have legitimate reasons for their exclusion such as preserving neutrality, reducing concerns of capture, limiting free-riding, or failing to meet reasonable requirements.[77] But in certain cases, organizations could be forced to admit outsiders. Such a remedy should be limited to cases in which SSOs (1) exclude rivals, (2) offer members a significant market advantage that they could not otherwise obtain, and (3) lack legitimate business reasons for their exclusion.[78]

The final concern deserves more thorough discussion. Industry members could exercise *monopsony* power that would depress the price of patented inputs.

MONOPSONY

The most frequent concern raised about SSOs is their potential to cause monopsony harms. Monopsony is the lesser-known mirror image to monopoly. Monopoly occurs when a seller has the power to restrict sales and thereby increase the price paid by consumers. Monopsony takes place when a powerful buyer, by limiting its purchases, reduces the price it pays to suppliers.[79]

This concern could apply to SSOs since licensing rules and royalty discussions could allow SSO members (the buyers) to force patent owners (the suppliers) to

---

75. *Id.* at 35–8.

76. Majoras, at 10. Relatedly, if the organization is only a sham for cartel-type activities, per se condemnation would be appropriate.

77. HOVENKAMP, JANIS & LEMLEY, at 35–21 to 35–22.

78. *Id.* at 35–23.

79. Jonathan M. Jacobson & Gary J. Dorman, *Joint Purchasing, Monopsony, and Antitrust*, 36 ANTITRUST BULL. 1, 5 (1991) [hereinafter Jacobson & Dorman, *Joint Purchasing*].

reduce the royalties they can charge. Technically, the activity in SSOs would resemble an *oligopsony* because it involves multiple buyers.[80] But I will employ the monopsony term because of its prevalence.

In settings in which SSO members have the power to reduce license prices below competitive levels, monopsony threatens two harms. First, it could have adverse effects on allocative efficiency, reducing the quantity and price of the input below competitive levels. Second, it could have effects on dynamic efficiency, reducing innovation. Before showing why these effects are not likely, I explore four characteristics of SSOs that dramatically reduce the monopsony concern.[81]

The first stems from the composition of the bodies. Standard setting organizations consist of not only licensees but also licensors. Some parties, in fact, may play both roles depending on the setting. The presence of licensors in the negotiation process diminishes the likelihood that SSOs would excessively reduce price.[82]

Second, the timing of interactions between licensees and suppliers reduces the possibility of monopsony. Before selection, SSO members do not know the standard that will be selected or the identity of the owner.[83] As a result, the organization deals not with a specified party but with an array of potential suppliers.

Third, the nature of SSO interactions minimizes monopsony concerns. The typical setting involves suppliers announcing their adherence to RAND terms or specification of maximum royalties. But such individual declarations do not resemble joint monopsony action depressing royalties. Antitrust concern also is lessened since unilateral announcements of licensing terms do not satisfy the concerted-action requirement of Section 1 of the Sherman Act.

Fourth, the power of patentee suppliers distinguishes SSOs from other potential monopsony settings. A party owning a patent essential to a standard's implementation has far more bargaining power than the typical seller confronting a monopsony. It could abstain from joining the SSO, refuse to license its patent, and hold up the standard. Any maximum royalties set by the SSO thus would not affect nonmember patentees. The voluntary nature of SSOs and importance of *every* essential patent reading onto a standard thus reduce the monopsony concern.

---

80. *Id.* at 6; *see also* J. Gregory Sidak, *Patent Holdup and Oligopsonistic Collusion in Standard-Setting Organizations*, at 17–18, http://ssrn.com/abstract=1081997 (distinguishing between monopsony, in which "a single firm purchases the entire market supply of the good," and oligopsony, in which "each of several firms purchases a substantial share of the market supply for an input").

81. For an argument that there is a greater risk of oligopsony than I discuss, see Sidak.

82. Gil Ohana et al., *Disclosure and Negotiation of Licensing Terms Prior to Adoption of Industry Standards: Preventing Another Patent Ambush?*, 24 EUROPEAN COMPETITION L. REV. 644, 654 (2003).

83. Mark A. Lemley, *Ten Things To Do About Patent Holdup of Standards (and One Not To)*, 48 B.C. L. REV. 149, 162 (2007) [hereinafter Lemley, *Patent Holdup*].

Relatedly, if SSO members reduce prices too much, patentees will be discouraged from joining the organization, making it less likely that it would know about potentially relevant patents.[84]

Aside from these four general characteristics, the primary harm linked to monopsony—reduced purchases—is absent in this setting. A brief detour into rudimentary economics shows that in monopsony cases, buyers' reduced purchases artificially depress price. The reason flows from the *upward-sloped supply curve*. A supply curve depicts the quantity of goods that a seller provides at a specified price. In the case of monopsony, the supply curve slopes upward because goods are scarce. In other words, buyers purchase the lowest-cost items first and higher-cost goods later.[85] Because buyers would pay more for additional units, the price rises as the purchases increase. For example, in the labor market, employers pay higher wages to employ additional workers because of constraints such as geography and talent.[86]

For our purposes, the relevant concern would be that SSO members are able to depress the price paid to patentees below the competitive level by cutting back on licensing. But a quick look at the supply curve reveals that monopsony does not explain such behavior. The supply curve for patented goods is flat. Nearly all the costs attributed to supplying patented items flow from the initial costs of creation, with a zero marginal cost of producing additional items.[87] As a result, buyers' reductions in purchased items would not lower the price received by the sellers. Because the supply curve is flat, any reduction in purchases does not affect price.

Casting for analogies, the scenario is less like a monopsony and more like an *all-or-nothing* scenario. In such a setting, buyers do not reduce their purchases but aggregate them and award them to a single seller, inviting the sellers to bid against each other.[88] The all-or-nothing label is explained by the consequences of the transaction: the winning bidder gets to supply all the buyers' purchases, while the others get nothing. In contrast to monopsony's reduction in social welfare, the all-or-nothing deal, by lowering the prices charged by sellers with market power, can improve welfare.[89]

---

84. Majoras, at 9.

85. Jonathan M. Jacobson & Gary J. Dorman, *Monopsony Revisited: A Comment on Blair & Harrison*, 37 ANTITRUST BULL. 151, 156 (1992).

86. Jacobson & Dorman, *Joint Purchasing*, at 13.

87. Hillary Greene, *Buyer Price-Fixing and Intellectual Property*, ¶ 42, 2008 DUKE L. & TECH. REV., http://intprop.law.duke.edu/documents/2008/Greene%20CLE%20Article.pdf. The presence of nontrivial transaction costs makes the conclusion modestly more nuanced.

88. Gail F. Levine, *B2Bs, E-Commerce, & the All-or-Nothing Deal*, 28 RUTGERS COMPUTER & TECH. L.J. 383, 402 (2002).

89. *Id.* at 403–06 (explaining that buyers can force sellers' prices down to marginal cost and that consumers could thereby benefit).

In the SSO setting, even if buyers reduce a supplier's price, they tend not to reduce the number of items purchased. In fact, disclosure and negotiations before a standard's selection are designed to *increase* its implementation, which would *expand* the number of licenses.[90] This is directly contrary to monopsony's goal.[91]

The primary concern of monopsony—the welfare loss of fewer inputs purchased—thus does not apply to IP. At the time of the activity, there is no static allocative loss of resources not being employed in their highest-value use.[92]

Nonetheless, there may be a dynamic, long-term concern. Dynamic efficiency contemplates the employment of resources in their highest-valued use over time. It is tightly linked to innovation. The concern with monopsony is that a reduction in price paid to patentees could lower innovation incentives. Future inventors might be dissuaded if they knew the royalties they could obtain would be reduced. Is such a result likely?

In the vast majority of cases, it is not. Innovators substantially benefit from having their patents reflected in standards widely adopted in an industry. Any effects of depressed licensing rates thus tend to be significantly outweighed by more numerous licenses. By reducing the number of standards, holdup threatens "a more immediate adverse impact on innovators' efforts."[93]

Because of innovation's importance and the *possibility* that it could be affected by SSO members' purchasing power, patentees should be allowed the opportunity to offer evidence of reduced innovation incentives. If they can introduce specific evidence that SSO members have buying power and that their joint depression of prices has reduced innovation incentives, such anticompetitive effects could be considered. But in nearly all cases, such a showing is not likely.

PROCOMPETITIVE JUSTIFICATIONS

SSOs

Despite their potential anticompetitive effects, SSOs more typically offer (as discussed throughout the chapter) an array of powerful procompetitive justifications.[94] First, they can improve product quality by collecting information related to safety

---

90. Ohana et al., at 654.

91. Preventing holdup also may align with patentee manufacturers' preference for first-mover advantages in arriving quickly on the market rather than high royalties.

92. J. Gregory Sidak & Daniel F. Spulber, *Deregulatory Takings and Breach of the Regulatory Contract*, 71 N.Y.U. L. Rev. 851, 935 (1996).

93. Ohana et al., at 654.

94. *See generally* Michael A. Carrier, *Why Antitrust Should Defer to the Intellectual Property Rules of Standard-Setting Organizations: A Commentary on Teece and Sherry*, 87 Minn. L. Rev. 2019 (2003).

and performance records.[95] Second, interoperability standards enable firms to use a common platform and can reduce price and enhance competition in the marketplace. Third, the standards contribute to a greater realization of network effects and prevent buyers from being stranded in a product that loses the standards war.[96] Fourth, they prevent holdup and create markets that might not otherwise exist.

Further strengthening the procompetitive benefits, the industries in which SSOs have developed are those with the greatest potential for bottlenecks, patent thickets, and thwarted innovation. A study conducted by Professor Mark Lemley demonstrated that SSOs have concentrated "in precisely those industries where the unconstrained enforcement of patents could be most damaging to innovation," namely, software, Internet, telecommunications, and semiconductors.[97] The danger of holdup is more pronounced in these industries since a single product may require licenses for hundreds or thousands of patents.[98]

Just as ominous, the industries are marked by cumulative innovation, with one generation's patented invention built on those of previous generations.[99] The clearing of patent thickets and fostering of cumulative innovation and new markets through SSOs offers perhaps the most powerful benefits for competition and innovation. Significant to begin with, the procompetitive benefits of SSOs are magnified in removing the potentially explosive landmines of the patent system.

IP Rules

Not only are the SSOs themselves procompetitive, but their IP rules are as well. The rules are designed to address the issue of holdup. As stated before, an SSO often can choose among an array of alternative technologies before a standard's selection. But after the standard has been chosen and the organization has invested in technologies to implement it, it has less flexibility to switch. At that point, participants can charge higher-than-expected royalties knowing that the members are not easily able to abandon the technology. As the example of the VITA SSO revealed, even promises to license patents on a reasonable and nondiscriminatory basis will not prevent holdup when the details are left vague and are the subject of dispute after the standard has been adopted. The cases involving failure to disclose even more strongly demonstrate the dangers of holdup. For this reason, search, disclosure, and licensing rules are procompetitive.

Search rules merely require SSO members to search for IP that might read on a standard. Most SSOs do not impose this obligation because of the burden it

---

95. HOVENKAMP, JANIS & LEMLEY, at 35–10.

96. Shapiro, at 88.

97. Lemley, *SSOs*, at 1954.

98. *Id.* at 1953; Lemley, *Patent Holdup*, at 150.

99. Scotchmer, *Standing on the Shoulders of Giants*, at 29.

would impose.[100] But even when they do, such an obligation would not lead to anticompetitive effects. Even if a broad obligation to search dissuades potential patentees from entering the organization, this does not constitute anticompetitive effect.

Disclosure rules inform SSO members deciding on a standard of the IP that would be implicated by the selection of certain standards. Disclosure rules generally differ from information-sharing arrangements that antitrust courts have condemned since the information divulged prevents the strategic hiding and ex post exploitation of IP. The American National Standards Institute recommends that all accredited standards bodies require early disclosure, which provides notice, gives an opportunity to evaluate the technology, and offers time to negotiate license terms.[101]

Licensing rules are even more essential in avoiding the holdup problem. They offer a procompetitive justification by circumventing a potential bottleneck and contributing to the creation of a product that might not otherwise exist. RAND licensing aims to address holdup by requiring patentees to agree, before the standard's selection, to reasonable licensing.

Because the requirement is vague, some SSOs have required participants to provide more specific terms, such as the maximum royalties they would charge. A simple announcement of terms under which patents would be licensed does not constitute an antitrust violation since there is no agreement between rivals. And even discussion of the terms in the SSO should be evaluated under the Rule of Reason. As Professor Mark Lemley explains, "[T]he parties are going to have to have these conversations individually or collectively anyway" and it is preferable to have them before the standard's adoption.[102]

In its Technology Transfer Guidelines, the European Commission recognized the benefits of SSO members negotiating licensing terms, stating that parties are "free to negotiate and fix royalties for the technology package and each technology's share of the royalties either before or after the standard is set." It explained that such agreement "is inherent in the establishment of the standard . . . and cannot in itself be considered restrictive of competition." And it highlighted the efficiencies from agreeing to royalties before the standard's

---

100. A thorough search is costly and time-consuming, particularly because of the evolving nature of standards under development and subjectivity involved in determining whether a patent reads on a standard. Anne Layne-Farrar, *Antitrust and Intellectual Property Rights: Assessing the Link Between Standards and Market Power*, 21 ANTITRUST 42, 45 (2007).

101. American National Standards Institute, *Guidelines for Implementation of the ANSI Patent Policy* 5 (2003), http://www.niso.org/committees/OpenURL/PATPOL.pdf; *see generally* Weiser, at 22.

102. Lemley, *Patent Holdup*, at 162.

adoption to "avoid the choice of the standard conferring a significant degree of market power."[103]

In U.S. law, the IP rules of SSOs bear some resemblance to other types of activity that have received substantial antitrust deference. In one case, the Supreme Court upheld blanket licenses that allowed licensees to perform any of the millions of copyrighted musical works in the package, thereby reducing transaction costs and creating "a different product."[104] In a second category, the antitrust agencies have upheld nearly all cross-license agreements and patent pools they have examined because they resolve bottlenecks among owners of blocking patents that could have otherwise prevented the use of products.[105]

PROPOSAL

Given SSOs' significant procompetitive justifications, courts and the antitrust agencies should consider their activity under the Rule of Reason. The sole exception would be SSO members' joint decision to fix prices for the goods they *sell* to consumers. Such activity is not needed for standards development and has severe anticompetitive effects. As a result, it should be per se illegal.

Three other actions should be closely monitored. The first involves the type of deception that occurred in the Dell and Unocal cases. This activity could demonstrate attempted monopolization under Section 2 of the Sherman Act. Such a claim requires a plaintiff to demonstrate "(1) that the defendant has engaged in predatory or anticompetitive conduct with (2) a specific intent to monopolize and (3) a dangerous probability of achieving monopoly power."[106] For our purposes, a plaintiff making this claim thus must prove factors such as causation (with the deception resulting in a standard's adoption or higher royalties), control of the market, and intentional conduct.[107]

---

103. Guidelines on the Application of Article 81 of the EC Treaty to Technology Transfer Agreements (EC) ¶ 225, 2004 O.J. (C 101) 1, 39, http://europa.eu/eur-lex/pri/en/oj/dat/2004/c_101/c_10120040427en00020042.pdf.

104. *Broadcast Music, Inc. v. Columbia Broadcasting System, Inc.*, 441 U.S. 1, 5, 20–22 (1979).

105. Letter from Joel I. Klein, Assistant Attorney General, Department of Justice to Gerrard R. Beeney, Sullivan & Cromwell (Dec. 16, 1998), http://www.usdoj.gov/atr/public/busreview/2121.htm (DVD patent pool); Letter from Joel I. Klein, Acting Assistant Attorney General, Department of Justice to Gerrard R. Beeney, Sullivan & Cromwell (June 26, 1997), http://www.usdoj.gov/atr/public/busreview/1170.htm (MPEG pool).

106. *Spectrum Sports, Inc. v. McQuillan*, 506 U.S. 447, 456 (1993).

107. HOVENKAMP, JANIS & LEMLEY, at 35–44 to 35–51. The case of manipulation similarly should require plaintiffs to demonstrate a subversion of the process that results in competitive harm. *Id.* at 35–36.

The second activity involves a boycott. A closed SSO of industry competitors should be opened when it excludes rivals, offers members a significant market advantage they could not otherwise obtain, and lacks a legitimate business reason for exclusion.[108]

The third action occurs when patentees demonstrate that SSO members have buying power and that their joint depression of prices has reduced innovation incentives. In that case, such an anticompetitive effect should be balanced against the SSO's procompetitive justifications. Such balancing between reduced innovation incentives and the prevention of holdup will admittedly be challenging. And it will not occur in many cases. But given the importance of the values on each side of the scale, courts must consider both. Given the demonstrated procompetitive effects and multiple hurdles to monopsony power, the justifications should prevail in nearly all cases. Nonetheless, a legitimate showing of reduced innovation incentives could conceivably carry the day.

Absent these situations, SSO activity should be upheld under the Rule of Reason. Standard setting organizations serve significant procompetitive purposes in fostering compatibility, enhancing competition, contributing to network effects, and creating markets that might not otherwise exist.[109] These benefits are even more potent given that the industries in which SSOs have developed are those with the greatest potential for bottlenecks and thwarted innovation. The IP rules of SSOs are procompetitive as well. Search, disclosure, and licensing rules eliminate ambiguity and prevent holdup, the most significant concern facing SSOs. For that reason, courts and the antitrust agencies should uphold nearly all such rules.

CONCLUSION

In short, the gathering of rivals in SSOs might, at first glance, present concerns for antitrust. Members in the organizations could boycott rivals. They could manipulate the process to hurt competitors. They could engage in downstream collusion, raising the price for consumers. And they could exercise buying power to reduce innovation incentives.

But in the vast majority of cases, these concerns will not be paramount. Standards usually increase competition and offer consumers a greater range of products.

---

108. *Id.* at 35–23.

109. Recognizing these benefits, Congress provided for Rule-of-Reason treatment (and a reduction in potential liability from treble to single damages) for standards-related activity. Standards Development Organization Advancement Act of 2004, Pub. L. No. 108–237, 118 Stat. 661, 15 U.S.C. §§ 4301–4305 (2004). The Act, however, was limited to formal SSOs (as opposed to informal consortia) and did not protect the organizations' members.

They increase network effects and allow the creation of products that might not otherwise be produced. And in markets that tend to coalesce around one product, jointly set standards are superior to the alternative of a dominant firm's de facto standard. For while de facto standards protected by IP allow a single firm to control a technology, SSOs allow multiple parties to make products complying with a standard.[110]

The IP rules of SSOs also are important in reducing holdup. A patentee's power may exponentially increase after the organization has adopted a standard and its members have invested in technologies to implement it. Requiring members to disclose relevant patents provides essential information to the SSO. Nailing down licensing terms increases this information and reduces surprise attributed to holdup.

Consumers will typically benefit from standard-setting and the IP rules of SSOs. As a result, courts and the agencies should apply Rule-of-Reason analysis to the activity. While they should carefully scrutinize boycotts, collusion in selling products, and stifled innovation, they should foster competition and innovation by upholding nearly all standard-setting activity.

---

110. Lemley, *SSOs*, at 1901; Gifford, at 359.

15. UNSETTLING DRUG PATENT SETTLEMENTS: A FRAMEWORK FOR PRESUMPTIVE ILLEGALITY

Hatch-Waxman Act 347
    General Purposes 347
    Competition-promoting Framework 351
    2003 Revisions 353
    Mixed Success 355
Cardizem 357
Schering-Plough 358
Tamoxifen 361
Analysis of Courts' Approaches 363
    Importance of Settlements 364
    Settlements and Innovation 365
    Presumption of Patent Validity 366
    Patent Scope 368
    Natural Status 369
Proposal 370
    Regulatory Regime: Existence and Equilibrium 371
    Regulatory Regime: Effectiveness 372
    Antitrust Harm 373
    Reverse Payments 377
    Rebuttal 378
Conclusion 382

Consumers spend billions of dollars on prescription drugs. Senior citizens choose between medicine and food. Federal and state governments suffer from rapidly growing expenses. General Motors estimates that it increases the price of its cars by $1,500 because of health-care costs.[1]

In short, a tidal wave of high drug prices is crashing across the U.S. economy. One of the primary culprits has been the increase in agreements by which brand-name drug manufacturers and generic firms have settled patent litigation. The framework for such agreements has been the Hatch-Waxman Act, which Congress enacted in 1984. One of the Act's goals was to provide incentives for generics to challenge brand-name patents. But brand firms have recently paid generics millions of dollars to drop their lawsuits and refrain from entering the market.

---

1. Eduardo Porter, *Japanese Cars, American Retirees*, N.Y. TIMES, May 19, 2006, at C1.

Of course, firms with valid patents can charge high prices and exclude competitors. That is the intended purpose of the patent system, and is especially needed for the difficult, expensive process of developing marketable drugs. At the same time, however, companies cannot lawfully use invalid patents to restrict competition. Challenges to invalid patents, in fact, benefit consumers and reduce prices.

Certain settlement agreements could be justified by objective assessments of the patent's validity. But in recent years, agreements have more frequently included large payments from brand patentees to generic challengers. These *reverse payments*, which differ from typical licensing payments that flow from challengers to patentees, may even exceed what the generic could have earned by entering the market. Further raising suspicion, many of the patents are not valid. In the 1990s, generics won nearly 75 percent of their challenges to patents on drugs such as Prozac, Zantac, Taxol, and Plantinol. Consumers saved almost ten billion dollars from the introduction of generic competition on these four products alone.[2]

Despite the concerns presented by reverse payment settlements, courts have recently blessed them. They have explained that the agreements reduce costs and increase innovation. They have referred to settlements as "natural by-products" of the Act. And they have pointed to patents' presumption of validity in demonstrating the agreements' reasonableness. Although scholars and the Federal Trade Commission (FTC), which enforces the antitrust laws in the drug industry, have voiced strong arguments against courts' leniency, these have fallen on judicial deaf ears.

In this chapter, I explain why settlement agreements with reverse payments should be presumptively illegal. I apply the framework that the Supreme Court articulated in *Verizon Communications v. Law Offices of Curtis V. Trinko,*[3] which underscored the importance in antitrust analysis of a regulatory regime covering the challenged activity. In particular, the Hatch-Waxman Act provides Congress's views on innovation and competition in the drug industry, freeing courts from the thorny task of reconciling the patent and antitrust laws.

By encouraging generic patent challenges but also providing for patent term extensions and marketing exclusivity periods, the Act offered a delicate balance between competition and innovation. Unfortunately, mechanisms that Congress employed to encourage patent challenges—such as an exclusivity period for the

---

2. *Generic Pharmaceuticals: Marketplace Access and Consumer Issues: Hearing Before the S. Comm. on Commerce, Science, & Transportation,* 107th Cong. 61 (2002) (statement of Kathleen D. Jaeger), http://frwebgate.access.gpo.gov/cgi-bin/getdoc.cgi?dbname=107_senate_hearings&docid=f:90155.pdf; *see generally* Prepared Statement of the Federal Trade Commission before the Senate Special Committee on Aging, *Barriers to Generic Entry,* at 10, http://www.ftc.gov/os/2006/07/P052103Barriersto GenericEntryTestimonySenate07202006.pdf [hereinafter *Barriers to Generic Entry*].

3. 540 U.S. 398 (2004).

first generic to challenge validity—have been twisted into barriers preventing competition. Antitrust can play a central role in resuscitating the drafters' intentions and promoting competition.

Reverse payments for generics to delay entering the market also are concerning because of the parties' aligned incentives. By delaying generic entry, the brand firm can increase its monopoly profits. It can then use a portion of these profits to pay the generic more than it would have received by entering the market. From an antitrust perspective, these payments for delay threaten to divide markets, a particularly egregious offense eliminating competition between rivals.

Given the Act's clear purpose to promote patent challenges, as well as the parties' aligned incentives and the severe anticompetitive potential of reverse payments, courts should treat such settlements as presumptively illegal. If the parties can demonstrate that the payments represent a reasonable assessment of litigation success, then they can rebut this presumption. If not, courts should conclude that the agreements violate the antitrust laws. Such a conclusion applies not only to final settlements, which dispose of patent litigation, but also interim settlements, which do not end the litigation but tend to prolong it and delay entry.

This chapter begins by introducing the Hatch-Waxman Act, exploring its purpose, text, and mixed success. It then discusses three representative cases illustrating courts' increased leniency toward reverse payment agreements. In justifying a framework for presumptive illegality, this chapter explains the importance of the relevant regulatory framework. It demonstrates the ineffectiveness of the Act's competition mechanisms. And it focuses on reverse payments, describing their uniquely concerning aspects and potentially severe anticompetitive harm. Finally, it shows how the settling parties can rebut the presumption of illegality.[4]

HATCH-WAXMAN ACT

General Purposes

In 1984, Congress enacted the Hatch-Waxman Amendments to the Food, Drug and Cosmetic Act (Hatch-Waxman Act).[5] In doing so, the legislature sought to increase generic competition and foster innovation.[6]

---

4. This chapter focuses on judicial, as opposed to legislative, solutions for reverse payments.

5. The Act was originally called the Waxman-Hatch Act. Kevin J. McGough, *Preserving the Compromise: The Plain Meaning of Waxman-Hatch Market Exclusivity*, 45 FOOD DRUG COSM. L.J. 487, 487 (1990).

6. Drug Price Competition and Patent Term Restoration Act of 1984, Pub. L. No. 98–417, 98 Stat. 1585 (1984), *codified as amended* at 21 U.S.C. § 355 (1994).

First, Congress sought to promote generic competition. Generic drugs have the same active ingredients, dosage, administration, performance, and safety as patented brand drugs.[7] Despite the equivalence, generic manufacturers were required, at the time of the Act, to engage in lengthy and expensive trials to demonstrate safety and effectiveness. The FDA approval process took several years, and because the required tests constituted infringement, generics could not begin the process during the patent term.[8] They therefore waited until the end of the term to begin these activities, which prevented them from entering the market until two or three years after the patent's expiration. At the time Congress enacted Hatch-Waxman, there was no generic equivalent for roughly 150 drugs whose patent term had lapsed.[9]

The drafters of the Act lamented the "practical extension" of the patentee's "monopoly position" beyond expiration.[10] Relatedly, they sought to ensure the provision of "low-cost, generic drugs for millions of Americans."[11] Generic competition would save consumers, as well as the federal and state governments, millions of dollars each year. And it would "do more to contain the cost of elderly care than perhaps anything else this Congress has passed."[12]

One of the tools used by the legislature to accelerate generic entry was a resuscitation of the experimental use defense. In the case of *Roche Products, Inc. v. Bolar Pharmaceutical Co.*, the Federal Circuit had held that the generic firm committed infringement by experimenting with the active ingredient in the brand's patented sleeping pill so as to facilitate FDA testing.[13] The court explained that the generic's use was "solely for business reasons and not for amusement, to satisfy idle curiosity, or for strictly philosophical inquiry." In addition, it refused to interpret the defense to cover "scientific inquiry" when "that inquiry has definite, cognizable, and not insubstantial commercial purposes."[14]

Congress reversed this holding in the Hatch-Waxman Act. It exempted from infringement the manufacture, use, or sale of a patented invention for uses "reasonably related to the development and submission of information" under a federal law regulating the manufacture, use, or sale of drugs.[15]

---

7. U.S. Dep't of Health & Human Servs., Food & Drug Admin., Center for Drug Eval. & Research, *Generic Drugs: Questions and Answers* (2007), http://www.fda.gov/buyon-lineguide/generics_q&a.htm.

8. Congressional Budget Office, *How Increased Competition from Generic Drugs Has Affected Prices and Returns in the Pharmaceutical Industry*, at 38 (1998) [CBO Study].

9. H.R. REP. No. 98–857, pt. 1, at 17 (1984), *reprinted in* 1984 U.S.C.C.A.N. 2647, 2650.

10. H.R. REP. No. 98–857, pt. 2, at 4 (1984), *reprinted in* 1984 U.S.C.C.A.N. 2686, 2688.

11. 130 CONG. REC. 24427 (Sept. 6, 1984) (statement of Rep. Waxman).

12. H.R. REP. No. 98-857, pt. 1, at 17.

13. 733 F.2d 858 (Fed. Cir. 1984).

14. *Id.* at 863.

15. 35 U.S.C. § 271(e)(1)(2004). In 2005, the Supreme Court broadly interpreted the exception, finding that it covered activities that did not ultimately lead to information

Congress also sought to promote generic competition by creating a new process for obtaining FDA approval. Before Hatch-Waxman, generic companies that offered products identical to approved drugs needed to independently prove safety and efficacy. One reason that generics chose not to bring products to the market after a patent's expiration was the expense and time involved in replicating clinical studies. As discussed in more detail in the next section, the Act created a new type of drug application that allowed the generic to rely on the brand's studies, thereby accelerating entry.

Also discussed below, the legislature increased competition by fashioning market exclusivity. In particular, it encouraged generics to challenge invalid or noninfringed patents by creating a 180-day period of marketing exclusivity for the first generic firm to do so.

In addition to promoting generic competition, the Act increased incentives for innovation. Before 1962, companies had only needed to demonstrate a drug's safety to gain FDA approval. But amendments to the Federal Food, Drug, and Cosmetic Act (FDCA) in 1962 required manufacturers to show not only that a drug was safe but also that it was effective for its intended use.[16] As a result, brand firms were required to undertake additional years of testing and clinical trials after the patent's issuance. Such a development delayed commercialization and substantially eroded the effective patent term.[17]

The industry thus faced an "innovation crisis." The number of new chemical entities entering human testing fell 81 percent from the late 1950s until the late 1970s.[18] New drug compounds and dosage forms also decreased. Firms' R&D declined because of increased investments but reduced returns.[19] And U.S. drug companies shifted their research overseas.[20]

Much of this crisis was traced to the decline in the *effective patent life*, the period between FDA approval and patent expiration. This period was reduced as manufacturers engaged in more extensive tests, delaying the drug's marketing.

---

included in an FDA submission. *Merck KGaA v. Integra Lifesciences I, Ltd.*, 545 U.S. 193, 207 (2005).

16. Elizabeth Stotland Weiswasser & Scott D. Danzis, *The Hatch-Waxman Act: History, Structure, and Legacy*, 71 ANTITRUST L.J. 585, 588 (2003).

17. *Id.*

18. Maureen S. May et al., *New Drug Development During and After a Period of Regulatory Change: Clinical Research Activity of Major United States Pharmaceutical Firms, 1958–1979*, 33 CLINICAL PHARMACOLOGY THERAPEUTICS 691, 691 (1983).

19. John R. Virts & J. Fred Weston, *Returns to Research and Development in the U.S. Pharmaceutical Industry*, 1 MANAGERIAL & DECISION ECON. 103, 110 (1980).

20. JOHN W. EGAN ET AL., ECONOMICS OF THE PHARMACEUTICAL INDUSTRY 105–06 (1982). *See generally* James J. Wheaton, *Generic Competition and Pharmaceutical Innovation: The Drug Price Competition and Patent Term Restoration Act of 1984*, 35 CATH. U. L. REV. 433, 450 (1986).

Before the 1962 amendments, the effective patent life nearly matched the 17-year patent term. By 1981, it had fallen to less than 7 years.[21]

The legislature thus extended the patent term. The extension currently consists of half the time the drug is in clinical trials plus the period spent awaiting FDA approval after trials. The extension can last up to five years and, together with the remaining patent term, can give the patentee up to 14 years of protection.[22]

Congress also provided for periods of market exclusivity not based on patents. A company that offers a drug with a new active ingredient is entitled to either four or five years of exclusivity.[23] Because the FDA cannot receive generic applications during this period, the practical exclusivity period is extended by another two years, the time it typically takes the FDA to approve an application.[24] Similarly, new clinical investigations essential to approval receive three years of exclusivity.[25] The FDA has applied this form of exclusivity to new dosage forms, new uses, and adoption of over-the-counter status.[26]

The Act's drafters emphasized the equilibrium between competition and innovation. Representative Henry Waxman underscored the "fundamental balance of the bill"[27] and the Energy and Commerce Committee Report explained that allowing early generic challenges "fairly balanced" the exclusionary rights of patent owners with the "rights of third parties" to contest validity and market products not covered by the patent.[28] Similarly, the Judiciary Committee Report concluded that the Committee "has merely done what the Congress has traditionally done" in IP law: "balance the need to stimulate innovation against the goal of furthering the public interest."[29]

In fact, the equilibrium was even more finely calibrated than the traditional balance between innovation and competition that underlies IP law. For Congress placed on the innovation side of the ledger not only patent term extensions but also (1) nonpatent market exclusivity for new chemical entities and new clinical investigations and (2) an automatic 30-month stay for brand firms that sued

---

21. Wheaton, at 451–52.

22. 35 U.S.C. § 156(c), (g)(6); *see generally* Weiswasser & Danzis, at 591.

23. 21 U.S.C. § 355(j)(5)(F)(ii). The exclusivity period is four years for generic filers certifying patent invalidity or non-infringement and five years for other generic filers.

24. JOHN R. THOMAS, PHARMACEUTICAL PATENT LAW 350 (2005). As described more fully below, other factors (including the brand firm's automatic stay and litigation) increase the delay.

25. 21 U.S.C. § 355(C)(3)(E)(iii).

26. Elizabeth H. Dickinson, *FDA's Role in Making Exclusivity Determinations*, 54 FOOD & DRUG L.J. 195, 201 (1999).

27. 130 CONG. REC. 24425 (Sept. 6, 1984) (statement of Rep. Waxman).

28. H.R. REP. No. 98–857, pt. 1, at 28.

29. H.R. REP. No. 98–857, pt. 2, at 30.

generics that had challenged the patent's invalidity or claimed noninfringement. According to one of the chief negotiators, the exclusivity period for new drugs was "the key to the compromise."[30]

In short, Congress responded to the problems of insufficient generic entry and inadequate innovation through a carefully calibrated balance among patent term extension, nonpatent exclusivity, and generic competition.

Competition-promoting Framework

Of the policies underlying Hatch-Waxman, generic competition has engendered the most attention and concern. The antitrust issues that have arisen under the statute have flowed from provisions intended to expedite generic entry. To understand the relevant framework, it is necessary to explore the provisions of the Act, as well as the process by which the U.S. Food and Drug Administration (FDA) approves drugs. Neither of these offer the simplest regimes ever created.

A company that wishes to market a new drug must receive approval from the FDA. To do so, it files a New Drug Application (NDA), which consists of thousands of pages and includes information on numerous categories, including clinical trial data.[31]

The Hatch-Waxman Act allows generic firms to avoid the expensive and lengthy NDA process by filing an Abbreviated New Drug Application (ANDA). To do this, the applicant must show that its drug possesses the same active ingredient, route of administration, bioequivalence (rate and extent of drug absorption), and other characteristics of the brand. If it can make this showing, it can rely on the brand's safety and effectiveness studies, dispensing with the need for independent preclinical or clinical studies.[32]

NDA applicants also are required to identify patents they believe would be infringed by the marketing of generic drugs.[33] When the FDA approves the NDA, it lists the patents in a publication known as the Orange Book.[34] Named for its orange cover (but now published in electronic form and accessible on the Internet), the publication contains a list of all the drugs approved for marketing in the United States.[35]

---

30. Alfred B. Engelberg, *Special Patent Provisions for Pharmaceuticals: Have They Outlived Their Usefulness?*, 39 IDEA 389, 406 (1999).

31. Federal Trade Commission, Generic Drug Entry Prior to Patent Expiration: An FTC Study, at 5, http://www.ftc.gov/os/2002/07/genericdrugstudy.pdf [hereinafter Generic Drug Study]; THOMAS, at 306.

32. Generic Drug Study, at 5.

33. THOMAS, at 15.

34. The technical name is "Approved Drug Products with Therapeutic Equivalence Evaluations." Electronic Orange Book, Jan. 2008, http://www.fda.gov/cder/ob/.

35. THOMAS, at 327.

An ANDA applicant must provide one of four certifications for each patent listed in the Orange Book relating to the relevant NDA. It can certify that

(I)   no patent information appears in the Orange Book,
(II)   the patent has expired,
(III) it will not seek approval until the patent expires, or
(IV)   the patent is invalid or will not be infringed by the generic drug.[36]

For the first two certifications, the FDA can approve the ANDA immediately. For the third, approval is granted when the patent expires. It is the fourth certification that has resulted in settlement agreements raising antitrust concern.

Upon filing such a certification, an ANDA applicant must provide notice within 20 days to the patent and NDA holders.[37] Such notice must detail support for its claim of invalidity or noninfringement.[38] If the patent holder (typically the brand firm) does not bring an infringement suit within 45 days, the FDA may approve the ANDA as soon as the regulatory requirements are satisfied.[39]

If, in contrast, the patent holder sues within 45 days, it receives an automatic 30-month stay of FDA approval. The stay operates like a preliminary injunction, preventing the ANDA applicant from marketing its product for a period of roughly 30 months (or less if a court determines that the patent is invalid or not infringed).[40] As a practical matter, the 30-month stay approximates the 25-month periods for (1) FDA approval of generic applicants filing paragraph IV certifications that are not sued and (2) the average period between the filing of a complaint and a district court decision.[41] Even though the generic has not entered the market, the paragraph IV certification is treated as an artificial act of infringement that allows the patentee to sue before entry.[42]

To encourage challenges to potentially invalid drug patents, the Act grants a 180-day period of marketing exclusivity to the first applicant filing a "substantially complete" ANDA with a paragraph IV certification.[43] During the period,

---

36. 21 U.S.C. § 355(j)(2)(A)(vii); *see generally* THOMAS, at 313.

37. 21 U.S.C. § 355(j)(2)(B)(ii),(iii). The 20-day limit was added in the 2003 amendments to the Act.

38. 21 U.S.C. § 355(j)(2)(B)(iv)(II).

39. 21 U.S.C. § 355(j)(5)(B)(iii).

40. *Id.* The period could extend an additional 12 months depending on when the generic filed its Paragraph IV certification. 21 U.S.C. § 355(j)(5)(F)(ii); *see generally* C. Scott Hemphill, *Paying for Delay: Pharmaceutical Patent Settlement as a Regulatory Design Problem*, 81 N.Y.U. L. REV. 1553, 1566 n.50 (2006).

41. Generic Drug Study, at 39.

42. 35 U.S.C. § 271(e)(2); *see generally Eli Lilly & Co. v. Medtronic, Inc.*, 496 U.S. 661 (1990).

43. 21 U.S.C. § 355(j)(5)(B)(iv).

which begins after the first commercial marketing of the drug, the FDA cannot approve other ANDAs for the same product.[44]

2003 Revisions

In 2003, Congress enacted the Medicare Prescription Drug, Improvement, and Modernization Act. Three of the Act's most important changes addressed abuse of the Hatch-Waxman Act by limiting patent holders to a single 30-month stay, establishing *forfeiture events* causing ANDA applicants to lose the exclusive 180-day marketing period, and requiring parties to provide notice of settlement agreements to the antitrust enforcement agencies.

The single 30-month stay provision was a "centerpiece" of the legislation, designed to "allow[] lower-priced generic products to enter the market more quickly."[45] Under the Hatch-Waxman Act, a brand firm could wait until a generic filed an ANDA and then list an additional patent in the Orange Book. If the generic then filed a paragraph IV certification, the brand could sue and receive another 30-month stay. As an example of such behavior, GlaxoSmithKline, by obtaining multiple 30-month stays, blocked generic competition against its anti-depressant drug Paxil for more than 5 years.[46]

The 2003 revisions addressed this problem by limiting the stays to patents submitted to the FDA before submission of the ANDA.[47] To be sure, multiple 30-month stays are still possible. For example, a generic could file paragraph III and paragraph IV certifications on different patents and then, before the submission of the ANDA, change the paragraph III designation to paragraph IV.[48] Nonetheless, the change has reduced the problem's frequency.

The second modification was designed to limit abuse of the 180-day exclusivity period. The Medicare Act created various forfeiture events that resulted in generics forfeiting their 180-day exclusivity period. The events include the generic's

- failing to market its drug within 75 days of FDA approval
- failing to market its drug within 75 days of a final judicial decision or consent decree finding the patent invalid or not infringed
- withdrawing its ANDA

---

44. Generic Drug Study, at 7. Until amended in 2003, the Hatch-Waxman Act included as a second trigger for the 180-day period a court decision finding invalidity or lack of infringement.

45. H.R. Conf. Rep. No. 108-391 (2004), *reprinted in* 2004 U.S.C.C.A.N. 1808, 2187.

46. Generic Drug Study, at 51.

47. 21 U.S.C. § 355(j)(5)(B)(iii).

48. U.S. Dep't of Health & Human Servs., Food & Drug Admin., Center for Drug Eval. & Research, *Guidance for Industry: Listed Drugs, 30–Month Stays, and Approval of ANDAs and 505(b)(2) Applications Under Hatch-Waxman, as Amended by the Medicare Prescription Drug, Improvement, and Modernization Act of 2003*, at 8–9 (Oct. 2004), http://www.fda.gov/cder/guidance/6174dft.pdf.

- failing to obtain tentative FDA approval within 30 months of the filing of the ANDA
- witnessing the expiration of the patents entitling the applicant to exclusivity
- entering into an agreement found to violate the antitrust laws[49]

A close reading of the statute shows that these "use it or lose it" provisions do not necessarily trigger forfeiture as quickly as might be assumed. Simplifying greatly, the statute provides that the first filer loses exclusivity if it fails to market the drug by the later of (1) 75 days after FDA approval and (2) 75 days after an appellate court decision finding invalidity or noninfringement.[50] The exclusivity period thus would extend to the subsequent court decision, which could occur long after the FDA's approval.

Nonetheless, the changes—together with the Federal Circuit's recent expansion of declaratory judgment actions—reduce the likelihood of complete bottlenecks. Before the amendments, a brand that entered an agreement with the first ANDA filer to refrain from entering the market could indefinitely forestall generic entry by not suing subsequent ANDA filers.[51] But the Federal Circuit in 2007 at least partially opened that bottleneck, making it easier for generics to file declaratory judgment actions against brand companies where (1) the brand listed patents in the Orange Book, (2) the generic filed a paragraph IV certification, and (3) the brand sued the generic on one or more of the patents.[52] Although courts have not addressed the availability of such actions when the brand does not sue the generic, the increased use of declaratory judgments could reduce bottlenecks.

Finally, the Act required brand and generic companies to file settlement agreements that concerned the 180-day exclusivity period or the production, sale, or marketing of a drug with the FTC and Department of Justice within ten days

---

49. 21 U.S.C. § 355(j)(5)(D)(i).

50. 21 U.S.C. § 355(j)(5)(D)(i)(I) (referring to "decision from which no appeal (other than a petition to the Supreme Court for a writ of certiorari) has been or can be taken that the patent is invalid or not infringed"); *see* Erica N. Andersen, Note, Schering *the Market: Analyzing the Debate over Reverse-Payment Settlements in the Wake of the Medicare Modernization Act of 2003 and In re* Tamoxifen Citrate Litigation, 93 IOWA L. REV. 1015, 1023–24 (2008); Prepared Statement of the FTC Before the Comm. on the Judiciary of the U.S. Senate, *Anticompetitive Patent Settlements in the Pharmaceutical Industry: The Benefits of a Legislative Solution*, at 17 (Jan. 17, 2007), http://www.ftc.gov/speeches/leibowitz/070117 anticompetitivepatentsettlements_senate.pdf. The forfeiture provisions apply only to ANDAs filed after December 8, 2003 for which no Paragraph IV certifications were filed before the December 8 date. Medicare Modernization Act, § 1102(b), 117 Stat. 2066, 2460 (2003).

51. Barriers to Generic Entry, at 21.

52. *Teva Pharmaceuticals USA, Inc. v. Novartis Pharmaceuticals Corp.*, 482 F.3d 1330, 1344 (Fed. Cir. 2007).

of the agreement.[53] Representative Waxman sought to ensure the enforcement of the antitrust laws by requiring disclosure of "secret, anticompetitive agreements."[54] Similarly, the Senate Judiciary Committee explained that the amendments were designed to "put an end to the exploitation" by which brand firms "abused the Hatch-Waxman law" by "agreeing with smaller rivals to delay or limit competition."[55]

Mixed Success

On the whole, the Hatch-Waxman Act has been successful in increasing generic entry. Generic drugs, which made up 19 percent of prescriptions for drug products in 1984, increased to 65 percent in 2008.[56] For the most popular drugs with expired patents, the share facing generic competition burgeoned from 35 percent in 1983 to almost 100 percent today.[57] And once a generic enters the market, the brand loses an average of 44 percent of its market, with one study finding generic penetration of approximately 75 percent after two months.[58]

These trends are amplified by health plans' encouragement or requirement of generic drugs.[59] Most states allow pharmacists that receive prescriptions for brand drugs to substitute generics. Medicaid policies and managed care plans also encourage such substitution.[60] And unlike the situation at the time of the Hatch-Waxman Act, when an average three-year gap existed between patent expiration and generic entry, generics today enter the market almost immediately at the end of the patent term.[61]

Generic entry also saves consumers billions of dollars each year. Because generics have far lower development costs, they sell the drugs at a significant discount. The first generic entrant prices its product, on average, 5 to 25 percent

---

53. Medicare Prescription Drug, Improvement, and Modernization Act of 2003, §§ 1112, 1113, Pub. L. No. 108–173, 117 Stat. 2066.

54. 146 Cong. Rec. E1538 (daily ed. Sept. 20, 2000).

55. S. Rep. No. 107–167, at 4 (2002).

56. Generic Pharmaceutical Association, *Frequently Asked Questions*, 2008, http://www.gphaonline.org/Content/NavigationMenu/AboutGenerics/FAQs/faqs2.htm.

57. CBO Study, at 37.

58. *Id.* at xiii (44 percent); Doug Long (IMS), *2003 Year in Review: Trends, Issues, Forecasts*, at 35 (2004), http://piapr.com/presentaciones/DougLong2003YIRPresentation.pdf (75 percent).

59. Alden F. Abbott & Suzanne T. Michel, *The Right Balance of Competition Policy and Intellectual Property Law: A Perspective on Settlements of Pharmaceutical Patent Litigation*, 46 IDEA 1, 24 (2005).

60. In re *Schering-Plough*, 2003 WL 22989651, Part II.B.2 (F.T.C. Dec. 8, 2003), vacated by *Schering-Plough Corp. v. FTC*, 402 F.3d 1056, 1058 (11th Cir. 2005).

61. CBO Study, at 38.

lower than the brand drug.[62] The presence of a second generic lowers the price to approximately half the brand price.[63] In markets in which 6 or more generics enter, the price falls to a quarter of the brand price.[64] One study found that the substitution of generic drugs saved purchasers of prescription drugs through retail pharmacies $8 to $10 billion in 1994.[65] Another survey showed that patients could save 52 percent in the daily costs of their medications by purchasing generic drugs.[66]

The Hatch-Waxman Act also has been successful in increasing the patent term. Nearly half of the top 20 "blockbuster" drugs in 1997 received extensions of at least 2 years.[67] The average period of marketing rose from approximately 9 years before Hatch-Waxman to about 11½ years in the early 1990s.[68]

Even though generic entry increased after the Act, prices also have recently increased. Prescription drug spending is the fastest growing segment of healthcare expenditures, increasing from approximately 6 percent in 1993 to almost 11 percent in 2003.[69] Senior citizens, despite making up only 13 percent of the population, account for 42 percent of all drug expenditures.[70] Between 2000 and 2004, the average price of the 100 most frequently dispensed retail prescriptions rose almost 25 percent, with the price for brand drugs rising three times faster than the price of generics.[71]

These price increases can be linked to agreements by which brand firms have settled patent infringement disputes by paying generics to abandon their challenges and delay entering the market. Just as concerning, the companies have more frequently employed these agreements when enforcers and courts look the other way. In particular, the use of reverse payments plummeted after the FTC first declared its concern with these agreements in 2000 and skyrocketed after the courts bestowed their blessing in 2005.

---

62. *Id.* at xiii; U.S. Dep't of Health & Human Servs., Food & Drug Admin., Center for Drug Eval. & Research, *Generic Competition and Drug Prices* (2006), http://www.fda.gov/CDER/ogd/generic_competition.htm.

63. *Id.*

64. *Id.*

65. CBO Study, at 35.

66. U.S. Dep't of Health & Human Servs., Food & Drug Admin., Center for Drug Eval. & Research, *Savings From Generic Drugs Purchased at Retail Pharmacies* (May 3, 2004), http://www.fda.gov/cder/consumerinfo/savingsfromgenericdrugs.htm.

67. Engelberg, at 426.

68. CBO Study, at 39. The figures for the post-Hatch-Waxman term are based on drugs approved between 1992 and 1995 that received an extension.

69. *Id.* at 1.

70. Families USA, *Cost Overdose: Growth in Drug Spending for the Elderly, 1992–2010,* at 2, July 2000, http://www.familiesusa.org/assets/pdfs/drugod852b.pdf.

71. U.S. Gov't Accountability Office, *Prescription Drugs: Price Trends for Frequently Used Brand and Generic Drugs from 2000 through 2004,* at 4, 10, GAO-05-779 (Aug. 2005).

In the years since the passage of the Hatch-Waxman Act, the drafters of the legislation have unequivocally expressed their disapproval of reverse payment settlements. Representative Waxman explained that such agreements were an "unfortunate, unintended consequence" of the Act that "turned . . . the law . . . on its head." Waxman emphasized that the purpose of the legislation was to promote generic competition, not allow generics "to exact a portion of a brand-name firm's monopoly profits in return for withholding entry into the market."[72]

Senator Orrin Hatch similarly found such agreements "appalling." Hatch "concede[d], as a drafter of the law, that we came up short in our draftsmanship." And his assessment mirrored that of Waxman in making clear that "[w]e did not wish to encourage situations where payments were made to generic firms not to sell generic drugs and not to allow multi-source generic competition."[73]

Three representative cases demonstrate courts' increasing leniency toward these agreements. In the first case, from 2003, the Sixth Circuit found the settlement to be per se illegal. But the next two, from 2005, applied much more deference.

CARDIZEM

The first case, *In re Cardizem CD Antitrust Litigation*, involved a drug used to treat angina and hypertension and to prevent heart attacks and strokes.[74] In November 1995, the U.S. Patent and Trademark Office (PTO) issued a patent for the prescription drug Cardizem CD to Carderm, which licensed it to Hoescht Marion Roussel. The next month, Andrx Pharmaceuticals filed the first paragraph IV certification, asserting that its product did not infringe any patents covering Cardizem. In January 1996, Hoechst and Carderm sued Andrx for patent infringement. The complaint did not seek damages or injunctive relief, but triggered a 30-month stay during which the FDA was not able to approve Andrx's ANDA.

In September 1997, the FDA tentatively approved Andrx's ANDA, indicating that it would finally approve the application when the 30-month stay expired in July 1998. Nine days after this announcement, the parties settled. Andrx agreed not to market a bioequivalent or generic version of Cardizem (even those not at issue in the litigation) in the United States until it obtained a favorable,

---

72. Brief for Representative Henry A. Waxman as Amicus Curiae in Support of Petitioner, *FTC v. Schering-Plough Corp. et al.*, 126 S. Ct. 2929, No. 05-273 (U.S. Sept. 30, 2005), 2005 WL 2462026; Sheryl Gay Stolberg & Jeff Gerth, *Medicine Merchants/Holding Down the Competition: Keeping Down the Competition; How Companies Stall Generics and Keep Themselves Healthy*, N.Y. Times, July 23, 2000, § 1, at 1.

73. 148 Cong. Rec. S7565, 7566 (daily ed. July 30, 2002) (statement of Sen. Hatch).

74. 332 F.3d 896 (6th Cir. 2003). The facts are taken from *id.* at 899–903.

unappealable determination that the patent was not infringed.[75] By filing the first Paragraph IV certification, Andrx received a 180-day period of marketing exclusivity. But by not entering the market, it never triggered this period, creating a bottleneck that blocked other Paragraph IV filers from receiving FDA approval. In exchange for this promise, Hoechst agreed to pay Andrx $40 million per year, which would increase to $100 million per year if a court determined that the patent was not infringed.[76]

The FDA issued its final approval of Andrx's ANDA in July 1998. Hoechst then began to pay Andrx to refrain from marketing the product. Two months later, Andrx reformulated its product, and the FDA approved this version the following year. Upon FDA approval, Hoechst and Andrx settled their infringement case, with Hoechst paying a final sum of $50 million, for total payments of roughly $90 million. Andrx then introduced its generic product, Cartia XT, which sold at a significantly lower price and captured a substantial share of the market.

The Sixth Circuit found that the agreement was per se illegal. It explained that the settlement guaranteed to Hoechst that "its only potential competitor" would "refrain from marketing its generic version of Cardizem CD even after it had obtained FDA approval." And it focused on the effect of the Hatch-Waxman Act. "By delaying Andrx's entry into the market," the court continued, "the agreement also delayed the entry of other generic competitors, who could not enter until the expiration of Andrx's 180-day period of marketing exclusivity, which Andrx had agreed not to relinquish or transfer." The court also was concerned that the agreement prevented Andrx from marketing products not covered by the patent. It concluded that the settlement was "a horizontal agreement to eliminate competition, . . . a classic example of a *per se* illegal restraint of trade."[77]

SCHERING-PLOUGH

The second case dealt with a product used to treat high blood pressure and congestive heart disease. Schering-Plough manufactured an "extended-release microencapsulated potassium chloride product, K-Dur 20." Although the active ingredient in K-Dur 20, potassium chloride, was not patentable, Schering owned a patent on the extended release coating of the drug.[78]

---

75. Andrx also could market its generic version if it entered into a license agreement with Hoechst or if Hoechst entered into a license agreement with a third party.

76. The $100 million payment also would be made if Hoechst dismissed the infringement case or failed to refile the case after a court ruling that did not determine issues of validity, enforcement, or infringement.

77. *Cardizem*, 332 F.3d at 907–08.

78. *Schering-Plough Corp. v. FTC*, 402 F.3d 1056, 1058 (11th Cir. 2005). The facts are taken from the opinion. *See id.* at 1058–62.

In 1995, Upsher-Smith Laboratories sought FDA approval to market a generic version of K-Dur 20. Schering sued Upsher for patent infringement, and the parties settled the case immediately before trial was to commence in June 1997. The parties agreed that Upsher would not enter the market until September 1, 2001 and that Schering would license other Upsher products. In particular, Schering received licenses to five Upsher products, including a sustained-release niacin product used to reduce cholesterol.

In 1995, ESI Lederle also sought to market a generic version of K-Dur 20. Schering sued ESI for patent infringement, and the parties settled in 1997. They agreed that ESI could enter the market on January 1, 2004 (almost three years before the patent was to expire) and that Schering would pay ESI $10 million if it received FDA approval by a certain date. Both Upsher and ESI remained off the market several years beyond their previous expectations.[79]

In 2001, the FTC filed an administrative complaint alleging that Schering's settlements with Upsher and ESI violated Section 5 of the Federal Trade Commission Act (FTC Act) and Section 1 of the Sherman Act. An Administrative Law Judge (ALJ) concluded that the settlements were lawful. The FTC's complaint counsel appealed this decision to the full Commission.

The Commission reversed the ALJ's decision and, in an exhaustive opinion, held that the settlements violated the FTC and Sherman Acts. It found that the licenses Schering paid to Upsher and ESI greatly exceeded the value of the products it received. Even though there were significant safety and market concerns with one product, Schering (1) did not include its knowledgeable employees in the negotiations, (2) failed to request sales projections or research relating to the drug, (3) never followed up on unfulfilled requests for information, and (4) did not object when Upsher suspended its work.[80] This lack of interest supported the Commission's conclusion that Schering paid the generics to delay entering the market.

More generally, the FTC explained that it would invalidate settlements by which "the generic receives anything of value and agrees to defer its own research, development, production or sales activities." The Commission created exceptions to this prohibition for an "agreed-on entry date, without cash payments" and for payments less than $2 million that could be linked to litigation costs.[81]

The Eleventh Circuit, in *Schering-Plough Corp. v. FTC*, reversed the FTC's condemnation. It concluded that "neither the rule of reason nor the per se analysis was appropriate" for the agreements. The emphasis on anticompetitive effects, in particular, was "ill-suited" for cases involving patents, which "[b]y their nature . . . cripple competition . . . [and] create an environment of exclusion."

79. Petition for a Writ of Certiorari, *FTC v. Schering-Plough Corp.*, at 8 (U.S. filed Aug. 2005) [hereinafter FTC Cert Petition].
80. In re *Schering-Plough Corp.*, 2003 WL 22989651, Part IV.
81. *Id.*, Parts II.B.4, VIII.

The court instead articulated a test that focused on "(1) the scope of the exclusionary potential of the patent; (2) the extent to which the agreements exceed that scope; and (3) the resulting anticompetitive effects."[82]

Pursuant to the first factor, the court found that Schering's patent gave it "the legal right to exclude Upsher and ESI from the market" until the generics proved the patent's invalidity or that their products did not infringe the patent. Neither of the firms alleged the patent's invalidity or claimed that the infringement suits were "shams."[83]

Regarding the second factor, the court found that the agreements did not restrict competition beyond the scope of the patent. It found Schering's payment to Upsher for unrelated products to be "a bona fide fair-value payment." And it found that the ESI settlement reflected 15 months of mediation as well as "the strength of Schering's case." The court concluded that the settlement terms were "within the patent's exclusionary power" and that patentees "should not be in a worse position" than other parties in settling lawsuits.[84]

On the third factor, the court found that any restrictions on competition were "ancillary restraints" necessary to settlement. The agreement between Schering and Upsher applied only to products covered by the patent at issue. More generally, the court stated that reverse payments were "a natural by-product of the Hatch-Waxman process" and that patent litigation resulted in "a litany of direct and indirect costs" and "decrease[d] . . . innovation" by increasing uncertainty in developing patented products.[85]

The court concluded that the agreements "fell well within the protections of the . . . patent" and thus were not illegal. In the end, the court stated, it "cannot be the sole basis for a violation of antitrust law" for a brand firm with a patent to pay a generic competitor.[86]

The FTC sought Supreme Court review of the Eleventh Circuit decision, and was backed by 34 states, the AARP, and a patent policy think tank.[87] Reflecting a rare disagreement between the agencies, the Justice Department recommended against granting certiorari. The agency suggested that the appropriate legal standard "should take into account the relative likelihood of success of the parties' claims."[88] The Supreme Court denied certiorari.

---

82. 402 F.3d at 1065–66.

83. *Id.* at 1066–68.

84. *Id.* at 1069–72.

85. *Id.* at 1073–75.

86. *Id.* at 1076.

87. Christopher M. Holman, *Do Reverse Payment Settlements Violate the Antitrust Laws?*, 23 SANTA CLARA COMPUTER & HIGH TECH. L.J. 489, 491 (2007).

88. Brief for the United States as Amicus Curiae, *FTC v. Schering-Plough Corp. et al.*, No. 05-273, at 11 (U.S. May 2006).

TAMOXIFEN

The third case involved tamoxifen, which was used to treat breast cancer and was "the most prescribed cancer drug in the world."[89] Imperial Chemical Industries (ICI) received a patent on tamoxifen in August 1985, and Zeneca, a former ICI subsidiary, then obtained the rights to the patent and manufactured the drug. In December 1985, Barr Laboratories filed an ANDA with the FDA, requesting approval to market a generic version of tamoxifen. In September 1987, Barr amended the ANDA to incorporate a paragraph IV certification.

In November 1987, ICI sued Barr and Barr's supplier for patent infringement. In April 1992, a district court declared ICI's patent invalid. It found that ICI had intentionally withheld crucial information from the PTO regarding safety and effectiveness tests. These tests showed hormonal effects "opposite to those sought in humans," which could have led to "unpredictable and . . . disastrous consequences."[90]

ICI appealed to the Federal Circuit, and while the appeal was pending, the parties entered into a settlement agreement. Zeneca agreed to pay Barr $21 million and Barr's supplier more than $45 million if Barr withdrew its challenge to Zeneca's patent. Barr also agreed, by switching its paragraph IV certification to paragraph III, not to enter the market until Zeneca's patent expired in 2002. And it promised to revert to a paragraph IV certification, which could delay other generic challenges if a court declared the patent invalid. Finally, the parties agreed to file a motion to vacate the judgment invalidating Zeneca's patent.

In addition to the challenges to the validity of Zeneca's patent, consumers filed 30 lawsuits targeting the agreement between Zeneca and Barr. They claimed that the agreement allowed the parties to circumvent the district court's invalidation of the patent. The district court, however, granted the defendant's motion to dismiss, in part because the agreement's termination of the litigation "cleared the field for other generic manufacturers to challenge the patent."[91] In fact, however, the settlement removed the most motivated challenger (the first-filing generic) and also delayed other generics' challenges.[92]

The Second Circuit began its analysis by explaining that reverse payments did not constitute per se violations. The court was "not unaware" of the "troubling dynamic" in the cases that "[t]he less sound the patent or the less clear the infringement . . . the more a rule permitting settlement is likely to benefit the patent holder." But its concerns were assuaged by relying on the presumption of

---

89. In re *Tamoxifen Citrate Antitrust Litig.*, 466 F.3d 187, 193 (2d Cir. 2006). The facts are taken from the opinion. *See id.* at 193–99.

90. *Imperial Chem. Indus. v. Barr Labs.*, 795 F. Supp. 619, 622 (S.D.N.Y.1992).

91. 466 F.3d at 197.

92. Hemphill, at 1584–86.

patent validity, which ensured that settlement was "merely an extension of the valid patent monopoly."[93]

On the issue whether reverse payments were "excessive," the court admitted that it seemed "suspicious" for a patentee to settle litigation against a potential generic manufacturer by paying "more than either party anticipates the manufacturer would earn by winning the lawsuit and entering the newly competitive market in competition with the patent holder." But it found the suspicion to "abate[] upon reflection."[94]

It concluded that as long as "the patent litigation is neither a sham nor otherwise baseless" or beyond the patent's scope, a patentee can enter into a settlement "to protect that to which it is presumably entitled: a lawful monopoly over the manufacture and distribution of the patented product." Zeneca's patent litigation, claimed the court, was not baseless or fraudulent.[95]

The court then found that the agreement's effects did not exceed the patent's scope. First, the settlement did not restrict the marketing of noninfringing products. Because Zeneca's patent "preclude[d] all generic versions of tamoxifen," any competing version "would . . . necessarily infringe the patent."[96] Second, by concluding litigation, the agreement "opened the . . . patent to immediate challenge by other potential generic[s]." Third, the settlement "did not entirely foreclose competition" since a license from Zeneca allowed Barr to market Zeneca's version of tamoxifen eight months after the agreement became effective. Even if the version distributed by Barr sold for only 5 percent less than Zeneca's version, the court found that "[t]his was competition nonetheless."[97]

In the end, the court affirmed the lower court's order granting the defendant's motion to dismiss.

Judge Pooler filed a vigorous dissent. She stated that the majority's "sham" requirement was "not soundly grounded" in precedent and was "insufficiently protective of the consumer interests safeguarded by the Hatch-Waxman Act and the antitrust laws." In particular, she pointed to the important public interest in "having the validity of patents litigated," especially "in light of the recent trend toward capping the maximum amounts insurers and public benefit plans will spend on medications." And she highlighted the difference between the interests of the parties and those of the public when "the patent has already been shown to be vulnerable to attack and the generic manufacturer is paid to keep its product off the market."[98]

---

93. 466 F.3d at 206, 211.
94. Id. at 208.
95. Id. at 208–09, 213.
96. Id. at 213–14.
97. Id. at 214–16.
98. Id. at 224, 226 (Pooler, J., dissenting).

Judge Pooler concluded that a reasonableness standard should apply. Such a standard would rely primarily on the patent's strength at the time of settlement and secondarily on factors such as the size of the payment, the amount the generic firm would earn during its exclusivity period, and other anticompetitive effects. She concluded that the plaintiffs' pleading was adequate to survive a motion to dismiss because of their claims that (1) the patent's invalidity determination would have been affirmed on appeal, (2) Barr "received more than it would have through a victory on appeal," and (3) Barr agreed to "deploy its paragraph IV certification to defeat other potential generic entrants." The judge concluded by contrasting the "factual record not yet in existence" in the case with the "full record" that courts had considered in other Hatch-Waxman cases.[99]

In sum, the *Cardizem* court applied the most aggressive scrutiny to reverse payment settlements. Such an approach made sense given that the agreement prevented the generic from entering the market even with products not covered by the patent. On the other hand, the *Schering* and *Tamoxifen* courts, as discussed in the next section, applied an excessively deferential analysis that failed to appreciate the relevant regulatory framework.

ANALYSIS OF COURTS' APPROACHES

These courts (and others) have justified their conclusions on policies of secondary importance. In addition, they have insufficiently recognized both the Hatch-Waxman framework and potential antitrust harm of reverse payment agreements.

The Hatch-Waxman Act reflects Congress's position on the balance between competition and innovation in the pharmaceutical industry. It was designed to solve specific problems. It addressed high drug prices and insufficient generic entry by promoting competition. It dealt with shortened effective patent terms resulting from changes in the FDA approval process by promoting innovation. This specific calibration displaces more general views on the patent and antitrust regimes.[100] Its explicit resolution is especially helpful given the difficulty of reconciling the patent and antitrust laws.

Recent courts, however, have ignored this specific guidance. They have taken upon themselves the Herculean task of reconciling competition and innovation. They have done this even though the legislature's preferred equilibrium appears before them on the silver platter of the Hatch-Waxman Act.

Courts, for example, have emphasized the benefits of settlement and, relatedly, the positive effects of settlements on innovation. At the same time,

---

99. *Id.* at 228, 232.
100. *See* Hemphill, at 1614.

they have ignored the competition benefits of challenges to invalid patents. This gets it exactly backward. Innovation-based arguments for settlement do not appear in the Act's text or legislative history. On the other hand, even a cursory consideration of the statute underscores the importance of patent challenges.

Fleshing out these errors, this section explores the five policies upon which courts have relied in justifying their deference to reverse payment agreements. These policies have emphasized (1) the importance of settlements, (2) the link between settlements and innovation, (3) the presumption of patent validity, (4) the scope of the patent, and (5) the "natural" status of reverse payments. An appreciation for the Hatch-Waxman framework demonstrates the secondary importance of these policies.

Importance of Settlements

First, courts have voiced a general policy in favor of settlement. They have recognized that settlements conserve resources, provide certainty that encourages investment, and result in licenses increasing competition.[101] Settlements are particularly beneficial for patent litigation, which is lengthy, complex, and costly.[102] For these reasons, the *Tamoxifen* court explained that "courts are bound to encourage settlements."[103] And the court in *Schering* found that "[t]he general policy of the law is to favor the settlement of litigation" and that "the policy extends to the settlement of patent infringement suits."[104]

But reverse payment agreements are not typical settlements. They are agreements that dispose of the validity and infringement challenges central to the Hatch-Waxman scheme. Any general preference in the law for settlement was displaced by the Act's specific framework.

A 180-day period of exclusivity for the first ANDA to challenge a patent only makes sense in the context of encouraging patent challenges. Moreover, the purpose of the exclusivity period, to ensure that a generic competitor could not "free ride" on a rival's litigation efforts before the first filer recovered litigation costs, is not promoted if the litigation never produces a judgment benefiting other generics.[105]

In addition, the 180-day period only applies to ANDA filers that seek to enter before the end of the patent term. It does not apply to certification challenges that target expired patents or delay approval until the end of the patent term.

---

101. In re *Schering-Plough Corp.*, 2003 WL 22989651, Part III; U.S. Dep't of Justice & Fed. Trade Comm'n, Antitrust Guidelines for the Licensing of Intellectual Property ¶ 2.3 (1995).

102. In 2007, in patent cases with more than $25 million at risk, each party faced a median expense of $5 million. AIPLA, *Report of the Economic Survey 2007*, at 25 (2007).

103. 466 F.3d at 202.

104. 402 F.3d at 1072.

105. Engelberg, at 423.

On the other side, the 30-month stay provision reveals patentees' incentives to file suit after receiving notice of a paragraph IV certification.[106]

Finally, the 180-day bounty itself demonstrates the unique nature of these agreements. General patent settlements do not prevent other competitors from challenging the patent. In these cases, even if the settling defendant agrees not to challenge the patent, many others often wait in the wings to do so. In contrast, the Hatch-Waxman bounty creates a regulatory barrier to entry that can significantly delay other patent challenges. Competition's central role is confirmed by the repulsion to reverse payments exhibited by Senator Hatch and Representative Waxman in the 2003 Medicare amendments debate.

In short, general patent-based policies in favor of settlements must give way to an industry-specific resolution that encourages patent challenges.

Settlements and Innovation

The second principle motivating courts is to defer to settlements so as not to harm incentives for innovation. The *Tamoxifen* court stated that rules "severely restricting" settlements could hamper the patent system's goals by increasing uncertainty and delaying innovation.[107] Similarly, the court in *Valley Drug Co. v. Geneva Pharmaceuticals, Inc.* concluded that reduced settlement options would raise enforcement costs and "impair . . . incentives for disclosure and innovation."[108] The court in *In re Ciprofloxacin Hydrochloride Antitrust Litigation* found that the inability of brand-name firms to "control or limit their risk" through settlements could "chill[] efforts to research and develop new drugs" and lead to "severe consequences for consumers."[109] And the *Schering* court found that "the caustic environment of patent litigation" could reduce innovation by increasing "the uncertainty around the drug manufacturer's ability to research, develop, and market the patented product."[110]

Any effects of settlements on innovation, however, are secondary in the context of the Hatch-Waxman Act. The Act, once again, offered a nuanced equilibrium between competition and innovation. To promote innovation, the drafters offered patent term extensions, nonpatent market exclusivity, and a 30-month stay of FDA approval for generics filing paragraph IV certifications. Nowhere in the Act or legislative history did the drafters ever link settlements to innovation. And since the Act's passage, the drafters' consistently negative reactions to such settlements have confirmed the absence of such a link.

---

106. FTC Cert Petition, at 4.
107. 466 F.3d 187, 203 (2d Cir. 2006).
108. 344 F.3d 1294, 1308 (11th Cir. 2003).
109. 261 F. Supp. 2d 188, 256 (E.D.N.Y. 2003).
110. 402 F.3d at 1075.

Presumption of Patent Validity

Third, courts have upheld settlement agreements based on a presumption of patent validity. Section 282 of the Patent Act states that patents "shall be presumed valid."[111] Courts have relied on this presumption to ascertain the validity that is so crucial to determining the appropriate antitrust treatment. A settlement that allows generic entry before the end of the term of a valid patent promises to accelerate competition. In contrast, a settlement delaying entry beyond the date the generic could have entered on an invalid patent could allow the firms to divide the market.

It is in this context that a substantive role for the procedural burden plays an outsized role. The *Tamoxifen* court, for example, found that the presumption of validity allows parties to settle "weak patent cases" even though "such settlements will inevitably protect patent monopolies that are, perhaps, undeserved."[112] And the *Schering* court relied on the presumption in concluding that a brand firm would not suffer antitrust liability for exclusionary activity unless generics were able to prove a patent's invalidity or noninfringement.[113]

Courts have also relied on the presumption in rebutting assertions by the FTC and commentators that patents are "probabilistic property rights" or rights to "try to exclude" (as opposed to "rights to exclude").[114] Such an argument highlights the uncertainty of patent rights and contends that settlements should not leave consumers in a worse position than they would have been through ongoing litigation. Consumers, in other words, have a "property right" to the competition that would have prevailed in litigation.[115]

But courts have rejected these arguments, which "undermine the presumption of validity that Congress afforded patents." They have found that settling parties are not required to "preserve the public's interest in lower prices." They have worried that the probabilistic approach would have adverse effects on patent licenses, "undermining the settled expectations of patentees and potential . . . licensees across countless industries." And they have made clear that "there is no support in the law" for "a public property right in the outcome of private lawsuits." Settling parties, in short, have "no duty to use patent-derived market power in a way that imposes the lowest monopoly rents on the consumer."[116]

---

111. 35 U.S.C. § 282 (2002).

112. 466 F.3d at 211.

113. 402 F.3d at 1066–67.

114. Cristofer Leffler & Keith Leffler, *Settling the Controversy Over Patent Settlements: Payments by the Patent Holder Should Be Per Se Illegal*, 21 Res. L & Econ. 475, 484 (2004); Mark A. Lemley & Carl Shapiro, *Probabilistic Patents*, 19 J. Econ. Persp. 75, 75–76 (2005); Carl Shapiro, *Antitrust Limits to Patent Settlements*, 34 Rand J. Econ. 391, 395 (2003); *see generally* Steven W. Day, *Leaving Room for Innovation: Rejecting the FTC's Stance Against Reverse Payments in* Schering-Plough v. FTC, 57 Case W. Res. L. Rev. 223, 233–36 (2006).

115. Shapiro, at 395–96.

116. In re *Ciprofloxacin Hydrochloride Antitrust Litig.*, 363 F. Supp. 2d 514, 531–33, 541 (E.D.N.Y. 2005).

For four separate reasons, however, the Patent Act's presumption of validity is entitled to far less weight than courts have accorded it. First, it is only a procedural evidentiary presumption.[117] Patentees cannot, for example, rely on the presumption as substantive evidence in preliminary injunction proceedings. As the Federal Circuit has explained, the presumption is a "procedural device" for allocating burdens of production and persuasion at trial, not "evidence which can be 'weighed' in determining likelihood of success" at the preliminary injunction stage.[118] "A presumption of validity," as scholars in a recent amicus brief colorfully analogized, "does not entitle a patentee to evade the test of patent litigation any more than a criminal defendant's presumption of innocence entitles him to avoid trial."[119]

Second, the presumption should be entitled to the *least* amount of deference in situations in which the parties enter agreements that prevent validity from even being challenged. Patent litigation plays an important role in testing weak patents and ensuring that the public does not suffer the adverse effects of invalid ones.[120] The Supreme Court has recognized such an objective in several cases that have allowed licensees to challenge validity.[121] The presumption of validity should be particularly weak when the activity at issue precludes the testing of patents.

Third, confirming the fragile status of the presumption, the Hatch-Waxman Act's text and legislative history demonstrate the importance of invalidity challenges. Increasing generic competition was a primary goal of the legislation. That is why Congress provided a 180-day bounty to the first generic to challenge a patent's invalidity. Settlements preventing patent challenges are a particularly inappropriate setting for the presumption.

Fourth, empirical studies have consistently shown that a significant percentage of granted patents are invalid. Surveys have found that

- courts invalidated 46 percent of patents between 1989 and 1996[122];
- the alleged infringer prevailed in 42 percent of the patent cases that reached trial between 1983 and 1999[123];

---

117. *Stratoflex, Inc. v. Aeroquip Corp.*, 713 F.2d 1530, 1534 (Fed. Cir. 1983).

118. *New Eng. Braiding Co. v. A.W. Chesterton Co.*, 970 F.2d 878, 882 (Fed. Cir. 1992); *see generally* Hemphill, at 1602 n.181.

119. Brief Amici Curiae of 28 Professors of Law, Business, and Economics in Support of Appellants, In re *Ciprofloxacin Hydrochloride Antitrust Litigation*, No. 2008–1097, at 11 (Fed. Cir. Jan. 25, 2008).

120. *Id.* at 12.

121. *MedImmune, Inc. v. Genentech, Inc.*, 127 S. Ct. 764 (2007); *Aronson v. Quick Point Pencil Co.*, 440 U.S. 257, 264 (1979); *United States v. Glaxo Group, Ltd.*, 410 U.S. 52, 57 (1973); *Lear, Inc. v. Adkins*, 395 U.S. 653, 670 (1969).

122. John R. Allison & Mark A. Lemley, *Empirical Evidence on the Validity of Litigated Patents*, 26 AIPLA Q.J. 185, 205 (1998) (survey limited to cases resulting in a final judgment of validity).

123. Kimberly A. Moore, *Judges, Juries, and Patent Cases—An Empirical Peek Inside the Black Box*, 99 MICH. L. REV. 365, 385 (2000).

- in patent cases between 2000 and 2004, courts found that 43 percent of patents were invalid and 75 percent were not infringed.[124]

In the context of generic challenges in particular, the rate of invalidity appears to be even higher. In a study of paragraph IV challenges between 1992 and 2000, the FTC found that the generic prevailed in 73 percent of the cases and that the brand-name companies won only 27 percent of the time.[125] These figures are consistent with a survey of Federal Circuit decisions from 2002 through 2004 that found that pharmaceutical patentees were successful on the merits in 30 percent of the cases.[126]

This invalidity rate is particularly concerning, and the potential anticompetitive effects especially staggering, given the importance of the drugs that have been the subject of lawsuits. In the FTC study of challenges between 1992 and 2000, sales were far higher in the cases in which brand firms sued generics. For the 75 drug products subject to litigation, the first generic applicant gained $190 million in median net sales the year it filed its ANDA. In contrast, most of the 29 new drug applications that were not subject to suit had net sales of less than $100 million in the year of filing.[127]

Lawsuits have been particularly prevalent on blockbuster drugs such as Cipro, Claritin, Paxil, Pravachol, Prilosec, Prozac, and Zoloft.[128] In fact, of the ten top-selling brand drugs in the United States in 2006, at least six (Nexium, Prevacid, Singulair, Effexor XR, Plavix, and Lexapro) were the subject of litigation under the Hatch-Waxman Act in 2008.[129]

Patent Scope
The fourth framework on which courts have relied involves the patent's scope. Courts have tended to uphold reverse payments as a type of activity falling within the scope of the patent.

The court in *Ciprofloxacin* found that a reverse payments agreement did not "restrain[] competition beyond the scope of the claims of the . . . patent" and thus

---

124. Inst. for Intellectual Prop. & Info. Law, Univ. of Houston Law Ctr., *Patstats: U.S. Patent Litigation Statistics, Decisions for 2000–2004*, ¶¶ 1–16, 23–24, http://www.patstats. org/Composite%20Table%20(2000-2004).html (last visited Feb. 8, 2008).

125. Generic Drug Study, at 10, 16.

126. Paul M. Janicke & LiLan Ren, *Who Wins Patent Infringement Cases?*, 34 AIPLA Quart. J. 1, 20 (2006).

127. FTC Drug Study, at 14.

128. *Id.* at 10–11; *see generally* Stephanie Greene, *A Prescription for Change: How the Medicare Act Revises Hatch-Waxman to Speed Market Entry of Generic Drugs*, 30 J. Corp. L. 309, 331 (2005).

129. Brief of Amicus Curiae Federal Trade Commission in Support of Appellants, In re *Ciprofloxacin Hydrochloride Antitrust Litigation*, No. 2008-1097, at 9 (Fed. Cir. Jan. 25, 2008).

did not create "injury to the market cognizable under existing antitrust law."[130] The court in *Schering* similarly concluded that reverse payments were "within the patent's exclusionary power."[131] The *Tamoxifen* court found that the settlement did not "unlawfully extend the reach" of the patent.[132] And the *Valley Drug* court sought to achieve "a suitable accommodation between antitrust law's free competition requirement and the patent regime's incentive system" by immunizing activity within the patent's scope.[133]

The concept of scope, however, cannot do all the work courts require of it. The overriding question in these cases is whether the patent is valid. If it is, then an agreement allowing entry before the end of the patent term is within the scope. But if the patent is not valid, there is no scope at all.[134] For that reason, judicial inquiries into the scope of the patent assume validity and thus eliminate antitrust concern. As stated above, the procedural presumption is not sufficient to prove substantive validity. In assuming the very validity it seeks to prove, therefore, scope is not an appropriate inquiry.

Natural Status

The fifth foundation on which courts have relied is the "natural" status of reverse payments under the Act. The *Schering* court explained that "[r]everse payments are a natural by-product of the Hatch-Waxman process" and that "patents, payments, and settlement are . . . all symbiotic components that must work together . . . for the larger abstract to succeed."[135] Similarly, the *Tamoxifen* court noted that reverse payments were "particularly to be expected in the drug-patent context because the Hatch-Waxman Act created an environment that encourages them."[136]

Courts are correct that reverse payments have accompanied settlement agreements under the Act. But that is a far cry from a conclusion that such a development is beneficial.[137] In fact, it may reflect no more than the parties' preference for sharing monopoly profits. To consider the point more broadly, we would not justify collusion in an industry based on rivals' effortlessly engaging in it. Similarly, the legality of reverse payment settlements in no way depends on their frequency.

---

130. In re *Ciprofloxacin Hydrochloride Antitrust Litig.*, 363 F. Supp. 2d 514, 535, 540 (E.D.N.Y. 2005).

131. 402 F.3d at 1072.

132. 466 F.3d at 213.

133. 344 F.3d at 1305.

134. Andersen, at 61.

135. 402 F.3d at 1074.

136. 466 F.3d at 206.

137. *See* Herbert Hovenkamp, Mark Janis, & Mark A. Lemley, *Anticompetitive Settlement of Intellectual Property Disputes*, 87 MINN. L. REV. 1719, 1758 (2003).

If the foundations of courts' reasoning are flawed, how should reverse payment settlements be analyzed? In the next section, I offer a new framework justifying the presumptive illegality of these agreements.

PROPOSAL

The framework I propose aims to bridge the gap between courts and commentators. As discussed above, courts have fastened on policies that are of secondary significance in the context of Hatch-Waxman. In contrast, the FTC and an array of commentators have sounded alarms about the concerning nature of reverse payment settlements. But to date, they have not articulated a construct on which courts have relied in invalidating the agreements. For example, a focus on a right to "try to exclude" runs headlong into the presumption of patent validity on which courts have been transfixed.

My argument for presumptive illegality has five elements:

(1) The existence of Hatch-Waxman's regulatory structure
(2) The regime's ineffectiveness in promoting patent challenges
(3) The severe anticompetitive harm of market allocation
(4) The uniquely concerning nature of reverse payments
(5) A rebuttal for reverse payments reflecting reasonable assessments of patent validity

Given the first four elements, the default position should be that such agreements are presumptively illegal. Because these agreements are not generally procompetitive in nature, deferential review under the Rule of Reason is not appropriate. And because some agreements could conceivably be justified if the reverse payments reflected the parties' reasonable assessments of patent validity, per se illegality also is not appropriate at this time.

A default position that reverse payments are presumptively anticompetitive recognizes the framework and increasing ineffectiveness of the Hatch-Waxman Act. It also acknowledges the potentially severe anticompetitive effects of reverse payment settlements, which are particularly suspicious given the aligned incentives of the parties and windfalls received by generics.

An error-costs analysis of settlements confirms the propriety of the presumptive illegality approach. There are two types of errors in the antitrust analysis of settlements. Courts committing Type I errors wrongfully punish lawful activity such as reasonable payments on valid patents. Type II errors, in contrast, wrongfully allow illegal activity such as excessive payments on invalid patents.

In encouraging settlements and giving effect to the presumption of patent validity, courts have sought to minimize Type I errors. In the process, however, they have increased the frequency of Type II errors. This is a mistake. The Hatch-Waxman framework was designed to encourage patent challenges, reduce delay in entering the market, and promote generic competition. Type II errors, in allowing parties to delay entry on invalid patents, fly in the face of the Act's text and intent. The Act's preference for Type I errors confirms the propriety of presumptive illegality.

Having situated the default position most generally, the chapter now fleshes out each of the elements of the framework.

Regulatory Regime: Existence and Equilibrium

The Supreme Court in *Verizon Communications Inc. v. Law Offices of Curtis V. Trinko, LLP* considered the effect of a regulatory regime on the application of the antitrust laws.[138] The Telecommunications Act of 1996 sought to break up local monopolies by requiring incumbent local exchange carriers (ILECs), which had state-provided monopolies in the provision of local phone service, to share their networks with competitors. The *Trinko* case arose when an AT&T customer alleged that Verizon discriminated against new entrants in the local market.[139]

The Court found that the 1996 Telecommunications Act "deter[red] and remed[ied] anticompetitive harm." As a result, it rejected the plaintiff's refusal-to-deal claim. The presence of the telecommunications regime significantly reduced "the additional benefit to competition provided by antitrust enforcement." In contrast, the Court continued, where "nothing built into the regulatory scheme . . . performs the antitrust function . . . the benefits of antitrust are worth its sometimes considerable disadvantages."[140]

In addition to considering the role of the telecommunications regime in fostering competition, the Court more generally described the relationship between antitrust and regulation. It explained that "[a]ntitrust analysis must always be attuned to the particular structure and circumstances of the industry at issue." In particular, courts must take "careful account" of "the pervasive federal and state regulation characteristic of the industry." The analysis also must "recognize and reflect the distinctive economic and legal setting of the regulated industry to which it applies."[141]

Consistent with this approach, the Court in *Credit Suisse Securities v. Billing* concluded that the securities law regime "implicitly precluded" the application of the antitrust laws. In *Billing*, securities buyers challenged practices by which underwriting firms forced them to buy additional shares, pay high commissions, and purchase less desirable securities. The Court explained that the conduct fell "squarely within the heartland of securities regulations" and that the Securities and Exchange Commission (SEC) had authority to supervise the activities and

---

138. 540 U.S. 398 (2004).
139. *See generally* Michael A. Carrier, *Of Trinko, Tea Leaves, and Intellectual Property*, 31 J. CORP. L. 357 (2006).
140. 540 U.S. at 411.
141. *Id.*

"continuously exercised" such authority. It also pointed to the "complex, detailed line" separating permitted from forbidden activity and the existence of activity that could be punished under the antitrust laws but upheld under the securities laws.[142]

Just as the telecommunications and securities regimes presented comprehensive frameworks, the Hatch-Waxman Act offered an exhaustive scheme that prescribed Congress's desired balance between competition and innovation in the drug industry. The drafters used patent term extensions, market exclusivity, and 30-month stays to foster innovation. And they created a market exclusivity period and revived the experimental use defense to promote generic competition. The Act, in short, constructed a delicate equilibrium that demonstrated the secondary relevance of settlement-related policies on which the courts have been riveted.

The drafters, for example, did not demonstrate any concern for the relationship between settlements and innovation. Innovation was an important objective of the statute, but it was fostered through other mechanisms, such as patent term extensions and nonpatent market exclusivity.

The Act's policy encouraging validity challenges also displaced a general preference for settlements. Looking at the marketplace in 1984, the drafters saw high drug prices and few generics. They sought to increase competition and obtain early generic entry by implementing a market exclusivity period to encourage challenges to invalid and noninfringed patents. Reserving this period for generics that wished to enter during the patent term confirmed the importance of early entry and concern with settlements delaying entry.

Comparing Hatch-Waxman to the telecommunications and securities regimes that the Supreme Court has recently considered uncovers modest differences in goals, from promoting competition (the Hatch-Waxman and telecommunications regimes) to disclosing information (securities regulation). Another disparity involves the identity of the parties enforcing the regimes. While the telecommunications and securities acts rely on federal regulators, Hatch-Waxman depends on generic firms challenging invalid patents. As described more fully in the next section, however, this enforcement mechanism has been gutted in recent years as settlements have markedly reduced the regime's effectiveness.

Regulatory Regime: Effectiveness

Before minimizing the need for antitrust, courts must find not only that a regulatory regime exists but also that it functions effectively.[143] In *Trinko*, Justice

---

142. 127 S. Ct. 2383, 2387, 2392–97 (2007).

143. A contrary position might show less concern with an ineffective regulatory regime, which could reflect a deliberate under-enforcement strategy rather than a need for antitrust oversight. See Phil Weiser, *The Relationship of Antitrust and Regulation in a Deregulatory Era*, at 21 (2005), http://papers.ssrn.com/sol3/papers.cfm?abstract_id=814945. But deliberate

Scalia explained that phone companies that provided local service were required to "be on good behavior" and not to discriminate in providing access to certain facilities before they could enter the long-distance market. In addition, firms that did not satisfy these conditions were subject to financial penalties, daily or weekly reporting requirements, and the suspension or revocation of long-distance approval.[144] In *Credit Suisse,* the Court noted the SEC's active enforcement, pointing as one example to its detailed definitions of "what underwriters may and may not do and say during their road shows" and bringing actions against underwriters who violated the regulations.[145]

In contrast, in the Hatch-Waxman setting, generic firms have recently been less effective in promoting competition. The drafters of the Act encouraged challenges to invalid or noninfringed patents. They believed that such challenges would lead to earlier market entry and lower prices for consumers. And they assumed that generics could enter the market immediately upon a judicial finding of invalidity.

Although generic entry has burgeoned in the quarter-century since Congress enacted the law, generics are increasingly not serving their designated function.[146] They are agreeing not to challenge patents and not to enter markets in exchange for payment. Many settlements even provide more money than the generic could have received by proving invalidity and entering the market.

The 180-day bounty, in particular, has been twisted from an incentive for the generic to challenge patents to a barrier to entry preventing challenge. By settling with the first to challenge under the 180-day bounty, the brand firm can significantly delay other generics' entrance into the market.

In short, the Hatch-Waxman Act's carefully balanced regulatory regime is not working as intended to promote competition.

Antitrust Harm

Just because the Act is not fulfilling its intended function does not mean that antitrust should offer assistance. As it turns out, however, the discipline can play a uniquely effective role in repairing Hatch-Waxman. Such a role is warranted given the severe anticompetitive dangers threatened by reverse payment settlements. Of all the types of business activity, agreements by which competitors divide markets threaten the most dangerous anticompetitive effects.

---

underenforcement does not appear likely in the Hatch-Waxman context, as revealed by the drafters' hostile reactions to reverse payment settlements.

144. 540 U.S. at 412–14. Even if the effectiveness of the telecommunications regime was weaker than the court anticipated, at least the regulators were engaging in some actions that promoted competition. *See* Carrier, at 369–70.

145. 127 S. Ct. at 2393.

146. *See also* Hemphill, at 1615; Herbert Hovenkamp, *Sensible Antitrust Rules for Pharmaceutical Competition,* 39 U.S.F. L. REV. 11, 19 (2004).

Why does market division present more competitive concern than monopolization, agreements between suppliers and dealers, and price fixing? Because it restricts *all* competition between the parties on *all* grounds. Even price fixing allows the parties to compete on factors other than price. Where competitors divide markets, in contrast, consumers are robbed of competition on all grounds.

The Supreme Court has explained that "[o]ne of the classic examples of a *per se* violation . . . is an agreement between competitors at the same level of the market structure to allocate territories in order to minimize competition."[147] Courts have consistently found territorial allocations among competitors to be per se illegal.[148] In *Palmer v. BRG of Georgia,* to pick one example, the Supreme Court applied per se illegality to an agreement by which competitors divided markets, agreeing not to compete in the other's territory.[149]

Settlement agreements by which brands pay generics not to enter the market threaten dangers similar to territorial market allocation. But instead of allocating geographic space, they allocate time, with the brand blocking all competition for a period of time.[150]

Nor is it a defense that settlements only block potential competitors not certain to enter the market. The D.C. Circuit in the *Microsoft* case asserted that "it would be inimical to the purpose of the Sherman Act to allow monopolists free reign to squash nascent, albeit unproven, competitors at will."[151] The leading antitrust treatise similarly explains that "the law does not condone the purchase of protection from uncertain competition any more than it condones the elimination of actual competition."[152]

The anticompetitive harm at issue has human consequences. Artificially high prices result in patients not filling prescriptions or splitting pills in half.[153] Decisions not to comply with doctors' orders because of high costs result in pain, more severe medical conditions, and even death.[154] Such harms are magnified by the blockbuster nature of many of the drugs at the center of reverse payment agreements.

---

147. *United States v. Topco Assocs., Inc.,* 405 U.S. 596, 608 (1972).

148. ABA SECTION OF ANTITRUST LAW, ANTITRUST LAW DEVELOPMENTS 103 (6th ed. 2007).

149. 498 U.S. 46, 49–50 (1990) (per curiam).

150. In re *Schering,* 2003 WL 22989651, Part II.A.

151. *United States v. Microsoft Corp.,* 253 F.3d 34, 79 (D.C. Cir. 2001) (en banc).

152. XII HERBERT HOVENKAMP, ANTITRUST LAW: AN ANALYSIS OF ANTITRUST PRINCIPLES AND THEIR APPLICATION ¶ 2030b, at 213 (2d ed. 2005).

153. Brief of Amicus Curiae The American Antitrust Institute in Support of Petitioners, In re *Tamoxifen Citrate Antitrust Litigation,* No. 06-830, at 8 (U.S. 2006).

154. Thomas Rice & Karen Y. Matsuoka, *The Impact of Cost-Sharing on Appropriate Utilization and Health Status: A Review of the Literature on Seniors,* 61 MED. CARE RES. & REV. 415, 420, 427–28 (2004).

Not all patent settlements, to be sure, constitute market allocation agreements. If a patent is valid and infringed, the patentee could rely on the patent itself to restrict competition. In that case, an agreement that allows a generic to enter before the end of the patent term could increase competition. On the other hand, if a patent is invalid or not infringed, there is no legitimate justification for delaying competition. In such a setting, the agreement serves as a cover for market allocation agreements.

The appropriate antitrust treatment of patent settlements thus depends on the validity of the patent and existence of infringement. But the most straightforward way to determine these issues, patent litigation, is not appropriate in this setting. Determining patent validity and infringement would require significant analysis and testimony on complex issues such as patent claim interpretation and infringement analysis. Such inquiries, which could take weeks, cannot easily be inserted as mini-trials within antitrust cases.

In addition, an analysis of the merits of the patent infringement case tends to be unreliable. After a case settles, the parties' interests become aligned, with a generic firm lacking the incentive to vigorously attack a patent's validity or an infringement claim. In the *Schering* case, the generic had initially certified that the brand's patent was invalid or not infringed by its product. After settlement, the generic's views "dramatically changed," with the chief financial officer testifying that because of the risk posed by infringement damages, the company would not market its drug until the litigation was concluded.[155]

But another option is available. Red flags of potential invalidity are raised when brands pay generics more than they ever could have gained by entering the market. Further hoisting such flags are the parties' aligned incentives. Because the brand makes more by keeping the generic out of the market than the two parties would make by competing in the market, the parties have an incentive to split the monopoly profits, making each better off than if the generic had entered. These shared monopoly profits come at the public's expense.

Other settlement provisions, such as royalty payments to the patentee, do not align incentives as directly. Instead, they reflect a compromise of the parties' assessments of litigation success. And they do not offer greater rewards than the generic could have received by winning its infringement case.[156]

In short, settlements allowing entry before the end of the term of a valid patent offer benefits for competition. On the other hand, agreements resolving litigation on invalid patents that delay generic entry harm competition. While a direct determination of patent validity may not be possible, a strong indicator of invalidity exists in the form of excessive payments. Absent proof of consideration for a brand's significant payment to a generic, the quid pro quo for the payment

---

155. In re *Schering Plough*, 2003 WL 22989651, Part II.C.

156. Thomas B. Leary, *Antitrust Issues in the Settlement of Pharmaceutical Patent Disputes, Part III*, 30 SEATTLE U. L. REV. 377, 391 (2007).

would appear to be the generic's agreement to defer entry beyond "the date that represents an otherwise reasonable litigation compromise."[157] Given the severe anticompetitive effects of market division, courts must search for such indicators.

Finally, two characteristics distinguish reverse payments from other regulatory activity and settlements. First, the remedies are more likely to lie within courts' expertise. The Supreme Court in *Trinko* worried about courts' ability to craft remedies for unilateral refusals to deal, for which they would need to determine the assets to be shared and price charged for the shared assets.[158] In contrast, courts are more likely to correctly analyze agreements between competitors.

They also are able to determine whether reverse payments represent an objective assessment of the transferred asset's value or an excessive payment to delay entry. Such an inquiry is easier than other obligations such as the reasonable royalty calculation in determining patent damages. Courts calculating reasonable royalties construct a hypothetical licensing negotiation to determine what the infringer would have paid, considering factors such as the rate for similar patents, the importance of the invention, and expert testimony.[159] In contrast to selecting a reasonable royalty from an infinite array of potential rates, the inquiry here begins with a single specified rate and asks whether it appears unreasonable. In the *Schering* case, the FTC demonstrated how to execute such an inquiry by exhaustively documenting the company's lack of interest in the transaction.[160]

The second characteristic is the unique ability of these agreements to create barriers to entry. Other settlements do not prevent third parties from challenging patents. In the Hatch-Waxman context, in contrast, they delay, if not prevent, other challenges. Moreover, after the brand firm settles with the first generic filer, subsequent generics would be less motivated to pursue a challenge since they would be further behind in the approval process, would not be entitled to the market exclusivity period, and would receive a return dependent on the outcome of the first filer's suit.[161] Such hurdles loom large given the costs of developing generic drugs and receiving FDA approval.

In short, Hatch-Waxman presents a regulatory regime that antitrust courts cannot avoid. The generic companies charged with enforcing the scheme are not effectively doing so. Antitrust can play a critical role in returning the statute to its intended purposes. In the process, it can punish the most concerning type of market activity, thereby promoting competition and benefiting consumers.

---

157. FTC Cert Petition, at 18.

158. HERBERT HOVENKAMP, THE ANTITRUST ENTERPRISE 247–48 (2005).

159. *Georgia-Pacific Corp. v. United States Plywood Corp.*, 318 F. Supp. 1116 (S.D.N.Y. 1970); *see generally* Mark A. Lemley & Carl Shapiro, *Patent Holdup and Royalty Stacking*, 85 TEX. L. REV. 1991, 2018–19 (2007).

160. In re *Schering-Plough Corp.*, 2003 WL 22989651, Part IV.

161. Hemphill, at 1586.

Reverse Payments

The antitrust harm of market division is even more pronounced in the context of reverse payments. Significant validity concerns are raised when a brand pays a generic more than it could have achieved by winning its lawsuit and entering the market. Reverse payments are particularly suspicious in aligning the parties' incentives. Sharing monopoly profits is more profitable for the brand and generic companies than competing for duopoly (and, as additional generics enter, even smaller) profits. In fact, the generic often gains more through settlement than through successful litigation. Generics have powerful incentives to file the first patent challenge but little incentive to pursue the litigation.[162]

Other types of agreements do not align the parties' incentives as directly. One example is a traditional licensing agreement by which a generic pays a brand to enter the market. This resembles the typical settlement that presents significantly less concern because it leads to more competition. And it presents different incentives, with the brand seeking higher royalties and the generic desiring lower payments.

Another example, though slightly more nuanced, involves the determination of the date of generic entry. Commentators have reasonably viewed the incentives of the parties as divergent, with a brand firm desiring late entry and a generic firm coveting early entry.[163] To the extent a generic firm prefers the certainty of an exclusivity period to its early commencement, the parties' incentives might be modestly more aligned.[164] The reverse payment scenario, in contrast, does not offer any deviation from wholly aligned incentives.

Finally, as an empirical matter, reverse payments do not appear necessary to settle disputes between brands and generics. These payments disappear when challenged and reappear when the antitrust coast is clear. Between 1992 and 1999, 8 of the 14 final settlements between brands and generic first-filers involved reverse payments.[165] In 2000, the FTC announced that it would challenge such settlements.[166] In the succeeding four years, between 2000 and 2004, *not one* of 20 reported agreements involved a brand firm paying a generic filer to delay

---

162. Leary, at 381.

163. Hovenkamp, Janis, & Lemley, at 1762.

164. Hemphill, at 1593.

165. Federal Trade Commission Bureau of Competition, *Agreements Filed with the Federal Trade Commission under the Medicare Prescription Drug, Improvement, and Modernization Act of 2003: Summary of Agreements Filed in FY 2005*, at 4 (Apr. 2006), http://www.ftc.gov/os/2006/04/fy2005drugsettlementsrpt.pdf.

166. Abbott Labs and Geneva Pharms., File No. 981-0395 (Statement of Chairman Robert Pitofsky and Commissioners Sheila F. Anthony, Mozelle W. Thompson, Orson Swindle, and Thomas B. Leary) (Mar. 16, 2000), http://www.ftc.gov/os/2000/03/hoe-schtandrxcommstmt.htm.

entering the market.[167] During this period, parties continued settling their disputes, but in ways less restrictive of competition, such as through licenses allowing early generic entry.

In 2005, after the *Schering* and *Tamoxifen* courts took a lenient view of these agreements, the reverse payment floodgates opened. In 2005, 3 of 11 final settlements (27 percent) between brand-name and generic firms included such payments. In 2006, 14 of 28 settlements (50 percent) contained these provisions.[168] And in 2007, 14 of 33 settlements (42 percent) included such compensation.[169] Equally concerning, in recent years roughly 70 to 80 percent of settlements between brand firms and first generic filers have involved reverse payments.[170]

Given all this background, payments from brands to generics that exceed what the generics could have gained by entering the market provide strong evidence of invalidity. In particular, they indicate a patentee's serious doubts about validity. The less likely a patent is valid, the more likely a patentee would make a large payment to a generic to prevent it from challenging the patent.

Rebuttal

The last four sections have shown that the appropriate default position for reverse payment settlements should be presumptive illegality. But because in certain cases payments could reflect an objective assessment of the patent's strength, the settling parties should have the opportunity to rebut this presumption. In offering such a rebuttal, I conservatively allow the parties to introduce arguments that have been offered in the economic literature. If judicial experience demonstrates that these arguments do not in fact justify the payments, then per se illegality might ultimately become a more appropriate treatment.

An agreement concerning the generic entry date, without any cash payment, often reflects the odds of the parties' success in patent litigation.[171] By way of example, if there were 10 years remaining in the patent term and the parties agreed

---

167. Federal Trade Commission Bureau of Competition, *Agreements Filed with the Federal Trade Commission under the Medicare Prescription Drug, Improvement, and Modernization Act of 2003: Summary of Agreements Filed in FY 2006*, at 4 (Apr. 2006), http://www.ftc.gov/os/2006/04/fy2005drugsettlementsrpt.pdf [hereinafter FY 2006 Agreements].

168. *Id.*

169. Federal Trade Commission Bureau of Competition, *Agreements Filed with the Federal Trade Commission under the Medicare Prescription Drug, Improvement, and Modernization Act of 2003: Summary of Agreements Filed in FY 2007*, at 3 (May 2008), http://www.ftc.gov/os/2008/05/mmaact.pdf [hereinafter FY 2007 Agreements].

170. *Id.* at 5 (11 of 16 agreements, or 69 percent); FY 2006 Agreements at 6 (9 of 11 agreements, or 82 percent).

171. Robert D. Willig & John P. Bigelow, *Antitrust Policy Toward Agreements that Settle Patent Litigation*, 49 ANTITRUST BULL. 655, 660 (2004).

there was a 60 percent chance that a court would uphold the patent's validity, the mean probable date of entry under litigation would occur in 6 years.[172]

A brand is likely to gain additional exclusivity by supplementing the parties' entry date agreement with a payment to the generic. Continuing the example above, the brand could pay the generic to gain an additional 3 years (for a total of 9 years) of exclusivity. The monopoly profits the brand earned in these 3 years would vastly exceed the reduced profits it would earn from sharing the market with the generic. Even with a payment to the generic, the brand would still come out ahead. And the generic would also benefit since the payment would exceed the profits it could have gained by entering the market.

In buying more exclusivity than the patent alone could provide, reverse payments tend not to reflect an objective assessment of validity. In most cases, the patentee would not pay more than its litigation costs unless it believed it was buying later generic entry than litigation would provide.[173] That may not be the case, however, when the parties can demonstrate the reasonableness of the payment. Four potential settings in which the parties could show this include (1) payments no higher than litigation costs, (2) "cash-strapped generics," (3) parties with asymmetric information, and (4) otherwise reasonable payments.

First, if the payment is no higher than litigation costs, it is more likely to represent an objective assessment of patent validity. Once the brand sues the generic, each side must pay litigation costs. A reverse payment that does not exceed these costs does not present significant concern since the parties would have been required to spend this money in any event.[174] Litigation costs include a party's out-of-pocket costs and attorneys' fees from the time of settlement until the end of the case.[175]

Second, cash-strapped generics need to receive cash quickly. As a result, they could insist on entry earlier than the mean probable date of entry.[176] But because the brand company does not share this view, the parties cannot reach a settlement solely along the dimension of time. The payment of money could bridge the gap, allowing the generic to accept a later entry date while providing it with needed cash.[177]

Third, informational asymmetries could justify reverse payments. One such asymmetry involves information about the patent's value. The brand firm could have better information than the generic about the state of the market and the

---

172. Marc G. Schildkraut, *Patent-Splitting Settlements and the Reverse Payment Fallacy*, 71 ANTITRUST L.J. 1033, 1043 (2004).

173. Shapiro, at 407–08.

174. The conclusion is slightly more nuanced since the brand also pays the generic's costs, which it would not otherwise have paid. Hemphill, at 1594–95.

175. Hovenkamp, Janis & Lemley, at 1760 n.177.

176. Schildkraut, at 1059.

177. *Id.* at 1059–63.

period of time the patent will have economic value.[178] When the patent's value is high, bargaining may not lead to agreement since the brand does not wish to cede its valuable monopoly and the generic insufficiently appreciates an offer for modestly earlier entry. In this scenario, a reverse payment could bridge the gap. Although the parties could disagree over the valuation of potential entry dates, they do not differ on the valuation of cash.[179]

Fourth, in a more general defense, the parties could demonstrate the reasonableness of any payments. Such a showing could rely on factors such as (1) sales projections, (2) market analyses, (3) payments for similar products, and (4) the brand's interest in the product and due diligence. In the *Schering* case, the FTC conducted an exhaustive analysis on the issue, ultimately concluding that Schering's licenses greatly exceeded the value of the products it received.[180]

Each of these four scenarios could conceivably occur. As a result, per se illegality is not (at least yet) an appropriate treatment for reverse payment settlements. But the identification of particular scenarios in which reverse payments could be justified is a far cry from a determination that they explain behavior in most cases. For that reason, commentators' arguments for why patentees might need to make reverse payments in certain situations does not demonstrate the propriety of Rule-of-Reason analysis as a default framework.

In fact, one model predicted that 92 percent of cases in which reverse payments were necessary to reach settlement were likely to reduce consumer welfare.[181] Among the cases in which reverse payments were needed, the surplus loss from inefficient settlements was nearly 30 times the surplus gain from efficient settlements.[182] And given the infrequent need for reverse payments to attain settlement, the model's authors concluded that less than one-half of 1 percent of efficient settlements would occur only because of reverse payments.

The Hatch-Waxman framework, drafters' intentions, severe anticompetitive harms of market allocation, and uniquely concerning nature of reverse payments counsel placing the burden on the settling parties to show the reasonableness of the payments. As a final justification for putting the burden on the defendants, the settling parties are most likely to have the relevant information in their possession.

The parties must demonstrate the reasonableness of the payments, typically by producing sufficient evidence to place the payment in one of the four recognized categories. As the FTC has suggested, they must show that the justifications are cognizable and plausible.[183] For example, if the parties rely on a defense

---

178. Willig & Bigelow, at 660.

179. *Id.* at 661.

180. In re *Schering-Plough Corp.*, 2003 WL 22989651, Part IV.

181. Leffler & Leffler, at 484.

182. *Id.*

183. In re *Schering-Plough*, 2003 WL 22989651, Part I.C.

of cash-starved generics, they must show that the generic actually was cash-starved and that the support resulted in the generic entering the market earlier than it otherwise would have.[184] If the parties can introduce such evidence, agencies and courts should uphold the settlement under the Rule of Reason. In such a case, the reasonableness of the payment reflects an objective likelihood of the patent's validity.

Putting the burden on the settling parties to demonstrate a payment's reasonableness also makes sense given the more nuanced agreements into which firms have recently entered. No longer are brand firms making simple cash payments for generics not to enter the market. Instead, they are paying generics for IP licenses, for the supply of raw materials or finished products, and for helping to promote products. They are paying milestones, up-front payments, and development fees for unrelated products. And, in the latest trend, they are agreeing not to launch authorized, brand-sponsored, generics.[185]

Many of these provisions—such as a supply agreement by which a brand pays a generic *even if it does not supply the product*—exceed the fair market value for the item.[186] Of particular concern, side payments appeared in nearly all the settlements that restrained generic entry but few of the settlements that did not.[187] Nor is the product provided by the generic typically even one that the brand had sought before the settlement.[188] In other words, it is becoming harder for plaintiffs to track down evidence of payments for delay.[189] To demonstrate the reasonableness of these side payments, it would be necessary for courts to examine product promotion expenses, supply invoices indicating the cost of raw materials, the value of IP licenses, and similar figures.[190]

It therefore makes sense to put the burden on the settling parties to provide evidence of the payments as well as their reasonableness. The parties would be more likely to possess this evidence and more likely to demonstrate the transaction's fair market value.

---

184. *Id.*, Part III.

185. FY 2007 Agreements, at 2; FY 2006 Agreements, at 4–5.

186. FY 2006 Agreements, at 5.

187. Prepared Statement of the FTC Before the Comm. on the Judiciary of the U.S. Senate, *Anticompetitive Patent Settlements in the Pharmaceutical Industry: The Benefits of a Legislative Solution*, at 17 (Jan. 17, 2007), http://www.ftc.gov/speeches/leibowitz/070117 anticompetitivepatentsettlements_senate.pdf.

188. C. Scott Hemphill, *Drug Patent Settlements Between Rivals: A Survey*, at 15 (2007), http://ssrn.com/abstract=969492.

189. For a recent attempt to do so, see the FTC's 2008 complaint against Cephalon, which alleged "side-term inducements" (such as licenses to IP, supply agreements, and codevelopment deals) to generics so they did not challenge its sleep-disorder drug Provigil. Complaint ¶ 56, *FTC v. Cephalon, Inc.*, No. 08-cv-2141-RBS (E.D. Pa.).

190. Andersen, at 72–74.

In short, the Act's preference for patent challenges, together with regulatory barriers to entry and the potential severe anticompetitive effects and uniquely concerning nature of reverse payments, supports a default position of presumptive illegality.

CONCLUSION

Reverse payment agreements present complicated behavior lying at the intersection of patents, antitrust, the FDA process, and the Hatch-Waxman Act. Courts have ignored the guidance provided by the Act in emphasizing policies such as the importance of settlements and presumption of patent validity.

In this chapter, I have shown the importance of Hatch-Waxman in providing Congress's specific views on the reconciliation of the patent and antitrust laws. The legislature's finely tuned equilibrium underscores the importance of generic competition and patent challenges and minimizes the policies favoring settlement. As the Supreme Court reminded us in *Trinko*, courts must consider the applicable regulatory regime in determining the appropriate antitrust scrutiny. Such consideration is particularly necessary given the Act's increasing ineffectiveness as reverse payment settlements reduce generic competition and patent challenges.

Antitrust can ameliorate this deficiency. Given the severe anticompetitive harm presented by market division and the significant validity questions presented by reverse payment agreements, aggressive antitrust scrutiny is appropriate. In fact, given the inability of antitrust courts to directly determine patent validity, the proxy of unjustified settlements provides the best available evidence of invalidity.

Courts should treat reverse payment settlements as presumptively anticompetitive. The settling parties can demonstrate that the payments are reasonable and reflect an objective assessment of the patent's validity. But in the vast majority of cases, presumptive illegality will resuscitate the generic competition at the heart of the Act. Given the importance of the drugs subject to reverse payments and the far-reaching effects of skyrocketing health care costs, a more justified and aggressive framework for such agreements would offer significant benefits.

CONCLUSION

This book has sought to transform the role of the law from innovation's distracted bystander to its avid promoter.

The ten proposals I offer improve the laws having the most direct effect on innovation. They encompass some of the most important and debated doctrines in copyright, patent, and antitrust law. They cover a wide swath of the economy, including the biotechnology, pharmaceutical, software, and electronics industries. They affect some of the hottest topics in innovation today, including BlackBerry devices, P2P software, and generic drugs. And they address topics of global appeal and consider the laws of Australia, China, the European Union, India, Japan, and Korea.

Throughout the book, I have crafted proposals that are calibrated to, and extend no further than necessary in addressing, various harms. For example, I conclude that the equilibrium on patented research tools displaces the need for action but calls for proposals if the situation changes. Recommendations on material transfers are cognizant of business realities, with academia and industry more likely to agree on publication restrictions than reach-through licenses that reserve rights to materials providers. And the proposal for post-grant oppositions introduces opposition fees and fee-shifting mechanisms that aim to deter frivolous challenges.

The proposals also are practical and realistic. Commentators sometimes offer complicated recommendations. But my proposals—covering, for example, *Sony*, statutory damages, the *eBay* framework, and settlements—are simple enough that courts can easily apply them. Other actors also can implement the recommendations. Congress can enact a post-grant opposition system and revise the DMCA. Universities can adopt model material transfer agreements. And the antitrust agencies can follow a predictable innovation markets framework.

The proposals also open the door to rich insights that have been advanced in the innovation literature. Two foster disruptive innovation—and seek to cultivate the next iPod, TiVo, or BitTorrent file-sharing software—by bolstering dual-use technology and abolishing mammoth statutory damage awards. Two others promote user innovation, modifying the DMCA to increase contributions to aftermarket products and laying the foundation for an experimental use defense based on scientists' creation of research tools.

As an added bonus, the proposals rescue Congress's intent. The drafters of the DMCA targeted pirates, not interoperable devices. Statutory damages assured adequate compensation, not stifled investment and innovation. The Hatch-Waxman Act encouraged generic competition, not settlements prohibiting patent challenges.

In writing this book, I have sought to embark upon a new era in the often chilly IP-antitrust relationship. Fresh from the 20th-century battles about which field was "superior," I offer a new, 21st-century road map that treats the laws as collaborators. Improving IP law reduces antitrust's burdens. Improving antitrust helps to cabin IP. Antitrust concepts of consumer demand and error costs help fix the DMCA, patent relief, and dual-use technologies. And IP concepts and industry-specific realities assist settlements, SSOs, and innovation markets.

Until now, measurement difficulties have kept innovation in the dark. Courts have shined their lights elsewhere—on price or copyright infringement. This book illuminates the light of innovation and shines it across an expansive range of business activity. The result: proposals that show just how much innovation has been neglected.

None of us like to lose our security blanket. We may be apprehensive about abandoning our crutches of price and creativity. But we have no choice. We must carve out a greater role for innovation in copyright, patent, and antitrust law. Our livelihoods and our economy demand no less.

INDEX

3G wireless systems, and patent pools, 96

3M Innovative Properties Co. v. Avery Denison Corp., 248

321 Studios, as victim of litigation asymmetry, 132

35 U.S.C. § 271(e), FDA Act, described, 260, 261n

AARP, 98, 360

A.B. Dick v. Henry, 74

abandoned research lines, 282

Abbreviated New Drug Application (ANDA), described, 351–352

Acacia, 235

access ban, defined, 179

Accolade, 174–176

Accolade, Sega Enterprises Ltd. v., 174–176, 178, 183, 197

Acid Pro, 50

acquisition of IP, as principle in IP Guidelines, 81

active inducement test, 136

Acuff-Rose Music, Inc., Campbell v., 176

Administrative Patent Judges (APJs), 225

aftermarkets
  defined, 164
  and monopolies, 197
  overview of, 170–171
  as potential monopolies, 64, 165
  as protected by DMCA, 184–184
  revenues obtained from, 171
  as threat to innovation, 54

Aging, Senate Special Committee on, 346n

AHP-American Cyanimid merger, 313n

AHRA (Audio Home Recording Act of 1992), 122

Aibo, robotic dog, 190, 196

Aibopet, 190

AIDS research, 255, 313

Aimster, 117, 132

Aimster case. *See In re Aimster Copyright Litigation*

AIPLA (American Intellectual Property Lawyers Association), 218

Alcoa, 63

Allied Tube & Conduit Corp. v. Indian Head, Inc., 93, 330–331

allocative efficiency, defined, 63, 65

all-or-nothing scenario, defined, 338

A&M Records, Inc. v. Napster, Inc., 115–116, 135–136, 137–138

Amazon.com, 27
  cloud computing, affected by, 143
  as disruptive innovation, 28
  new technology, use of, 142
  promotion innovation of, 52

Amerge, 315

America Online, 178

America Online Instant Messaging Service, 116

American Antitrust Institute, 95n

American Bar Association Section of IP Law, 227–228

American Home Products-American Cyanamid merger, 92

American Intellectual Property Lawyers Association (AIPLA), 218

American Inventors Protection Act (1999), 212

American National Standards Institute (ANSI), 326, 341

American Patents Development Corp., Carbice Corp. of America v., 75

American Society of Mechanical Engineers v. Hydrolevel Corp., 93, 331

American Society of Sanitary Engineering case. *See In re American Society of Sanitary Engineering*

American Tobacco, 67

ANDA (Abbreviated New Drug Application), described, 351–352

Anderson, Chris, 141

Andrx Pharmaceuticals, 357–358

ANSI (American National Standards Institute), 326, 341

anticommons
    defined, 53, 253
    infringement, as causing, 256
    overview of, 255–256, 268
    and "tragedy of the commons,"
        53n, 256n
anticompetitive effects
    pharmaceutical companies and, 98–99
    reverse payments and, 98
    and SSOs, 335–336
Anti-Trust Acts, 75
*Antitrust Guidelines for the Licensing of
    Intellectual Property. See* IP Guidelines
antitrust law
    agreements and, 56–58
    benefits of, 67–68
    and consumer demand, 7
    copyrights *vs.*, 173–174
    cost of, 68
    Crandall and Winston, theories
        of, 65–66
    DMCA and, 165
    economic growth and, 65
    economic theories, 63–66
    effect on innovation, overview of, 3–4,
        5–6, 9–10
    error-costs analysis, overview of, 7
    flaws of, 64–66
    history of, 61–64
    innovation and, 68–69, 292
    innovative efficiency, as primary
        goal of, 65
    IP law, in conflict with, 4, 71–73
    market power and, 194
    mergers and, 59–61
    monopolies and, 58–59
    need for, 65
    overview, 55–61
    patent law *vs.*, 8
    regulation, relationship with, 371
    repeal of, for export cartels, 67
    secret language of, 16
    states' role in, 61n
    and trade secrets, 22
    view of standards, 324
Antitrust Modernization Commission,
    overview of, 5–6
AOL. *See* America Online
AOL Time Warner's Reprise Records, 125

Apache, as user innovation, 29
API (application programming
    interface), 167
APJs (Administrative Patent Judges),
    225, 225n
Appalachian Coals, Inc. v. United States, 62
Apple, 50, 87
application programming interface (API),
    defined, 167
appropriability
    defined, 302
    and innovation markets, 302–303
    and monopoly, 302
*Approved Drug Products with Therapeutic
    Equivalence Evaluations. See* Orange
    Book
Arnold, Schwinn, & Co., United States v., 78
Arrow, Kenneth, 298
Article 82. *See* Treaty Establishing the
    European Community (EC Treaty)
*Aspen Highlands Skiing Corp., Aspen Skiing
    Co. v.,* 58
*Aspen Skiing Co. v. Aspen Highlands Skiing
    Corp.,* 58
assembly code, defined, 168
Astra-Zeneca, 318–319
ATMI, Inc., Praxair, Inc. v., 242,
    246, 252
AT&T, 371
Audio Home Recording Act of 1992
    (AHRA), 122
Australia, 166, 176, 182, 263
authorized generics, defined, 98
author's life plus 70 years, 41, 46, 103
Aventis, 317
*Avery Denison Corp., 3M Innovative
    Properties Co. v.,* 248

Bahrain, 166
Bainwol, Rich, 155
Baker, Jonathan, 67–68
balance of hardships, 241, 244–249
Barnes and Noble, 27
Barnett, Thomas, 94, 334
Barr Laboratories, 361–362
basic input-output system (BIOS), 175
Battle.net, 188–189, 196
Baxter-Immuno merger, 92, 313,
    316–318, 321

Bayh-Dole Act, 202–203
  commercializing patents, role in, 272
  and material transfer agreements, 284
  and the NIH, 274
  preamble amended (2000), 273–274
  proposed reform of, 254, 268, 271–275,
    271n, 278
  purpose of, 257, 271–272
BearShare, 119
Bell, Alexander Graham, 129
Bentham, Jeremy, 45
Berkey Photo, Inc. v. Eastman
  Kodak Co., 78
Bessen, James, 49
Betamax VCR, 41, 106, 107, 108, 109,
  323–324
Bibster, and P2P, 139
bid rigging, defined, 56
Billing, Credit Suisse Securities v., 371, 373
Biogen, 314
biomedical research, and the NIH, 274
BIOS (basic input-output system), 175
biotechnology
  in Australia, study on, 263
  bottlenecks created by patents, 53,
    202–203, 264
  defined, 254
  experimental use defense and harm,
    263–264
  in Germany, study on, 263
  in Japan, study on, 263
  and licensing, 264
  patents, empirical study on, 262
  research tools, overview of, 254–255
  role of patents in innovation, 47
BitTorrent, 28, 125, 139–140
Black & Decker, Inc. v. Robert Bosch Tool
  Corporation, 240, 245
black box testing, defined, 168n
BlackBerry, 8, 231–232, 234, 250
Blackmun, Justice Harry, 110–111
blanket licenses, 72, 78
Bliley, Tom, 183
Blizzard case. See Davidson Associates v.
  Jung
Blizzard Entertainment, 140, 188–189
block booking, defined, 76
blockbuster drugs, 356, 368
"blocking patent" inventions, 269n

Blood Products Advisory Committee of
  the Center for Biologics Evaluation and
  Research, 317n
Blu-Ray technology, 9, 324, 327
BMG, 124, 159
BMI Music, Inc. v. Columbia Broadcasting,
  Inc., 78
BnetD, 188–189, 196
Board of Patent Appeals and
  Interferences, 212, 225, 232n
Board of Trade of Chicago v. United States, 57
Boiler and Pressure Vessel Code (SSO), 331
Bolar Pharmaceutical Co., Roche Products,
  Inc. v., 258–259, 260, 348
bonds, posting, 154
Bork, Robert, 63
Bosch Tool Corporation, Black & Decker, Inc.
  v., 240, 245
Boskin, Michael, 32
bottlenecks
  created by blocking patents, 342
  created by patent cases, 53, 253
  generic vs. brand drugs, 354
  and market power, 252
  in university-industry relationships, 267
Bowman, Ward, 72
boycotts
  as per se illegal, 62
  and SSOs, 343
BRCA genes, 255
breast cancer research, 255, 267, 361–363
Breyer, Justice Stephen, 118, 238
BRG of Georgia, Palmer v., 374
Broadcom Corp. v. Qualcomm, Inc., 332n
Brooktrout, Inc. v. Eicon Networks
  Corp., 240
Buffalo Technology Inc., Commonwealth
  Scientific and Industrial Research
  Organisation v., 240, 241, 247, 251, 252
burden-shifting, pros and cons of, 57
Bureau of Economic Analysis, 30
Bureau of Labor Statistics, 30
Bush, President George W., 285
business climate, role in innovation, 24

California Air Resources Board, 329,
  331–332
California Dental Association v. FTC, 57
Campana, Thomas, Jr., 231–232

Campbell, Eric, empirical studies by, 281–285

Campbell v. Acuff-Rose Music, Inc., 176

cancer research, 255, 267, 318–319, 361–363

Canon photocopiers, as disruptive innovation, 28

Caouette, Jonathan, 50

Carbice Corp. of America v. American Patents Development Corp., 75

Carderm, 357

Cardizem case. *See In re Cardizem CD Antitrust Litigation*

cartels, 67, 336n

Cartia XT, 358

CD-4, 313–314

CD sales
 MP3.com and, 153–155
 music artists and, 124–125
 popularity of, 177
 P2P and, 119–122, 130
 recording industry, dependence on, 124n

Cephalon, 38n

Chamberlain Group, Inc. v. Skylink Technologies, Inc., 186–187, 195n, 197

Change Exchange, Telequip Corp. v., 241, 248

Charles Schwab, as disruptive innovation, 28

Cherry Auction, Fonovisa v., 109

Chesterfield v. United States, 258

Chicago School of Economics, 2n, 63, 64, 66, 78

Chile, 166

China, 166, 181, 270

Christensen, Clayton, 10, 27, 28, 126

Ciba-Geigy-Sandoz merger, 92, 313n

CinemaNow, 124

Cipro, 368

Ciprofloxacin case. *See In re Ciprofloxacin Hydrochloride Antitrust Litigation*

circumvent, defined, 180

Cisco, 330

Civil War, business after, 61

claim construction, defined, 37–38, 202

Claritin, 368

Clayton Act, 61n, 62, 74

client-server model, 111–112

Clinton administration, and DMCA, 179, 184

cloning, gene, 254, 268

cloud computing, 143–144

Codes of Fair Competition, 67

Cohen-Boyer, 254, 268

collusion
 and antitrust law, 65–66
 cost of preventing, 68
 danger of, 307

Colombia, 166

Columbia Broadcasting, Inc., BMI Music, Inc. v., 78

Comcast, 235

commentary, as copyright infringement defense, 42

Commission (Magill), RTE & ITP v., 90–91

Comm'n of the European Cmtys., Microsoft Corp. v., 89–92, 167

common-law defense, overview of, 257–260

Commonwealth Scientific and Industrial Research Organisation (CSIRO), 240

Commonwealth Scientific and Industrial Research Organisation v. Buffalo Technology Inc., 240, 241, 247, 251, 252

community colleges, as disruptive innovation, 28

company atmosphere, role in innovation, 23–24

competition
 irreparable harm and, 244–247
 as per se illegal, 374
 procompetitive justifications of SSOs, 339–342
 purpose of, 84n
 See also anticompetitive effects

competitive harm
 and market concentration, 312
 and R&D, 308

complex *vs.* discrete innovation, 26

compulsory license, as copyright infringement defense, 42

computer software
 anticompetitive uses of, 170
 bottlenecks created by patents, 53
 client-server model, overview of, 111–112
 and copyright, overview of, 171–174
 copyright protection granted, 21, 40, 172

decompiled object code, importance of, 168
file sharing, 111–115, 119, 122, 139–140
General Public License (GPL), 50–51, 188
interoperability, importance of, 170, 173
lock-in, defined, 329–330
open source movement, 50–51
overview of, 167–168
and post-grant opposition time frame, 220
price, affordable, 112–113
as protected by DMCA, 163–165
reverse engineering and, 166, 168–170, 176
and standards, 324n–325n
technological *vs.* legal protection, 176
as utilitarian, 173
conglomerate mergers, defined, 59n
Congress
    Federal Trade Commission (FTC), enacted by, 62
    intent in establishing DMCA, 165, 182–183, 193, 194
    intent in statutory damage remedies, overview, 147–148
    IP reform, role in, 79–80, 244
    new technologies, legislating, 110, 122–123, 144–145
    post-grant opposition, reform legislation for, 217–218
    statutory damages, reasons for implementing, 150–152
    statutory damages, upper limit, as recognized by, 152
Connectix Corporation, Sony Computer Entertainment v., 174, 175–176, 178, 183, 196, 197
Connor, John, 68
Constitution, U.S.
    Congress, power granted to, 110, 244
    Copyright Clause, 124
    and natural-rights theories, 44
    and utilitarian theory, 45
consumer demand
    and antitrust law, 7
    DMCA, importance in, 194–195
Continental TV v. GTE Sylvania, 56, 57, 63, 78, 85

contract law, role in innovation, 24
contributory infringement
    Aimster guilty of, 117
    defined, 38, 41, 108
    example of, 75
    Grokster not guilty of, 117
    Napster guilty of, 116–117
    Patent Act (1952), effect on, 76
    venture capitalists and, 157
CONTU (National Commission on New Technological Uses of Copyrighted Works), 172
convergent medical technologies, defined, 233
coordinated effects theory, defined, 60
Copyright Act, 83, 161, 175, 195n
    of 1790, 41, 149n
    of 1856, 149n
    of 1870, 40
    of 1909, 149–153
    of 1976, 40, 41, 150, 152
    of 1980, 172–174
    defined, 39–40
Copyright Clause of Constitution, 124
copyright estoppel, as copyright infringement defense, 42
copyright law
    effect on innovation, overview of, 3, 6–7
    secret language of, 16
copyrights
    author's life plus 70 years, 41, 46, 103
    client-server computing model and, 112
    creativity, as enhanced by, 126
    dangers of, 54
    duration of, 40–41, 46–47
    exclusion, as the foundation of, 72
    expression *vs.* ideas, protection of, 173
    hindsight, 138
    history of, 177
    importance of, 102–103
    infringement, remedies for, 43
    infringement of, 41–43
    infringement suit, defenses in, 41–43
    IP law, role of, 49–52
    Microsoft, used as defense, 88
    misuse, as copyright infringement defense, 42
    off-shore companies and, 124
    protection, defined, 39–40

copyrights (*cont.*)
rights, described, 40
vs. antitrust principles, 173–174
vs. patents, 40, 173
core-component analysis
described, 247
and inadequate legal remedy,
246–248
"corporate death penalty," 158
corporate law, role in innovation, 24
Costa Rica, 166
Council on Competitiveness, 23
Court of First Instance, described, 89n
courts
antitrust cases, favoring of, 76–77
Congressional reforms, effect of on,
79–80
economics, role of in IP decisions, 78
experimental use, as defense,
restrictions on, 39
intellectual property (IP), favoring of,
73–74, 78–83
patent immunity, disfavoring
of, 74–76
patent law, as guidance for copyright
infringement, 41
Sherman Act, grappling with meaning
of, 62
sources consulted by, 38
statutory damages, upper limit, as
recognized by, 152
Crandall, Robert, 65–66
creation, ease of, as function of copyright,
50–51
Creative Commons, described, 51
Creative Commons licenses, 50–51
creativity *vs.* innovation, 119–128
Credit Suisse Securities v. Billing, 371, 373
cre-loxP mouse, 254
criticism, as copyright infringement
defense, 42
cross-licensing
attacked by court, 76
in complex innovation, 27
as principle in IP Guidelines, 81
upheld by antitrust agencies, 342
See also licensing
CSIRO (Commonwealth Scientific and
Industrial Research Organisation), 240

cumulative innovation, 26
defined, 53
Cutter, Whittemore v., 257–258

D'Arby, Terence Trent (Sananda
Maitreya), 125
"darknets," 124
*Data General v. Grumman Systems Support
Corp.*, 82–83
Dave Matthews Band, 125
Davidson Associates (Blizzard
Entertainment), 140, 188–189
Davidson Associates v. Jung, 187–189,
190, 196
deadweight loss
defined, 53
vitamin sales, as example of, 68
decentralization, as affected by copyright
law, 54
deception, SSO cases involving, 330,
331–332
decompiled object code, importance
of, 168
defacto standard setting, defined, 325, 344
Dell, 93
Dell case. *See In re Dell*
democracy, as affected by copyright
law, 54
Denison, Edward, 32
Department of Justice, U.S.
Antitrust Division, VITA case, 94,
333–334
and *Antitrust Guidelines for the Licensing
of Intellectual Property*, 81
drug agreements and, 354–355
and *Horizontal Merger Guidelines*, 59
innovation-market case, 312n
mergers and, 67, 296
patent pool complaints and, 96
Department of Labor, U.S., 32
Department of Transportation, 67
Depression, Great, effect on
business, 62
designing around the invention, 269
Detkin, Peter, 234
development, as stage of innovation, 20
Diablo (video game), 188
diffusion, as stage of innovation, 20
digital fingerprinting, 123, 137

Digital Millennium Copyright Act (DMCA)
 aftermarkets, effect on, 164–166, 184–185
 amendment, proposed, 193–194
 and *Chamberlain*, 195n
 exemptions, 180–181
 international implications of, 181–182
 legislative history of, 182–184
 limitations of, 7, 194–197
 overview of, 5, 6, 11
 purpose of, 40, 122, 163–164, 179, 193–194
 Section 1201, 179–181, 185–186, 189
 as supporting user innovation, 30
 text of, 179–181
 as threat to innovation, 54
 triennial exemption review, 190–192
digital piracy
 danger to online businesses, 178
 and DMCA, 163–164
 dongles, 192
digital rights management (DRM), 123, 1770–178
digital subscriber line (DSL), 113
digital watermarks, 123
Direct TV, 235
Director, Aaron, 63n
disclosure, disseminating inventive concepts, role in, 269
disclosure rules, defined, 327, 341
discovery, as stage of innovation, 20
discrete *vs.* complex innovation, 26
disruptive innovation
 difficulties facing, 102–103
 new technology as, 126–28
 vs. sustaining innovation, 27–28
dissemination, as function of copyright, 52
distribution of tools (per DMCA), defined, 180
DMCA. *See* Digital Millennium Copyright Act (DMCA)
DNA, 254, 266
doctrine of equivalents, defined, 38
Dodge, Don, 127
Dominican Republic, 166
dongles, defined, 192
downloading music. *See* P2P (peer-to-peer)

drastic *vs.* nondrastic innovation, 301
DRM (digital rights management), 123
drugs
 brand drugs, reason for high cost of, 356
 cost of, 345–346, 355–356
 generic. *See* generic drugs
 human cost of, 374
 See also biotechnology; pharmaceutical industry
DSL (digital subscriber line), 113
dual-use technologies
 examples of, 105, 106, 134
 importance of, 105–106
 infringement cases, overview of, 105–108
 overview of, 6–7, 11
 secondary liability, case examples of, 109–111, 115–119
 statutory damages, elimination of, 102
 statutory damages remedies for infringement of, 43, 54
 as supporting radical innovation, 29
Dugan v. Lear Avia, Inc., 258
Duke University, 259–260
Duke University, Madey v., 259–260, 262
duopolies, 377
DuPont, 254, 265
DVD-ROM, and patent pools, 95, 96
DVDs, high-definition, 9, 324
DVRs, 239, 241, 249
dynamic efficiency, defined, 339

E. Bement & Sons v. National Harrow Co., 73
EAST (Examiner's Automated Search Tool), 207
Eastman Kodak, 64, 78–79, 83–84
Eastman Kodak Co., Berkey Photo, Inc. v., 78
Eastman Kodak Co., Image Technical Services, Inc. v., 83–84
Eastman Kodak Co. v. Image Technical Services, Inc., 64
eBay
 as an aggregator, 142
 as disruptive innovation, 28
 promotion innovation of, 52

eBay v. MercExchange
  holdup and, 328n
  injunctive relief and, 8, 200, 201, 232,
    233, 237–239, 242, 244, 249
  monetary damages and, 39
  patent infringement relief and, 202, 383
  right to exclude and, 248, 251
EC Treaty. *See* Treaty Establishing the
  European Community (EC Treaty)
EchoStar, 235, 239
Echostar Communications Corp., TiVo Inc.
  v., 239, 241, 245, 249
economic growth
  antitrust law and, 65
  relationship to innovation, 31–33, 49
economic theories, antitrust, 63–66
economics, role in court IP decisions, 78
Economist magazine, 272
economy
  role in innovation, 24, 32–33
  standards, role of, 324
Edison, Thomas, 129
education system
  patent fees for, 223
  role in innovation, 23
educational use, as copyright infringement
  defense, 42
EFF (Electronic Frontier Foundation),
  156n, 191
effective patent life, defined, 349–350
Effexor XR, 368
efficiencies
  defined, 65n
  and mergers, 309–311
  types of, 65
EGFR inhibitors, 318–319, 319n–320n
Eicon Networks Corp., Brooktrout,
  Inc. v., 240
Eisenberg, Rebecca, 255–256, 272
El Salvador, 166
Electronic Frontier Foundation (EFF),
  156n, 191
Ellickson, Robert, 266
Embrex, Inc. v. Service Engineering
  Corp., 259
EMI, 124
enablement
  defined, 224
  as patent requirement, 36

Energy and Commerce Committee
  Report, 350
entertainment industry
  and digital rights management, 177–178
  DMCA, role in enacting, 164
  and *Grokster* case, 117
  promotion and new technology, 141
  threatened by innovation, 107–108, 131
  VCR use, objection to, 110
  See also movie industry; music industry;
    recording industry
entrepreneurship, as stage of
  innovation, 20
ephemeral copies, as copyright
  infringement defense, 42
Epidermal Growth Factor receptor
  tyrosine kinase (EGFR) inhibitors,
  318–319, 319n–320n
equitable estoppel, as copyright
  infringement defense, 42
Erbitux, 319
error-costs asymmetry, 106, 128,
  131, 133, 145
ESI Lederle, 359–360
ESTs (expressed sequence tags), 255
Ethernet, defined, 334
EU. *See* European Union (EU)
Eureka Specialty Co., Heaton-Pennisular
  Button-Fastener Co. v., 73
European Commission, Microsoft, case
  against, 89–92, 167
European Court of Justice, 89n, 90–91
European Patent Office, 221, 222
European Union Copyright Directive, 181
European Union (EU), 44
  Court of First Instance, described, 89n
  free trade agreements with U.S., 166
  law *vs.* U.S. law, 90
  Microsoft, case against, 89–92
  and post-grant opposition time frame,
    221, 225
  Technology Transfer Guidelines, 341–342
European Union Software Directive
  (1991), 176
evergreening, defined, 98
ex parte reexaminations
  defined, 211–212
  of patents, 211–212
  and post-grant opposition threshold, 218

Examiner's Answer, 208n
Examiner's Automated Search Tool
    (EAST), 207
examiners (PTO)
    court findings, effect of workload
        on, 37, 200
    evaluation of, 208
    job description, 36–37, 207–208, 209
    workload of, 201, 229
exclusion, antitrust laws and, 72
exclusive rights, need for, 45–46
exclusivity period
    defined, 350, 350n
    and Medicare Modernization Act, 353
Expedia, as disruptive innovation, 28
experimental use
    as common-law defense, 257–260, 257n
    by Federal Circuit, 267
    as patent infringement defense, 39, 253
    statutory exemption, 260–261
    universal application of, 270–271
experimentation, and patent infringement,
    256–257
experimentation on the invention
    defined, 254
    and patented research tools, 268,
        269–271
exports, antitrust laws repealed for, 67
expressed sequence tags (ESTs), 255
expression, as protected by copyright, 173

Facebook, 124, 144
"failing firms" defense, 311
fair use, 152
    as affected by DMCA, 166, 195
    as copyright infringement defense, 42
    and reverse engineering, 164
    in Sega case, 175
    and timing for post-grant
        opposition, 220
false negative (Type II error), 130, 370–371
false positive (Type I error), 130, 370–371
FastTrack, 115, 117
FCC (Federal Communications
    Commission), 134
FDA. See Food and Drug Administration
    (FDA)
FDA Act. See Federal Food, Drug, and
    Cosmetic Act (FDA Act)

Federal Circuit
    and Board of Patent Appeals and
        Interferences, 212, 225, 232n
    on claim construction, 202
    description of, 8, 39, 80
    on experimental use, 202, 254,
        258–260, 267, 348
    on experimentation on the patented
        invention, 270
    and Hatch-Waxman Act revisions, 354
    and identity of requesters, 228n
    on injunctive relief, 39, 232, 236–239
    on patent and antitrust laws, 72
    patentee and antitrust immunity, 84
    and pharmaceutical patentees, 368
    on software patentability, 172
    and SSOs, 332
    on statutory exemption, 260–261, 261n
    and Supreme Court, 200, 202
    on validity, 367
    on willful infringement, 201, 216,
        250–251
    See also specific cases
Federal Communications Commission
    (FCC), 134
Federal Courts Improvement Act (1982),
    78, 80
Federal Food, Drug, and Cosmetic Act
    (FDA Act)
    35 U.S.C. § 271(e), described, 260
    before Hatch-Waxman Act, 349–350
    review process, overview of, 304–306
federal funding. See funding, government
Federal Trade Commission Act (1914), 62,
    95, 293
Federal Trade Commission (FTC)
    and Antitrust Guidelines for the Licensing
        of Intellectual Property, 81
    "Chairman," use of explained, 95n,
        329n
    enacted by Congress, 62
    and Genzyme-Novazyme merger,
        295–296
    and Horizontal Merger Guidelines, 59
    patent pool complaints and, 96
    pharmaceutical companies, lawsuits
        against, 92, 312–322
    and post-grant opposition
        reform, 218

Federal Trade Commission (FTC) (*cont.*)
  purpose of, 346
  Section 5, 335, 359
  SSO lawsuits and, 93–95, 334–335
fee system, for patent opposition, 222–223
FEL (free electron laser), 259–260
Fibrin sealant, 316
field-of-use restrictions, as patent license
  restriction, defined, 72
file sharing
  litigation involving, 115–119, 122
  P2P as mode of, 111–115, 139–140
  See also P2P (peer-to-peer)
financing. *See* funding
fingerprinting, digital, 123, 137
Finland, 23
Firefox, Mozilla, 29, 111
"first office actions on merits,"
  defined, 208
first sale doctrine
  as copyright infringement defense, 42
  defined, 281
first-sale doctrine, as patent infringement
  defense, 38
Fisher, William, 122–123
Fonovisa v. Cherry Auction, 109
Food and Drug Administration (FDA)
  petitions denied by, 99
  stages of review, 296, 351
Ford, Henry, 28
Foreign Patent Access System
  (FPAS), 207
forfeiture events, 353
four-factor test
  as applied, 239–244
  overview of, 238, 244, 250–251, 252
Fox News, 140
FPAS (Foreign Patent Access
  System), 207
France, 32
fraud
  on Copyright Office, as copyright
    infringement defense, 42
  defined, 98
  liability limited to, 85
  willful, and antitrust immunity, 84
free electron laser (FEL), 259–260
free expression, as affected by
  DMCA, 166

free riders
  defined, 4
  taking advantage of innovation, 46
free riding, 210
free speech, as affected by copyright
  law, 54
free trade agreements, and DMCA, 166
Free Trade Area of the Americas
  (FTAA), 166
FTC. *See* Federal Trade Commission
  (FTC)
FTC, California Dental Association v., 57
FTC, Schering-Plough Corp. v., 97–98,
  358–360, 363, 364, 365, 366, 369, 375,
  376, 378
"functionally novel" innovations, 28, 165
funding
  government
    and material transfer agreements
      (MTAs), 284
    and the NIH, 274
    and noncommercial use of
      inventions, 271–272
    as replacing patent incentives,
      273–274
    role in innovation, 22–23
    of stem cell research, 285
    and uniform biological MTAs
      (UBMTAs), 287–288
    of university research, 271
  role in innovation, 24
  See also investment

game theory of economics, defined, 64
garage door opener (GDO), Chamberlain,
  186–187
GarageBand, 50
GATT (General Agreement on Tariffs and
  Trade), 36n
GDP. *See* gross domestic product (GDP)
gene cloning, 254, 268
Genentech, Medimmune v., 200–201
General Agreement on Tariffs and Trade
  (GATT), 36n
General Electric, United States v., 75
General Motors, 312n, 345
General Public License (GPL), 50–51, 188
generic drugs
  authorized, defined, 98

bounties for, 367, 373
in *Cardizem* case, 357–358
and competition, 373
entry date, importance of, 378–380
first filing, importance of, 377–378
and Hatch-Waxman Act, 347–357
monopolies, importance of, 377
and reverse payments, 377–382
in *Schering-Plough* case, 358–360, 366, 375
in *Tamoxifen* case, 361–363
and validity, 368
vs. brand-name drugs, 97–98, 99
Genesis, Sega, 174
Geneva Pharmaceuticals, Inc., Valley Drug Co. v., 365, 369
Genzyme-Novazyme merger, 295–296, 310–311, 313, 320–322
Germany, West, 32, 221, 262, 263, 270
Gillette, King, 170
Ginsburg, Justice Ruth Bader, 118, 238
GlaxoSmithKline, 353
Glaxo-Wellcome merger, 92, 301, 308n, 312n, 313, 314–316, 321
Glaxo-Wellcome—SmithKlineBeecham merger, 92, 308n, 313n
global. *See* international
GlobalSantaFe Corp., 239, 249
GlobalSantaFe Corp., Transocean Offshore Deepwater Drilling, Inc. v., 239, 240, 241, 245, 247, 249
Gmail, 24, 143
GNU, 188, 188n
Gnutella, 115, 117
good cause, in post-grant opposition, 227
Good Technology, 232
Google
 atmosphere good for innovation, 23–24
 cloud computing, affected by, 143
 as disruptive innovation, 28
 how its search engine works, 111, 142
 Viacom copyright infringement suit, 147
government, measurement of innovation, 30
government funding. *See* funding, government
GPL (General Public License), 50–51, 188

grantbacks
 as one of Nine No-No's, 77
 as patent license restriction, defined, 72
Grateful Dead, 125
Great Baltimore Fire (1904), 323
Great Depression, effect on business, 62
Grinnell Corp., United States v., 58
Grokster, 115, 117, 118, 119, 137
Grokster, MGM v., 41, 115, 117–119, 126, 129, 135–136, 139, 159
Groove Networks, and P2P, 139
gross domestic product (GDP)
 role in innovation, 22–23
 See also economic growth
"growth accounting," defined, 31
Grumman Systems Support Corp., Data General v., 82–83
G.S. Suppiger Co., Morton Salt Co. v., 74–75
GTE Sylvania, Continental TV v., 56, 57, 63, 78, 85
Guatemala, 166
Guidelines for the Licensing of Intellectual Property. See IP Guidelines
Guild, Sawin v., 258

Haemacure, 317
Harbour, Pamela, 320
Hart-Scott-Rodino Antitrust Improvements Act (1976), 59
Harvard, 254
Hatch, Orrin, 357, 365
Hatch-Waxman Act (1984)
 2003 revisions, 353–355
 agreements and, 98
 brand-name *vs.* generic drugs, 97, 200–201
 competition and, 351–353
 and generic drug entry, success of, 355–357
 overview of, 9
 and patent challenges, 370, 372–373
 purpose of, 345–346, 347–351, 363
 as regulatory regime, 293
 regulatory structure of, 370, 371–372
 reverse payments, cases involving, 357–363
 Waxman-Hatch Act (former name), 347n

HD-DVD, 9, 327
HDTV, and performance standard, 325
Heart, 125
Heaton-Pennisular Button-Fastener Co. v. Eureka Specialty Co., 73
Hegel, George, 44
Heller, Michael, 255–256
Hemaseel, 317
Henry, A.B. Dick v., 74
high-definition TV (HDTV), and performance standard, 325
historical evidence of patent law and innovation, 49
HIV research, 255, 313
Hoescht Marion Roussel, 357–358
holdup, patent, 328–330, 340, 344
Honduras, 166
Hong Kong, 176
Horizontal Merger Guidelines (1992, 1997)
  competitive harm and, 306–308
  described, 303
  efficiencies and, 309–311
  innovation markets and, 93, 292, 296
  market concentration and, 304–306
  market entry and, 308–309
  mergers and, 59
  Schumpeterian defense and, 311–312
horizontal mergers, defined, 59
horizontal restraints, as principle in IP Guidelines, 81
Hotz, George, 191
House and Senate Judiciary Committee, 183, 350
House Commerce Committee, 183, 190–191
House of Representatives, U.S., 148
5HT-ID, 314
human embryonic stem cell research, 255, 284–285
human talent, role in innovation, 23
Hummer Winblad, 157
Hunter, Dan, 49, 51
hybrid P2P, defined, 114
Hydrolevel Corp., American Society of Mechanical Engineers v., 93, 331

IBM, 79, 129
IBM computers, 177–178
ICI (Imperial Chemical Industries), 361

idea-expression dichotomy, as copyright infringement defense, 42
ideas, as protected by copyright, 173
IE. *See* Internet Explorer (IE)
IEEE (Institute of Electric and Electronic Engineers), 326
Illinois Tool Works, Inc. v. Independent Ink, Inc., 81–82
IM (instant messaging), as hybrid P2P, 114
Image Technical Services, Inc., Eastman Kodak Co. v., 64
Image Technical Services, Inc. v. Eastman Kodak Co., 83–84
Imclone, 318–319
Immuno, 317, 318
iMovie, 50
Imperial Chemical Industries (ICI), 361
Implant Innovations, Inc., Nobelpharma AB v., 80
IMS Health GmbH & Co. OHG v. NDC Health GmbH & Co. KG, 91
In re Aimster Copyright Litigation, 115, 116–117, 130, 133, 136–139
In re American Society of Sanitary Engineering, 93
In re Cardizem CD Antitrust Litigation, 97, 357–358, 363
In re Ciprofloxacin Hydrochloride Antitrust Litigation, 365, 368–369
In re Dell, 93, 331, 342
In re Independent Service Organizations Antitrust Litigation (Xerox), 80, 84–85
In re Rambus, 94, 332
In re Seagate Technology, LLC, 201, 216, 250
In re Tamoxifen Citrate Antitrust Litigation, 98, 361–363, 364, 365, 366, 369, 378
inadequate legal remedy, and core-component analysis, 246–248
incentive theory, 45
incentives
  and lowered prices, 339
  and market concentration, 307
  for patents, 273–274
incremental *vs.* radical innovation, 26–27
INDC Health GmbH & Co. KG, MS Health GmbH & Co. OHG v., 91

Independent Ink, Inc., Illinois Tool Works, Inc. v., 81–82
independent service organizations (ISOs), 83, 84
India, 176
Indian Head, Inc., Allied Tube & Conduit Corp. v., 93, 330–331
Induce Act (Inducing Infringement of Copyrights Act), 123n
industry and universities, relationships of, 264–267, 288–290
inequitable conduct, as patent infringement defense, 38
infringement
  and blocking technology, 137
  claims, importance of, 37–38
  contributory, defined, 38
  of copyrights, 41–43
  as defined by William Robinson, 258
  and experimentation, 256–257
  importance, 37–38
  literal, defined, 38
  overview of, 7–8
  of patents, 37–39
  quantifiable costs of, 128–129
  remedies, overview of, 235–236
  remedies for, 39
  willful. *See* willful infringement
injunctions, permanent, 238–239
injunctive relief
  balance of hardships, 241, 248–249
  and competition, lack of, 245–246
  in *eBay* case, 237–239
  examples of, 231–232, 233–235, 239–244
  in Federal Circuit, overview of, 236–237
  four-factor test
    as applied, 239–244
    overview of, 238, 244, 250–251, 252
  inadequate legal remedy
    defined, 246
    example cases of, 240, 242–243, 245
    irreparable harm and, 246–246
  irreparable harm
    competition and, 244–246
    example cases of, 239–240, 242, 245
  problem of, 233–235
  public interest, 241, 249–250
  when appropriate, 232–233

inkjet printers
  and aftermarkets, 171
  as disruptive innovation, 28
  in *Lexmark* case, 185–186
Innovate America (report), 23
innovation
  in Aibo incident, 190
  and antitrust law, 68–69, 292
  copyrights, importance of, 102–103
  creativity vs., 119–128
  defined, 2, 19
  DMCA, as threat to, 165
  and economic growth, 31–33, 49
  examples of, 24–25
  "functionally novel," 28
  global context, overview of, 11–12
  Internet, role of, 51–52
  IP, role of, 47
  laws affecting, overview of, 3–4
  and license restrictions, 268n
  measurement of, 30–31
  promotion of, 142–144
  and R&D, 297, 298, 299, 301–302
  secondary liability, as threat to, 54
  as speculative, 297, 298, 299
  stages of, 20
  statutory damages remedy, as threat to, 43
  subjects of, 20–22
  types of, 26–29
  why neglected, 2
innovation asymmetry, 106, 128–130, 133, 144
innovation markets
  antitrust lawsuits and, 92–93
  appropriability and, 302–303
  critiques of, 297–298
  described, 93
  drastic vs. nondrastic innovation, 301
  and market entry, 308
  mergers challenged, 312–322
  overview of, 9, 297
  pharmaceutical companies and, 92
  product vs. process innovation, 300–301
  technology and, 301–303
  as unnecessary, 297, 298, 299
  U.S. Department of Justice case, 312n
innovative efficiency, defined, 65
innovative markets, defined, 60

298 INNOVATION FOR THE 21ST CENTURY

instant messaging (IM), as hybrid
P2P, 114
Instant Messaging Service, America
Online, 116
Institute of Electric and Electronic
Engineers (IEEE), 326
Integra Lifesciences I, Ltd., Merck KGaA v.,
260–261
Intel, 234–235
Intellectual Property and Communications
Omnibus Reform Act (1999), 213n
intellectual property (IP) law
antitrust law, in conflict with, 71–73
defined, 35
IP Guidelines, 80, 81–82, 292, 297
market power of, 71n
and material transfer agreements
(MTAs), 283–284
as not being used effectively, 54
period of disfavor, 74–77
periods of dominance, 73–74,
78–83
as public good, 46
rationales for, 43–46
reverse engineering, role of, 197
role of, in innovation, 47
utilitarianism and legislation of, 45
vs. antitrust law, overview of, 4, 5–6
intent tests, 84n
inter parte reexaminations
defined, 212–213
estoppel provisions, 228
and post-grant opposition
threshold, 218
time frame for, 227
interbrand, defined, 56
interface (interoperability) standards,
defined, 326
interface specifications, defined, 167
international
DMCA, effect of in trade, 166
innovation, global context of, 11–12
translation of Creative Commons
licenses, 51
International Salt Co. v. United States,
76, 77
Internet
cloud computing, 143–144
role in innovation, 51–52

royalty-free licensing, defined, 328
search, overview of, 111–112
and standard setting, 326–327
video downloads, 139–140
See also World Wide Web
Internet Archive, and P2P, 139
Internet Explorer (IE)
as client software, 111
copyright and, 138
in *United States v. Microsoft,* 87
interoperability
in *Davidson* case, 187–189
defined, 167, 181
in DMCA exemptions, 181
examples of, 170
software, as important to, 173
interoperability (interface) standards,
defined, 326
intrabrand, defined, 56
Intuit, 28
invalid patents
benefits to challenges, 346
harm of, 221
litigation over, 209–211
market power and, 229
invention
"blocking patent" inventions, 269n
claim construction, importance of,
37–38
designing around, 269
experimentation on the invention,
defined, 254
patents, importance of, 244
process of, 45–46
as stage of innovation, 20
unforeseen benefits of, 129
investment
lawsuits, fear of, 133
liability of investors, 156–157
and post-grant opposition, 216
as stage of innovation, 20
venture capitalists, role in
innovation, 24
See also funding
IP. *See* intellectual property (IP) law
IP Guidelines, 80, 81–82, 292, 297
iPhone, 191, 195
iPods, 102, 129
Iressa, 319

irreparable harm
    competition and, 244–247
    example cases of, 239–240, 242, 245
    inadequate legal remedy, 246–248
ISOs (independent service organizations),
    83, 84
Israel, 23
iTunes, 123, 125, 127, 141, 143

Japan, 23, 32, 166, 182, 214, 222, 263,
    270, 316
Japanese Patent Act, 270
Java, 87
Java Virtual Machine, 87
JEDEC, 94
joint ventures, as per se illegal, 62
Jones, Charles, 32
Joost, 28, 139
Jordan, 166
Jung, Davidson Associates v., 187–189,
    190, 196

KaZaA, 115, 124
K-Dur 20, 358–360
Kennedy, Justice, 238
keyboard, QWERTY, and defacto
    standard, 325
keys (for software), defined, 178
Kitch, Edmund, 45
Knogo, 312n
knowledge, in "growth accounting," 32
Kodak. *See* Eastman Kodak
Korea. *See* South Korea
Korean Patent Law, 270
Kovacic, William, 95, 335
KSR v. Teleflex, 200

labor theory and IP, 43–44
laches, as copyright infringement defense, 42
Lake Michigan, 236
Lande, Robert, 68
lasers, and patent pools, 96
last.fm, 143
Lastowka, Greg, 49, 51
Lau, Lawrence, 32
law, as secret code, 16
*Law Offices of Curtis V. Trinko, Verizon
    Communications v.*, 9, 58, 98, 293, 346,
    371, 372–373, 376, 382

"law on the books" *vs.* "law on the
    ground," 202
Lear Avia, Inc., Dugan v., 258
legal remedy, inadequate
    defined, 246
    example cases of, 240, 242–243, 245
    irreparable harm and, 246–248
Lehman, Bruce, 184
Lemley, Mark, 134, 160, 340
Lexapro, 368
*Lexmark International, Inc. v. Static Control
    Components, Inc.*, 185–186, 193
libraries, use by, as copyright
    infringement defense, 42
license restrictions
    and innovation, 268n
    Microsoft accused of, 88
licensee veto power, as one of Nine
    No-No's, 77
licensing
    in biotechnology, 264
    exclusive, 77n
    as principle in IP Guidelines, 81
    reach-through license, defined,
        280, 289n
    restrictions on, 72
    as vital to innovation, 20
    See also cross-licensing
licensing rules, defined, 327, 340
LimeWire, 119
Line Material Co., United States v., 76–77
LionShare, and P2P, 139
litigation asymmetry, 106, 128, 131–133
local area network, 240
Locke, John, 43–44
lock-in, 329–330
lock-out code, defined, 170
Loew's, United States v., 76, 77, 82
Long Tail concept, 141
LSDs (lysosomal storage disorders),
    310–311, 321

Mac Office, 87
Macrovision, 136n
Madey, John, 259–260
Madey v. Duke University, 259–260, 262
Maitreya, Sananda (Terence Trent
    D'Arby), 125
Majoras, Deborah, 95, 329, 335, 336

Malthus, Thomas, 31n
mandatory limited disclosure, 226
manipulation, SSO cases involving,
    330–331
manufacturer *vs.* user innovation, 28–29
market allocation agreements
    anticompetitive harm of, 370, 373–376
    defined, 56
    as per se illegal, 62
market concentration
    and competitive harm, 312
    and incentives, 307
    and mergers, 304–306
    and preclinical development, 305–306
    and suppression, 307–308
market dominance, role of patents in,
    48–49
market entry
    and mergers, 308–309
    odds of Phase III firms succeeding,
        309n
market power
    and antitrust, 194
    invalid patents and, 229
    and monopolies, 197
    as principle in IP Guidelines, 81–82
    as protected by DMCA, 184, 194
market power presumption, 81–82
material transfer agreements (MTAs)
    costs of, 286
    dangers of, 281–284
    overview of, 8, 279–281
    uniform biological MTA (UBMTA),
        286–287, 289–290
Maxalt, 315
Media Player, Windows, 89
Medicare Prescription Drug,
    Improvement, and Modernization Act
    (Medicare Modernization Act), 353, 365
Medimmune v. Genentech, 200–201
*Mega Lift Systems LLC, MGM Well Services,
    Inc. v.*, 239, 245
*MercExchange, eBay v. See eBay v.
    MercExchange*
Merck, 315–316
Merck KGaA v. Integra Lifesciences I, Ltd.,
    260–261
*Mercoid Corp. v. Mid-Continent Investment
    Co.*, 75–76

merger doctrine, as copyright
    infringement defense, 42
*Merger Guidelines. See Horizontal Merger
    Guidelines*
mergers
    anticompetitive, cost of preventing, 68
    and antitrust law, 59–61, 63, 65–66
    and competitive harm, 306–308
    and efficiencies, 309–311
    "failing firms" defense, 311
    in innovation markets, 312–322
    and market concentration, 304–306
    and market entry, 308–309
    and monopolies, 296
        danger of, 296
    nine products involving FTC, 301n
    of pharmaceutical companies, examples
        of, 92
    and Schumpeterian defense, 311–312
    size of firms, importance of,
        311–312
Merritt, Judge Gilbert, 186
"Mertonian ethos," defined, 257
Meurer, Michael, 49
Meyer, David, 60n
MGM v. Grokster, 41, 115, 117–119, 126,
    129, 135–136, 139, 159
*MGM Well Services, Inc. v. Mega Lift
    Systems LLC*, 239, 245
Microsoft, 61n, 87–92, 134
    willful infringement and *Microsoft*
        case, 250n
    See also Windows, Microsoft
Microsoft Corp., United States v., 49,
    87–89, 226, 374
*Microsoft Corp. v. Comm'n of the European
    Cmtys.*, 89–92, 167
Microsoft Corp., z4 Technologies, Inc. v., 235,
    242–243, 245, 247, 249, 250
*Mid-Continent Investment Co., Mercoid
    Corp. v.*, 75–76
migraine treatments, 314–316, 316n
Mill, John Stuart, 45
Milwaukee, 236
misappropriation, and reverse
    engineering, 172
Model 39 remote opener, Skylink, 187
Model T, as disruptive innovation, 28
modularity, defined, 167–168

monopolies
and aftermarkets, 197
and antitrust law, 58–59, 65–66
and appropriability, 302
cost of preventing, 68
defined, 58
in Glaxo-Wellcome merger, 308n
and market power, 197
and mergers, danger of, 296
Microsoft as, 88
patents and, 52–53
profit sharing *vs.* duopolies, 377
and refusal to license, 82–85
in telecommunications, 371, 372
utilitarianism theory, effect on, 45
monopsony
defined, 336
harms and SSOs, 336–339, 343
oligopsony, defined, 337
in *Soundview* case, 333
"moral rights" theory and IP, 44n
Morocco, 166
Morpheus software, 117
Morton Salt Co. v. G.S. Suppiger Co.,
74–75
Motion Picture Association of America
(MPAA), 107, 134
*Motion Picture Patents Co. v. Universal Film
Manufacturing Co.*, 74, 75
movie industry
encoding VHS recordings, 136n
home entertainment, affecting revenue
of, 108
infringement, in 1930s, 151
threatened by innovation, 107–108
vs. TV innovations, 134
See also entertainment industry
Movielink, 124
Mozilla Firefox, 29, 111
MP3
described, 114n
and iTunes, 141
Napster, use of, 114
and Pioneer Inno, 155
and recording studio subscription
services, 127n
small inventors and, 132
MPAA (Motion Picture Association of
America), 107, 134

MP3.com lawsuit, 153–155, 156, 159,
160, 161
MPEG-2, and patent pools, 95, 96
MPEG Layer-3. *See* MP3
*MS Health GmbH & Co. OHG v. INDC
Health GmbH & Co. KG*, 91
MTAs. *See* material transfer agreements
(MTAs)
Muris, Timothy, 295–296, 320
music downloading. *See* P2P
(peer-to-peer)
music industry
and disruptive innovation, 102
need for copyrights, 50
threatened by innovation, 107
See also entertainment industry;
recording industry
Music Jukebox, 143
MusicNet, 127n
MusicShare, 115–116
Myozyme, 321
Myriad Pharmaceuticals, 255, 267
MySpace, 124, 125, 143

naked restraints, 62
nanotechnology, defined, 233n
Napster, 178
contributory infringement, guilty of,
116–117
as disruptive innovation, 102
how it worked, 116
as hybrid P2P, 114
RIAA (Recording Industry of America),
meetings with, 127
sued by recording industry, 10
and venture capitalists, 133, 157
as victim of litigation asymmetry, 132
Napster, Inc., A&M Records, Inc. v., 115–116,
135–136, 137–138
NASA, 140
National Academy of Science, and
post-grant opposition reform, 218
National Commission on New
Technological Uses of Copyrighted
Works (CONTU), 172
National Cooperative Research Act
(NCRA), 78, 79, 85
National Cooperative Research and
Production Act (NCRPA), 79n

*National Harrow Co., E. Bement &
Sons v.,* 73
National Income and Products
Accounts, 30
National Industrial Recovery Act, 67
National Institute of Standards and
Technology, 326
National Institutes of Health (NIH), 267,
273, 274–275, 286, 287, 288, 309n
National Research Council of the National
Academies, 262
National Science Foundation (NSF), 287
natural-rights theories and IP, 43–44
NCRA (National Cooperative Research
Act), 78, 79, 85
NCRPA (National Cooperative Research
and Production Act), 79n
NDA (New Drug Application), 305,
351–352
N-Data (Negotiated Data Solutions),
94–95, 334–335
*NDC Health GmbH & Co. KG, IMS Health
GmbH & Co. OHG v.,* 91
Negotiated Data Solutions (N-Data),
94–95, 334–335
neoclassical microeconomics,
defined, 63
Netanel, Neil, 122–123
Netflix, 142
Netherlands, 270, 270n
Netherlands, Patent Act of 1995, 270n
network effects market, defined,
48–49, 324
New Drug Application (NDA), 305,
351–352
New Technologies Products (NTP),
231–232, 234, 250
Newman, Judge Pauline, 270
news reporting, as copyright infringement
defense, 42
Nexium, 368
Nicaragua, 166
NIH. *See* National Institutes of Health
(NIH)
NIH Public Access Policy, 289n
Nine No-No's, 77, 292
*Nine Points to Consider in Licensing
University Technology,* 275
Nintendo, 174

*Nobelpharma AB v. Implant Innovations,
Inc.,* 80
Nokia, 232
nondrastic *vs.* drastic innovation, 301
nonexclusivity, defined, 46
nonobviousness
as criticized by Antitrust Modernization
Commission, 5–6
as patent requirement, 36
nonpracticing entity, 234–235, 248
nonprofit institutions
and Bayh-Dole Act, 287
NIH model contract, 288
and noncommercial research, 254
patent fees for, 223
use of patented material, 271n
nonrivalrousness, defined, 46
norms, described, 265–266
Northwest, 67
Novazyme, 295–296, 310–311
novelty, as patent requirement, 36
NSF (National Science Foundation), 287
NTP (New Technologies Products),
231–232, 234, 250

object code, defined, 167
O'Connor, Justice Sandra Day, 111
O'Connor, Sean, 285
off-shore companies, and copyright
infringement, 124
oligopsony, defined, 337
Oman, 166
Omrix, 317
oncomouse, 254
open source movement, 50–51
OpenNap, 118
Orange Book, 99, 351–352, 351n, 353, 354
organizational structure, role in
innovation, 23–24
Orphan Drug Act, 320
OSI, 319
Ostrom, Elinor, 266n
Outfoxed (documentary), 140

package licensing, mandatory, as one of
Nine No-No's, 77
Paice LLC v. Toyota Motor Corp., 235, 242,
243, 246, 248, 250
Palmer v. BRG of Georgia, 374

Panama, 166
Pandora, 143
parody, as copyright infringement
    defense, 42
Patent Act (1952), 76, 238, 366, 367
Patent and Trademark Law Amendments
    Act (1980). *See* Bayh-Dole Act
Patent and Trademark Office. *See* U.S.
    Patent and Trademark Office (PTO)
patent law
    effect on innovation, overview of, 3, 7–8
    misuse, as patent infringement
        defense, 38
    misuse, defined, 79
    secret language of, 16
    software, role in protecting, 172
    vs. antitrust law, 8
Patent Misuse Reform Act (1988), 78, 79,
    80, 82, 85
patent pools
    antitrust lawsuits and, 95–97, 99, 342
    defined, 72
    and holdup, 324n
    as monopoly, 73
    as principle in IP Guidelines, 81
patent system
    boundaries, need for, 202
    challenges facing, 200–203
    European system *vs.* U.S., 217
    exclusion, as the foundation of, 72
    fee system, 222–223
    immunity, decline of, 74–76
    invalid patents. *See* invalid patents
    litigation, 209–211
    purpose of, 20, 205, 346
    reform legislation, 217–218
    validity. *See* validity
patent trolls, 35, 200, 234
patentable subject matter, as patent
    requirement, 36
patentees
    and antitrust immunity, 84
    compensation for infringement, 236
    pharmaceutical, 368
    protection of, 212
    royalty payments, for drug
        patentees, 375
    and SSO prices, 338
    as winners in validity litigation, 210

patents
    application, requirements for, 36
    application process, 36–37, 206–209
    "bounty" for patentability
        information, 217n
    as business strategy, 48–49
    dangers of, 52–53
    enablement, defined, 224
    essential *vs.* substitute, 96
    expiration of, 222
    free riding, 210
    holdup, 328–330, 340, 344
    incentives for, 273–274
    infringement of, 37–38
    infringement suit, defenses in, 38–39
    IP law, role of, 47–49
    issued, reexamination of, 211–213
    multiple, 233, 247n
    noncommercial use of, 258
    remedies, overview of, 235–236
    research tools, role in creating, 276
    restrictions of licensees, 72
    subject matter, defined, 224
    utility, defined, 223–224
    vs. copyrights, 40, 173
    written description, defined, 224
Patents Depend on Quality Act of
    2006, 219
Paxil, 353, 368
PCR (polymerase chain reaction)
    technology, 254, 268
Peer-to-Peer Community Patent
    Review, 215
peer-to-peer (P2P). *See* P2P (peer-to-peer)
Penn State University, and P2P, 139
PEP (Printer Engine Program), Lexmark,
    185–186
peptides, 260
per se analysis *vs.* Rule-of-Reason, 63–64
performance standards, defined, 325
personhood theory and IP, 44
Peru, 166
petitions, as delay tactic, 99
Pfizer, 315–316
Pfizer-Warner-Lambert merger, 92, 313,
    318–319, 322
pharmaceutical industry
    "bricks," defined, 91
    in German, study on, 263

pharmaceutical industry (*cont.*)
  innovation market mergers, 312–313
  in Japan, study on, 263
  mergers, reasons for, 310
  petitions, as delay tactic, 99
  and post-grant opposition time
    frame, 220
  preclinical development, overview of,
    304–306, 305n
  R&D, role in innovation, 299, 300
  role of patents in innovation, 47,
    292–293
  settlement agreements, 97–98
  See also drugs
Pharming, 321n
Philippines, 176
photocopiers, and copyright
  infringement, 138
photorefractive keratectomy (PRK) lasers,
  and patent pools, 96
Pioneer Inno, 155
piracy. *See* digital piracy
Plantinol, 346
Platform for Privacy Preferences, 330
Plavix, 368
Playstation, Sony, 175–176
polymer, defined, 233n
Pompe disease, 295–296, 310–311,
  320–321
Pooler, Judge, 362–363
Posner, Judge Richard, 63, 136
Post-Chicago School, 63
post-grant opposition system
  appeals, 225
  estoppel, 228
  evidentiary showing, 224–225
  fee system, 222–223
  form of opposition, 225–227
  investment, effect on, 216
  judges and, 225
  overview of, 7–8, 205, 213–218
  recommendations for, 383
  reform needed, 202
  requester, identity of, 227–228
  and small business, 216–217
  threshold for, 218–219
  time frame for filing, 219–223, 225
postsale restrictions, as one of Nine
  No-No's, 77

potential competition, defined, 298
Power Box radio chargers, 240
P2P (peer-to-peer), 102
  benefits of, 113–114, 139–142
  CD sales and, 119–122
  commercial development halted, 119
  defining characteristics of, 113
  as disruptive innovation, 28
  distribution of, 139–140
  legal cases defining use of, 115–119
  music artists, use of by, 124–125
  as new business model, 6
  overview of, 111–115
  promotion of, 141–142
  types of, 114–115
  use of, increasing, 124
Pravachol, 368
Praxair, Inc. v. ATMI, Inc., 242, 246, 252
preclinical development, overview of,
  304–306, 305n
predatory pricing, defined, 59
President's Commission on the Patent
  System, 222n
PressPlay, 127n
Prevacid, 368
price fixing
  beneficial, example of, 56n
  coal producers and, 62
  cost of preventing, 68
  defined, 56
  as lawful, 74
  as per se illegal, 62
  by SSOs, 330, 332–333, 342, 343
price specification for licensees, as one of
  Nine No-No's, 77
prices, as set by Supreme Court, 56
Printer Engine Program (PEP), Lexmark,
  185–186
printer ink cartridges, DMCA and, 163
prior art
  defined, 206
  in examiners' search, 36
prior use right, as patent infringement
  defense, 39
Prioritizing Resources and Organization
  for Intellectual Property (PRO IP) Act
  of 2008, 148
process *vs.* product innovation, 300–301,
  300n

production, as function of copyright, 51–52
productive efficiency, defined, 65
promotion, as function of copyright, 52
property rights, need for, 45
prosecution history, defined, 38
Prozac, 346, 368
PTO. See U.S. Patent and Trademark
    Office (PTO)
PTO's *Utility Guidelines*, 256n
public good
    IP as, 46
    post-grant opposition and, 217n
    problem of, 210
Public Health Service, 286
public interest, 241, 249–250
public use, as copyright infringement
    defense, 42
publication restrictions, of science
    research, 283, 288–289

Qualcomm, Inc., Broadcom Corp. v., 332n
quantity restrictions, as patent license
    restriction, defined, 72
quick-look analysis, 57
QWERTY keyboard, and defacto
    standard, 325

Rader, Judge Randall, 259, 261n
radical innovation
    and software industry, 169
    vs. incremental innovation, 26–27
Radin, Margaret, 44
radio
    secondary liability and, 152–153
    XM radio lawsuit, 155–156
Rai, Arti, 272
Rambus, 329–330, 332
Rambus case. See In re Rambus
RAND (reasonable and
    nondiscriminatory) terms
    IP licensing, 324, 327–328
    and monopsony, 337
    reasonable royalties, 327–328, 341
reach-through license, defined, 280, 289n
Reagan administration, 60
RealNetworks, 134
reasonable and nondiscriminatory
    (RAND) terms. See RAND (reasonable
    and nondiscriminatory) terms

recording industry
    CD sales, dependence on, 124n
    Napster, response to, 127
    Napster, sued by, 10
    subscription services, 127n
    See also entertainment industry; music
        industry
Recording Industry of America (RIAA)
    and declining CD sales, 121–122
    file-sharing suits, 119, 122
    MP3.com lawsuit, role in, 153–155
    Napster, meetings with, 127
    new technology, grappling with,
        127–128
    statutory damages recovered, example
        of, 159
    XM radio lawsuit, 155–156
RecordTV.com, as victim of litigation
    asymmetry, 132
Reese, Tony, 134, 138
reexamination process
    proposal for reform, 223–224
    *See also ex parte reexaminations; inter
        parte reexaminations*
refusal to license
    near–per se legality, 84–85
    as patent misuse, 80
    role in IP, 82–85
refusals to deal, defined, 59
Register of Copyrights
    1961 Report of, 150–151
    triennial exemption review of DMCA,
        190–192
Relpax, 315
Rembrandt, 95n
remedies. *See also specific types;* statutory
    damages
repair defense, as patent infringement
    defense, 38
ReplayTV, 131, 133
Report of the NIH Working Group on
    Research Tools, 287–288
Reprise Records, 125
reputation harms, 245
Research in Motion (RIM), 231–232
research tools, patented
    access to, need for, 8, 11, 202–203
    accessibility of, 8, 11
    in biotechnology, 254–255

research tools, patented (*cont.*)
dangers of, 255–256
described, 254
empirical studies on use of, 261–267
and experimentation on the invention, 268, 269–271
infringement, as causing, 256
and patent incentives, 273n
patents, role in creation of, 276
royalty payments on, 269
and user innovation, 30, 254, 268, 275–277, 278
reverse doctrine of equivalents, as patent infringement defense, 39
reverse engineering
aftermarkets, as means to compete in, 171
in *Chamberlain* case, 186–187
as copyright infringement defense, 42–43, 164
defined, 164
and DMCA, 164
as limiting IP, 197
overview of, 168–170
in *Sega* case, 174–176
reverse payments
anticompetitive effects, 98, 347
brand-name *vs.* generic drugs, 97, 99
defined, 9, 346
as distinguished from other types of settlements, 376
in drug company settlements, 346–347
harm of, 363
and Hatch-Waxman Act, 360
importance of, 364–365
and innovation, 365
and Medicare Modernization Act, 365
natural status of, 369–370
and patent scope, 368–369
patent validity and, 366–368, 370, 378–382
as per se illegal, 361, 380
as presumptively illegal, 346, 347, 370, 377–378
and Rule of Reason, 381
in *Tamoxifen* case, 360–361
upheld by courts, 368
use of, 356
Rhapsody, 142

RIAA. *See* Recording Industry of America (RIAA)
Ricardo, David, 31n
Riggs, William, 277
right to exclude
defined, 71
importance to patents, 84
RIM (Research in Motion), 231–232
Robert Bosch Tool Corporation, Black & Decker, Inc. v., 240, 245
Roberts, Chief Justice John G., 238
Robertson, Michael, 154
Robinson, William, 258
robotic dog (Aibo), 190
Roche Products, Inc. v. Bolar Pharmaceutical Co., 258–259, 260, 348
Roche-Genentech merger, 92, 313–314, 322
Rockwell International Corporation, Townsend v., 84–85
rolling code, defined, 187
Romer, Paul, 32
Rosen, Hillary, 127
royalty payments
in CD sales, 125
compulsory, as one of Nine No-No's, 77
for drug patentees, 375
and injunctive relief, 236n
in Negotiated Data Solutions (N-Data) case, 234–335
as patent license restriction, defined, 72
on research tools, 269
SSOs and, 324, 333–334, 337–338
and Unocal, 329
royalty-free licensing, defined, 328
RTE & ITP v. Commission (Magill), 90–91
Rule of Reason
agreements, applied to, 56–58
defined, 57
joint ventures, applied to, 292
licensing arrangements, applied to, 292
in National Cooperative Research Act (1984), 79
patent misuse, applied to, 292
price fixing, applied to, 292
as principle in IP Guidelines, 81
and reverse payments, 381
and SSOs, 334, 341, 342, 343, 343n, 344
vs. per se analysis, 63–64
Ruth v. Stearns-Roger Manufacturing Co., 258

sales territories, exclusive, as per se
illegal, 62
Sawin v. Guild, 258
Scalia, Justice Antonin, 238, 372–373
SCC (Static Control Components),
185–186
scenes-à-faire, as copyright infringement
defense, 42
Schering-Plough Corp. v. FTC, 97–98,
358–360, 363, 364, 365, 366, 369, 375,
376, 378
Schumpeter, Joseph, 102, 298, 311
Schumpeterian defense, 296, 316, 318, 321
science, research
abandoned research lines, 282
as affected by DMCA, 166
and common-law defense, 257
materials, delays in receiving, 282
publication restrictions, 283
"Science and the Useful Arts," 124, 244
scientists, research
access to patented research tools, need
for, 8, 11, 202–203
and material transfer agreements
(MTAs), 279–280
self-reporting, bias of, 262n
scope, patent
importance of, 37, 85
reverse payments and, 368–369
Scour.com, as victim of litigation
asymmetry, 132
Seagate case. *See In re Seagate
Technology, LLC*
Sealagen, 317
search rules, defined, 340–341, 341n
SEC (Securities and Exchange
Commission), 59n, 371, 373
secondary liability
defined, 41, 108
examples of cases involving, 108–111
Grokster case *vs. Napster* case, outcomes
of, 135–136
needing revision, 102–103
statutory damages and, 158–160
statutory standards for, 118n
as threat to innovation, 54, 132
Secretary of Commerce, U.S., 30–31
Securities and Exchange Commission
(SEC), 59n, 371, 373

Security+ GDO, Chamberlain, 187
Sega Enterprises Ltd. v. Accolade, 174–176,
178, 183, 197
selection, as function of copyright, 51
self-reporting, bias of, 262n
Senate Judiciary Committee, 355
Senate Special Committee on
Aging, 346n
Sensormatic, 312n
sham litigation
and antitrust immunity, 84
defined, 98
liability limited to, 85
shareholders. *See* investment
Shasta County, California, 266
Sherman Act, 74, 77
1890, 61, 67, 73
Section 1, 58, 61, 78, 83, 337, 359
Section 2, 61, 82, 83, 84, 342
Singapore, 166, 176
Singulair, 368
size, of merging firms, 311–312
*Skylink Technologies, Inc.,
Chamberlain Group, Inc. v.*, 186–187,
195n, 197
Skype, 28, 139
small business
and antitrust law, 63
and mergers, 311–312
patent fees for, 223
and patent incentives, 274n
post-grant opposition and, 216–217
size of merging firms, 311–312
in *TiVo* case, 241
Smith, Adam, 31n, 324
Smith & Nephew, Inc. v. Synthes, 239,
240, 245
SmithKlineBeecham, 301
merger with Glaxo-Wellcome, 92,
308n, 313n
*Socony-Vacuum Oil Co.,
United States v.*, 62
software. *See* computer software
Solow, Robert, 31–32
SonicBlue, as victim of litigation
asymmetry, 132
Sonny Bono Copyright Term Extension
Act (1998), 41
Sony, 50, 124, 190, 196, 323, 324

Sony Computer Entertainment v. Connectix Corporation, 174, 175–176, 178, 183, 196, 197
Sony Corporation of America v. Universal City Studios
and *Aimster*, 117
Betamax VCR, importance of, 106, 107, 108
contributory infringement and, 136
error-costs asymmetry and, 145
evaluation of, 133–135
and *Grokster* case, 117–119, 136, 159
innovation asymmetry and, 133, 144
litigation described, 109–111
and *Napster* case, 116
and non-infringing uses, 6, 41
and reverse engineering, 178
secondary liability test, 102
vicarious liability and, 136
Sony Electronics, Inc. v. Soundview Technologies, Inc., 332–333
Soulseek, and P2P, 139
Soundview Technologies, Inc., Sony Electronics, Inc. v., 332–333
source code, defined, 167
Sousa, John Philip, 107
Souter, Justice David, 238
South Korea, 23, 166, 214, 270
Southern States Equipment, 76–77
sovereign immunity doctrine, 264n
specification, defined, 38
spillovers, defined, 302
spoof files, defined, 114n
spyware, 114
SSOs. *See* standard-setting organizations (SSOs)
Standard Oil, 67
Standard Sanitary Manufacturing Co. v. United States, 74
standards
absence of, results of, 323
defined, 323
wars, 327
standard-setting organizations (SSOs)
anticompetitive effects, 335–336
antitrust lawsuits and, 93–95, 99, 330–332
Boiler and Pressure Vessel Code, 331
closed, 336

deception, cases involving, 330, 331–332
and IP rules, 327–328, 340–342
manipulation, cases involving, 330–331
monopsony harms and, 333, 336–339, 343
Negotiated Data Solutions (N-Data) case, 334–335
overview of, 9–10
price fixing by, 330, 332–333, 342, 343
procompetitive justifications, 339–342
and Rule of Reason, 334, 341, 342, 343, 343n, 344
types of, 325–327
VITA case, 333–334
Stanford University, 259
staple article of commerce doctrine, 109–110
StarCraft (video game), 188
Static Control Components, Inc., Lexmark International, Inc. v., 185–186, 193
Static Control Components (SCC), 185–186
statutory damages
as "corporate death penalty," 158
and fair use defense, 152
law, review of, 148–149
legislative history of, 149–153
limiting, proposal for, 160–161
overview of, 6–7, 11
purpose of, 150–151, 158
rationale for, 158–159
as remedy for copyright infringement, overview of, 43, 147–148
secondary liability and, 158–160
as supporting radical innovation, 29–30
as threat to innovation, 43, 102–103
upper limit recognized, 152
when appropriate, 251
Stearns-Roger Manufacturing Co., Ruth v., 258
stem cell research, 255, 284–285
Stevens, Justice John Paul, 238
"sticky information," 11, 276
Story, Justice Joseph, 257–258
Strandburg, Katherine, 276
StreamCast, 117, 118, 119, 137
Summit-VISX, patent pool, 96
Sun, 87
superpeer P2P, defined, 114

supersedeas bonds, 154
suppression, and market concentration,
307–308
Supreme Court decisions
antitrust, role of, 58, 64, 331
Chicago School of Economics
reasoning, 63, 66
competition, 78, 374
contributory infringement, 106,
117–188, 133, 159, 178
experimental use defense, 348n–349n
fair use, 176
Federal Circuit, 200, 202
free riding, 210
holdup, 328n
injunctive relief, 238–239, 242, 252
innovation, 252
market power, 81–82
merger cases, 59
monetary damages, 39
monopoly, 73–74, 165, 197
prices, as set by, 56
regulatory regime, importance of, 9, 98,
293, 346, 371, 382
software as patentable, 172
SSOs, 342
staple article of commerce doctrine,
109–110
statutory exemption, 260–261
tying, 88
utilitarian theory, 45
validity, 367
vertical agreements, 46
See also specific cases
sustaining *vs.* disruptive innovation, 27–28
Synchronized Multimedia Integration
Language, 330
Synpac, 321n
Synthes, Smith & Nephew, Inc. v., 239,
240, 245

tamoxifen, 361–363
Tamoxifen case. *See In re Tamoxifen Citrate
Antitrust Litigation*
Taq DNA polymerase, 255
Tarceva, 319
Tarnation (movie), 50
taxes, role in innovation, 24
Taxol, 346

technological protection measures (TPMs)
in Australian law, 182
in Chinese law, 181–182
in Japanese law, 182
legal protection of, 178
in video game market, 196
See also digital rights management
(DRM)
technology
as disruptive innovation, 126–128
and drug industry, 302
in "growth accounting," 32
and infringement, 137
in protecting digital copyrights, 123
technology market, defined, 60
technology spillovers, defined, 216
Technology Transfer Guidelines (EU),
341–342
TechSearch, 234–235
Telecommunications Act (1996),
58, 293, 371
telecommunications monopolies,
371, 372
Teleflex, KSR v., 200
telephone networks, and performance
standard, 325
Telequip Corp. v. Change Exchange,
241, 248
territorial restrictions, as patent license
restriction, defined, 72
theaters, secondary liability and, 152–153
third parties, harm to, 243, 250
Thomas, John, 217n
Thompson, Mozelle, 296, 320
Thomson, James, 284–285
tie-outs, defined, 77
Tila Tequila, 125
time zones, 323
Tisseel, 317
TiVo, 6, 239
*TiVo Inc. v. Echostar Communications
Corp.*, 239, 241, 245, 249
Toner Loading Program (TLP), Lexmark,
185–186
tort law, role in innovation, 24
Toshiba, 324
Tower of Babel, 323
*Townsend v. Rockwell International
Corporation*, 84–85

Toyota Motor Corp., Paice LLC v., 235, 242, 243, 246, 248, 250
TPMs. *See* technological protection measures (TPMs)
trade secrets
 and antitrust law, 22
 effect on innovation, 21–22
Trademark Trial and Appeal Board, described, 227n
trademarks, effect on innovation, 21
Trade-Related Aspects of Intellectual Property (TRIPs), 35–36, 271n
trafficking provision, DMCA, 180, 189
"tragedy of the commons," 53n, 256n
Trans World Airlines (TWA), 67
Transocean Offshore Deepwater Drilling, Inc. v. GlobalSantaFe Corp., 239, 240, 241, 245, 247, 249
Travelocity, as disruptive innovation, 28
Treaty Establishing the European Community (EC Treaty), Article 82, 89, 90, 92
triennial exemption review, DMCA, 190–192
Trinko case. *See Verizon Communications v. Law Offices of Curtis V. Trinko*
TRIPs (Trade-Related Aspects of Intellectual Property), 35–36, 271n
trolls. *See* patent trolls
trusts, after Civil War, 61
TurboTax, as disruptive innovation, 28
TV
 online, 139
 vs. movie industry, 134
TWA (Trans World Airlines), 67
tying
 and antitrust immunity, 84
 Clayton Act, effect on, 74
 defined, 59, 88
 liability limited to, 85
 in market power presumption, 82
 Microsoft accused of, 88, 89
 as one of Nine No-No's, 77
 as patent misuse, 80
 penalized, 76
 as per se illegal, 62, 76
Type I and Type II errors, 130, 370–371

UBMTA (uniform biological MTA), 286–287, 289–290
U.K., 32, 270
Underwriter's Laboratory, 326
uniform biological MTA (UBMTA), 286–287, 289–290
unilateral competitive effects, defined, 307
unilateral effects theory, defined, 60
Union Oil Company of California (Unocal), 93, 329, 331–332, 342
United Kingdom, 32, 270
United Shoe, 63
United States, Appalachian Coals, Inc. v., 62
United States, Chesterfield v., 258
United States, International Salt Co. v., 76, 77
United States, Standard Sanitary Manufacturing Co. v., 74
United States v. Arnold, Schwinn, & Co., 78
United States v. General Electric, 75
United States v. Grinnell Corp., 58
United States v. Line Material Co., 76–77
United States v. Loew's, 76, 77, 82
United States v. Microsoft Corp., 49, 87–89, 226, 374
United States v. Socony-Vacuum Oil Co., 62
Universal City Studios, 109
Universal City Studios, Sony Corporation of America v. See Sony Corporation of America v. Universal City Studios
Universal Film Manufacturing Co., Motion Picture Patents Co. v., 74, 75
Universal (recording label), 124
universities
 Bayh-Dole Act and patenting, 272, 275
 and experimental use defense, 253
 federal funding and, 271
 industry, relationships with, 264–267, 288–289
 and noncommercial research, 254
 patent fees for, 223
 patent trolls, use of, 234
 and process innovation, 300n
 and sovereign immunity doctrine, 264n
 and stifled innovation, 267
 use of patented material, 271n
University of Hawaii, 259
University of Wisconsin, 284–285

Unocal (Union Oil Company of
California), 93, 329, 331–332, 342
unpatented products, sale of, as one of
Nine No-No's, 77
unreasonable agreements, 62
Upjohn-Pharmacia merger, 92, 312n, 313n
Upsher-Smith Laboratories, 359–360
upward-sloped supply curve, defined, 338
U.S. Constitution. See Constitution, U.S.
U.S. Court of Appeals for the Federal
Circuit, 200
U.S. Department of Justice. See
Department of Justice, U.S.
U.S. Department of Labor, 32
U.S. Department of Transportation, 67
U.S. law vs. law in European Union, 90
U.S. Patent and Trademark Office (PTO)
Board of Patent Appeals and
Interferences, 212, 225, 232n
"bounty" for patentability
information, 217n
invalid patents and, 208–209
patent applications, requirements for,
36–37, 206–209
patent competitors and, 205
Patents Depend on Quality Act
of 2006, 219
and post-grant opposition reform, 218
third-party prior art and, 215n
Utility Guidelines, 256n
See also examiners (PTO)
U.S. Secretary of Commerce, 30–31
useful article doctrine, as copyright
infringement defense, 42
user vs. manufacturer innovation, 28–29
USPTO. See U.S. Patent and Trademark
Office (PTO)
utilitarian theory, and IP, 45–46
utility
defined, 223–224
as patent requirement, 36
Utility Guidelines (PTO), 256n

Valenti, Jack, 6, 107
validity
patentees as winners, 210
and post-grant opposition, 223–224
and reverse payments, 366–368, 370,
378–382

See also invalid patents
Valley Drug Co. v. Geneva Pharmaceuticals,
Inc., 365, 369
VARA (Visual Arts Rights Act), 44
V-chip, 332
VCR
Betamax, 41, 106, 107, 108, 109,
323–324
digital, 131
lawful use of, court found, 133
as new business model, 6
unforeseen uses of, 129, 130
VCR dates, replacing moviegoing, 107
Vectibix, 319
veil piercing, 157
venture capitalists. See investment
Verizon Communications v. Law Offices of
Curtis V. Trinko, 9, 58, 98, 293, 346,
371, 372–373, 376, 382
vertical agreements, defined, 56
vertical mergers, defined, 59n
vertical nonprice restraints
defined, 56
as per se illegal, 62
and Rule-of-Reason, 63
vertical territorial restraints, as per se
illegal, 78
Viacom, 147
vicarious liability
defined, 41, 108
Napster guilty of, 116
Video Electronics Standards
Association, 331
video game systems, and copyright law,
174–176
Virtual Game Station, Connectix,
175–176
Visual Arts Rights Act (VARA), 44
VITA (SSO), 94
VITA (VMEbus International Trade
Association), 333–334, 340
Vitex, 317, 318
Vivendi Universal, 155n
VL-bus, 331
VMEbus International Trade Association
(VITA), 333–334, 340
von Hippel, Eric, 11, 28–29,
275–276, 277
von Lohmann, Fred, 156n

Wal-Mart, 123
Walsh, John, empirical studies by, 261–263, 264, 281–284
Walt Disney Productions, and Sony, 109
WarCraft (video game), 188
WARF (Wisconsin Alumni Research Foundation), 285
Warner Brothers (recording label), 124
watermarks, electronic digital, 123
Waxman, Henry, 350, 355, 357, 365
Waxman-Hatch Act. See Hatch-Waxman Act (1984)
Web-Based Examiner Search Tool (WEST), 207
West Germany, 32, 221, 262, 263, 270
WEST (Web-Based Examiner Search Tool), 207
Whittemore v. Cutter, 257–258
WiCell Research Institute, 285
Wilco, 125
willful infringement
    and eBay case, 250n
    and Microsoft case, 250n
    and NTP (Blackberry) case, 250n
    overview of, 6–7
    remedies for, 43
    standard raised for, 201
    vs. innocent infringement, 160
    See also infringement
Windows, Microsoft
    and defacto standard, 325, 327
    Internet Explorer. See Internet Explorer (IE)
    in Microsoft lawsuits, 87–92, 167, 242–243, 249
Windows Media Player, 89
Winston, Clifford, 65–66
Winwood, Steve, 125

WIPO (World Intellectual Property Organization) Copyright Treaty, 179, 181
Wired (magazine), 141
wireless local area network (WLAN), 240
Wisconsin Alumni Research Foundation (WARF), 285
withheld materials, 281–282
WLAN (wireless local area network), 240
work group servers, defined, 89–90
World Intellectual Property Organization (WIPO) Copyright Treaty, 179, 181
World of Warcraft (game), 140
World Trade Organization (WTO), 36n, 271n
World Wide Web
    client-server model, as example of, 111
    consortium, 326, 330
    in 1990s, 138
    See also Internet
written description, defined, 224
WTO (World Trade Organization), 36n, 271n

Xerox case. See In re Independent Service Organizations Antitrust Litigation (Xerox)
XM radio lawsuit, 155–156

Yahoo!, 143
YouTube, 6, 52, 142, 143, 147

z4 Technologies, Inc. v. Microsoft Corp., 235, 242–243, 245, 247, 249, 250
Zantac, 346
Zeneca, 315–316, 361–362
ZF Friedrichshafen AG, 312n
Zoloft, 368
Zomig, 315

LaVergne, TN USA
29 March 2011
222022LV00001B/3/P